MODERN URBAN HISTORY RESEARCH IN EUROPE, USA AND JAPAN
A Handbook

Modern Urban History Research in Europe, USA and Japan

A Handbook

Edited by
CHRISTIAN ENGELI
and
HORST MATZERATH

BERG

Oxford / New York / Munich

Distributed exclusively in the US and Canada by
St. Martin's Press, New York

Published in 1989 by
Berg Publishers Limited
77 Morrell Avenue, Oxford OX4 1NQ, UK
165 Taber Avenue, Providence, RI 02906, USA
Westermühlstraße 26, 8000 München 5, FRG

© Berg Publishers 1989

British Library Cataloguing in Publication Data
Modern urban history research in Europe;
  U. S. A. and Japan : a handbook.
  1. Urban regions, history
  I. Engeli, Christian II. Matzerath, Horst
909'.09732
ISBN 0–85496–040–6

Library of Congress Cataloging-in-Publication Data
Modern urban history research in Europe,
  USA, and Japan.
  1. Cities and towns—History. 2. Cities
and towns—Historiography. I. Engeli,
Christian. II. Matzerath, Horst.
HT113.M63 1989   307.7'6   88–7911
ISBN 0–85496–040–6

Printed in Great Britain by Billing & Sons Ltd, Worcester

Contents

Contents

Contents

Preface

This volume aims at providing a basis for international cooperation in the field of urban history; at the same time, being a result of such cooperation. Colleagues from all over the world responded willingly to our request for collaboration in compiling this manual — a sign in itself of a desire for such cooperation; a sign also that it promises to be successful.

Inevitably, completion of this work was subject to the particular difficulties and imponderables involved in international cooperation, and was further complicated by our intention of simultaneously presenting English and German versions so as to reach a wider circle of readers. We regret that this has led to a delay in publication.

Finally, it is our pleasant duty to express our thanks to many people: first of all, to Beate Hoerkens and Isabell Stade of the "Deutsches Institut für Urbanistik", who edited the contributions. It is entirely due to their tireless efforts that manuscripts originally differing greatly in form and content can be presented here in a uniform manner. We should further like to thank Ruth Stanley, who was involved in the project from its inception as translator, and Mary Carroll, who was responsible for imposing editorial consistency between the English and the German text, published by Kohlhammer Verlag, Stuttgart.

We also have to thank Ágnes Ságvári — who assisted us at the beginning of the project with advice and by providing contacts — as well as many other colleagues whose names are not mentioned here and who, in various ways, supported this work and helped bring it to fruition.

This volume arose as a project funded by the Volkswagenwerk Foundation, which has selected "The History and Future of European Towns" for one of its main areas of sponsorship. For this reason, we owe special thanks to the Foundation — not only for its financial support, but also for its understanding and cooperation.

Dr Christian Engeli
Dr Horst Matzerath
Berlin, April 1989

CHRISTIAN ENGELI AND HORST MATZERATH

Introduction
Modern Urban History Research in Europe, the USA and Japan*

A. Aims and Concept

The last few decades have witnessed a rapidly growing universal interest in the town, resulting from the recognition that the town is a phenomenon of central importance in our society, and that the transformations characterised by the term "urbanisation" represent one of the most important processes in the development of the modern world. There is, however, less awareness of the details of this process, of the factors that provided crucial impulses for its development, of the turning points demarcating significant phases in this process, and of the present state of its development.

These issues also invite the question: what were the conditions that gave rise to the manifold problems which confront towns in virtually every country? Finally, it also remains to be seen whether developments observed in towns are of a general, i.e. universal, nature, whether they reveal specific national characteristics, or whether they can only be usefully treated in the local context of each individual town. Just as the study of what is individual or unique to a town presupposes a knowledge of the development of the town in the regional and national context, so the peculiarities of a nation's process of urbanisation can only be brought out through comparative international studies. Moreover, in this age of town-twinning, with its burgeoning of European and international organisations, urban history is presented with many opportunities to draw atten-

* Translated by Ruth Stanley

1

tion to points of similarity in a common history.

This book attempts to establish a basis for defining the position of the modern town by tracing its historical development in a number of countries. The research reports (Part I) are intended to provide a basic sketch of the development of research in the past few decades with respect to the most important aspects of the history of the modern town, and to show which methodological approaches have been at the forefront of the discussion, and which facilities have been available to urban-history researchers in different countries. These reports place special emphasis on those developments that may be regarded as characteristic of the process of urbanisation. The aim of the editors has been to enable researchers into urban history to profit from the approaches, central themes and methods applied by researchers in other countries. Furthermore, the aim has been to provide an approach to international co-operation in comparative research. The bibliographies in Part II provide access to scientific facilities. The English translations lower the initial language barrier, though knowledge of the relevant language remains a prerequisite for any serious study of the foreign literature and developments in other countries.

A survey of international urban history research is only possible for a limited number of countries and only significant if the comparison is restricted to a certain number of cases. Varying systematic criteria might be used for the purposes of selection: countries where the process of urbanisation is especially advanced; a comparative study of urbanisation under different political and economic systems (Western, capitalist; Eastern, communist; developing countries); a specific geographical area. We selected the principle of a geographical nexus for several reasons. Despite all the differences between the individual countries of Europe, this area shares certain cultural and historical similarities which not only explain these countries' interest in each other, but also provide bases for comparisons. At the same time, however, this area includes a broad spectrum of differing development processes, a spectrum running from the rapid and early industrialisation and urbanisation of countries such as England to the later industrialisation and slow process of urbanisation of the states of Southern and South-Eastern Europe. A further aim was to include some communist countries of Europe as examples of the socialist-planned economy type of urbanisation, or at least as examples of Marxist historiography, an aim only partially fulfilled. Inclusion of the United States of America, the largest and most important of the Western capitalist industrialised countries, one which has experienced an intensive process of urbanisation and one, moreover, where urbanisation research is especially advanced, seemed imperative. Finally, Japan was included as an example from a different culture, similarly characterised by a late, but also an especially intensive, process of industrialisation and urbanisation, and as a country connected in numerous ways with Europe and North America.

A bibliographical survey has been provided for each European country, giving this book the character of a systematic work of reference. The choice of countries represented by the research surveys in Part I resulted from the consideration that the separate regions of Europe should each be represented by at least one example: Great Britain for the British Isles, Spain for the Iberian Peninsula, Italy for Southern Europe, Czechoslovakia and Hungary for Eastern Europe, and Sweden for Scandinavia. The Western area of mainland Europe is comparatively strongly represented — by France, the Netherlands, the Federal Republic of Germany, Switzerland and Austria. The fact that this region forms a geographical area with numerous unifying relations, making it particularly suited to illustrating various developments, seemed to justify this choice. (The socialist-planned economy development and Marxist urban historiography were to have been more strongly represented, with additional research reports on the Soviet Union, Poland and the German Democratic Republic but these were not forthcoming.)

The long period of time elapsing between completion of some of the manuscripts (1985) and this book's going to press is a result of conditions familiar to all editors, particularly those who have worked with an international team of contributors.

The ambiguity inherent in the concept of "modern urban history research" is intentional. The subject of the research reports is modern urban history: roughly speaking, urban history in the period 1850–1950 or, in some cases, to the present. In European countries this means a demarcation from the town of the Middle Ages and the early modern period. Where the line was to be drawn in individual cases, whether it depended on political events, or on economic and social developments, was left to the individual contributors. The reports also deal with modern urban history in the sense that they emphasise newer questions and methods, whereby gaps in research and desiderata are also clearly pointed out. The development of research in recent decades is necessarily of central interest.

3

To give a certain unity and comparability of the entries and to make the book easier to use contributors were asked to concentrate on the following topics:

institutions and scientific facilities;
general presentations and research surveys (as well as the development of research in individual fields such as the concept of the town and the urban systems);
politics, the law and constitution;
population and social structure;
the development of architecture and town planning;
economy and transport;
culture and science;
the churches.

In addition, mention is to be made of the most important local studies.

So far as the research reports of Part I are concerned this scheme has necessarily been modified according to the circumstances and the research developments in each country; these modifications must be understood and accepted as a consequence of the tremendous variation in the significance of urban history and the extent to which it is organised in the respective countries. The bibliographies in Part II have, however, remained, as befits their character, as a reference work for comparative research. In order to avoid repetition of bibliographical details between the research report and the bibliography for one and the same country, footnotes have been avoided where possible in the research reports; bibliographical details of the literature referred to in these reports are to be found in Part II. The research report from France is an exception: the literature cited in this report is completely different from that in the bibliography. The numbers in the text refer, therefore, not to the bibliography in Part II but to the notes following the report itself. Japan also proves to be an exception: literature references are marked with two numbers. The first of these refers to the notes following the research report in the original Japanese version (in Japanese characters), the second to the bibliography in Part II.

B. Possibilities and Problems of the Comparative Approach

Urban history has two dimensions; that of how towns developed, and that of reflection and analysis. Though the subject of this book is the research process in individual countries, the nature and the intensity of the urban process must — or so one would expect — also be reflected in the extent to which the phenomenon is made the subject of scholarly research. In general, there is a relatively clear relation between the degree of urbanisation and urban history research: countries such as the United States and England, for example, with a marked urbanisation tendency, show a marked awareness of the problems of urbanisation at a relatively early stage, an awareness that is reflected in historical research. In countries such as Spain and Hungary, by contrast, where the process of urbanisation has been comparatively weaker and later, research has not yet developed so far. However, this relationship is not so direct as might appear at first sight: urban history research is extremely lively in Austria, although this country occupies at best a middle position so far as urbanisation is concerned.

The reports of this volume, taken as a whole, provide a general outline of the current state of urban history research in international comparison. This book can merely be an attempt to identify some of the most important principles of the development with references to individual countries having exemplary character only. Thus the findings presented in the national reports have, of necessity, been subjected to renewed generalisation. Needless to say the reader is master of his own system of control: reading the reports himself.

The character of urban history research is not only to be viewed as a reflection of the actual development of the process of urbanisation; clearly, it also depends significantly on the scientific development of the discipline in each country, not least on the discipline's openness and its receptivity towards other disciplines. The fact that in almost every country an intensive study of urbanisation did not occur until relatively late in the development process is a further argument against an all too straightforward relationship between the state of research and the degree of urbanisation.

Urban history is fed by very different traditions; and within each individual country, too, interest in urban history has always had specific motivations and been subject to modifications resulting, in part, from political developments, in part from processes within the discipline of history. Thus, in the case of Czechoslovakia, attention is drawn to the difference between the bourgeoisie's interest in the historiography of the 19th-century town, and Marxist historiography in the period after the Second World War. The report on the

Federal Republic of Germany examines more closely the development of various phases of urban history; in the case of Spain, a development of research approaches from positivism via functionalism to a Marxist-influenced approach is emphasised. And reference is made, finally, to the influence of the protest movement of 1968 on urban history research in France.

Most of the articles show clearly that interest in the history of the modern town and the process of urbanisation in individual countries has not proceeded from historical science, but that history has rather received decisive impulses from other disciplines dealing with problems of the town in a more immediate and topical way. This applies above all to the influence of geography, but also to town planning and architecture, law, more recently also to demography and sociology and, finally, to ethnography and cultural science. In contrast, economics has had little influence, except in cases such as that of the Federal Republic of Germany or in the context of Marxist approaches. It is worth noting that the influence of political science on urban history is not even mentioned.

Corresponding to variations in the development of urban history, the organisation of historical research also differs greatly from country to country. While two journals of urban history are published in the United States, no organisation for this field of study exists there. Great Britain possesses a scholarly organisation for urban history, the Urban History Group, as well as a scholarly journal. In Austria, points of concentration for the field of modern urban history exist in the "Arbeitskreis für Stadtgeschichtsforschung" and the "Ludwig-Boltzmann-Institut für Stadtgeschichtsforschung", although neither of these institutions is specialised in modern urban history. In the Federal Republic of Germany, there are a number of such institutions and above all, the "Institut für vergleichende Städtegeschichte" represents urban-history research, although here, too, interest has so far been concentrated more on the pre-industrial town. The "Deutsches Institut für Urbanistik" regularly publishes a journal on modern urban history, "Informationen zur modernen Stadtgeschichte", and another urban history review with the somewhat misleading title "Die alte Stadt" is also published there. Journals of urban history exist in a number of other countries such as Japan, the United States, Great Britain, Austria, France, Italy, and the Netherlands. The extent to which facilities such as town atlases, municipal records or published sources on urban history are available varies greatly from one country to another. France possesses a comprehensive manual for this field — the multi-volume *Histoire de la France urbaine*. In other countries — Switzerland and Spain, for example — such an infrastructure is largely lacking.

The problem of finding a precise definition for the concept of the town — especially for that of the 20th century — is a central problem of urban history research everywhere. In the Federal Republic of Germany, reference is made to the "hopeless ambiguity" of the concept. Similarly, British urban history research is criticised for having failed to clarify satisfactorily the historical significance of the phenomenon of the town. The individual contributors mention different criteria to define the concept which, not infrequently, compete with one another within an individual country: legal status, size (with differing limits), settlement forms. Thus, in Japan, for example, there has been a transition from the initial concept of the town, based on legal status, to a definition based on size, with the lower limit currently at 50,000 inhabitants. In the United States controversy on the character of the town has led to a pragmatic definition with the main fields of urban history research being defined and delineated.

The countries in this book reveal vastly different points of emphasis in individual areas of urban history research. The growth of the urban population, the central element of the urbanisation process and, at the same time, the one which can most easily be grasped, can count on lively interest in all the countries included here. But this is not true, to the same extent, of the causes and factors of growth such as, for example, migration.

In the United States, interest is concentrated on social history and, within this field, mainly on class structure. In Austria it is the lack of such studies which is stressed as a deficit of urban history research. Within research on social classes, special attention is generally given to the working class — not only in socialist countries. In social history, in particular, there is a divergence of interests that appear to be conditioned partly by individual countries' specific problems. Vertical mobility, racial discrimination, assimilation of immigrants and class formation are named as central themes of research in the United States; studies on individual town quarters are raised as a special characteristic of Swiss urban history; in Japan's case the need is stressed for studies of specific social groups — children, the handicapped, Koreans and those subject to discrimination. In many countries it appears that interest in the life,

7

world and mentality of the urban population has grown in recent years.

The development of the urban system, of inner-urban structures and of processes in the relations between towns and their surrounding areas, including the suburbs, have in nearly all countries been studied mainly by geographers; as geographers have developed a genetic approach analysing the long-term development of spatial structures, this is often still the case. Increasingly, though, urban historians have incorporated into their own research elements of geographical analysis to both questions and methods. The same applies — though by no means to the same extent — to questions of urban building and housing development in the context of the history of urban building and town planning, housing development and architecture. In general, these disciplines have only recently begun to develop an interest in the historical development of the modern town. Historians' interest in the structures of urban building and housing development is increasingly related to an interest in the economic conditions of building development and its social consequences.

The treatment of the economy, traffic and transport, and the urban infrastructure varies greatly from one country to another. In countries where research is based on Marxist methods of thought and explanation, the relationship between economic development and urban development is an essential element in the interpretation of historical development as a whole. To what extent this axiom has passed from a general deduction and been incorporated into empirical analyses — in studies of economic mechanisms such as land prices, for example, or analyses of the influence of economic interests on the process of urban development — is a different matter. The preference given to private initiative rather than public involvement in the United States could provide a starting point for fruitful comparisons with countries whose urban development has been more strongly determined by public decisions, whether at national or local government level.

There appears to be a particularly marked divergence of research interest in individual countries to the institutional conditions of urban development (law, politics and the administration). In the research reports on several countries — England, the Netherlands, Austria, Switzerland and Spain — it is pointed out that this is a barely developed area. In the United States' case, on the other hand, it is stated that for a long time historians' interest in the town related exclusively to its political history. In the Federal Republic of Germany, too, it can be said that local government development has been one of the central themes of modern urban history research. In this connection, the relationship between town and state is undoubtedly an important aspect, and one that is discussed in the report on Japan. Similarly, it plays a central role — also with respect to the development of urban history research — in the report on France.

In most countries, there has until now been very little research into urban culture and the cultural life of the town; this deficit is explicitly mentioned in the reports on Great Britain, Spain and Hungary. In the United States, however, greater interest has been taken in cultural history. The changed orientation there — away from a structural towards a more strongly cultural analysis of urban social history — probably corresponds to a wider trend evident in many countries. It coincides with the attention given to the history of everyday life and urban mentalities, mentioned above. Another expression of this is the development of "urban ethnology", described in the article on Japan. The "history of everyday life" which in recent years has found broader support in Europe, attracting the interest of many non-professional historians, also approaches the topic at this level, mainly in studying the experiences of the lower classes in the industrial and urban milieu. It appears that researchers with this approach are more interested in the class-based conditions of such experiences rather than their urban or non-urban character.

In numerous countries the history of the capital plays a central role in national urban history, even though it is generally recognised that the capital city is usually something of an exception within the urban system. This over-emphasis arises with a certain inevitability in the case of a centralistic organisation of the state, as in France. However, the same tendency is also emphasised in countries such as Austria and Czechoslovakia. It can result from a *de facto* preponderance of the capital in comparison with other towns and cities, or from a concentration of research and scientific institutions in the capital city.

In virtually all countries with a longer tradition of urban history, a peculiar dichotomy between older and newer urban history has developed. The tendency is that the older urban history appears more influenced by questions of political and cultural history, while an interest in social and economic history tends to predominate in the more recent urban history. Modern urban history research has

9

concentrated in most countries on the 19th-century town; only in a few cases, such as the Federal Republic of Germany, have researchers already begun to pay more attention to the 20th century. The report on Japan names the 1930s as the beginning of a period that, in general, is comparatively under-researched.

It can be seen from the research reports that urban development and the process of urbanisation have varied greatly from one country to another. The period when urbanisation took place, and the tempo at which this development proceeded, was as different from one country to the next as is the degree of urbanisation reached today. The important role of industrialisation in this process is shown clearly in many of the reports; however, it is also clear that industrialisation was not the sole cause of urbanisation. Thus, in Italy, modern urban history is not associated with industrialisation, a process which did not start until around the turn of the century. In the case of Switzerland, market functions are emphasised as a central factor in the urbanisation process, whereas industrialisation largely occurred in rural areas. In the Netherlands, too, industrialisation is seen to have had a minor significance for the urbanisation process.

C. The Function and Position of Modern Urban History

In almost all the reports there is reference to the fact that, despite its variety, urban history has not yet become an independent discipline in its own right within historical science, but in some countries there are indications that it is developing into such a discipline. This process seems most advanced in the United States, where urban history is an established part of the historian's university education. In Great Britain, the development of the discipline reached a certain conclusion with the founding of a chair of urban history; in this phase, however, the development was too closely associated with one individual, H. I. Dyos, although his legacy has now been taken up by a generation of younger historians.

The reasons for this state of affairs are undoubtedly to be seen partly in the fact that — as many contributors emphasise — modern urban history is a young discipline which has not yet developed its definitive form. It is certainly also the case that some of the scholarly works dealing with urban phenomena do not pursue an interest in urban history, nor do they take the town as their frame of reference;

instead, in the context of case studies, they merely view the town as a section of society as a whole. But essentially the causes lie deeper than this: they have to do with the difficulty of clearly defining the concept of the town, a difficulty arising from the wealth of aspects embodied in the concept, and to which reference has already been made. This problem is exacerbated by the fact that, as a result of the very process of urbanisation, the phenomenon of the town is less and less susceptible to an unambiguous demarcation from its surroundings. The "Randstad" in the Netherlands and the "Ruhrgebiet" in Germany are particularly drastic examples of urban sprawl. Discussions of such phenomena as urban conurbations, sub-urbanisation, counter-urbanisation, the crisis of the town and de-urbanisation, also raise for the historian the question of the possibilities of modern urban history, and to what extent its existence as a discipline is justified. Above all, for the urban historian the question arising from this is whether the town in the industrial age must already be viewed as a historical phenomenon, one belonging to an earlier phase of development that has already reached its conclusion and been superseded by a new phase — the role of the town in a post-industrial society. Until the contours of such a post-industrial society are more clearly discernible, it will hardly be possible to speak in a meaningful way about the role of the town in this society or about the significance of urban history research in clarifying this process.

For the time being, modern urban history sees itself challenged in a fruitful way, on the one hand, by practical politics and, on the other, by other disciplines concerned with the town. To this extent, the social and political problems of individual countries have also been reflected in urban history research: the conservation and preservation of monuments, planning, the reconstruction of town quarters, and the problems of the town and its surrounding areas have provided impulses for scientific discussions in numerous countries, and also led to historical analyses of such topics. If the immediate practical relevance of such studies is not always apparent at first sight, they nevertheless contribute in various ways to a heightened awareness of the problems, to the ability to recognise solutions and subject proposals to critical scrutiny. The example of the United States, where historians have discussed racial problems and immigration, or themes relating to women's history, shows how variously they can respond to topical subjects in an attempt to shed light on their longer-term causes and determinants. In this connection, urban history researchers in Japan have already dealt with the history of environmental pollution.

It is precisely the attempt to grasp the variety of urban phenomena, to investigate urban developments, including problematic issues, and to seek contact with neighbouring disciplines, that has led, beside the reasons already mentioned, to urban history's lack of clear contours as a sub-discipline. This problem is reflected in most of the reports — in, for example, complaints about the ramifications of urban history (Hungary), or about the lack of theory and method (Federal Republic of Germany, Japan, Switzerland). The failure of "New Urban History" in the United States, a concept that was advanced with far-reaching aspirations, shows very clearly that even in the most favourable circumstances, urban history will establish itself as an independent discipline only as a result of a longer-term process of development. For the time being, the variety of methodological approaches and questions resulting from intensive contact with neighbouring disciplines and from direct contact with practical problems has proved to be enlivening and enriching, not only for urban history, but for history in general.

Urban history in each country is confronted by the fundamental question of the path along which urban history research should go. Depending on the present state of development, the answers may differ greatly and mean many things: a deepening of the historical dimension in individual disciplines; the cooperation of individual disciplines concerned with the town; an extension of urban history research; an organisational and/or institutional association of efforts in the field of urban history; the founding of a sub-discipline of urban history.

Proceeding from the town as a phenomenon of decentralisation within a system, the answer will not be seen to lie in centralistic solutions; rather, it is hoped, that a pluralistic approach would lead to a favourable development of urban history research, as is being aimed for in the United States on the basis of experience. Taken as a whole, the reports show in which respects modern urban history in the individual countries could be improved:

— an improvement of scientific facilities (bibliographies, municipal records, town atlases, collections of source materials),
— a greater degree of institutionalisation, with national organisations specialised in urban history,
— an improvement in the possibilities of communication (urban history journals, the publication of series on urban history,

conferences),
— the development of research strategies and concepts (including financial support),
— more intensive relations with neighbouring disciplines,
— methodological receptiveness and greater reflexion of methodology,
— inclusion of additional dimensions of urban development that have scarcely drawn attention to date, such as urban culture,
— a stronger orientation towards the realities of urban development and the problems of the towns.

PART I

Research Reports

List of Authors

Editors
Christian Engeli, Research Scientist at the "Deutsches Institut für Urbanistik", Berlin (West).
Horst Matzerath, Research Scientist at the Archives of the City of Cologne and Lecturer at Duisburg University.

Austria
Renate Banik-Schweitzer, Research Scientist at the Archives of the City of Vienna.
Gerhard Meißl, Research Scientist at the Archives of the City of Vienna.

Czechoslovakia
Jan Havránek, Lecturer, Research Scientist at the Archives of Prague University.
Jiří Pešek, Research Scientist at the Archives of Prague University.

Federal Republic of Germany
Jürgen Reulecke, Professor of Modern History at Siegen University.

France
Francois Bédarida, Director of the "Institut d'Histoire du Temps Présent", Paris.

Great Britain
Anthony Sutcliffe, Professor at the Centre for Urban History, Leicester University.

Hungary
Sándor Gyimesi, Professor of History at the Karl-Marx-University, Budapest.

Italy
Alberto Caracciolo, Professor at the Institute of History, Rome University.

Japan
Ryuichi Narita, Associate Professor of Japanese History at Tokyo University.
Kinichi Ogura, Professor of Economic History at Tokyo University.
Akio Yoshie, Associate Professor of Japanese History at Tokyo University.

The Netherlands
Herman A. Diederiks, Lecturer of Social History at Leiden University.

Spain
Fernando de Téran, Professor of Urban Planning at the Polytechnic University, Madrid.

Sweden
Lars Nilson, Research Scientist at the Institute of History, Stockholm University.

Switzerland
Bruno Fritzsche, Professor of History at Zürich University.

United States of America
Kathleen N. Conzen, Professor of America Urban History at Chicago University.
Michael H. Ebner, Professor of American Social and Urban History at the Lake Forest College, Ill.

RENATE BANIK-SCHWEITZER AND GERHARD MEIßL

Austria*°

A.   Questions, Methods, Organisation

The recent bibliography listing literature published on Austrian
towns up to 1981(8) reveals that urban history research in Austria
focused on medieval and early modern towns until very recently.
Only about a third of the publications deal with urban development
in the 19th and 20th centuries. The last few years have witnessed
an increase in work concerned with modern times, however; and
the bibliographic appendices for 1982 and 1983 show that at least
half of the studies devoted to urban history relate to the
19th and 20th centuries. This gratifying development is impaired
only by the fact that, despite the rising tendency, not more than
one-fifth of these studies falls into the category of "modern" urban
history dealing, for example, with questions and methods of "new"
regional history rather than those of traditional areal studies.

This situation must be seen in conjunction with the way the study
of history was dominated by historicism, by a hermeneutic interest
in the actions of eminent personalities, in grand strategy and isolated events. Structural factors were studied chiefly in relation to
institutions in the context of constitutional and legal history. Austrian works on urban history were written in the tradition of historical areal studies, seldom reaching beyond a detailed and precise
description of individual phenomena to engage in an analysis of
structures and processes or to form types, as called for in this
country by O. Brunner. Critical debates on the issues, methods and
interpretive concepts of the modern social sciences took place later

---

* Translated by Ruth Stanley
° Numbers in brackets in this chapter refer to entries in the bibliography on pp.
243–62 of this volume.

in Austria than in the Federal Republic of Germany and other Western countries, and the accompanying theoretical discussions were far less intense. The aim of research in the social sciences, namely to structure social facts and developments from the most comprehensive theoretical constructs possible, using causal models and the like, had to be reconciled with the historian's claim to illuminate and interpret the unique attributes of historical events, social groups and individuals, and to show how their forms and actions were moulded by contemporary conditions, ideas and behaviour.

Thus, historians committed to this approach, if they were not to lapse into a sociological reductionism that could not do justice to historical reality, were confronted with modifying the concepts derived from the social sciences in the light of their historical material; they were compelled to use synchronic and diachronic comparisons to emphasise the nature of social facts as arising in a process of development, and to draw attention to "simultaneity of the non-simultaneous". Studies adopting this approach — research on economic development, on changes in social structure or living conditions, or on the process of political democratisation, etc. — are none too numerous in Austria, but have appeared more frequently since the mid-1970s. So such historians used the example of the town to expound their theories, and the studies are to be counted as modern urban history research in the broader sense. To the extent that these subjects have been approached by comprehending socio-economic change in the last 200 years explicitly as a process of urbanisation, or by analysing this change using concepts of regional history, viewing the urban phenomena under investigation in interdependence with macrosocial structures and processes, they are to be classified as modern urban history in the narrower sense.

Despite a certain element of scattering, the following focal research areas in modern urban history in Austria can be defined: social ecology, local government, demography (above all research on the long-term development of urban family structures), housing and, in recent times, urban lifestyles also. In recent years, a combination of new research approaches and methods have given rise to a few studies that largely satisfy the requirements of "new" regional history.

The bulk of socio-ecological studies on Austrian towns has not resulted from the research interests of historians, but of geographers. For a long time, economic and social geographers mainly examined towns in the context of their surroundings following W. Christaller's concept of central places. Then, encouraged by H. Bobek and, in particular, by E. Lichtenberger, interest turned in the 1960s to an analysis of intra-urban structures, and the concepts and methods developed by American social ecologists since the 1920s were applied to the situation in Austria. A series of dissertations on Austrian towns appeared dealing principally with the existing state of development, at best including the most recent past. They had the merit, however, that their standardised terminology and data categories, and their use of quantifying data, meant it was possible to compare different regional units in the same period of time. The disadvantage of modern social ecology — its lack of theory concerning social change — hindered the application of its methods in historical research for a long time and has still not been entirely overcome. Efforts to integrate methods of social ecology into a concept of social change are now concentrated on work being done on the Historical Atlas of Vienna.

To begin with, focus on local government evolved from a renewed interest in this subject in the 1960s and 1970s, when modern social problems — urban renewal, marginal groups, environmental problems — became manifest above all in the local sphere. Added to this local government, as practised in Vienna prior to the Second World War, was such that many people assumed that a more detailed study of it would prove worthwhile in offering an alternative to modern local government, which was going through a crisis. In-depth analyses of social welfare policies, especially housing policy, were published and, for the first time, their effects on the living conditions of the population were examined. The first two volumes (60) of a planned series on the modern history of Vienna appeared in 1985. These deal with local government in Vienna from 1740 to 1934 and pursue new research aims with fresh methods (analyses of budgets and election results, correlation between changes in social structure and local government).

The two research fields of family structure and housing owe their existence to an ambitious research project, or rather a special research activity of the Institute for Economic and Social History at Vienna University. In the framework of the so-called "family project", the development of family structures since the end of the 19th century in different urban and rural test areas was analysed quantitatively first of all using population census returns, conscription lists, parish registers, etc. In many publications, the results were studied in connection with the development of the organisation of production and the reproductive sphere, as indicated by quantitative data. In the latter study, points of contact were established with housing, which through studies on housing policy is also related to local government.

Studies on housing, largely conducted by the Institute at Vienna University, deal almost exclusively with Vienna — not only because of the location of the Institute, but also because Vienna, as the only old, large city in present-day Austria, is the most suitable for examining the long line of capitalist housing production and utilisation.

Proceeding from a systematic analysis, based on quantitative data of the economic factors affecting the production and distribution of housing, many more relevant new sub-disciplines have been systematically developed within the formulated theoretical framework. Thus, for example, the combined result of several studies has been an overall analysis of housing policy in Vienna from its beginnings in the late 19th century until the present. While the housing market has not yet been adequately studied, living conditions and alternative forms of housing have aroused greater interest. Most recently, housing has been analysed as an aspect of the urban lifestyle, as "history from below" from the perspective of the inhabitants. The necessary qualitative data have been gleaned from contemporary investigations and first-hand reports and also, where possible, from narrative interviews using the methods of oral history.

The most recent field of research, urban lifestyle, owes its development to an ever-growing interest in writing history afresh from the perspective of society. This interest has been encouraged not least by historians who have occupied themselves with the history of underprivileged groups such as workers and women; but it has also been encouraged by modern political grass-roots movements seeking historical information to help them in arguing their case and in finding their identity.

Since the largely quantitative methods of the new social history are barely suitable for a grasp of specific lifeworlds, most studies of urban lifestyles make use of qualitative methods, among them the analysis of contemporary investigations and reports, as mentioned above, of discourses that bring out modes of exercising power, and narrative interviews as used by oral history. Even if the representatives of oral history are still frequently accused of producing research results lacking in representativeness, and the "barefoot historians" of the "dig where you stand" school are accused of lacking professionalism, an overall grasp of their subject, and knowledge of structural relationships, these methods are, nevertheless, probably irreplaceable in research on the lifestyles of the silent majority of the population, on collective mentalities, etc.

Research into urban lifestyles is currently concentrated at the Institute for Economic and Social History at Vienna University, and also at the university's "Institut für Volkskunde", which has been applying the methods of oral history for some time. These two institutes have been co-operating in this area ever since a more sociological orientation in research activities asserted itself in the "Institut für Volkskunde". At about the same time, the Historical Institute of Salzburg University and two independent groups of researchers, one with ties to Graz University, the other connected with Vienna University, began working in this field. Research work is concentrated on the city of Vienna and on towns in industrial conurbations (Fohnsdorf and Eisenerz in Styria and Wiener Neustadt in Lower Austria).

There is no coherent form of organisation for research on modern urban history in Austria. Research activity is carried out by different institutions and groups; these influence research in varying degrees and in an uncoordinated fashion, less through a common commitment to long-term programmes than through traditional preferences for specific methods and fields of research.

Among the most important research institutions and groups are:
— the town and state archives,
— historical associations of towns and localities,
— the Commission for Economic, Social and Urban History of the Austrian Academy of Sciences,
— the Ludwig Boltzmann Institute for Urban History Research,
— institutes at universities and colleges of higher education,
— independent research groups working on projects financed by diverse institutions.

From the point of view of method, closer relations exist among the first four of these groups and institutions on the one hand, and between the latter two, on the other.

On the whole, the research activity of archives is oriented towards the care, ordering, documentation and presentation of their material. The main emphasis of research activity is on the Middle Ages, as the archives are generally especially rich in material for this period and the questions of researchers are frequently tailored to suit the material available. However, the systematic issues treated by modern urban history neither result from the archive material available, nor can they be dealt with using the material of a single institution.

The research activity of the Ludwig Boltzmann Institute for Urban History Research, with departments in Linz and Vienna, is influenced by a similar approach. The main function of the central office in Linz is a documentation covering all historical epochs of urban history sources, and the compilation of a bibliography on the history of Austrian towns (8). The branch in Vienna publishes the Austrian atlas of towns (*Städteatlas*) (19) on the model of the German one; this is chiefly a cartographic source book documenting the development of towns in Austria up to the beginning of industrialisation. Only the *Historical Atlas of Vienna* (14), also published by the Vienna branch of the Ludwig Boltzmann Institute, deviates from this approach. A thematic atlas with data interpretation in volumes of commentary and with its main emphasis on the 19th and 20th centuries, it relies on the questions and methods of modern urban history research.

The main function of the Austrian Working Group on Urban History Research ("Österreichischer Arbeitskreis für Stadtgeschichtsforschung"), founded before the Ludwig Boltzmann Institute for Urban History Research, lies in organising conferences on urban history and publishing their results. Through its personnel (to some extent identical with that of the Ludwig Boltzmann Institute), it is also closer to the medieval period than to research on modern urban history, and up until now it has organised only two conferences dealing with urban development in the 19th and 20th centuries (23/24). Historical associations of towns and localities also have close connections with archives; this is revealed not only in the composition of their directorates, but also in their research activities, which are, on the whole, oriented towards the questions dealt with by areal studies or local history and geography.

The main task performed by the Commission for Economic, Social and Urban History of the Austrian Academy of Sciences consists in editing and publishing the multi-volume Austrian *Städtebuch* (13) on the basis of a rigid scheme of compilation giving little room to more recent questions of urban history.

Modern urban history research is thus concentrated in the universities and there, revealingly, in institutes that have not been influenced by traditional areal studies and, consequently, have not found themselves in the same methodological cul-de-sac. From the areas of social geography, economic and social history, and ethnography have come the new, comprehensive questions that initiated modern urban history research. However, until now, such a main field of research has not been institutionalised at the universities. A large part of the innovative research is done in habilitations and dissertations. However, this does not guarantee continuous research activity with long-term planning and consistent quality.

The same applies to groups of independent researchers who are closely associated with the universities to the extent that their members are often graduates who can neither find permanent employment at the universities nor embark immediately after graduation upon a career and who, financed by public grants or by private foundations, frequently continue to work on topics with which they have already dealt while at university.

Outside the narrower area of historical institutions, research is also carried out by institutes that are concerned mainly with analyses of the present-day social system but are also interested in at least the medium-term historical development, such as the "Österreichische Institut für Wirtschaftsforschung", the "Institut für Höhere Studien", the "Kommunalwissenschaftliche Dokumentationszentrum", the "Institut für Stadtforschung", the "Österreichische Institut für Raumplanung" and others. Although these institutes often fail to provide a wealth of detail, they nevertheless frequently offer methodological approaches and suggestions of interest to modern historical science. However, as they are interested in topical problems, continuous historical research can not be expected of them.

Modern urban history research in Austria has made obvious progress; however, not least because of its institutional fragmentation, it has not yet become firmly established as a field of study in its own right within modern history. The institutionalisation of the subject, and a new concept of urban history's role as part of "new" regional history in E. Hanisch's (21) sense, could bring modern urban history research closer to this goal.

B. The Development of Individual Fields of Research

(a) *The Concept of the Town and Types of Town*

Scarcely any work has been done directly on "the concept of the town", "municipal law" and "urban system" in the 19th and 20th centuries, although studies on other topics have dealt with these in passing. A comparative study of Berlin, Vienna and Budapest in the 19th century, by R. Banik-Schweitzer and G. Meißl (82), is a contribution to the topic of "town types". In a comparison of statistical data on employment structure and industry, this study has shown that all three cities, despite considerable differences in size and the fact that their development was not simultaneous, are to be counted as industrial metropolises.

(b) *Politics, Law and Constitution*

Hardly any studies are available on questions relating to the municipal constitution in the 19th and 20th centuries, probably because such questions have lost much of their importance in comparison with the medieval period. W. H. Hubbard's (30) study on the development of the municipal constitution of Graz from 1869 to 1918 is an exception. In comprehensive and complex new studies on local government, such as that in the new political history of Vienna from 1740 to 1934, by M. Seliger and K. Ucakar (60), the development of the town constitution is always dealt with at length.

There are also few specialised studies on the relationship between town and state, but one exception is a study on the relationship between local government and the constitutional state in Vienna during the liberal epoch. For the rest, state and local politics are usually still studied separately. However, some analyses of local government are already seeking to bring out its dependence on, or opposition to, state politics. The new political history of Vienna mentioned above is explicit in setting itself this goal in its detailed analysis of the changing relationship between the commune and the state as a whole. By contrast, there is far more literature in the field of municipal administration (functions, organisation, finance, poor law, welfare and public relief). Nevertheless, the state of research in some central areas is unsatisfactory. There exists a short history of municipal administration (26) dealing mainly with Vienna, and a few studies on various periods of local government characterised in each case by the domination of a different political party. But, up to now, there have been no systematic analyses of the long-term development of municipal administration. The new political history of Vienna, already mentioned, is the first work to contribute to filling this gap.

The topic of local government finance has also been studied very little. Apart from a dissertation published many years ago on the budgetary and financial policies of Graz since the Second World War, there is only one short study on the budget of Vienna in the liberal era (65). Again, the only detailed and long-term budget analysis of an Austrian town is to be found in the new political history of Vienna by M. Seliger and K. Ucakar (60), where it forms one of the central categories of analysis.

Among the various fields of local government activity, "housing" and "welfare" have aroused the most interest. The latter has been dealt with in a series of dissertations at Vienna University, but these have not been included in the bibliography. The information gained in such studies has been included in some publications surveying this topic. There is hardly any literature on other areas of local government activity.

Local government politics — politicians, political parties, associations — is the best worked field from a quantitative point of view; so far as quality is concerned, it leaves much to be desired. Complex studies dealing with wider regions are, in general, to be valued more highly than the more detailed, specialised studies of local areas. Still unmatched in some sections is the multi-volume work, by C. A. Gulik (44), on Austria's road to fascism, published shortly after the Second World War. He chiefly examines the policies of Austrian Social Democracy, which concentrated heavily on Vienna, and an entire volume of this work is dedicated to local government in Vienna in the interwar years. A. Rabinbach (55) has recently published a study, based on his dissertation (published in 1973), of the crisis-ridden development of the Social Democratic Party until the Civil War in 1934; in this context he also deals with local government politics in Vienna.

Recently, M. Seliger has given much attention to municipal politics in Vienna; together with K. Ucakar, he published in 1985 the two-volume political history of Vienna 1740–1934, mentioned above (60). As preliminary studies for this work, Seliger had already published a study on the liberal parties within the local council ("Gemeinderat") of Vienna from 1861 to 1895 (65), a comprehensive study of the Social Democratic Party in local government in the prewar and interwar years (published in part) (58), the history of Vienna's separation from Lower Austria in 1922 and, together with K. Ucakar, in the context of the *Historical Atlas of Vienna*, the first detailed quantitative analysis of elections in Vienna from 1848 to 1932, including the development of electoral law and the socio-economic structure of the electorate (59).

In general, it may be said of research into the history of political parties that there has been more on the labour movement and labour parties, particularly the Social Democratic Party, than on the bourgeois parties. Here too, however, there is a preponderance of studies on the state as a whole (47/51/55). Nevertheless, as Vienna was the centre of the Austrian labour movement, and as local government in the capital was the main field of activity for the Social Democrats in the interwar years, state and local politics are largely identical in this period.

The same applies to a study on the origins of the Christian Social Party (50), which in this period was, above all, a "Viennese" party. For the same reason, the first studies (by J. W. Boyer) on changes in the bourgeoisie's electoral behaviour in connection with the development of the Christian Social Party, concentrate on Vienna (38/39). Although works have been published on the Christian labour movement (54), and a short essay on the Christian Social Party in the interwar years (61) also exists, there is no comprehensive systematic history of this party in the period under discussion. Studies on the liberal and German National parties, on which there are as yet only a few works on individual aspects (49/65), would also be desirable. Recently, G. Botz has worked on various aspects of National Socialist policy relevant to the field of local government (35).

The most recent studies on party history reveal an increasing trend towards regionalisation and the inclusion of socio-economic criteria (37). However, studies limited to individual towns are still rare. Important preliminary work for a more complex history of local politics and political parties has been done in studies on the personnel structures of local councils and the so-called "Bürgermeisterbücher" (mayors' records). The persons comprising the local council of Vienna from 1860 to 1895 have been studied in a series of dissertations (45/46/53); two analogous works on the local council of Linz from 1880 to 1934 deal with consecutive periods (63/64). Mayors' records also exist for these two cities (40/43).

Monographs on the associations, clubs and other groupings

closely connected with various parties are also comparatively numerous but are largely written from the standpoint of institutional history. Again, it is the associations with ties to the Social Democratic Party that have been more thoroughly researched. Here the gamut runs from the "Republikanischer Schutzbund" and the trade union and cooperative movements (57/198/199), through the Social Democratic youth movement and the student (68) and protest (37) movements to the "Arbeitersportverein" (56). On the bourgeois side, there is a dissertation on associations in Vienna in the Pre-March period (1815–1848), a study of some liberal associations and one — a contribution to the early history of the Christian Social Party — on Viennese Catholic associations.

(c) Population and Social Structure

The achievement of the older works on this subject, largely deriving from traditional areal studies, rested chiefly on an exact description of regional conditions. The credit for having developed an interest, over and above this, in an analytical approach, in structures, processes, comparisons and the formation of types, must go in Austria above all to Otto Brunner. Quantitative studies able to build on a tradition of working with statistical material already developed under the Monarchy, also rarely exceeded the limits of description, in this case using numerical examples. Quantitative social geography does not lack theoretical concepts or a well-developed set of analytical tools, but it does lack a grasp of specific historical facts and thus of the modifications necessary to its explanatory scheme if it is to be used in historical analysis. Beginning in the early 1970s, however, economic and social history has increasingly adopted the methods of modern social science, and this has led to some impressive results, especially in studies on the population and social structure of towns using (computer) analyses of mass data — the published results of the official statistics, conscription lists, parish registers, etc. The first survey of work so produced in interdisciplinary cooperation with sociologists, statisticians and social geographers, has been provided by H. Helczmanovski (75).

A systematic summary of population growth in Austrian cities has not yet been written. Only a few studies exist on the development in some towns, or in towns in the context of larger regional units. The course of population growth in Vienna since the end of the 18th century, differentiated according to suburbs and boroughs, has been documented by F. Baltzarek (69). Interesting for its method is a contribution by R. Gisser which determines the regional differentiation in population growth by calculating the concentration of population in the Austrian provinces (74); indirectly, this provides evidence for the increase in urbanisation in the second half of the 19th century.

There are not a great many urban history studies on demographic development in the narrower sense. However, mention should be made of a data collection, still in manuscript form, on Vienna from the 18th century until the interwar years (72), on the presentation of the geographical distribution of demographic characteristics in the *Historical Atlas of Vienna* (14), and of a few studies of population movement. Studies on historical demography and family research, which have been carried out in Austria since around the early 1970s, have proved particularly fruitful for urban history research. They combine the aspiration of analysing demographic data systematically in the context of overall socio-economic change with the development of new types of (mass) sources, the application of new (often computer-based) quantitative methods and the adoption or modification of social science theories. The results of the relevant studies, of which there are already a large number, do not always correspond. Thus, a new analysis of the raw data of the 1857 population census in Graz has led to an emphasis on the significance of demographic factors as a cause of change in household structures (76). While historians at the Institute for Economic and Social History of Vienna University, where — in a long-term project on comparative research into historical family structures — Vienna is the main object of study along with other Austrian towns, see the development of new forms of organisation of production as the decisive factor influencing changes in family structures, and, in particular, giving rise to the development of the working-class family (70/71/78/80).

The phenomenon of regional mobility has until now seldom been dealt with. More frequently it has arisen in the context of the above-mentioned research on family history or in studies on the problems, so acute in Austria, of nationalities and minorities (103/107). At any rate, we can deduce from conscription lists from Vienna in the Pre-March period (67) that in the manufacturing age, when there was a big demand for skilled textile workers on the Viennese labour market, immigration from Southern Germany and Italy was more significant than in the second half of the 19th century, when the capital mainly attracted poorly qualified migrants from the Sudeten. Material on the development of religious structure is mainly to be found in studies on the condition of the Jewish minority (88/89/108/131).

Questions relating to occupational structure and the changes it has experienced have only recently been systematically studied. On the basis of the population censuses from 1869 to 1960, the shift in favour of the tertiary sector has been brought out in more detail in the case of Vienna and a few other larger Austrian towns (98/123). The *Historical Atlas of Vienna* (14), and a differentiated comparison of Vienna, Berlin and Budapest, have provided an analysis of changes in occupational structure also dealing with the secondary sector in connection with the rise of industrial forms of production. It has been shown that Vienna's development up to the First World War was similar to that of the industrial metropolis Berlin, even if less dynamic (212).

Compared with research on medieval and early modern towns, research on the social and income structure of towns since the industrialisation has not yet progressed very far (87). There are virtually no analyses of the process of social mobility. Better researched is the condition of individual strata such as the higher nobility (134), the lower classes (105), and craftsmen (242). Interest in the genesis and development of industrial society since the early 19th century, an interest which has grown in recent years, has undoubtedly led to special attention being paid to the stratum most immediately affected by these vast changes, the urban proletariat. Here too, a critical examination of the social sciences led to the formulation of more precise questions, concepts and methods, and so to better-founded information — for example, with respect to changes in forms of work in the specific conditions of economic development found in the towns (95/104/117/120/121), or the development of the labour movement from its roots among craftsmen and liberals to an organisation of skilled industrial workers and intellectuals (94/96/106/133).

The growth of social history prompted a change of emphasis towards previously rather neglected questions such as collective phenomena, life conditions and behavioural forms of broad segments of the population, and this has led, in the most recent past, to an increased interest in the history of everyday life. Concentrating mainly on the reproductive sphere, an attempt is being made to grasp the experiences, mentalities and forms of expression of mainly underprivileged and, according to traditional research criteria, "inarticulate" social groups, of whom, until now, historians have barely taken note. Now, with the help of new topics such as forms of nutrition, leisure activities, holidays, etc., their experience is to be grasped and, through the analysis of new types of sources — worker (auto)biographies, (pictorial) documents, utensils, etc. — and through the use of oral history, those involved are to find expression as historical actors. Among the studies relevant to urban history, which have increased especially in recent years, only a few will be mentioned here as examples: studies on consumer behaviour (130), an analysis of the reading matter of domestic servants (137), and numerous studies of working-class culture in the field of tension between middle-class standards and the opposing world of the proletariat (92/116/119).

(d)   Architectural Development

Apart from a publication on the Viennese garden city movement (150), there are no monographs of town planning concepts. To the extent that this topic is dealt with at all, it occurs in biographies of architects and town planners (for example, on C. Sitte and O. Wagner, etc.).

Art historical studies dominate in the field of urban architecture. Since R. Wagner-Rieger's (156) rehabilitation of historicism, studies of Vienna have concentrated on the 19th and 20th centuries. Thus, extensive tribute has been paid to the architectural achievements of historicism in a multi-volume work on the Vienna "Ringstraße" (157).

The shift of research interest to a different period also encouraged art historical studies of a new type; these went beyond the analysis of façade styles to a study of interior and exterior forms, and the function of individual buildings or ensembles in the social context in which they developed. Among such studies are the work by M. Reissberger (203) on the "Ringstraßenpalais" designed by the architect T. Hansen, a study on the development of worker housing by P. Haiko (143) and, by both the above-named authors, a study of the "superblocks" of Red Vienna (144). However, the majority of works on town architecture have a more documentary character. Among them is a three-volume work on Austrian architecture in the 20th century by F. Achleitner (140), which includes not only the buildings of this period but also earlier buildings of cultural significance. The volumes of the Austrian "Kunsttopographie" are also to be counted among such works, as are those by H. Koepf documenting aesthetically important buildings to provide a basis for preservation measures (147).

Art and cultural historians are also beginning to take note of industrial architecture. Beside a work on utility buildings in Vienna (158), there exists a study on industrial monuments in Graz (152) and the first volume (including Vienna) of a two-volume work on industrial monuments in Austria (159). The first attempt to go beyond a documentation of buildings is offered by H. Sterk's two-volume work on industrial culture in Austria (154), which also deals with many urban industrial buildings. In addition, there are many studies dealing with the development of urban architecture in individual buildings or ensembles. As an example, the monograph series on public buildings, streets and squares in Vienna, edited by P. Pötschner (149), may be mentioned.

The history of town planning is chiefly dealt with in studies by scholars connected with the institutes for town planning at the Technical Universities of Vienna and Graz as well as at the "Akademie der Bildenden Künste" in Vienna. They mostly concentrate on describing the contents of individual projects and the history of their development and realisation. Not until recently have historians started to analyse planning as a political process, e.g. in works by M. Seliger and K. Ucakar (60), or by L. Redl and H. Wösendorfer (151). A similar understanding of planning is revealed in the approach adopted in some dissertations on this subject (148/150).

There are numerous studies on the development of housing estates, which are mostly written from the standpoint of settlement geographers. Of these studies, only a selection could be included in the bibliography. They mostly analyse a cross-section of economic, construction and social data taken from the recent past with the aim of constructing a sociogeographic type for the towns studied. Today's structure is seldom grasped as the result of development processes. Among the works of this kind, one of the best is H. Bobek's and E. Lichtenberger's study of the architectural and spatial development of Vienna since the mid-19th century (164).

With his study of settlement forms, A. Klaar represents his own school of research, assigning certain settlement forms to various epochs of development. The maps he has devised showing the ages of buildings in Austrian towns (18) provide the necessary empirical basis for this. Some technical dissertations give more attention to settlement genetics; in so doing, however, they neglect social and political aspects (178/183).

Besides these works there are numerous monographs on individual towns; these are mainly descriptive histories of events. Exceptions to this are two recently published works on Fohnsdorf (176) and Eisenerz (173), two mining towns in the crisis-ridden industrial area of Upper Styria. In these works, urban history was, for the first time, written as a different form of the history of control, as the history of the subjection of the local population to company strategies and an ever more rationalised enterprise organisation that even intrudes into the reproductive sphere.

Among numerous individual aspects, the topic of land prices must be highlighted. It has been dealt with in a study of the Viennese Old City by E. Lichtenberger (177) as well as in a more theoretical work by P. Feldbauer (188), who analyses land prices as determinants of urban development. The empirical material for both these works was derived from the same contemporary investigation carried out in Vienna in the second half of the 19th century.

Two main approaches can be distinguished in studies on town districts; the first includes works in social geography, mostly dissertations, which deal with the inner differentiation in towns and make frequent use of the techniques of analysis developed by American social ecologists (161/170/177). The majority of these works are cross-section analyses. A synthesis of cross-section and longitudinal-section analyses is offered in a work on the sociogeographic structure of Vienna from 1869 to 1934 by R. Banik-Schweitzer (162), and by a comparative study of Berlin, Vienna and Budapest by the same author (23).

The second approach follows more the tradition of local history and geography. Thus, for example, suburbs of Vienna have been studied in a series of dissertations (165). It did not prove possible to maintain a uniform plan for this research, however. New methodological impulses may be expected from the school of history of everyday life and from the "new" regional history. Information on urban infrastructure has previously been provided mainly by technical monographs, frequently published on the occasion of anniversaries. As a sub-discipline of local government, infrastructure is dealt with in two works mentioned above, by R. Banik-Schweitzer (65), and by M. Seliger and K. Ucakar (60).

Studies on the development of town planning have, in the past decade, mostly concentrated on housing policy. The greater part of them deal with Vienna; only recently have larger studies on other Austrian towns and regions been published (195). So far as Vienna is concerned, the topic of housing policy has been dealt with for all periods. From studies on the beginnings of housing reform in the liberal era, the scope extends through housing policy from 1892 to 1914, housing policy in Red Vienna (58/186) (and the suppressed alternative of a social economy) (198/199), and housing policy in Vienna under the National Socialists (187) and up to the housing policy of the Social Democrats from 1945 to 1975 (204).

The production of housing and the housing market in the first half of the 19th century have been touched on in a study of mass housing in Pre-March Vienna (1815–48) (69); various publications (188) deal at length with this theme for the second half of the 19th century, and a dissertation treats it in the period from 1919 to 1934 (185).

Studies on the agents of housing construction are also comparatively numerous. Council housing in Vienna in the interwar years has attracted the most attention (191/194), and cooperative building has also received attention (184/189/192/198). The old problem of "high versus low building" has been studied in detail from the point of view of the political expectations associated with building types and the actual possibilities of different living forms. Against a positive evaluation of the superblocks of Red Vienna, recent criticism has pointed to the socially conservative concept behind the "red fortresses" (80/116). The political and cultural ambivalence of this housing concept had been recognised much earlier because all political tendencies had claimed it as their own. Various exemplary cases have been used to investigate anarchist tendencies, cooperative and social economy concepts (189/198/199), and conservative and fascistic models (184/202).

Studies also exist on types of houses and flats. True, art historical studies predominate so far as bourgeois living accommodation is concerned, while typological studies on worker housing predominate (208). Nevertheless, house and flat types have recently been examined increasingly from the viewpoint of housing culture (190/200). Here, there is a fluid transition to studies on living conditions. Interest in this subject in Austria has, until now, largely concentrated on the proletariat (80/193/197), and middle-class living conditions have hardly been studied (206).

(e) Industry and Transport

Two main methodological approaches have been adopted in dealing with problems of industry location. The first is represented by economic geographers, whose method builds on W. Christaller's theory of central places. A large number of dissertations in economic geography exist, studying various regions with this descriptive-typifying method. More progressive new studies, such as those by H. Bobek and M. Fesl (214), or by H. Bobek and J. Steinbach (215), have abandoned typification on the basis of prescribed categories in favour of measuring relations (e.g., interconnections of labour markets) with which, in particular, the catchment areas of towns or urban regions can be demarcated. However, the necessary data are mostly not available for such investigations into earlier periods.

The second approach is represented by regional economics; starting from the siting theories of J.H.v. Thünen and A. Weber, it deals with problems of siting from the viewpoint of business and national economics. Thus, two studies analysing the regional distribution of GNP were able to establish the higher level of productivity in towns as against rural areas (225/226), and a study of Bohemia's industrial development in the 19th century was able to show that location of industry is dependent in Thünen's sense on the extension of the transport system (236).

Common to the majority of the works mentioned is that they provide cross-sectional analysis, but do not study processes. Not until recently have attempts been made to study location of industry from the view of the geographical requirements of the production process (232); for this, use has also been made of newer hypotheses of the debate on imperialism (211).

For a long time it was second-generation émigré Austrians (N. Gross, P. Bairoch, R. Rudolph, H. Freudenberger, J. Komlos, etc.) who wrote the economic history of Austria in accordance with new methodological requirements. For about the past few years, Austrian studies have also been published by K. Rothschild (241), H. Matis (231) and others, that fulfil these requirements. However, there are still no good-quality surveys of the economic development of individual towns. The new economic history of Vienna by G. Chaloupek and M. Wagner (218) is a first step towards closing this gap. There are, however, already some works which use more advanced methods and which deal with sub-disciplines of the economic development of individual towns. The questions, which have so far aroused most interest, are the development of urban industry and the fate of craftsmen under the increasing domination of the industrial system (97/120/242). R. Banik-Schweitzer and G. Meißl's (212) study of the industrial development of Vienna, statistically the best-founded work, was able to show that Vienna, like Berlin and Budapest, is to be counted among the category of the industrial metropolis, and that shortly before the First World War it was the most dynamic industrial region in the Austrian half of the Empire.

On the basis of long-term estimates of GNP for the Austrian half of the Empire, R. Sandgruber attempts to calculate its distribution in the crown lands (244). This study also provides evidence of the particularly dynamic growth of the Viennese region shortly before the First World War. The same author also calculates an index of retail prices in Vienna from 1800 to 1914 (237), as well as further economic indicators for the capital (243).

More numerous than studies of the economic development of individual towns, are works on the regional or urban development of individual industries, or company histories. Among the latter, E. März's history of the "Creditanstalt" (229) particularly deserves special mention because its analysis of national economic policy goes far beyond the normal in such studies.

The first comprehensive analysis of economic policy at the local government level is to be found in the earlier-mentioned economic history of Vienna by G. Chaloupek and M. Wagner (218). Individual aspects of this subject are dealt with in the work by M. Seliger and K. Ucakar (60); local infrastructure policies are treated in a study by R. Banik-Schweitzer (65).

At present, the only monographs existing on local enterprises are purely descriptive; they do not rise above the level of commemorative publications and for this reason have not been included in the bibliography. Surveys such as the political history of Vienna by Seliger and Ucakar (60), or Chaloupek and Wagner's (218) economic history of Vienna do, however, deal with local enterprises in the more general context of the local economic system.

There is a wide, largely technically-oriented fund of literature on means of transport, but this has not been included in the bibliography. By contrast, historical analyses of the transport system are few. A few studies deal with the development of the Viennese transport system (252/254/255); there is an essay dealing with, among other things, transport policy in Vienna from 1870 to 1895

(65), and a few studies on the effect of transport systems in influencing the location of industry (212/236/244). There are some recent studies analysing tourism in towns in the well-known tourism regions of Western Austria (253); by contrast, there are still no studies on the development of urban tourism in the 19th century.

(f) Culture and Science and Churches

Since Austria's identity is still largely defined with reference to the cultural achievements of the past, works on cultural history are far more numerous than works on the history of science. Symptomatic of this is the title of one of the works listed here: "Warum war es in Österreich um die Naturwissenschaften so schlecht bestellt?" (Why were the natural sciences in Austria in such a bad way?) (261). The answer given is that promotion of science did not serve to enhance the domination of the true wielders of power in the state, the feudal forces, and therefore did not occur. Since the aristocracy influenced politics in Austria far more even than in Germany, efforts were not made to secure domination through achieving economic pre-eminence, which would have presupposed scientific research, but rather through maintaining privileges. This end was served by affirmative cultural achievements — music, visual arts, theatre — as long as these were not intellectual and so might have questioned the system of domination. While it is true that Austria did not lack modern industry, it was this very industry (e.g. the electrical industry) that was largely under foreign ownership; and basic research was carried out where the companies had their headquarters. Nor was there any lack of scientific talent, which was best able to develop in the sphere of medicine and which, in its traditional form as the technique of physical health, was useful to the state (the army) and was least hindered by society. But the history of natural sciences, philosophy and also the social sciences at Austrian universities, was one of destruction and suppression, both under the monarchy and in the First Republic, in which, unofficially but not ineffectively, the same forces were at work as before 1918.

The interest of American authors has been aroused by the irrationality of political and cultural life in Austria, encouraged by the persistence of feudal domination; these authors have recently dealt with Austrian cultural history, usually equated with Viennese cultural history. Works by W. J. McGrath (275) and C. E. Schorske (284) point to the connections between late romantic art and irrationalist populist politics in the form of antisemitism, on the part both of the German Nationals ("Schönerer") and the Christian Socialists ("Lueger"), and also in the form of Zionism ("Herzl"). These works see the development of such politics fostered by the absence of a strong liberal higher bourgeoisie oriented towards humanist enlightenment and scientific thought. Another work, by A. Janik and S. Toulmin (269), also refers to these connections; it interprets the "Vienna Circle's" orientation towards logical positivism and linguistic philosophy as a result of the introversion in which the bourgeoisie, largely lacking political power, took refuge.

A fairly broad spectrum of the history of Austrian thought is covered in the work by W. M. Johnston (271). He fails, however, to treat social structures in relation to their economic basis, and this leads to some errors of judgement. Such mistakes are avoided in the works of the two Austrians, E. Winter (290/292) and A. Fuchs (264), whose works are less broadly conceived.

Foreign authors have been heavily involved in the writing of Viennese cultural history, with the result that their specific interest in Vienna — the outstanding achievements of high culture in the *fin de siècle* — has also strongly influenced the approach of Austrian research into cultural history. Thus, the major exhibition "Dream and Reality — Vienna 1870–1930" presents the city mainly as a cultural achievement of the bourgeoisie, largely neglecting the social and economic basis. The exhibition catalogue (287), which deals with more individual aspects of urban reality than are shown in the exhibition, can not dispel this impression, since here, too, the achievements of high culture are greatly over-represented.

Besides the historical writing that concentrates on an analysis of the bourgeoisie's high culture and its social determinants, another approach has long been followed — researching the culture of the lower strata. At first this was largely in the form of the history of institutions. Thus, for example, there are some works on organisations for worker education and schooling (258/273/286/289). Only recently has working-class culture outside such institutions been studied. A starting-point was provided by the works mentioned above (116/198/199/200) in which again and again references to the discrepancies between the aims and strategies of the labour movement or of labour parties, and the reality of proletarian life, are to be found. A large exhibition on proletarian culture in the interwar period, held in 1981, contributed a great deal towards establishing this field of research (119). For the time being, the cultural history of the bourgeoisie has nothing similar to offer. The history of bourgeois — and aristocratic — culture of everyday life has not yet been written. This may have something to do with the fact that the contribution of Jewish culture — at least to the cultural life of Vienna — has up to now been a taboo subject. However, there are indications that here, too, progress is being made. The most recent research approach follows the Swedish "dig where you stand" concept (91), the aim of which is that those who were formerly the objects of historical research find their own history and thus themselves.

C. Summary

This short survey has shown that modern research on urban history in Austria has managed to catch up with the international state of development in some areas, but that there are still large gaps in research, if only with respect to methods. This is partly because a country the size of Austria does not have the personnel or the necessary material resources to work with equal intensity on all the sub-disciplines of the subject. It is also because modern urban history research had to overcome considerable resistance on the part of traditional areal studies — a conflict which is by no means over.

Among the relatively well-researched fields are to be counted, as mentioned in the introduction, local government, family research, history of labour, social ecology, housing, and — to the extent that one can already say this of a relatively new field — the history of everyday life of the lower classes. The most serious gap in research, because it has the gravest consequences, is probably to be seen in the field of class and strata analysis and of social mobility. The persistent use of incorrect or at least unclear concepts detracts from the validity of all works in social and cultural history that rely on such concepts. Most other gaps in research appear, in contrast, to be less dubious structurally.

A further weakness of modern urban history research in Austria is its striking concentration on Vienna. This is to be explained both by the concentration of research institutes there and by the importance of the capital, both as a paradigm and as a centre of research. But Vienna only embodies one type of town; all the others have, up to now, been ignored. The two monographs on Fohnsdorf and Eisenerz, however, herald a change in the spread of research among types and regions.

Interest in the region as a field of research, which has grown in the past few years, can be of great use to the future development of urban history research. But care must be taken that the precise working-out of local economic structures, living conditions, political relations, etc., do not degenerate into a self-obsessed love of detail. Rather, it must be systematically related to the development of neighbouring towns, the social system in its entirety, and to comparable towns. It is after all the task of history, not only to bring out that which is unique, but also, placing it in the specific historical context determining it, to use comprehensive structures and processes to analyse and explain the unique.

JAN HAVRÁNEK AND JIŘI PEŠEK

Czechoslovakia*

A. Early Research

The study of urban history has a long tradition in Czechoslovakia. Beginning in 1861, when the Czech bourgeoisie was victorious in the city council elections in Prague and elsewhere in central Bohemia, Czech historians could rely on the support of these town councils when studying their history. Of course, decades passed before histories of these towns were written. In this respect, Prague held the central position. V. V. Tomek, the first Czech professor of history at Charles University, wrote a traditional and detailed history of Prague up to the year 1609 in 12 volumes (186). Similar descriptive town histories of many Bohemian and Moravian towns were published between 1890 and 1950. Undoubtedly the most thorough of these, which deals with social as well as political developments, is the history of Pelhřimov in five volumes by J. Dobiáš (175). This work, however, deals with events only up to 1648. The period of the Counter Reformation was not very popular among Czech historians, and the Bohemian German historians also paid it little attention.

The history of the modern town — as opposed to the history of the old town — was, until the Second World War, mainly beyond the field of interest of historians. During the interwar period, a few serious preparatory works were written, for example a history of the Prague city government from 1848 by M. V. Kratochvíl (50), who later became a famous writer of historical novels. Not historians, but specialists in art history, architecture, urban studies and geography dealt with modern urban history, especially the history of Prague,

* Numbers in brackets in this chapter refer to entries in the bibliography on pp. 277–292 of this volume.

during the 19th and 20th centuries. Among the books by art historians, special mention must be made of those of Z. Wirth (23). They contain pictures documenting the development of Prague architecture in the 19th century. A unique source documenting the life of Prague during the last 200 years are six books (one volume for each of the old quarters), published under the title *Zmizelá Praha* between 1945 and 1948 (187). They contain pictures (mostly photographs and descriptions) of streets and buildings destroyed in the last two centuries including those destroyed during the Second World War; war damage in Prague, however, was not great.

Among the geographical works on Prague published in the 1940s are two dealing with the geography of Prague in a broader context, including the historical perspective. Their authors were the German geographer O. Lehovec (183) and the Czech geographer J. Král (181). A study of social history and much information will be found in the portraits of 18th century Prague society and its lifestyle by A. Novotný (149–151). The 1820s and 1830s are dealt with in the work of N. Melniková-Papousková (146) as well as in Z. Nejedlý's biography of Smetana (148) that describes life in Prague in 1839 and 1840.

Whereas in these books, urban history is studied as a part of general Czech cultural history, for the specialists in urban studies it has another meaning: they study it as the factor that has shaped the living conditions of the contemporary inhabitants of the towns. With this aspect in mind, the architect P. Janák wrote a book about the development, over a period of 100 years, of tenement housing in Prague (83); K. Teige and J. Kroha wrote analytical studies of the changing style of dwellings, looking more towards future developments (104).

This short survey of the main trends in previous research on urban history shows what traditions could be drawn on in the work of the last 30 years. Some of the above-mentioned scholars (Nejedlý, Teige, Kroha) were strongly influenced by Marxist concepts of history and this is one reason why their work has found so many followers among historians and urban planners since the 1950s, when historical research began to concentrate on the modern town, industry and workers.

B.   Recent History Research

(a)   Centres of Urban History Research

During the last 30 years, town history in the Czech provinces has been greatly influenced by the research findings of five related disciplines (the development in Slovakia is similar but not identical):

1. the history of the working class and its organisations, above all its political organisations, since the beginning of the 1950s;
2. urban studies and town sociology, which has made significant contributions since the beginning of the 1960s;
3. historical demography, which in the last 20 years has been very successful, thanks to the cooperation between demographers and historians;
4. ethnography, which in the last 15 years has studied intensively the lifestyle of the urban working class in past and present times;
5. art history, which has always studied the modern architecture of towns and cities from many aspects, and which in the last decade intensified its endeavours.

Because there did not exist — and still does not exist — any centre coordinating the research of urban history, it is understandable that such research was influenced by the questions posed by these related disciplines. Nevertheless, the tradition of describing past events accurately from source material, which had found expression in works on urban history written during the first half of the 20th century and in the preceding period, was also successfully applied to modern urban history.

Since the beginning of the 20th century the archives of towns and cities have been the natural centres of both research and publishing of scholarly works on urban history. Since the 19th century, the Prague city archive has been used by its directors, who were often also professors of history at the university, as a centre of historical training; seminars were held there and students could work with original documents. The first periodical dealing with the history of Prague, *Sborník příspěvků k dějinám hlavního města Prahy* (5), founded in 1907, in which detailed studies on the urban history of Prague appeared, was published by this archive. By 1938 eight volumes had been published, initially edited by J. Čelakovský and later by V. Vojtíšek. This tradition of a journal on the urban history of Prague was revived in 1965 and since then (with two interruptions) one volume has been published annually under the title *Pražský sborník historický* (edited by F. Holec) (6). This yearbook contains five to ten articles (with summaries in German) as well as reviews and reports that provide systematic information about the entire field of Prague city history, book reviews dealing selectively with the history of other towns and cities in Czechoslovakia, and notes drawing the reader's attention to important recent foreign publications in the field. About one-third of the articles are on modern urban history, and at two to three yearly intervals complete bibliographies of the literature on the history of Prague are published (12). Since 1980, the same archive has published a second journal, *Documenta Pragensia* (7), which mainly publishes new research results of specialists employed in this archive.

In the first half of the 20th century, town and city archives became centres of research in Brno, Bratislava, Plzeň and Cheb, mostly due to initiatives of their directors. In the second half of the century, the city archive of Ostrava became important as well. In Brno, a journal for local history was published until 1970 and may be reissued (1); in Ostrava, such a journal is still published (3).

As centres of regional historiography two research centres have held important positions during the last 15 to 20 years — the Department of regional history at Palacký University in Olomouc, originally headed by L. Hosák and now by J. Bartoš, and the Silesian Institute of the Czechoslovak Academy of Sciences ("Slezský ústav ČSAV") in Opava, directed by J. Vytiska, who succeeded O. Káňa 15 years ago. The orientation of the research of these two institutes is different. The Olomouc group concentrates on a systematic historical topography of Moravia, oriented predominantly towards modern local history and continuing the series *Moravská vlastivěda* (15), published before the Second World War, and which concentrated on Medieval and Early Modern history. This modern topography, arranged according to the administrative units of 1948, has appeared since 1967 under the title *Historický místopis Moravy a Slezska 1848–1960*. In these volumes each town and village has a chapter devoted to it, providing information on administrative, economic (including, for example, the size of different enterprises according to the number of employees), social, political (electoral results since 1920) and cultural characteristics.

The three collective authors mostly worked with published sources to characterise the economic, social, national, political and cultural development of each town or village in the years from 1848 to 1948 (on occasion up to 1960). Each of the sections is followed chronologically, and each volume is devoted to several (three to four) political regions. For each region an extensive analysis of its economic structure and development is added. Political circumstances and political and other organisations are thoroughly analysed; the school system, the cultural organisations and their perspectives are likewise described. An extensive bibliography of literature on local history is given at the end of each chapter. The chief editor of this series, J. Bartoš, used his experience from working on local history to publish a manual on historiography, particularly for local history writers (24).

The Silesian Institute, which from the start has focused on local history, has, since the 1960s, extended its scope to include research on other industrialised areas, concentrating particularly on questions relating to demography and social history, first of the coalmining region of Ostrava, and, in the 1970s, of Northwestern Bohemia. A result of this research was an exemplary social history by J. Matějček (88). The activity of the institute has recently been extended to cover Slovakia. During recent years the Silesian Institute's research team has concentrated on the development after 1945, and on voters' behaviour at the polls between the First and Second World Wars. The computerised analysis of population statistics of these regions produced interesting results.

In Slovakia, too, research on urban history was concentrated primarily in the archives of important towns, especially the city archive of Bratislava. In addition, E. Hruška published, also in Bratislava, an important study of worldwide town building of the past (113). This work, with 1,540 illustrations, written from an architect's point of view, traces the development of the town as a form of human settlement from prehistoric times into the future. The author concentrates, however, on the development of the European town from the Middle Ages onwards and especially on changes in the 20th century.

A few institutions, such as architecture faculties at technical universities, encourage broader comparative studies on urban development in Czechoslovakia as a whole (sometimes comparing this with developments abroad), and publish the results of such research. But the main supporters of urban history research are local governments — especially the city councils of larger cities or historical towns with many old monuments — which support the publication of works on local history. In the past few decades, many such studies of good, sometimes even of excellent, scholarly standards, have been published.

(b)   Individual Fields of Research and Disciplines

The key question — what is the town, how is it defined? — was easily answered for those local units that originated in the Middle Ages and obtained town privileges, and also for those few that obtained these privileges later, up to the beginning of the modern industrial, capitalist era. The legal status of the town was granted to them by the King as head of the state. The problem of defining the town not only from the legal, but also from the sociological point of view arose in the 20th century. For example, in 1930 the smallest town in Bohemia, Rabštějn nad Střelou, had 344 inhabitants, whereas the most populous village, Kročehlavy (*de facto* a proletarian suburb of Kladno) had more than 10,000 inhabitants. Historical works, written after 1945, frequently use the term "modern town" (or "city"; in Czech "mesto", is used for both) for any settlement, regardless of its legal status, with the sociological characteristics of a capitalist town.

The problems of transition are the theme of an essay by L. Kobylková: "The transition of the medieval town into the 'historical nucleus' of the city in the period of the Industrial Revolution" (39). The author compares data on the geographic, economic, social and demographic character of six important towns in Bohemia and Moravia (22) (Plzeň, České Budějovice, Jihlava, Jindřichův Hradec, Liberec, Prostějov) during the 19th century. In preparation for a broader, comparative international study of this problem, the author studied Western European literature and published an informative article about it (29). This problem of transition was one of the topics dealt with in studies by sociologists (30/90), economic historians (31), social historians (35) and historical demographers (81/85/98); however, it was the main point of interest only in the works of urban scholars like J. Hrůza (36); P. Janák (83); O. Dostál (17) *et al.* In all these studies the authors concentrated on the social function of the town. The origins of the modern town and city were considered in connection with the process of industrialisation.

The jurists were interested in questions concerning the special legal position of the towns in the early modern period, the political role of their self-governing authorities (52/53), their relations to the authority of the state (43) and other legal problems connected with self-government. A monograph by J. Klabouch on the history of self-government in the Austrian half of the Dual Monarchy (Cisleithania), regarded as the standard work on this question, occupies a special position in the literature on the legal history of towns (49). In geographical monographs, especially the works of V. Häufler, towns and cities are studied in relation to their environment (75).

The history of the labour movement (14) has been closely connected with the history of towns for two reasons: first, in the 19th century the workers were primarily concentrated in cities and towns; secondly, Marxist historiography has endeavoured to view the political history of the working class in connection with its social history and, to a lesser degree, with its economic history. The conclusions of many monographs on this movement, written since the 1950s, strongly influenced a work on Prague's history published in 1964 (178). This work deals extensively with modern urban history, one half of it being concerned with the last 100 years. To some degree a model work, it strongly influenced histories of towns and cities published in the following two decades. These excellent monographs were primarily based on the analysis of source materials and contained many previously unknown or neglected facts.

A new history of Bratislava, the capital of Slovakia, was published in 1966; the 1978 edition expanded the section on modern history (160). A new history of Brno (164) focused mainly on the modern political history of the city. A detailed history of Plzeň (176/177) up to 1948 is available in three volumes, and it contains much information about the city's schools and cultural life. Other analytical articles on the local history of Plzeň can be found in *Minulostí Západočeského kraje* (4), a journal for the history of Western Bohemia. Many articles about the modern history of other Bohemian towns are to be found in various journals for local history (37). Monographs on the modern political history of Bohemian towns are relatively rare (166/167). For Moravia, though, in addition to the works on Brno, there are many studies on modern urban history written in the last 15 to 20 years. Initially, interest was concentrated on Ostrava where a monograph on the history of the city (173) followed a series of analytical articles on its origins as a modern industrial centre. The articles concentrated especially on the immigration of its population (92/93). The journal for the city history of

Ostrava has published two bibliographical surveys of literature about the city and its region (8/9). In the past decade histories of other towns in this area, concentrated predominantly on the modern period, have appeared (168–174). Historical monographs on other towns in various parts of Moravia were published in the 1970s, and there is much attention to the modern period (188–192).

In the last 15 years some very thorough works on the history of Slovak towns have been published, focusing on modern social history. Some books describe the social changes in towns which, after attaining great importance in the Middle Ages, were stagnant throughout the 19th century, and have experienced a revival only in recent decades (193–199).

The modern history of Bratislava has been studied thoroughly and from many viewpoints (157–163), while for Kŏsice (population 200,000), the second largest Slovak city, only the preparatory work for further studies, and a thorough bibliography on the town's modern political history has been completed (11).

The impulse for studying Prague's modern city history, encouraged by the publication in 1964 of a work on the town's history, led to many works on the history of Prague's working class (89) and socialist labour movement (60), including a chronological survey of its development up to 1921 (49). This year, in which the Communist Party of Czechoslovakia was founded, is described in detail in a book using quotations from journals and other sources as well as many photographs to reconstruct very impressively the atmosphere of the city in that important year (180). The electoral results in Prague after 1918 have been analysed in detail (V. Ledvinka/51). As regards the election of 1907, the first held under universal suffrage, an attempt was made to fix the social basis of different political parties founded on a detailed analysis of population statistics of the various constituencies from both a social and ethnic point of view (J. Havranek/45). The results of these analytical studies were later compared with a similar analysis of the Viennese electorate in the same election (46). Monographs on the development of the city administration of Prague from 1922 to 1965 have also been published (Merta/55/56).

The orientation of Marxist historiography towards the history of the working class not only led to detailed descriptions of the histories of its political organisations in the towns, but also to many attempts to describe the whole social structure of modern towns and cities. Works on town history published in the 1960s and 1970s have provided much useful material on the social history of Czechoslovakia which can also be used in comparative studies on developments in neighbouring Central European countries. For foreign students, it is useful that many of these town histories include summaries in German and Russian, sometimes in French or English, and occasionally in Polish and Hungarian.

Urban studies and sociology of towns and cities have always taken historical aspects into account in their treatment of the subject matter; of course, the function of the town in the life of the whole country today can be understood only in the context of the changes in its economic function since the beginning of modern, industrial, capitalist society. In this respect, conclusions drawn by economic historians are very important. The economic situation of the Bohemian towns in the 18th century has been carefully studied in a few sophisticated articles (P. Bělina/121/122; A. Míka/132). Another study produced new insights into early industrialisation in Prague in connection with the role of industry in the town's life (Z. Míka/133). In many articles and books the role of the Industrial Revolution in transforming towns in various regions of Czechoslovakia has been illustrated (P. Hapàk/32; M. Myška/40; L. Tajták/42). These studies, together with the demographic studies cited below, represent an important contribution on the part of Czechoslovak historiography to the analysis of the social changes in urban societies brought about by the Industrial Revolution in Europe. The expansion of industry and its crisis-ridden development had special significance for the most important industrial centre of Bohemia — Prague. Some articles consider the development of Prague's industrial branches (F. Dudek/125; O. Smrček/139), others study the industrialisation of Prague in a broader context (P. Horská-Vrbová/127). P. Horská-Vrbová also wrote an article on urbanisation in Bohemia, published in English (34). The connection between the renewed industrial development of the socialist era and urban life has so far only been dealt with in case studies (129).

The history of public transport, especially of mass-transport, interests not only specialists, but many amateurs, too. The close collaboration of these two groups saved many technical monuments and resulted in useful articles and books, many with instructive illustrations. The opening of the Prague Metro was an appropriate occasion for a book on the history of the capital city transport system (134). A book on the history of city transport in Ostrava has also been published (124). It was followed last year by an illustrated survey of the history of city transport, including a discussion of technical progress in the construction of tramways, buses and trolley buses — in all cities and towns of Czechoslovakia in which tramways once existed (130). In some respects, none of the newer publications can fully replace F. Roubík's survey of the history of mass transport (137), which studies urban transport in the context of the general development of passenger transport.

Other institutions in the Prague infrastructure have been the subject of historians' studies, including, in recent decades, histories of the city water supply (123), the market-hall (128) and the pawnbrokers (126). Some of these books are popular histories, which ensure them better access to the general reader, but this does not diminish the reliability of the information they contain. They are written, however, primarily for those readers who seek confirmation of the memories of their youth.

Not the past but the future is the central interest of authors of urban monographs; urban history interests them only to the extent that it has helped to form the contemporary town. Among these authors we find architects of previous generations whose works are now treated as a part of classic urban theory, for example, the book of K. Honzík (142) and B. Fuchs (111). O. Nový (41) is, in this respect, the most important representative of the middle generation. The sociological viewpoint is represented by the works of J. Musil (28), which are concerned also with international aspects, and by the works of authors' collectives headed by him (30). Numerous books by J. Hrůza are either theoretical in orientation (38), consider the future (114), or describe the urban theories of the old utopians (37). His encyclopaedia of contemporary urban studies contains much important information on the modern theory and practice of town planning and construction (25).

The problems of urban history have also been dealt with by specialists in historical geography. Their most significant publications consisted of two volumes in their journal *Historická geografie*, which concentrated on the problems of the geographic development of the Prague agglomeration in the past centuries (179). The plans of the towns are an important source for an analysis of their development. In the journal are articles discussing the geographic development of the whole agglomeration, together with those that trace the development of different industrial branches in the city. Most of the articles providing information on the city infrastructure are oriented towards the present, the only exception being an article on the history of Prague hospitals. All have resumés in German and English; two volumes of the journal have been published in English.

Articles giving a general survey of the history of Slovak towns between the wars (33), analysing the economy of the town governments in southern Bohemia (136), or bringing data from the communal statistics on developments in Prague since 1945 (20) have similar character. City maps are an important source for the interpretation of urban development in the 19th century. V. Hlavsa published a catalogue of old maps of Prague with an analysis of their reliability as source material (20), and an informative article on building activities in different parts of Prague during the second half of the 19th century, supplemented by many maps (112). A sociogeographic method was used in an analysis of building activities (P. Matějů/116) since the 1930s. A popular history of Prague suburbs was published in 1955 (120). It was followed by an analytical study of the oldest of them (Z. Míka/117), that was based on primary sources from the city archive; similar studies for other suburbs are being prepared. The difficult problems connected with the negotiations between the Prague city council and representatives of the important suburbs from the beginning of the 20th century until their unification in "Velká Praha" (Greater Prague) in 1922 have been described by F. Holec (47). The history of Prague streets, including all the name changes, prepared in handbook form by four authors, is much used by those interested in Prague's history (110).

Historical demography, which has achieved significant research results in Czechoslovakia since the 1960s, successfully traced the changes in the structure and behaviour of the town population of Prague and Ostrava during the last two centuries. Using the parish registers in Prague, it was possible to make the first detailed analyses of the 18th century (95), including a detailed analysis of the infant mortality rate at the end of the century (103). J. Havránek, using census data from 79 microwards, studied data on the structure of families and single persons of different social, national and religious groups in the second half of the 19th century (78). He came to the conclusion that there were important differences in the demographic behaviour of different classes and social groups. From this analysis important characteristics of the living conditions of Prague proletarian families in 1900 were also derived (80). Among the publications considering the population development in the 20th century (86), there is one which focuses on the development of Prague (84).

For Plzeň, there is an analysis of population and housing condi-

tions in the suburb, Starý Plzenec (M. Bělohlávek/64), and in Brno,
J. Janák studied the anti-immigration measures used — without
much success — by the authorities around 1850 (82). J. Havránek
published a description of workers', particularly miners', immigration to Northern and Western Bohemia in the last decades of the
19th century (77). He attempted to trace the consequences of this
immigration for the changing national and social structure of the
population of important towns in the area. The problems connected
with workers' immigration into the mining and industrial areas and
their importance for the changing social and national character of
the districts were studied with impressive results by M. Myška(91),
L. Dokoupil (69/70) and B. Pitronová (97), who concentrated on the
coal-basin of Ostrava and Karviná. Not only historians but also
demographers have studied carefully the historical aspects of demographic questions. The works of V. Srb and M. Kučera (86) are
surveys with special stress on coefficients of fertility and mortality,
whereas M. Hampl (76) considers the changes in population concentration in the last 100 years.

The work of Czech ethnographers in recent decades has been
strongly oriented towards the lifestyle and customs of the urban
population of Bohemia, especially of the working class. Their research methods, consisting of oral history and the documentation of
daily life based on photographs, clothing and furnishings, were
combined with source material from the archives and the popular
press to reach highly interesting conclusions. The first articles
provided information about the development of proletarian housing
in Brno (72). In the 1970s Prague ethnographers, led by A. Robek
(99), began studying the Prague proletariat; their conclusions were
published in a well-illustrated monograph on proletarian life and
culture since 1848. Most of the authors, M. Moravcová (dressing,
demography), J. Šťastná (diet), F. Vančík (housing), J. Svobodová
(family life), O. Skalníková (customs, social life) published preparatory studies based on sources in a journal of workers' ethnography,
Etnografie dělnictva, and to some extent also in a traditional journal of
Czech ethnography, *Český lid*. In addition to this work, a short
monograph on the proletarian suburb, Žižkov, was prepared by F.
Vančík (105). Articles on the way of life of the lower classes in urban
society have been written by other authors as well (102/65). Recently, the life of the lumpenproletariat has been the subject of
historio-sociological study (96).

Art historians, especially those who study the history of architecture, have not neglected the economic and social history of the towns and cities. This is shown in an older history of modern Czech architecture by J. Koula (145), and in a well-illustrated history of Czech architecture (19). The contemporary series of monographs on the art history of Bohemian and Moravian towns, for example Kutná Hora, Tábor, Slavonice, Loket, focuses on the older architecture. Among the four volumes on the history of the visual arts in Prague, however, two deal with the 19th and 20th centuries. The history of Prague architecture in the 19th century is described by D. Líbal and E. Poche (185), and in the 20th century by M. Benešová and O. Nový (179). The yearbook, *Staletá Praha* (154/155/156), published by the Prague Authority for the Preservation of Artistic Monuments, has produced three volumes with articles on monuments built in the last two centuries. Architects and urban planners have published an introductory book with many illustrations and maps (109). In discussing experiences of the past, especially developments of the last century, they sought inspiration for further development of the city.

In recent years art historians have inspired close cooperation between specialists of different disciplines in studying 19th and 20th century history. Regular conferences in Plzeň are organised for this purpose. In 1982, the role of towns and cities in 19th-century Czech culture was the theme of the conference (147). These conferences are an example of cooperation between specialists, mostly young ones, in economic, social, political and cultural history.

The careful analysis of paintings and novels provided useful material on the social structure of Czech towns in the 19th century and the historical analysis of sources helped to reconstruct the changing structure of the consumption of cultural products. From all this, interesting new conclusions may be drawn that are useful for comparative studies of the development of modern European urban society.

JÜRGEN REULECKE

Federal Republic of Germany*°

Scholarly interest in urban history and the development of modern towns is a tradition which has existed in Germany for almost 180 years. The motives and underlying reasons for this interest, the aspects on which research has concentrated and the intensity of this study have changed in such a way in this time, however, that any attempt to paint a brief, comprehensive historiographical picture must of necessity result in only a rough sketch and blurred outlines. In addition to this, a clearly defined subdiscipline of "urban history", with its own methodology and an unmistakable line of research, has still not really been able to establish itself within the "guild" of German historians, despite various approaches and a steadily increasing number of publications on the subject. In accord with the fact that, due to its "almost hopeless ambiguity" (Stoob/ 12), the concept of the "town" is largely resistant to comprehensive definition, and the "town" as an object of research offers a large number of possible approaches, it was, from the outset, by no means only historical experts who determined the course of research on urban history; indeed, for a long time, they played only a secondary role. At first glance, urban history research carried out so far in Germany reveals, as one of its special characteristics, a wide spectrum of involved disciplines. Except for a few historians who tended to be working in isolation, even before the First World War, jurists and economists, geographers, social scientists and ethnologists, architects, art historians and town planners dealt with individual

* Translated by Ruth Stanley
° Numbers in brackets in this chapter refer to entries in the bibliography on pp. 305–326 of this volume.

aspects of urban history relevant to their research, which was mostly not historical but related to the present. The spectrum of interested neighbouring disciplines has increased steadily since then, particularly in the last decades: demographers, historians of medicine and technology, ecologists and others have also provided important contributions to the analysis of the development and formation of the modern town, from their own standpoint and using their own methodological instruments.

Very roughly speaking, three periods may be distinguished which, each in its own way, showed a particular interest in urban history, or in which the questions dealt with by urban history experienced a remarkable extension. These periods were the decades 1820 to 1830 and 1890 to 1900, and the 1970s and 1980s. It appears that in times of unpredictable social change in which contemporaries experience a stronger feeling of crisis, reflection on history and, in particular, on the historical qualities and roots of the immediate environment — and in the bourgeois age, that means particularly the town — are more strongly developed than in periods of general upsurge and positive expectations of the future.

A. Lines of Research Development

The first impulse to research urban history came from legal scholars. The founding of the so-called Historical School of Law by F. C. Savigny and K. F. Eichhorn around 1820 encouraged — not least through the influence of a romantic world-view against the background of a politically much-fragmented Germany — the notion of a historically attestable "law-forming common spirit of the German nation" (Treitschke), which was alleged to have developed early in medieval town constitutions and urban self-government. During a period in which traditional values imparting meaning and order to the world of estates were rapidly becoming defunct, representatives of the Germanist branch of the Historical School, first K. F. Eichhorn, later especially G. Beseler, attempted to prove, through research based for the first time on an extensive use of source material, that the "old truly Germanic principles of freedom", above all freedom of agreement and the cooperative union of independent individuals in the community of the people ("Volksgemeinschaft"), also lent themselves to solving current problems. From the outset, this view narrowed research on urban history, which at the same time was burdened by an ideological function that continued to have effect over a long period. An especially significant limitation was the fact that, to begin with, interest focused exclusively on the medieval town, and essentially on its legal status and internal legal structures. Moreover, it became clear that those taking part in this debate, because of their idealised view of the bourgeois society to be created and, to some extent, consciously rejecting the ideas of the Enlightenment, pursued only those aspects which lent themselves to practical realisation in political activity. The article on towns and town statutes in the famous *Staatslexikon* by K. Rotteck and K. Welcker is impressive evidence of this, as is the argument of the legal historian, Germanist and moderate liberal representative to the Paulskirche National Assembly in 1848, G. Beseler, who saw in the town guild and cooperative system of the Middle Ages the true "German law" institutions from which a general citizenry of the state could develop to build a "dam against the despotism both of the masters and of the masses".

G. Beseler was the teacher of O. von Gierke, who then became prominent in the German Empire through extensive works on the history of cooperative law. Starting out from the results of his research, he demanded (in a similar fashion, but more pointedly than his contemporary R. von Gneist, whose concept of self-government relied very heavily on English history) the independence and autonomous responsibility of communal self-government *vis-à-vis* the state. To this extent he helped the typical characteristics of Pre-March urban history research to survive. He also oriented his research on the Middle Ages towards current disputes and wished to bring his influence to bear specifically on a revival and extension of the autonomous organisation of town citizens, carrying on from Stein's municipal reform in 1808. O. von Gierke, in turn, had considerable influence on H. Preuß, a specialist in public law, who carried the Historical School's conception of self-government (which had been widened and to some extent more radically formulated) into the 20th century by overcoming the dualism of state and citizens' community that had been emphasised in the debates on the legal origins of the town. He declared both forms of government and administration to be an expression of the same cooperative principle. He thus initiated the disputes over local self-government that were carried on in the final phase of the Weimar Republic.

Altogether, it may be said of the first phase of urban history research and its effects up to the First World War that the approach was essentially restricted to the question of the development of the town and the specific origins of town constitutions in the 9th to the 14th centuries. So, besides the representatives and epigones of the Historical School, this was also the approach of such historians of constitutional law as G. L. v. Maurer, W. Arnold, K. W. Nitsch and A. Heusler. Only occasionally was the medieval town's market function, later emphasised by theoreticians of the market such as A. Schultz, E. Gothein and R. Sohm, as well as the historian G. v. Below, also taken into consideration.

The line of development described above, very strongly motivated by the historical argument of a concept of self-government alleged to be specifically German, was considerably widened around 1890 to 1900 by new factors making for an interest in urban history and impulses provided by other disciplines of scholarship; at the same time, however, problems outside the field of scholarship again played a part. Industrial urbanisation with its far-reaching social consequences had changed the urban sphere of life, the field of day-to-day political activity of the liberal bourgeoisie, which, under the Empire, was largely excluded from government of the state to such an extent that, once again, there seemed to be a need for reflection on the basis of urban bourgeois existence and the threats to which it was subject. Moreover, the educated bourgeoisie ("Bildungsbürgertum") was suffering a crisis of identity for many other reasons which we cannot enter into here. In the debate which now began and which was again strongly influenced by ideology, a number of fundamentally different positions may be identified. One took up older (agrarian) romantic and anti-urban ideas which had been advanced by W. H. Riehl in the 1850s and now found their way into various conceptions of social biology. Another — a position to which, besides the public lawyers, historians in particular were committed — attempted once again to derive arguments for the form of modern urban life, and life in the state in general, from research on the original function of the town in the Middle Ages and in the early modern period. The question of the origins of town development was an explosive one to the extent that the answer to it also promised to provide the justification for either an organic or a seigneurial conception of the state. In the context of these disputes, the interpretative models of the origin of the town grew considerably in number. Thus, the disputatious historian G. v. Below, in opposition to the hitherto prevailing interpretation based on legal history, advanced the theory that the existence of a market was the primary constituent factor of a town, from which a stronger defensive system, i.e. the compulsion to fortify, resulted. Writings on urban history published by historians, although still concentrating on the Middle Ages and, at most, the early modern period, reached a first height in this connection.

At the same time, however, increased efforts were made to examine the process of urbanisation more purposefully, to interpret this process with more optimism for the future and to influence it through planning. Important impulses were provided here by urban planners, by architects and by the discipline of urban sociology that was beginning to develop. Large exhibitions on towns, such as the one in Berlin in 1910, well-attended congresses such as the Congress on Urban Systems held in Düsseldorf in 1912, and numerous collections of programmatic essays were aimed at enlightening public opinion on the possibilities and prospects for planned and well-conceived urbanisation. A stock-taking of scholarship on how the modern town came into being was an essential part of this and was particularly appreciated by representatives of the so-called Younger Historical School of Political Economy, who now occupied themselves more intensively with research on the town and urban history. A large number of scholarly works, in particular dissertations, especially on current economic and social problems of the modern town, resulted from this commitment. Many details of urban development under the influence of industrialisation were dealt with, often using statistical material; however, the approach was mainly descriptive, and treated the subject largely in isolation from more comprehensive analytical concepts. Even so, these were important first steps towards empirical social research, which would be taken up again at a very much later stage, after the Second World War.

Nevertheless, the first theoretical approaches are also to be found in this period; they developed from the need to work out the corresponding structural characteristics of the widely varied outward forms of the town, and to seek out the laws of urban development. The most significant of these attempts was made by M. Weber, whom we are probably right to regard as standing at "the beginning of modern urban research" (C. Haase) in Germany. Weber was not so much interested in the town as an independent central object of research in its own right, but rather in using the example of urban development, as only one of many, to shed light on the overall process of social development, lasting over many centuries and reaching its peak in industrialisation. To this purpose he defined the characteristic peculiarities of different types of town by making functional, temporal and world-historical distinctions. The structural typology of the (Western) town that he developed has continued to be influential right down to present-day discussions of urban history, above all in medieval town history. Among the characteristics of the medieval town (fortifications, associative character, partial judicial and administrative autonomy, market), M. Weber, too, emphasised the market function, for him the very constituent element of the town's special character. Besides economic criteria, however, political and social criteria were also included in the definition of town types, but these were clearly subordinate to the economic aspects.

A second significant attempt to grasp the character of the town from the view of society as a whole was made by W. Sombart, who, in the context of reflections on the theory of capitalism, also saw the economic functions of the town as being of foremost importance. His contribution to a clarification of terminology through "interpretative-analytical" town concepts widened this narrow perspective in the direction of a complex, more layered concept. Also noteworthy are the approaches to a more comprehensive grasp of the town in social theory undertaken by G. Simmel and F. Tönnies. They also took the enormous changes in society as a whole as their starting point and attempted to make a connection between the mentality of the modern inhabitant of a large city and his forms of living, and basic types of human interaction.

Parallel to the currents mentioned above, which had a decisive influence on German urban history research practically up until the eruption of National Socialism, there ran — and still runs today — another line of tradition springing from local and cultural history. For a long time, however, both these disciplines were hardly noticed by university historians because of the strong fixation on political history and the history of ideas that dominated in the universities, and because of the critical attitude towards social and economic sciences. Also worthy of mention are the diverse forms of engagement of a large number of active — and often amateur — researchers in local history, who joined together in local and regional history associations in the second half of the 19th century. However, their initial contribution to urban history must be judged as a mixed one: in these clubs, preservation of a patriotic cultural heritage, a view of the past that was often uncritical and strongly romantic, vague notions of national characteristics ("Volkstum") and a strongly developed local patriotism were mixed with antiquarian curiosity, with the educated bourgeoisie's efforts to assert itself, and with special interests of different kinds — such as, for example, in genealogy or numismatics. The problems of the industrial age were largely excluded; nevertheless, modern research in urban history owes something to these efforts, despite their many problematical limitations. Besides being the harbourers of older town chronicles, often rich in material, the local history associations were also the centre not only of efforts to preserve and collect many sources on urban history which might otherwise have been lost, but also of impulses to establish museums for ethnology and the history of technology, and particularly regional and local archives in which bequests and endowments could be housed.

All the different traditions of urban history mentioned above — to a greater or lesser extent — dominated research on urban history in the Weimar Republic. Besides intensive continuing research on the medieval town's legal and constitutional aspects, studies of the ideas and institutions of self-government again received a great deal of attention, especially regarding their achievements in the 19th century following Stein's municipal reforms in Prussia. The special emphasis on this topic was connected with resistance to the strong centralising efforts with which the Weimar state limited the competence of urban self-government in a growing number of areas. Besides this, there was, however, also a significant new theoretical approach, which was to be taken up after the Second World War mainly by urban geographers: this was the theory of central places developed by W. Christaller (55). The explicit animosity of National Socialism towards large cities, its "blood and soil" romanticism, the pathos of its antiurbanism and its glorification of the peasantry as the "life source of the Nordic race" put an end, for the time being, to a further scholarly development of modern urban history research in Germany. At most, pessimistic descriptions of urbanisation and crassly biological works were published, intending to prove that life in large cities led to the deracination and disorientation of human beings. An exception to the highly questionable concentration on this aspect was the publication of the first two volumes of the *Deutsches Städtebuch* (edited by E. Keyser) in 1939 and 1941; it was then continued from 1952 onwards (9).

During the first two decades after the Second World War there was a considerable extension of the scope of questions dealt with and the methods of investigation used in social scientists' and geographers' urban research and, once again, in medieval urban history. But, with few exceptions, there is little evidence at first of new attempts at historical research on modern towns and industrial urbanisation, and much less evidence of modern historians, in general, devoting any greater degree of attention to this topic. Sociologists were primarily concerned with studies of communities; prompted by American models, they dealt with social and ecological differentiations in the towns and with informal social relations, and the factors of community integration.

After the authorities of the centralised state had been discredited, a concern with possible self-determination and codetermination in local areas was natural, especially as the need to rebuild the towns and cities destroyed in the war, to integrate refugees from Eastern Europe and to reintegrate evacuees caused them to be seen as areas of special social focus. At the same time, a very active subdiscipline of geography developed: urban geography began taking an intensive interest in functional and structural aspects of the urban system. W. Christaller's theory of central places was taken up again and supplemented by a more strongly genetic viewpoint. Research into medieval history also experienced a change in the 1950s. The approach that had dominated until then of viewing the "town in the legal sense" was overcome and greater attention was given to the economic and cultural significance of the town and, in particular, to the development of an urban bourgeoisie. In analyses of the medieval town, the grant of municipal rights was included in a mass of differing criteria "which has a different composition in individual periods and regions: criteria become less important, or are developed further, or new criteria are added; there are shifts in the priority rating of the criteria" (E. Ennen/57). Parallel to these various forms of urban research, communal sciences — some research institutes had flourished in the Weimar Republic — were reorganised. They began research aimed at a systematic study of the interrelations between municipal law, local government and municipal financial and economic relations; here, however, the jurists' viewpoint dominated throughout and for a long time the subject was not really able to develop a clear profile because of the strong orientation towards legal practice.

After the Second World War, in contrast to the wide interest in the town in other social sciences, topics of urban history were not taken up by modern historians until very much later and, on the whole, tended to be tackled hesitantly. As late as 1962 H. Herzfeld expressed his astonishment, in view of the abundance of tasks for the historian in the field of modern urban research, that "this 'green meadow' of attractive topics has been so obstinately ignored" (25). This situation was connected with the traditional commitments of German historiography, which continued to be influential for a long time, and with the particular way in which this burdensome legacy was finally overcome. As early as 1949, at the first Historians' Congress after the Second World War, G. Ritter pointed out that German historians, through their "one-sided attention to political history and an all too sublimated history of ideas have become positively backward". He acknowledged that they — and he — were experiencing a certain "helplessness in face of the phenomena of modern mass society and the complicated problems of modern economic life". During the following years, which were characterised by a new conservatism, his call for self-criticism met with virtually no response from the "guild" of modern historians. They consistently maintained their traditional interest in knowledge oriented towards the political history of events and ideas; and "individualising and hermeneutic methods" (J. Kocka) continued to be used.

Nevertheless, during this period, this paradigm came gradually but with increasing effectiveness to be called into question; in a sense this development was initiated from the fringes of the historical sciences. At the end of the 1950s, W. Conze had taken up O. Brunner's ideas and proposed the concept of "structural history" to describe a historical approach which looked at internal structures, at determinants and objectivisations of historical and social reality, and which emphasised supra-individual conditions and processes rather than the individual human being and his actions, and collective rather than individual phenomena. Concerning method, he suggested widening the traditional hermeneutic approach by using quantifying, typologising and comparative methods, and by co-operating with the systematic social sciences. W. Conze saw urban history research as a particularly worthwhile variation of structural history studies, "for the 'historic structure' of a town presents itself to us as a unit which is relatively easily grasped, which can be viewed as self-contained and which nevertheless . . . contains all the diverse problems of modern structural change" (W. Conze in W.

Köllmann/279). The most important work from this circle, W. Köllmann's *Sozialgeschichte der Stadt Barmen im 19. Jahrhundert*, published in 1960, took up impulses from community sociology and also the programmatic new orientation of the structural history school, and developed them further. This significant attempt at an integrative grasp of urban economic and social structures, which also took account of political consciousness-forming, was influenced by the works of O. Brunner and W. Conze and, above all, by W. Brepohl's attempt to develop an ethnology of industrial cities, and G. Ipsen's (62) reflections on the theory and typology of urban development. Besides taking up new impulses from community sociology and social or structural history, which was gradually gaining more notice, German urban history research also took up questions which had attracted attention before the Third Reich. The problem of local government, i.e. the relationship of tension between centralist and federalist structural elements, also had a determining influence on the period of reconstruction, and so it was natural that the development of the ideas and institutions of municipal government, as well as the threats to which it was subject, should again receive greater attention. Additional impulses for urban history were provided by economic history, which began researching the regional peculiarities and local forms of industrialisation. Regional studies, individual monographs with the accent on economic history, were also published at this time. These are also important references to local economic conditions in a few articles published to celebrate the anniversaries of chambers of commerce. At the same time, W. Brepohl attempted to use empirical social research, material on local history, and questions raised by ethnologists as a basis for establishing the effects of urbanisation on mentalities in the Ruhr, an area with particularly large conurbations.

Nevertheless, in the 1960s scholarly contributions on the development of the modern town, its institutions, and a town system characterised by urbanisation, were rare. Even if, in this period, the impulses provided by the above-mentioned pioneers of modern research in German urban history were being taken up here and there and were gradually beginning to bear fruit, viewed as a whole, they did not at first leave many traces in modern German history. A cause of this was the imminent generation-change: the rising generation of historians had a new, increasingly conspicuous orientation. They concentrated their attention on social and structural problems of a different dimension, as becomes apparent in their considerable engagement in the controversy — provoked by F. Fischer's *Deutschlands Griff nach des Weltmacht* (published 1961) — over the extent of German responsibility for the outbreak of the First World War. Questions of the "deeper problem of social and political power" and of the consequences of the time-lag between economic modernisation on the one hand, and social and political modernisation on the other, played a central part in the German Empire. To this extent, German history in the 1960s was definitely a phase in which the older "Historismus" was gradually superseded by a new orientation, which proceeded more from theoretical premises and comprehensive explanatory models. In this new orientation, the wealth of the general topics now being countenanced under the concept of "social history" at first pushed interest in the "green meadow" of modern urban history into the background. Even in the journal *Archiv für Kommunalwissenschaften* (1), which has appeared since 1962 and which was expressly intended to provide a forum for discussion for historians, too, as its co-editor, H. Herzfeld, emphasised in the first volume, only a few articles may be found dealing unequivocally with urban history.

Perhaps one can say that in the period up to the end of the 1960s, the time was not yet ripe for an interest in possibly all-too-cumbersome details, in local peculiarities, in the tension between "above" and "below". Instead, younger historians were influenced by the notion that including theories of sociology, political science and economics in historical analysis could lead to a "historical social science" saturated by theory, and, with the help of new analytical methods, the tradition of "Historismus" could be overcome, or at least greatly modified. There is no doubt that the historical landscape was considerably altered by these approaches, without their proving fruitful for urban history until the 1970s.

B.   The State of Current Research

From the end of the 1960s onwards, a great expansion of the universities in the Federal Republic of Germany took place, and the number of students rose considerably. Besides the expansion of traditional universities, new ones were founded and enlarged, particularly in the most populous and heavily urbanised "Land", North Rhine-Westphalia. The science of history also changed in appearance through the establishment of new institutes and the appointment of a larger number of younger historians to newly created chairs. The social history approach, and especially concern with individual aspects of the general process of modernisation from the early 19th century onwards, found many more supporters. In the following period, it had a decisive influence on discussions in the field of history. From here, strong impulses were provided for research in modern urban history, as may be seen from two events that took place as early as 1970: first, for the first time at a Historians' Congress (the biennial meeting of West German historians), on 3 April, 1970, in Cologne there was a special section on urban history — revealingly, on problems of local government in the 19th century. Secondly, in October, 1970, the German Institute of Urban Studies ("Deutsches Institut für Urbanistik") began publishing the *Informationen zur modernen Stadtgeschichte*, edited by C. Engeli (3). This publication was intended, as was stated programmatically in Volume I, to counteract the fragmentation and considerable "methodical isolation" of urban history, defined here as the "history of a comprehensive process of urbanisation". Moreover, in the same year, H. Stoob founded the Institute of Comparative Historical Urban Research at the University of Münster. At first, this Institute directed its attention to towns before 1800, but it then began increasingly to carry out research on urban development in the age of industrialisation. Since 1975, it has been the centre of a special area of research supported by the German Research Society, and geographers and ethnologists are also involved with it; it concentrates mainly on "spatial structure — social structure — culture" as well as town-country relations and religious movements in towns. A working group on the historical development of urban areas, formed in 1973, which had its genesis in the "Akademie für Raumforschung" in Hanover, was more strongly influenced by urban and rural planning. In addition, since the early 1970s regional study groups, which until then had mainly dealt with medieval towns, have been extending their research interests to include the 19th and 20th centuries; an example is the working group on south-west German urban history research founded in 1960 under the influence of E. Maschke and J. Sydow. And finally, in 1974, besides all these existing groups, a further important group was founded: the Study Group for Urban History Research, Urban Sociology and Preservation of Monuments; its general secretary is O. Borst. Since its foundation, this group has organised an annual International Conference on Towns; it publishes a journal for urban history, urban sociology and the preservation of monuments. It has appeared under the title *Die alte Stadt* (2) since 1978.

Once again, in 1974 and 1980, sections of the historians' congresses were concerned with urban history themes. Moreover, the number of dissertations and theses for diplomas and state examinations with their main emphasis on local history has grown since 1970, the more so since a wealth of new impulses on research in urban history has been provided by expanding subdisciplines, such as labour movement history, history of the political parties, demographic history and family history. Also, the opportunity arose of applying new methodological approaches — above all the new computer systems to process mass data — in the analysis of such complex but, at the same time, surveyable regions as individual towns.

The urban history themes and fields of study which, in the course of the 1970s, were chiefly dealt with — exclusively by younger historians — may be roughly divided into three areas:

In the first place, a renewed attention to problems of urban self-government may be observed; however, the main aim was to link general political development with structures and leading persons in the local political field of forces; a start was made at least in studying these problems against the background of the social and economic context of each individual town. Several authors dealt with the influence of parties, social groups and, finally, of National Socialism on political life in the local sphere. Of the many detailed problems of urban self-government in the course of the last 100 years, the financial basis, crucial for the strength of self-government, was treated in greater detail; and, in addition, the administration of communal services and local social services began to attract attention.

A second group of researchers took up topics directed at analysing economic and demographic conditions in towns and, in this way, treating the general processes of urbanisation and internal migration in exemplary cases in more detail than previously. It is obvious that, in studies of this kind, the boundaries between economic, social and demographic history are fluid, and, in some cases, the main points of emphasis lay more in the economic, and others more in the social sphere. Research on social changes attempted, besides registering specific local peculiarities, to analyse the conflicts resulting from this major change and the efforts to solve them in each case. Here, special mention must be made of the various impulses provided by W. Köllmann. During the 1970s — partly following directly his work, partly stimulated by W. Fischer and W. Conze and also by the historical theory of modernisation — a larger number of studies were made on the development of individual towns and of the entire town-country relationship under the influence of industrialisation and various other modernisation processes. A number of historical studies of individual dominating large enterprises also resulted — in a certain sense as a by-product — in new information on the history of the towns researched.

The third area, most clearly identifiable in West German research on urban history since the late 1970s, results from two approaches directly inspired by social history. It is surprising that, despite the contacts between urban history and empirical social research in the 1950s, hardly any attempts worth mentioning were made at a historical grasp of the dimensions of experience in urban existence. Both structural history, which concentrated on the analysis of the interrelation of supra-individual influences and social phenomena, and also the more strongly theory-oriented social history research of the 1970s were at first concerned to establish the long-term trends of social development and the mechanisms that took effect at the macro-social level. The question of urbanisation was viewed in this context, and where specific studies on towns were included in the treatment of the theme, they not infrequently had an exemplary or indeed purely illustrative function. Paradoxically, the interest in the town as a sphere of experience, which was roused only a few years ago, did not follow on from research traditions to be found in this country; to a far greater extent it was the result of English, American and, sometimes, French studies. The two new approaches, which found a lively response within a short time and very quickly gained criticism, may, on the one hand, be characterised by the concept of the "history of everyday life", and on the other, they may be seen in connection with the American concept of "new urban history", oriented towards strict social science methods. The line of research described only vaguely as "history of everyday life" or "social history from below" sought now, at last, to look at the sufferings, experiences and learning processes, the value orientations and behavioural patterns of individuals, and their complex relationships to the general political, social and economic framework. In this, they discovered, particularly in the field of urban history, instantly rewarding objects of study, and the freshness of their approach, their resourcefulness in discovering new source materials, are a consolation sometimes for the undeniable conceptional weaknesses of the "culturalist approach". Living conditions, household, family life and leisure activities, seen against the background of the urban or neighbourhood environment, began to attract interest, as did the development and specific forms of social segregation, mental processes of adjustment and differentiation of social groups as a result of urbanisation, the forms of articulation of social protest and the expression of social conflicts. In comparison with the thoroughly variegated picture of the "history of everyday life", the reception of the questions and methods of "new urban history" and related concepts is not as well developed, but the phase of initial discussion, which received additional impulses from urban history studies by young American scholars in Germany and Austria, has now been left behind. The results of efforts to introduce quantifying urban history in the Federal Republic of Germany, usually related to social and ecological questions, can not now be in dispute; they already show that many points of contact exist between this approach and the history of everyday life — even though the methods and the sources used are to some extent radically opposed — as indeed the boundaries between these methods and the first two areas on which attention has been concentrated are also fluid.

The last observation is made with particular reference to some collections of essays on urban history that have come onto the market in the last few years. The sum of the numerous individual articles in these volumes do not by any means amount to a self-contained overall picture of the modern development of German towns, but it does at least enable us to draw up an interim balance. From this balance some of the main trends in recent urban history research become clear, and, at the same time, it shows the questions still remaining to be answered and the problem fields on which up to now not enough light has been shed.

From the standpoint of methods and strategy, four trends are striking:

1. an increasing involvement of detailed research on urban history in the general process of urbanisation;
2. the extension of the historical gaze to dimensions of life in the towns which, until now, have received little or no attention;
3. a clear willingness to cooperate with neighbouring disciplines, which also, to some extent, have discovered a greater need for a more comprehensive historical treatment of their special questions and concerns; and

4. the trend towards international comparisons as well as towards including results of foreign research and methodological impulses.

Of still greater significance, however, are new orientations in the contents of research and extensions of the existing spectrum of research. Although we can not give a complete picture here, attention is drawn to the following important thematic concerns on which research on urban history has concentrated in the past few years:

1. The methods, objects and aims of research into urban history, but also of the historiography of urban history, have been made the subject of an increasingly wide-ranging debate. In this, their didactic components (i.e. the significance and the mode of disseminating the results of urban history in schools, in local politics, in urban conservation as a means of gaining or maintaining "regional identity", etc.) is being increasingly discussed.

2. There are indications that the spectrum of urban self-government, the specific manifestations of urban constitutions, the various enactments determining the scope of local politics, are increasingly being viewed in connection with spatial and temporal categories of a mental nature. As a result, the varying respective room for manoeuvre, the areas of experience, socialisation and planning, as well as "social" times (simultaneities and dissimultaneities), differentiated by social stratum, come into view. New knowledge of the dynamics of urban societies and society as a whole in the process of urbanisation may then be derived from the establishment of a juxtaposition and partial opposition of different spaces and times.

3. In this context, numerous references to processes of mobility and adjustment, to phenomena of levelling and, on the other hand, also of differentiation, have resulted at the same time: the spectrum of research reaches from the purely demographic analysis of the urban population via studies on geographical and social mobility to investigations of differing living and health conditions and income differentials as well as leisure habits and political articulation (e.g. at elections) in urban districts. Furthermore, increasing attention is being given to the strategies and activities with which the dominating circles tried to overcome or suppress the threatening divergencies arising from a sometimes headlong urbanisation.

4. Building on the areas of settlement, land-use, urban architecture, the principles as well as the effects in reality of planning policy etc. are no longer treated and presented in isolation but rather in the

context of the dominant conceptions and power structures of urban society and society as a whole, i.e. the question of social and economic reasons underlying appropriation, use and mastering of space is raised. The extension of urban infrastructures, for example, no longer appears merely as an application of technological innovations or as an organisational problem, but as an answer to the challenges of social policy, hygiene and industrial capitalism. It is precisely in looking at the development of land prices, urban budget and tax systems, as well as the diffusion of specific forms of living accommodation (e.g. tenement houses), that the "town as business" (G. Fehl/185) is revealed in many different senses of the term.

5. Since for the past few years economic historians have increasingly viewed the region as the "essential operative territorial unit for industrialisation" (S. Pollard/224) and Christaller's "theory of central places" (55), which has been considerably developed by urban geographers, has also started to be of interest to urban historiography, relations between the town and the surrounding area and the site functions of the towns in the regions increasingly appear in a new light. This is mainly with respect to economics, but also, in a rudimentary manner, with respect to the diffusion of urban living forms and the development of an "urbanity" in society as a whole that is no longer associated only with large towns.

6. The last aspect leads to the role of the (large) town as a centre of culture and science, and also, at the same time, as a context for a particular sociocultural milieu, giving the "town dweller" a specific identity, admittedly differentiated both according to social stratum as well as, for example, according to the culture of the individual's neighbourhood, church community, youth and family, but nevertheless unmistakable within society as a whole. In this field, modern ethnology, which nowadays views itself as "empirical cultural science", and political science interested in history and favouring the concept of "political culture", have provided impulses. In this context, the critical analysis of urban ideologies, which in the past have provided highly contradictory concepts, have sometimes had a considerable effect on public life. In other words, an approach through the history of ideas, has gained ground, not in isolation, but, for example, in connection with studies in the history of mentalities on experiences of place and patterns of identification of town dwellers.

Besides this short characterisation of the newer trends that I regard as particularly important (relating less to topics which have already been extensively treated and more to those which, in some cases, have only just come onto the urban historian's horizon), it must also be observed that the traditional questions are being pursued further with new sources and methods of analysis, and that local historiography has developed considerably — often on the occasion of a town's anniversary — through histories, historical picture books and chronicles of individual towns and communities. However, in this area, remarkable products and rather dubious ones exist side by side, since all too often the authors are governed not by a solid and cautious approach to the topic with the intention of providing enlightenment, but rather by the mass production of glossy wares that sell well and, above all, are intended to satisfy the public's nostalgic yearnings.

C. Prospects of Urban History Research

Viewed as a whole, the spectrum of modern German research on urban history has become very much more complex in the past few years than it was in the first two and a half decades following the end of the Second World War. This is not least connected with the fact that modern urban history and historical research on urbanisation is increasingly seen as two sides of the same coin, and the interrelations between them are gradually growing ever closer. Admittedly, it must be emphasised that we are mostly dealing with first steps in this direction, not with research strategies that are already widely followed and generally accepted. The lack of an unmistakable research profile for urban history, mentioned at the beginning of this article, proves disadvantageous in this connection; despite a bundle of individual offers, there is a lack of a reasonably self-contained theoretical framework "of medium range", capable of including both the specific developments in individual towns and the causes and manifestations of urbanisation in the context of comprehensive processes of social change in the past two centuries. Moreover, it is revealing that the facets of town and urbanisation history of the 19th century (i.e. of the epoch of industrialisation in the narrower sense) are comparatively well researched even though many questions are still open; this is not the case with the manifestations of deurbanisation in the 20th century. Proceeding from this observation, it appears to be thoroughly appropriate that epochs and characteristic features of urban development in modern times should not be seen exclusively from the standpoint of urbanisation as a part of the process of "modernisation"; rather, from the comparison with town systems in other societies and cultures, additional categories of interpretation and classification may be won. Indeed, our knowledge of urban development since the First World War is noticeably smaller than for the period before 1914; gaps in research predominate here, and they grow larger the closer we come to the present. To this extent, present-day research on urban history in the Federal Republic of Germany may be characterised as a branch of scholarship marked by colour and variety; it is still in the middle of a process of change, and thus its outlines are not very clear, but for that reason it has many possibilities and prospects.

FRANÇOIS BÉDARIDA AND GILLES JEANNOT

France*°

A. Problematics and Methodology: The Pluralism of Approaches

Although French historians have, by predilection, generally tended towards the study of pre-industrial towns we have noted, in the last quarter century, an increase in the number of works dedicated to towns of the 19th century and of the first half of the 20th century. Signs of a broadening in the field of urban history should therefore be recognised along with an inclination of social science research on towns to be orientated towards history. On the one hand, geographers, sociologists and architects have submerged themselves in archives, and on the other, historians, even if this entails criticising them, have started borrowing concepts from other social sciences. Thus a sort of cohabitation, if not a genuine interdisciplinary coherence, has been established between those studying urban research.

(a)   The Slow Germination of Urban History

It is perhaps appropriate to attribute two specific traits of urban research since the beginning of this century to the relatively late urban development in France. The first is the rareness of studies, and the second, the ambition of the questions posed. The central question, at least in its implicit formulation, is "What is the town in its functions and in its dynamics?" A simple analysis of the present is not enough to provide an answer, so history must be looked to for illumination and explanations.

* Translated by Rose-Marie Couture.
° Numbers in this text do not refer to the bibliography but to the annotations at the end of this report.

Geographers were the first to pave the way. In 1911 R. Blanchard published his work on Grenoble, a classic today, in which he analysed the mechanisms elucidating the rhythms, causes and effects of urban growth.[1] This work inaugurated a long series of monographs, which, at first, imitated this model.[2] There was then an attempt to deepen the analysis by placing the town in the economic, global and social systems. This is particularly true of recent studies devoted to the great metropolises.[3] Shortly after the Second World War, G. Chabot and then P. George sought to promote panoramic views and propositions of synthesis of the urban fact in general.[4]

Whereas jurists were principally content with formal descriptions of institutions, the majority of town planners were preoccupied with according a large area to history. In the period between the two world wars, M. Poëte, along with P. Lavedan, who initiated a new chapter in art history with his work on town planning,[5] proclaimed a great ambition. Inspired by Geddes and Bergson, he proposed a vision of the town as a material and spiritual totality which should be studied in its evolution in the same fashion as a living organism.[6]

On the historians' side, after H. Pirenne, who was able to imbue a real social and human dimension into the network of texts and institutions,[7] L. Febvre and M. Bloch immediately made their journal the *Annales d'histoire économique et sociale* accessible to urban history. This interest by the "*Annales* school" was soon confirmed and amplified brilliantly by F. Braudel in his thesis on the Mediterranean which was published in successive editions of *Afterthoughts on Material Civilisation and Capitalism*. However, it is important to note that inquiries instigated in this manner are, as a rule, limited to the Middle Ages and — except for the 19th and 20th centuries — to the modern period. Indeed, it was a historian not associated with this trend, L. Chevalier, who took the initiative of tackling a study of the working class in Paris during the first half of the 19th century. By according an important place to demography, he relegated economic matters. From this methodological reasoning he moved towards a concept which established an analogy between urban and biological life; henceforth inhabitants' modes of behaviour, social habitus, mental attitudes, and political activities could be interpreted as repercussions of biological forces.[8]

Even though the limits of a town/country distinction have become evident since these preliminary works, the town continues to elude definition. More often than not the metaphor of a living organism is applied to the town to define it: this is the case with M. Poëte, whose language systematises this representation (tissue, artery, heart . . .), and also with L. Chevalier. This is also true with adherents of a functionalist approach, be they geographers (A. Demangeon) or historians (L. Febvre). If, at its inception, this approach seemed to dissect the town by distinguishing organs corresponding to functions, it remains animated by the search for a final synthesis in the tradition of Durkheim, Malinowsky and Mauss.[9] Town planners and engineers, inspired by Le Corbusier's model, later pursued an inverse procedure in their works. Le Corbusier's model, the finality of which, straining towards action, comprehends differentiating the diverse functions of the town and then treating them as many specific problems.[10]

Since the 1960s these general (and more often than not metaphorical) descriptions of the town and its evolution have been less successful. Nevertheless similar designs in Y. Barel's town-system[11] or in the town-language of semiologists can be seen.[12] Transfer of knowledge from sciences in expansion, such as biology or linguistics, are always seductive, but do they not neglect to pose the initial question: by what authority may one think of the town as a system or as a language?

B. From Knowledge to Action : The State, Social Demands and Urban Research

Along with the "urban revolution" which transformed the face of France during the 1950s and 1960s, research on towns also changed in rhythm and dimension, statute and finality. No longer the object of patiently and wisely elaborated academic studies, it became rather a societal venture flowing into the practices of political and town planning. Due to the impulse of growth, social demand asserted itself. On the one hand, the constitution of a unified discipline, which would make grand statements on the urban phenomenon, was renounced to the benefit of attempted exchanges and the construction of a knowledge which would appeal to different disciplines contributing to it. On the other hand, an endeavour to associate knowledge to action was expected in order to answer concrete and urgent needs. The urgencies of the day took command. In terms of research, the hour of interdisciplinarity and commissioning struck. The orders of the state abounded. A first symptom was the creation of the Centre for Urban Research (CRU) in 1962, which was then followed by a systematic policy of commissioned research conducted by the Ministry of Urban Affairs, the Ministry of Transport, the Planning Commission and other public authorities concerned with urbanisation.

Even if research has, on a parallel basis, been informed by development sustained in university circles, it is important to stress the impact and significance of the relatively new mode of investigation represented by commissioned research. The latter, which functions on the basis of invitations to tender or by means of conventions entrusted directly to research organisations or research departments, is in effect characterised:

— by its mode of legitimisation: pertinence is more important than excellence;

— by its conditions of production: one-year or two-year contracts, the constitution of teams, often mobile (hence a precarious situation for researchers, modified, however, by an ambience of growth and optimism), a propensity to regroup according to tendencies;

— by a relative abundance of funding (especially in the first years).

A peculiar tonality in French urban research has resulted from this: inventiveness, rapid evolution of problematics — sometimes pleasant, sometimes controversial discussions between the disciplines — but also ideological rigidity and an absence of capitalisation of results.

(a) From the Technical to the Political

Appealing to works in the social sciences to elucidate the decisions of public authorities implies a gap between study and reflection on the one hand, and realisation on the other. This is one of the functions of the apparatus for forecasting political and town planning of territory in a country such as France, and it explains why the Planning Commission having had to resolve the housing problem (1st and 2nd plan 1946–57), was obliged to tackle the problem of imbalance between Paris and the provinces — an issue about which J.-F. Gravier set off warning bells shortly after the war in an incisive, though controversial book.[13]

These administrative preoccupations, paired up with those of geographers, traditionally bound to problems of hierarchy and urban skeletons, which now began to stimulate theories such as W. Christaller's theory of central places and F. Perroux's poles of growth. This is why studies undertaken systematically on the country's urban network endeavoured to make clear the "metropoles of equilibrium" policy, the aim of which was to reconstitute structuralising regional centres starting with eight cities (5th plan 1966–70).[14] As far as the policy of new cities is concerned, conceived around 1965 (and realised in the following years), it was in part inspired by the works of sociologists.[15]

Studies on the cost of growth and on urban grievances consequently contributed to making the optimal position of medium-sized towns evident and accompanied the policy of assisting them in their development at the time of the 6th plan (1971–75).[16] On the occasion of the "country contracts" ("contrats de pays"), and in the same decentralising vein, interest turned towards small towns and the "region of towns".[17] However, in relation to the ambitions of a voluntary geography, it is questionable whether the state's planned economy actions are not henceforth reduced to the simple movement of accompanying natural evolution[18] without the staying power of studies conducted — shedding light on the relations of the town and its environment — permitting political and town planners to understand better the internal mechanisms of urban morphology and citizens' aspirations.

During the 1960s research on urban planning started making great progress. Anxious to accelerate the passage of rural France to urban France, the state abandoned aid to construction and housing so as to invest in collective equipment, particularly transport, a trend stimulated by the 5th plan and the creation of the Ministry of Equipment. The Bridges and Roadways Authorities are at the heart of this apparatus; a body of agents whose practical and symbolical efficiency is based on technicality and rationality.

In a very functionalist perspective, researchers' interest turned towards models of how the town develops and functions, as well as to programming techniques concerning equipment. In this case, one witnessed the triumph of quantitative and empiric approaches, the "urban games" (in which attempts to represent the strategies of various actors and partners in the urban world were made), calculations on the estimated demands of transportation or the evolution of property prices, the whole directly inspired by American models.[19] Success, however, was short-lived as these works ran slap into double criticism. First, they required a mass of data for limited results. Secondly, they were reproached for being content to mask orientations or decisions taken independently with "scientism" — especially concerning the automobile's development[20] — and, in a more general manner, for imprisoning citizens' existence in a standardised and repressive functionalism.[21]

There was an even more significant fact. By abandoning these models, the need to take a certain historic density into account was recognised in urban development. The town no longer appeared as a mere technical domain where rationally planned equipment would be enough to answer specific needs and whose growth could be defined by mathematical models. Its future could no longer be dissociated from society's future as a whole.

In addition to this criticism, there was the will of many of those in administration to understand the crisis of May 1968. Due to this, the preoccupation of reflecting urban matters in the larger context of society became apparent in the subjects offered for tender since the summer of 1968. The 6th plan (1971–1975) marks a period of pomp in urban research which allows little place for historians but a great deal for history.

In urban research, where sociology then predominated, there were three principal currents at centre stage: the sociology of organisations, Marxism, M. Foucault's thought (especially as relayed by the works of CERFI).

1. Relying on the thought of M. Crozier (*The Bureaucratic Phenomenon*) and on that of P. Grémion (*Peripheral Power*) the sociology of organisations applies the description of bureaucratic mechanisms, which characterise other sectors of social life, to the urban phenomenon. Far from the passage of a decision to its execution being smooth, the numerous restraints on change must be taken into account, such as the strategy of groups or individuals in the administration, obstacles inherited from the past, etc. In this tenor, J.-C. Thoenig's work can be cited. In a historical study, he exposed the power of the Bridges and Roadways Authorities which was based on an ideology of progress and rationality.[22]

2. On the Marxist side two key words have inspired urban research — theorising and historicising. M. Castells is the most notable thinker here.[23] Starting from the criticism of the Chicago School, Castells reproaches American sociologists for defining facts which do nothing but translate a process of

rapid industrialisation in a market economy without voluntary social control as characteristic of urban culture (Wirth) or of urban ecology (Burgess). In the same vein, he considers the work of French sociologists to be unsatisfactory as they use empiric categories, such as socio-professional categories, as if they were concepts, or who confirm correlations between communal history and land use without being able to impart the underlying theory. M. Castells encountered this theory in Althusser's and de Poulantzas' structuralist reading on Marxism — reading which in particular lends merit to the role of ideological practices and urban struggles. Aside from this tendency, other Marxist interpretations — that of J. Lojkine for example — are inspired by a more orthodox economism.

This Marxist current has contributed to renewing the analysis of the property question[24] by demonstrating that the market is structured by a double confrontation: the confrontation between property proprietors and constructors, which determines construction costs; and the confrontation between employers and wage-earners, which determines the share of salary apportioned to rent.[25] Thus, the profits of capitalist construction in the property sector is the motor of the increase in the value of property rather than the strategy of small proprietors. In other ways, though, the domination of entrepreneurial strategies are stressed — Usinor at Dunkerque, for example[26] — or of state strategies[27] in urban planning. At the same time urban struggles, although they constitute a relatively marginal phenomenon, have been much studied because some people expected an explosion of societal contradictions in the urban crisis.

Thus, beyond the broadening of the town-function to the town-system, the town finds itself re-situated in an historic perspective. In this perspective the trends animating it and its evolutionary laws reflect the structures of its mode of production. The town itself has today become the strategic 'locus' of society's future development.[28]

3. The third current, greatly influenced by M. Foucault's thought: that in which the framework of CERFI (Centre for Study and Research on Institutional Formation),[29] and based on a reflection of history, questioned once again the evidence of needs which were supposed to be answered by

collective equipment and, in a larger context, the organisation of the town and urban life.

In *The Geneology of Morals*, Nietzsche denounced those who, starting from punishment as a goal, had turned it into an origin, whereas for him "every goal, every utility are but symptoms indicating that a will for power has seized something less powerful than itself and has imposed a function of its own design upon it". Likewise, for the researchers at CERFI, public equipment does not respond to a pre-existing need. It is created by a forceful blow of the will for "territorial fixation" or "normalisation" on the part of the state.[30] The archetype of this forceful blow is the "great imprisonment" of madmen in the classical epoch described by M. Foucault: scarcely a specific answer to the eternal problem of madness, but rather its act of birth. From that moment on, historic practice, instead of seeking auto-differentiation or the realisation of a concept already germinated at the origin, must illuminate a discontinuous series of forceful blows. "Geneaologies" determine the nature of ruptures which mark the birth of different types of collective equipment: housing estates, schools, hospitals, stadiums . . .[31]

So, for CERFI, and equally for Marxist thought, there is no autonomous question of the town per se. The town may be comprehended only in the light of a genuine philosophy of history. Naturally, this leads to vast enquiries concerning the state and the individual, society and liberty.[32]

(b) From the Local to the Patrimonial

In view of the economic crisis and the stabilisation of the urban thrust, there has been a transition from the management of growth to the management of constructed space. This heralds the beginning of the rehabilitation of old districts and historic centres (Nora Report, 1975), and of the large units built in the 1950s and 1960s ("Habitat and Social Life" Procedure, 1977). Simultaneously the witness of the ebb of systems, of structuralism and of Marxism, for example, can be seen.

Not only has funding for social science research on the urban phenomenon diminished perceptibly, but the radiant myth of a radical and simultaneous solution to urban problems, and social and economic problems ("change your town, change your life") has also declined. Public authorities now assign more modest objectives to commissioned research: how to adapt to the crisis, remedies for urban pathology.

The three dominant features of the late 1970s and early 1980s are of interest for local and daily aspects, a blossoming and revival of architectural studies, and the significance of ethnology. Concurrently there is a preference for micro-studies and monographs in lieu of ambitious theoretical constructions.

1. The study of daily life in an urban environment — the object of a research subprogramme in the 6th plan — was intended to improve understanding of how everyday social relations are facilitated, impeded or transformed by the organisation of urban space.[33] However, this postulation — of executive action based on peoples' daily existence — is again questioned in the posterity of older works (H. Lefebvre, the situationists, P. Sansot), which brought to light micro-practices of appropriation or of the deviant adaption of space. The daily aspect appears in a new light. It is neither a reflection of dominant modes of alienation nor an expansion of the "quality of life" programmed by town planners. The agoras have been forsaken for other sociable places, it is realised, and the inhabitants' pedestrian paths, constituted by moments of attention or neglect of the environment, of acknowledgement or of rejection, are not reducible to a geometric outline,[34] recognising that a certain value exists in the time spent in public transport.[35]

This insistence on the irreducibility of individual practices in the face of town planners' intentions, constitutes an extreme form of criticism of systems. However, we have easily been able to demonstrate the specificity of districts and the associative life animating them, and which then informs the entire town. The local level has thus come to be privileged: the point where urbanisation meets decentralisation, which has been popular in minds since the end of the 1970s and in action since 1982.[36] The "local object", be it a place (building, district, town) or a social group, asserts itself with researchers (especially sociologists and political scientists) as much as with decision-makers, to the point that the notion of "local development" has come to supplant that of urban development in the 9th plan (1984–1988).[37]

2. A major innovation in the last 12 years is the full-force entry of architects into the field of urban history. Although architectural history has traditionally been a sub-section of art history, limiting itself to describing, classifying and explaining masterpieces, it has now, along with social sciences (economy, sociology, social psy-

chology, etc.,) become the centre of gravity. For, if space is to a certain extent the product of social relations, it has in relation to them a specific existence, since it is simultaneously the pre-existing locality in which they are organised and one of their most important ventures. Hence it is suitable to adopt a double strategy: on the one hand, to seek the information necessary for understanding the formation of constructed space in the history of social relations, and on the other, to enrich the knowledge of social relations by analysing spatial configurations.[38] Minor architecture is also accorded a place of honour and dissected with a typo-morphological method borrowed from the Italians[39] and which consists of locating regularities in parcelling or construction procedures.

Whereas this method permits a rediscovery of the notion of "urban architecture", studies so conducted provide an opportunity to show the mediating role of architecture, between social demands and constructed form: an argument for the discussion presently perturbing the profession concerning the relationship between history and architectural creation. It is all more pertinent since there is an attempt to redefine, if not to rehabilitate, the professional status of the architect, and the architect's education is undergoing a profound renewal. If architects were forced to cede responsibility to engineers during the large phase of urban growth, they are now devoting themselves to recovering a social function — hence the will to reconcile architecture and the town through largely historical reflection.[40] Furthermore, it is the deliberate policy of public authorities to favour research by associating architecture with social sciences. Contrary to other organisations, which commission research to explain administrative choices, CORDA (Orientation Committee for Research and Development in Architecture) and SRA (Service for Research on Architecture) have been set up with the specific goal of complementing the teaching of architecture and of opening pathways with the humanities and, more specifically, with history in the name of the past-present continuum.[41] Nevertheless, it should be noted that these new developments in the history of towns are largely due to architects enthusiastically entering the field of historical research — they have even become great archival consumers — rather than to professional historians whose redeployment relating to the history of architectural creation remains limited.[42]

3. Since 1980 urban ethnology has been subject to an undeniable renewal.[43] Overcoming the methodological and epistemologi-

cal difficulties raised by the double decentring of their discipline in relation to its original scope (loss of distance of exotic societies and of the stability of rural societies), ethnologists have discerned how the town in its history is rich in accumulations of layers and archaeological depths, rich also in memory inscribed as much in its voids as in its constructed spaces rather than being merely a locality of movement and forgetting.

By once again taking up ethnology's favourite themes — places of sociability, parties and demonstrations, families and ethnic groups — and by questioning the manner in which groups strike roots, research has articulated itself around the notion of local identity, that is to say, the modes of being in relation to the world and in relation to others — the product of a certain history and experience which permit self-definition with reference to locality. The reference to the past serves more to characterise features singular to the present than to deduce mechanisms opening to the future. And the intention of preserving an "ethnological patrimony" even becomes explicit in the works realised for the Ministry of Culture.

However, in the face of the fine reception of accumulation which confines to an inventory of patrimony, especially in certain works by architects who are signatories of the declaration of Brussels, in the face of mistrust with regard to all generalisations, it should be reaffirmed that knowledge of the town, regardless of how precise and rigorous the constantly multiplying monographs may be, rests on the synthesis of the cultural and the technical, the architectural and the spatial, the social and the economical.

(c) What Direction is Urban History Taking?

In this context, it seems that an evolution in the last few years revolves around the following axes:

1. That which is at issue bears less on themes and methods than on the finality of studies on the urban past. The aim of history has recently been to understand this past so as to master the future. The former has in effect meant reclaiming the determinants, be they invariable (Marxist thought), or multiple and interactive ("Annales school"), or yet again it meant researching "geneaologies" (CERFI), or inertias (the "long haul"). In short, it was above all an endeavour to capture a movement. However, after the rationalistic intoxication of the years of great growth, and after a wise return to the management of existing towns, the feeling arose that the Num-

ber One problem was no longer one of re-inventing the town, but one of a town that was already there. This town, an entity of constructions, an entanglement of networks, an agglomeration of multiple and diverse groups, is an accumulation town, and intelligence and mastery of it proceed as much from the patient and laborious analysis of the past as of the present.

2. The first lesson to be deduced from the publication of a special issue of Annales ESC published in 1970, "History and Urbanisation", was that the history of the town is multiform. The desire to point out differences, to submerge oneself in the past so as to make new questions emerge rather than to confirm any particular theory, is encountered again in the magazine *Urbi* (even though this magazine's articles are concerned with a distant past and paradoxically not a single one deals with 19th or 20th century French history). The same is true also of many recent historical works on modes of urban life, on districts, on migrations and even more so on the construction of the town.[44] The interest in the history of urban politics can thus be explained; without being a "lesson", but rather a specific "reading", it permits the beginning of a dialogue with other disciplines and a better understanding of the interplay of contemporary urbanism.[45] Whether a long or a short time is at stake, the historian makes an effort to patiently untangle the threads of old operations, to measure the significance of actors and of the socioeconomic context, to bring the mechanisms of regulation to light while still insisting on local and temporal specifics, to take the diversity and complexity of phenomenon into account which are juxtaposed without ever effacing the past.[46]

3. If historians have participated in activities of commissioned research in the field of urban studies, it is important to recognise that they did so in a rather restrained fashion. Playing a major part in scientific production, the urban history of universities has therefore continued to follow a relatively autonomous path. Research on objectives closely dependent on the economy should not be opposed to academic knowledge independent of momentary needs and the constraints of action. However, bulkheads and unwieldiness are persistent. Even so, interactions between fundamental and applied research have not ceased to make progress.

4. The remaining and more profound question is that of the specifics of the contemporary town as an object. The problem of synthesis is posed acutely whether it pertains to the 19th century city or to the 20th century city. This is, in fact, what surfaces in the most

impressive French accomplishment of the last few years: the two volumes of *The History of Urban France*, the first dealing with the years 1840 to 1950, the second to the years from 1950 to 1980.[47] The question remains — how can research conducted with such different viewpoints and in such diverse fields — demography, economy, anthropology, sociology, culture, politics, etc. — be amassed as a whole? Is there not a risk of juxtaposing rather than composing? As someone outstanding in the field lucidly recognises: "In certain respects it is less a matter of diverse realities than a matter of different views of one unique reality".[48] At the present stage of urban history and if being imprisoned by inclusive and mutilating theories is to be avoided, can anyone do better?

Notes

(1) *R. Blanchard*, Grenoble. Étude de géographie urbaine, Paris, 1911.

(2) *J. Levainville*, Rouen. Étude d'une agglomération urbaine, Paris, 1913; *P. Arbos*, Clermont-Ferrand, Clermont, 1930; *A. Demangeon*, Paris, la ville et sa banlieue, Paris, 1933.

(3) *E. Dalmasso*, Milan capitale économique de l'Italie, Aix-Marseille, 1970; *C. Chaline*, La métropole londonienne. Croissance et planification urbaine, Paris, 1973; *G. Burgel*, Athènes. Étude de la croissance d'une capitale méditerranéenne, Lille, 1975.

(4) *G. Chabot*, Les villes, Paris, 1948; *P. George*, La ville et le fait urbain à travers le monde, Paris, 1952.

(5) *P. Lavedan*, Histoire de l'urbanisme, 3 vols., Paris, 1926–52.

(6) *M. Poëte*, Une vie de cité. Paris de sa naissance à nos jours, 4 vols., Paris 1924–1931; *G. Bardet*, for many years director of the "Institut d'Urbanisme de l'Université de Paris", was influenced by this view; see his Problèmes d'urbanisme, Paris, 1941.

(7) *H. Pirenne*, Medieval Cities, Princeton, 1925.

(8) *L. Chevalier*, Classes laborieuses et classes dangereuses à Paris pendant la première moitié du XIXème siècle, Paris, 1958. In her work on the same subject, *A. Daumard* adopts a completely different approach. She concentrates on the social structure and on ownership of real property.

(9) See *P. Claval*, Les mythes fondateurs des sciences humaines, Paris, 1980, p.164.

(10) In fact, these two functional approaches are not identical. In the case

of the human sciences, it is a methodological approach to analysis and interpretation ("there is no organ which does not have a function"), whereas *Le Corbusier* provides a prioristic definition: Man has certain needs and the town has to fulfil these needs. *Cerda*, who traces the history of the town purely by reference to the development of the traffic system, understands history in *Le Corbusier's* sense.

(11) *Y. Barel*, La vielle médiévale, Paris, 1975; *Prospective et analyse de système*, Paris, 1971.

(12) *F. Choay* ed., Le sens de la ville, Paris, 1972.

(13) *J.-F. Gravier*, Paris et le désert français, Paris, 1947.

(14) *J. Hautreux, J. Lecourt and M. Rochefort*, Le niveau supérieur de l'armature urbaine française, Paris, 1963 (Commissariat du Plan); *M. Rochefort*, L'Organisation urbaine de l'Alsace, Strasburg, 1960; *R. Dugrand*, Villes et campagnes du Bas-Languedoc, Paris, 1963; *Y. Babonaux*, Villes et régions de la Loire moyenne, Tours, 1966.

(15) Especially *P. H. Chombart de Lauwe* and his collaborators.

(16) *P. Pinchemel, A. Valiki and J. Gozzi*, Niveau optimal des villes, Lille, 1969; *J. L. Piveteau, P. Claval and J. E. Roullier*, Déséconomies et nuisances liées à la croissance urbaine, in: Bulletin de la Société Neuchâteloise de Géographie, 1974, pp. 1–30; *D. Faudry*, Les coûts de l'urbanisation. Critique d'un concept et éléments d'une nouvelle problématique, Paris, 1975; *DATAR*, Scénario pour les villes moyennes, Paris, 1972; *J. Lajugie*, Les villes moyennes, Paris, 1974.

(17) *G. Veyret-Vernier*, Plaidoyer pour les moyennes et petites villes, in: Revue de Géographie Alpine, 1969, pp. 5–24; *Colloque sur les petites villes*, in: Bulletin de l'Association des Géographes Français, no. 400/401 (1972), pp. 267–298; *DATAR*, Région urbain, région de villes, in: Travaux et Recherches de Prospective, no. 44 (1973); *J. Destandeau*, Régions de villes, Paris, 1975.

(18) See *G. Burgel*, in: Histoire de la France urbaine. Vol. V, Paris, 1985, pp. 177–186.

(19) A survey is provided by *P. Merlin*, Méthodes quantitatives et espace urbain, Paris, 1973; *A. Bailly*, L'Organisation urbaine. Théories et modèles, Paris, 1975; *J. de La Brunetière, R. Prudhomme and G. Dupuy*, Les jeux de simulation urbanistique, Paris, 1972; *E. Préteceille*, Jeux, modèles, simulation, Paris, 1972.

(20) *G. Dupuy*, Une technique de planification au service de l'automobile, Paris, 1975.

(21) This has been criticised above all by *J. Dreyfus*, La ville disciplinaire, Paris, 1976.

(22) *J.-C. Thoenig*, L'ère des technocrates. Le cas des Ponts et Chaussées, Paris, 1973. Thoenig shows how an occupational group that once possessed a key position in agrarian society later became a driving force behind the urbanisation process; in so doing, it substituted

modernity and rationality for the traditional standards of human life.

(23) In an article that forms the point of departure for this new approach: 'Y-a-t-il une sociologie urbaine?', in: Sociologie du Travail, 1968, pp. 72–90; see also *M. Castells*, La question urbaine, Paris, 1973.

(24) *C. Topalov*, Capital et propriété foncière. Introduction à l'étude des politiques foncières, Paris, 1973; *A. Lipietz*, Le tribut foncier, Paris, 1974.

(25) *M. Conan and J. M. Le Floch*, La recherche urbaine. Essai de rapport de conjoncture, in: Bulldoc, no. 50 (1975).

(26) *M. Castells and F. Godard*, Monopolville. Analyse des rapports entre l'entreprise, l'Etat et l'urbain, Paris and The Hague, 1974.

(27) *J. Lojkine*, Le marxisme, l'Etat et la question urbaine, Paris, 1977; *La politique urbaine dans la région parisienne 1945–1972*, Paris 1972; La politique urbaine dans la région lyonnaise, Paris, 1973.

(28) Unfortunately, examples illustrating these theoretical discussions are not provided for the period prior to 1945–1975. As an expression of this approach, cf. the low importance attached to urban history in the periodical *Espaces et Sociétés*.

(29) Originally the concern was to determine the appointment of the "new towns" (*villes nouvelles*), taking account of specific local requirements in each case.

(30) The first term is taken from *G. Deleuze and F. Guattari*, L'anti-Oedipe, Paris, 1975, the second from *M. Foucault*, Surveiller et punir (translated by Alan Sheridan as: Discipline and Punish: The Birth of the Prison, London, 1977); all the authors collaborate in CERFI.

(31) *L. Murard und P. Zylbermann*, Le petit travailleur infatigable, in: Recherches, no. 25 (1976); *L'halaine des faubourgs*, in: Recherches, no. 29 (1977); see also *Fonctionalisme en dérive*, in: Traverses, no. 4 (1976).

(32) Cf. the assessment of CERFI's efforts in *F. Fourquet*, L'accumulation du pouvoir ou le désir d'Etat, Paris, 1982.

(33) *Délégation Générale à la Recherche Scientifique et Technique (DGRST)* and *Ministère de l'Équipement*, Recherche urbaine. Compterendu d'activité au 1er janvier 1973, Paris, 1973, p. 223.

(34) Cf. the stimulating attempt to provide a phenomenological description of urban development in *J. F. Augoyard*, Pas à pas. Essai sur le cheminement quotidien en milieu urbain, Paris, 1979; *P. Sansot*, La poétique de la ville, Paris, 1973; *A. Cauquelin*, La ville la nuit, Paris, 1977.

(35) *M. Bonnet*, Le temps dans le métro. Du plein ou du vide, in: Annales de la recherche urbaine, no. 5 (1979), pp. 171–195.

(36) On decentralisation, municipal government and local society, cf. the announcements by DGRST, *Ministère de l'Intérieur* and DATAR. Cf. also the special issues of *Annales de la recherche urbaine*, no. 10/11 and *Espaces et Sociétés*, nos. 20/21 (1977) and nos. 34–39 (1981).

(37) So far as the quality of relations between the state and local administrat-

ive districts (*communes*) is concerned, there is no fundamental difference between the urban and the rural milieu. Both are the cases of "développement local", cf. *IXème Plan, Développement urbain*, Paris, 1983.

(38) *B. Huet and C. Devillers*, Le Creusot. Naissance et développement d'une ville industrielle (1782–1914), Paris, 1981, p. 9.

(39) Especially *Muratori, Aymonino, Rossi.*

(40) One-third of the studies are historical; cf. *B. Queysanne*, La recherche en histoire. Quelques réflexions, in: Cahiers de la recherche architecturale, no. 13 (1983), pp. 34–35.

(41) CORDA existed from 1972 to 1979 and was followed by SRA in 1980.

(42) Very generally speaking, historians participate little in current urban research; in the period from 1978 to 1984, less than 20 out of a total of 889 research studies recorded by the Centre de Documentation sur l'Urbanisme were by historians.

(43) The first studies, by *C. Pétonnet*, Ces gens-là, Paris, 1968, and *J. Monod*, Les barjots. Essai d'ethnologie des bandes de jeunes, Paris 1968, published in the 1960s, found no echo. As evidence of the change in attitude since 1980, see the special issue of various periodicals that have since been published: *Anthropologie culturelle dans le champ urbain*, in: Ethnologie Française, 1982; *Anthropologie urbaine*, in: L'Homme, 1982; *Ethnologie urbaine*, in: Terrain, 1984.

(44) Cf. the two anthologies edited by *M. Garden* and *Y. Lequin* as well as the results of the hearings of experts in the Centre d'Histoire Économique et Sociale de la Région Lyonnaise, *Construire la ville* and *Habiter la ville*, Lyon, 1983–1985; cf., too, the special issue of *Mouvement Social*, 1982, on life in the quartiers.

(45) On the contemporary period, cf. *Les politiques urbaines en France depuis 1945*, in: Bulletin de l'Institut d'Histoire du Temps Présent, 1984, Compl. Vol.

(46) Cf. *M. Garden*, Construire la ville, p. IV. This approach has also been adopted by scholars in disciplines other than history. Cf. the development in the work of *J. Lojkine*; in the case of Paris and Lyon, he posits the total subordination of local politics to the dictates of the state; however, his most recent works on Lille relativise this position by noting influences deriving from the traditions of Catholic social teaching and of socialism: Le marxisme et les recherches urbaines, in: Économie et Humanisme, no. 252 (1980, pp. 24–32). Cf. also the comparison of the Marxist concept of spatial development as determined exclusively by socioeconomic mechanisms with the historical evidence, in: *A. Vant*, Imagerie et urbanisation. Recherches sur l'exemple stéphanois, Diss. Lyon, 1982.

(47) See the bibliography, p. 341, no. 48.

(48) *M. Agulhon*, Histoire de la France urbaine, Vol. IV, Paris, 1983, Introduction, p. 11.

ANTHONY SUTCLIFFE

Great Britain*

A. The Study of Modern Urban History

Britain led Europe, and the rest of the world, into the process of industrial urbanisation. The proportion of the population living in urban areas reached 80% on the eve of the First World War, well in advance of any other industrialising country. Subsequently, urbanisation stabilised at this level, allowing other industrialising countries to catch up. However, their urbanisation levels have also tended to stabilise in the region of 80 to 85%, suggesting that Britain had, as early as 1914, reached the maximum effective level of urbanisation attainable in industrial society. Meanwhile, Britain had gone on to lead the world in the transformation of established industrial cities to meet 20th century requirements. This leadership was increasingly undermined by the country's relative economic decline in the 20th century. First in North America, and later on the Continent of Europe, per capita national incomes rose to the point where the resources devoted to the creation, maintenance and transformation of the urban environment exceeded those available in Britain. However, Britain retains an important accumulation of knowledge on urban affairs. One element of this is the study of urban history, which has been more extensively pursued in Britain than anywhere else in the world except the United States.

Urban history began to emerge as a self-conscious field of study in Britain after the Second World War. As it did so, it partially incorporated three existing traditions which had already generated a substantial body of writings on the history of towns. These were the venerable antiquarian and topographical traditions, which had

* Numbers in brackets in this chapter refer to entries in the bibliography on pp. 375–385 of this volume.

reached full maturity in the 18th and 19th centuries, and the study of local aspects of the history of public policy which had emerged at the end of the 19th century under the principal influence of S. and B. Webb (58). It was, however, economic history which provided the main dynamic of growth after 1945. Thanks to its continuous development since the 1880s, British economic history was now at the peak of its explanatory power. With interest moving from the Industrial Revolution and economic fluctuations towards the human implications of economic development, towns began figuring on the agenda of a growing number of historians who sought to grasp the totality of the industrial existence within a convenient spatial framework. This aspiration had the further effect of encouraging economic historians to draw their theoretical inspiration from the full range of the social sciences, and not just from economics. From here it was but a short step to the idea of a comprehensive, integrating urban history in which historians and social scientists could share in recreating what was arguably the axial experience of the British industrial era.

The taking of this step can be dated with a degree of precision unusual in historiography. In 1962, H. J. Dyos, an economic historian teaching at the University of Leicester, convened an informal meeting of scholars with urban interests from among his fellow members of the Economic History Society. From these modest beginnings grew the Urban History Group, which, in the late 1960s and the early 1970s, became perhaps the most productive and stimulating interdisciplinary forum in the whole of British historical studies. Conferences, meetings and publications multiplied, and adherents were drawn in from a widening range of fields and disciplines. With American urban history, the origins of which dated back to the 1930s, also passing through a period of enhanced activity, Anglo-Saxon urban historians led the world for a while. In the later 1970s, however, doubt and disintegration set in.

The main weakness of the broad British school of urban historians led by Dyos was that it was never able satisfactorily to define the historical significance of the urban phenomenon. In the absence of such a definition, the towns were merely a container or backdrop for the interplay of broader historical forces. Only in the study of the physical creation of the urban environment did a distinctive urban history theory and praxis emerge. Despite its origins in the Economic History Society, in association with which it continues to hold its annual meeting, the Urban History Group failed to promote a concerted study of the urban economy. Meanwhile, social history had emerged as the main growth area of British historiography. Fostered for a while by the Urban History Group, it struck out on its own in the mid-1970s leaving urban history significantly denuded, and increasingly under attack from social historians and theorists as a chimera or irrelevance. These difficulties were compounded by the premature death of H. J. Dyos in 1978, since which time British urban history has been going through a period of reappraisal which has produced no definitive results as yet. Meanwhile, some of Britain's largest cities have entered a period of manifest economic decline which may reflect the country's passage into a post-industrial era which will transform the functions and characteristics of urban areas. Thus from the confidence of the post-war years, Britain has moved into a new age of uncertainty, and urban history has moved with it.

B. Organisation, Resources and Aids

The bulk of research on modern British urban history emanates from historical, geographical, sociological, political and architectural departments in universities and polytechnics. There is one research centre, the centre for Urban History, founded at the University of Leicester by Professor Peter Clark in 1986. Two funded research programmes have generated a considerable volume of published material. *The Victoria History of the Counties of England*, which is directed by C. R. Elrington from the Institute of Historical Research at the University of London, has shown great interest in the urban dimension of local and regional history in recent years. *The Survey of London*, directed by F. Sheppard, is a topographical exercise financed by the former Greater London Council. A number of municipalities have commissioned town and city biographies, the most notable being the three-volume *History of Birmingham* (182/183/184); and initiatives by members of local universities have produced from time to time a concentration of research on individual towns, often expressed in a collection of essays such as the recent volume on Leeds edited by D. Fraser (193). There is, however, no multi-volume urban history of Great Britain on the lines of the *Histoire de la France urbaine*. In 1970, the London publisher, Edward Arnold, inaugurated a series of monographs, "Studies in Urban History", under the general editorship of H. J. Dyos, but no further volumes have been commissioned since 1978. There is no British journal of urban history similar to the *Journal of Urban History* or *Storia Urbana*. There are few urban history textbooks, but the Oxford University Press is building up an informal series of survey volumes of English urban history on a chronological basis, with works by S. Reynolds (42), P. J. Corfield (35) and P. J. Waller (44) already in print. Leicester University Press published a number of volumes in the series *Themes in Urban History*, a collection of abridged versions of recent university theses planned by H. J. Dyos and edited after his death by D. Fraser, in the early 1980s, but no further volumes are envisaged.

Very few university and polytechnic courses deal exclusively and explicitly with urban history, but the Open University's courses on Urban Development and Urban Change and Conflict, which are studied throughout the country, have been influential in arousing interest in the field as a teaching subject. There are many courses in local history, and in the history of town planning and architecture, which include urban material (see A. C. Hepburn/28). Since the death of H. J. Dyos, Britain's first Professor of Urban History, there have been no designated chairs in the subject.

This lack of formal organisation and explicit urban history publications reflects the collaborative strategy for the development of urban history favoured by H. J. Dyos and expressed in the work of the Urban History Group. The original *Urban History Newsletter*, issued by Dyos from 1963, was replaced in 1974 by the *Urban History Yearbook* (5), published by Leicester University Press. The yearbook is primarily methodological and bibliographical in content, functioning as a guide to a plethora of work, more or less closely related to the concerns of urban history, embodied in publications and theses. Its future secure under the editorship of D. J. Reeder, the *Urban History Yearbook* remains the principal embodiment in print of British urban history, with the Urban History Group providing the main focus in terms of conferences and meetings. Thus urban history proceeds on the course set by H. J. Dyos, bringing together historians and social scientists from a variety of fields within an interdisciplinary framework in which the relevance of their work to urban concerns can be distinguished.

So influential has the Dyos approach been in Britain that a new generation of specialised scholarly groups has been created within the general field of urban history since the 1970s. They include the Planning History Group, the Pre-Modern Towns Group, and the

Construction History Group. Urban history is also a major concern of the Historical Geography Research Group which meets under the aegis of the Institute of British Geographers. The work of the Planning History Group focuses on the 20th century which is still somewhat neglected by other urban historians, and it publishes a *Planning History Bulletin* (2) from the University of Birmingham. A scholarly journal, *Planning Perspectives* (3) was launched in 1986. Much work by urban historical geographers appears in the pages of the *Journal of Historical Geography* (1). The Urban History Group is now trying to establish links between these organisations, but it is too early to assess the results of its initiative.

Meanwhile, much research and documentary material relevant to urban history appears as a result of local and regional initiatives. Britain has a strong tradition of antiquarian, archaeological and historical societies which, however confined their original interests, have published large quantities of scholarly work in the general field of history in recent decades (see E. L. C. Mullins/8). Local and regional historical journals such as *Northern History* have proliferated since the 1950s. Some of them, such as the *Bulletin of Local History, East Midland Region*, publish the work of amateur historians, much of which is of a very high quality. The interests of amateur historians also predominate in the pages of a national journal, *The Local Historian*. As time passes, these local and regional institutions devote increasing attention to the history of the industrial era, including its urban dimension.

Resources for the study of modern British urban history are concentrated in the town and city collections of archives which are located in most cases in the municipal reference libraries. Much recent material relating to urban government is still in the hands of the municipalities themselves but research access is normally granted except for near-contemporary records. National surveys of municipal holdings have been undertaken by P. Laxton, of Liverpool University's Department of Geography, and (for planning history records) by M. Simpson, of the Department of History, University College, Swansea, on behalf of the Planning History Group. An official review of municipal archives is currently being mounted by the Department of the Environment.

The county archives do contain a measure of material relevant to the urban history of the 19th and 20th centuries, though they are more useful for earlier periods. On the other hand, the main archive collections of the central government, concentrated in the English and Scottish Public Record Offices in London and Edinburgh, respectively, contain quantities of material relevant to towns in the industrial period, reflecting the developing central supervision of urban affairs which rapid urbanisation tended to generate. Both offices publish a series of guides and other introductions to their collections [see H. N. Blakiston and Public Record Office (17)]. Additions to local and regional archives are monitored and listed by the Royal Commission on Historical Manuscripts, which maintains an invaluable consultative facility — the National Register of Archives, in London. Private archives, such as the records of the great urban landowners, can be readily traced by this means. F. Ranger provides a basic guide to British record repositories (18).

An outstanding source of printed material is the published proceedings of the British parliament which fall into two main categories: the debates of the House of Commons and the House of Lords, which are recorded verbatim in the *Debates* series (often popularly referred to as *Hansard*), and the proceedings and papers of parliamentary committees, commissions and government departments which are published in the *Sessional Papers* (sometimes referred to as [British] *Parliamentary Papers* or "blue books"). Manuscript parliamentary records can be consulted at the House of Lords Record Office, at the Palace of Westminster. A number of lists and guides to these proceedings have appeared over the years, and the most convenient initial access to them is through Bond's guide. Another valuable source of printed material, much of it drawn from the national archives, is the volumes published by a number of local, county and regional record societies (see E. L. C. Mullins/16).

There are no methodological guides as such to the researching of urban history, but urban historians can draw much enlightenment from a number of handbooks on research into local history aimed primarily at amateur historians. Particularly useful are those of F. G. Emmison (15), W. B. Stephens (19), A. Rogers (11) and P. Riden (10). J. West (20) has provided a valuable guide to town records. The *Urban History Yearbook* (5) contains a number of methodological articles, and reference should also be made to two volumes deriving from conferences of the Urban History Group, *The Study of Urban History* (22), and *The Pursuit of Urban History* (24). Historical geographers should consult *Area*. The main bibliography of urban history is that of G. H. Martin and S. C. McIntyre (7), which continues the much earlier compilation of Gross. A further compilation by G. H. Martin is in preparation, but, in the meantime, the annual, cumulative bibliography of urban history in the *Urban History Yearbook* provides extensive coverage. G. H. Martin's succinct bibliography in the *Guide international d'histoire urbaine* (29) remains of great value. A. Sutcliffe's (9) bibliography of the history of urban and regional planning includes many British titles.

C. Research: Results and Issues

For the purposes of this survey, modern British urban history is taken as beginning in the mid-18th century when the industrialisation process originated. Research on the history of British towns and urbanisation since this period has concentrated on two major areas. These are: the creation of the physical environment, and social history. The study of urban politics and government has been less prominent, except in so far as it has related to the control and improvement of the environment as, for instance, in the history of public health, municipal housing, slum clearance, and urban and regional planning. The productive economies of urban areas, and changes in mentalities associated with the urban phenomenon, have been relatively neglected. Chronologically, the main emphasis of research has been on the period 1815 to 1914.

Urban history is so much an amalgam of the experiences of individual towns and cities that general surveys are very difficult to write, particularly in the absence of systematic and comprehensive statistical analysis of the British urban network and of the economic and social structures of its component units. However, the urban geographers are well on the way to filling this gap. H. C. Darby (31), and R. A. Dodgshon and R. A. Butlin (32), have constructed comprehensive studies of the changing geography of England and Wales which, in the modern period, pay full attention to the growth and articulation of urban areas. B. T. Robson (43) has provided a speculative but stimulating disquisition on the dynamics of urban growth, with particular reference to 19th-century England. The 20th-century urban network, less thoroughly studied as yet, can nevertheless be approached through D. Donnison and P. Soto (37), and P. Hall (129). H. Carter's (30) introduction to urban historical geography contains much British material. These studies reveal a progressive concentration of Britain's rapidly growing population during the 19th century, with the urban hierarchy increasingly dominated by London and a number of large manufacturing and seaport conurbations. In the 20th century there has been a gradual shift towards deconcentration into urbanised regions, culminating in recent years in the depopulation of the central cities of the conurbations. The evolution of manufacturing industry, which favoured large cities in the later 19th century, but subsequently encountered growing external diseconomies there, appears to have been fundamental to this development.

The impact of these growing towns on the landscape is the subject of a lively and wide-ranging discussion by B. Trinder (177). The emergence of the town of the industrial era as a physical entity is surveyed by G. Burke (102), and (with an emphasis on architecture) by D. W. Lloyd (138). J. Burnett's (103) study of housing history, even broader than its title suggests, amounts to a general essay on the physical development of the modern English town with due reference to social and policy aspects. More oriented towards public policy and planning, but nevertheless providing a general introduction to the development of the urban environment, are G. E. Cherry (109) and W. Ashworth (95). Taken as a whole, these studies chart an improving urban environment in which the increasing intervention of public authority has generally been beneficent in its effects. This ameliorist tradition in British urban history has recently been challenged, principally in the fields of housing and planning history, which will be discussed later.

None of the studies mentioned so far has much to say about Scotland, but the gap is now being filled by Scottish historians themselves. I. H. Adams (33) has written a pioneering survey, and the collective volume edited by G. Gordon and B. Dicks (27) is expected to be the first of a series. Scottish urban history is in many respects *sui generis*. Scotland had its own system of urban administration and the multi-storey housing which characterised its larger cities had more in common with the continent of Europe than with England. R. G. Rodger (148) has shown how tenement housing was the product of lower *per capita* incomes and the distinctive institutions of Scottish land tenure.

Wales, for its part, did not maintain a separate urban administrative system and most English statistical surveys and other official inquiries, including the Census, incorporate Wales. However, Wales generated few large towns and has not been extensively studied by urban historians. Mention should be made, nevertheless, of the efforts of the historical geographer, H. Carter, as reflected for instance in his studies of Merthyr Tydfil with S. Wheatley (66), and

of M. J. Daunton's biography of Cardiff (186), — the most important to date to be devoted to a Welsh city.

Survey volumes of periods of British urban history since the
beginning of industrialisation were almost unknown until recently.
Some, like those of D. Read (41) and P. J. Waller (44), are social
histories of periods so recent that their authors have chosen to make
urban life their central theme. P. J. Corfield (35), however, has
produced a thorough study of towns and urbanisation in 18th-
century England, which is complemented by M. J. Daunton's (36)
briefer review of the links between towns and industrialisation in the
18th century. These works confirm that much of the manufacturing
growth of the second half of the 18th century occurred outside the
established towns, close to sources of water power and minerals. The
towns prospered nevertheless as centres of commerce, professional
services, artisanal activities, consumption and leisure. P. Borsay
(64) has even identified an 'urban renaissance' in the late 17th and
early 18th centuries, which reached its culmination in the emergence
of spas and resorts such as Bath, Buxton and Brighton. After 1800
steam power and improved road and canal communications, later
enhanced by the railways, allowed mechanised manufacturing to
expand readily in the towns and the urbanisation process consequently accelerated. The level of urbanisation rose via a century-
long S-curve from around one-third in 1800 to about four-fifths in
1900, with growth favouring the largest cities, London at their head.

A phenomenon of this magnitude can scarcely be ignored by
historians but it is also a daunting challenge. R. Lawton, a historical
geographer provides the pithiest review of the 'age of great cities'
which was in the 19th century (39). Significant differences between
the leading cities of the period provide the central theme of A.
Briggs's influential volume of essays, *Victorian Cities* (34). Ten years
later, in *The Victorian City*, H. J. Dyos and M. Wolff (23) brought a
constellation of talents to bear on the problem. These individual and
collective surveys have clearly established the rich diversity of
19th-century towns and cities as social phenomena, but a unifying
theory and analysis are still lacking. Moreover, the economic dynamic of Victorian urbanisation remains under-researched, partly
perhaps because of the apparent inevitability of the process. Little
effort has been made by economic historians to follow up the lines of
inquiry suggested by the economic geographer, A. Pred (175).
Instead, the study of spatial dynamics has concentrated on regions,
as for instance in the work of E. H. Hunt (168) and C. H. Lee (170).

Much of this high-quality material is incidentally relevant to towns, but much more could be done from an explicitly urban perspective. For the time being, urban historians are discouraged from making the necessary commitment of time and effort partly by their awareness, encouraged by scholars such as E. A. Wrigley (46) and P. Abrams (166), that the regional dimension may offer greater insight into the spatial aspects of historical processes than can the urban dimension.

As we move forward into the 20th century, D. Fraser (38) provides a useful survey of the Edwardian period, but thereafter there are no general urban history surveys. However, general studies of social history continue perforce to have an urban focus, such as H. Perkin's (172) review of the period from the 1890s to the present. More volumes of this type are planned in the social history series produced by the London publisher, Hutchinson.

It is often suggested that the production of effective general surveys must await the appearance of more local studies in urban history. Much work of this type, some of it of antiquarian nature, appears yearly, but the exemplar of a modern city history is generally taken to be A. Briggs's (182) second volume in the *History of Birmingham* series, which is flanked by the work of C. Gill (183), and of A. Sutcliffe and R. Smith (184). A. Briggs's emphasis on social history is echoed in S. Pollard's study of labour in Sheffield (173), which is broader than its title suggests, and in J. Simmons's history of Leicester (194). Leeds has recently been covered by a collective volume edited by D. Fraser (193), and 19th-century Bradford now has an effective portrait from the pen of J. Reynolds(185). F. Hill's history of Lincoln (195) is an outstanding treatment of a smaller town. S. G. Checkland's reflections on the dynamics of the history of industrial Glasgow (189) are bound to prompt much further work, both on Glasgow and on other manufacturing cities. A. Gibb's (190) study must count as an early product of that stimulus, with its emphasis on urban policy. Among the ports, G. Jackson's on Hull (192) and A. Temple Patterson's on Southampton (200) are the outstanding studies. K. Richardson's chronicle of Coventry's development (187) is notable for its strongly contemporary emphasis.

Among the studies stressing the economic history of towns in the early stages of their industrialisation, the early work of T. C. Barker and J. R. Harris on St. Helens (199), and of W. H. Chaloner on Crewe (188), still stand out, for more recent emphasis on social history has partially discouraged further exercises of this type.

However, it may be — paradoxically enough — that the very growth of urban history has discouraged the town biography by its emphasis on comparative processes and structures. The study of London, universally recognised as *sui generis*, should of course surmount such conceptual obstacles, but the main problem here is the size and complexity of what was for so long the world's largest city. F. Sheppard (197) has produced an effective portrait of London in the first half of the 19th century, but the planned series on the history of London, of which it forms a part, is still incomplete. Meanwhile D. J. Olsen (142), L. C. B. Seaman (92) and A. A. Jackson (136) have written evocative portraits of the physical aspects of London in the 19th and 20th centuries, and M. D. George's (75) social history is still of value for the 18th century. P. L. Garside's (196) recent essay concentrates on the 20th century but sets it in a longer perspective drawing on much recent work. Also emphasising the 20th century, and the physical form of London, is the richly illustrated work of G. Weightman and S. Humphries (198).

It needs, of course, to be stressed that the paucity of urban biographies is offset by the great volume of material on individual towns embedded in the thematic work to which we shall now turn. The study of aspects and themes of urban history is one of the great strengths of the British tradition because, due partly to the inspiration of H. J. Dyos, so many economic, social and political historians were attracted to the urban scene, particularly in the 19th century, as a quarry of material for their investigations of general historical processes. The investigation of 19th-century urban workers' housing grew, for instance, out of the "standard-of-living controversy" which exercised so many economic historians in the 1960s. Ultimately, housing history was to become a field of inquiry in its own right, as a facet of the study of town building with which our discussion of these thematic approaches will begin.

The study of modern town building grew out of the history of architecture, mainly because of the involvement of distinguished architects in the creation of the residential townscape in Bath, Edinburgh, London and other centres of fashion during the "Augustan age" of the 18th century when the principles of Palladian design were belatedly applied to the layout and building of British towns. The work of the architectural historian, J. Summerson (154), provided the main link between architectural and urban history, though it was preceded to some degree by that of the Danish architectural and planning historian, S. E. Rasmussen (145), D. J. Olsen's (143) study of some of the "great estates" of London's West End echoed J. Summerson's emphasis on the habitat of the rich as an artistic creation, but he was more interested than J. Summerson in the economics of the subdivision and building processes. A similar emphasis on the practical aspects imbued the study of the building of classical Edinburgh by economic historian A. J. Youngson (165). The growing interests in the finance and administration of urban property prompted historians to delve more deeply into the records of the great landowners. They proved uniquely rich because of the widespread adoption in England since the 16th century of the urban-building lease, a device which avoided the alienation of land held in settled estates, but which, by the 18th century, was in widespread use even by non-aristocratic landowners. The leasehold system not generally obtained in Europe by the 19th century, allowed the original owner to maintain a direct interest in his property until it reverted to him on the expiry of the lease. The resulting archives provided a mine of information for C. W. Chalklin (107) when he shifted the emphasis of town-building studies in the early industrial era to provincial towns noted for their utilitarian rather than aesthetic townscapes. In doing so, he confirmed that the early industrial town-building process was essentially an amalgam of multiple small-scale enterprises. Even the landowners, who alone were potentially in a position to shape whole urban districts, often delegated the work of subdivision to small developers who handled a few sites at a time. Only the biggest aristocratic landowners maintained a permanent involvement, which was often associated with a political participation in urban affairs, an area of activity which has recently been elucidated with great vigour and perception by D. Cannadine in an influential monograph (105) and a volume of essays (106). Because it was conducted on such a small scale, usually without the production of lasting records, the work of builders and building financiers in the 19th century is very obscure. P. J. Aspinall (96) has done some useful work on the structure of the building industry in a number of towns, indicating only a very slight tendency towards a concentration of activity in the later part of the century. H. J. Dyos (122) has shown that, as might be expected, the scale of building activity in London was somewhat larger than in the provinces. C. G. Powell's (174) survey of the British building industry in the 19th and 20th centuries, which draws fully on these and other studies, shows that much remains to be done, but the sheer labour and sometimes frustration involved in work in this area are a serious deterrent.

We are, nevertheless, already in possession of a picture of the 19th-century town-building process which is one of prolific, multi-faceted activity, scarcely influenced by the embryonic public authorities of the day except through the developing building regulations recently charted by S. M. Gaskell (128), and shaped by large landowners only in the richest residential neighbourhoods of the most fashionable towns. The early physical results of this process are clearly visible in M. D. Lobel's (12) excellent collection of town maps, reconstructed to show the groundplans of English towns in about 1800. Apparently there was no shortage of capital and enterprise for residential building until the later 19th century, when Britain began to move towards the large-scale, subsidised public housing which has done so much to shape its cities in the 20th century (which will be discussed below). There was a persistent preference among housing consumers for single-family houses. Incomes among manual workers were so low during the early stages of industrialisation that the resulting house form, typical of the manu-facturing and transport centres of the Midlands and North between the 1780s and the mid-1800s, was the back-to-back terrace house, normally of two storeys. The genesis and development of this rudimentary type of workers' housing have been fully investigated — in the case of Leeds, by M. D. Beresford (98). Of course, the poorest workers could not afford even houses as small as these, and the resulting phenomenon of the cellar-dwelling has been analysed in respect of Liverpool by I. C. Taylor (160). In London, back-to-back housing was prohibited under the unique Building Acts which regulated construction there, and the poor normally occupied rooms in larger, older houses. The spread of building regulations to the provincial towns from the 1840s resulted in the standardisation of a superior type of terraced house incorporating a back yard or garden and allowing through-ventilation. S. Muthesius (141) has provided a full study of this 'bye-law terrace' principally from an architectural point of view, while M. J. Daunton's (115) study of mass housing in the later 19th century concentrates on social and economic aspects. C. A. Forster (127), provides a useful case-study of Hull. In London, land values were so high that the second half of the 19th century saw a big growth of tenement housing, which in the working-class sector was built principally by the philanthropic trusts and limited divi-dend companies, which have been studied by J. N. Tarn (159). Meanwhile, the terraced house fell from favour among the better-off, and was replaced by the villa, which can be pursued into the 20th century through the work of A. A. Jackson (136), and A. M. Edwards (125). However, much study remains to be done on 20th-century private housing, and the main collections of essays in this field, edited by S. D. Chapman (108), A. Sutcliffe (155), and M. A. Simpson and T. H. Lloyd (152) concentrate on the 19th century.

The rise of the villa was largely a function of the suburbanisation process, the origins of which lay in the 18th century in the case of London and the largest industrial cities, but which did not begin to transform the British urban townscape until the middle and later decades of that century. At the core of suburbanisation were the changes occurring in the commercial and manufacturing centres of the cities, but these have been surprisingly little investigated. J. R. Kellett's (169) study of the impact of railways on city centres remains outstanding, and there is a good survey of the depopulation and commercialisation of the City of London by D. F. Stevens (153). The transport improvements associated with suburbanisation have been well summarised in a recent article by T. C. Barker, following the massive study of London's transport which he and M. Robbins co-authored (167). J. P. McKay's (171) internationally comparative study of tramway electrification suggests that suburbanisation did not become a mass phenomenon until the 1890s, and reinforces D. Ward's (162) warning about misleading backward extrapolations into the 19th century of 20th-century urban forms. Nevertheless, there remains plenty of peripheral expansion — and the associated changes in attitude — to study in the 19th century.

The principal exemplar of the suburban case study is H. J. Dyos's portrait of Camberwell (122), but almost as influential is F. M. L. Thompson's (191) biography of another London suburb, Hampstead. F. M. L. Thompson has gone on to edit a volume of essays on suburbanisation by younger scholars (161). H. C. Prince (144) and M. A. Simpson (176), dealing with London and Glasgow, respectively, provide useful surveys of the development of entire suburban sectors. There is no nationwide study of the suburbanisation process but D. Reeder (85) provides a recent review of the question in a published lecture delivered in the H. J. Dyos Memorial Lecture series. A problem of suburbanisation studies is the difficulty of distinguishing true suburbs from peripheral growth of a non-suburban nature, particularly where working-class and lower-middle-class housing development is concerned. Indeed, historical interest may well be switching towards more general urban processes in the later 19th century, rendering traditional suburban studies obsolete.

As the Victorian middle-classes suburbanised, they became increasingly concerned about the poorest parts of the cities which they had left. These poor areas came to be identified as "slums" and with them there was perceived a "slum problem" which was one of the major stimuli to the growth of public intervention in the workings of large cities in the later 19th century. Significantly, H. J. Dyos detected a close economic link between the suburb and the slum, implicit in his 1968 article on the slums of London (72) and fully explicit in a stimulating essay on slum and suburb which he wrote with D. Reeder (124). However, the best-detailed analysis of slum formation is G. S. Jones's study of the East End of London (77) in the 1880s, when high unemployment, the casualisation of labour, and rising rents produced an acute social crisis. The generally ineffectual reaction of the authorities to the London slum problem has been investigated by A. S. Wohl (163). What it was like to live in a Salford slum emerges from the semi-autobiographical account of R. Roberts (87), C. G. Pooley's (86) analysis of individual life experiences in Liverpool, and R. Samuel's (90) innovative exercise in oral history. Links between the 19th-century slum and the "inner city problem" of today are traced in a stimulating fashion by M. Hebbert (132).

This concentration of attention on the two extremes of suburb and slum has left virtually unexplored the greater part of the Victorian city which was neither suburb nor slum, but which housed, in mediocre conditions, the large numbers of skilled and semi-skilled workers, and the rapidly expanding group of white-collar workers who were employed primarily in the service sector. M. J. Daunton (115) has pointed to this important gap and has made an admirable effort to fill it, and D. Englander (73) provides a valuable study of landlord-tenant relations. However, much remains to be done. Fortunately, the students of urban social structures have shed light on these intermediate groups, and it is to their work that we shall now turn.

The availability of a decennial national Census from 1801 permits the investigation of social structures during the 19th century with a precision which is quite impossible for earlier periods. However, the manuscript records of the Census are available to researchers only after a lapse of 100 years and so can shed no light on the end of the 19th and 20th centuries. Moreover, the early Censuses were crude and inaccurate, and satisfactory research using them is not possible before 1841 or even 1851. These practical limitations have produced a narrow "window" through which a great volume of research effort has poured, with spectacular results. The outstanding study of household structure is M. Anderson's (61) on Preston which, supported by L. Lees's (79) more recent survey of the settlement of Irish immigrants in London, has stressed the adaptation of migrants to conditions in large towns rather than the disruption of their personal lives. Great poverty and hardship nevertheless remained, and emerge from W. A. Armstrong's (62) general survey of the social structure of York, a model of its kind. Hardship contributed to the acute class antagonisms which J. Foster (74) has detected in Oldham in the 1840s in an influential and controversial study of class in three English towns during the early stages of industrialisation. Cities as the specific locus of class formation also provide the central theme of R. Q. Gray's (76) study of skilled workers in Edinburgh, and G. Crossick's (67) comparable work on artisans in south London. Both these analyses emphasise the internal generation of class attitudes, but P. Joyce's (78) study of Lancashire mill towns in the second half of the 19th century suggests that employer paternalism remained an important influence on worker attitudes at any rate until the 1890s. E. Roberts (86), too, is drawing attention to the late 19th and early 20th centuries with her work on living standards.

Until recently, the preoccupations of British social and labour historians with the working class discouraged study of the urban middle classes, but this gap is now being filled by a cohort of younger historians led by W. D. Rubinstein and R. J. Morris. W. D. Rubinstein (89) has been particularly interested in the distribution of personal wealth both spatially and between occupational groups. He has shown that industrialists were not, as a class, as rich as merchants, financiers and landowners, and that personal wealth was heavily concentrated in London. R. J. Morris (81) has shown how the middle classes maintained a hegemony over 19th-century towns through exclusive institutions and thus, to some degree, reconstructed the towns and their society in their own image. G. Crossick (67) for his part, has now turned his attention from skilled manual workers to the lower middle class.

British historians, in contrast to their counterparts in the American "new urban history", are more interested in social structures than in social mobility, partly because the attitudes which have moulded the British sociopolitical system since the later 19th century have evidently derived from slowly changing mass social formations rather than from the chimera of individual upward mobility which helped discourage the emergence of a monolithic labour movement in the United States. The lower level of foreign immigration into Britain almost certainly enhanced working-class cohesion. Such foreign immigration as occurred located principally in the larger cities, but its implications for urban society as a whole are only now being investigated, as for instance in the work of C. G. Pooley (84) and J. Walvin (93), together with that of L. Lees (79), already cited. The residential location of the social classes, and indicators thereof such as spatial patterns of marriage, are principally the concern of historical geographers such as R. Dennis (71). For all this, British study of the social articulation of urban areas is still overshadowed by American work, partly because of its paucity of studies of social and residential mobility.

Study of urban social life and customs has concentrated on the working classes in recent years, partly owing to the influence of the 'social control' paradigm in British social history since the later 1960s. The main feature of the century is the abandonment by many manual workers of formal religious observance when they moved into the towns, which caused considerable concern to middle-class contemporaries and prompted the various religious denominations to take counter-measures. None of these was very successful (though the Roman Catholic Church enjoyed considerable success in retaining the loyalty of Irish immigrants to English cities), but the sheer size of the effort has attracted historians such as E. R. Wickham (181). More recently an interest has sprung up in religious sociology, with H. McLeod (180) as its outstanding exponent. Spatial aspects of religious observance are discussed by B. I. Coleman (178). In Scotland, links between religion and politics have aroused much historical attention, for instance in the work of A. A. MacLaren (179). Of course, among the biggest discouragements to working-class religious observance were poverty and long working hours, but enough time remained to them to engage in recreations, of which the middle classes and the authorities disapproved, to prompt formal efforts to direct their superfluous energies into more acceptable channels. The work of H. Cunningham (70) and P. Bailey (63) provides the quickest access to the debate on 19th-century leisure. Holidays away from home had a distinct urban expression in the form of the seaside resort, the development of which has been charted by J. K. Walton (45).

Our survey now begins turning to the relatively neglected 20th century. The main emphasis in this period is on public policy, reflecting an expansion of the institutions and scope of urban administration in the later 19th century, and the urban location of the major social problems which have been tackled in the 20th-century progress towards the "Welfare State". However, because urban government started to expand from its rudimentary beginnings early on in the industrialisation process, we shall begin our account in the first half of the 19th century, when the expanding towns started to generate alarming problems of public order and public health. This phase attracted the scholarly attention of S. and B. Webb (58) over half a century ago, and their work still enjoys an unimpeachable authority. More recent surveys of the growth of local government have been provided by historians such as K. B. Smellie (57) and B. Keith-Lucas (52). Public health, perhaps the main stimulus to public administrative activity, has been investigated by an army of scholars, but the best access to their work is the up-to-date survey by A. S. Wohl (59). The widening scope of urban government in the later 19th century, and political influences thereon, are discussed principally by D. Fraser (47), E. P. Hennock (51), A. Offer (54), and J. R. Kellett (53). D. Owen (55) and T. Hart (50) provide valuable case studies, of London and Glasgow respectively. London government, of course, was transformed by the creation of the London County Council in 1889. While a new history of the L. C. C. is in preparation by a group of London scholars, the older official history by I. G. Gibbon and R. W. Bell (49) remains of value. W. A. Robson's (56) polemical history is still of interest, though it has been recently overshadowed by the definitive study of metropolitan government by K. Young and P. L. Garside (60). These latter works, of course, include extensive consideration of the twentieth century towards which the L. C. C., with its progressive policies, indubitably pointed. However, studies of urban administration devoted exclusively to the years after 1914 are rare; the later essays in D. Fraser's *History of Modern Leeds* (193) provide an example.

The 20th century, nevertheless, brought important extensions of the scope of urban government and two of these — municipal housing, and urban and regional planning — have attracted considerable historical attention. The study of planning has emerged partly from analysis of the history of 19th-century architecture, with the essays on model communities by W. Creese (113) and the C. and R. Bells (97) exemplifying this line of evolution. However,

19th-century urban architecture has been an important area of study in its own right, mainly because the Victorian failure to develop "modern" styles has intrigued historians at least since the publication of K. Clark's (112) great essay on the Gothic Revival. The best general surveys of 19th-century British architecture, most of which was urban, are by R. F. Jordan (137) and by R. Dixon and S. Muthesius (119). Recently, growing respect has been shown for Victorian architecture both in terms of its artistic and utilitarian quality, and of the validity of the motivations and objectives of its designers and their clients. C. Cunningham's (114) study of town halls stresses their functional aspects and C. Dellheim (117) emphasises the value of the past and its forms as legitimating forces in Victorian society. A number of authors have pointed to a gradual transition towards modernity, A. Service (149) providing a good example of such a study. Q. Hughes (135), D. Sharp (150), F. Worsdall (164) and D. Hickman (133), dealing with Liverpool, Manchester, Glasgow and Birmingham, respectively, have produced excellent urban architectural histories, based on individual analysis of surviving buildings. However, so many outstanding buildings of the industrial era have been lost through redevelopment that it is appropriate to mention that H. Hobhouse (134) has produced a valuable alternative architectural history of London, based on buildings which have disappeared.

It was towards the end of the 19th century that socialistic architects such as R. Unwin began to advocate the application of architectural skills to the habitat of the poorer classes through town planning. However, planning was also associated with a programme of urban economic reform which before 1914 sought primarily to secure cheaper land for workers' housing, partly through the provision of cheaper and more extensive transport. Thus surveyors and engineers became involved in town planning, to produce a composite profession which has set its mark on 20th-century Britain. The rise of the town-planning profession and the work of some of its leading exponents has been well charted in two books by G. E. Cherry (109/110), while A. Sutcliffe's *Towards the Planned City* (155) sets the origins of British planning in an international perspective.

After the First World War town planning achieved rather less than its advocates had hoped, but it revived after the Second World War when comprehensive national institutions of urban and rural planning were set up and a "New Towns" programme was inaugurated. The New Towns strategy, unique in the world, has found it hard to adapt to fluctuating circumstances since the 1950s, as M. Aldridge (94) has shown, but it has nevertheless attracted a considerable degree of scholarly attention, some of it historical. The parallel strategy of the containment of established urban areas by the imposition of green belts has been fully evaluated by P. Hall (129), who has demonstrated that in the long run the general patterns of urban growth have continued to be shaped principally by market forces rather than by public policy. However, where public policy has encountered its severest criticisms has been in the field of public housing and the urban redevelopment with which, in many cases, it has been associated. The irony of this assessment lies in the fact that between the two world wars, when town planning stagnated, the emergence of public housing as a key element in British municipal policy provided the main sphere for the activity of the planners. M. Bowley's (101) survey of the evolution of public housing policy remains of great value, while M. Swenarton (158) has aroused much controversy with his suggestion that the central government's leap into subsidised housing in 1919 was an anti-revolutionary measure. In the 1930s the emphasis switched from peripheral housing to slum clearance and A. Ravetz (146) provides a fine study of Quarry Hill, Leeds, the largest of the multi-storey estates of the 1930s. Much less work has been done on low-density housing between the wars, but an Italian scholar, D. Calabi (104), is setting a fine example to British housing historians, and M. J. Daunton's volume of essays (116) includes three balanced case studies of individual localities.

After the Second World War, British public housing moved into a predominantly high-rise phase which marked the 1950s and 1960s in particular. L. Esher (126), who participated in this episode, provides a sympathetic account, but A. Ravetz (147) is scathing in her criticisms. P. Hall's (130) stimulating model of the "planning disaster" with its related case studies helps to explain how major errors of planning policy are virtually impossible to avoid. P. Dunleavy (121) also is primarily interested in the limitations on political and administrative initiative. J. Melling (139) and S. Merrett (140), however, in their discussions of the dynamics of housing policy, stress that the defects and errors are rooted in the contradictions of modern urban capitalism. Marxist and Weberian scholars of this type, following the recent example of Manuel Castells, will no doubt continue to turn towards historical research, and it is to be hoped that a fuller appreciation of the dynamics of the urban economy will emerge therefrom.

D. Conclusion

We have thus returned to one of our initial judgments, that the *economic* history of British towns and cities has been neglected. Given that towns exist primarily because their qualities of accessible location and concentration give them a comparative advantage in the production of goods and services, any study of urban history which neglects this production function is bound to be incomplete, however important the functions of the town in the sphere of reproduction. Moreover, without this analysis of the economic dimension of urban history, it will be impossible to define the historical significance of the urban dimension in modern British history — another weakness to which we referred initially. There can be no doubt about the volume of work which touches on aspects of the history of modern British towns and cities — and indeed there could be no other result in a country which has so long been so heavily urbanised. Moreover, as time passes, more work will appear on the period since 1914, which is relatively neglected at present. However, no true development of British urban history can occur without a reinforcement of the essential underpinning theory which must identify what is distinctive about the nature of urban areas. In the current state of historical research in general, it seems likely that the greatest progress will be made in two fields: first, that of the political economy of towns and cities; and second, that of the cultural forms associated with urban existence. In the former area, towns can be viewed principally as units of production, but the fundamental relationships between public and private activity which urban concentration tends to generate can be distinguished and emphasised. In the latter area, the town is viewed principally as an agent or locus of reproduction. Thus the study of urban history offers the opportunity to bring together the historical investigation of production and of reproduction more readily than do many other historical fields, as we can already glimpse in the work of a younger generation of historians including scholars such as P. Joyce (78), G. S. Jones (77) and J. Melling (139). Let us not forget, however, that the association of production and reproduction in the study of individual towns and of urban history in general was marked out in the early 1960s by A. Briggs (34), and complemented by H. G. Dyos's emphasis on the urban existence as a comprehensive experience. Thus British urban historiography can be regarded as maintaining an essential continuity in comparison with which some of the weaknesses or omissions mentioned in this review may justifiably be regarded as temporary or superficial.

SÁNDOR GYIMESI

Hungary*

A. Questions and Methods

Several disciplines are involved in studying the history of town development and urbanisation in Hungary in the 19th and 20th centuries. Besides historical science much research in this field has been done by urbanology, which comprises the geography of settlements and their organisation as well as town construction. In the theoretical foundation it is plainly settlement geography that should receive primacy. In this respect the work of T. Mendöl helped urban research gain independence and acquire its theoretical basis (47). Researchers still apply his system of categories or at least use it as a starting point, and it is often the subject of theoretical debates.

Opinion among researchers is divided over T. Mendöl 's definition of the settlement as the working and dwelling place of a group of people. T. Mendöl (48) himself disregarded spatial unity, holding that the provincial places of residence of workers commuting daily to their places of work in Budapest also belong to the capital. The Urbanology Subcommittee of the Hungarian Academy of Sciences has recently emphasised territorial contiguity while others think they have found a proper definition in the regularly used functional unity of the place of residence, place of work, institutions, etc.

Mendöl favoured the functional approach and distinguished the town from other settlements as a seat of central functions. He means by that all those functions not found in each place, i.e. both functions of central places in Christaller's sense and so-called special functions of supra-regional character. The town in this sense is not

* Numbers in brackets in this chapter refer to entries in the bibliography on pp. 401–408 of this volume.

the same as in the administrative sense: it either extends beyond its boundaries (agglomeration) or is more restricted than they are. For the latter, T. Mendöl takes the example of towns in the Great Hungarian Plain (Kecskemét, Nagykőrös, etc). These towns have three morphological units arranged in different zones with the nucleus of the town in the centre surrounded by the rural (village) zone, while the third zone consists of the inhabited areas on the outskirts, that is, the adjacent, detached farms. T. Mendöl did not include the latter two in the territory of the town, but measured its real size by the urban nucleus alone.

As opposed to T. Mendöl and relying on the functional view, F. Erdei (33) defined the theory of the so-called agricultural town. In his opinion the towns of the Great Hungarian Plain represent a peculiar Hungarian type, morphologically different from Western European towns. In these towns, the detached farms mean agricultural farms, i.e. the work-place, they have regular contact with the town and form an organic part of it. (Originally, the detached farm was only a place of residence while people also kept their town houses for a long time).

Even today there is no single definition of the town as a seat of central functions. Currently, Hungarian urban geography distinguishes three groups of functions: local functions (concerning only the population of the settlement, meeting everyday demands and having no regional or supra-regional character); basic functions (these are practically the same as the functions of central places); and special functions (reaching beyond the area of the town and often also referred to as "singular" functions in the literature). In the strict sense, only the second set of functions makes a settlement a town. Against the geographical application of this principle, statisticians and economists argue that productive activity, which is usually a special function, is not really taken into account. They suggest that settlements should be graded according to the share of GNP produced in the town. The present state of statistical science does not permit this to be directly measured, so indexes should be gained by aggregating representative values — the number of active wage earners, the value of retail turnover, for example.

From these discussions, it emerges that three approaches should be distinguished: settlement hierarchy, the state of development, and the functional approach. Settlement geography defines hierarchical position according to the role the settlement plays in the urban network depending on the level of functions (e.g. county town, seat of the district court). In this classification, production is only indirectly taken into account as a town-shaping force. It is regarded as a factor which determines only the order of magnitude, not the hierarchy.

The notion of the state of development is defined by the nature and level of the services the town can offer its citizens. (It can be measured by, for example, the average area of accommodation per head, size of shops, consumption of electricity, etc.)

There are two ways of studying urban functions and functional types: occupational structure and study of the gravity zones. The analysis of E. Lettrich (24/45) typified the occupational structure with the help of a triangular diagram comparing the proportions of three groups — those employed in agriculture, in industry and in the service sector. As regards the number of people employed in the service sector she identified the three most typical classes of town:

1. rural settlements where the proportion of agricultural wage earners is 55% or higher
2. settlements where people have homes at two different places at the same time (and where the three sectors are in more or less equal proportion) and
3. urban settlements (where the proportion of agricultural wage-earners is under one-third).

The type distinguished by the occupational structure is not entirely the same as the functional type — the number of commuters and pensioners, for example, may cause divergences between the two — but they are closely related to each other. The former is especially suitable for comparing regions at different levels of development and for characterising a longer period.

Recent research shows that there is a higher correlation between urbanisation and occupational structure than between urbanisation and the state of development measured by the share of GNP.

The study of gravity zones developed in parallel with agglomeration research. Two basic methods of exploration are applied in Hungary today: the gravitational model and empirical surveys. The gravitational model uses various weights (population, institutions, the number of people employed in commerce, etc.). The empirical surveys concentrate on the town. They either set out from the supply capacity of the town and examine how many people, besides the town's population, can be supplied by the different activities, or attempt to scan to what extent people from the provinces take advantage of town services. The latter has mainly been measured using the data of different institutions. Attempts have been made to interview samples of the rural population, but owing to their subjective approach they proved unreliable when checked.

The same towns were surveyed in the different regions of Hungary by both the gravitational and the empirical method. While in regions of the Great Hungarian Plain, the two types of investigation produced the same results, in the northern, more industrialised areas the gravitational method gave a less authentic picture.

The practice of settlement and town planning owes a great debt to geographical theory and investigation, but has treated the methods of town and settlement classification in a practical and analytical way. Even today the conditions for declaring a settlement a town follow this pattern: a gravity zone of at least 10,000 people, of whom at least 5,000 live in the urban central part; the proportion of people employed in industry or in the service sector must amount to at least 75% of the total; and among secondary institutions, a town must have an ambulance station, a polyclinic for specialist consultation, a secondary school and a network of specialised shops.

So settlement policy viewed the problem of towns within the whole settlement network from the point of view of industrial development and the supply of the population. Thus, with respect to transport, the primary (basic) supply — general practitioner, primary school, shop, etc. — must be within reach in up to 15 minutes; secondary (middle grade) supply — specialist doctors, secondary school, special shops — in up to 40 minutes; and the highest grade supply in up to 180 minutes. Among the researchers in this province, I. Perényi (49) used three aspects in his classification:

1. the number of inhabitants (with a lower limit of 20,000),
2. occupation (agricultural, mixed and industrial),
3. centres of a large region.

In view of the present situation and also of the plan for developing the settlement network made in 1963 and amended in 1970, G. Köszegfalvi and J. Kóródi (43) classified the 67 towns of the country — with the exception of Budapest, always treated as a special case — as follows: five very important centres of the highest grade, 14 main centres, 36 centres of middle grade (two industrial, one agricultural, nine former county towns, and the rest administrative centres), eight industrial towns without any central role, and four former administrative centres.

Mention must be made of the statistical enquiry by M. Fórizs in 1960 (35), which assigned the 62 provincial towns of the time to four development categories according to seven criteria (size of the area, number of inhabitants, central administrative function, roles in retail trade, education, and health care, and the proportion of industrial wage earners).

Thus there is no unified standpoint for classification, only outlines within which each investigation selects the appropriate perspectives. It should also be noted here that the analyses of the gravity zones and agglomeration levels are like cross-sections in not reflecting changes over time. When time phases are examined, that is, when the historical aspects are also considered, only the size of population and the occupational structure are analysed. However, the gravity zone analysis gained from the different sections also gathers some important materials that are useful for historical research. The formation of agglomerations has also raised problems in the field of administration, and researchers tend to think that the sphere subordinated to administration will provide a solution.

Historical research in the stricter sense generally used administrative and legal categories. Towns in Hungary have always been divided into two categories according to their legal status: before 1871 there were country (market) towns and royal (free) boroughs, later these were corporate towns and municipal towns, and, after 1949, towns classed as districts and towns classed as within county rank. In some cases, especially in research on the period after 1870, in addition to these categories, settlements with a population of more than 10,000 or over 20,000 were also counted as towns. The classification, especially when applied to the period before 1970, had two basic defects. On the one hand, the towns had acquired their status very much earlier, so that it no longer reflected the actual state of development; on the other hand, if royal free boroughs are assessed, the urbanisation level of the country will appear much lower than it was in reality; but if the nearly 700 market towns are counted, the figure obtained far exceeds reality. Z. Dávid (32) was the first to attempt setting up a more complex classification system using the combination of legal status and number of inhabitants. Z. Dávid investigated settlements in two different periods, in 1785 and in 1828. He used his own criteria to select market towns with a population exceeding 2,000 drawing on administrative, economic and cultural aspects, the employment structure of the population and urban architecture. To the royal free boroughs he added the most outstanding settlements of this kind hoping to arrive at a more authentic figure of towns in Hungary.

It was S. Gyimesi (36) who first attempted a historical application of the functional town conception of urban geography. Gyimesi selected and classified those settlements that could be regarded as towns in Hungary in the first half of the 19th century with the help of four functional groups (administrative, cultural, commercial or industrial production, and supply) on the basis of the occupational distribution of the population and the institutions of the settlement. Again on a functional basis, V. Bácskai and L. Nagy (26) started examining the town network of Hungary at the beginning of the 19th century. They started by examining those settlements which, during the national tax assessment of 1828, were named by villagers as the places at which they regularly went to market. Computers were employed to investigate the newly discovered market districts. Using a factor analysis based on data gained from the tax evaluation, five groups could be identified which, in the authors' opinion, corresponded, on the whole, with the functional criteria common to towns. This number of towns is much smaller than those indicated in Z. Dávid's (32) or S. Gyimesi's (36) analyses.

The functional selection of towns is still limited to a narrow circle and only yields good research results from the first half of the 19th century. Most of the investigations, even geographical and statistical ones, are restricted to functional and other types of analysis of towns that are recognised as such in the administrative sense, i.e. settlements officially designated as towns.

B. Research Development in Individual Fields

In recent decades, research on urban history has developed in several directions. Within historical research in the strict sense, S. Gyimesi (37) has studied the characteristics of town development during the period of transition from feudalism to capitalism in comparison with European development up to the 1870s. He has pointed out that two major factors played an important role in the position of towns during that period: first, agricultural commodity production and trade — including the emergence of links with international trade — and second, the development of public administration which became a greater force in the urbanisation process. In this period, commercial and agricultural towns made great headway and they also took over some administrative and cultural functions. Industry, however, did not yet play an important role in the development of towns, often being located at agricultural production sites. In his study on town development after 1945, I. Berend T. (31) examined another transitional period. He established that the large-scale industrialisation of the country after 1948 brought about a great increase in urbanisation, and development of the infrastructure was unable to keep abreast of the rapid increase in the urban population. Despite efforts to decentralise industry, the role of the Budapest conurbation increased steadily and, with the decline in agricultural industry, the development of the old agricultural towns was also halted.

L. Ruzsás (50) analysed the development of towns in Transdanubia and Southern Hungary in the 18th and 19th centuries. In one region he emphasised the delayed growth of industrial and commercial centres and, in the other, the importance of grain production and trade.

As to the different sub-sections of urban history, the most popular research topic seems to be the social and political development of urban society. This is partly due to the growing attention given to social history in the last 20 years. Mention must be made of the work of K. Vörös (68), who made a major breakthrough in this field when studying the social composition of the Budapest "virilists" between 1873 and 1917. (After the beginning of capitalism in Hungary only half of the municipal legislators were elected, while the other half were made up of the highest taxpayers, called "virilists".) Based on his analysis, similar research was done on Hódmezövásárhely and Debrecen, providing important information about the composition, character and enterprises of the bourgeois elite.

V. Bácskai (52) has done research of a similar kind on the mobility of householders in the city of Pest. Z. Tóth (66) has attempted to examine changes in the style of living and types of social adjustment in small towns during the time of the bourgeois transition by making use of wills and inventories of estates.

Two statistical sources must also be mentioned here: one is a methodical collection of statistical data concerning society and economic life in Budapest in the last 100 years, the other is an analysis of the mobility of the urban population after 1945 based on a survey. The results of the latter have also been elaborated in a study concentrating on the mobility of different generations, educational and vocational qualifications, and the effect of mobility on demographic trends.

Among the problems of urban self-government and administration three issues have been of major concern to researchers. The first is the conflict between the old feudal self-government and the centralising bureaucratic aims of enlightened absolutism and the landowners, who wanted to defend their privileges against the towns. Here, mention must be made of a study and source-book by G. Bónis (54) on the internal administrative system of Pest and Buda, a work by A. Csizmadia (57) on the legal status of ecclesiastical market towns, and several studies by I. Orosz (63) treating the conflicts between the wine-growing market towns in the Tokay district and the power of landowners.

The second major issue is the strivings of the Hungarian Age of Reforms (1825–1848) for capitalist transformation, the problems of settling the legal status and organisation of towns. Many works deal with the arguments and decrees concerning the towns in the legislation of the Age of Reforms and the War of Independence in 1948 and 1949. Some others analyse the conditions of the different towns, for example a work by G. Komoróczy (60) on the public administration of Debrecen, and one by Ö. Both (55) on the criminal jurisdiction of Szeged.

The third major problem is the adjustment of town administration to the modern state and the legal and social issues this involves. Nevertheless, it is a somewhat neglected field and few works have been published apart from a book by P. Hársfalvi (59) about the conditions of Nyiregyháza.

As far as different aspects of economic life in towns are concerned, research on guild industry has made the best progress. Besides a comprehensive work by G. Eperjessy (72) on market towns, several other studies treat the issues of guildship in Pest and Debrecen. Great help is given to historical research by the national guild cadastre which records all the guild charters found in the country according to their year of issue, the trade in question and their locations. Urban industry in the manufacturing era has largely only been studied for Budapest. Two titles on urban history deserve attention: a work by V. Sándor (77) on the Budapest milling industry, and a collection of studies edited by G. Ránki (76) on the industrial history of Debrecen. A book on the 400-year history of the Debrecen Press, written by K. Benda and K. Irinyi (70), represents a transition towards cultural history. This is a neglected field; few works have been published apart from urban historical monographs. Monographs on ecclesiastical history appear to be even rarer.

Most research on urban history, even the above-mentioned independently published works, continues on from town monographs. Studies on the history of Budapest are an exception in this respect.

The first plans for a modern monograph on Budapest were made in the 1930s. A series of studies was begun entitled "Tanulmányok Budapest Multjából" (Studies on the Past of Budapest) to publish findings and results. The monograph was never completed, but the series was revived in the 1950s. The volumes contained several essays on the 19th and 20th centuries and the findings of international urban history also gained access. Some of the more recent volumes of the Budapest historical monograph (since 1978) deal with the 18th and 19th centuries. A volume dealing with the post-1945 period is still in preparation. Research on the history of Budapest (78) encouraged the publication of several prominent works of urban history, among them a five-volume collection of source material from the 18th and 20th centuries, and a concise summary of the history of Budapest in English and German (both edited by Á. Ságvári), and also a seven-volume bibliography (12).

The great headway made by local history since the 1960s gave an impetus to the publication of monographs on the history of several provincial towns. The standard of these works varies; the best among them are the monographs on the so-called "Haidu" towns (Eastern Hungary). Two undertakings of major importance have been started: historical monograph series on Debrecen and Szeged, each in five volumes. So far the first volume has been published on the history of Szeged and the second on Debrecen. The latter covers the first half of the 19th century.

The historical monographs on Budapest, Szeged and Debrecen are being written by a group of qualified experts. The different chapters comprise the issues of demographic conditions, the settlement structure, economy, society, culture, town administration, town policy, etc. These works do not deal much with the history of architecture, but some other publications have done so.

Apart from historical monographs on different towns from their beginnings up to the present, most works analyse only a certain period in the history of a town. Two outstanding pieces are a book by G. Komoróczy (60) on Debrecen in the Age of Reforms and a study of Györ in the mid-19th century by P. Balász (80).

This list may suggest that, apart from the monographs, urban historical problems of the 20th century were a rather neglected field of historical research. These issues have been given greater attention by urban geography, which, though it is mainly concerned with changes after 1945, often goes back to the first half of the century or even to 1869, the year in which regular statistical surveys started. Research into the 19th century is of limited value because it traces the history only of towns in the present territory of the country, and often uses only demographic aspects. The urbanisation processes of the 20th century have mainly been explored by E. Lettrich (44/45). She distinguishes two processes of urbanisation from the turn of the century to 1949, and post-1949, the year regarded as a turning-point with respect to mobility, regional concentration of the population, changes in demographic attitude, occupations, housing conditions and the relationships between towns and rural areas.

Besides the large number of studies analysing different problems of urbanisation, attention must be called to the several monographs on towns written from a geographical viewpoint. In addition to the works of E. Lettrich, P. Beluszky's (30) book on the gravity zone of Nyiregyhaza is outstanding also from a methodological aspect.

As mentioned earlier, research into settlement geography is also closely connected with the development of settlements and town planning. An excellent publication on the conditions of rural towns supports these studies in both their theoretical foundation and with empirical data. Besides an introduction on urban history (still invaluable today), the volume discusses the territorial conditions, the population and population density of the 62 provincial towns from 1869 to the present day, economic, cultural and administrative features, and supply. A separate chapter is devoted to the history of town planning from the beginning of the 19th century to the present day. The volumes *Hungarian Towns* and *The Counties and Towns of Hungary* can be regarded as the continuation of the collection on provincial towns. These, however, merit attention only as data collections and do not come up to the standard of the former work.

Urban history works on town planning and townscape form a separate group. Courses on the history of town planning included in architectural training were the starting-point for these studies. In the 1950s first plans were made to compile a comprehensive work that was to analyse the process of settlement development in line with the aspects of town planning, explore its laws and define the role of historical values in modern settlement planning. However, it soon became evident that a great deal more preparatory work would be required for such a collection. To meet this long-felt need, monographs were written on the history of town planning. The methodology of the research was elaborated by I. Valló and V. Borbiró (81), who tested it in their work on the town planning of Győr. The study on town planning in Gyór was followed by two similar volumes. Meanwhile, research on the history of architecture from another point of view had also started. On the initiative of the Ministry of Housing and Public Construction, a national survey of the country's historic monuments started in 1951. The results of the surveys were used in two publications: the *Hungarian Historic Monuments* and *Townscape and Monuments*. These monographs dealing with town planning and monuments pay great attention to the 19th century. The volumes are richly illustrated with pictures and maps and form a useful and attractive part of urban historical research. As research on historical monuments developed, it came to put increasing emphasis on the analysis of historic town centres in its investigation of town planning history. L. Gerő (69) and P. Granasztói were leaders in this field.

C. Conclusion

Research on urban history in Hungary is quite extensive and its achievements provide a fair basis for more comprehensive historical works outlining the main features of urbanisation and urban development. But detailed, comprehensive work on urban history is still needed.

Researchers of urban history in Hungary generally know and apply relevant international findings and methods. The most well-known and exploited fields dealt with settlement geography and town planning. In spite of the strengthening of social history, sociological aspects are not dominant, partly because sociology disregards the temporal aspect which is a basic condition of the historical conception. There has been little systematic analysis of the internal infrastructure (public utilities, etc.). However, it is the fragmentary nature of urban historical research that causes the greatest problems, and the elaboration of a detailed, comprehensive work on urban history would require the harmonisation of the different points of view which are still lacking.

ALBERTO CARACCIOLO

Italy*°

A. Changes in Methods and Trends

As in many other countries, "urban history" as such (and under this name) is a very new discipline. Consequently, its methodology is as yet rather uncertain, and the organisation of research is weak. This situation and its recent development will be discussed in the following pages.

Overall, one can suggest that research in this field has greatly changed in the last 20 to 25 years. This change dates from the report by E. Sestan, presented in 1960 at the 11th International Congress of the Historical Sciences in Stockholm, on the commune-city in Italy: it is only since then that there has been a growing interest in the history of the modern Italian city, that is, city formation in the last two centuries. Clearly, whilst a strong interest in the analysis of the historical city and the medieval period persists, the extremely rapid urbanisation of Italy over the past 20 to 30 years due to the predominately industrial character of contemporary settlement has meant that the historiography of the city has become an "historiography of modernisation". The conference held on Capri in 1983, which was promoted by the "Gramsci Institute" and the "Maison des Sciences de l'Homme" (of which the proceedings are shortly to be published) is a good example of these new developments: modern and contemporary capital cities ranging from Portugal to Hungary were studied within both interdisciplinary and comparative frameworks. Thus, these are signs that Italian urban historiography is moving away from provincialism and indifference to methodology.

---

* Translated by Elizabeth White.
° Numbers in brackets in this chapter refer to entries in the bibliography on pp. 417–426 of this volume.

B. The Development of Studies in Individual Research Fields

(a) Typology, Definition, Image

The debate on the significance and typology of the modern city has always been very much conditioned in Italy by comparisons with the medieval period and with the flowering of the communes as city-states. As early as 1858, a famous essay by C. Cattaneo (42) emphasised the Italian characteristic of strong continuity of experience through successive settlements in both their formal and social configuration. In many cases, therefore, discussion of the modern city has become involved with the concept of the city itself, with discussions of the relationships over a long period with the countryside, and with the bourgeoisie as a characterising class.

The distinction between this more distant history and modern realities was finally stated in clear and ordered terms in a conference in 1973 at Sorrento entitled "From the Pre-industrial to the Capitalist City" (A. Caracciolo/20). Many studies have since followed, making use of the same concept of periods according to which, apart from specific differences relating to individual areas and countries, the "modern city" as such is considered to date back two centuries in connection with the origins and expansion of the first industrial revolution. Work co-ordinated by P. Rossi on "The City as a Political Institution" (52) can be accepted as an example of a similar concept of historical periods which, in addition, takes into account the other extremely important preceding transformation — the birth of the great national and absolutist states.

However, it cannot be said that overall there have been many significant results in methodology or works of great originality on definitions. In general, most studies have reproduced the proposals and interpretations already put forward in other countries by sociologists, urbanists, demographers and political scientists. In the last 20 or 30 years many foreign authors have been translated, beginning with certain classics — from M. Weber (first translated in 1950 but finally obtaining success in the 1979 edition) to E. Howard (1962), from J. Gottmann (1970) via L. Mumford (1963 and 1970) and C. Sitte (1981) to the selection of the work of F. Choay (*The City: Utopia and Reality*, 1973). There has, however, been continuous acknowledgement of new works, particularly those in English.

On the basis of these cultural influences there have been several general works on the "image" of the city (P. Sica, *et al.*/45); attempts at typology (A. Pizzorno/33; A. Aquarone/28); general works from the viewpoints of urbanism and planning (C. Aymonino/36; L. Benevolo/38; C. Tafuri/46; and others), or from more distant and more "ideological" viewpoints (M. Cacciari/39; A. Caracciolo/10). At other times discussions on synthesis and approaches to the city phenomenon have been found in general historical or cultural works paying greater attention to the past: for example the Italian *Encyclopaedia Einaudi* has, in the last ten years, included several entries, which have the scale and depth of authentic essays of some length, with titles such as housing, environment, city, settlement, population, region, space, territory, and village.

(b)   Politics, Administration, Institutions

The political approach to the history of the modern city developed from the period of confrontation of 1968 and later. This produced, above all, occasional publications linked to enquiries about the growth and configuration of conurbations in Italy today, the elements of exploitation and class discrimination that they contain, and the rebellion and revolution which can breed there. This approach, with its roots especially in certain leftist movements and the university faculties of architecture, had a short life, and achieved only modest scientific results. Among the few exceptions are the works of F. Ferrarotti and his group, linked to the journal *La Critica Sociologica*.

Independent of these trends, the connection between the city and its political administration was studied in the context of the history of the capitals of pre-unified and united Italy. For example, the obviously political and practical question of the "choice" of Rome in 1861 to 1871 has been repeatedly analysed (first in an essay by F. Chabod, then by A. Caracciolo/56, and by various authors in "Roma Capitale"/58); this, in fact, was the end of a pluralistic situation in a country where Turin, Milan, Venice, Genoa, Florence and Naples also had long traditions as capitals. Throughout the 20th century, the gradual domination of Rome, through its political, administrative and cultural centralisation — despite the resistance of other centres, especially Milan as an economic capital — has been, and still remains, the object of much discussion.

Political historians have in recent years studied municipal affairs in a distinct and often very technical manner, differing from the approach of other scholars. Over the last 20 years the analysis of legal institutions and of government at a local level has become more important, especially in connection with the general political question of unity and its aftermath, in a broader context than simply the history of urban centres. Individual authors, however, like P. Calandra (47), S. Cassese (48), E. Rotelli (53), and various institutes such as the "Institute for Studies of Public Administration" (ISAP, Milan) have traced the development of "communal and provincial" laws (and, from 1970, "regional" as well) during the reign of Victor Emmanuel II and the period of the Republic. Today there are a growing number of young scholars examining such legislation in its practical applications and in relation to certain particular urban societies.

The literature is rather sparse and is in the form of preliminary monographs on those institutional and administrative aspects which accompanied the stages of modern urbanisation in an Italy which, around 1900, had an industrial basis for development. The topics which have attracted interest in Italy at that period are the trend towards municipalisation of many public services, the debate about public housing and public intervention in hygiene and sanitation. At the beginning of this century it was through such questions that the maturity of a town, and also the capacity of the working and artisan classes to promote forms of self-government, could be judged. The centralised, totalitarian management of local administration in the Fascist period hindered the studies of that period, and the new republican regime has ended up concentrating its legalistic attention on regions rather than communes.

(c) Demography and Social Structure

Historical-demographic studies in Italy have a certain positivist tradition, which developed in the 19th and 20th centuries under scholars such as P. Castiglioni, F. Corridore, F. Coletti, W. Giusti and G. Mortara. During the interwar years, a committee for the study of population problems worked on historical sources: using the same initials (CISP), a group of scholars of the new generation was formed about 1970. Since then, there has been a tremendous increase in work, both on a macro- and micro-demographic level, often involving urban and social history. One of the first examples of solid interdisciplinary work was the book by A. Mioni and C. Carozzi, *L'Italia in Formazione* (15) published in 1970 and updated since then. In some years there was a review of research results at the conference of the Italian Society of Historical Demography (SIDES) in Assisi.

The SIDES conference of 1980 was entirely given over to the theme "La demografia storica delle città italiane" (The Historical Demography of Italian Cities). It opened with three papers on different specialist areas: M. Berengo lecturing on history, L. Gambi on geography and E. Sonnino on demography — proof of the existence of communication between methodologies and approaches. For many cities, and also for many provinces and regions, particularly in the South of Italy, local historical series have been produced. Less aggregate analyses, at the level of family, occupation and social position have also been developed. For example, a conference in Trieste in 1983 collected dozens of contributions and stimulated great debate about family structures and relationships. This conference was attended by many scholars from abroad, and Italian historical (and also urban) demography compared favourably with studies carried out in other countries.

In the analysis of the social configuration of urban areas, there is a certain emphasis on villages and small to medium-sized centres. It is anthropologists (many of whom are foreign, such as Blok, Davis and Schneider, who all did case studies in Italy) who have produced some of the most interesting contributions in recent years. There were several pioneering monographs around 1960; for example A. Pizzorno on a small industrial commune in Lombardy (64) and P. Ugolini on a rural village of Lazio (67). But recently, work has become more abundant, embracing the ideas of "micro-history" which are especially evident in the review "Quaderni Storici", and urbanistic approaches such as those put forward by E. Guidoni in the review "Storia della Città".

There has also been a recent increase in studies of neighbourhoods, groups and social classes in the larger Italian cities, or in towns in the process of expanding industrially and demographically: in general, though, their approach can be said to belong to "social history" rather than "urban history". The residential working-class areas of Milan, Turin, and the Venice-Marghera agglomeration, the working class suburbs of Rome, functional change in the historic centres of Bologna, Florence and Naples — all have been analysed as they are of great importance to planners and administrators. Overall, there has been a great increase in the way Italy has changed, at different levels of cities and settlements, from a predominantly rural country to — for the first time in the 1950s — an urban one, with hierarchies of cities varying in size and regional typology.

(d)   Territory: Urban and Regional Organisation

In 1958 a conference on "City and Countryside" was held in Milan for social scientists. Amongst other things, this led to an important review of existing studies in Italy, or those linked with international research, on the organisation of territory from the social and historic viewpoint. The proceedings, published by the "Associazione Italiana Scienze Sociali" (AISS) in 1959, serve only as a starting point, a move away from the generic tradition of studies on territory which had previously prevailed, especially at the level of regions or regional states. Meanwhile, a chain of regional institutes was founded, dedicated to socio-economic studies (among the first were l'ILSES in Milan and CRURES in Perugia). Offices were also established for studying territory, linked, in 1970, with autonomous administrative bodies called "Ente Regione". In a situation where university departments of geography produce, on the whole, traditional research of little importance, the institutes, which grew up in a period of political-administrative awareness, contributed, either directly or indirectly, to the historical analysis of settlement phenomena.

The geographical configuration of Italy has always emphasised the problem of transport, and that was already clear to the ruling liberal class which completed the national railway network in 1860. Recent studies on the railways from their private development up to nationalisation (at the beginning of the 20th century), electrification (in the 1930s), reconstruction and competition with the motorway network (especially in the 1950s) have helped to link the history of the city with the country's geographical nature. This was a determining factor in long-distance linkages and in inter-settlement transport networks organised according to a complex hierarchy. More and more frequently, studies have taken on a spatial dimension, in relation, for example, to southern Italy (F. Compagna/73). There has been a trend towards metropolitan conurbations and the city-region (F. Archibugi/69) and a growth in the historical axes of urbanisation (C. Carozzi and R. Rozzi/71).

(e)   The Economy and Development Factors

It is difficult to isolate the history of the city from economic history, in general, and from its scientific literature. In Italy a characteristic element is that industrialisation, which occurred late, was concentrated among the large cities of the "triangle" of the north-west of the country — Turin, Milan and Genoa. This is an example of the so-called "dualism" phenomenon, described by economists, such as V. Lutz and P. Saraceno, as a model of economic development which is neither aggregated nor balanced.

In the same light, can be explained the keen interest shown by Italian historiography in the labour factor in comparison to other factors of production. In recent years there have been many papers on internal migration as well as foreign migration, concentrating particularly on growth centres such as Prato, Biella, Marghera, Schio, etc., and there have been some attempts at synthesis (e.g. A. Treves/81). And, in addition, statistical material has recently been reviewed in a critical manner (O. Vitali/82).

(f)   Cities as Places of Civilian Life and Local History

It is not right to label as "urban history" every paper dwelling on a particular cultural institution or a particular city. There are, for example, published lists of academies or public libraries which were in existence at various times in individual places, just as there are endless studies of monuments, palaces, works of art and churches, but they will not be discussed here. It is more useful to point out that some popularity has been achieved, and is still being achieved, by books and entire series devoted to the complex history of a city throughout the centuries —history in which both formal and cultural elements have their place.

The work, which is still the most famous — and most lengthy (17 volumes!) — is the *History of Milan*, edited by G. Treccani, and published in the 1950s. It starts at the most ancient settlements and goes up to 1918 using essays and various types of research — which sometimes verge on folklore — or concern erudite minutiae or on other occasions, lack an overall theme. However, it represents a summary of useful information which is often well documented and illustrated. Moreover, Milan had a long and important history as the capital of a duchy (and for a certain time as a kingdom), which distinguished it from so many other smaller cities, the histories of which were published at more or less the same time. In analogous form is the *History of Naples* (10 volumes, 1967–1971). Equally lengthy histories, although less detailed, were also written on Venice, Rome and other cities.

These recent studies and publications can be considered as the latest phase of what was, in Italy, the powerful 19th century current of "local history". It was a positivist tradition aimed at revealing civil history as opposed to ecclesiastical history, often starting from pre-Roman settlements or Roman municipalities, then dealing with medieval communes, and ending with the "Risorgimento". Combined in that tradition were learned styles of narrative and analysis, as well as apologias for famous citizens dictated by a strong hagiographical objective in which the "city" remained more or less in the background. Nevertheless, some elements of this "local history" in recent decades have developed along more critical and valid lines (C. Violante/27), becoming a useful point of reference in the development of modern historical-urban researches.

C. Synthesis of the Present Research Situation

In Italy the term "storia urbana" with a specific application in accordance with the term "urban history" has, therefore, had meaning only in the past 20 years. It is in this period that, despite persistent fissiparous tendencies questioning every author and historical problem posed, an acceptable level of coherence has been reached. The early 1970s saw the consolidation of links with research in other countries, especially Britain (due to the influence of H. J. Dyos and his group). In addition, out of the problems of economic development, of industrial take-off, and of the Italian "miracle", came the desire to examine the specific role of urban centres in their various stages and in specific regional areas.

Today, the state of historical-scientific analysis in Italy is advanced and complex. It has three main avenues — the question of urban land use and the construction business (including considerations of conservation and ecology); the question of forms, models and decisions on development and urban infrastructure; and the question of human activity in contemporary urban settlements (occupation and free time, community activity, political and cultural expressions, neighbourhoods, transport networks and traffic, etc.). These are the themes now being examined and elaborated upon; worthwhile work is being produced, with a true historical approach. It is the development of these themes that will lead to a more satisfactory fusion between the disciplines which compete for the title "urban history".

RYUICHI NARITA, KINICHI OGURA AND AKIO YOSHIE

Japan*°△

A. Growing Interest in the Town and its History

Rapid urbanisation, accelerated by the Japanese economic boom in the 1960s, brought fundamental changes in the political, social and economic functions of the town, as well as in the relations between town and country. Seen in historical perspective, Japanese towns, like the Japanese economy, grew too quickly in a relatively short period of time. Urban problems have developed into national problems; they have become factors with a decisive influence on the quality of life of both the urban and the rural population. Current urban problems have become a subject of study in a variety of disciplines that examine them from differing viewpoints.

But the town as the living space of human beings has grown historically, and representatives of special disciplines thus ask about the historical development of it, particularly the modern town since industrialisation. The following report will, therefore, review the most important studies from various disciplines on the character of the town and on urban problems. This will be followed by a discussion of various historical studies of the town. Here, a division into three periods of time will be made, and the study will concentrate on works on urban development until the end of the Second World War.

More than anyone else, the economist K. Miyamoto has had great

* Translated from German by Ruth Stanley.
° The authors would like to thank their colleague H. Ishizuka for his great assistance in formulating the manuscript.
△ In this text there are always two references: the first relates to the bibliography on pp. 427–435 of this volume, the second to the notes in Japanese characters at the end of this report.

influence on the questions and the methods of research into urban history. His main work, *Toshikeizairon* (Studies on the urban economy, 1980) (105)[1] concentrates on the capitalist development in towns. He examines the basic concept of the "town" and also touches on urban problems and town politics. In this work, towns in Japan are compared with towns in the United States, and urban theories are systematically presented.

Present-day urban problems of land, accommodation, traffic, water supply and sewage system, waste disposal, public service institutions, environmental pollution, accidents, finance and administration, have also been studied by T. Shibata, (47),[2] who offers a survey of the history of the Japanese town and urban problems. The political scientist T. Oshima (70)[3] has explained political structures in the modern Japanese town from the point of view of local self-government and has dealt extensively with the municipal government of Tokyo at the end of the Meiji period (1868–1912).

The architect E. Inagaki (97)[4] has dealt with the development of modern architecture in Japan and has shown, with abundant documentation, the connection between urban development and building activity for the period from the Meiji Restoration (1868) until Japan's defeat in the Second World War (1945).

Urban geographers have also given attention to the historical process of urbanisation; but there is still no exchange of views or cooperation with historians. The study by K. Fujioka (44),[5] for example, on urban topography, provides many valuable ideas. In a historical journal M. Yamada (49)[6] has reported on the history of research into urban geography. Ethnology, too, which up to now has largely been concerned with the "Jomin" (the common people), has recently opened up a new field of research, "urban ethnology"; N. Miyata (116)[7] may be named as a representative of this field. In addition, the historical journal *Rekishikoron* has published a special issue on "Ethnology in the Town" (119).[8]

In literary criticism, too, the town has been the subject of much discussion in recent times. A. Maeda (114)[9] has treated the topic "Town and Literature" in Japanese novels of the modern period up to the present. K. Isoda (111)[10] has traced the change in Tokyo thought since the end of the Tokugawa shogunate.

T. Yamamoto's (120)[11] book cannot be placed in any particular category, but deserves a mention here; as a social educator, Yamamoto studied the "true conditions of moral conversion activities in the town and their spiritual structure" in Tokyo in the second decade of the 20th century.

The history of prefectures and communities also provides rich material on urban history. R. Azusaka (4)[12] has published a bibliography on local history. The centenary celebrations of the Meiji Restoration (1868) in 1968 provided an excellent opportunity to collect material on local history, as will be the centenary of the institution of the Municipal Regulations (1889) when it is celebrated this year. Most of the works published to date are official descriptions of constitutional and institutional changes, with isolated analyses of urban history. Recently, however, the part played in publication by historians has increased, and historical studies with a scholarly foundation have appeared, as the examples of the works on Yokohama (133),[13] Amagasaki (122),[14] the district of Nakani in Tokyo (127)[15] and Tokyo itself (128)[16] show. Also worthy of mention is Abiko, where the publication of the town's history developed from a citizens' cultural movement. They planned the publication themselves, carried out the investigations, and wrote down their results (121).[17] Studies on local history have also been undertaken by parliaments and educational institutions.

Urban history research and writing that takes the various individual fields into account and treats the town as a complex, is still rare. H. Ishizuka[18] must be named as a pioneer in this field. In 1973, his study on the structure of the modern Japanese town and its transformation in connection with the industrialising policy of the Meiji regime was published (103). In 1977, he undertook a successful attempt to present the social and economic history of Tokyo (10). The main theme of his study was the development of capitalism and the outbreak of urban problems from the eve of the Meiji Restoration until the great earthquake in Kanto (1923); in it, the author attempts to examine the development from the ordinary people's viewpoint. He thus concentrates not only on urban merchants and capitalist entrepreneurs, but also on artisans and small traders, on apprentices and workers, on white-collar workers and even slum dwellers. Industrial pollution, epidemics, traffic and housing problems, the life of the people, and social movements, are all dealt with in this study. Although his work is a case study on the imperial capital, the essential character of the Japanese town is superbly presented.

T. Hashimoto (28/46/57)[19] has developed his own ideas on urban history. He has attempted to explain urbanisation in connection with the demographic development, the development of industry, and labour migration, and he must be credited with having treated the process of urbanisation in connection with migration movements.

Studies dealing with urbanisation from the viewpoint of environmental pollution are widespread. On this H. Koyama (24)[20] has remarked: "The formation of the modern town of Osaka, a pioneer of Japanese capitalism, signified at the same time the development of the first town to pollute the environment". Koyama has also edited a collection of documents on environmental pollution problems in Osaka in the Showa period up to the war (1926–1941). The study by Y. Oda (108)[21] is also one of the few works studying urban pollution; research up to now has concentrated on the disposal of industrial sewage from the Ashio mines. Besides this, there exist a few collections of documents and chronological tables presenting historical data (22/23).[22]

While economic and social historians have made efforts to provide a framework for urban history, research has also been undertaken for more detailed study of urbanisation and its effects in a specific town or region. For the industrial region of Keihin, a study by M. Yamada (91)[23] is available, investigating the urban problems there from 1900 to the 1940s. The study concentrates mainly on the problems that arose following the great earthquake in Kanto, the Second World War, and the construction of a dam for the harbour town of Yokohama and its neighbouring towns. On Tokyo, a study on *Town Structure and Town Planning*[24] has been published; it is distinguished by an interdisciplinary co-operation that has been rare up to now. Besides this, the special issue of the journal *Rekishitecho*, on "The Taisho Era in Tokyo: Cultural Reflections" (131)[25] and the special edition of the historical journal *Rekishihyoron* on "Power and the People in the Formative Years of the Imperial Capital" (129)[26] deserve special mention. Studies on Osaka have been gathered in a collection of articles (126)[27] and in a special issue of a journal.[28] On Kobe, the journal *Rekishikoron* has dealt with the special topic of "The modern history of Kobe" (125).[29] This volume reveals a trend towards dealing with urban history both as economic and social history, and as local history. The journal *Rekishikoron* has dealt with the theme of "The Town in Modern Japan" and, in so doing, anticipated the interest in urban history, although the period covered did not extend beyond the 1920s.[30] Since then, urban history as social history, and comparative urban history, have come to be at the centre of the discussion. Over and above this, many studies exist that do not place the town as an object of research at the centre of investigation, but which nevertheless can contribute much to urban history if read from a particular standpoint. Think, for example, of works on the history of educational institutions, the labour movement, and medical care. In addition, a growing interest in urban history in the above-mentioned fields may likewise be observed.

B. The Period of Transition from the Feudal to the Modern Town

Most modern Japanese towns originated in feudal fortified towns of the 16th century. In 1878, ten years after the Meiji Restoration, the number of towns with a population of more than 10,000 amounted to 100. Three large towns — the historic capitals Tokyo (previously called Edo), Kyoto and Osaka — headed the population table, followed by a number of older, princely fortified towns — Nagoya, Kanazawa, Hiroshima, Wakayama, Sendai, etc. A survey on the process of transformation from the feudal to the modern town can be found in the work of T. Furushima (45)[31] and F. Unno (48),[32] who have attempted a description with reference to the development of capitalism. They have pointed out that the towns that originated in the period of the Tokugawa shogunate evolved new elements and conditions under capitalism and became modern towns; in this process, capitalism certainly encouraged the development of new industrial towns, but "urban trade in various goods, characteristic of traditional craftsmen", remained at the centre of the urban economy.

On 1 April, 1889, new municipal and parish regulations based on the Prussian model became law; 39 new towns were created. While in law no minimum population requirement was associated with municipal status, most towns had more than 30,000 inhabitants. Nowadays, municipal status is conditional upon a population of more than 50,000. Self-government in 19th-century towns was considerably limited; in reality, they were constituted "from above". Studies on this problem have been published by H. Kikegawa (58),[33] but further research extending beyond his results has yet to be undertaken. Problems such as the meaning of the new regulations for the people, and their reaction to them, have not been studied. It remains a task of future research to investigate local self-government in connection with the history of popular autonomy. In this regard, it should be pointed out that, in contrast to the European town, where a bourgeois class had developed before the establishment of self-government, the Japanese town showed strong authoritarian features.

In the past few years studies have been appearing on the everyday life of the urban population and urban cultural history. Novel aspects and questions are raised and a new picture of urban living is presented. Among these works is the study by S. Ogi (117/118).[34] Using Tokyo as an example, he attempts to portray "not only food, clothing and housing, but also the productive, social, educational, spiritual, and recreational life — in short, the organic cohesion of popular life in its entirety." His presentation, with a wealth of material, covers such problems as marriage and divorce, education and health. While all aspects of urban life are superbly portrayed in this study, the "organic cohesion" remains unsatisfactory, since the individual aspects are treated separately. Of interest in this work, however, is the proposal to revise the usual division into chronological periods; thus the author asserts that the 15 former urban districts of Tokyo experienced a period of independence from the 1st until about the 22nd year of the Meiji regime (1868 until roughly 1889). He designates it as the "Tokei period", in contradiction to the earlier Edo period and the later Tokyo period. Moreover, the author argues against the view of Tokyo as a predecessor of "Bunmei Kaika" (civilisation and enlightenment, meaning Europeanisation); and he emphasises its continuity with the former Edo. Problems of the formation of a new urban ruling stratum, of discrimination and popular movements, however, lay outside his interest. As a further representative of the new direction, we may cite N. Kawazoe (112),[35] who has concentrated his attention on "flowers as urban culture", connecting the town with the country, and has described the floral landscapes of the garden cities of Edo and Tokyo in the Meiji period. These two authors laid the foundations of the new direction in research.

The transition from the feudal to the modern town is also one of the main themes of the history of architecture and building. In this connection, T. Hatsuda (95)[36] has given attention to buildings in the Japanese-European style, built by master builders and apprentices using the traditional techniques of the Edo period, and with the transformation of building complexes. In his study, he rejects the view that the architect alone creates "architecture and the town", and, in his description of basic trends in architecture and town planning, attempts to view the town through the eyes of those master builders and the apprentices, as well as the ordinary people supporting them. Mention must also be made of T. Fujimori (92).[37] His work deals with the planning of the brick streets of the Ginza, Tokyo fire precautions in the first ten years of the Meiji regime, the reform of the urban districts, the concentration of state offices as well as with town planning in Tokyo in the first half of the Meiji period and its transformation. These topics had already been dealt with but it was the author's intention to view the Meiji regime's plan for Tokyo as a whole. He deals also with the method and ideas of town planning with reference to political conflicts and economic problems. This work is valuable for the discovery of new materials and the reproduction of the plan in an appendix, just as much as for its original commentary. It can be viewed as an excellent study on the history of town planning. Fault could be found with the fact that town planners are at the centre of this study, the contribution of individual town dwellers not to mention that of popular movements, has been neglected although town planning must surely have caused tension between the rulers and the ruled.

The point of divergence in economic and social historians' awareness of problems is found in their answer to the questions of whether Tokyo continued to develop in the tradition of Edo during the Meiji period, or whether there was a break in development. S. Ogi and N. Kawazoe, like T. Hatsuda and T. Fujimori, regard Tokyo's development more as a continuous process; on the other hand, H. Ishizuka (30)[38] asserts that Tokyo in the Meiji period with its zones of foreign settlements, was a town of a "semi-colonial type", and that the numerous town plans can be seen as an "attempt to convert Tokyo into a West European town". He points out that Tokyo was later transformed into a town of the "Fukoku Kyohei" (rich state and strong army) type. T. Mikuriya's research results have also contributed to this subject. A debate has developed between H. Ishizuka, T. Fujimori and T. Mikuriya (93).[39] A continuation of this dialogue with wider participation would be desirable.

For the above-mentioned period of time, urban popular movement has proved a little-worked field. It is, therefore, a task of research to shed light on the development of the "Jiyu-Minken" (freedom and civil rights) movement in the towns, and the specific content and the actual state of the "Toshi-Minken" (municipal civil rights) movement. This problem has been dealt with, to some extent, concerning Tokyo, Osaka and Kyoto, as well as important harbour towns with foreign settlements such as Yokohama and Kobe. There is, however, still a lack of such studies of the medium-sized and small provincial towns.

In the period from the beginning of the Industrial Revolution until the First World War and shortly thereafter, the modern town developed rapidly. By 1913, the number of towns had reached 69, and town development continued increasing. Towns of a new type appeared, such as the industrial towns of Yahata (1917) and Kawasaki (1924), the mining town of Omuta (1917), and the naval ports of Kure (1902), Sasebo (1902) and Yokosuka (1907). In the great cities of Tokyo and Osaka the population increased. Research on this rapid urbanisation has only recently been undertaken, and there is a lack of studies presenting this process as a whole. Apart from earlier-mentioned works, which approach the problem from the perspective of economic and social history, there are no studies on this period. There are some individual studies, but they do not contribute to a classification of urbanisation. To put it differently: at present, it is not urbanisation itself that is being studied, but rather the problems it brought with it.

We have already observed that there is a need for studies on the lower strata of urban society. C. Nishida[40] has been working on this important problem for some time and has edited two collections of documents (84/86). M. Sumiya (88)[41] has studied the urban lower classes with reference to the history of wage earners. On the basis of his findings, M. Tsuda (90)[42] embarked on a study of Tokyo society from the end of the Meiji period until the beginning of the Taisho period (1912–1926). For this, he analysed the "Saimin Kobetsu Chosa" (population census of the poor) and other extensive material, studied individual occupations, the standard of living, the reasons and conditions for movement to, and settlement in, cities, and came close to the actual situation. K. Nakagawa (83)[43] has studied the subsequent Taisho period. In his sweeping analysis covering the years from 1890 to 1931, he reaches the conclusion that, during that time, the lifestyle of urban society underwent a great transformation.

In honour of G. Yokoyama, to whom research on the lower strata of urban society owes much, it was planned to publish his complete works in four volumes, as well as an additional special volume. However, only two volumes have appeared (77).[44] C. Nishida (85)[45]

has compiled a bibliography of his publications and Y. Tachibana
(89)[46] has written his biography. On the Taisho period, the work of
T. Kagawa, the leader of the social movement, dealing with the
psychology of the poor (80),[47] is of great importance; yet no one has
so far attempted to analyse his findings with reference to urban
history, nor do there exist any collections of documents for this
period. The discovery of new material, as well as biographies of T.
Kagawa, Y. Kusama and others would be desirable. A bibliography
of literature on slums in modern Japan, including information on the
libraries in possession of such literature, would be very valuable for
research (8/12).[48]

H. Ishizuka (79)[49] and T. Hashimoto (57)[50] have written essays
remarkable for their methodological approach. H. Ishizuka started
taking a greater interest in the lower strata through studying living
conditions and epidemics (cholera) spread through the water
supply. He emphasised those urban problems affecting the entire
population, such as the problem of housing, frequent outbreaks of
fire, and the drastic rise in epidemics. He placed these topics in the
context of the formation of the towns and of municipal politics, and
attempted to write an urban history. Hashimoto was, as mentioned
above, interested in the connection between urbanisation and popular movements and, using the example of the provincial town of
Kanazawa, illustrated the characteristics of the lower strata of
society and their modes of behaviour in the Meiji and Taisho
periods. He concentrated on the gilding craft as the traditional trade
of this town, studying the conditions of work and the consciousness
of the lower class employed in this craft, analysing their participation in the rice revolt of 1918. Both these works started as studies of
provincial towns, but the investigations are limited to the rice revolt
and the great earthquake in Kanto (1923).

M. Miyachi (62)[51] describes the condition of Tokyo's urban
population on the basis of a wealth of material. He deals with the
period after the Russo-Japanese War (1904–1905) up to the First
World War (1914–1918), describing it as a "time of unrest in the
urban population" from which various popular movements developed. His work, in which the "extreme insecurity in the urban
districts, never seen before or after this period", is described in
connection with the living conditions of the lower strata (from
whence came the supporters of the popular movements) has had a
considerable influence on the further development of research into
urban history in this period. Whereas M. Miyachi was interested in

popular movements of the lower classes, and their work and services, K. Eguchi (52)[52] studied the old middle class of the urban population. He has mainly investigated the small tradesmen's and artisans' movement for abolition of taxes, and has described the movements of the urban petty bourgeoisie in the years from 1890 to 1930. Although the old middle class formed the widest stratum of the urban population, they were largely neglected until K. Eguchi started his studies. He was interested in the old middle class not so much to place its history in the context of urban history, as to investigate the possibility of forming a unified front. But what was the situation with regard to the new middle class? Even before the First World War, attention had been drawn to the development of this class, yet research on the movements of the new middle class, on its living conditions and consciousness, has only recently begun. On the white-collar workers' movement, there exists only the detailed study by M. Noda (68).[53] Stimulating ideas on this topic may also be found in H. Hamaguchi's (54)[54] study, and in numerous publications of the Japanese Society for the Study of Daily Life[55] that treat urbanisation in passing.

The urban popular movement is relatively well covered until the rice revolt, but thereafter the movement developed in numerous directions. There were movements for the regulation of leases and rents, for a reduction in gas charges and charges for public baths, against corruption, and for tax rebates; however, there is a lack of studies on these movements. So far as the popular movement after the rice revolt is concerned, there is a wealth of research on the workers' and peasants' movement, as well as on the proletarian party and the socialist movement. Nevertheless, research cannot be limited to these, but should direct attention to the variety of popular movements. The variety of these movements in the towns is nothing other than a phenomenon called into being by urbanisation, and researchers into urban history will be unable to make further progress without studying this phenomenon.

There are many areas remaining for future research, including investigations into the residents' and citizens' movements. It was a characteristic of the democratic movement of the Taisho period that the inhabitants of certain regions protested against environmental pollution and took action against the pricing policies of public utilities, such as the gas, electricity, and tram companies. These actions reveal the behaviour of the urban population and their consciousness with respect to urban problems as citizens of the town, and, for the urban popular movement, they were of the utmost importance. So far, only studies by S. Okuda (69)[56] and R. Narita (67)[57] have been published: Okuda's deals with the movements in Kobe during the economic crises in the Showa period; Narita's studies revolve around the actions affecting municipal utility companies in the second and third decades of the 20th century. Thus, researchers still have the task of shedding light on the problems which confronted the urban popular movements. In the Industrial Revolution, urban problems increased; they grew still more dramatically in the continuing urbanisation during the First World War. Especially in the 1920s, the phenomenon of urban sprawl was very marked as a consequence of urban growth into the surrounding areas; equally acute were traffic, waste-disposal and sewage problems. Crime spread, especially those offences typical of urban areas. Studies on environmental pollution, which increased with the development of monopoly capitalism, as well as on the urban problems of this period, have yet to be undertaken. In Tokyo, a Society for the Study of Municipal Government has been founded to study the activities of local government. Studies by K. Harada (55),[58] Y. Kojita (60)[59] and A. Shibamura (72)[60] on the political history of Osaka have recently been published. In comparison with this field of research, more studies are available on urban culture. H. Minami (115)[61] has made a detailed study of mass culture under the influence of the invention of the mass media and the appearance of the middle class. The complete works of W. Kon (113),[62] who observed the customs and lifestyle of ordinary people, must also be mentioned. In addition, many first-hand accounts of urban entertainment, customs, and practices have been published, but cannot be individually named here.

It was during the years from 1910 to 1930 that municipal politics attained full development. Studies on the lives of people, who played a crucial role in municipal politics, made great progress. H. Mizobe (63)[63] re-examined, from a new angle, Y. Tsurumi's biography of S. Goto. A. Shibamura (71)[64] wrote about H. Seki, S. Watanabe and Y. Sadayuki (75)[65] on H. Ikeda, and R. Narita (66)[66] on D. Tagawa. Municipal law has been studied by S. Akagi (50),[67] S. Takagi (74)[68] and A. Nakamura (64),[69] all of whom have dealt with town planning law. Y. Watanabe (76)[70] and R. Suzuki (73),[71] have studied municipal law, focusing on land leasing and tenement housing. Based on these research findings, S. Fukuoka (53)[72] has analysed the cooperative building societies, the "garden city" idea, the outlines of Tokyo's municipal government, the reconstruction plan following the great Kanto earthquake, and has traced the process of development and disintegration in municipal politics. He concentrates mainly on the connection between municipal politics and the state's bureaucratic, governmental structure but he does not consider municipal politics in the relationship of tension with the people.

A future task of research would be to discuss the basic approach and the character of municipal politics in the Taisho period with reference to ordinary people. Concerning this, the work of Y. Kojita (59)[73] deserves mention; in an original essay he attempts to explain party politics as resulting from the transfer of land taxes and from urban problems.

The exacerbation of urban problems called for urban social welfare. At first, self-help organisations developed among the people; later the municipal authorities and the state took on responsibility for care of the poor and for other social welfare institutions. Many works have been published on the history of social welfare, and K. Yoshida (110)[74] is a leader in this area. However, historical studies on the social services have not yet been placed within urbanisation, nor has a link been created with urban history. Nevertheless, the work of M. Omori (109)[75] is worthy of mention; it discusses the system of welfare commissioners and attempts to grasp the reorganisation of the urban government system. R. Narita (107)[76] has written a biography of T. Kato, who began by providing medical care for the population; later he extended the welfare measures for the urban population to include food, legal advice and communal living. With the foundation of a "commune", he ventured an experiment in the history of town planning. These two authors are named here because, basing their work on research findings in the history of social welfare, they have moved towards the study of urban history. These attempts have only recently been undertaken, and it could constitute an enrichment of urban history if more data, reports, and persons discussed in the history of social welfare, were included in urban history research. It would also be enhanced if a new catalogue of urban problems was drawn up, demonstrating the variety of urban welfare measures.

A new field of research would be the evaluation of the significance of the town for children, for disabled people, and for the Koreans resident in Japan, and other groups suffering discrimination. At the present time, there exists a bibliography on the history of social welfare which could provide a starting point (6).[77] Reports from the municipal governments of Osaka and Kyoto dating from this period are also available as reprints (81).[78]

On 1 September 1923, the great earthquake in Kanto and the imperial capital Tokyo occurred. Y. Kurabayashi (7)[79] has published a bibliography of the works that have appeared on this catastrophe. The bibliography is currently being continued, and permits a survey of this terrible disaster. The disastrous effects were more the result of human failings than of natural causes if the fact that the secondary damage caused by fire was enormous is taken into account. The destruction of buildings and the infrastructure cast the urban population into great misery, and urban problems erupted. The authorities' reports, studies, and statistics, newspaper reports and documents collected by journalists, notes and first-hand reports from the people, all abundant, form a "treasure chest of urban history". Among the human misfortune immediately following the earthquake, the panic massacring of Koreans, socialists and anarchists must be counted. This action also deserves analysing with reference to urban history. Works on the reconstruction of Tokyo have been written by R. Narita (99),[80] T. Kodama (104),[81] R. Iwami (98),[82] and N. Mochida (106),[83] but further research would be desirable.

Urban history has been considerably less well researched for the time from the beginning of the Showa period until the end of the Second World War. During the boom of heavy industry and arms manufacture, the towns of Niihama (1937), Hitachi (1939) and Tachikawa (1940) sprang up, and, during that time, urban problems multiplied and worsened. The concentration of the population in the cities led to the development of new satellite cities on their outskirts; town planning became an emergency measure and a form of country planning. With the exception of a few fields, the transformation of the towns at this time has until now attracted little scholarly attention.

Research work on the control of the town by the state has yielded two successful studies. The work of S. Akagi (50)[84] studies the situation in the imperial metropolis Tokyo from 1925 to 1943. He places the control exercised over the urban population in the context of his analyses of popular movements for a purge of municipal government, for regulation of elections, for a general mobilisation of national consciousness and support for the imperial government. He also deals with the function of the "Chonaikai" (town-quarter association) and the "Tonarigumi" (neighbourhood association) as units exercising control over the people, showing that they played an important role as pure or pseudo-cells of Tenno fascism (god-emperor fascism). These associations, recreated as important posts, were central to the hierarchy of authority of empire-prefecture-urban district — "Chonaikai-Tonarigumi" — household-individual. This study has, at a stroke, filled a gap in research. In this context, it is remarkable that the movement for greater urban autonomy had the opposite effect to that desired: the entrenchment of the constitution of the imperial metropolis with its authoritarian orientation. S. Akagi's interest concentrates on the administration's bureaucratic government and on the logic of the institutions that characterised the urban constitution. He does not discuss the various movements and the actual situation of the "Chonaikai" and "Tonarigumi."

By contrast, R. Akimoto (51)[85] has attempted to grasp the trends of urban control in the context of confrontation with the people. On the basis of documents created by the people themselves, he has been able to show that the influence of the "Chonaikai" and "Tonarigumi" as an apparatus to unify the people, reached into the furthest corners of everyday life. This study shows clearly how the logic of control analysed by S. Akagi penetrated deep into the life of the people and how this control affected the actual situation. R. Akimoto also deals with people's lives in periods of want, the destruction through air raids, and evacuation measures, so that his work has the character of a life history of the urban population. A new study on the "Chonaikai" has been published recently by G. Nakayam (65).[86]

During the Second World War, towns were heavily damaged during air raids, and, in the past few years, a movement to collect documentation of these experiences has developed. New facts have come to light and research has made progress; however, air raids have not been discussed with reference to urban problems, although through them, many people were killed by explosive and incendiary bombs, buildings were burnt down and cities totally destroyed — and these facts were nothing other than pressing "urban problems."

On the situation in the country as a whole, a ten-volume work with documents has appeared (100),[87] and R. Harada (94)[88] has published a two-volume work. Documents on individual cities such as Tokyo, Yokohama, Kawasaki, Hachioji and Tachikawa, have been collected by citizens' cultural movements (123/124/132/134).[89] It must be mentioned that the writer K. Saotome (101)[90] has collected first-hand accounts of the air raids, and that the historians S. Imai (96),[91] H. Koyama,[92] and M. Yoshida[93] have discovered new material and embarked on a scholarly analysis of it. The research carried out by these historians points the way for urban history, and it would be desirable for research on the process of reconstruction to be carried further from this point of view. Urban history research in the field of urban catastrophes could thus fulfil a new, important task — to help prevent such catastrophes and to contribute to peace.

C.   Methodological Approaches in Research

The modern town and its problems have become a subject of research for various disciplines. Correspondingly, different branches of scholarship are asking questions, the solution of which is of interdisciplinary interest. In historical research on the modern town, various approaches to methodological procedures have therefore been developed. The current state of the discussion in the field of research on urban history in Japan will be summarised below. Essentially, this discussion concentrates on four issues: the definition of the town; the theoretical approach; the integration of urban history into the history of a region; and the connection between urban history and world history.

(a)   The Definition of the Town

The economic and social significance of the town underwent a fundamental transformation in the course of industrialisation. Corresponding to the political and social development that accompanied the modernisation of the Japanese state, a fundamental change in the institutional and legal relations between town and country took place. Functional characteristics decisive for the distinction between town and country in the pre-industrial age are no longer capable of defining the modern town. The town lost its monopoly on trade and manufacturing, and new branches of industry chose rural locations. The motorisation of transport made it possible for a great many people to live at the periphery of towns and in rural areas. The town as a densely populated living area lost importance. This applies above all to the town centre, which is still the centre of urban life, but has virtually no residential population.

Thus, it is necessary to develop new conceptual tools for historical research on the town that can be used to grasp the reality of the town before and after industrialisation.

(b)   *Theoretical Considerations*

Depending on the questions of concern to individual authors, structural and functional aspects, institutional and administrative facets, or a phenomenological approach to everyday urban life have been selected in presentations of the historical development of the town. The historical development of a town can not, however, be ascertained on the basis of a single phenomenon, and for this reason it will be necessary in future to take more account of differing theoretical considerations in presentations of urban history. By taking account of differing theoretical approaches, historical studies on urban research could also make a greater contribution to the current urban research of other disciplines.

(c)   *Urban History as a Part of Regional History*

The typology of a town proceeds mainly from structural and functional characteristics; in this, it is assumed that the structure of a town depends on the function it exercises in a particular "region". The historical development of a town can only be grasped in the context of the reciprocal influences of individual towns in their region; for the function of a town in a given region can only develop out of these reciprocal influences. In future, the description of the historical development of one or more towns must take greater account of the history of the region.

(d)   *Urban History in the Context of World History*

In many modern Japanese towns, European influences on the formation of the urban landscape are, even today, unmistakable; the Marunouchi business district in Tokyo, built in brick at the end of the last century on the model of London, may serve as an example. Similar business districts and areas inhabited by foreigners may also be found in harbour towns such as Yokohama and Kobe, and give the urban landscape a special character. Such towns, in which European influences have had a decisive importance for the formation of the urban landscape, are thus designated as semi-colonial. Similar, but often more obvious examples are other Asian cities such as Calcutta, Delhi and Singapore. This approach shows that the world-historical aspect can not be ignored in describing an urban landscape. The world-historical aspect serves also to assess the importance of Edo (present-day Tokyo) in the 17th century, when, as the capital of the Tokugawa shogunate, Edo already had more than 1,000,000 inhabitants. Tendencies to concentrate on the political and administrative functions of the capital were strengthened by the Meiji regime's efforts to modernise the country as well as the capital. The history of Tokyo is an essential part of Japan's history of modernisation, and can only be explained in the historical context of world history.

Notes

(1) 宮本憲一『都市経済論―共同生活条件の政治経済学―』筑摩書房1980年。
(2) 柴田徳衛『現代都市論』東京大学出版会1967年(第1版), 1976年(第2版)。
(3) 大島太郎『官僚国家と地方自治』未来社 1981年。
(4) 稲垣栄三『日本の近代建築 その成立過程』丸善 1959年、鹿島出版会 1979年(再版)。
(5) 藤岡謙二郎『日本の都市 その特質と地域的問題点』大明堂 1968年。
(6) 山田誠「都市研究と地理学」、『日本史研究』200号 1979年。
(7) 宮田登『都市民俗学の課題』未来社 1982年。
(8) 『歴史公論』92号 1983年
(9) 前田愛『都市空間のなかの文学』筑摩書房 1982年。
(10) 磯田光一『思想としての東京―近代文学史論ノート―』国文社 1978年。
(11) 山本恒夫『近代日本都市教化史研究』黎明書房 1972年。
(12) 阿津坂林太郎編『地方史文献総合目録』上巻(戦前編) 1970年、下巻(戦後編) 1972年、索引 1975年、いずれも巌南堂書店。
(13) 『横浜市史』5巻9冊、資料編18冊、有隣堂 1958~1982年。
(14) 『尼崎市史』11巻・別巻 1966~1983年。
(15) 『中野区史』昭和編3巻、資料編3巻、1971~1978年。
(16) 『東京百年史』6巻・別巻 1972~1979年。
(17) 高木繁吉「地方史研究の始源をみつめて 市民の手で創る我孫子市史の軌跡」、『地方史研究』167号 1980年。
(18) 石塚裕道『日本資本主義成立史研究―明治国家と殖産興業政策―』吉川弘文館 1973年、『東京の社会経済史―資本主義と都市問題―』紀伊国屋書店 1977年。
(19) 橋本哲哉「大正デモクラシー期における都市の形成について」、『金沢大学法文学部論

集経済学編』22号 1975年、「都市化と民衆運動」、『岩波講座日本歴史17、近代4』
1976年、「日露戦後の都市化と労働力の移動」、『日本史研究』200号 1979年。

(20) 小山仁示『戦前昭和期大阪の公害問題資料』ミネルヴァ書房 1973年。

(21) 小田康徳『近代日本の公害問題―史的形成過程の研究―』世界思想社 1983年。

(22) 神岡浪子編『資料近代日本の公害』新人物往来社 1971年。神奈川県立川崎図書館編
『京浜工業地帯公害問題資料集』1973年。飯島伸子編著『公害および労働災害年表』
公害対策技術同友会 1970年。同『改訂公害・労災・職業病年表』公害対策技術同友会
1979年。

(23) 山田操『京浜都市問題史』恒星社厚生閣 1974年。

(24) 東京都立大学都市研究会編『都市構造と都市計画』東京大学出版会 1968年。

(25) 『歴史手帳』5巻1号 1977年。

(26) 『歴史評論』405号 1984年。

(27) 大阪歴史学会編『近代大阪の歴史的展開』吉川弘文館 1976年。

(28) 「都市大阪の史的究明」、『歴史評論』393号 1983年。

(29) 『歴史手帳』9巻2号 1981年。

(30) 『歴史公論』90号 1983年。

(31) 古島敏雄「明治期における都市の動向」、地方史研究協議会編『幕末・明治期における
都市と農村―日本の町Ⅲ―』雄山閣 1961年。

(32) 海野福寿「明治初年・都市研究の二三の問題」同上所収、「工業発展と都市の動向―職
業統計を手がかりとして―」、古島敏雄・和歌森太郎・木村礎編『郷土史研究講座7・
明治大正郷土史研究法』朝倉書店 1971年。

(33) 亀卦川浩『明治地方制度成立史』柏書房 1967年。『自治五十年史 制度編』良書普及会
1940年。

(34) 小木新造『東京庶民生活史研究』日本放送出版協会 1979年。『東京時代―江戸と東京
の間で―』日本放送出版協会 1980年。

(35) 川添登『東京の原風景―都市と田園との交流―』日本放送出版協会 1979年。

(36) 初田亨『都市の明治―路上からの建築史―』筑摩書房 1981年。

(37) 藤森照信『明治の東京計画』岩波書店 1982年。

(38) 石塚裕道『「東京史」研究の方法論序説』国連大学 1979年。

(39) 「シンポジウム明治の東京計画」、東京都立大学『総合都市研究』19号、1983年、御厨貴
「明治国家形成と都市計画」(１)(２)、『東京都立大学法学会雑誌』23-1・2、1982年。

(40) 西田長寿編『都市下層社会 明治前期労働事情』新生社 1949年、同編『明治前期の都市
下層社会』光生社 1970年。

(41) 隅谷三喜男『日本賃労働史論』東京大学出版会 1955年。

(42) 津田真澂『日本の都市下層社会』ミネルヴァ書房 1972年。内務省地方局・社会局編
津田真澂解説『細民調査統計表』慶応書房 1971年復刻。

(43) 中川清「戦前における都市下層の展開―東京市の場合―」上下、『三田学会雑誌』71巻3
～4号 1978年、『戦前東京の都市下層』国連大学 1982年。

(44) 『横山源之助全集』第1・3巻 明治文献 1972～1974年。

(45) 西田長寿「横山源之助『日本の下層社会』の成立」、『歴史学研究』161号、1953年。

(46) 立花雄一『評伝 横山源之助―底辺社・文学・労働運動―』創樹社 1979年。

(47) 賀川豊彦『貧民心理の研究』

(48) 生瀬克己『近代日本スラム関係文献所在目録』、桃山学院大学『総合研究所報』17巻
1号、1981年、日本住宅協会編「スラムに関する文献目録」、『住宅』15-5～17-1、
1966年5月～1968年1月。

(49) 石塚裕道『都市下層社会と「細民」住居論』国連大学 1980年、『東京の都市スラムと公衆衛生問題』国連大学 1981年。

(50) 橋本哲哉『地方都市の下層民衆と民衆暴動』国連大学 1980年。

(51) 宮地正人『日露戦後政治史の研究―帝国主義形成期の都市と農村―』東京大学出版会 1973年。

(52) 江口圭一『都市小ブルジョア運動史の研究』未来社 1976年。

(53) 野田正穂「戦前におけるサラリーマンの組合運動」(1)～(14)、『銀行労働時報』1960年～1961年。

(54) 浜口晴彦『社会の組織化―近代化にともなう思想対立の位相―』早稲田大学出版部 1980年。

(55) 日本生活学会編『生活学』第1冊～、ドメス出版 1975年～。

(56) 奥田修三「昭和恐慌期の市民闘争―兵庫県における借家争議・電燈争議を中心として―」、『立命館大学人文科学研究所紀要』10号、1961年。

(57) 成田龍一「大正デモクラシー期の都市住民運動―東京市における―」、『地方史研究』167号、1980年。

(58) 原田敬一「都市支配の構造―地域秩序の担手たち―」、『歴史評論』393号、1983年。「都市支配の再編成―日露戦後の大阪市政改革運動をめぐって―」、『ヒストリア』101号、1983年。

(59) 小路田泰直「日本帝国主義成立期の都市政策―地方改良運動をめぐって―」、『歴史評論』393号、1983年。

(60) 芝村篤樹「1920年代初頭の大阪市政―大阪市会の動向を中心に―」、『ヒストリア』100号、1983年。

(61) 南博編『大正文化』勁草書房 1965年。

(62) 川添登、竹内芳太郎・吉坂隆正・加藤角一・内井乃生編『今和次郎集』9冊ドメス出版 1971～1972年。

(63) 溝部英章「後藤新平論 闘争的世界像と"理性の独裁"」(一)(二)、『法学論叢』100巻2号、101巻2号、1976年～1977年。

(64) 芝村篤樹「関一における都市政策の歴史的意義」、前掲『近代大阪の歴史的展開』吉川弘文館 1976年。

(65) 渡辺俊一・定行恭宏「池田宏伝・試論」、『土地住宅問題』56～67号(61号を除く)、1979年～1980年。

(66) 成田龍一「田川大吉郎の都市論 その形成過程」、『歴史評論』330号、1977年。

(67) 赤木須留喜「都市計画の計画性」、前掲『都市構造と都市計画』東京大学出版会 1968年。

(68) 高木鉦作「都市計画法」、鵜飼信成・福島正夫・川島武宜・辻清明編『講座日本近代法発達史9』、勁草書房 1960年。

(69) 中邨章「大正八年・都市計画法再考―都市計画区域と都市計画地方委員会の政治的断面―」、沖田哲也・中邨章・竹下譲編『地方自治と都市政策』学陽書房 1981年。

(70) 渡辺洋三『土地建物の法律制度』、上、中、東京大学出版会 1960年～1962年。

(71) 鈴木禄弥「借地借家法」、前掲『講座日本近代法発達史11』勁草書房 1967年。

(72) 福岡峻治「大正期の都市政策―住宅・都市計画構想の展開―」(一)(二)(三)、『東京都立大学法学会雑誌』11巻2号、12巻1号、13巻1号、1971年～1972年。

(73) 小路田泰直「『政党政治』の基礎構造―都市と地租移譲問題―」、『日本史研究』235号、1982年。

(74) 吉田久一『現代社会事業史研究』勁草書房 1979年。

⑺ 大森実「都市社会事業成立期における中間層と民本主義―大阪府方面委員制度の成立をめぐって」、『ヒストリア』97号、1982年。

⑺ 成田龍一『加藤時次郎』不二出版 1983年。

⑺ 近代日本社会事業史文献目録編集委員会編『近代日本社会事業史文献目録』日本生命済生会 1971年。

⑺ 大阪市役所編『労働調査報告』14冊、大阪市立中央図書館 1975年～1981年。
京都市社会課編『調査報告』10冊、文学出版 1978年。

⑺ 倉林義正『関東大震災(1923)関連主要文献目録』(3の1)一橋大学経済研究所 1982年。

⑻ 成田龍一「『帝都』復興をめぐる都市論の興起と変質」、東京歴史科学研究会編『転換期の歴史学』合同出版 1979年。

⑻ 小玉徹「震災復興と〈助成会社〉―東京再開発をめぐる財政・土地問題と諸階層」、『日本史研究』245号、1983年。

⑻ 岩見良太郎『土地区画整理の研究』自治体研究社 1978年。

⑻ 持田信樹「後藤新平と震災復興事業―〈慢性不況〉下の都市スペンディング」、東京大学『社会科学研究』35巻2号、1983年。

⑻ 赤木須留喜『東京都制の研究―普選下の東京市政の構造―』未来社 1977年。

⑻ 秋元律郎『戦争と民衆―太平洋戦争下の都市生活―』学陽書房 1974年。

⑻ 中川剛『町内会―日本人の自治感覚―』中央公論社 1980年。

⑻ 日本の空襲編集委員会編『日本の空襲』10巻 三省堂 1980年～1981年。

⑻ 原田良次『日本大空襲―本土制空基地隊員の日記―』上下、中央公論社1973年～1980年。

⑻ 東京空襲を記録する会編『東京大空襲・戦災誌』5巻、講談社 1973年～1974年、横浜市・横浜の空襲を記録する会編『横浜の空襲と戦災』6巻、横浜市、1975年～1977年、川崎市編・刊行『川崎空襲・戦災の記録』3巻、1974年～1975年、八王子空襲を記録する会編・刊行『盆地は火の海―八王子大空襲体験記録』3冊、1980年～1983年。立川市文芸同好会編・刊行『立川空襲の記録』4冊、1972年～1976年。

⑼ 早乙女勝元『東京大空襲 昭和20年3月10日の記録』岩波書店 1971年。

⑼ 今井清一『大空襲5月29日 第2次大戦と横浜』有隣堂 1981年。

⑼ 小山仁示「太平洋戦争下の大阪空襲について」、柴田実先生古稀記念『日本文化史論叢』同会 1976年、「米軍資料による第1次大阪大空襲」、海溪昇教授退官記念『日本近代の成立と展開』思文閣出版 1984年。

⑼ 吉田守男「京都小空襲論」、『日本史研究』251号、1983年。

HERMAN A. DIEDERIKS

The Netherlands*°

In the Netherlands, for centuries a highly urbanised country, urban history as a separate branch of the study of history has scarcely been developed. A number of things have been written about cities, but mainly from the perspective of local history. Consequently, no specific journal of urban history is published in the Netherlands. A survey of Dutch urban history has, however, been printed in the English journal, *Urban History Yearbook* (3), published since 1974 in Leicester. Based on the most prominent publications, the article gives an impression of the entire period since the late Middle Ages.

Articles published on the subject of urban history are found, for the most part, in journals of economic and social history, as well as in historic geographical journals. A good example is the somewhat older *Economisch Historisch Jaarboek* (*Economic Historical Yearbook*), published since 1971 under the title *Economisch- en Sociaal Historisch Jaarboek* (*Economic and Social Historical Yearbook*). The *Tijdschrift voor Sociale Geschiedenis* (*Journal of Social History*), first published in 1975, is an example of a newer journal in which many articles on urban history can be found. Certain aspects of urban development have also been discussed in the periodical published by the recently established Industrial Archeology Society, as well as in the journal *Historische Geografie* (*Historical Geography*). A number of articles published in these journals will be discussed later.

At this point, a remark should be made concerning the interpretation of the 19th and 20th centuries. The fact is that the modern city in the Netherlands did not appear until the second half of the 19th century. Nevertheless, the entire 19th century has been chosen as

* Translated by Judith L. Smyth.
° Numbers in brackets in this chapter refer to entries in the bibliography on pp. 440–453 of this volume.

the chronological context here, also because of the high degree of continuity found in the Netherlands. Many old cities developed into modern ones during the course of the 19th and 20th centuries.

A number of books and articles concentrating on urban history in the Netherlands during the 19th and 20th centuries will be discussed under various headings. The present bibliography reviews studies published in the course of approximately the last ten years, taking into account those which have appeared since 1976.

A. Introduction

A bibliography of urban history was published in 1978 (2). On the basis of judicial historic and demographic criteria, municipal rights and population numbers, 188 cities were included. The history of each of these cities is dealt with from early times until 1940.

Besides this, archive material pertaining to urban history has become more accessible by the publication of archive overviews since 1979.

The series *Overzichten van de Archieven en Verzamelingen in de Openbare Archiefbewaarplaatsen in Nederland* (*Overviews of the Archives and Collections in Public Archive Depositories in the Netherlands*) (8), has been published since 1979 under the auspices of the Association of Archivists in the Netherlands, Samson Publishing, Alphen aan de Rijn. The inventories are arranged according to province, with the exception of Part VIII, which deals only with Amsterdam, and Part IX, which describes the collection of the General Public Record Office. This series is the first and most important introduction to the Dutch archives. Information is given on each archive, how it is inventoried, and whether it includes a complete inventory or simply a tentative catalogue listing.

The series also contains information on the location and opening hours of the various archives. The overviews indicate which collections can be found in the Provincial Government Archives and which in the Municipal Archives, the latter, of course, being the most interesting to the urban historian.

Current bibliographies on a number of cities are also published. Reviews of books and articles concerning the history of Amsterdam and based on information obtained from the library of the Amsterdam Municipal Archive are printed regularly in the regional historic geographical magazine *Ons Amsterdam*. Sometimes a single bibliography of one particular city will be published as, for example, that in 1978 on the city of Doetinchem on the Yssel (1).

B. The Process of Urbanisation

The process of urbanisation in the Netherlands during the 19th and 20th centuries was characterised by the absence of large cities and a decentralised growth. The Netherlands was, and still is, an urbanised country without cities.

During the 18th century, Amsterdam still dominated the urban system, although Rotterdam and The Hague began challenging that position during the 19th and 20th centuries. The reason for this decentralised growth lies in a decentralisation of functions: Rotterdam serving as a seaport, The Hague as the centre of politics, and Amsterdam as the focal point of financial and cultural activity (11). The growth of Amsterdam stagnated until the middle of the 19th century and did not revive until after 1880.

The rapidly growing cities were the specialised ones, as, for example, Rotterdam with its harbour and the textile cities of Enschede and Tilburg. Amsterdam was specialised in capital-intensive sectors of the economy so that population growth, in general, was slower than in cities having labour-intensive branches of industry (9). In comparison with England and Germany, modern urbanisation in the Netherlands generally lagged behind, influenced partly by a late industrialisation. Nevertheless, the "old cities", those arising during the late Middle Ages, were the first to show signs of growth, subsequently followed by the new industrial towns in the South and East. In addition, growth occurred in clusters of interrelated, functionally complementary cities (10).

An analysis of the factors relevant to the growth of cities indicates that industrialisation definitely was not the most important factor. In research on 117 urban municipalities, political and financial processes, as well as relationships between these cities and surrounding areas, have been studied. Between 1899 and 1930 various, partially integrated urban systems arose. The nature of the system determined, in part, the rate of growth in the cities composing the system (28).

The phenomenon of suburbanisation had already begun to appear at the end of the 19th century, developing further during the period between the two world wars, and especially after the Second

World War. Partially generated by the need for better housing, migration from the cities to outlying communities began, but, due to decentralised industrialisation, travelling from the cities to work in surrounding areas also occurred. This led to urban agglomeration as early as the 1930s. After 1945, the number of inhabitants of large cities declined, though this decrease would later be compensated by the influx of foreign migratory workers (12).

Some authors divide the urbanisation process during the 19th and 20th centuries into two stages. The period from 1815 to 1870 is considered to have been characterised by the development of the separate city, but, due to the lack of good means of communication, an integrated urban system did not develop.

Although urbanisation occurred mainly in the western part of the Netherlands, the "randstad", and although this area has received the most attention from researchers, more interest has been shown lately in other parts of the country.

During the first stage, that of the separate city, Groningen in the north east was the largest city, having a population of less than 40,000 in 1869. Centres of growth were the cities of Noord-Brabant and Limburg which benefited from the temporary affiliation (1815–1830) of the Southern Netherlands. Through the affiliation they became more centrally situated. After the Belgian Revolt they profited from their position as military bases. It is generally assumed that 17th and 18th century ramparts were an obstacle to urban expansion during the 19th century, but, in most cities, sufficient space was available within these walls. In Noord-Brabant, the most notable growth before 1870 took place in the textile city of Tilburg. Taken as a whole, the urban population outside the "randstad" area grew only slightly before 1870. Only after this date, and particularly after 1945, did urbanisation outside the "randstad" area develop further. This process took place in clusters of cities, and here, once again, decentralised growth prevailed.

Not all cities which had flourished within the urban system during the 16th and 17th centuries did so again in the 19th century. Particularly in peripheral areas, such as parts of Noord-Holland and Zeeland, a number of cities lost their former functions and acquired nothing new to replace them. In the Noord-Holland city of Enkhuizen, for example, there were numerous farms within city limits at the beginning of the 19th century (125). Middelburg, the capital of Zeeland, noted in 1935 for its glorious past, struggles along today as an administrative and market town with an architectural open-air museum. This situation was also changed by the devastating effects of war on the city in 1940 (131).

C. Individual Fields of Research

(a)   *Developments in Urban Physical Planning*

The term urban development here refers mainly to the physical spatial processes which took place in the cities during the 19th and 20th centuries. These processes have been progressively placed within a legislative context, particularly since the 1960s. In 1961, the Monuments Act was passed; between 1962 and 1965, the Physical Planning Act went into effect; and finally, in 1984, the Urban and Village Renewal Act was approved. Maps and atlases provide an excellent means for following these developments. An interesting question is, "Which changes in inner-city functions took place during the 17th and 18th centuries?" These changes can clearly be traced with the help of the first cadastral maps, most of which date from the middle of the 19th century. R. Smook selected 36 cities and, using the oldest available cadastral and current maps, has analysed the changes that occurred in these cities. On a third map, changes that had taken place over the course of more than a century were noted. The construction of railways and railway stations, the laying-out of parks, the creation of industrial zones, and urban expansion were sketched on this third series of maps. Although Smook doesn't present a complete historical analysis, his book does provide a useful inventory (85).

The development of cities and their distribution throughout the country depends a great deal on the means of available communication. In the 19th century, railways played a crucial part. A dissertation published by the Technological Institute in Delft includes a systematic inventory of all main and local railways, describing how particular railway lines were laid out and why certain routes were chosen (74).

Research has been done on the role played by trains and trams in "randstad" and suburban development, namely in the Amsterdam area from 1870 to 1914. A revolutionary development and expansion of public transport began in 1900, but, despite this, the process of suburbanisation was a selective one. Amsterdam opted for inexpensive accommodation for low-income groups, thereby producing a good deal of relatively poor quality housing (115).

Research has been carried out on the relationship between urban structure before the 19th century, and city areas created between 1860 and 1900. The most important example is that provided by the city of Arnhem. The question is whether the development of urban communities should be seen as a continuous process. Was 19th century urban design based on the physical structure of the historic city? The main issue in this respect is how physical characteristics dating from the recent, as well as the distant, past, can be retained during the process of urban renewal (86).

Urban physical structure can also be analysed by studying individual buildings. Numbered housing is a prerequisite necessary for this type of research. House numbering was generally introduced in Dutch cities during the 18th century, specifically in 1795 when a system of population registration was developed at the insistence of the French, who invaded the Netherlands in that year. Many of the numbering systems set up at that time were later revised, resulting in a synthesis of the older and more recent systems. A study has been made of how the original house numbering system in Amsterdam was realised (65).

Many studies on the physical structure of Amsterdam have been published. For the purpose of census-taking, a standardised system of district classification was developed, allowing the social stratification of the city to be reconstructed. So, to what extent was Amsterdam a "socially stratified" city at the beginning of the 19th century? Did the poor live with the poor and the rich with the rich? A reorganisation of the original classification scheme into ten districts indicates that there was a certain amount of division along social lines. Various social groups inhabited the medieval core of the city, while the area defined by the ring of concentric canals may be referred to as "distinguished". Areas on the outskirts of the city, such as the Jordaan and the eastern and western islands, definitely exhibit a number of characteristics of working-class neighbourhoods (30). Although the Jews never lived in actual ghettos, they were densely concentrated in certain areas, and, despite their formal emancipation in 1796, they continued to live close together, carrying on their traditional professions during the first three decades of the 19th century (34). Did new neighbourhoods for the élite also emerge later in the 19th century? From 1870 to 1900, city forming did take place within the historic core of the city. Were the élite driven to new areas because of this? Three areas were laid out for the purpose of housing the upper-class, two on the east side of the city (the Plantage and the Sarphati neighbourhoods) and one on the south side (surrounding the Vondel Park). Only the latter can be called a success (69). Nevertheless, the old ring of canals retained its enormous attraction for Amsterdam's élite, certainly until 1900. An analysis of part of the new élite Vondel Park and Vondel Street area reveals that it was inhabited mainly by successors to the old patrician class, together with members of the newly formed upper-middle-class, and, to a much lesser extent, by the "haute juiverie", newly affluent German immigrants and those who had made their fortune in Indonesia (27).

An analysis of the development of Amsterdam since 1900 leads to the conclusion that town planning is almost impossible because of the problem of suburbanisation, and that only in combination with regional planning can results be achieved. Amsterdam served as an example in this analysis, which focuses attention on the solution of the garden city, Berlage's General Plan of Expansion of 1934, and plans developed during the 1960s (75).

L. Pincoff's activities in Rotterdam illustrate how the structure of a city can be determined by one individual. The achievements of this developer from 1849 to 1879 are spectacular. He founded the Rotterdam Business Association and commissioned the digging of a number of harbours on the south bank of the Maas. Although he was later exposed for his fraudulent practises, the facilities developed under his direction endured and played an important part in the development of Rotterdam as a modern world harbour (132).

The history of urban expansion during the 19th and 20th centuries is also concerned with the construction of new sections directly surrounding the old historic core. In some old cities, like Leiden for example, modern urban expansion did not begin until the end of the 19th century (79). Many working-class neighbourhoods were developed during the first half of the 20th century, particularly in the period between the two world wars. The Noorderkwartier and the Kooi, for example, were layed out on the northern and eastern city limits of 17th century Leiden. Housing societies played an extremely important part in this enterprise. During the period between the wars, the socialist-oriented housing society "De Eendracht" was especially active in constructing high quality housing in the Kooi area, which was designed to surround a public park. This neighbourhood is popularly known as the "Red Village" (55). Comparable urban areas were built, among other places, in Utrecht and

Groningen (45). At what precise moment did municipal governments become actively concerned with housing construction, and specifically with workers' housing? The Housing Act of 1901, which stated that for every proposed project, exact and officially approved plans were required, offered for the first time the means by which municipal governments could regulate building activities. Before this Act went into effect, intervention occurred only incidentally. Leeuwarden, the capital of the Province of Friesland, grew from 16,504 inhabitants in 1811 to 29,690 in 1899, during which time some unregulated housing construction took place. The development of the railway in 1865 provided the city with an excuse to intervene in this process (128).

(b)   Urban Architecture

As an overview of architectural styles and the architects associated with them, H.J.F. de Roy van Zuydewijn's illustrated review should be mentioned. He provides a survey of 19th and 20th century building in Amsterdam, arranged according to style and architect, opening with the neoclassical at the beginning of the 19th century and concluding with the Delft school, particularly influential from 1930 to 1940. It is a useful inventory of urban architectural history, covering a time during which the city quadrupled in size (84).

The one architect most responsible for the appearance of Amsterdam as it is today is P.J.H. Cuypers (1827–1921), designer of the Central Station and the Rijks Museum. A study of Cuypers' work in Amsterdam to celebrate the centennial of the Rijks Museum was published in 1985. Special attention was paid to his homes on Vondel Street and the six Roman Catholic churches designed by him, two of which have since been demolished (78). An active group of architects formed the Amsterdam school, which was responsible for many buildings in the city between 1910 and 1930. The Maritime House on the Prins Hendrikkade, situated diagonally across from the Central Station, and the Tuschinski Theater are two splendid examples of their work (70). An Italian study, also translated into Dutch, describes a number of developments in urban planning and, in particular, architectural developments between 1870 and 1940 (72). The debates on the Housing Act of 1901, the General Plan of Expansion of 1934, and new ideas on workers' housing are all discussed.

Some information is available on individual buildings and the plans which led up to them. In 1840, the decision was taken to demolish the Amsterdam Bourse, built in the 17th century by the master builder H. de Keyser. It was to be replaced by a new stock exchange, and a design competition was organised. An article about this competition and the choice of the best design was published in the 1984 Amsterdam Yearbook, *Amstelodamum* (87).

An important contribution to urban history today is being made by industrial archeologists. A number of typical urban commercial buildings are being studied. Inventories have been made, for example, of factories built during the 19th century in one of the older parts of Amsterdam, the "island" of Oostenburg, where engine and shipbuilding industries developed during the last century (111). A tentative inventory has also been done on the city of Leiden (96).

A thorough description of the long construction history of the present Amsterdam Historical Museum is presented in the series *Dutch Monuments of History and Art*. This building was originally used partly as a monastery, later becoming an orphanage in the 20th century (80). The Binnengasthuis memorial volume is also worth mentioning. This hospital was enlarged mainly during the 19th century and rebuilt as a university hospital, a function it fulfilled until 1981 (56).

A number of inventories has been completed recently on certain specific types of buildings. In 1982, a list was compiled of harbour buildings, such as warehouses, sheds, office buildings and refineries, still to be found in Rotterdam. Many of these buildings date from the 19th century (76). Rotterdam's industrial heritage has also been studied and a survey report was published in 1983 (82).

(c) Demography

Few specifically demographic studies have been published. There are, however, a number of publications on the Ancien Regime which, to some extent, include the beginning of the 19th century. Nusteling has made a reconstruction of Amsterdam's population and employment during the lengthy period from 1540 to 1860. His study centres on the entire population and its purchasing power, but, due to the lack of complete population figures for the preceding period, it is concerned mainly with the years between 1622 and 1795. Census figures became available after 1795. The study includes numerous appendices which provide additional information for the period after 1860. Data on wages, for example, are given until

1910 and price indexes until 1912 (58).

Marriage registration in Amsterdam during the Ancien Regime has been extensively studied and the information used for research on migration patterns. The registers of proposed marriages during the first decade of the 19th century have been analysed in order to gain insight into the problem of migrant integration in Amsterdam society (31), a process in which partner choice played a key part (32).

The amount of attention given to cities from around 1800 can be attributed largely to the abundance of statistical information available on this period, thanks to the French occupiers. The first population census in 1795 was followed by a religious census in 1809. The population of Amsterdam declined drastically by approximately 18% between 1795 and 1815. Initially, this was due to a drop in immigration, but during the incorporation in the Napoleonic Empire, in which Amsterdam became the third city of the Empire, the population decline was aggravated by mass emigration (33). It was not until the middle of the 19th century that the population again reached the level of that at the end of the 18th century. Utrecht, a relatively large city at that time (some 40,000 inhabitants in 1826), has also been studied. The market, which was visited regularly by wealthy farmers from the surrounding countryside, provided, along with the university and the garrison, the economic basis for the city's existence. Economic variables, such as rye prices, show little or no statistical connection with demographic developments from 1771 to 1825 (43). Whereas the population of Amsterdam greatly decreased at the beginning of the 19th century, the town of Schiedam proved an exception, with a population increase caused by its flourishing distilling industry. A complete census of all households, including demographic and economic data such as the one taken in Schiedam in 1807 for tax-collection purposes, allows the historian to study the 19th century household structure from a demographic and economic perspective (63). A similar study has been done on the rapidly developing port of Rotterdam from 1810 to 1880 (37), and mortality rates for some cities have also been examined. Since 1774, causes of death have been recorded in Amsterdam and changes in the patterns of mortality over the lengthy period from 1774 to 1930 have been discussed in an article on the subject. The question raised was the degree to which hygiene measures, such as improvements of drinking water supplies, led to changes in these patterns. A decline in the number of deaths caused by intestinal diseases did, however, decrease before safer drinking water had become available. In trying to find an explanation, emphasis has been placed on improved foodstuffs, particularly the potato (47). In a study of the relationship between causes of death and social inequality in the Netherlands from 1850 to 1940, data for a number of cities, such as The Hague, Amsterdam, Hilversum, Rotterdam, Dordrecht, Arnhem and Nijmegen, have been compiled. Special emphasis has been placed on the relationship between the socio-economic position of the head of the household and infant and child mortality rates (61).

Little research has been done on internal migration within cities. An exception, however, is a limited study of population mobility in a number of sections of Leiden during the last decade of the 19th century, and between the wars. A much higher degree of mobility was discovered during the 1930s. People moved more often than in the 19th century, some even returning to their old homes during the ten years covered by the study (36).

Very little is being done on urban family reconstruction. One study has been made, though, of changes in fertility patterns in the Noord-Brabant's city of Breda from 1850 to 1940, based on family reconstruction. Changes in fertility were related to such factors as occupation, religion and child mortality. Cohorts born during the periods 1840 to 1869, 1870 to 1879, and 1880 to 1890 have been included in the study (39).

(d)   Economic Structure

Surveys of the general urban economic structure in the Netherlands are not available. The total economic structure or specific segments of this structure have, however, been analysed for certain cities. Most of the studies on Amsterdam focus on the beginning of the 19th century. A study of the economic structure centred on which sectors, in the early 19th century, should be seen as generating, and which as servicing, indicates that next to the commercial sector, which stagnated at that time, certain industrial branches, such as sugar refining and tobacco processing, should be considered generating sectors of the economy (95).

A special segment of the economic structure is the labour market. There appears to be a contradiction between high wages and mass unemployment in Amsterdam during the first half of the 19th century. The labour market was clearly segmented in Amsterdam between 1800 and 1865, characterised by a fluctuating demand for labour (120). Characteristic of that segmentation was the control of the diamond industry by the Jews, the domination of the Germans in the sugar refineries, and the large number of migratory construction workers from the province of Brabant. The fluctuating demand for labour was met with by a flexible labour force, immigrants, and migratory workers coming from traditional sectors of the economy still prevalent in the eastern Netherlands and Germany. This stream of workers filled gaps caused by the high urban mortality rate, and provided the growth sectors of the economy with labour. Thus, in Amsterdam, with its many modern sectors, two parts of a dual economy converged. This situation continued until approximately 1830.

Two separate labour markets have also been noted in Amsterdam's construction business until about 1870. One of these was the traditional artisan market with its fixed wages, with workers employed mainly in repair work and rebuilding. The second was the modern construction sector, primarily composed of migratory workers employed in the construction of new buildings. During the 1860s and 70s, the artisan sector disintegrated, due partially to the population increase, and hence urban expansion. At this point. the threatened artisans began forming labour unions which can be seen as a reaction to their precarious position (105).

Amsterdam was, of course, primarily a commercial centre, based on trade from the Baltic Sea since the 16th century. From 1725 to 1780, the same level of trade was almost reached as during the golden age of the 17th century. This situation, however, did not recur in Amsterdam after the establishment of national independence in 1813, as indicated by the statistics available until 1824 (104). Amsterdam was also a centre of timber trading in the 18th century and important auctions were held there. Although Amsterdam lost its prominent position in this area after 1808, price records continuing into the 20th century provide insight into this trade (112).

Licence registers, which were a way of taxing businesses, provide an opportunity for studying changes in urban economic structures. The licence registers for Leeuwarden, the capital of agrarian Friesland, have been studied for 1870, 1880 and 1890; the effects of the disastrous agricultural crisis of 1880–1890 can be clearly seen in the Leeuwarden registers. Between 1870 and 1880 the number of businesses, particularly in the trade sector, showed an enormous increase (127).

Licence registers have also been used in analysing the economic development of Delft in the 19th century. Although Delft functioned mainly as a regional service centre around 1820, industry became significantly more important, with special emphasis on the part played by the military establishment. After 1880, industry's generating role prevailed over that of the regional service function, and the founding of the Technological Institute in 1900 provided a new element in the economic structure of the city (123).

The diamond industry gained a more prominent place in Amsterdam's economic structure during the 19th century, particularly during the second half (118).

One of the typical age-old urban industries was beer brewing, especially in the southern provinces of the Netherlands, and many local breweries continued in business during the 19th and 20th centuries. A review article has been published on brewing techniques, concerned specifically with a brewery in Maastricht, capital of the province of Limburg (130). The Maastricht Historical Society commissioned a survey of brewing history in Maastricht in which the introduction of Beieren brewing in the 19th century is treated (129).

Archaeologists have given much attention to the development of the metal industry. Although the development of The Hague is conventionally ascribed to the location of the national government there, this impression is not entirely correct. At an early stage, The Hague was a centre of the heavy metal industry. A copper mill was started in 1824 and a foundry was added later. In particular, a large amount of street furniture (e.g. lantern posts and bridge railings) was produced. A lead and zinc mill built in Utrecht in 1866 proved such a public nuisance that it was eventually closed, although not until the early 1980s (106).

Shipbuilding and maintenance are among the most important activities in the Rotterdam harbour area. A society for the operation of a slipway was founded in 1840. With the help of a steam engine, ships were towed up the slipway for repairs. The slipway was closed in 1895, due to the disappearance of sailing vessels and the increasing size of steamships, as well as the competition from public docks and the unfavourable location of the slipway (90).

Smaller cities also tried to develop better seaway connections. Groningen, capital of the province of Groningen, constructed the Eems Canal in 1876, and Scandanavian timber, English coal, and

Russian and Prussian grain all reached the city by way of this canal. However, Groningen failed to become a port of any significance because of the many obstructions ships encountered in the canal (92).

Quite often, the introduction of machinery — particularly machine factories — took place in the cities. A useful guide for tracing the mechanisation route from town to town is an interim report published with the aid of the Institute of Technology in Eindhoven (4).

(e) Cities and Energy Supply

During the 19th century energy in Dutch cities was supplied increasingly by gas and later by electricity, making the use of gas and electric motors possible. Nevertheless, horsepower was used to operate mills in Amsterdam until 1919; the last one to work in this way was a hulling mill. An article dealing with the entire period from 1519 to 1919 describes how horsepower was used in every type of industry: diamond cutting, butter churning, goldwire fabrication, on dredging machines, in malt mills, drilling mills, fulling mills, gunpowder mills, white-lead mills, and sugar refineries (102).

In most cities, gas was supplied by privately owned companies, many of which were English or used English capital. Gas was introduced in Amsterdam in 1825, and in 1885 the Imperial Continental Gas Association opened its new installation, the Wester Gasworks (114).

Gasworks were not appropriated by Amsterdam's city government until 1898. The first city to exploit this source of energy itself was Leiden, which began using gas in 1848 mainly for streetlighting. Technical and organisational problems impeded the start of this project (117), but Leiden had set the example for other towns in the Netherlands. Obviously, if a concessionaire was able to make a profit on gas sales, cities themselves could do so. In all 20 cities had gasworks by about 1900, and ownership was transferred into city hands (107). Breda hesitated between the choice of city or private ownership. A private company had made a proposal in 1845, but it was not until 1858 that a city-owned gasworks went into operation, mainly supplying streetlighting. Profits rose and the price of gas per cubic metre was lowered accordingly. Gas was produced on the premises of the gasworks until 1947, and subsequently provided solely by the National State Mines from 1953 to the 1970s when the mines closed and the change was made to natural gas (89). From 1844 to 1874, The Hague was committed to a concession granted to a private firm, thus preventing city operation until the contract expired (94). Electricity did not become available until a much later date; the introduction and distribution of this type of energy can be seen, along with telephone, gas and water facilities, as an infrastructural urban innovation. At the time of its introduction, most of the utilities were publically owned. A number of uses for electricity paralleled those of gas, meaning that relative price differences between the two became important, as was the case in the city of Groningen (108).

(*f*)   *The Social Structure*

The problem of social structure has been studied from the aspect of social stratification alone and in relation to social mobility. Studies on social stratification have predominated and only gradually have monographs dealing with the problem of upward mobility become available.

In 1976, a report causing some discussion was published on a study of the social structure of the Netherlands around 1850. It included various data on the provinces and larger cities. The categories used were: upper middle-class, lower middle-class, (farmers), working class, and lumpenproletariat, thereby quartering the urban social structure. In 1850, the processes of industrialisation and modernisation in the Netherlands had barely begun. One of the most salient features mentioned by the authors is that whereas skilled labourers represented only 0.3% of the national work force, they comprised 2.2% of that of Amsterdam. Unskilled labourers represented 3.5% of the national work force against 13.7% in Amsterdam (42). Although general census taken since 1795 provide data on the entire population, specific occupational census have only been taken since 1849; and since this type of census information is almost indispensable in the analysis of social stratification, descriptions of social structure at the beginning of the 19th century tend to be somewhat imprecise. A report of this kind was written in 1812 by the mayor of Amsterdam, W. van Brienen, in which he describes the various social strata to be found in Amsterdam at that time, including the habits and customs of different social groups (54).

Aside from this, polling registers have also been studied so as to analyse the composition of the upper classes and changes in this structure. Voting took place indirectly, so that the local urban element can easily be discerned. Since 1815, all males above the age of 23, who paid a certain amount of real estate and personal property tax, had the right to vote. The tax amount varied according to the town. In 1848, the Constitution was revised, including changes in voting laws. An analysis of those inhabitants of Delft having the right to vote in 1849 and 1850 shows that it was the lower middle-class (formerly the shopkeepers' and tradesmen's class) which was allowed to vote, and that in a static class society, conservative voting behaviour can be attributed to this group (15). Around 1850, the right to vote was no longer reserved for the privileged or so-called "respectable" class. In urban areas, besides public officials, merchants, professional men, and those of independent means, a number of shopkeepers, artisans, innkeepers and bakers also gained the right to vote.

On the basis of this data it is possible to determine the degree of equality or inequality in the level of welfare in each city. A statistic comparison can be made by using the Lorenz curve and the Theil index. Using this method, it becomes clear that Amsterdam was more prosperous than Rotterdam, due to improvement in the situation in Amsterdam since 1817. This is not surprising, since 1817 was a year of economic crisis (23). After 1895, the rate of economic growth accelerated in the Netherlands, raising the question as to whether this led to an increase or a decrease in income differences in Amsterdam. In answering, it becomes evident that immigration and emigration did not play a major part. This would have meant that the well-to-do had moved away, thereby influencing the level of affluence. This clearly had little effect. Whereas industrialisation continued at an accelerated pace after 1895, the social changes deriving from this process did not manifest themselves until the 20th century. Income inequality did not begin to decrease rapidly until the 1920s. At this time it dropped by 40% in comparison with the period preceding the First World War. A similar situation occurred after the Second World War when, during the 1950s, a decrease in comparison with the period right before that war took place (53).

About 1850, the upper middle-class dominated Amsterdam socially and politically, it was almost a "closed society" practically inaccessible to those from the lower classes. Scarcely anyone succeeded in entering the select circle by means of a "good match" or by any other means. During the 19th century, however, the chances for upward social mobility increased, due to economic developments. More people from simple backgrounds were able to approach the level of prosperity of the upper classes; but did these newcomers thereby gain entry into society circles? Did the traditional and commercial, financial elite mix socially or inter-marry with the new industrial elite? This is one of the main questions posed in a recent study. And besides this, a characterisation sketch of both the traditional and the new elite is given covering such topics as the sort of professions they practised, their religious convictions, the neighbourhoods in which they lived and how they related to the rest of society.

The initial data for this study were supplied by polling registers for the parliamentary elections between 1854 and 1894. Random samples were taken from the registers, and data were collected from such sources as the Municipal Register, deeds and certificates from the Registrar's Office, and membership lists from cultural societies (68).

Covering approximately the same period, the elite in the southern city of Maastricht has also been analysed. This city had a French oriented upper-class which still maintained connections with the countryside, but which also included new industrial families. Maastricht has been called the first industrial city of the Netherlands. During the process of industrialisation, part of the established elite left the city, and their place was taken by similar upper-class families coming from other areas, showing that there was more of a geographic than social mobility. The elite included members of the new industrial class, merchants, lawyers, medical professionals and retired military officers, the presence of the latter relating to the fact that Maastricht had a large military base (26).

(g) *Poverty, Social Problems and Socialism*

During the 19th and 20th centuries, Amsterdam was the most turbulent city in the Netherlands. But, in general, the country was a model of tranquillity in comparison to surrounding countries, and what unrest there was was concentrated in Amsterdam. In 1835 there was a tax revolt in the city, which resulted in the resignation of the mayor. Following a number of other riots, the Jordaan Revolt occurred in 1934 as a spontaneous reaction to a cut in unemployment benefits. It was, however, not the social aspect, i.e. public resistance, which triggered off the tax revolt of 1835 (19). The main impetus for the riot came, rather, from small landlords who induced the populace with gin and money. One hundred years later the Jordaan Revolt occurred during the lowest point in the period of depression between the two world wars. Reduced unemployment benefits provoked a spontaneous riot in the Jordaan, a working-class neighbourhood; six people were killed and many others wounded. The riot was a more or less spontaneous response on the part of desperate, unemployed labourers (14).

Although large numbers of paupers living from charity were concentrated in the urban areas of the western Netherlands in the early 19th century, a multitude of beggars also inhabited the towns in the more rural surroundings of the east and northeast. Charity settlements, aimed at rehabilitating urban paupers and beggars by providing jobs in (cottage) textile industry and farming, were established in the northeast. City governments paid for the upkeep of those sent to the settlements. Accounts of these transactions, which can be found in Municipal Archives, allow the historian to examine the situation more thoroughly. This has been done for the city of Groningen, and based on data covering 1823 to 1870, the researchers concluded that a class of professional beggars existed at that time (46).

Cities struggled throughout the entire 19th century with problems of poverty and relief for the poor. Part of the poor relief was provided by church parishes, but much still remained to be done by city governments. At a time when city funds were already heavily drawn on, the problem of whether or not the relief recipient and his family had a right to financial aid became more and more acute. In 1853, a control system employing volunteers to visit the poor was set up in Elberfeld, Germany. Each volunteer had charge of five families, thereby establishing a system of direct control. This system was temporarily used in Leeuwarden between 1893 and 1913. After the devastating agricultural crisis, the number of those on poor relief rose sharply. The system — referred to as the Elbersfeld system because of its origin — failed to work in Leeuwarden because of the aggressiveness of the poor toward the volunteer supervisors. Besides that, the volunteers had no say as to whom should or should not be granted aid. City authorities reserved this power for themselves (50).

In 1976, an extensive study was published on the living and working conditions of labourers in a small provincial capital, 's-Hertogenbosch, between 1850 and about 1900. Den Bosch had nearly 21,000 inhabitants in 1850 and 30,517 in 1899. Not only was the town a centre of regional trade, it also served as a government administration centre and had a military base as well. Den Bosch's importance as a trade centre declined during the 19th century. Small-scale enterprises, including cottage industries, dominated manufacturing, which began expanding in about 1900. The fastest growing industries were cigar manufacturing, shoe manufacturing, printing, food processing and the metal industry. During the second half of the 19th century, living conditions of Den Bosch's workers improved. The Catholic Church dominated labour organisations so that the cigar makers' strike did not meet with a favourable reception (41).

To what extent seamen can be included in the urban labour market remains unclear. It can be argued that because of the predominance of regularly scheduled freight shipping in the harbour of Amsterdam, the seamen working out of that port can be counted as inhabitants of the city, whereas this is not the case with Rotterdam's seamen, who were chiefly employed in tramp shipping. Besides this, Rotterdam seamen were difficult to organise in a trade union. Taking into consideration the isolation and consequential solidarity among seamen, it is quite likely that they went on strike quite readily. The seaman's strike of 1911 indicates that this is not always conducive to achieving the desired results (22).

The same distinction between Amsterdam and Rotterdam can also be made with regard to dock workers. Up until the First World War, dock workers in Rotterdam were not as willing to strike as those in Amsterdam. Although the number of strikes in the former city increased, these should be seen as acts of desperation (99). Shortly after the Second World War, a number of strikes broke out among dock workers in Amsterdam and Rotterdam. The communist oriented "Eenheidsvak centrale", the United Labour Union, played a particularly important part in the strikes (93).

A sympathetic reaction by employers to social problems, such as housing, was more the exception than the rule. One such unusual man was J. C. van Marken, founder of Gist Manufacturing in Delft. In 1882, he began construction on a residential park for the workers in his factory. The project was named Agneta Park, in honour of his wife, and was completed in 1885. In his factory, van Marken had also made a number of arrangements to improve the social welfare of his workers. Agneta Park consisted not only of workers' housing, but van Marken also had a spacious home for himself built in the middle of it. Not all the factory workers were equally happy with this situation (88). While discussing the "Refinement Offensive" on the part of the middle and upper class, the People's Housing Movement should also be mentioned. One such housing project was founded in Leiden by a group of wealthy, left-wing liberals for the purpose of "refining" the city's working-class (52).

Urban history also relies on the techniques of "oral history".

Much attention has been given to the daily lives of the unemployed between the wars. A research report has been published on a working-class neighbourhood in Utrecht and the reaction of its inhabitants to the crisis of the 1930s. In general, the reaction was more one of resignation than revolt. The three trade unions active in Utrecht at that time cared for their unemployed members and taught them a certain amount of class consciousness (57).

Prostitution is one of the problems faced by urban communities. This phenomenon, of course, is not new to cities, but in former times it was not considered to be a great social and moral problem. The development of middle-class morality and the growth of medical knowledge during the 19th century led to an intolerant attitude toward prostitution. The increase in medical knowledge brought with it the necessity of registering prostitutes, and these registers provide a source of information for historians interested in this phenomenon. A study on regimentation and the effect of medical examinations in Zwolle, the provincial capital of Overijssel, has been published. Geographical mobility of the prostitutes was studied also and found to be quite high because of the frequency of compulsory medical examinations (48). A study on prostitution in Utrecht reveals that a change in organisation took place in about 1865. The officially registered women frequently came from areas farther away from the town, and the number of officially registered brothels decreased (64).

During the 1930s, sociologists studied marginal urban groups, and a number of these studies have since been reprinted. Impressions are given of the occupational life of Chinese peanut vendors, girls employed in the garment industry, and various pedlars during the Great Depression (25).

A sociographic study carried out from the perspective of contemporary problems in the 1980s on urban working-class neighbourhoods has also been done. Not only the present characteristics and structure are discussed, but also the historical growth of these areas. Furthermore, the book contains a list of the principal working-class neighbourhoods found in Dutch cities (62).

The development of socialism may certainly be described as an urban phenomenon. A review of the Social Democratic League — "Sociaal-Democratische Bond" — traces its origins back to Amsterdam in 1878. From there the league spread to Haarlem, Rotterdam, Leiden and the rest of the country. The core of the league was concentrated in the larger cities and it was not until 1888 that it began gaining a following in rural areas. The first members were educated craftsmen who rebelled primarily against the increasingly impersonal and more business-like relationships between employers and workers. Around 1890, the league began to take a more radical approach, influenced to a large extent by urban unemployment, and grew into a movement of discontented workers (18).

Maastricht has been cited as the first industrial city of the Netherlands. Large factories became situated there even before 1850. The organised labour movement, however, did not develop until a relatively late date. This is sometimes explained by referring to the fact that potteries and glassworks provided excellent workers' benefits. Nevertheless, the activities of the socialist, Vliegen, during the 1890s led to the organisation of a socialist movement in Maastricht. After this activist leader had left the city, the movement disintegrated, however. Furthermore, the Roman Catholics had come to the conclusion that there were, indeed, a number of pressing social problems with which they should deal if they did not wish to forfeit labour support to the socialists (21).

Information on local socialist politics can be gained by examining the studies made of prominent figures in the Socialist Movement. One of these, on whom a biography has been written, is the journalist and politician P. L. Tak (1848–1907). In 1899, he became a member of the Social Democratic Labour Party, the revisionist successor to the Social Democratic League. He was active in the Co-operative Movement and joined the city council in 1904. At the time of his inauguration, the number of socialist council members doubled from three to six (16).

(h) Mentality

The development of socialism can be viewed from the perspective of the history of mentalities. Education, the press, religious and community life should, in any case, be included in this category. A study on architectural training in Amsterdam from 1820 to 1844 has been published (83). Another study, printed as an article, has been done on popular conceptions among large groups of urban newspaper readers. Three major Rotterdam newspapers were selected, each having its own distinct type of reading public. Rotterdam was the first city in the Netherlands to have a pluri-form press. Local newspapers have been published since 1880, when the city began to expand rapidly. The three newspapers were the Roman Catholic *Maasbode*, the "elite" *Nieuwe Rotterdamsche Courant* and the local *Rotter-*

dams Newsblad (121).

With urban expansion, churches found themselves faced with a number of organisational problems. Should the Calvinist Church community be divided to meet the needs of growing urban populations? Would growth and an increase in scale affect the organisation to such an extent that members would lose their say in church matters? It was decided, in The Hague for example, to divide the community on the grounds that smaller communities would be better able to cope with urban problems. The question remained as to whether there should be one or more church councils (122).

The mentality found in old working-class neighbourhoods differs from that of the new "garden cities". The latter are inhabited by more highly skilled and better unionised workers, as, for example, in Leiden, particularly in the Kooi area, which was built just outside the old city limits between the world wars (35).

(i)   Urban Government

How does city government policy come about; which institutions influence this process? In a city such as Amsterdam with its own university, it would be expected that the department of social sciences at the university would have some influence on city council policy (77). An important aspect, of course, concerns city finances. At the time of the Republic, each city was more or less autonomous. After the establishment of the monarchy in 1815, the situation became much more centralised. The main source of city income was the surcharge placed on state taxes, mainly commodities tax, during the first decades of the 19th century. When the new Municipal Corporations Act, which granted more autonomy to municipal governments, went into effect in 1851, the principle of a surtax maintained. Municipal governments acquired a number of the duties, which were previously the responsibility of the national state government, as shown by the Poor Law of 1854 and the Elementary Education Act of 1857. Local excise tax was abolished in 1865, and a number of municipal governments resorted to poll taxes, thus pointing out the differences between municipalities (20).

The responsibility for maintaining public health was also a source of tension between local and city governments on the one hand, and provincial and national state governments on the other. While local "Collegia Medica" existed at the time of the Ancien Régime and were succeeded by local committees for the Inspection of Public

Health during the French occupation, a centralised system of public health care was not organised until the establishment of the monarchy in 1815. The provinces also played a part in this process. The great epidemic diseases of the 19th century, such as cholera, etc., forced local and national authorities to adopt control measures. Local authorities, however, remained responsible for the enforcement of public health policies. The cholera epidemic of 1832, the first in a series which continued until 1866, may be seen as a test case (29).

In 1965, an extensive study of the development of Amsterdam's public health care was published (67). The causes of the high death rate until about 1880, as well as the factors leading to a quick drop in this figure after that date, are examined in this study. Not only are sanitary conditions and the causes of death and disease taken into account, but the availability of medical facilities is also discussed. The author argues that an explanation of the causes of a declining death rate since 1880 must be sought in cultural factors, the most important of which he considers to be an awareness of modern hygiene notions among urban dwellers. Similar studies on cities other than Amsterdam are rare. The city of Groningen is an exception, however. There, too, death rates dropped after 1877. Hygiene facilities, such as running water, improved medical knowledge and its application, and in particular, higher incomes for a larger portion of the population, and the consequently improved nutrition are all mentioned as the important factors (51).

Anniversary commemorations of the introduction of such urban innovations as drinking water facilities are often the occasion for publications. The Amsterdam Waterworks commissioned a popular historical survey of drinking water facilities during the past 700 years. Emphasis is placed on the period after 1851, at which time a commercial company began piping spring water from the dunes to Amsterdam for sale there (100). The Marketing Board also celebrated its 50th anniversary with a commemoration publication. The first 100 pages of the book are devoted to the period from 1300 to 1815, and the remainder to the development of markets and their organisation since 1815 (103).

One of the urban services on which there should be more information is the police force. A more systematic study of the development of police forces in the 19th century has recently begun, but the results are still forthcoming. It is known, however, that an expansion of the police force and its duties took place mainly during the last decades of the 19th century. In 1841, for example, the strength of the police force was the same as in 1800 — four police commissioners and 56 officers for every 200,000 inhabitants (17).

D. Conclusions

Based on publications printed mainly during the past ten years, a number of aspects of Dutch urban history during the 19th and 20th centuries have been reviewed. A thorough survey has not been attempted here. It has become evident that the historical phenomenon of urbanisation is being studied mainly from the perspective of social and economic history, as well as from that of historical geography. The political aspect and the viewpoint of the historian of mentalities are inadequately represented. The most prominent historical journals in the Netherlands have been reviewed here and the results are considerable. Still, much remains to be done. Studies on social stratification and social mobility are still too few in number. Demography, particularly the aspect of migration, deserves more attention. Municipal government policy and public facilities still form, to a large extent, a blind spot. Extensive monographical studies on the process of urbanisation, in general, and more specific studies of its various aspects are virtually non-existent. The studies mentioned here are, for the most part, limited in range and deal mainly with local subjects. In short, much remains to be done before the urban landscape of the Netherlands during the 19th and 20th centuries has been completely surveyed. Once this has been accomplished, a fruitful analysis of urban development in relation to broader social processes can truly begin.

FERNANDO DE TERÁN AND MARTIN BASSOLS

Spain*

A. Questions, Methods, Organisation

It can not be claimed that studies on urban history have become a coherent and systematic discipline in Spain. Nor can it be claimed that a unitary institutional organisation for such studies exists. On the contrary, it may be stated that investigation in this field has developed in a diversified and heterogeneous way, from various disciplinary spheres (general history, geography, economics, sociology, demography, architecture, engineering, law, etc.) that have long shown an interest in urban phenomena and their development. Thus, the fundamental point to be made when talking about urban history in Spain is the extremely fragmentary and sparse nature of the subject.

On the whole it can be said, that professional historians, engaged in the description or the interpretation of very general processes or in the treatment of highly specific details, have not paid special attention to the subject of the city, although there are exceptions. But these exceptions are fewer if we narrow the sphere and pass from urban history to modern urban history, that is, to urban history after industrialisation. We find then that most of the investigation devoted to this subject has been carried out by scholars who did not initially come from the sphere of history, but who, from their respective disciplines, felt the need to study the processes of the historical development of urban phenomena in their most varied aspects. The result is fragmentation, dispersion and heterogeneity, with a multitude of viewpoints and approaches, which hinders a

* Numbers in brackets in this chapter refer to entries in the bibliography on pp. 496–510 of this volume.

synthesised presentation.

On the other hand, in view of the fragmentary and incomplete character of these views, we have to use as a referential framework some general historical studies which do not constitute urban history in themselves, but which rather provide us with a basis indispensable for an understanding of the history of the city. These are studies of the political, economic and social history of Spain, thanks to which it is possible to appreciate the role played by the city in the general history of the country and the way political, economic and social processes have affected the history of the city.*

Specific aspects of the spatial evolution of the urban phenomenon (system and urban hierarchy, country-city relationship) have been researched above all by geographers and economists, whereas in researching urban spatial organisation proper, including the morphological aspects — types of cities, urban form, spatial growth, housing, and urban architecture — geographers have worked with architects and art historians.

Geographers and economists, together with demographers and sociologists, have also been interested in the aspects of population and social structure, land uses and prices, economic activities and functions. Furthermore, geographers, sociologists and general historians have dealt with the more obviously political aspects (parties, organisations, elections) and with the political-administrative aspects, both financial and legal, in collaboration with jurists. Urban

---

* The most important of these studies are listed below since they could not be included under the headings provided in the general bibliography on urban history in Spain.

Banco de Bilbao, La España des las Autonomías, Madrid, 1981 (=Self-administration in Spain).

Banco de España, Ensayos sobre la economía española a mediados del siglo XIX, Madrid, 1970 (=Articles on Spain's economy in the mid-19th century).

Clavera, J. et al., Capitalismo español (1939–1959), Madrid, 1973 (=Spanish capitalism).

Sánchez Albornoz, N., España hace un siglo: una economía dual, Barcelona, 1968 (=Spain one hundred years ago: a dual economy).

Tortella, G., Los orígenes del capitalismo en España. Banca, industria y ferrocarriles en el siglo XIX, Madrid, 1973 (=The origins of capitalism in Spain: Banks, industry and railways in the 19th century).

Vicens Vives, J., Historia económica de España, Barcelona, 1955 (Economic history of Spain).

Vicens Vives, J., Historia social y económica de España y América, Vol. IV: Burguesía, industrialización, obrerismo, Barcelona, 1959 (=Social and economic history of Spain and Latin America, Vol. IV: The middle class, industrialisation and the workers' movement).

planning aspects have been dealt with mainly by architects and jurists, and the urban infrastructure aspects by engineers and economists.

The process has followed a similar course in all these spheres: initially, those who pioneered such research, adopting conceptual and methodological approaches similar to those existing at any given time in other European countries, were few. German and French influences were the strongest in the 1930s and 1940s, giving way later — in the 1950s and 1960s — to the British and North American, and, in the 1970s to Italian trends.

Little by little, individual research assumed a broader basis through pupils, followers and new scholars; institutional conditions were established which, although they have not necessarily been very favourable to research, have at least permitted the formalisation and definition of the disciplines involved. In this sense, the universities have played and are playing the most important role, for such research was pioneered by university lecturers and is largely continued by university departments. But it is also necessary to point out the existence of some non-university centres at which studies related to urban history have been carried out, such as some Institutes of the "Consejo Superior de Investigaciones Científicas" and the "Instituto de Estudios de Administración Local", which publish their own journals. There have also been important contributions by private organisations, such as foundations and research departments of the large banks.

Owing to the great variety and heterogeneity of disciplinary approaches mentioned above, it is difficult to establish general similarities in the conceptual and methodological approaches employed by all the disciplines involved in research into modern urban history. Nevertheless, it seems that, in very general terms, a common evolution can be detected in several of those disciplines. This evolution proceeded from general approaches with an empirical basis and a rather intuitive interpretation. Later on (in the 1950s and 1960s), it passed to a stage distinguished by a functionalist interpretation, aspiring to gathering large amounts of mostly statistical information. Emphasis was placed on an exalted attempt at being scientifically objective, finding serious fault with the subjectivity of the previous stage. Afterwards, or at the same time (in the 1960s and 1970s) Marxist-oriented approaches took over. Their interest lay in demonstrating the relation between the ways of organising urban space and the political systems of economic and social organisation (applications of the Marxist theory of the origin of the capitalist city). Finally, at present, is the phase in which a certain inflation of Marxist interpretations and language is giving way to an epistemological and methodological plurality. In this situation, there seems to be an increasing interest in studying the physiognomy, morphology, genesis and configuration of fragments of urban space. At the same time, there is an attempt to dispense with broad general explanations, which interrelate all the spatial and social aspects and place excessive faith in the explanatory value of statistics.

Within this complex panorama, the fields more extensively researched from the mid-1970s to the mid-1980s have been those concerning demography, social and functional structure and spatial evolution. The country's urban system as a whole, and features of regional or subregional systems, are also receiving attention. The fields of urban typology, planning, land prices, infrastructures, cultural facilities and legislation have also been studied, but to a lesser degree. Still less attention has been paid to municipal politics and finance.

In general terms, it can be said that there are a few works only offering successful syntheses of urban history. They range from monographs on specific cases (local research) to the broad interpretative views of the general historical process the nation has undergone. As already mentioned, these general histories do not directly refer to urban phenomena, which, however, appear reflected in relation to the economic, demographic, sociological, etc., perspectives on which these views are based.

B. The Development of Individual Fields of Research

In the years before the outbreak of the Civil War (1936–1939) the first studies of urban history were carried out in Spain. Architects began to show more interest in understanding the evolution of the city over a period of time and in the chronological series of its plans, in order to undertake planning, which had become imperative because of the legislation of 1924 (Municipal Statute). Very simple studies of development (a succession of commented historical plans) or historic-descriptive reports were seen as a part of the basic information for town planning and were included in the programme of the School of Architecture in Madrid (100). These years also saw the publication of the perceptive analyses of the first Spanish urban historian, the architecture teacher Torres Balbás. His work, primarily concerned with the presence of the Arabic element in Spanish cities, does not refer to the modern city, which appears after industrialisation, but his name must be mentioned as that of a pioneer and a teacher who exerted a deep and lasting influence.

The definition and measurement of the urban, as a category opposed to the rural, as well as the measurement of the level of urbanisation in Spain, its variation through time, and the identification of types of cities, are all subjects which started to be researched in the years after the Civil War by geographers, economists and sociologists on the basis of the population censuses. There was an interesting precursor in a publication by the State Office of Social Action and Emigration (85), which offered a first approach to the demographic history of the country. Some of the first works were merely descriptive (34). Later on purely statistical criteria were used (80/81/84/86/89/90). Finally introduced were economic criteria of functional specialisation and of domination, following to a certain extent North American models such as those of J. Diez Nicolás (31/32/72/73), R. M. Majoral (82), H. C. Capel (69/70), M. Ferrer and A. Precedo (77) and J. Martin and A. de Miguel (83). A good summary, updated to 1980, can be found in J. Bosque Maurel's work (26).

The study of the national system of cities, urban hierarchy, as well as territorial distribution of population and activities, has essentially been developed by geographers and economists. A pioneer in these studies is the economist R. Perpiná, who started his research during the 1930s. Influenced at the very beginning by the German ideas of the same period about economic structure, he later paid a good deal of attention to Spain's modern economic history, and to the role cities have played in it (36/37/88). Later, other scholars such as H. C. Capel (28/29) and I. M. Ivaristi (35) also devoted their attention to this subject, which, moreover, received special attention from several official institutions during the preparation of the Third Economic and Social Development Plan (1971). The Plan had a good monograph on the current state of towns and regions in Spain with reference to their historical development (39). Some research had been conducted as preparation for the Plan and the findings were published (41). Both the monograph and this research provide new information about functional hierarchy in the system of cities and about the typology and delimitation of rural, urban and metropolitan areas. In general terms it can be said that this is a fairly well-covered field, inseparably linked to that of population and social structure. A good synthesis can be found in M. Ferrer Regales' work (33), in which he presents a typology of Spanish cities according to their demographic size, a definition of the general structure of the Spanish urban system, and an extensive analysis of the spatial organisation of industry. On the other hand, the planning experience of economic development, which has now become history, has also received attention (104/109/115).

Both the historical evolution of the Spanish population and the process of demographic concentration in cities, are realities, an understanding of which is indispensable in order to establish the definitions and characterisations that have been referred to. Most of the research mentioned above is based on demographic studies which supply knowledge about the history of urban population growth and variations in the social and economic structures of Spanish cities. But there are, in addition, other studies which concentrate more on purely demographic aspects, such as A. Garcia Barbancho's research on migration in Spain (78/79), and the interesting general historic view offered by J. Nadal (86/87). In the same sphere mention may be made of the Spanish Association of Historic Demography which was founded in 1983.

But, apart from this general research, there is another kind of more specific investigation, which forms another very important group of contribution to the historical study of the demographic and social aspects of Spanish urban reality. It is the monographs on cities (local research), mainly the work of geographers. There are already many such studies, dealing with the formative process of a city (or parts of it), paying attention to the relationship between spatial development and urban morphology on the one hand, and, on the other, demographic evolution and economic, social and functional structure. Very often a historical analysis of the power structures and their influence upon the spatial configuration, is included. Frequently, geographers try to ascertain who was in control of the city, what the motors of its economy were, and what the society living in it was like. In some cases, they endeavour to show how economic and social events are reflected in spatial organisation. They seek a correspondence between spatial structure and urban morphology as a reflection of the struggles among social groups in that space. This is because such research has often been carried out from more or less explicitly Marxist standpoints, but not all such studies illustrate this approach. The pioneering investigations of M. de Terán could rather be included in a school related to what is nowadays called "human geography" (163/172). More recent research has emphasised the formal aspects.

The proliferation of this kind of specialised research into cities makes it necessary to select a few to give a representative overview. Attention is thus drawn to studies on Bilbao (160), Burgos (161), Cáceres (162), Cuenca (164), Gijón (165/166), Guadalajara (167), Murcia (174), Oviedo (175), Santa Cruz de Tenerife (178), Sogovia (179), Valladolid (182/183), Vigo (184) and Zaragoza (185).

As already stated, not only do all these works include a historical analysis of the demographic, economic and social aspects; one of their most important distinguishing features is the study of the historical evolution of spatial development. They analyse the historical evolution of urban growth and the various stages of the city's morphological transformations and reorganisations, especially its transition from pre-industrial to modern conditions and, in detail, the last phases of the urban explosion resulting from the economic development of the 1960s.

Moreover, this analysis often contributes to the study of the forms of land division, the distribution of property and the evolution of its economic value. It investigates and reveals the variety of land uses, carrying out a functional analysis of economic activities. The historical evolution of hydraulic and road infrastructures has often been treated, and a relatively detailed account of the various planning stages of the city is often given. In some cases, the study also includes an outline of the historical development of housing and its salient features, and reference is usually made to the architectural characteristics common to the city, its landscape and visual appearance. A concrete study of relevant urban features such as streets, squares and public spaces can be found as well. Interest in studying some of these elements, or all of them in a city, as well as the urban transformations caused by their alteration, is the characteristic feature of some monographs, including those by M. de Terán (119), R. Mas (140), L. Moya (144), D. Brandis and R. Mas (170), E. Ruiz Palomeque (171) and M. de Terán (172). Greater emphasis on the morphological and spatial aspects and less attention to the demographic, economic and social aspects serve to distinguish some of the recent investigations, carried out mainly by architects. These can be added to the above list: Barcelona (157/158), La Coruña (168/169), San Sebastián (177) and Valladolid (181). Architects are now showing a remarkable interest in questions of urban history, together with restoration, reconstruction and the redesigning of the old parts of cities.

But, apart from the important contribution of data thus furnished by researching into specific cases, we can also find some syntheses which seek to offer complete views of the urban evolution in Spain. Thus, for instance, Capel (130) gives a general picture of the most characteristic stages in the historical formation of Spanish urban reality, which are manifested in the various fragments that make up the collage of our present-day cities. M. de Solá-Morales (150), I. de Solá-Morales (149) and R. Moneo (143) also offer overall views of some key periods in the formation process of Spanish cities, an effort whose most important forerunner is P. Bidagor (94).

On the history of urban planning, there is comprehensive and detailed general research collected in a book of considerable scope by F. de Terán (119). Some other works that are more schematic or more monographic in their approach to the subject, or cover a shorter period of time, are those by E. de Alarcón (91), P. Bidagor (95), G. Blein (96), O. Bohigas (97), G. R. Collins et al. (99), A. Herrero (137), E. Larrodera (103), J. Martínez Sarandeses (105), V. Martorell et al. (106), M. Ribas Piera (108), C. Sambricio (147), R. Urena (121), M. Valenzuela (122), a work from the city-administration of Madrid (92) and several publications by F. de Terán (114/115/116/118/120/151).

The history of infrastructures is, as stated earlier, a subject frequently discussed in local research monographs, and there are very few general studies of it, except those that deal with intercity infrastructures, such as the road network (138/141), the railway network (125/132/155), and the telecommunications network (129/142/146). As a valuable forerunner, there is a general history of public works in Spain until the end of the 19th century by P. Alzola (124). On the other hand, there are several local studies of some infrastructural systems in certain cities. For instance, there are good historical studies of the creation of Madrid's water supply (145), its approaches (136) and railway stations (123). Added to that engineers have, in recent years, started taking an interest in historical research on these topics, and the history of public works having been introduced as a subject in some schools of civil engineering.

Investigations into the organisation and the legal system of cities have been carried out in Spain within the framework of various academic disciplines integrated in the faculties of law. Even though legal historians have paid some general attention to the evolution of local legislation, it has mainly been the discipline of administrative law that has dealt with the study of urban legal history, sometimes through monographs, at other times within the framework of the general study of institutions. In recent decades, administrative law has given rise to the appearance of two disciplines that are steadily establishing a clear profile: municipal law and urban law.

The development of legal history has essentially followed an institutionalist course, influenced by German ideas of the past century, neglecting until recently more modern historical periods. As an antecedent, L. García Valdeavellano's work can be cited. This is the most solid research into the origins and the organisation of Spanish cities, even though it refers only to the medieval period.

On the other hand, administrative law was initially oriented towards interpretation of the legal stipulations in their historical development in the matter of local system and city planning. Later on it attempted to integrate legal aspects with the economic and social context, trying to offer an overall history. The first efforts in this direction are found in two excellent works by A. Posada (63/64).

The urban explosion that Spain experienced from 1950 onwards brought about an increasing interest in the history of urban law. In 1950, the "Instituto de Estudios de Administración Local" published a compilation of historical texts, as well as description of the course of development of Spanish urban legislation (54). M. Bassols' fundamental work (47) presents exhaustive research into the historical development of urban legislation, connected with socio-economic conditions, and with the ideas and the theoretical conception of town planning. P. Arnanz's (44) and L. Parejo's (62) works follow the same line.

The historical study of administrative organisation is more copious and difficult to synthesise. Mention may be made of the work of I. Beneyto (48), R. Larrainzar (56) and M. Baena (46). The relationship between state administration and local organisation has been researched by L. Morell Ocana (60), and the subject of municipal finance by R. Rodríguez Monino (65), G. Coloma Martí (49) and I. Moral Ruiz (59). There are also important and exhaustive bibliographies (50/53/61).

The current panorama of investigation in urban history from the legal viewpoint shows a new methodology distinguished by an attempt to incorporate the complementary approaches of political science and philosophy, as well as of economics and sociology. This enrichment may lead to a deepening of urban history through local research which has not been brought about from the legal viewpoint. A historical view of urban law has become an important subject in Spanish law faculties.

Forms of municipal government and the political life of institutions, in relation to the operation of the political parties, have received attention in recent works of general history and monographs on specific subjects, periods or situations (45/51/57/58/66/67).

Other subjects to which attention should be paid — if urban history is accepted as a composite field of study — and which have been sorely neglected to date, or been given unequal attention in local research into individual cities. Such subjects include industry and trade in the city, public services, municipal enterprises, urban transport planning, cultural facilities, the press, parochial planning of the Catholic Church, etc. These topics still lack comprehensive and comparative research.

C. Conclusions

All this points to the conclusion (as anticipated at the beginning) that urban history in Spain does not exist as an autonomous discipline and that historical studies related to town planning and the city are a heterogeneous mass which has been accumulated from different and unintegrated disciplinary spheres. It is significant that there is no complete, systematic and comprehensive work presenting the history of Spanish cities, nor is there a journal specifically devoted to this subject, nor have any bibliographies dealing exclusively with urban history been compiled.

Individual fields of modern urban history have been researched. Some are well covered and others have been virtually neglected.

Among the well-covered areas are the overall system of cities and their distribution, urban population, migration and urban growth. The subjects of planning, spatial evolution of cities and social and functional structure are also well covered, but a general study of the types of cities and the forms of their evolution and development is lacking. There is a good deal of local research but it is not systematised in a synthesis. The field of cultural activities and services has not been researched either. There are analyses of the current situation and forecasts on future shortcomings, but no studies on the historical development leading to these problems. Historical research into the evolution of urban infrastructures is also lacking. The relationship between urban history and political movements and the role of the parties or the church have not been studied, and are topics of awaiting future researchers.

The last few years have witnessed greater interest in the historical aspects of the city and city planning. This could well mean that the time may be ripe for a combined effort to integrate the scattered and individual research projects. The forerunner of this was the Symposium on City Planning and Urban History organised in 1980 by the art historian A. Bonet. It seems that the time has arrived to organise the establishment of a true discipline of urban history in Spain, in so far as this goal may be attainable. We are aware that the difficulties are great, as has been observed in the course followed by other countries since the Leicester Congress in 1966.

LARS NILSSON

Sweden*°

A. The Organising Framework

Urban historians in Sweden were successful in finding comprehensive organisational forms for their work at an early stage. On 7 June 1919, representatives from "Svenska Stadsförbundet" (the Swedish Municipal Confederation), individual cities and the historical discipline at the universities, assembled at the stock exchange in Stockholm to found an institute for the study of urban history. The initiative came from the Municipal Confederation, and the institute was intended to form a special division within the confederation. The idea of furthering research in urban history within the framework of the Municipal Confederation had apparently existed since its foundation in 1908, but it was only when the historians N. Herlitz and N. Ahnlund took an interest in the project that its realisation became feasible. One of the reasons for the founding of the Institute of Urban History was the desire to raise the quality of research within the discipline. Ahnlund and Herlitz compared Swedish research with that in Finland and Germany and concluded that Swedish research did not attain the same level of quality. An improvement considered desirable in light of the expected increase in urban monographs during the 1920s and 1930s, when several cities were scheduled to celebrate their 300th and 350th anniversaries. Ahnlund and Herlitz noted that signs of improvement could already be observed.

The Institute of Urban History was thus founded in 1919 as a section within the Swedish Municipal Confederation. The organiser

* Translated by Marie-Louise Rodén.
° Numbers in brackets in this chapter refer to entries in the bibliography on pp. 511–526 of this volume.

and driving force behind the institute was Y. Larsson. The idea of founding such an institute seems to have been of purely Swedish origin; foreign prototypes for such organisations simply did not exist. In Norway and Finland, institutes for the study of local history were founded approximately a decade later, but they had different methods and goals. In many other countries, comprehensive organisations within modern urban history were founded only during the 1960s or later. The International Commission for Urban History saw the light at the Conference for World History in Rome in 1955. It was also during the 1950s that an American Urban History Group was established.

The task of the Institute has been defined as furthering research within urban history by organising, registering and publishing source material on the history of Swedish cities. Other continuing tasks have been to follow and inform about current research and to note and present recently published literature within the field of urban and local history. The Institute also has its own series for the publication of research results.

B.   The Breakthrough in Scholarly Research

Local descriptions of individual cities were fairly widespread as early as the 18th century. These studies, however, usually lacked historical perspective and for the most part contain curious anecdotes of the most diverse origin. They can hardly be described as scientific. The embryo of a scientific investigation of the history of cities is found only towards the end of the 19th century. C. T. Odhner was a pioneer in this field; he systematised information from various local descriptions during the 1860s and so placed them in a scientific context (41). Odhner's major interest was the constitutional perspective, and he sought to achieve a history of local ordinances. After Odhner's pioneering work, a series of studies followed during the 1870s and 1880s, which were oriented towards economic and urban history (Forssell/31), and which, during the 20th century, found a continuation in E. Heckscher's (32/112) studies in urban history. As is easily understood, it was the civic organisation of an earlier period — the Middle Ages, 16th and 17th centuries — which became the focus of scholarly interest at the turn of the century.

The breakthrough of Swedish urban history in scholarly research can be dated to the 1920s. Ever since that time, the subject has had a predominantly monographic emphasis. The breakthrough is seen, for example, in the urban monographs concerning Sundsvall (N. Ahnlund/145), Umeå (B. Steckzén/147) and Göteborg (H. Almquist/124), but even in more broadly defined studies by, for example, N. Herlitz *Svensk stadsförvaltning på 1830–talet* (Swedish Municipal Administration during the 1830s) (33), E. Heckscher *Den ekonomiska innebörden av 1500– och 1600–talens svenska stadsgrundningar* (The economic implications of the founding of Swedish cities during the 16th and 17th centuries) (112) and A. Schück *Studier rörande det svenska stadsväsendets uppkomst och tidigaste utveckling* (Studies concerning the development of the Swedish civic organisation) (42). Other features of this breakthrough were the foundation of the Institute for Urban History and the establishment of a Chair in Urban History in 1927. This position was created thanks to a donation from the City of Stockholm and was intended to be held by a scholar who focused especially on Stockholm's own history. N. Ahnlund was appointed as first holder of the Chair in Urban History.

An important goal for N. Herlitz — the first director of the Institute of Urban History — was an attempt to improve the professional quality of monographs in urban history. This could be achieved, he argued, by placing the development of the individual city in a larger context and by relating it to relevant traits in a broader social development. Herlitz further emphasised that urban history was one part of a broader historical development and that increased research in this field would eventually enrich the historical discipline as a whole. But, to give both urban history and the historical discipline, in general, greater relevance, according to Herlitz, they must also be linked to contemporary life.

The tendency towards an emphasis on monographs, which was established during the 1920s, has continued to dominate Swedish urban history. Urban history has largely been synonymous with the history of individual cities. The study of the urbanising process has mainly been left to representatives of other disciplines, primarily geographers, who have often worked with a short time-frame. Urban government and administration have been the primary interest within the monographic tradition. Trade and industry, settlement, social conditions, demography, cultural life and even additional aspects are often taken into account, but are seldom treated in an analytical or systematic manner. There is, moreover, no real integration of the various subject fields taken up within respective urban histories. Each field is treated internally without taking into consideration what is happening in other areas. The goal for this type of monograph is to give the most comprehensive picture possible of the life and development of the individual city, with a point of emphasis on government and administration. It could be called "traditional monographs". They have had an ideographic and narrative character, but seldom realise the goals formulated by Herlitz. The traditional monographs are stamped by their breadth and versatility.

The urban monographs produced during the 1920s, 1930s and 1940s most often concern the city before the middle of the 19th century, that is, before large-scale industrialisation began affecting the appearance and development of the Swedish city. The most important work about the modern industrialising city produced during this period is a study by the geographer W. William-Olsson, *Huvuddragen av Stockholms geografiska utveckling 1850–1930* (Central Aspects in Stockholm's Geographic Development, 1850–1930) published in 1937 (109).

C. Svensk Stad ("Swedish Towns")

Around the year 1950 certain new and interesting features can be found within Swedish urban history. The interest in discussing content, research strategies and level of professionalism increased once more. A generalising perspective was adopted in several contexts. A larger work concerning the urbanisation process in Sweden from 1911 to 1950 by G. Ahlberg was published in 1952 (47). Also, at the beginning of the 1950s, the impressive work *Svensk Stad* ("Swedish Towns") (20) which encompassed several disciplines, appeared. At the institutional level a second Chair in Urban History at Stockholm University was established in addition to the already existing professor's chair. This first chair, moreover, became an "ordinary" professorship in history when Ahnlund retired a few years later.

Svensk Stad occupies a special place within the humanistic disciplines in Sweden. It was one of the first humanistic research projects and was organised on an interdisciplinary basis. The institutional base for the project was the Department of Art History at Uppsala University and the director of the project was G. Paulsson. Art historians, ethnologists, architects and sociologists all participated in the project. No historians were included, however, if one of Paulsson's closest co-workers, B. Hanssen, is not counted as part of this group. Hanssen is probably, side by side with Paulsson, the single scholar most important for the work's successful completion. According to one calculation by D. Gaunt (23), Hanssen is responsible for 35–40% of all the text in *Svensk Stad*, which was published under the name of a single author Paulsson.

Svensk Stad was given a very broad format. There are detailed accounts of individual traits in home decoration, and questions concerning the development of densely populated areas, social strata, classifications and typologies of densely populated areas are even taken up. The 19th century city is in the foreground, and therefore the origin and structure of the modern industrialised city. The empirical studies focus on the smaller and medium-sized cities, while the larger cities are not taken up at all. In terms of its choice of subject, *Svensk Stad* is strongly oriented towards the discussion of dwellings, which was a central issue in Sweden's social debate of the 1940s. Aspects of daily life treated in this study include the organisation of residences, furniture and home decorations. In addition, *Svensk Stad* contains several regional monographs describing both older urban communities and the industrial towns and station communities which sprang up during the 19th century. The interest in densely populated areas in addition to the formal cities is quite marked, and *Svensk Stad* is something of a pioneering work in this sense. The contributions made have not, however, had any noticeable consequences within the discipline itself. Even today, it seems that very little research has been done on densely populated areas other than cities. Another topic which is covered in *Svensk Stad* is social ecology, i.e. studies of where in the city various social strata have had their dwellings. In a Weberian spirit, the leaders of the project had a predilection for ideal types such as "the agrarian market town", "the bourgeois merchant town", "the industrialised city", and "complementary societies".

The aspiration towards generalising statements and explanations, which distinguished Herlitz and certain other historical researchers in urban development active around 1920, can also be found in Paulsson and his closest co-workers in *Svensk Stad*. In the preface to the first edition (1950), it is said that a city is partly the consequence of general technological, social and economic processes which all work in the same direction, and partly a historical place with living conditions which have been determined by the region's own internal prerequisities, which are not shared by all other cities. The city is thus attributed both general and specific qualities, and it takes on a distinct form through the co-operation of various forces. These different forces are found in a condition of dynamic equilibrium, that is, a constantly shifting position of equilibrium. The tool which makes possible an analysis of the city as a whole, is, according to *Svensk Stad*, M. Weber's concept of ideal types. The type "permits the reflection of the transitory in conformity to law, and makes that which conforms to law into an apparent concretion". The research perspective laid out in the preface to *Svensk Stad* is thus essentially different from the manner in which urban history has usually been treated in Sweden.

The publication of *Svensk Stad* did not lead to an intensification of urban historical research. The book was well received, but without great enthusiasm. Research in urban history continued at this time, around 1950, primarily in the spirit of the traditional urban monograph. It was only during the 1970s that *Svensk Stad* received greater attention and began to be published in new editions.

An additional element in the development of urban history in about 1950 was, as has been mentioned above, the establishment of a new special chair in Urban History at Stockholm University. This position was also joined to that of director of the Institute of Urban History. It is interesting to note how the new professor — F. Lindberg — regarded his discipline. The city is, he says in an article from 1951 (18), a phenomenon worthy of study for its own sake, and it must be treated as a unified organism, for otherwise one can not capture the diversity which the city represents. The object of study is in the first place the individual city, either the city as such or else phenomena within the city. Lindberg makes the argument for a kind of total history of the individual city, but his definition also includes research surrounding the urbanisation process on a general level as well as locally or regionally limited investigations of various social phenomena. According to Lindberg, two types of phenomena represent the core of this discipline: first, the economic preconditions for the existence, flourishing and decline of cities; and second, questions which touch upon the development of local ordinances, administration and politics. Lindberg also emphasised the need for an interdisciplinary perspective as well as for comparison and synthesis within modern urban research. Several of the viewpoints articulated by Lindberg at this time were eventually put into practice by other scholars during the 1970s.

D. Urban History after 1970

Around 1970 new tendencies in the scholarly development of Swedish urban history could be observed as the volume of research significantly increased. On the institutional level, I. Hammarström succeeded F. Lindberg as Professor in Urban History. It is easy to trace foreign influence behind several of the new developments of the 1970s, as well as the effect of general changes within the historical discipline. The interest in social, demographic and economic history increased, as is well known, in the entire Anglo-Saxon world during the 1960s. This interest gave rise to a series of locally and regionally oriented studies. These studies were partly the result of the difficulty in carrying out empirical research for the new themes on a national level. They therefore required adjustment to a local scale. The shift in subject matter generated an increasing number of studies which were limited to individual cities or other local communities. The developments within the historical discipline brought with them an increased theoretical and methodical awareness and level of curiosity. Within Swedish urban history this meant that the generalising perspective, which had previously been advocated by, for example, N. Herlitz and the authors of *Svensk Stad* was taken up once again.

The American "New Urban History" represented an outflow of the new tendencies within the historical discipline. "New Urban History" almost exclusively occupied itself with social and geographic mobility, and very soon affected Swedish historical research, where questions surrounding patterns of mobility were given a high priority towards the end of the 1960s. The project for the study of popular movements as well as the group for migration research within the Department of History at Uppsala University studied migrations from an historical perspective and with various cities as research object. Among those influenced by "New Urban History" were M. Eriksson and S. Åkerman (52), H. Norman (74), B. Öhngren (75) and B. Kronborg and T. Nilsson (68). The Swedish mobility investigations mentioned here would, in T. Hershberg's terminology, come under the heading "urban as site". The city is not the real object of study. It simply constitutes the space where events or processes are played out. The actual focus of investigation in these studies was patterns of mobility and support for popular movements.

This type of urban-related research — structural studies —

developed strongly at the beginning of the 1970s. It marked the transition from the more traditional emphasis on administration and government towards a social history of the city. In addition to the research projects described, several others focusing on social, demographic and economic variables in an urban space, were active at this time. During the latter part of the 1970s the level of intensity decreased somewhat in favour of research concerning the history of settlements and buildings. Progress in this field was clearly reflected in the founding of a special journal, *Bebyggelsehistorisk Tidskrift* (1).

In the area of urban monographs, a new format was tested during the 1970s — the thematic monograph — in addition to the traditional, comprehensive monograph. While the traditional monographs were usually the product of a single author, the thematic monographs were organised within the context of research projects and the authors were drawn from various academic disciplines. In a thematic monograph the authors consciously refrain from trying to give a comprehensive picture of the city's development. Instead, a certain theme is chosen and explored in depth. In this manner, there are possibilities for analysis and explanations of causality which go beyond the level that can be attained by the traditional monograph. Through the medium of the chosen theme, the scholar attempts to analyse and explain essential traits in the development of the city. The object of research is the city itself; it is the development of the city which is to be explained and made comprehensible. In this respect, the thematic monograph is essentially different from a structural study. In a structural study, the city only provides the physical frame for the analysis, while in a thematic monograph the city itself is the object of the study. The thematic approach can most clearly be seen in the city monographs concerning Nyköping (139), Enköping (122) and Kalmar (131) as well as the regional history of Vindeln (150).

The research concerning the history of Kalmar was conducted, under Hammarström's direction, on the basis of a model which was intended to elucidate the relationship of the individual city to and its interplay with the surrounding society. The comparative approach was very strongly marked. In terms of subject matter, the individual contributions concentrate on the themes "economic life and population", while very little attention is given to the administration and government of the city. The orientation in subject matter is founded on the conception that the city primarily draws its identity from its functional composition and its functional tasks in society. A similar programmatic explanation is given in the regional history of Vindeln. Here, the goal of the study is described as the analysis of how changes in the surrounding world (regionally, nationally, internationally) affect the local community and how the community then adjusts to these changes. Society on a local level is, moreover, perceived as having its own internal structures which function in relative independence of external change.

A somewhat different approach to the city as a research object can be seen in the history of Enköping. S. Dahlgren (122) the chief editor, emphasises that the city is primarily a political entity and that the question of how residents organise and maintain local concerns is what gives the city its identity. The focus of interest is mainly that of traditional urban history, i.e. the government and administration of the city.

The thematic monographs were thus a new feature in urban historical literature of the 1970s, even if the majority of monographs still maintained the traditional format. Another new element was that the presentations were to a much greater degree, occupied with the modern industrialist city. The older works often end with the beginning of industrialisation towards the mid-19th century and the coming into force of communal law in 1862. But one of the larger projects initiated during the 1970s nevertheless focuses upon the older Swedish city. The project in question is called "The Medieval City — the consequences of the early urbanisation process for contemporary planning".

Swedish urban history developed in several directions during the 1970s and was characterised by great diversity at this time. This was the era of "New Urban History" — inspired municipal studies at the side of research in building and settlement as well as social, demographic and economic studies of individual communities. Thematic monographs and traditional urban monographs were produced, but there were even more general studies of the urbanisation process. Examples of such works are T. Falk's *Urban Sweden* (53), and B. Öhngren's report *Urbaniseringen i Sverige 1840–1920* (19). The growing interest in urban history and the increasing research volume was also manifested in co-operation among the Scandinavian countries. The principal theme of the meeting for Scandinavian historians in Trondheim in 1977 was the urbanisation process from the Middle Ages until the First World War. At the following meeting of Scandinavian historians in Jyväskylä in 1981, there was a follow-up with a special section devoted to urbanisation in Northern

Europe after the First World War. A new feature in the co-operation among Scandinavian historians was the initiation of conferences on local history during the 1970s. The first conference was arranged through Danish initiative in 1970; this has been followed by meetings every third year (25).

One aspect of the reorientation in urban history during the 1970s is that theoretical and methodical questions have received greater attention. Interdisciplinary aspects have also been emphasised and have had an effect on actual research. The importance of studying a given city in relation to its environment has often been pointed out. In practical terms, this has most often taken the form of studies of immigration to and emigration from various cities. Widespread popular interest in local history in all its forms also developed strongly during the 1970s. Many of the monographs and regional descriptions which were produced during this decade were the work of non-professional researchers with a great interest and strong feeling for their own region's culture and history.

It is difficult to point to a defined and unified direction in research in urban history during the last several decades. On the part of the Institute of Urban History and of the Chair in Urban and Regional History, however, a noticeable move towards comparative urban history, where the principal interest has been the growth, structure and development of the modern industrialised city and densely populated areas. Another goal has been to actively engage historians in research on the urbanisation process during various epochs. The latter ambition has now been realised in the form of two research projects concerning Swedish urbanisation from the 16th century up to 1980.

E. Conclusion

During the three periods under consideration — the 1920s, around 1950 and after 1970 — the dominating monographic tradition has been augmented by an increased effort in coming to terms with the more comprehensive processes and conditions which cause urban development, stagnation and change. It is also primarily during these three periods that discussions concerning scientific method, identity, strategy and approach, are encountered.

The development of the 1970s is markedly different from that of the 1920s as well as that which took place around 1950. There is a considerably larger volume of research, an increased diversity in choice of topic and a greater interest in research surrounding the industrialised city. The relationship of a city to its environment has become one method for obtaining new knowledge about the city itself, urban conditions and the urbanisation process. Several new aspects, primarily the fields of settlement, demography, social and economic history have received attention and have thus been added to the traditional domain of urban history, i.e. local government and administration.

BRUNO FRITZSCHE

Switzerland*°

A. Questions and Methodology

To evaluate the state of research in modern urban history, it would
seem appropriate to look at this research in connection with the
stages of urban history itself.
The old Swiss Confederation, which collapsed in 1798, included
seven city states besides the five Länder. The internal structure and
constitution of these cities differed greatly, but common to all was
that they made a subject area for themselves out of their catchment
area and hinterland. Political sovereignty was exercised exclusively
by citizens of the towns, and, eventually, there emerged from these
circles a few great families who effectively ruled the towns.
The 50 years of political changes that began in 1798 and were
completed, with the adoption of a new Federal Constitution, in
1848, saw a struggle for freedom and equality, not against king and
nobility, but of subjects against full citizens, of the country against
the town. It took place in various stages, reaching a climax in the
1830s. In this period of "regeneration", the towns finally lost their
predominant position vis-à-vis the country. The visible expression of
this on the whole bloodless revolution was the razing of the town
walls at the insistence of the rural population. Only in Basel did
these conflicts finally lead to a separation of the town from the
former subject area, which was constituted as the autonomous
half-canton of Basel-Land in 1833. It is revealing that Basel did not
demolish its city walls until much later — after 1859 — and then as
a result of urban growth.

* Translated by Ruth Stanley
° Numbers in brackets in this chapter refer to entries in the bibliography on pp.
527–532 of this volume.

Finally, the Federal Constitution of 1848 stipulated in the article on equality (Article 4): "In Switzerland there exist no local privileges". Thereafter, the interest of historians waned, as they were mainly oriented towards political history. Typical of this is the wayward history of Bern by R. Feller, which goes up to 1798 in four volumes, and then ends abruptly (67). Feller did, it is true, continue his history of Bern after 1798, but only from a sense of duty, as the flat and unenthusiastic presentation reveals (68). The motto — "Bärn, du edle Schwyzerstärn" (Bern, you noble star of Switzerland) — applies only up to 1798, and along with Bern, the stars of the other once-proud city republics were also extinguished.

The town's loss of its predominant position during the period of regeneration is well researched within the framework of general political development, and has been presented in literature which was mostly published some time ago. In the later development, towns are, in the constitutional sense, political entities like any other. Specifically, urban political issues arise only in certain limited areas; the distinction, relevant in property law and in politics, between the old community of citizens and the modern community of inhabitants, continued far into the 19th century. In the field of administration, towns are sometimes subject to special regulations (e.g., building laws that apply only to "urban conditions"), or are equipped with special competence (e.g., their own police corps). Extending the administrative area through incorporation, and the political procedures connected with this process, affected mainly, but neither exclusively nor universally, the urban communities. Political organisation is regulated by the cantonal constitution: in principle it was the same for all communities. But from an early stage the towns, because of their size, started summoning town parliaments instead of communal assemblies as the legislative body, and transferred executive powers to full-time representatives.

These and similar political aspects have been dealt with in various local studies. There is hesitation, however, in calling this urban history research in the true sense, for such studies only examine special cases of political structures and contribute little to a general understanding of urban development in the 19th century. Since there is no longer any fundamental political difference between urban and rural communities, preoccupation with political questions and methods of political history are inappropriate. So, what approaches and methods should a modern urban history adopt? This methodological discussion has scarcely, at best sketchily, been taken up, although discussions in other countries have provided many impulses. Social and economic historians, in whose field the development of towns, no longer politically predominant but gaining ever-increasing socio-economic significance, would lie, have not yet undertaken a systematic study of the topic.

This may be connected with the fact that the stereotype of "rural Switzerland" has been cultivated very adroitly and for an extremely long time, not only in the tourist industry, but also in the national consciousness. This idyllic view is right to the extent that, although Switzerland became an industrial nation early, it had a relatively low degree of urbanisation in the 19th century (3). The official definition of a town in Switzerland is a community with 10,000 or more inhabitants. On this definition, in 1850 there were eight towns in Switzerland, in 1910 there were 26, and in 1980, 96. In 1850, roughly one person in 15 lived in a town, in 1910 one in four, and today almost half the population does so. This relatively low urbanisation is explained by the fact that the textile industry, the most important sector of production in terms of net product and number of persons employed, tended, for various reasons, to be found in rural locations, as did the important watch-making industry, and by the fact that Switzerland, poor in raw materials, has no coal, iron and steel industries to form large conurbations.

This should not, however, obscure the fact that, following the considerable thrust of urbanisation after 1885 — closely connected with the rise in long-term economic growth — problems of urban living became acute in Switzerland. The evidence of this is in the statistical investigations into housing conditions which began in the 1890s. A number of towns set up their own "statistical bureaux" around this time, whose function was to continuously register the pulse of urban development. The age of statistics relating to inner-urban processes thus begins around 1890 and provides extensive source material of which, as yet, little use has been made by historians; for earlier periods overall figures, such as those provided by the population censuses from 1850 onwards, have to be mainly relied upon.

In the very epoch in which it was threatened, the image of rural Switzerland was energetically refurbished. National unity was presented in the "village Suisse" of the National Exhibition in Geneva (1896); and the "Dörfli", an architectural representation of the idyll of rural life, became the main attraction of the National Exhibitions in Bern (1914) and Zurich (1939). This recourse to rural values also found expression in the attempt to settle a new generation of "worker farmers" on the peripheries of the towns, and in projects which followed the model of the English garden city in trying to bring the countryside into the town. Behind this anti-urban movement lay the attempt, seldom stated explicitly, to stabilise the social system which appeared threatened by the town — or more exactly, by the concentration of the lower classes in the proletarian districts. These were a stronghold of a radical labour movement, which did not properly develop until the urban growth after 1885.

These comments indicate some desiderata for research on urban history, arising from the specifically Swiss situation:

1. The connection often postulated between industrialisation and urbanisation is doubtful. Swiss towns of the 19th century are not typical industrial towns, but developed as nodal points in the expanding transport network, while factories are largely to be found in rural areas.

2. For this reason, the connection between urbanisation and market economy, between urban system and transport system, deserves special emphasis. It is well known that the construction of the (initially private) railway lines was due to rivalries between towns, but the dialectical process of urban growth and growth of the transport system has never been systematically studied, least of all in connection with the developing hierarchy of towns so far as spatial economy is concerned.

3. Swiss towns are not towns of factory workers; nevertheless, the labour movement originated in the towns and was concentrated on them. It is revealing, for example, that the national general strike of 1918 originated in the towns and the strike call was followed almost exclusively in the larger towns although, as is known, the rural areas were equally as heavily industrialised. These are clear indications that an explanation of the labour movement must not only take the situation at the place of work into account: at least as much consideration must be given to urban conditions of life. This, too, is a topic which has only just begun to receive attention.

The connection between social protest and urban living conditions was clearer to contemporaries than it is to present-day historians. This is shown, for example, by the attempts already mentioned to prevent a concentration of the lower classes by a "back-to-the-land" ideology. But developments then took a different turn: with the coming of state-subsidised municipal housing, introduced hesitantly in 1898 and attaining significant proportions only after 1918, urban living conditions improved and, at the same time, social controls were facilitated. Moreover, the situation became less tense in the inter-war years in that the towns, in a period of weak economic growth, only expanded slowly (annual growth rates 1888–1910, 3.6%; 1920–1941, 1.2%). The long period of growth after the Second World War has brought with it a new thrust of urbanisation, which can only be measured unsatisfactorily with the usual statistical criteria. If in 1980, 43.4% of the population lived in towns, this refers to communities with at least 10,000 inhabitants, which have usually long since grown beyond their political boundaries. Since 1930, the constantly changing concept of agglomeration has been applied to the totality of communities which are economically oriented towards one town. In 1980, 61.5% of the population lived in urban agglomerations. The thrust of urbanisation or suburbanisation, which accompanied the recent economic boom and led to a sort of ribbon development covering large parts of the country's non-mountainous area, again prompted political reactions, this time at the national level. Development planning, which was enshrined in the constitution in 1969, has up to now produced above all an abundance of figures which provide contemporary and future historians with extensive data (62).

Current problems may also have encouraged an interest in urban history. The results so far, however, relate mostly to individual examples in the fields of demography (population growth and structure) and social questions (social strata, social segregation, municipal housing). There are no comprehensive analytical studies of the significance of the towns for economic growth and transport policy; questions relating to the siting of industry have, at best, been touched upon by economists and traced back a few years or decades. Altogether, the student of urban history in Switzerland will not get by without taking other fields of scholarship into account in order to form an idea of the various lines of research: geographers have been concerned with geopolitical dynamics and with transport; ethnological studies have investigated urban living conditions; architecture and town planning have mainly been studied by art historians; sociologists have provided some studies which are also interesting from the historian's point of view, as is shown by the bibliographical survey below. This survey can make no claims to completeness, since given the paucity of historical studies, it has been necessary to include other fields of scholarship.

Taken as a whole, this compilation shows that there is a not insignificant body of literature dealing in one way or another with the town in the 19th and 20th centuries. But no comprehensive survey exists and, what is more serious, there is no agreement on the questions to be asked, the methods to be applied, or the topics on which research is most urgently needed. Co-ordination is difficult because the historical profession has no institutions for the study of the town: there is no Chair, no institute, no association for urban history.

B. State of Research

Although there is no Chair of urban history, the department of architecture of the Swiss Technical University in Zurich has a Chair in the history of town planning. Research is carried out in the institute for the History and Theory of Architecture connected with this; it publishes its own series of monographs. Naturally, the methods and approaches are those used in the history of art and architecture; the main emphasis has, until now, been on the medieval and pre-industrial town. However, efforts are being made to take the industrial towns of the 19th and 20th centuries more into account.

Like the institutions, the research aids for urban history are extremely meagre. The working group proposed by the International Association of Historians in 1955 in Rome has borne little fruit in Switzerland, in contrast to other countries. Paul Guyer published a bibliography of urban history in 1960; it is revealing that the 763 works listed deal almost exclusively with the pre-industrial epoch (1). No journal of urban history exists; one is most likely to find articles on the subject in architecture journals (40/42).

The accessibility of rich source material contained in individual town's archives varies tremendously; the city archives of Zurich and Basel (where the city canton's archives are also the state archives), have been made available in a model fashion.

Noteworthy, since it is not a matter of course, is the fact that these archives have also preserved mass data such as registers of inhabitants, returns from the population censuses, etc. However, an analysis of these sources will be an arduous task only possible with the help of electronic data-processing methods. The register of Zurich's inhabitants from 1865 to 1880 has been prepared for machine reading with financial support from the Swiss National Fund for the Promotion of Scientific Research (20). Various analyses are currently being made of these data, which are generally available for purposes of research (24). The Committees of Enquiry into Housing Conditions on Basel (16), Bern (27) and Zurich (35), for example, provide statistical data on an aggregate basis from the 1890s onwards, as do the publications of various communal statistical offices including once again Basel, Bern and Zurich. The Institute for the History and Theory of Architecture collects architects' papers, etc., and projects on town and district planning might be found in this collection. Documents of an important association of architects (CIAM) in the years between the wars have also been published (53).

A short report on the state of research into modern urban history appeared in 1976 in the Swiss *Zeitschrift für Geschichte*, dealing mainly with what remains to be done in the field (6). U. Gyr has published a report on the situation of research into urban culture in Switzerland, which reaches very similar conclusions, from an ethnologist's point of view, to those of this survey: that the field of urban research in the Switzerland of rural ideals is still largely undeveloped (5). Nevertheless, some of the beginnings that have been made are also of interest to the historian, and greater activity in this field is to be expected.

The town's loss of political predominance between 1798 and 1848 has been dealt with in its political aspects, mainly in older literature (2). Communal politics and the political-administrative organisation after 1848 have roused little interest, except where fundamental changes were involved, for example, in the case of incorporations which, in Switzerland, where communal autonomy is strongly emphasised, led to political processes which were always out of the ordinary and generally drawn-out (51). Comparative studies of urban building regulations and town budgets would be desirable contributions from political historians; on these topics, there exist only older — and often out-of-date — studies (60).

Demographic studies on town growth face a problem in that such statistical data for Switzerland as a whole exist only from the 1870s onwards. Earlier data on marriages, births and deaths can be gathered from parish registers, but this is a time-consuming process and possibly only feasible for towns of a medium size. H. Buri has done such work on Lucerne from 1700 to 1850 (17). W. Schüpbach has traced Lucerne's demographic development from 1850 to 1914, making a very careful interpretation of it in the context of urban health policy (provision of accommodation, health regulations, professionalisation of medicine and the hospitals) (34). A weakness of all urban demography studies is the fact that, owing to lack of data, the migratory movements, which had such a decisive influence on growth, can not be measured. Only from the 1890s do figures on internal migration exist for various cities, including Lucerne; they show clearly that net immigration, which for certain periods could at best be calculated as the difference between total and natural population growth, only accounts for a small fraction of total migration. H. Wolfensberger has written on the statistical and demographic aspects of immigration to Zurich from 1893 onwards (39), and P. Alteslander's dissertation contains a wealth of information on sociological aspects of this immigration (12).

Although in the small Swiss towns of the 19th century there could be no spectacular slum districts, a clear differentiation of urban districts according to social strata is discernible. The phenomenon of social segregation has been demonstrated and described in studies of Zurich (21), Basel (14), Bern, (38) and Lucerne (15). An ambitious sociological study, largely dealing with the present-day situation, takes Bern as an example and tries to explain the spatial structure of social segregation on the basis of the well-known model of Park and Burgess (22). Other authors are explicit in finding no support for the Chicago model, an example of which is K. Kreis' study of the development and living conditions of the Zurich working-class district of Aussersihl (26).

The fact that towns may be divided into different areas which are clearly distinguishable sociologically, provides the justification for studies of individual districts. Using the methods of geographers, M. Rupp has studied the changes in building and, hence, also the socio-economic changes in the Länggasse in Bern, a district inhabited by the lower middle class (50). In a more conventional framework, P. Guyer has described the history of the villa suburb

Zurich-Enge (46), and A.Hebeisen that of the working-class district of Lorraine in Bern (47). A disadvantage of some of these studies is that they often neglect to view the (in itself important) investigation of small structures and interwoven relationships in a larger context. The social profiles of various districts that these studies enable us to draw, prompt the question whether the experience of housing and environmental conditions specific to a certain social stratum (i.e, the socialisation dependent on membership of that stratum), led to norms and value judgements peculiar to it, and whether this socialisation became a central element of social conflict in the industrial society then taking shape (9).

Some ethnological studies are concerned with individual aspects of the urban way of life, including the historical context (25). In his 500-page, many-faceted monograph on St. Gallen in the 19th century, the art historian P. Röllin has attempted to grasp the totality of visual impressions in the town as a living space "between homeland and foreign country, between tradition and progress" (49). G. Heller's dissertation, "Propre, en ordre", which is refreshingly witty, not only in the title (and in the cover picture by M. Leiter), studies bodily hygiene and cleanliness in the home, not only as a medical requirement, but also in its significance as a means of discipline and training for an orderly bourgeois life in urban society (23). A. Ulrich studies a not-so-clean subject — prostitutes and brothels in Zurich — in the context of the sexual morality of the 19th century (37). B. Furrer examines entertainment in Zurich in the same period (64).

The most recent studies of individual districts seem to have concentrated on working-class areas; in Zurich, this is the former proletarian suburb of Aussersihl. Besides the study by K. Kreis mentioned above, H. Looser has also made a study of this district (30). In addition, various projects are in progress, and there even exists a Historical Association Aussersihl, one of the aims of which is to document "the history of everyday life in Aussersihl". These studies of the everyday life of the lower classes, undoubtedly in-fluenced, in part, by fashionable trends, will be of great value if they can be integrated into social history as a whole, and if it is not forgotten that proletarian districts and other parts of the town complement each other. Aussersihl is also the subject of a remark-able dissertation by H. P. Bärtschi entitled "Industrialisierung, Eisenbahnschlachten und Städtebau" (43). An enormous amount of material is provided but it seems, in part, to be lacking integration.

Nevertheless, it is highly laudable that an architect has not contented himself with formal, aesthetic and technical aspects of town planning, but rather sets this "contribution to the history of architecture and technology" within the political, social and economic framework.

This is the very point at which historians often find older studies by art historians to be deficient — studies for which he or she is nevertheless grateful since, with few exceptions (56), there are few historical works on town planning and building policy. Above all, the series, *Inventar der neueren Schweizer Architektur* (INSA), must be mentioned. Published by the Society for the History of Swiss Art, with financial support from the Swiss National Fund for the Promotion of Scientific Research, three volumes have appeared so far. The series aims to provide an inventory of historic buildings from 1850 to 1920 in the towns and main areas of the cantons. The first volume also contains a short article and a bibliography on town planning in Switzerland (65). The inventories of the individual towns, which contain a great deal of material on individual buildings, are each prefaced by a historical introduction, a chronological table and notes on town planning. O. Birkner's book on building and housing in Switzerland from 1850 to 1920 is largely devoted to an art-historical assessment; this applies to both parts of the book, on types of building and architectural styles (4). The introductory section on building materials provides, from an unaccustomed viewpoint, insights into economic and technological development. Thus, for example, the list of representative buildings constructed from various types of stone recalls the transport revolution which, as a contemporary put it, first made possible "the splendid conveyance of ashlars". O. Birkner has also written a shorter work on building and housing in Basel, which examines the early planning for various districts (13). In the wake of a wave of nostalgia and the rediscovery of early photography, a whole series of picture books on 19th-century towns has appeared; they are rich in visual material but usually modest so far as historical content is concerned (60/69/71/74).

There is a good deal of older literature on technical aspects of urban infrastructure, gas and electricity works, water works and sewerage, all of which were often, in the initial phase, privately run. The same applies to the tramways, to which mainly amateur railway enthusiasts have turned their attention. So far as new studies in the field of urban infrastructure are concerned, mention should be made of E. Suter's dissertation on the Zurich water supply (36), and of a study by M. Haeflinger, who interprets the introduction of a centralised water supply in Basel as a process of civilisation (in the sense in which that term is used by N. Elias) (10).

The "housing question", a burning issue at the turn of the century which gave rise to a flood of articles and pamphlets, has hardly been studied by historians. A few monographs have been written on philanthropic housing programmes; these are easy to cover, but quantitatively of little importance (18). With respect to municipal housing on a communal or co-operative basis, reference must be made to an older study, which provides a good overview (31).

The influence of land prices on urban structure is the subject of an article which takes Bern as an example (44), and which draws on an older dissertation by Hebeisen (48). Hebeisen's is the only study, apart from that by K. Kreis, that examines land prices systematically over a longer period of time. Further studies would be desirable; they would require the arduous task of collecting data from land registers and handwritten records of changes to the registers. Various statistical bureaux have published land prices since the turn of the century; however, they mostly relate to newly developed agricultural land that has not yet been built on. Since it is in the nature of things that such plots are to be found at an ever-increasing distance from the centre, dissimilar situations, that is, dissimilar properties are compared throughout, and the index of land prices appears increasingly distorted. M. Vieli has suggested a practical method for correcting this error (55). His results relate to the recent past (1932–1964), and his methods should be considered for historical works on earlier periods.

Many of the studies just mentioned also deal with economic aspects of urban development, but there are few monographs dealing specifically with economic history. H. Bauer has published a book, commissioned by the Basel Chamber of Commerce, on the economic history of Basel in the last 100 years; it concentrates on the main areas of economic activity in Basel (silk ribbon, chemical industry, transport) on the basis of local history (58). P. Stolz's dissertation on Basel's economy in the early period of industrialisation has a more sophisticated scholarly approach (63). He has also written an article sketching some lines of development of Basel's urban economy (54). In it, he discusses the possibility of research in the context of the well-known Export-Base Theory, but the application of such a model has yet to be made. The macro-economic significance of the Swiss towns has not yet been studied; a few economists have provided contributions on siting questions in the context of spatial economics theory. The fact that a dissertation on industrial conurbations in Switzerland comes to the conclusion that "the basic pattern of the siting structure of Swiss industry is to be explained historically, i.e. natural siting conditions are nowadays less important than created ones" only goes to show how important it would be to make a historical study of the problem (59).

Besides the works already mentioned, which have been singled out because of especially interesting aspects, there is a number of further monographs on towns, for example on Bern (45), Geneva (70), Winterthur (73) and the little town of Rapperswil (72). In addition, numerous other studies investigate urban areas without focusing attention on specifically urban problems. Nevertheless, they can shed light on important aspects of urbanisation research. As examples, two works which are useful in this respect are: M. Schaffner's dissertation on the working-class population of Basel (32) and C. Müller's dissertation on entrepreneurs and workers in Baden (11).

In connection with tracts on regional, transport and energy planning, which have been published and have acquired political significance in the past ten years, a tremendous amount of scholarly work has been stimulated or commissioned; a central position in this process is occupied by the Institute for Local, Regional and National Planning at the Swiss Technical University in Zurich. Even though these studies deal with the present or the future, it is still worth the historian's while to pay attention to them, less for their — usually inadequate — historical retrospects than for the stimuli their methods provide on subjects such as agglomeration effects in industry (57), on the change from migration from rural areas to an exodus from the cities (19), and on relationships between road networks and economic spatial development.

C. Outlook

It seems to us to be important for the future of urban history research in Switzerland that greater attention be given to methodological and theoretical considerations. As this survey has shown, there is no lack of interesting individual studies; what is lacking is a comprehensive concept to make disparate local histories into a body of research on urban history.

KATHLEEN NEILS CONZEN AND MICHAEL H. EBNER

The United States*

A. General Trends in Research

The study of urban history in the United States will reach its half century in 1990 with the 50th anniversary of the publication of A. M. Schlesinger, Sr.'s "The City in American History" (38). With its assertion that "the city, no less than the frontier, has been a major factor in American civilisation", this article symbolically launched urban history as a legitimate realm of scholarly inquiry. By the early 1950s, a small core of practitioners was supporting a newsletter and pioneering the first university courses in the field; by the 1960s, the urban history course was becoming a fixture in the university curriculum, dissertations in the field were multiplying and a lengthening list of conferences and publications attested to its popularity and intellectual fertility (B. McKelvey/59; D. W. Hoover/55). Today, in the American Historical Association's Guide to Departments of History 1983–1984, some 236 historians across the country list urban history as a field of specialisation.

While numerous practitioners are also to be found within other academic disciplines and beyond the confines of academe, the field retains the close links to social history and to the individualistic tradition of university-based research that nurtured its initial strivings. Sociology, economics, geography, and most recently cultural anthropology, have proved the most influential cognate disciplines. The field supports two specialised academic journals, but no formal organisation, no independent research institutes, and relatively few large-scale group research projects. Nor have urban historians been able to generate much consensus regarding the scope and definition

* Numbers in brackets in this chapter refer to entries in the bibliography on pp. 533–550 of this volume.

of the field, let alone methodological or interpretive agreement. The extent to which such a lack of consensus continues to be regarded as troubling, is evident in the fact that since 1980 no fewer than ten distinct articles have been published, each assessing the evolution of American urban history and setting forth programmatic statements about its immediate prospects (K. N. Conzen/45/46/47; M. H. Ebner/48; D. S. Gardner/52; D. Schaffer/62; T. Hershberg/53; R. A. Mohl/60; B. M. Stave/66; D. F. White/69).

The profusion of such articles reflects longstanding divisions within the ranks of urban historians. Central to the debate is the distinction between the role of urbanisation within the national history of the United States, and the history of American urban places and urban life. A. M. Schlesinger, himself, foreshadowed the former perspective when he structured his 1933 history of late-19th century America around the argument that "underlying all the varied developments that made up American life was the momentous shift of the centre of national equilibrium from the countryside to the city" (38, p. 435). A number of pioneers produced significant studies in a similar vein (C. Bridenbaugh/73/74; R. C. Wade/103), but the admonitions of E. E. Lampard, beginning in 1955, to study urban history from what economists would regard as a macro perspective — that is, examining the causes, concomitants and consequences of the urban phenomenon on a national and even international scale — went long unheeded (30/31/32/56/57/58).

Instead, American urban history evolved in two distinct directions, both largely dependent upon monographic "case study" analysis of particular locales. This circumstance is at least partially attributable to the physical size of the nation, the numbers and diverse types of cities within its borders, and the decentralised locations of both scholars and archival material. The first direction, the biographical, characterised much of the scholarship of the 1940s and 1950s. Its goal was the chronological history of individual cities (e.g. C. Green/27; B. L. Pierce/300; R. G. Osterweis/306; B. Still/304) or sets of cities (e.g. W. Belcher/71; R. C. Wade/103) with urban history simply the sum total of trends common to all cities (e.g. B. McKelvey/33). These studies drew from the conventions of national history-writing their primary concern to chart and explain demographic, economic, and political growth, and from an older 19th-century tradition of amateur local history the belief in "progress" and successful problem-solving as their central theme.

Partly for these reasons, and partly because chronological coverage was frequently achieved at the expense of in-depth analysis, the biographical approach proved less satisfactory as new concerns surfaced in the 1960s. Indisputably affected by the milieu of their times — large-scale urban redevelopment, the riots in America's cities, the unpopular war in Southeast Asia — historians tended to abandon celebration of urban success for careful analysis of the roots of modern-day social and economic afflictions. Newly available governmental sources of funding supported many of these studies; new awareness of the analytical tools and models of the social sciences gave them their interpretive structure; for help in data analysis many (though far from all) turned to the new technology of the computer. Because the sources to which they turned were frequently highly detailed and complex, most urban history books and articles exemplifying this problem-oriented approach were framed to study a specific topic within the setting of a single community during a limited span of time.

Generally this scholarship has pursued one of two directions. Although both derived from the continuing division among urban historians noted above, the distinctions reached the point of making them appear independent of one another. One direction examined specific urban problems of national dimensions, such as ethnic politics, public health, education, policing, or mass transit within the context of a particular city's historical evolution (e.g. J. M. Allswang/108; S. Galishoff/165; R. Mohl/185; S. K. Troen/292; R. Lane/182; C. W. Cheape/243). Directly informed by contemporary perceptions of urban problems, these case studies frequently drew upon other social sciences for methodological and interpretive models and, in contrast to the biographical school, were concerned with the individual city not for itself but as a site within which broader national processes could be observed.

The other direction placed emphasis not on immediate problems of service delivery but rather on underlying urban social structures, in order to clarify long-standing debates within national historiography regarding such issues as social mobility, racial discrimination, immigrant assimilation, or class formation. It took much of its inspiration from path-breaking books on Newburyport and Boston by S. Thernstrom (196/197), which pioneered ways of using quantitative analysis to make a range of systematic source materials little used before — manuscript census schedules, tax rolls, city directories and vital records — yield abundant data on the behaviour of ordinary urban dwellers. Largely inspired by a conference on

19th-century cities held during 1968 at Yale University, historians working in this mode adopted the rubric of "new urban history" to describe what they saw as an effort to deepen "understanding of the lives of men and women living in dense urban settlements undergoing explosive growth and structural transformation" (S. Thernstrom and R. Sennett/198).

That rubric proved to be confusing, controversial and short-lived. The basic problem was that much of the research examined a single concern — social mobility in local settings (e.g. H. P. Chudacoff/154; P. Decker/161; C. Griffen and S. Griffen/167; T. Kessner/180). Yet critics had severe reservations regarding both the reliability of the data and the ability of locally confined studies to address what was a process national in scope. Moreover, it was quickly recognised that, in practice, most of the studies took little account either of the distinctly urban quality of the mobility processes they were attempting to study, or of the specific character of the cities in which they were set (M. H. Frisch/164; S. M. Blumin/146). Clearly, the "new urban history" did not encompass even a fraction of what might theoretically be regarded as urban history; indeed, its claims to be "urban" at all were questionable. As S. Thernstrom soon noted, "most of the subjects that have preoccupied the new urban historians are not confined to the city, and should not be approached as if they were" (67, p. 361). This was followed a few years later by his even more emphatic statement: "I've stopped labelling myself an urban historian at all" (B. M. Stave/65, p. 230).

Such disclaimers of urban orientation may have finished some of the criticism directed at the mobility studies, but they did little to rescue the field of American urban history, itself, from the disarray into which criticism of the exaggerated claims of the "new urban history" had cast it. There was real danger, in fact, of throwing the baby out with the bathwater and ignoring very positive developments in American urban historiography. For one thing, students of urban social structure soon turned from efforts to simply quantify behaviour to more sophisticated attempts to probe the social influence of both structural constraints and cultural values, work that is opening up major new questions for the urban historian (e.g. O. Zunz/207; S. M. Blumin/147; D. H. Doyle/162). Just as significant, it can be argued that much of the debate over the "new urban history" was a red herring that, in its obsession with studies that were not really urban in focus, distracted attention from a rapidly growing collection of shelf work clearly central to urban history by any definition.

The scope and tendencies of this work can be discerned in a compilation made up of some 338 monographs published during 1983, books that are to be found in most urban history course bibliographies. Almost one in four (23.4%) was published in the four years 1980 to 83 alone, with close to half (47.9%) having appeared in the 1970s, compared to 18.3% in the 1960s, 4.7% in the 1950s, 3.3% in the 1940s, and 2.4% in the 1930s. Telling, is the fact that 67.5% (228) of all these monographs were set in a single city framework, a tendency that is, if anything, increasing: 66.4% (172) of the pre-1980 studies were so designed, compared with 73.4% (58) of the studies published in the early 1980s. Also notable is the shifting regional setting of the monographs. Before 1980, some 54% of the 180 monographs with a specific regional setting dealt with the Northeast, 26% with the North Central region, 14% with the South, and 6% with the West; by the early 1980s, the rising urban role of the sunbelt was reflected in the fact that the South and the West each were the focus of 17% of the monographs with a specific regional setting, while the shares of the Northeast and North Central regions declined to 47% and 19%, respectively.

Changes in topical focus index the emergence of new concerns and the fading of old. Studies of urban social history continue to dominate the list, but whereas nine of the monographs published in the 1960s and 1970s can be classified as mobility studies, only two such books were published in the early 1980s. Studies of ethnic and racial minorities remain popular, but Hispanics are now receiving significant attention for the first time. The early popularity of studies of city boosterism and urban rivalry has faded, but there is renewed interest in tracing the development of regional urban networks, with four studies of the south and southwest appearing between 1930 and 1983. Moreover, urban historians are clearly expanding their horizons beyond the boundaries of the central city. Only three of the 13 studies of suburbs or metropolitan areas were published by 1971, but since 1977 an additional ten monographs have appeared. Other topics altogether overlooked now receive attention. Until 1975 there were no studies of sports, recreation and leisure framed in the tradition of urban history, but nine monographs — coinciding with a rising interest in popular culture — are now available in this area. The flourishing field of American legal history has yielded three monographs since 1975 that readily lend themselves to the literature of urban history, and there are signs that renewed interest in the history of urban government and finance is joining the long-standing preoccupation with urban political history.

A significant proportion of these studies was originally framed as doctoral dissertations. Current trends in dissertation research suggest that the field of urban history will continue to remain a productive one for at least some time to come. The annual number of Ph.D. dissertations with an evident urban history focus, according to the listings provided by the *Journal of American History* since 1976, has fluctuated fairly randomly between 73 and 96 for the last six years, at a time when the total number of history dissertations completed has declined significantly. Social history topics have proved consistently the most popular, increasing from an average of 40% of the annual total of urban-related dissertations from 1976 through 1979, to 46% in the 1980 to 1983 period. Studies of ethnic and racial minorities make up well over half of this total; mobility studies have been declining, while studies of the family and women, and of class formation, have been growing in number. Reflecting the heightened concern for values noted above, cultural history is also increasingly popular, with its share of the total dissertations rising from 5.3% in the initial four-year period, to 10.5% in the following four years. Studies of topics related to urban infrastructure and the physical growth of the city have averaged around 9 to 11% of the total over the entire period, while urban social services and reform have been attracting fewer scholars, dissertations dropping from an average of 16.7% of the total to 12.5%, as is also the case with studies of city growth and urbanisation (from 17.5% to 15%) and politics and government (from 9% to 6.7%).

These publication and dissertation statistics indicate that urban history research in the United States is alive and well, despite the much-publicised discrediting of the "new urban history". Much of the work remains without a clear urban conceptual framework, a fact that continues to leave many in the field uneasy: Americans appear to be no less eclectic than other English-speaking urban historians (A. F. Artibise and G. A. Stelter/4), but are less comfortable in their eclecticism. If nothing else, however, the American debate over the "urban-ness" of the "new urban history" has produced some public agreement on a pragmatic definition of the subject as encompassing the three major issue-complexes of national urbanisation, city-building and governing, and social processes as they occur in urban settings (T. Hershberg/53; K. N. Conzen/47). Moreover, although there is no dominant theoretical approach, nor any clearly recognisable "schools" of American urban history (despite the important training role of universities such as Harvard, Chicago and Columbia during the formative years of the 1960s), implicit modernisation theory, as popularised by L. Mumford and the Chicago School of Sociology, provides a fairly standard basis for both texts and monographs in the field (for intellectual genealogies, consult B. M. Stave/65; see also the comments of D. S. Smith/64). Both Mumford's negative interpretation of the chaotic impact of modern technological change upon the city, and the Chicago School's efforts to detail the specific consequences of urban expansion on both personality and community (L. Mumford/36; R. E. Park, E. W. Burgess and R. D. McKenzie/37), found resonance in attempts by urban historians to construct a basic interpretive framework and periodisation for the field (O. Handlin/28; R. C. Wade/40/41; E. E. Lampard/31/56/57/58). The most specific of these schema, S. B. Warner's (42) interpretation of urban development through the succession of differing urban environments (mercantile, early industrial, mature industrial, post-industrial) created by changes in city size and economy in the course of industrialisation, has probably had the greatest influence upon both research and textbook treatments (e.g. D. R. Goldfield and B. R. Brownell/26). Equally influential has been Warner's emphasis on the enduring American bias towards private, rather than public solutions for urban problems (42) (see also Z. L. Miller/35), and the insistence of R. Wiebe (44) and S. P. Hays (29) on the significance of the late 19th century dissolution of localistic community orientations. There is also a growing interest in the implications of Marxist theory for urban history (M. H. Ebner/48). A brief review of several areas within American urban history can serve to illustrate some of the interpretive issues raised by this recent work.

B. Development in Individual Fields

(a) *Urban Definitions and Urban Systems*

The problem of defining urban places has received relatively little attention from American urban historians. (The British usage of the term "town" does not have an American counterpart. A "town", in American parlance, is a small settlement towards the lower end of the urban hierarchy; "city" technically refers to places with urban charters, and, in common usage, to larger urban places.) Most accept a simplistic combination of census-based demographic criteria and the political criterion of incorporation. The issue has come to the fore only in the context of the debate over the degree of colonial and 19th century urbanisation in the south. Where some scholars attempted to assess the causes and consequences — cultural and political as well as economic — of southern under-urbanisation (J. G. Rainbolt/97), others attempted to argue that the only problem lies in the historian's inability to recognise an urban place in a crossroads collection of stores and warehouses (J. A. Ernst and R. Merrens/80). By focusing attention on a functional definition of urban places, this controversy encouraged significant research linking differing levels of urbanisation and systems of cities to the varying marketing needs of staple crops, as in the case of the urbanisation that accompanied the mid-18th century transition from tobacco to wheat-growing in the Cheseapeake Bay region (C. Earle and R. Hoffman/79; J. M. Price/96; R. D. Mitchell/91; J. T. Lemon/85).

The fact that the American urban system was expanding through space as well as over time through most of the 19th century has posed a special set of problems for students of modern American urban history. F. J. Turner's classic "Frontier Thesis" had interpreted the city in essentially central-place terms as the last stage of frontier settlement, emerging only after phases of hunting and trapping, backwoods subsistence agriculture, and maturing farm settlement. R. C. Wade (103), by contrast, argued that cities in the Ohio Valley were "spearheads" of frontier settlement, preceding all but the earliest frontiersmen into newly opened territory to serve as critical control and exchange points for western settlement. Subsequent work has confirmed similar urban patterns on other frontiers, traced the economic role of frontier cities with greater sophistication, and begun to sort out the patterns of investment that created them (K. Wheeler/105; R. Lotchin/87; J. Rubin/99; J. Haeger/83).

Other work has sought to explain the relative growth or decline of individual cities within the urban system. Favourite explanations have centred upon the role of entrepreneurial enterprise in capitalising upon locational advantage through the acquisition of new transportation linkages; they tend to stress the importance of "city boosting" — that is, promotion of the city by its businessmen — "urban imperialism" and city rivalries as factors in encouraging growth (W. Belcher/71; H. N. Scheiber/100; C. N. Glaab/81; B.

Brownell/75.) Economic historians have paid particular attention to the influence of industrialisation upon patterns of urbanisation, and are making clear the extent to which the growth of the major coastal metropolises in the early 19th century was linked to local hinterland development rather than interregional trade (J. G. Williamson and J. A. Swanson/106; S. S. Crowther/78; D. Lindstrom/86). Also receiving recent attention are the changing contexts of 20th century urbanisation, particularly the rise of the so-called "Sunbelt Cities" (C. Abbott/70; G. D. Nash/93; D. R. Goldfield/82) and the influence of the federal government on the location of 20th century urban growth (R. Lotchin/88).

In general, however, historians have left systematic work on the changing overall structure and character of the urban system to the historical geographer. Like historians, geographers have been concerned to account for the origins and expansion of the urban system, but have also given more explicit consideration to its hierarchical structure and functions, and to regional differences. J. E. Vance (102), for example, formulated a "mercantile model" of the extension into new settlement regions of chains of cities acting as wholesaling depots, which served as the initial basis for fuller urban penetration. E. K. Muller (92) traced the subsequent filling out of the urban system in the hinterland of such regional metropolises as the needs of long-distance trade to begin with, then local trade, and then the processing of agricultural goods with each in turn creating differential patterns of urban growth and functional specialisation. J. C. Hudson (84) documented the extent to which corporate decision influenced the pattern of initial urban distribution in areas settled in the latter part of the 19th century. A. R. Pred (94/95), with his model of circular and cumulative growth, attempted to explain why the large coastal mercantile metropolises were able to absorb most of the growth generated by the industrial revolution as well, and to document the way in which the spatial biases in information circulation permitted them to maintain dominance over regional systems of cities. Nevertheless, D. Ward (104) and D. R. Meyer (89) have suggested how limitations in 19th century transportation technology permitted new national metropolises to emerge in the west, their infant manufactures protected by a "tariff of distance" from eastern competition. On the basis of this work, and his own efforts to trace shifting patterns of metropolitan influence, M. P. Conzen (76/77) postulated three major phases in the evolution of the urban system in the 19th century, and began to delineate major urban regions and the functional and hierarchical distributions of individual cities within those regions.

This work on the evolution of the American urban system, despite the fact that much of it is stronger on theory than data, has implications of considerable significance, not only for the history of urbanisation but also for understanding how developments within individual cities were influenced by the city's role within the urban system. Nevertheless, it is yet to be integrated into the central interpretive frameworks of urban history. Urban historians have only started to explore the development of local urban systems (R. B. Miller/90; F. X. Blouin/72), and have seldom made use of a city's functional role as a critical analytical variable in any but the most impressionistic fashion.

(b)   Municipal Law, Governance and Politics

By contrast, the city as polity has commanded substantial attention in the literature of American urban history and yielded an abundance of studies. Very recently this area of investigation has achieved renewed sophistication, influenced by the important role of social history within the "new" urban history. "Precisely what is lacking", E. E. Lampard stated more than a decade ago (B. M. Stave/137), "is good political history of American cities . . . political in the larger sense, not just elections and running for office, who governs, but the nature of local government." Rather than portraying politics and governance in a narrowly-conceived framework which examines individuals and their personalities engaged in the electoral process, emphasis has turned to questions of structure, organisation, and behaviour as propounded by S. P. Hays (125). Although too much ignored at the time of its publication, the reassessment of New York City's Boss Tweed by S. J. Mandelbaum (128) anticipated such lines of investigation. The most up-to-date assessment of ongoing developments in the literature is provided in an essay-review by J. C. Teaford (140).

The classic portrayal of urban politics was informed by the boss-reformer dichotomy. This tradition originated in the work of Lord J. Bryce, taking its cue from his 1888 dictum: "There is no denying that the government of cities is one of the conspicuous failures of the United States." The impulse was further advanced by the journalistic exposés of corruption of L. Steffens, who wrote about the shame of the cities and their elected officials during the pre-First

World War years. Such studies of municipal government were inclined to portray the political setting as involving a continuing electoral struggle between the forces of good and evil (E. W. Griffith/117/118/119; C. R. Adrian and E. Griffith/107). But as historical studies of individual bosses and reformers multiplied, the simple moralistic dichotomy has yielded to increasingly sophisticated analyses of structural conditions encouraging bossism, functions performed by urban bosses, bases of electoral support, variations in motives and programmes among different strains of reform, and areas of overlap between bossism and reform (W. R. Miller/130; B. M. Stave/136; M. Shefter/135; J. M. Allswang/108; M. G. Holli/126; J. D. Buenker/111 — for a review of this literature see D. R. Colburn and G. E. Pozzetta/112; note also the M. G. Holli and P. A. Jones compendium of biographical information on big city mayors/127). In the process, as A. Bridges' (110) recent analysis of the emergence of machine politics in antebellum New York demonstrates, such work is showing how American political culture, itself, helped shape distinctively American patterns of urban social relations as well.

But the late 20th-century realisation of enduring governmental crisis in the nation's cities has also drawn historical attention to the very foundations of American urban government (M. H. Ebner/113). J. C. Teaford (139) turned to its earliest origins, examining the English antecedents of municipal government and tracing them to 1825. His main concern was the transformation spawned by the libertarian ideological fulcrum of the American Revolution. Municipal regulation of the economy, by and large a common practice in colonial society, was abandoned amid sharp criticism that it constituted an inhibiting force in the buoyant, developing marketplace. An important case study by H. Hartog (124) examines New York City, 1730 to 1870, from the vantage point of legal history, focusing on the continuing tensions between the provisions of the city charter, the authority of the state legislature, and the influence of the judicial process. The growing urban role of the federal government in the 20th century is also receiving more attention (M. I. Gelfand/116; P. S. Funigiello/115).

Also noteworthy are monographs that examine key institutional aspects of urban government. J. C. Teaford (141) takes direct issue with the Bryce thesis of "conspicuous failure." He argues that when historians study the accomplishments as well as the failures of American urban government during the second half of the 19th century, the record is often as positive as in any other western nation of the time. B. R. Rice (133) turns attention to the Progressive Era, analysing the underlying reasons leading to the popularity of government by commission, while M. S. Schiesl (134) traces the changing emphases within progressive urban reform over time. K. Fox (114) has written an illuminating study of the multi-faceted efforts to improve municipal government betwen 1890 and 1937, including an account of how federal legislation influenced this process. In studying the growth of public utilities within Houston, 1830–1915, H. L. Platt (132) devotes substantial attention to that city's legal integument and thereby underscores the intertwining of political and technological history, to which A. D. Anderson (109) adds a stress on fiscal considerations as well. Such concerns also inform a recent collection of essays on urban environmental history (M. V. Melosi/129; see also E. P. Moehring/61).

When to these concerns is added a social scientifically informed analysis of traditional questions about the distribution of political power in the American city, the result is the major redirection in the political focus of urban history evident in the work of D. C. Hammack (120/121/122). Eschewing the boss-and-reform dichotomy, he formulates a sophisticated analysis of the political decision-making process. Hammack favours a multi-causal explanation, taking issue with longstanding shibboleths about elite domination of the sources of power. His test cases, all based in New York City, include the formation of Greater New York City, mayoral politics, the construction of the subway system, and school centralisation. Whether or not one entirely accepts his thesis about the widening entrée to power, the broad scope of this research is proving instrumental in directing attention to basic historical questions about politics and governance which require a framework informed by social analysis (A. Sutcliffe/138; G. V. Harris/123; E. J. Watts/142).

(c) Population and Social Structure

Historians addressing problems of urban population and social structure have taken much of their cue from 19th-century worries that urban industrial growth posed a fatal challenge to the survival of republican institutions and community cohesion. How did urban Americans maintain social order in the face of growing economic inequality, population heterogeneity and new bases of wealth? Some sought to answer this question with research on more or less repressive instruments of social control, such as religion, charitable and reform organisations, or the police (P. Johnson/177; P. Boyer/152; R. Lane/182; J. C. Schneider/195). The "new urban historians", however, followed the lead of early 20th-century sociologists in turning to the social structure for their answer, which they found in the processes of social mobility and immigrant assimilation.

Their major initial focus was on the measurement of social mobility during the period of industrialisation (1850–1910) for which manuscript census and city directory data were readily available. Linking the various sources made it possible to trace individual careers over time and, thus, to estimate levels of geographical, occupational and other kinds of mobility, as well as the variables presumably influencing the process. Such research (S. Thernstrom /196/197; H. P. Chudacoff/154; P. Decker/161; C. Griffen and F. S. Griffen/167) made clear the great and increasing disparities of wealth and life chances within American cities during the period, the close association of such disparities with ethnic origin and race, and the very high levels of geographical mobility, especially at the lower end of the social ladder. Yet these studies also found that while chances for spectacular social mobility were statistically slim, upward mobility generally outweighed downward mobility regardless of class for those who persisted in one place, that levels of intergenerational social mobility were even higher, and that ethnic differences narrowed over time. While early studies sought to explain mobility differentials through individual-level variables, such as religion, literacy, and family background, hypothesising little place-to-place variation (S. Thernstrom/197), it soon became clear that different levels of opportunity available in various sectors of the economy under the rapidly shifting conditions of industrialisation played a major role (C. Griffen and S. Griffen/167; T. Hershberg/174). Most historians saw in the social mobility findings a major mechanism by which social order was maintained in the industrialising city: those who stayed could expect at least limited success within the existing system, while the discontented did not remain long enough to create lasting disruption.

O. Handlin (171/172) had earlier applied similar logic to the immigrant experience, arguing that although the massive inpouring of alien workers after the mid-19th century generated critical cultural conflict, the strength of ethnic attachments actually helped maintain social order: the American city first forced the immigrants to construct segregated communities that eased the initial shock of acculturation and prepared them for the economic opportunity that ejected them into the American "mainstream". By the 1960s historians were challenging this assimilation model from two directions. One group argued that physically segregated ethnic communities were never common in American cities and thus that the process operated differently than hypothesised (H. P. Chudacoff/ 155; S. B. Warner and C. B. Burke/204), while the other insisted that its outcome was better understood as ethnic maintenance than assimilation (R. Vecoli/201). Both issues were quickly addressed with the data and methods of the "new urban history", though the debates remain unresolved. Case studies have probed the circumstances under which immigrant ghettos developed and their role in immigrant adaptation (K. N. Conzen/157; O. Zunz/207), assessed the influence of structural factors and particularly cultural values in differential group mobility patterns (J. Barton/144; T. Kessner/180; J. Bodnar/149), emphasised the role of the family as the critical carrier of ethnic culture (V. Yans-McLaughlin/206; T. K. Hareven/173), and traced the gradual transformation of cultural values, social patterns, and ethnic identification from one generation to the next (D. Cinel/156). Central to much of this work is the insistence on the autonomous ability of immigrants to actively influence the terms on which they adapted to the industrial city.

Similar approaches, modified by greater emphasis on the negative consequences of racial prejudice, characterise the growing body of work on Hispanic communities in American cities (R. Griswold del Castillo/168; A. Camarillo/153; R. Romo/192; M. T. Garcia/166). By contrast, studies of black urban communities remain heavily focused on the external forces (including violence) that created the segregated ghetto and constrained life within it in ways unknown to immigrant groups (D. M. Katzman/179; W. Tuttle/200; T. L. Philpott/189), though early insistence (G. Osofsky/187) on the enduring sameness of ghetto oppression has yielded to a more textured understanding of variation with place and time (H. M. Rabinowitz/191; J. W. Blassingame/145; K. L. Kusmer/181; A. R. Hirsch/175). There have been recent efforts to look more closely at the internal dynamics of black ghetto life and black culture, mainly in order to understand better how institutionalised prejudice was translated into specific constraints on occupational patterns, community organisation, and family life (E. Pleck/190; T. Hershberg/174; and, particularly, J. Bodnar, R. Simon and M. Weber/ 150). The desperation of the black urban ghettos, however, has left few historians of the black community with the luxury of joining immigration historians in celebrating cultural autonomy (but see J. Borchert/151). Indeed, J. W. Trotter (199) has recently argued the necessity of interpreting the 20th-century black urban experience in class rather than exclusively racial/ethnic terms.

The increasing tendency to turn from structural to cultural analysis in urban social history is, however, a general one. The vogue for mobility studies had largely ended by the mid-1970s as methodological and conceptual limitations became increasingly clear. Critics noted that the level of error in linkages was high; that the individual city was an inappropriate locus within which to measure mobility within a national system; and, most importantly, that both the measurement of mobility levels and the implications derived from them assumed the existence of a social structure whose actual dimensions remained largely unexplored. Historians have turned, therefore, to delineating the shape of the urban social structure and to how it was perceived by individual urban dwellers, and in the process have laid to rest the older consensual models of urban social order. Most of this work has continued to focus on the era of industrialisation. While M. B. Katz (178) and his associates discerned the "crystallisation" of a new class system in the clarity with which census- and directory-based data separated the privileged from the remainder of urban society, E. P. Thompson's concern for the cultural basis of class formation has proved more contagious. Led by H. G. Gutman (170), urban history has joined hands with labour history to explore the development of working-class consciousness and its relationship to ethnicity and political ideology (B. Laurice/183; J. Cumbler/159; A. Dawley/160; P. Faler/163; S. Wilentz/205). This has stimulated parallel interest in the coalescence of an urban middle-class culture defined by domesticity, evangelical religion, and leisure-time activities distinctive from those of the working class (P. Johnson/177; M. P. Ryan/194; R. Rosenzweig/193). There is also significant recent work on the emergence and transformation of a distinctive urban upper class (E. D. Baltzell/143; E. Pessen/188; F. C. Jaher/176).

This historiography remains very incomplete, however. The large-scale, rural-to-urban migration of white Americans is virtually unexplored (see J. Modell/184 for a suggestion of the interpretive possibilities such work might yield), and urban history is only beginning to assimilate findings on demographic transition (M. Vinovskis/202; A. M. Guest and S. Tolnay/169). Only recently has the rapidly growing body of research in women's history attempted to weigh the specifically urban dimensions of women's experience. Most work is highly empirical. Generalisation and theoretical understanding are elusive — even the massive Philadelphia Social History Project has failed to produce more than a highly schematic interpretation of the overall process of social change in that city. Reliance upon the local case study means that the extent of variation across the urban system evades analysis. G. Nash's (186) long-term, comparative study of colonial urban social change and political evolution has not found its 19th-century counterpart, and urban social history has barely acknowledged the 20th century.

Nevertheless, urban social history has moved well beyond its initial preoccupation with the basis of social order to a nuanced examination of social changes accompanying industrialisation, and perhaps to the beginnings of a new synthesis linking such changes to other aspects of civic life as well. In particular, the middle decades of the 19th century are emerging as an important transitional phase during which a broad-based "proletarian" republican culture resting on the skilled workman may have dominated the public life of industrialising cities organised mainly on the basis of ethnicity, until the maturing industrial order generated a new and more formalistic conception of community along with the emergence of elite control, mass culture, and class and race as the critical defining variables (F. G. Couvares/158; O. Zunz/207; S. M. Blumin/146; M. H. Frisch/164).

(d)   *Urban Planning and Physical Development*

To the extent that historical work on American urban planning has moved beyond the purely architectural evaluation of specific plans, it has tended to concentrate upon either the history of the planning profession or planning as an aspect of urban political reform (see E. L. Birch/212). M. Scott's (233) monumental history of the profession remains a fundamental point of departure. Much of the work probes the relative weakness of formal planning in American urban development, stressing the continued dominance of essentially privatist, market-oriented values in shaping the physical structure of the American city. J. W. Reps (230), in a monumental series of volumes, has identified the main principles guiding the initial (usually private) platting of American cities; others have traced the role of market forces in subsequent redevelopment (M. W. White-hill/237; G. W. Condit/215; M. P. Conzen/216).

A much larger body of research has sought to isolate the factors that shaped the late 19th century emergence of the formal planning profession, conditioned the terms on which it slowly gained public acceptance, and contributed to the form of its impact on the American city (S. Buder/213; S. K. Schulz and C. McShane/232; J. A. Peterson/228/229). Studies of individual planners form an important part of this literature (T. S. Hines/220; A. Fein/217). This literature celebrates the vision and scope of early American city planning, while also documenting its tardiness in adding considerations of social justice to those of aesthetics and efficiency, and its forced subservience to the wishes of private developers (A. Sutcliffe/ 234). The idealistic planning ventures of the 1920s and 1930s have received significant attention (R. Lubove/225; D. Schaffer/231; J. L. Arnold/209), but R. A. Caro's (214) massive biography of Robert Moses better illuminates the combination of transmuted reform impulses, market considerations, and federal involvement that has played the dominant role in 20th-century American city planning.

Few urban historians, however, have sought to emulate R. Lubove's (226) pioneering study of how private and public factors intertwined to shape a particular city's environmental development (see also J. Kahn/222; C. Abbott/208). Consequently, the physical history of American cities has been left largely to the architectural historians (J. M. Fitch/218; C. Lockwood/223; D. S. Tucci/235), though housing is proving an exception. The values American urbanites sought to express in their homes (G. Wright/238; D. Hayden/219), their relative success in achieving them (R. G. Barrows/210; J. Tygiel/236), and the constraints imposed by these values on the development of public housing for the poor (R. Lubove/224; A. Jackson/221; J. F. Bauman/211) have all received significant attention. There is as yet, however, nothing like a fully satisfactory history of American urban housing as it varied from city to city over time.

(e) Transport and Spatial Structure

Most historical research on the physical character of American cities, including its infrastructure, has had a closer affinity to social rather than to planning history. Social scientists, while debating the relative merits of concentric, zonal, or multiple nuclei models, in explaining urban spatial structure (G. A. Theodorson/268), have generally agreed that American urban neighbourhoods have exhibited strong patterns of ethnic and racial, as well as, class segregation, in which social status increases with distance from the city centre. In an important series of articles in the 1960s, L. F. Schnore (259) argued that this distinctive American pattern was the product of a transformation from an earlier pre-industrial pattern of mixed land uses and social statuses and central elite concentration. This transformation, S. B. Warner (270) documented in a study of Boston suburban development, was a consequence of new modes of intra-urban transportation that encouraged the selective decentralisation of more affluent urban residents under conditions of rural idealisation, small-scale unregulated housing markets, and routine extension of urban infrastructures into newly developing residential areas. A critical precondition for this decentralisation, as S. B. Warner (269) noted in a subsequent study of Philadelphia, was the separation of workplace and residence that accompanied industrial revolution, to which D. Ward (203) added the role of differentially expanding sectors of the central business district in setting in motion constant processes of neighbourhood transition.

Subsequent research has shown the general applicability of this model of spatial transformation for other cities and periods (H. M. Mayer and R. C. Wade/253; J. Tarr/266; B. Blackmar/243; R. M. Fogelson/249; H. L. Preston/258), explored its social consequences (R. Sennett/261; P. Johnson/177), and probed its limitations. R. D. Simon (262), for example, has demonstrated how the political system permitted some working-class neighbourhoods to resist services that would increase the costs of home ownership, while T. Hershberg (174) and his collaborators have argued that the specific form of industrial development in Philadelphia encouraged the spatial structuring of that city in the 19th century as a patchwork of occupationally defined "mill villages" that precluded other kinds of social segregation. O. Zunz (207), on the other hand, insists that in Detroit, at least, ethnicity took predominance over class, occupation and race in structuring urban space until the industrial order matured in the early 20th century. This disagreement may stem from methodological differences; it probably also reflects distinct regional or functional patterns within the 19th century urban system (K. N. Conzen 245).

Most of this work has followed Warner in taking the form of the urban transportation system as a given. But urban historians are now beginning to focus directly on the economic, entrepreneurial, and political factors influencing city-to-city variation in the innovation of mass transit as well as other public services (C. W. Cheape/244; A. D. Anderson/239; H. Platt/257; G. H. Daniels and M. H. Rose/246; S. M. Hoy and M. C. Robinson/250 provide an exhaustive bibliography of research on urban infrastructure development more generally). Technological determinism as an explanation for the decline and motorisation of mass transit is similarly in retreat (S. Mallach/252; G. Yago/271; D. St Clair/263; P. Barrett/ 240).

Because most central cities have been unable to expand their political boundaries to capture much of the 20th century metropolitan growth, suburban development is an important part of American urban history, and one that is now attracting heightened interest. Recent publications include work on metropolitan governmental fragmentation (C. J. Teaford/267), on suburban planning experiments (J. L. Arnold/209; D. Schaffer/231), and on the development of individual suburbs and suburban systems (Z. Miller/ 254; C. A. O'Connor/256; H. Binford/242; M. H. Ebner/ 248). S. R. Stilgoe (264) has written a popularised, conceptually limited article-length survey, but K. T. Jackson's much-awaited book (251) will place the American suburban experience into broad chronological and comparative perspective for the first time. Among urban history surveys, D. R. Goldfield and B. A. Brownell (26) provide a welcome metropolitan context for studying suburbs. Two anthologies are available, one (P. C. Dolce/247) examining the suburban tradition thematically, the other (S. Schwartz and D. Prosser/260), geographically localised in its focus on New Jersey.

Much of the scholarship on the suburban tradition has been organised chronologically and draws upon comparisons with English and Continental antecedents. Though adjustments must be made for region, four overlapping stages of American suburban development seem evident: (i) the romantic suburb for affluent commuters, 1815–1850; (ii) the domesticated, middle-class suburb, 1850–1890; (iii) the modern, socially variegated suburb, 1890–1920; and (iv) the automobile suburb since 1920. The counterurbanisation that B. J. L. Berry (241) has identified as characteristic of the late 20th century is the latest manifestation of the process of population deconcentration. This classificatory sequence can provide a systematic understanding of consequential social, economic and technological benchmarks, regardless of whether the focus is on a specific community, a network of suburbs or suburbanisation within a regional, national, or comparative setting (P. O. Muller/255).

Social history themes and problematic, rather than celebratory interpretations, dominate much of suburban history. Most studies continue to echo S. B. Warner's indictment (270) of the so-called "streetcar suburb" and its successors (in contrast to the romantic suburb of the pre-Civil War era) as "centreless," lacking in "public life," and adding to the fragmentation of civic life in the metropolis. Suburbanisation created "closed social cells" (P. O. Muller/255) residential in function, homogenous in population, consensual in government, uncongested in physical form, that in abandoning the city fostered what K. T. Jackson (251) labels the "North American pattern" of "peripheral affluence and central despair". Though few suburbs fully lived up to this ideal, there is still little historical work on the functional and social complexity within suburbia (but see H. Binford/242).

(f)   Urban Culture

The growing interest in cultural approaches to urban history has inevitably influenced recent treatments of urban cultural institutions and conceptions of urbanity. There is a plethora of institutional histories of individual schools, churches, museums and voluntary organisations in city after city, generally narrative in character and laudatory in intent. By the 1960s, such institutional histories were joined by more carefully conceptualised studies attempting to assess the changing functions of such institutions within the American urban milieu. They often concentrated on elite actors, emphasising the negative consequences of the prevailing privatist ethos for American urban cultural development and stressing social control as a motive for cultural innovation. A case in point is the sophisticated body of research on the evolution of the urban public school (S. K. Schultz/289; S. K. Troen/292; D. B. Tyack/293; C. F. Kaestle/280; M. Lazerson/282; D. Ravitch/287); research on the voluntary efforts that created the major institutions of high culture in American cities has stressed similar themes (H. L. Horowitz/279; K. D. McCarthy/284).

But the "new" urban history's commitment to history "from the bottom up" also generated a rising interest in the development of an autonomous urban popular culture, exemplified in everything from sports to department stores to drinking habits to commercial amusements (S. A. Reiss/288; G. Barth/272; P. Duis/274; J. F. Kasson/281; L. A. Erenberg/275). The multiplication of such studies has fed a growing awareness of the role of cultural institutions in shaping class consciousness, and hence, in the work of scholars like R. Story (291), H. P. Ryan (194), S. M. Blumin (148) and R. Rosenzweig (193), is stimulating a renewed integration of social and cultural urban history. At the same time, comparative work is making evident the role of local culture in city-to-city variations in politics and governance (W. H. Pease and J. H. Pease/286). The broader, more anthropological conception of culture on which such work rests has also supported renewed examination of the M. and L. Whites' (297) classic interpretation of anti-urbanism in American thought, revealing a more complex set of attitudes toward the city than previously recognised and a distinctively American kind of urbanity (T. Bender/273; P. D. Goist/276; P. B. Hales/277; G. Barth/272; A. Lees/283).

For all its growing volume and interpretive complexity, however, research on the cultural history of American cities has thus far eluded comprehensive synthesis. The most promising effort remains N. Harris' (278) proposed four-part periodisation postulating a transformation from the imitative cosmopolitanism of the colonial elites; to a popular, integrating, participative culture in the decades separating the Revolution and the Civil War; to an emphasis on certification and segmentation accompanying the great era of institution-building in the later 19th and early 20th centuries; to, finally, the modern era in which the growth of the mass media and the new legitimacy of pluralism are undermining not only traditional forms of urban culture, but even the dependence of formal cultural institutions upon the city itself. But despite its obvious relevance to recent interpretations of urban social structure and governmental evolution, the Harris schema has been largely ignored by urban historians, remaining, like a good deal of the work on urban cultural institutions, more securely embedded within the American studies mode than within the accepted canons of the urban history field.

C. Conclusion

Urban historians in the United States, having absorbed the troubling methodological lessons of the last 20 years, approach the future less selfconsciously. The editor of the *Journal of Urban History* (1) marked the first decade of publication with an editorial assessment in November 1984, matter-of-factly remarking that beyond a certain point the quest for a definitive approach becomes "both useless and a bit boring" (B. Brownell/23). There now exists an intellectual environment that disdains single-minded agendas and instead encourages a pluralistic approach to scholarship. B. M. Stave (66), in addressing an international assembly on "A View from the United States", correctly poses the prospect of several alternative approaches looming. If this newly discovered tolerance endures it will be reflected in scholarship that explores a wide variety of concerns, some altogether new and others resurrected.

Any number of possibilities can be touched upon, albeit briefly, in the quest to anticipate the immediate future of American urban history. Reflecting a debate already in process among social historians in the United States as well as England (e.g. R. W. Fogel and G. R. Elton/49), more attention will be devoted to writing in the narrative genre. S. B. Warner's most recent book (296) already reflects such a turn. Increased attention to cultural interpretations, derivative of the anthropological tradition associated with the scholarship of C. Geertz, is yet another possibility (R. M. Morse and G. A. Stelter/285; R. G. Walter/294). An early, if tentative, example of such an approach is provided by S. B. Warner's use of urban imagery to explore the tension between social reality and modern values (296). Yet another tendency, growing out of the ongoing international communication among urban historians, is a tendency to compare urban subjects in their American context with those of other cultures (W. R. Miller/130; G. Yago/271; A. Lees/283). Studies taking the urban landscape itself as the dependent variable will provide a meeting ground for urban historians, geographers and architectural historians (J. R. Stilgoe/265; E. K. Muller/227), and encourage the trend towards the involvement of urban historians in practical matters of current policy (D. F. White/69). Finally, politically infused questions about urban power and society, no doubt informed by competing ideological starting points, will continue to stand prominent in the literature of American urban history.

What kinds of new synthesis or theory this fecund proliferation of sub-fields will engender is more difficult to predict. American urban history will, no doubt, always respond more readily to the immediate issues of the day than to the abstract demands of model-building or theory-testing, and will remain resistant to any single imposed perspective. Yet many of the diverse strains within urban history today are unified by a search for common cultural values and structural constraints influencing American urban development. If urban historians can cultivate an equal sensitivity to variation by region and city function, and remain open to international comparison, then even the theorisers within the profession need not despair for the future of the field.

CHRISTIAN ENGELI AND HORST MATZERATH

International Modern History Research*°

"International" may mean a number of different things in the context of urban history research: a transfer of research methods and results to other countries, comparative international studies in individual countries, personalised or institutionalised contacts among historians in two or more countries — for example, at conferences, or joint projects in which historians or institutions in different countries participate. Only when these various aspects are viewed as a whole is it possible to judge whether and to what extent an international urban history research that is more than the sum of national research results, may be spoken of.

A number of interpretative approaches exists whose validity is not limited to national developments. Among them are the Marxist concept of the antagonism between town and country, derived from the development of capitalism, W. Sombart's concept of the town in capitalism, and the distinction drawn by M. Weber between Oriental and Occidental towns. L. Mumford's view of the town as part of the historical process of mankind's development or, conversely, decadence theories such as those of O. Spengler, also possess a global character. The modernisation theory of the 1960s and 1970s (e.g. K. W. Deutsch, D. Lerner) sees the town, and hence urbanisation, as one of the central expressions of a purposive development process such as has occurred in an exemplary way in the industrialised capitalist countries of the West. Modernisation theory is the only one of these approaches to possess a comparative dimension in

* Translated by Ruth Stanley
° Numbers in brackets in this chapter refer to entries in the bibliography on pp. 563–575 of this volume.

the true sense. It uses quantifying models to place the stages of development reached in individual countries in relation to one another so as to measure their degree of modernity.

Several of the concepts dealing with the process of town development also have a general character. Among them may be counted the socio-ecological model of the Chicago School (R. E. Park/ E. W. Burgess), W. Christaller's concept of centrality, location theories such as those advanced by A. Weber and his followers, Sorokin and Zimmermann's concept of a town–country continuum, and H. Hoyt's theory of land values. Many of these theories and concepts were developed in relation to specific cases, then generalised and applied to other cases. However, these global theories, models and concepts have led to comparative international research at most in geography, in sociology and in planning and spatial sciences, but not in the field of urban history. Nevertheless, they form a potential — for comparative urban history research, too — permitting comparative research in the narrower sense to be carried out.

The beginnings of empirical international urban history research may be traced back to the end of the 19th century. As early as 1899, A. F. Weber presented a compilation of statistical material on population development and on important aspects of population structure; on the basis of this material, he also carried out comparative analyses (21). His book was not totally ignored, but the debate was not continued with the same intensity, so that when a second edition of the work was published in the 1960s, it amounted to a rediscovery. In France, E. Levasseur and P. Meuriot had already compiled a similar collection of comparative material on urban development before A. F. Weber did so (17/132). In these early collections of statistical sources, a basic problem inherent in scholarly studies on the town, urban development and the process of urbanisation is already apparent. The problem of the definition of the town and, in the case of collections of statistical material, above all the difficulty of setting significant thresholds for drawing a distinction between town and country.

Thereafter, statisticians, geographers, demographers, sociologists and economists attempted to determine the scope and intensity of the process of urban development. H. Haufe's approach (15) in 1936 was to study the development of the relation between town and country in the 19th and 20th centuries, using processed demographic data. L. Mecking (112), in a work published in 1949, concentrated on the development of large cities, one of the most significant aspects of the modern process of urban development. In addition, in 1959 a list of all the urban conurbations in the world was drawn up, this being one of the more recent phenomena in the worldwide process of urbanisation (23).

Efforts to define the urbanisation process more precisely — at least so far as demographic aspects are concerned — have led to the development, since the 1950s, of numerous data collections on the development of the urban population, covering different periods of time and with differing thresholds. The collection of material edited by R. Mols in the 1950s relates to the 14th to 18th centuries (20); B. R. Mitchell's time series covers the period from 1750 to 1970 (19); P. Flora's data extends from the beginning of the 19th century to the 1960s (13); the data collection compiled by the United Nations in 1969 relates to the period 1920 to the year 2000 (14); a second, published in 1972, covers the period from 1950 to 1970 (22); T. Chandler and G. Fox, in their work, cover a period of 3,000 years (11). These and other collections of statistical data can often be combined only with difficulty, revealing as they do considerable differences with respect both to the definition of the town and to the thresholds set and the way in which the data are aggregated. In this connection, I. D. Löwinger's study on the definition of the town in individual countries has proved helpful (99).

International comparative historical research began relatively late in the field of urban history. Important impulses in this direction can be traced back to the 1960s, above all to conferences with international participation whose results were adopted in many countries. The American O. Handlin (53) and the Englishman H. J. Dyos (45) were figures symbolising this new development; they not only convincingly embodied the new aspiration to write modern urban history in their own work, but also actively encouraged international exchange. International conferences proved during the next 20 years to be the most effective instrument of an international exchange of ideas and experience, and the beginning of international co-operation. This applies to sections on urban history at international historical conferences such as, for example, the one in Stuttgart in 1985. However, international conferences concentrating on special topics of modern urban history research have proved even more fruitful. A fixed venue for such meetings has not yet been established. Some of these conferences have taken place in Paris at the "Maison des Sciences de l'Homme", others in Münster in association with the "Institut für vergleichende Städtegeschichte"

(H. Jäger/54; H. J. Teuteberg/41). One of the most important of these conferences was the Dyos Memorial Conference held in Leicester in 1980, which documented the progress made in research since the first conference in 1966 (D. Fraser and A. Sutcliffe/46). In addition, a number of conferences since the 1970s have brought together representatives of countries in particular areas, for example the conferences of the "Österreichischer Arbeitskreis für Stadtgeschichtsforschung" dealing with Central European towns in the 19th and 20th centuries (W. Rausch/58/59), the 1978 Stockholm Conference on Scandinavia (I. Hammarström and T. Hall/52), that of the English Urban History Group, bringing together urban historians from English-speaking countries, and the conference held in Montreal for Francophone historians. A conference held in Freiburg concentrated, in particular, on Eastern and South-Eastern Europe (M. Glettler, H. Haumann and G. Schramm/50). Mention must also be made of international conferences and co-operation in the context of the Planning History Group. These conferences have dealt with topics ranging from general problems of urbanisation to questions of urban architecture and planning (London, 1977 and 1980), living conditions (*inter alia*, Venice, 1983), economic factors of urban development (Cracow, 1987), planned towns (Lucca, 1977) and colonial towns (Leiden, 1980). In these, as in several other conferences with international participation over the past ten years, "international" generally referred to the fact that those participating came from different countries, and that topics from various countries were discussed; comparative analyses in the strict sense were not elaborated.

It has not only been through such conferences, however, that a transfer of scientific methods and questions has taken place but also through a greater degree of exchange among scholars in different countries. Foundations and institutions in one country enable scholars to carry out research in another, or foreign scholars to visit their country for research purposes. The exchange programmes of individual universities also contribute to this. In a number of cases it has led to methodological approaches being applied to themes or problems of the host country, thus enriching the scholarly discussion there, or, conversely, knowledge and experiences of the host country have proved fruitful to research in another country. This applies, for example, to the studies on the German towns of Cologne and Koblenz carried out by the French historians P. Ayçoberry (186) and E. François (187), as well as to the studies by the Canadian historian W. H. Hubbard (183) on Graz in Austria.

In this way, two particular currents within modern urban history have strongly influenced the scholarly discussion, not only in the countries in which they originated. The first of these is the concept of "New Urban History" that had its origins in a conference held at Yale University, New Haven, in 1968 (S. Thernstrom and R. Sennett/67). The aspiration of writing urban history that is grounded in the social sciences, adopts an interdisciplinary approach, combining theory with historical material, and oriented towards the experiences of ordinary people in their society — all this, presented under an attractive short title, explains the appeal of New Urban History outside the United States, too. In the meantime, the limitations of the concept, which, so far as practical work is concerned, has essentially resulted in studies of mobility, have been subjected to a critical examination precisely in the United States. The French social history school of the "Annales" has also exercised a strong attraction extending beyond the borders of the country.

The undeniable progress made by modern urban history research in recent decades has so far led only to few results in international comparative urban history research. This discussion has been most intense in one specific, though very important area of modern urban development, namely that of the metropolises and the capital cities. In the cosmopolis or metropolis — the discussion has now advanced further, to the megalopolis — are concentrated in a specific way, the problems of national development and problems which also extend beyond the national context. For a long time, this subject was mainly dealt with by geographers; recently, the debate has also been taken up by historians. P. Hall's survey of "world cities" (109) appeared as early as 1966. The most comprehensive treatment of this topic is to be found in a volume edited by A. Sutcliffe presenting the results of a conference held in Brighton in 1980. This volume contrasts the most important examples of modern metropolises and also deals with the image of the metropolis presented in contemporary scholarship and art (119). A further publication compares Berlin, Vienna and Budapest (R. Banik-Schweitzer/102), while Berlin, London, Paris and New York have twice been the subject of comparative studies (K. Schwarz/118; H.-J. Ewers, J. B. Goddard and H. Matzerath/108). The subject of the metropolis overlaps to some extent with that of the capital city, since it is largely the same cities that are the subject of research in both cases. On the other hand, a number of countries have one or two metropolises that are not identical with the capital city; moreover, studies of capital cities tend to concentrate more on political developments. As early as 1971, the French historian P. P. Sagave compared and contrasted the cultural and political development of the German and French capitals (115). In 1980, the Hungarian historian A. Ságvári published an anthology on the capital cities of Europe (116); T. Schnieder and G. Brunn published a work entitled *Hauptstädte in europäischen Nationalstaaten* (117) in 1983, while T. Hall's study on planning in European capitals (144) appeared in 1986.

Study of the overall course of the urbanisation process is beginning to shift from the level of macro-sociological approaches, such as those adopted in the context of research on modernisation theory, to that of historical analysis. Research surveys compiled by leading representatives of urban history and historical geography have contributed fundamentally to the opening up of the field of comparative urban history research (O. Handlin/31; H. J. Dyos/28; E. E. Lampard/35; K. Bosl/74; P. Schöller/37). L. H. Lees and P. Hohenberg, in their work, traced historical development over a very long period of time, from 1000 to 1851. They distinguish between three phases, the last of which being the industrial age (90). They reach the conclusion that there is no fundamental break between the earlier development of towns and that of the industrial age, and that, as a whole, the town system has proved extremely stable. At about the same time, J. de Vries published a work (97) which also treated the whole of Europe (but excluding Russia and South-East Europe). However, this study is confined to a more limited period of time. He distinguishes four sub-systems within Europe (the Mediterranean, the Central European, the North-West European and the East European urban systems), each characterised by different developments. Altogether, J. de Vries ascertains a remarkable degree of continuity in the development of the town system. H. Stoob's studies on the formation of town in the industrial age (100) also show that the urban network was not fundamentally altered by industrialisation. Different emphases result from studies on the development of town sizes (P. Bairoch/124), on urban population growth (H. Matzerath/131) and on internal urban structures; above all the second half of the 19th century is then revealed as a period of particularly intense change.

It becomes apparent that international comparative research has been initiated with respect to the basic problems of the urbanisation process. Besides the question of the structure as a whole, individual aspects of the urbanisation process are also increasingly being studied. Thus, for example, comparisons have been made of different countries, as of Scandinavia (G. Authén Blom/70; Nordisk lokalhistoria/57) and of the overall development in Germany and Japan (H. Matzerath/ K. Ogura/91); comparative studies of suburban development in Sweden and the United States have been made (D. R. Goldfield/98), and of the forms of social-spatial development in Berlin, Vienna and Budapest (R. Banik-Schweitzer/102). The comparative approach has proved especially productive in studies on the attitude to towns and cities, which have established that — regardless of the intensity of the urbanisation process — attitudes to and views on the town have developed very differently (A. Lees/173/174; C. E. Schorske/177). In addition, the image of the town in literature and art in various countries has been subjected to a closer examination in recent decades.

So far as individual aspects of urban history research are concerned, in general only the beginnings of comparative analysis and international co-operation have been made. An exception to this is the history of town planning. There are comprehensive surveys of the development of modern planning (L. Benevolo/135/136) and publications on the history of town planning (F. Choay/140; G. E. Cherry/139; M. Garden/Y. Lequin/143; A. Sutcliffe/150/151/152). In addition, works have been published on the development of ideas and conceptions in town planning (F. Bollerey/137; N. Bullock and J. Read/138; R. Fishman/142; B. Miller Lane/146). And there are publications concentrating on particular aspects of architectural and spatial development, such as a comparison of the suburbs of Leipzig and Prague (K. Czok/141).

A wide range of studies is open to future work in comparative urban history research. Virtually untreated, from the comparative viewpoint, is the field of municipal constitutions and local government, including questions of municipal administration, the role of the mayor and political parties and municipal finances. An interesting aspect of this topic — the local government policies of the European labour movement — was the subject of an international conference in Grignano, near Trieste, in 1983; a different aspect has been studied by J. Havránek in a comparison of electoral behaviour in Vienna and Prague (123). The need to take the structures and conditions of the state and the constitution as a whole into consideration presents an additional difficulty in this field.

A further area for comparative studies is the development of municipal functions, in particular the technical infrastructure. Hence J. P. McKay has studied the development of urban mass transport, trams and omnibuses in Europe (161), while G. Yago has made a comparative study of a specific phase in the development of suburban passenger transport systems in Germany and the United States as well as, more specifically, a comparison of passenger transport in Chicago and Frankfurt (166). J. von Simson has compared water supply and sewage systems in Berlin, London and Paris in the 19th century (148). However, all these are at most the beginnings of a more systematic study of the technical infrastructure. In the whole area of municipal social and health policy, hardly any approaches to comparative research have so far been developed.

In view of the fact that in many countries research on urban social history is relatively far advanced, it must come as a surprise that there are so few comparative studies in this very field. Among the exceptions are works by M. Niehuss (133), who has studied the working population in a German and an Austrian town, and M. Glettler (128), who has studied the emigration of Hungarian Slavs to Pittsburgh, Vienna and Budapest, although more in the context of the history of national minorities than that of urban history. It appears that the specific nature of the materials and methods poses a particular problem for comparative work in this field. The same applies to comparative empirical studies on the economic development of towns; here, too, there have been only few beginnings (P. Bairoch/154).

The approaches towards an institutionalisation of modern urban history are as yet weak. The clearest of them is the "Commission internationale pour l'Histoire des Villes", which was founded in 1955, although it concentrates on medieval and early modern towns. The "Institut für vergleichende Städtegeschichte" in Münster, the "Maison de Sciences de l'Homme" in Paris, and the "Ludwig-Boltzmann-Institut für Stadtgeschichtsforschung" in Linz, have taken on important functions in organising international conferences and creating contacts. The same applies to the English Urban History Group. In addition, in 1983 the German Volkswagenwerk Foundation took the decision to make "The History and Future of European Towns" one of its main fields of sponsorship. The Centre for Urban History, established at Leicester University in 1985, runs joint research projects with urban historians in France, Belgium, the Netherlands and the Federal Republic of Germany. Nevertheless, a strengthening of co-operation in comparative studies in modern urban history would be helped if a firmer institutional grounding for such studies existed. This could be in the framework of the "Commission internationale" through the creation of a permanent working group or through one of the institutions already existing in any country taking on this task.

Comparative research also presupposes the development and extension of the tools of research. A scholarly journal for international comparative urban history research does not exist as yet; the functions it might fulfil in this sphere have so far been assumed mainly by the *Urban History Yearbook* (5). In view of constant advances, especially in the field of modern urban history, bibliographies quickly become out of date. This is the case with older surveys such as those by P. Dawson and S. B. Warner (7) and by E. Pfeil (8). The most important instrument in this field is still the survey edited by P. Wolff in 1977 (10). As to be expected, the most useful bibliographies are those surveying literature on individual aspects, such as A. Sutcliffe's bibliography on planning (9). A bibliography on modern urban history in Scandinavia was published as early as 1960 (6). Other instruments of research, above all collections of source materials, could result from more intense co-operation among scholars. In the field of demography, for example, the existing approaches could be compiled in a manual of comparative historical demography. Similar plans in the field of economic development or social history would appear to be utopian for the time being; they would first require comparative empirical studies, in the course of which the question would have to be clarified as to how far time series could be constructed and to what extent they could be made amenable to international comparison. However, a collection of source materials on the legal bases of municipal constitutions in individual countries would appear both desirable and practicable — for example, on the model of the collection edited by W. Haus and A. Krebsbach and published in 1967, *Gemeindeordnungen in Europa* (16), which documents the law in force.

The state and development of urban history in the individual countries form a central condition of comparative research. This means, first, that urban history must have reached a certain level in order to participate in an international dialogue. It also means that, within each country, tools of research must be elaborated for the local level which will also provide international comparative research with an appropriate basis. This point applies not least to the compilation of national bibliographies, town atlases, and manuals on urban history. The "Commission internationale" has encouraged the compilation of urban history bibliographies and has also drawn up guidelines for the edition on which national town atlasses are to be based.

The plea for more intense co-operation and co-ordination, and the need for efforts in this field to be more firmly institutionalised, must draw on the possibilities offered by existing institutions; it is they which have brought forth the variety of approaches existing today. International comparative research will, to begin with, continue to be concentrated on the European and "Atlantic" area. Within this framework, clear points of emphasis are recognisable, either among countries with a common language (English, French, German), or among countries belonging to a particular region (Scandinavia), or because of historical relations (Austria and her Eastern neighbours). But comparative urban history should also remain open to other contexts; to comparisons with former colonies or with countries of the Third World, and to comparisons with urban development in the Eastern bloc countries. It is true that, at present, these topics are still primarily subjects studied by political scientists, sociologists and geographers but historians will also have to address themselves to these questions.

PART II

Bibliographies

System

A. Urban History Institutions

B. Aids to Research

    (a) – Urban History Journals
    (b) – Bibliographies
    (c) – Handbooks on Urban History
    (d) – Atlases on Urban History and Urban Development
    (e) – Urban History Sources

C. Research Reports

    (a) – General Surveys
    (b) – Surveys of Individual Fields of Urban Research

D. Literature on Individual Areas of Urban History Research

    (a) – Concept and Definition of Town and Town Types
    (b) – Politics, Law and Statutes
    (c) – Population and Social Structure
    (d) – Town Planning, Housing
    (e) – Economy and Transport
    (f) – Arts and Sciences, Churches

E. Local Studies (a representative selection)

RENATE BANIK-SCHWEITZER AND GERHARD MEIßL

Austria

A. Urban History Institutions

Kommission für Wirtschafts-, Sozial- und Stadtgeschichte der Österreichischen Akademie der Wissenschaften, founded in 1961, based in Vienna.

Ludwig Boltzmann Institut für Stadtgeschichtsforschung (formerly "Forschungsstelle für Stadtgeschichtsforschung", founded in 1975; based in Linz), founded in 1976, based in Linz; subsidiary (city atlases) founded in 1977, based in Vienna.

Österreichischer Arbeitskreis für Stadtgeschichtsforschung, founded in 1969, based in Linz.

B. Aids to Research

(a)   Urban History Journals

1. *Pro Civitate Austriae*, 1985 ff., ed. W. Rausch, Linz, published biannually.
2. *Historisches Jahrbuch der Stadt Graz*, 1968 ff., pub. by Magistrat der Landeshauptstadt Graz.
3. *Historisches Jahrbuch der Stadt Linz*, 1955 ff., pub. by Stadt Linz.
4. *Forschungen und Beiträge zur Wiener Stadtgeschichte*, 1978 ff., ed. F. Czeike.
5. *Jahrbuch des Vereins für die Geschichte der Stadt Wien*, 1939 ff., ed. P. Csendes.
6. *Wiener Geschichtsblätter*, 1946 ff., ed. F. Czeike; published quarterly.
7. *Wiener Schriften*, 1955 ff., pub. by Amt für Kultur und Volksbildung der Stadt Wien.

(b)   Bibliographies (a selection)

8. *Bibliographie zur Geschichte der Städte Österreichs*, ed. W. Rausch, Linz, 1984.
9. *Durdik, Ch.*, Bibliographischer Abriß zur Bevölkerungs- und Sozialstatistik der Habsburgmonarchie im 19. Jahrhundert, Vienna, 1975.

10. *Gugitz, G.*, Bibliographie zur Geschichte und Stadtkunde von Wien (including sources and notes on secondary literature), Vols. 1–5, Vienna, 1947–1962.

11. *Katzinger, W.*, Österreichische Städtebibliographie 1970–1983, Linz, 1978 ff. (continued annually).

12. *Schweitzer, R.*, Österreichische Bibliographie für Städtebau und Raumplanung 1850–1918, Vienna, 1971 (Series of the Institut für Städtebau, Raumplanung und Raumordnung at the Technische Hochschule Wien, Vol. 17).

(c)   Handbooks on Urban History (a selection)

13. *Österreichisches Städtebuch*, ed. A. Hoffmann, Vol. 1: Die Städte *Oberösterreichs*, Vienna, 1968; Vol. 2: Die Städte des *Burgenlandes*, Vienna, 1970; Vol. 3: Die Städte *Vorarlbergs*, Vienna, 1973; Vol. 4: Die Städte *Niederösterreichs*, 2 vols., Vienna, 1976 and 1982; Vol. 5: Die Städte *Tirols*, Part 1, Vienna, 1980.

(d)   Atlases on Urban History and Urban Development

14. *Historischer Atlas von Wien*, 1st–3rd issues, Vienna, 1981–1987.

15. *Atlas von Niederösterreich*, Vienna, 1951–1958.

16. *Atlas der Republik Österreich*, ed. H. Bobek, 1st–6th issues Vienna, 1961–1980.

17. *Atlas der historischen Schutzzonen in Österreich.* 1. Städte und Märkte, published by Bundesdenkmalamt, Graz, 1970.

18. *Klaar, A.*, Baualterpläne österreichischer Städte, 1st–4th issues Vienna, 1972–1979.

19. *Österreichischer Städteatlas*, 1st–3rd issues Vienna, 1982–1988.

(e)   Urban History Sources

—

C.   Research Reports

(a)   General Surveys

20. *Baltzarek, F.*, Regional- und Stadtgeschichte im Spannungsfeld zwischen traditioneller historischer Landeskunde und Sozial- und Wirtschaftswissenschaften, in Jahrbuch des Vereins für die Geschichte der Stadt Wien, Year 34 (1978), pp. 438–459.

21. *Hanisch, E.*, Regionale Zeitgeschichte. Einige theoretische und methodologische Überlegungen, in Zeitgeschichte, Year 7 (1979/80), pp. 39–60.

22. *Meißl, G.*, Moderne Stadtgeschichte in Österreich: Zur Forschungssituation in den 1980er Jahren, in Zeitgeschichte, Year 14 (1986/87), pp. 89–97.

(b) Surveys of Individual Fields of Urban Research

23. *Die Städte Mitteleuropas im 19. Jahrhundert*, ed. W. Rausch, Linz, 1983 (Beiträge zur Geschichte der Städte Mitteleuropas, Vol. VII).
24. *Die Städte Mitteleuropas im 20. Jahrhundert*, ed. W. Rausch, Linz, 1984 (Beiträge zur Geschichte der Städte Mitteleuropas, Vol. VIII).

D. Literature on Individual Areas of Urban History Research

(a) Concept and Definition of Town and Town Types

—

(b) Politics, Law and Statutes

● Communal Statutes and Administration

25. *Botz, G.*, Wohnungspolitik und Judendeportation in Wien 1938–1945. Zur Funktion des Antisemitismus als Ersatz nationalsozialistischer Kommunalpolitik, Vienna and Salzburg, 1975 (Veröffentlichungen des Historischen Instituts der Universität Salzburg, Vol. 13).
26. *Czeike, F.*, Liberale, christlichsoziale und sozialdemokratische Kommunalpolitik (1861–1934). Dargestellt am Beispiel der Gemeinde Wien, Vienna, 1962.
27. *Czeike, F.*, Wirtschafts- und Sozialpolitik der Gemeinde Wien 1919–1934. 2 vols. Vienna, 1958/59 (Wiener Schriften Vols. 6 and 11).
28. *Ebert, K.*, Die Anfänge der modernen Sozialpolitik in Österreich. Die Taaffesche Sozialgesetzgebung für die Arbeiter im Rahmen der Gewerbeordnungsreform (1879–1885), Vienna, 1975.
29. *Feldbauer, P.*, Kinderelend in Wien. Von der Armenpflege zur Jugendfürsorge, Vienna, 1980.
30. *Hubbard, W. H.*, Die Entwicklung der Grazer Stadtverfassung 1869–1918, in Historisches Jahrbuch der Stadt Graz, Year 4 (1971), pp. 7–46.
31. *Klabouch, J.*, Die Gemeindeselbstverwaltung in Österreich 1848–1918, Vienna, 1968.

32. *Stekl, H.,* Österreichs Zucht- und Arbeitshäuser 1671–1920. Institutionen zwischen Fürsorge und Strafvollzug, Vienna, 1978 (Sozial- und wirtschaftshistorische Studien Vol. 12).

33. *Talos, E.,* Staatliche Sozialpolitik in Österreich. Rekonstruktion und Analyse, Vienna, 1981.

34. *Walter, F.,* Österreichische Verfassungs- und Verwaltungsgeschichte von 1500 bis 1955, Vienna, Cologne and Graz, 1972.

● Communal Politics

35. *Botz, G.,* Wien vom "Anschluß" zum Krieg. Nationalsozialistische Machtübernahme und politisch-soziale Umgestaltung am Beispiel der Stadt Wien 1938/39, Vienna and Munich, 1978.

36. *Botz, G., G. Brandstetter* and *M. Pollak,* Im Schatten der Arbeiterbewegung. Zur Geschichte des Anarchismus in Österreich und Deutschland, Vienna, 1977.

37. *Botz, G., et al.,* eds., Bewegung und Klasse. Studien zur österreichischen Arbeitergeschichte, Vienna, Munich and Zurich, 1978.

38. *Boyer, J. W.,* Political Radicalism in Late Imperial Vienna. Origins of the Christian Social Movement 1848–1897, Chicago and London, 1981.

39. *Boyer, J. W.,* Veränderungen im politischer. Leben Wiens. Die Großstadt Wien, der Radikalismus der Beamten und die Wahlen von 1891, in Jahrbuch des Vereins für die Geschichte der Stadt Wien, Year 36 (1980), pp. 95–173 and Year 37 (1981), pp. 117–176.

40. *Czeike, F.,* Wien und seine Bürgermeister. Sieben Jahrhunderte Wiener Stadtgeschichte, Vienna, 1974.

41. *Flanner, K.,* Wiener Neustadt im Ständestaat. Arbeiteropposition 1933–1938, Vienna, 1983 (Materialien zur Arbeiterbewegung, Vol. 31).

42. *Gerlich, P.,* and *H. Kramer,* Abgeordnete in der Parteiendemokratie. Eine empirische Untersuchung des Wiener Gemeinderates und Landtages, Vienna, 1969.

43. *Grüll, G.,* Das Linzer Bürgermeisterbuch, Linz, 1959.

44. *Gulick, C. A.,* Österreich von Habsburg zu Hitler, 5 vols., Vienna, 1950.

45. *Hahnkamper, G. M.,* Der Wiener Gemeinderat zwischen 1861 und 1864, phil. Diss., Vienna, 1973.

46. *Hausner, E.,* Die Tätigkeit des Wiener Gemeinderates in den Jahren 1884–1888, phil. Diss., Vienna, 1974.

47. *Hautmann, H.,* and *R. Kropf,* Die österreichische Arbeiterbewegung vom Vormärz bis 1945. Sozialökonomische Ursprünge ihrer Ideologie und Politik, 2nd ed., Vienna, 1976 (Schriftenreihe des Ludwig Boltzmann Instituts für Geschichte der Arbeiterbewegung, Vol. 4).

48. *Hawlik, J.,* Die politischen Parteien Deutschösterreichs bei der Wahl zur konstituierenden Nationalversammlung 1919, phil. Diss., Vienna, 1971.

49. *Holleis, E.*, Die Sozialpolitische Partei. Sozialliberale Bestrebungen in Wien um 1900, Vienna, 1978.

50. *Knoll, R.*, Zur Tradition der christlichsozialen Partei Ihre Früh- und Entwicklungsgeschichte bis zu den Reichsratswahlen 1907, Vienna, Cologne and Graz, 1973 (Studien zur Geschichte der österreichisch-ungarischen Monarchie, Vol. 13).

51. *Kulemann, P.*, Am Beispiel des Austromarxismus. Sozialdemokratische Arbeiterbewegung in Österreich von Hainfeld bis zur Dollfuß-Diktatur, Hamburg, 1979.

52. *Maderthaner, W.*, Kommunalpolitik im Roten Wien. Ein Literaturbericht, in Archiv für Sozialgeschichte, Year 25 (1985), pp. 239–250.

53. *Patzer, F.*, Der Wiener Gemeinderat 1918–1934. Ein Beitrag zur Geschichte der Stadt Wien und ihrer Volksvertretung, Vienna, 1961 (Wiener Schriften, Vol. 15).

54. *Pelinka, A.*, Stand oder Klasse? Die christliche Arbeiterbewegung Österreichs 1933 bis 1938, Vienna, 1972.

55. *Rabinbach, A.*, The Crisis of Austrian Socialism. From Red Vienna to Civil War 1927–1934, Chicago and London, 1983.

56. *Schobesberger, H., and F. Mayrhofer*, Geschichte der Linzer Arbeiter-Turn- und Sportbewegung (1903–1934), in Historisches Jahrbuch der Stadt Linz, 1977, pp. 233–346.

57. *Seibert, F.*, Die Konsumgenossenschaften in Österreich (Materialien zur Arbeiterbewegung 11), Vienna, 1978.

58. *Seliger, M.*, Sozialdemokratie und Kommunalpolitik in Wien. Zu einigen Aspekten sozialdemokratischer Politik in der Vorrund Zwischenkriegzeit, Vienna, 1980 (Wiener Schriften, Vol. 49).

59. *Seliger, M., and K. Ucakar*, Wahlrecht und Wählerverhalten in Wien 1848–1932. Privilegien, Partizipationsdruck und Sozialstruktur, Vienna, 1984 (Kommentare zum Historsichen Atlas von Wien, Vol. 3).

60. *Seliger, M., and K. Ucakar*, Wien. Politische Geschichte 1740–1934. Entwicklung und Bestimmungskräfte großstädtischer Politik, 2 vols., Vienna, 1985.

61. *Staudinger, A.*, Christlichsoziale Partei, in E. Weinzierl and K. Skalnik. Österreich 1918–1938. Geschichte der Ersten Republik, Vol. 1, Graz, Vienna and Cologne 1983, pp. 249–276.

62. *Talos, E., and W. Neugebauer*, eds., "Austrofaschismus". Beiträge über Politik, Ökonomie und Kultur 1934–1938, Vienna, 1984.

63. *Tweraser, K.*, Der Linzer Gemeinderat 1880–1914. Glanz und Elend bürgerlicher Herrschaft, in Historisches Jahrbuch der Stadt Linz, 1979, pp. 293–241.

64. *Tweraser, K.*, Der Linzer Gemeinderat 1914–1934. Krise der parlamentarischen Demokratie, in Historisches Jahrbuch der Stadt Linz 1980, pp. 199–274.

65. *Wien in der liberalen Ära*, Vienna, 1978 (Forschungen und Beiträge zur Wiener Stadtgeschichte, Vol. 1).

66. *Wien 1938*, Vienna, 1978 (Forschungen und Beiträge zur Wiener Stadtgeschichte, Vol. 2).

67. *Wien im Vormärz*, Vienna, 1980 (Forschungen und Beiträge zur Wiener Stadtgeschichte, Vol. 8).

68. *Zoitl, H.*, Kampf um Gleichberechtigung. Die sozialdemokratische Studentenbewegung in Wien 1914–1925, phil. Diss., Salzburg, 1977.

(c) Population and Social Structure

● Population

69. *Baltzarek, F.*, Das territoriale und bevölkerungsmäßige Wachstum der Großstadt Wien im 17., 18. und 19. Jahrhundert. Mit Beobachtungen zur Entwicklung der Wiener Vorstädte und Vororte, in Wiener Geschichtsblätter, Year 35 (1980), pp. 1–30.

70. *Ehmer, J.*, Familie und Klasse. Zur Entstehung der Arbeiterfamilie in Wien, in M. Mitterauer and R. Sieder, eds., Historische Familienforschung, Frankfurt/M., 1982, pp. 300–325.

71. *Ehmer, J.*, Familienstruktur und Arbeitsorganisation im frühindustriellen Wien, Vienna, 1980 (Sozial- und wirtschaftshistorische Studien, Vol. 13).

72. *Ehmer, J., H. Hold and B. Leuchtenmüller*, Demographische Daten für Wien, Vienna, 1976 (unpublished).

73. *Faßmann, H.*, Zur Altersverteilung und Zuwanderungsstruktur der Wiener Bevölkerung um die Mitte des 19. Jahrhunderts, in Wiener Geschichtsblätter, Year 35 (1980), pp. 124–149.

74. *Gisser, R.*, Konzentration und Relokation der Bevölkerung Österreichs auf Hauptregions- und Bezirksebene, in Sozialwissenschaften in der Stadtplanung, Vienna, 1976, pp. 51–53 (Der Aufbau, Vol. 5).

75. *Helczmanovszki, H.*, ed., Beiträge zur Bevölkerungs- und Sozialgeschichte Österreichs, Vienna, 1973.

76. *Hubbard, W. H.*, Städtische Haushaltsstruktur um die Mitte des 19. Jahrhunderts (Graz), in W. H. Schröder, ed., Moderne Stadtgeschichte, Stuttgart, 1979, pp. 198–216 (Historisch-Sozialwissenschaftliche Forschungen, Vol. 8).

77. *Kössler, M.*, Die Innsbrucker Bevölkerung von 1851–1950, unter besonderer Berücksichtigung der Zuwanderung von 1901–1931, phil. Diss., Innsbruck, 1955.

78. *Mitterauer, M.*, Auswirkungen von Urbanisierung und Frühindustrialisierung auf die Familienverfassung an Beispielen des österreichischen Raumes, in W. Conze, ed., Sozialgeschichte der Familie in der Neuzeit Europas, Stuttgart, 1976, pp. 53–145.

79. *Otruba, G.,* and *L. S. Rutschka,* Die Herkunft der Wiener Bevölkerung in den letzten hundertfünfzig Jahren, in Jahrbuch des Vereins für die Geschichte der Stadt Wien, Year 13 (1958), pp. 227–274.

80. *Pirhofer, G.,* and *R. Sieder,* Zur Konstitution der Arbeiterfamilie im Roten Wien: Familienpolitik, Kulturreform, Alltag und Ästhetik, in M. Mitterauer and R. Sieder, eds., Historische Familienforschung, Frankfurt/M., 1982, pp. 326–368.

● Social Structure

81. *Alltag in Wien seit 1948.* Katalog zur Sonderausstellung des österreichischen Gesellschafts- und Wirtschaftsmuseums, Vienna, 1979.

82. *Banik-Schweitzer, R., et al.,* Zeit der Metropolen. Berlin – Wien – Budapest 1850–1914, in Beiträge zur historischen Sozialunde, year 16(1986), p. 1–30.

83. *Bevölkerungsstruktur und religiöse Praxis in Eisenstadt,* Vienna, 1968.

84. *Bolognese-Leuchtenmüller, B.,* Bevölkerungsentwicklung und Berufsstruktur. Gesundheits- und Fürsorgewesen in Österreich 1750–1918, Vienna, 1978 (Materialien zur Wirtschafts- und Sozialgeschichte, Vol. 1).

85. *Botz, G.,* and *J. Weidenholzer,* eds., Mündliche Geschichte und Arbeiterbewegung. Eine Einführung in Arbeitsweise und Themenbereiche der Geschichte "geschichtsloser" Sozialgruppen, Vienna, Graz and Cologne, 1983 (Materialien zur Historischen Sozialwissenschaft, Vol. 2).

86. *Brousek, K. M.,* Die Wiener Tschechen zwischen den beiden Weltkriegen, unter besonderer Berücksichtigung des Turnvereins "Sokol", phil. Diss., Vienna, 1977.

87. *Brunner, O.,* Neue Wege der Verfassungs- und Sozialgeschichte, 2nd ed., Göttingen, 1968.

88. *Bunzl, J.,* Arbeiterbewegung, "Judenfrage" und Antisemitismus. Am Beispiel des Wiener Bezirks Leopoldstadt, in G. Botz *et al.,* eds., Bewegung und Klasse, Vienna, 1978, pp. 743–764.

89. *Bunzl, J.,* and *B. Marin,* Antisemitismus in Österreich. Sozialhistorische und soziologische Studien, Innsbruck, 1983 (Vergleichende Gesellschaftsgeschichte und politische Ideengeschichte der Neuzeit, Vol. 3).

90. *Czeike, F.,* and *W. Lugsch,* Studien zur Sozialgeschichte von Ottakring und Hernals, Vienna, 1955 (Wiener Schriften, Vol. 2).

91. *Ehalt, H. C.,* ed., Geschichte von unten. Fragestellungen, Methoden und Projekte einer Geschichte des Alltags, Vienna, Cologne and Graz, 1984 (Kulturstudien, Vol. 1).

92. *Ehalt, H. C., G. Heiß* and *H. Stekl,* eds., Glücklich ist, wer vergißt . . . ? Das andere Wien um 1900, Vienna, 1986 (Kulturstudien, Vol. 6).

93. *Ehalt, H. C., U. Knittler-Lux* and *H. Konrad,* eds., Geschichtswerkstatt –

Stadtteilarbeit – Aktionsforschung, Vienna, 1984.

94. *Ehmer, J.*, Rote Fahnen – Blauer Montag. Soziale Bedingungen von Aktions- und Organisationsformen der frühen Wiener Arbeiterbewegung, in D. Puls, ed., Wahrnehmungsformen und Protestverhalten. Studien zur Lage der Unterschichten im 18. und 19. Jahrhundert, Frankfurt/M. 1979, pp. 143–174.

95. *Ehmer, J.*, Frauenarbeit und Arbeiterfamilie in Wien. Vom Vormärz bis 1934, in H. -U. Wehler, ed., Frauen in der Geschichte des 19. und 20. Jahrhunderts. Geschichte und Gesellschaft, Year 7 (1981), No. 3/4, pp. 438–473.

96. *Ehmer, J.*, Vaterlandslose Gesellen und respektable Familienväter. Entwicklungsformen der Arbeiterfamilie im internationalen Vergleich 1850–1930, in H. Konrad, ed., Die deutsche und die österreichische Arbeiterbewegung zur Zeit der Zweiten Internationale. Protokoll des bilateralen Symposiums DDR-Österreich 1981 in Linz, Vienna, 1982, pp. 109–153 (Materialien zur Arbeiterbewegung, Vol. 24).

97. *Ehmer, J.*, Schuster zwischen Handwerk und Fabrik. Zum Verhältnis von sozialem Profil und politisch-organisatorischem Verhalten einer Berufsgruppe, in H. Konrad and W. Maderthaner, eds., Neuere Studien zur Arbeitergeschichte, Vol. 1: Beiträge zur Wirtschafts- und Sozialgeschichte, Vienna, 1984, pp. 3–23 (Materialien zur Arbeiterbewegung, Vol. 35).

98. *Faßmann, H.*, Die Struktur der Arbeitskräfte im historischen Wandel. Ein sektoraler Vergleich Wien 1857–1971, in M. Haller and W. Müller, eds., Beschäftigungssystem im gesellschaftlichen Wandel, Frankfurt and New York, 1983, pp. 76–96.

99. *Fellner, G.*, Antisemitismus in Salzburg 1918–1938, Vienna and Salzburg, 1979 (Veröffentlichungen des Historischen Instituts der Universität Salzburg, Vol. 15).

100. *Fielhauer, H.*, and *O. Bockhorn*, eds., Die andere Kultur. Volkskunde, Sozialwissenschaften und Arbeiterkultur. Ein Tagungsbericht, Vienna, 1982.

101. *Fritzl, H.*, Materialien zur Fabriksgesellschaft. Über Arbeitsteilung, Arbeitsorganisation und produktionstechnologische Veränderungen in der österreichischen Elektroindustrie von 1880 bis 1914, grund- und integrativwiss. Diss., Vienna, 1979.

102. *Glaser, A.*, Die Arbeits- und Lebenssituation der Arbeiterfrau, Vienna, 1975.

103. *Glettler, M.*, Die Wiener Tschechen um 1900, Munich and Vienna, 1972.

104. *Hahn, S.*, Fabrikordnung. Zu den Bedingungen industrieller Arbeit und berufsspezifischen Bewußtseins. Am Beispiel der Wiener Neustädter Lokomotivfabrik und der Daimler-Motoren-Gesellschaft 1890–1914, phil. Diss., Vienna, 1984.

105. *Hann, M.*, Die Unterschichten Wiens im Vormärz. Soziale Kategorien im Umbruch von der ständischen zur Industriegesellschaft, phil. Diss., Vienna, 1984.

106. *Häusler, W.*, Von der Massenarmut zur Arbeiterbewegung. Demokratie und soziale Frage in der Wiener Revolution von 1848, Vienna and Munich, 1979.

107. *Himmel, M.*, Die Italiener in Wien 1815–1848. Studien zu ihrer Sozialstruktur, phil. Diss., Vienna, 1972.

108. *Hruschka, H.*, Die Geschichte der Juden in Krems an der Donau von den Anfängen bis 1938, geisteswiss. Diss., Vienna, 1979.

109. *Hubbard, W. H.*, Binnenwanderung und berufliche Mobilität in Graz um die Mitte des 19. Jahrhunderts, in H. J. Teuteberg, ed., Urbanisierung im 19. und 20. Jahrhundert. Historische und geographische Aspekte, Cologne and Vienna, 1983, pp. 117–129 (Städteforschung, Vol. A 16).

110. *Hubbard, W. H.*, Auf dem Weg zur Großstadt. Eine Sozialgeschichte der Stadt Graz 1850–1914, Vienna, 1984 (Sozial- und wirtschaftshistorische Schriften, vol. 14).

111. *Internationale Tagung der Historiker der Arbeiterbewegung* – Sonderkonferenz Arbeiterkultur in Österreich 1918–1945, 1981 (ITH-Tagungsbericht, Vol. 16).

112. *Knittler, H.*, Abriß einer Wirtschafts- und Sozialgeschichte der Doppelstadt Krems-Stein, in Ausstellung 1000 Jahre Kunst in Krems, Krems, 1971, pp. 43–73.

113. *Konkolik, S. E.*, Studien zur Geschichte der Wiener aus den Ländern der böhmischen Krone in der ersten Hälfte des 19. Jahrhunderts, phil. Diss., Vienna, 1972.

114. *Kopecky, G.*, Frauenarbeit in der Zwischenkriegszeit, phil. Diss., Vienna, 1980.

115. *Kulturjahrbuch.* Wiener Beiträge zur Kulturwissenschaft und Kulturpolitik, ed. O. Bockhorn *et al.*, Vienna, 1982 ff.

116. *Langewiesche, D.*, Zur Freizeit des Arbeiters. Bildungsbestrebungen und Freizeitgestaltung österreichischer Arbeiter im Kaiserreich und in der Ersten Republik, Stuttgart, 1980.

117. *Lausecker, S.*, Vor- und frühindustrielle Produktionsformen am Beispiel der Seiden- und Baumwollindustrie in Wien und Niederösterreich (1740–1848), phil. Diss., Vienna, 1975.

118. *Löw, A.*, Die soziale Zusammensetzung der Wiener Juden nach den Trauungs- und Geburtsmatrikeln, 1784–1848, phil. Diss., Vienna, 1951.

119. *Maimann, H.*, ed., Mit uns zieht die neue Zeit. Arbeiterkultur in Österreich 1918–1934, Vienna, 1981.

120. *Meißl, G.*, Industriearbeit in Wien 1870–1913. Die zeitgenössische Industriestatistik als Quelle für die Analyse industriebetrieblicher

Standortentwicklung und Arbeitsorganisation, in Jahrbuch des vereins für die Geschichte der Stadt Wien, Year 36 (1980), pp. 174–229.

121. *Meißl, G.*, Minutenpolitik. Die Anfänge der "Wissenschaftlichen Betriebsführung" am Beispiel der Wiener Elektroindustrie vor dem Ersten Weltkrieg, in H. Konrad and W. Maderthaner, eds., Neuere Studien zur Arbeitergeschichte Vol. 1: Beiträge zur Wirtschafts- und Sozialgeschichte, Vienna, 1984, pp. 41–100 (Materialien zur Arbeiterbewegung, Vol. 35).

122. *Mesch, M.*, Arbeiterexistenz in der Spätgründerzeit. Gewerkschaften und Lohnentwicklung in Österreich 1890–1914, Vienna, 1984 (Materialien zur Arbeiterbewegung, Vol. 33).

123. *Möller, J. P. H.*, Wandel der Berufsstruktur in Österreich zwischen 1869 und 1961. Versuch einer Darstellung wirtschaftssektoraler Entwicklungstendenzen anhand berufstatistischer Aufzeichnungen, Vienna, 1974 (Dissertationen der Johannes-Kepler-Hochschule Linz, Vol. 2).

124. *Niehuss, M.*, Arbeiterschaft in Krieg und Inflation. Soziale Schichtung und Lage der Arbeiter in Augsburg und Linz 1910 bis 1925, Berlin and New York, 1985 (Veröffentlichungen der Historischen Kommission zu Berlin, Vol. 59).

125. *Olexinski, H.*, Die Geschichte der Armen- und Krankenpflege in Kärnten, unter besonderer Berücksichtigung der Klagenfurter Versorgungsanstalten, phil. Diss., Vienna, 1969.

126. *Papp, M.*, Wiener Arbeiterhaushalte um 1900. Studien zur Kultur und Lebensweise im privaten Reproduktionsbereich, phil. Diss., Vienna, 1980.

127. *Pfeisinger, G.*, Die Revolution von 1848 in Graz, Vienna, 1986 (Materialien zur Arbeiterbewegung, Vol. 42).

128. *Rozenblit, M. L.*, The Jews of Vienna 1867–1914. Assimilation and Identity, Albany, N. Y., 1983.

129. *Sablik, K.*, Julius Tandler. Mediziner und Sozialreformer, Vienna, 1983.

130. *Sandgruber, R.*, Die Anfänge der Konsumgesellschaft. Konsumgüterverbrauch, Lebensstandard und Alltagskultur in Österreich im 18. und 19. Jahrhundert, Vienna, 1982 (Sozial- und wirtschaftshistorische Studien, Vol. 15).

131. *Salzer-Eibenstein, G. W.*, Die Geschichte der Grazer Juden von ihren Anfängen bis Anfang des 20. Jahrhunderts, Graz, 1970.

132. *Scheuch, M.*, Die wirtschaftliche und soziale Lage der Industriearbeiter und die Entwicklung der Arbeiterbewegung in Vorarlberg von den Anfängen bis 1918, phil. Diss., Vienna, 1960.

133. *Steiner, H.*, Die Arbeiterbewegung Österreichs 1867 bis 1889. Beiträge zu ihrer Geschichte von der Gründung des Wiener Arbeiterbildungsvereines bis zum Einigungsparteitag in Hainfeld, Vienna, 1964.

134. *Stekl, H.*, Österreichs Aristokratie im Vormärz. Herrschaftsstil und Lebensformen der Fürstenhäuser Liechtenstein und Schwarzenberg, Vienna, 1973 (Sozial- und wirtschaftshistorische Studien, Vol. 2).

135. *Ströbel, B.*, Die Ernährung der Unterschichten in Wien im Zeitraum 1820 bis 1870, geisteswiss. Diss., Vienna, 1979.

136. *Suppan, A.*, Die österreichischen Volksgruppen. Tendenzen ihrer gesellschaftlichen Entwicklung im 20. Jahrhundert, Vienna, 1983.

137. *Tichy, M.*, Alltag und Traum. Leben und Lektüre der Wiener Dienstmädchen um die Jahrhundertwende, Vienna, Cologne and Graz, 1984 (Kulturstudien, Vol. 3).

138. *Wilder, F.*, Allgemeine und jüdische Emigration nach dem Zweiten Weltkrieg, mit Berücksichtigung der Juden Wiens, phil. Diss., Vienna, 1977.

139. *Zupfer, W.*, Zum kulturellen Wandel der Wiener Vororte Währing, Weinhaus, Gersthof und Pötzleinsdorf im neunzehnten Jahrhundert. Volkskundliche Beiträge zu einer Theorie der Urbanisierung, phil. Diss., Vienna, 1971.

(d) Town Planning and Housing

● Town Planning, Urban Architecture

140. *Achleitner, F.*, Österreichische Architektur im 20. Jahrhundert, Salzburg and Vienna, 1983.

141. *Doblhamer, G.*, Die Stadtplanung in Oberösterreich von 1850 bis 1938, Vienna, 1972 (Schriftenreihe des Instituts für Städtebau, Raumplanung und Raumordnung an der Technischen Hochschule Wien, Vol. 18).

142. *Fischer, F.*, Die Grünflächenpolitik Wiens bis zum Ende des Ersten Weltkrieges, Vienna, 1971 (Schriftenreihe des Instituts für Städtebau, Raumplanung und Raumordnung an der Technischen Hochschule Wien, Vol. 15).

143. *Haiko, P.*, Wiener Arbeiterwohnhäuser 1848–1934, in Kritische Berichte ANABAS, Year 5 (1977), No. 4/5, pp. 26–50.

144. *Haiko, P.* and *M. Reissberger*, Die Wohnhausbauten der Gemeinde Wien 1919–1934, in Archithese, 1974, No. 12, p. 49 ff.

145. *Haiko, P.* and *H. Stekl*, Architektur in der industriellen Gesellschaft, in H. Stekl, ed., Architektur und Gesellschaft von der Antike bis zur Gegenwart, Salzburg, 1980, pp. 251–341 (Geschichte und Sozialkunde, Vol. 6).

146. *Kapner, G.*, Architektur als Psychotherapie. Über die Rezeption von Stadtbildern in Romanen des 20. Jahrhunderts, Cologne and Vienna, 1984.

147. *Koepf, H.*, Stadtbaukunst in Innsbruck (1976); Krems-Stein (1975); Linz

(1975); Salzburg (1975); Niederösterreich (1977); Oberösterreich (1972); Steiermark und Kärnten (1974); Österreich (1972).

148. *Mayer, W.*, Gebietsänderungen im Raume Wien 1850–1910 und die Debatten um das Entstehen eines Generalregulierungsplanes von Wien, phil. Diss., Vienna, 1973.

149. *Pötschner, P.*, ed., Wiener Geschichtsbücher, Vol. 1–18, Vienna and Hamburg, 1970–1976.

150. *Posch, W.*, Lebensraum Wien. Die Beziehungen zwischen Politik und Stadtplanung 1918–1954, techn. Diss., Graz, 1976.

151. *Redl, L.*, and *H. Wösendorfer*, Die Donauinsel. Ein Beispiel politischer Planung in Wien, Vienna, 1980.

152. *Roth, P. W.*, Grazer Industriedenkmäler, Graz, 1978.

153. *Steinböck, W.*, Wien und Berlin in der Architektur des Klassizismus. Untersuchung über stilgeschichtliche und geistesgeschichtliche Voraussetzungen der Monumentalarchitektur Berlins und Wiens in der Zeit von 1780 und 1830, phil. Diss., Graz, 1960.

154. *Sterk, H.*, Industriekultur in Österreich. Der Wandel in Architektur, Kunst und Gesellschaft im Fabrikszeitalter, Vol. 1: 1750–1873, Vienna, 1984; Vol. 2: 1873–1918, Vienna, 1985; Vol. 3: 1918–1938, Vienna, 1986.

155. *Stokreiter, F.*, Die Entwicklung der Stadtplanung in Niederösterreich von der Mitte des 19. Jahrhunderts bis 1938, techn. Diss., Vienna, 1974.

156. *Wagner-Rieger, R.*, Wiens Architektur im 19. Jahrhundert, Vienna, 1970.

157. *Wagner-Rieger, R.*, ed., Die Wiener Ringstraße – Bild einer Epoche. Vols. I, VI, Graz and Cologne 1969/70; Vols. II–V, VII–XI, Wiesbaden, 1972–1980.

158. *Waissenberger, R.*, Wiener Nutzbauten des 19. Jahrhunderts als Beispiele zukunftsweisenden Bauens, Vienna and Munich, 1977 (Wiener Schriften, Vol. 38).

159. *Wehdorn, M.* and *U. Georgeacopol-Winischhofer*, Baudenkmäler der Technik und Industrie in Österreich., Vol. 1: Wien, Niederösterreich, Burgenland, Cologne and Vienna, 1984.

160. *Werkner, P.*, Villenarchitektur der Gründerzeit in Innsbruck, geisteswiss. Diss., Innsbruck, 1978.

● Settlement Development

161. *Backé, B.*, Die sozialräumliche Differenzierung in Floridsdorf, Vienna, 1968 (Dissertationen der Universität Wien, Vol. 9).

162. *Banik-Schweitzer, R.*, Zur sozialräumlichen Gliederung Wiens 1869–1934, Vienna, 1982 (Schriftenreihe des Instituts für Stadtforschung, Vol. 63).

163. *Bauer, H.*, Entwicklung der Infrastruktur Wiens 1891–1938, Vienna,

1974.

164. *Bobek, H.* and *E. Lichtenberger,* Wien. Bauliche Gestalt und Entwicklung seit der Mitte des 19. Jahrhunderts, Vienna and Cologne, 1966.

165. *Bodzenta, E.,* Meidling 1797–1890. Sein Wandel vom Dorf zum Großstadtbezirk, phil. Diss., Vienna, 1952.

166. *Deák, E.,* Das Städtewesen der Länder der ungarischen Krone (1780–1918). Part I: Allgemeine Bestimmung der Städte und der städtischen Siedlungen, Vienna, 1979.

167. *Deutsch, Ch.,* Beiträge zur Wirtschafts- und Sozialgeschichte der ehemaligen Wiener Vorstadt Margareten 1680–1829, phil. Diss., Vienna, 1969.

168. *Dimitriou, S.,* Stadterweiterungen von Graz. Gründerzeit (1854–1914), Graz and Vienna, 1979 (Publikationsreihe des Grazer Stadtmuseums Vol. 2).

169. *Franz, K.,* Die Innsbrucker Altstadt, naturwiss. Diss., Innsbruck, 1977.

170. *Gisser, R.,* Ökologische Segregation der Berufsschichten in Großstädten, in L. Rosenmayr and S. Höllinger, eds., Soziologie. Forschung in Österreich, Vienna, Cologne and Graz, 1969, pp. 199–219.

171. *Gossenreiter, J.,* Die funktionelle Gliederung von Graz, phil. Diss., Graz, 1961.

172. *Hubbard, W. H.,* Der Wachstumsprozeß in den österreichischen Großstädten 1869–1910, in P. C. Ludz, ed., Soziologie und Sozialgeschichte, Opladen, 1973, pp. 386–418.

173. *Hwaletz, O., et al.,* Bergmann oder Werkssoldat. Eisenerz als Fallbeispiel industrieller Politik. Dokumente und Analysen über die Österreichisch-Alpine Montangesellschaft in der Zwischenkriegszeit, Graz, 1984.

174. *Kainrath, W., F. Kubelka-Bondy* and *F. Kuzmich,* Die alltägliche Stadterneuerung. Drei Jahrhunderte Bauen und Planen in einem Wiener Außenbezirk, Vienna, 1984.

175. *Kunze, E.,* Das Städtedreieck Krems-Stein-Mautern. Seine Strukturentwicklung seit 1750, mit besonderer Berücksichtigung der sozialgeographischen Entwicklung, phil. Diss., Vienna, 1967.

176. *Lackner, H.,* and *K. Stocker,* eds., Fohnsdorf. Aufstieg und Krise einer österreichischen Kohlenbergwerksgemeinde in der Region Aichfeld-Murboden, Graz, 1982 (Interdisziplinäre Studien der Projektgruppe Fohnsdorf Aichfeld-Murboden, Vol. 1).

177. *Lichtenberger, E.,* Die Wiener Altstadt. Von der mittelalterlichen Bürgerstadt zur City, Vienna, 1977.

178. *Melicher, T.,* Die städtebauliche Entwicklung im Bereich der ehemaligen Befestigungsanlagen. Gezeigt an den sechs größten österreichischen Städten. Graz, Klagenfurt, Salzburg, Wien, Innsbruck und Linz zwischen 1800 und 1900, techn. Diss., Vienna, 1965.

179. *Nieuwolt, S.,* Die funktionelle Gliederung von Wien, in Geographische

Jahresberichte aus Österreich, Year 27 (1957/1958), pp. 1–60.

180. *Salzer-Eibenstein, G.*, Eisenerz. Die räumliche, funktionelle und wirtschaftliche Entwicklung und Gliederung der Stadtgemeinde, phil. Diss., Graz, 1970.

181. *Scherzinger, W.*, Die sozialräumliche Gliederung der Stadt Klagenfurt, phil. Diss., Vienna, 1970.

182. *Schweitzer, R.*, Die Entwicklung Favoritens zum Arbeiterbezirk in Wiener Geschichtsblätter, Year 29 (1974), pp. 253–263.

183. *Simlinger, R.*, Wiens Wachstum seit dem Niederreißen der Festungsmauern (1858–1914), techn. Diss., Vienna, 1965.

● Housing

184. *Altfahrt, M., et al.*, Die Zukunft liegt in der Vergangenheit. Studien zum Siedlungswesen der Zwischenkriegszeit, Vienna, 1983 (Forschungen und Beiträge zur Wiener Stadtgeschichte, Vol. 12).

185. *Bartl, F.*, Wohnungsproduktion und Wohnungsmarkt in Wien 1918–1938, phil. Diss., Vienna, 1980.

186. *Bauböck, R.*, Wohnungspolitik im Sozialdemokratischen Wien 1919–1934, Vienna, 1979 (Geschichte und Sozialkunde, vol. 4).

187. *Botz, G.*, Wohnungspolitik und Judendeportation in Wien 1938 bis 1945, Vienna and Salzburg, 1975.

188. *Feldbauer, P.*, Stadtwachstum und Wohnungsnot. Determinanten unzureichender Wohnungsversorgung in Wien 1848 bis 1914, Vienna, 1977 (Sozial- und wirtschaftshistorische Studien, Vol. 9).

189. *Förster, W.*, Die Wiener Gemeinde- und Genossenschaftssiedlungen vor dem Zweiten Weltkrieg. Arbeiterwohnungsbau und Gartenstadtbewegung, techn. Diss., Graz, 1978.

190. *Friedler, G.*, Über das Verhältnis von Wohnung und Wohnfolgeeinrichtungen, dargestellt an Hand der "Wiener Superblocks" und der neuen Wiener Stadtrandsiedlungen "Neukagran" und "Großfeldsiedlung", Berlin, 1973.

191. *Hautmann, H.*, and *R. Hautmann*, Die Gemeindebauten des Roten Wien 1919–1934, Vienna, 1980.

192. *Hösl, W.*, Die Anfänge der gemeinnützigen und genossenschaftlichen Bautätigkeit in Wien, phil. Diss., Vienna, 1979.

193. *John, M.*, Wohnverhältnisse Sozialer Unterschichten im Wien Kaiser Franz Josephs, Vienna, 1984 (Materialien zur Arbeiterbewegung, 32).

194. *Krauss, K.*, and *J. Schlandt*, Der Wiener Gemeindewohnungsbau–ein sozialdemokratisches Programm, in H. Helms, J. Janssen, eds., Kapitalistischer Städtebau, Neuwied and Berlin, 1971, pp. 113–124.

195. *Lackner, H.*, Der soziale Wohnbau in der Steiermark 1938–1945, Graz, 1984 (Forschung zur geschichtlichen Landeskunde der Steiermark, Vol. XXXIV).

196. *Lichtblau, A.*, Wiener Wohnungspolitik 1892–1919, Vienna, 1984 (Österreichische Texte zur Gesellschaftskritik, vol. 19).

197. *Niethammer, L.*, ed., Wohnen im Wandel. Beiträge zur Geschichte des Alltags in der bürgerlichen Gesellschaft, Wuppertal, 1979.

198. *Novy, K.*, Selbsthilfe als Reformbewegung. Der Kampf der Wiener Siedler nach dem 1. Weltkrieg, in Arch+, No. 55, (1981), pp. 26–40.

199. *Novy, K.*, Der Wiener Gemeindewohnungsbau: "Sozialisierung von unten". Oder: Zur verdrängten Dimension der Gemeinwirtschaft als Gegenökonomie, in Arch+, No. 45 (1979), pp. 9–25.

200. *Pirhofer, G.*, Linien einer kulturpolitischen Auseinandersetzung in der Geschichte des Wiener Arbeiterwohnbaues, in Wiener Geschichtsblätter Year 33, (1978), pp. 1–23.

201. *Pirhofer, G.*, and *G. Uhlig*, Selbsthilfe und Wohnungsbau. In der Periode der Integration (50er Jahre) und des "Lagers" (20er Jahre), in Arch+, No. 33, (1977), pp. 4–11.

202. *Posch, W.*, Die Wiener Gartenstadtbewegung. Reformversuch zwischen erster und zweiter Gründerzeit, Vienna, 1981.

203. *Reissberger, M.*, Theophil Hansens Zinspalais – künstlerische, gesellschaftliche und ökonomische Bedingtheiten eines Bautypus, in Umbau, Nos. 6/7 (1983), pp. 49–88.

204. *Rizy, L.*, Schwerpunkte sozialistischer Wohnungspolitik 1945–1975. Mieterschutz und flankierende Maßnahmen, kommunaler Wohnbau, Wohnbauförderung — unter besonderer Berücksichtigung des Raumes Wien, welth. Diss., Vienna, 1979.

205. *Schweitzer, R.*, Der staatlich geförderte, der kommunale und der gemeinnützige Wohnungs- und Siedlungsbau in Östrreich bis 1945, techn. Diss., Vienna, 1972.

206. *Stekl, H.*, Die Entstehung bürgerlicher Wohnkultur, in Beiträge zur Historischen Sozialkunde, Year 9 (1979), No. 3., pp. 51–56.

207. *Wagner-Rieger, R.*, Das Wiener Bürgerhaus des Barock und Klassizismus, Vienna, 1957.

208. *Wantra, W.*, Das Wiener Zinshaus. Eine entwicklungsgeschichtliche Studie mit ausschließlicher Berücksichtigung der zweckbaulichen Formen, techn. Diss., Vienna, 1953.

(e)   Economy and Transport

• Economy

209. *Baltzarek, F.*, Die Geschichte der Wiener Börse, Vienna, 1973.

210. *Bandion, E.*, Das Wiener Gewerbe und die Wiener Industrie im Rahmen der österreichischen Monarchie in der ersten Hälfte des neunzehnten Jahrhunderts, phil. Diss., Vienna, 1949.

211. *Banik-Schweitzer, R.*, Der Beitrag der vergleichenden Regional- und

Stadtgeschichtsforschung zur Differenzierung gesamtstaatlicher Wirtschaftsentwicklung im 19. Jahrhundert, in Bericht über den sechzehnten österreichischen Historikertag in Krems/Donau, Vienna, 1985, pp. 728–735.

212. *Banik-Schweitzer, R.*, and *G. Meißl*, Industriestadt Wien. Die Durchsetzung der industriellen Marktproduktion in der Habsburgerresidenz, Vienna, 1983 (Forschungen und Berichte zur Wiener Stadtgeschichte, Vol. 11).

213. *Bittner, M.*, Die wirtschaftliche und soziale Entwicklung von Linz, wirtschaftswiss. Diss., Innsbruck, 1957.

214. *Bobek, H.* and *M. Fesl*, Das System der Zentralen Orte Österreichs. Eine empirische Untersuchung, Vienna and Cologne, 1978 (Schriften der Kommission für Raumforschung der Österreichischen Akademie der Wissenschaften, Vol. 3).

215. *Bobek, H.* and *J. Steinbach*, Die Regionalstruktur der Industrie Österreichs, Vienna, 1975.

216. *Brusatti, A.*, ed., Die wirtschaftliche Entwicklung, Vienna, 1973 (Die Habsburgermonarchie 1848–1918, Vol. 1).

217. *Büttner, R.*, St. Pölten als Standort industrieller und großgewerblicher Produktion seit 1850, St. Pölten, 1972 (Veröffentlichungen des Kulturamts der Stadt St. Pölten, Vol. 5).

218. *Chaloupek, G.*, and *M. Wagner*, Wien. Wirtschaftsgeschichte 1740–1938, 2 vols., Vienna, n.d.

219. *Fendt, J.*, Die Textilindustrie Oberösterreichs. Untersuchung über die Entwicklung, Bedeutung und strukturellen Verhältnisse eines Industriezweiges, Vienna, 1978 (Dissertationen der Johannes-Kepler Universität Linz, Vol. 12).

220. *Fiereder, H.*, Reichswerke "Hermann Göring" in Österreich (1938–1945), Vienna and Salzburg 1983 (Veröffentlichungen des Historischen Instituts der Universität Salzburg, Vol. 16).

221. *Grallinger, T.*, Weiz und die Elin Union. Bedeutung eines Großbetriebes für eine Kleinstadt, Vienna, 1974.

222. *Hinteregger, R., K. Müller*, and *E. Staudinger*, Auf dem Wege in die Freiheit, Graz, 1984.

223. *Hoffmann, A.*, and *E. M. Meixner*, Wirtschaftsgeschichte des Landes Oberösterreich, 2 vols., Salzburg and Linz, 1952.

224. *Hopfgartner, A.*, Geschichte der Schuhmacherzunft in Innsbruck von den Anfängen bis zur Einführung der Gewerbefreiheit im Jahre 1859, Innsbruck, 1979 (Veröffentlichungen des Innsbrucker Stadtarchivs, N. F., Vol. 10).

225. *Keil D.*, and *A. Lach*, Wirtschaftliche Dynamik österreichischer Stadtregionen. Struktur und Entwicklung, Vienna and Munich, 1975 (Schriftenreihe des Instituts für Stadtforschung, Vol. 32).

226. *Keil, D.*, and *P. Schneidewind*, Die Wirtschaft der österreichischen

Stadtregionen. Struktur und Entwicklung (Schriftenreihe des Instituts für Stadtforschung 66), Vienna and Munich, 1979.

227. *Kepplinger, H.*, Quantitative Aspekte der Industrialisierung von Wien (1870–1890), in B. Perfahl, Marx oder Lassalle? Zur ideologischen Position der österreichischen Arbeiterbewegung 1869–1889, Vienna, 1982, pp. 265–315 (Materialien zur Arbeiterbewegung Vol. 21).

228. *Lettner, F.*, Die Industriestandorte in Oberösterreich. Ein Beitrag zur Darstellung der Industrialisierung Oberösterreichs, staatswiss. Diss., Vienna, 1958.

229. *März, E.*, Österreichische Bankpolitik in der Zeit der großen Wende 1913–1923. Am Beispiel der Creditanstalt für Handel und Gewerbe, Vienna, 1981.

230. *März, E.*, Österreichische Industrie- und Bankpolitik in der Zeit Franz Josephs I., Vienna, 1968.

231. *Matis, H.*, Österreichs Wirtschaft 1848–1913, Berlin, 1973.

232. *Meißl, G.*, Vorüberlegungen zu einer historischen Theorie der industriellen Standortwahl am Beispiel der österreichischen Entwicklung bis zum Ersten Weltkrieg, in Bericht über den sechzehnten österreichischen Historikertag in Krems/Donau, Vienna, 1985, pp. 736–742.

233. *Meixner, E. M.*, Linz 1945–1960. Industrie, Gewerbe, Handel, Verkehr, Geldwesen, Linz, 1962 (Studien zur Linzer Stadtforschung, Vol. 1).

234. *Merk, G.*, Zwei Pioniere der österreichischen Industrie. Alois Miesbach und Heinrich Drasche, Vienna, 1966.

235. *Mosser, A.*, Die Industrieaktiengesellschaft in Österreich 1880–1913, Vienna, 1980 (Studien zur Geschichte der österreichisch-ungarischen Monarchie, Vol. XVIII).

236. *Mosser, A.*, Raumabhängigkeit und Konzentrationsinteresse in der industriellen Entwicklung Österreichs bis 1914, in Bohemia, Year 17 (1976), pp. 136–192.

237. *Mühlpeck, V., R. Sandgruber* and *H. Woitek*, Index der Verbraucherpreise 1800–1914. Eine Rückberechnung für Wien und den Gebietsstand des heutigen Österreichs, in Geschichte und Ergebnisse der zentralen amtlichen Statistik in Österreich 1829–1979, Vienna, 1979, pp. 649–688 (Beiträge zur österreichischen Statistik, Vol. 550).

238. *Otruba, G.*, Quantitative, strukturelle und regionale Dynamik des Industrialisierungsprozesses in Österreich-Ungarn vom Ausgang des 18. Jahrhunderts bis zum Ausbruch des Ersten Weltkrieges, in Schriften des Vereins für Socialpolitik, N. F., Year 83 (1975), pp. 105–163.

239. *Otruba, G.* and *R. Kropf*, Die Entwicklung von Bergbau und Industrie in Oberösterreich. Von der Manufakturepoche bis zur Frühindustrialisierung, in Oberösterreichische Heimatblätter, Year 23 (1969), pp. 3–19; Industrietopographie, pp. 70–85.

240. *Prettenkofer, J.*, Die Reichswerke für Erzbergbau und Eisenhütten

"Hermann Göring", Linz. Der Ausbau der Linzer Werke während der Kriegsjahre und die Folgen für die österreichische Volkswirtschaft, Welthandel Diss., Vienna, 1975.

241. *Rothschild, K. W.*, Wurzeln und Triebkräfte der österreichischen Wirtschaftsstruktur, in W. Weber, ed., Österreichs Wirtschaftsstruktur gestern – heute – morgen, Vol. 1 Berlin, 1961, pp. 1–157.

242. *Salmeyer, C.*, Das gewerbliche Kleinbürgertum in Wien. Zu seiner wirtschaftlichen und politischen Entwicklung in der 2. Hälfte des 19. Jahrhunderts, phil. Diss., Vienna, 1980.

243. *Sandgruber, R.*, Wirtschaftsdaten für Wien. Von der Mitte des 18. Jahrhunderts bis 1938, Vienna, 1974 (unpublished).

244. *Sandgruber, R.*, Wirtschaftswachstum, Energie und Verkehr in Österreich 1840–1913, in H. Kellenbenz, ed., Wirtschaftliches Wachstum, Energie und Verkehr vom Mittelalter bis ins 19. Jahrhundert, Stuttgart and New York, 1978, pp. 69–93 (Forschungen zur Sozial- und Wirtschaftsgeschichte, Vol. 22).

245. *Santner, E.*, Handwerk und Gewerbe in Innsbruck in der ersten Hälfte des 19. Jahrhunderts, phil. Diss., Innsbruck, 1976.

246. *Steinbach, J.*, Vergleichende Betrachtung der Wirtschaftsstruktur von Wels, Villach und Leoben, phil. Diss., Vienna, 1968.

247. *Tremel F.*, Wirtschafts- und Sozialgeschichte Österreichs. Von den Anfängen bis 1955, Vienna, 1969.

248. *Tremel F.*, Der Bergbau als städtebildende Kraft in der Steiermark und in Kärnten, Vienna, 1968 (Leobner grüne Hefte, No. 109).

249. *Wiesbauer, H.*, Die österreichischen Aktiengesellschaften 1918–1938, Soz. wiss. Diss., Linz, 1977.

250. *Zatschek, H.*, Handwerk und Gewerbe in Wien. Von den Anfängen bis zur Erteilung der Gewerbefreiheit im Jahre 1859, Vienna, 1949.

● Traffic

251. *Krobot, W., H. Sternhart and F. Slezak*, Straßenbahn in Wien — vorgestern und übermorgen, Vienna, 1972.

252. *Kurz E.*, Die städtebauliche Entwicklung der Stadt Wien in Beziehung zum Verkehr, techn. Diss., Aachen, 1979.

253. *Schönthaler, W.*, Der Fremdenverkehr in der Tiroler Landeshauptstadt Innsbruck. Eine historisch-ökonomische und soziologische Untersuchung, Innsbruck, 1963 (Tiroler Wirtschaftsstudien, Vol. 18).

254. *Sengelin, W.*, Wiener Verkehrsplanungen in der franzisko-josephinischen Ära, phil. Diss., Vienna, 1980.

255. *Uhl, W.*, Zur Entwicklung des Wiener Stadtverkehrs seit dem 19. Jahrhundert, Mainz, 1973.

(f) Arts and Sciences, Churches

256. *Arbeiterbewegung*, Koloniale Frage und Befreiungsbewegung bis zum Ende des 1. Weltkrieges. Arbeiterbildung unter den Bedingungen des Kapitalismus, Vienna, 1981 (ITH-Tagungsberichte, Vol. 2).

257. *Auer, M.*, Die Ordensniederlassungen des 19. Jahrhunderts in Innsbruck, phil. Diss., Innsbruck, 1948.

258. *Baron, G.*, Der Beginn. Die Anfänge der Arbeiterbildungsvereine in Oberösterreich, Linz, 1971.

259. *Berner, P., E. Brix and W. Mantl*, eds., Wien um 1900. Aufbruch in die Moderne, Vienna, 1986.

260. *Broda, E.*, Ludwig Boltzmann, Albert Einstein und Franz Joseph, in Wiener Geschichtsblätter, Year 38 (1983), pp. 109–119.

261. *Broda, E.*, Warum war es in Österreich um die Naturwissenschaft so schlecht bestellt?, in Wiener Geschichtsblätter, Year 34 (1979), pp. 89–107.

262. *Bruder-Bezzel, A.*, Alfred Adler. Die Entstehungsgeschichte einer Theorie im historischen Milieu Wiens, Göttingen, 1983.

263. *Eygruber, G.*, Die Arbeiterseelsorge in Steyr um die Wende vom 19. zum 20. Jahrhundert, Vienna, 1981.

264. *Fuchs, A.*, Geistige Strömungen in Österreich 1867–1918, Vienna, 1978.

265. *Gorsen, P.*, Zur Dialektik des Funktionalismus heute. Das Beispiel des kommunalen Wohnbaus im Wien der zwanziger Jahre, in Habermas, ed., Stichworte zur "Geistigen Situation der Zeit", Vol. 1, Frankfurt M., 1979, pp. 688–706.

266. *Haider, A.*, Geschichte des Stadttheaters St. Pölten von 1820–1975, Grund- und integrativwiss. Diss., Vienna, 1978.

267. *Heger, W.*, Die Grazer Kulturpolitik im Zeitalter des Liberalismus 1867–1914, phil. Diss., Vienna, 1971.

268. *Hölzl, S.*, Studien zum Pflichtschulwesen in Tirol 1774–1806, in Tiroler Heimat, Vol. 38 (1975), pp. 91–138; Vol. 39 (1976), pp. 43–90.

269. *Janik, A.*, and *Toulmin S.*, Wittgensteins Wien, Munich and Vienna, 1984.

270. *Janz, R.-P.* and *K. Laermann*, Arthur Schnitzler: Zur Diagnose des Wiener Bürgertums im Fin de Siècle, Stuttgart, 1977.

271. *Johnston, W. M.*, Österreichische Kultur- und Geistesgeschichte. Gesellschaft und Ideen im Donauraum 1848–1938, Vienna, Graz and Cologne, 1974.

272. *Das Junge Wien*. Österreichische Literatur- und Kunstkritik 1887–1902, 2 Vols., Tübingen, 1976.

273. *Langhof, K.*, Mit uns zieht die neue Zeit. Pädagogik und Arbeiterbewegung am Beispiel der österreichischen Kinderfreunde, Bochum, 1983.

274. *Leyrer, M.*, Das Klagenfurter Stadttheater zur Biedermeierzeit, phil. Diss., Vienna, 1950.

275. *McGrath, W. J.*, Dionysian Art and Populist Politics in Austria, New Haven, 1974.

276. *Mecenseffy, G.*, Geschichte des Protestantismus in Österreich, Graz, Vienna and Cologne, 1956.

277. *Ofner, J.*, Zur Geschichte des Schulwesens der Stadt Steyr im 18. und 19. Jahrhundert (1750–1869). Ein Beitrag zur oberösterreichischen Schulgeschichte, in Veröffentlichungen des Kulturamtes der Stadt Steyr, Vol. 1 (1949), pp. 3–52.

278. *Ott, B.*, Die Kulturpolitik der Gemeinde Wien 1919–1934, phil. Diss., Vienna, 1969.

279. *Pfabigan, A.*, ed., Ornament und Askese im Zeitgeist des Wien der Jahrhundertwende, Vienna, 1985.

280. *Pfoser, A.*, Literatur und Austromarxismus, Vienna, 1980.

281. *Pieber, M.*, Die Geschichte des Volksbildungswesens in Wien, Vienna, 1979.

282. *Prossnitz, G.*, Das Salzburger Theater von 1892–1944, phil. Diss., Vienna, 1965.

283. *Reichmayr, J.*, and *E. Wiesbauer*, Das Verhältnis von Sozialdemokratie und Psychoanalyse in Österreich zwischen 1900 und 1938, in W. Huber, ed., Beiträge zur Geschichte der Psychoanalyse in Österreich, Vienna and Salzburg, 1978.

284. *Schorske, C. E.*, Wien. Geist und Gesellschaft im Fin de Siècle, Frankfurt/M., 1982.

285. *Stadler, F.*, ed., Arbeiterbildung in der Zwischenkriegszeit. Otto Neurath – Gerd Arntz, Vienna and Munich, 1982.

286. *Staudinger, E.*, Die Bildungs- und Fachvereine der Steiermark von 1848 bis 1973, phil. Diss., Graz, 1977.

287. *Traum und Wirklichkeit.* Wien 1870–1930, Vienna, 1985.

288. *Waissenberger, R.*, ed., Wien 1890–1920, Vienna and Heidelberg, 1984.

289. *Weidenholzer, J.*, Auf dem Weg zum neuen Menschen. Bildungs- und Kulturarbeit der österreichischen Sozialdemokratie in der Ersten Republik, Vienna, 1982.

290. *Winter, E.*, Barock, Absolutismus und Aufklärung in der Donaumonarchie, Vienna, 1971.

291. *Winter, E.*, Revolution, Neoabsolutismus und Liberalismus in der Donaumonarchie, Vienna, 1969.

292. *Winter, E.*, Romantismus, Restauration und Frühliberalismus im österreichischen Vormärz, Vienna, 1968.

E. Local Studies (a representative selection)

See the *Bibliographie zur Geschichte der Städte Österreichs*, listed under Item 8.

HERMAN A. DIEDERIKS

Belgium

A. Urban History Institutions

—

B. Aids to Research

—

(a) Urban History Journals

—

(b) Bibliographies

1. *Bauwens, P.*, and *E. Tellier*, Documents d'archives relatifs à Huy et sa région, Brussels, 1981 (Archives de l'Etat à Huy).
2. *Blockmanns, F.*, Archives anciennes de la ville d'Anvers. Inventaire des actes notariés, Antwerp, 1948.
3. *Bouesse, J.*, Essai de bibliographie historique générale et sélective des Namurois: Comté de Namur. Département de Sambre et Meuse. Province de Namur, Namur, n.d.
4. *Bourguignon, M.*, Inventaire des Archives de l'Assistance publique de la ville de Louvain, Tongeren, 1933.
5. *Bulletin critique d'histoire de Belgique et du Grand Duché de Luxemburg*, 1973–1975.
6. *Cuvelier, J.*, Inventaire des Archives de la ville de Louvain, 3 vols., n.p. 1929–1932.
7. *Denys, J., J. Buntnix* and *A. Stoop*, Ville de Saint-Nicolas. Inventaire des archives anciennes, Sint Niklaas, 1957.
8. *Diederick, I. L. A.*, Inventaire analytique et chronologique des chartes et documents appartenant aux Archives de la ville d'Ypres, 7 vols., Bruges, 1853–1868.

9. *Fourdin, E.*, Inventaire analytique des archives de la ville d'Ath, 2 vols., Brussels, 1873.

10. *Haeghen, V. van der*, Inventaire des archives de la ville de Gand. Catalogue méthodique général, Gent, 1896.

11. *Haelewyn, R.*, Inventaire des archives anciennes de la ville de Torhout, Torhout, 1960.

12. *Haelewyn, R.*, Inventaire des archives modernes de la ville des Torhout, Regimes français et hollandais, Torhout, 1971.

13. *Herdt, R. de*, Bibliographie van de Geschiedenis van Gent 1978–1979, in Handelingen van de Maatschappij voor Geschiedenis en Oudheden te Gent, Vol. XXXIII (1979), pp. 261–284 (=Bibliography of the history of Gent) (1978–1979).

14. *Houtrice, A. van*, Bibliographie de l'histoire de Bruges, n.p., 1972.

15. *Laar, A. van*, Bibliographie de l'histoire de la ville d'Anvers, 2 vols., Antwerp and Brussels, n.d.

16. *Panorama de l'histoire brugeoise depuis Duclos*, 1910, Bruges, 1972.

17. *Pergameni, C.*, Les archives historiques de la ville de Bruxelles, Brussels, 1943.

18. *Rod, R. de*, Ville de Malines. Inventaire des registres paroissiaux et des registres de l'etat civil jusqu'en 1829, Malines, 1949–1950.

19. *Verbeemen, J.*, Inventaire des archives de Seigneurs et de la ville de Diest, 2 vols., Brussels, 1961–1962.

20. *Wyffels, A.*, Ville de Tielt. Inventaire des archives anciennes, Tielt, 1962.

21. *Wymans, G.*, Inventaire des archives de la ville de Lessines. 1373–1943, Brussels, 1967.

(c)   Handbooks on Urban History

—

(d)   Atlases on Urban History and Urban Development

22. *Buinemans, R.*, and *G. van Cauwenbergh*, Nieuwe atlas van Antwerpen. Evolutie van een stedelijk landschap van 1850 tot heden, Brussels, 1981 (=New atlas of Antwerp. Evolution of an urban landscape from 1850 to today).

23. *Munier, W. A. J.*, Historische Atlas van Limburg en aangrenzende gebieden. 2nd series, Kerkhistorische kaarten, kerkelijke circumscriptie van de tegenwoordige provincie Limburg en de omliggende gebieden. 1801–1821, Asse, 1978 (= Atlas of Limburg and surrounding areas. 2nd series: church history maps, church descriptions of the present-day province of Limburg and its environs, 1801–1821).

24. *Vandermaelen, P.*, Dictionnaire géographique de la province d'Anvers,

Brussels, 1970.

(e) Urban History Sources

25. *Fairon, E.*, Regestes de la cité de Liège, 5 vols., Liège, 1933–1940.

26. *Gilliodts-van Severen, L.*, Mémoriaux de Bruges. Recueil de textes et analyses de documents concernant l'etat social de cette ville du XVe au XIXe siècle, 2 vols., Bruges, 1913–1920.

27. *Nieuwenhuyzen, K.*, Antwerpen, gefotografeerd in de 19e eeuw, Amsterdam 1976 (=Antwerp, photographed in the 19th century).

C. Research Reports

(a) General Surveys

28. *Gerin, P.*, L'Histoire des institutions belges de l'époque contemporaine. Avenir et possibilités. Bronnen voor de geschiedenis van instellingen in België, n.p., 1977.

29. *Pirenne, H.*, Les villes et les institutions urbaines, 2 vols., Paris and Brussels, 1939.

30. *Le problème des grandes agglomérations en Belgique.* Colloque organisé le 17 nov. et le 1er déc. 1956, Brussels, 1957.

31. *Volder, N. de*, Sociale geschiedenis van België, 2 vols., Mechelen, 1964 (=A social history of Belgium).

32. *Vollans, E. C.*, Urban development in Belgium since 1830, in Urbanization and its problems. Essays in honour of E. W. Gilbert, Oxford, 1968.

(b) Surveys of Individual Fields of Urban Research

—

D. Literature on Individual Areas of Urban History Research

—

(a) Concept and Definition of Town and Town Types

—

(b) Politics, Law and Statutes

33. *Aiken, M.*, and *R. Depre*, Policy and Politics in Belgian Cities, in Past and Present, 1980, pp. 73–106.

34. *Audenhoven, M. van*, De geschiedenis van den gemeentefinancien III:

Van de grote economische crisis der jaren dertig tot de tweede wereldoorlog. Gemeentekrediet van België, n.p., 1983 (=The history of local finances III: From the Depression in the thirties to World War II).

35. *Delhage, J. P.*, La presse politique d'Ath des origines à 1914, Louvain, 1974.

36. *Geet, W. van*, and *J. Delphine*, De gendarmerie te Antwerpen 1830–1977, Antwerp, 1978 (=The police in Antwerp, 1830–1977).

37. *Gubin, E.*, Bruxelles au XIXe siècle. Berceau d'un flamingantisme démocratique 1840–1873, Brussels, 1979.

38. *Pyck, M.*, Het Torhouts vredegerecht (1878–1978). Een vergeten eeuwviering, in: Het Houtland Jaarboek, n.p., 1978 (=The Torhout Peace Tribunal (1878-1978). A forgotten 100th anniversary).

39. *Suetens, L. P.*, Public Participation in Belgium, in Town Planning Review, Vol. 52 (1981), pp. 267–273.

40. *Weverke, H. van*, Les villes belges. Histoire des institutions économiques et sociales, in La ville. Recueils de la Société Jean Bodin, Vol. VII, Brussels, 1955.

41. *Witte, E.*, Luttes pour le pouvoir politique autour des principales villes belges 1830–1848, 2 vols., Brussels 1973.

(c)   Population and Social Structure

42. *Abeele, A. van den*, Hongeroproer te Brugge 2 en 3 mart 1847. Een breukpunt tijdens de "ellende der Vlaanders", in Handelingen van het Genootschap voor de Geschiedenis van Brugge, Vol. CXIX (1982), pp. 131–192 (=Starvation uprising of Bruges on 2nd and 3rd of March 1847. A turning point in the "misery of the Fleming").

43. *Belder, J. de*, De Gentse textielarbeiders in de 19de en 20ste eeuw, in Tijdschrift voor Geschiedenis, Vol. 92 (1979), pp. 187–192 (=Gent textile workers in the 19th and 20th centuries).

44. *Belder, J. de*, Nogmaals de Gentse textielarbeiders, in Tijdschrift voor Geschiedenis, Vol. 93 (1980), pp. 557–579 (=Gent textile workers again).

45. *Belder, J. de*, Les origines sociales de la bourgeoisie aisée de Bruxelles en 1914, in Revue Belge d'Histoire Contemporaine, Vols. III (1972) and IV (1973).

46. *Blockmanns, F.*, Les origines du régime corporatif officiel à Anvers, in Bijdragen voor de Geschiedenis der Nederlanden, Vol. VIII (1954).

47. *Cosemanns, A.*, Bijdrage tot de demografische en sociale geschiedenis van Brussel 1796–1846, Brussels, 1966 (=Contribution to the demographic and social history of Brussels 1796–1846).

48. *Dumont, G. H.*, and *A. Uyttebrouck*, Bruxelles, mille ans de vie quotidienne, Brussels, 1980.

49. *Eenoo, R. van*, Histoire du mouvement ouvrier à Bruges. 1864–1914,

Louvain and Paris, 1959.

50. *Flagothier-Musin, L.*, La grève générale de 1913 dans l'arrondissement de Liège. Analyse quantitative, in Belgisch Tijdschrift voor Nieuwste Geschiedenis, Vol. XIII (1981), pp. 313–338.

51. *Gadeyne, G.*, De plaatselijke commissies van geneeskundig toezicht in Oost-Vlaanderen. 1818–1830, in Handelingen voor de Maatschappij voor Geschiedenis en Oudheden te Gent, Vol. XXXIII (1979), pp. 175–200 (=The local commissions of the medical supervisor in East Flanders. 1818–1830).

52. *Haegen, H. van der*, and *R. de Vos*, De choleraepidemie te Leuven in 1849, in Driemaamdelijks Tijdschrift van het Gemeentekrediet van België, 1980, pp. 197–200 (=The cholera epidemic in Louvain in 1849).

53. *Lis, C.*, Les conditions de logement et l'assainissement d'impasses à Anvers au milieu du XIXe siècle comme mesure des oppositions de classes, in Revue Belge d'Histoire Contemporaine, Vol. I (1969).

54. *Lul, A. van*, Enkele demografische aspekten van het arrondissement Aalst, in Land van Aalst, Vol. I (1949), pp. 68–79 (=Some demographic aspects of the arrondissement Aalst).

55. *Mareschal, J.M.*, Étude démographique de Torguy de 1910–1947, in Pays Gaumais, Vol. IX (1948), pp. 91–100.

56. *Moreau, G.*, La corrélation entre le milieu social et professionel et le choix de religion à Tournai, in Sources de l'Histoire Religieuse de la Belgique, Louvrain, 1968 (Bibliothèque de la Revue d'Histoire Ecclésiastique, Vol. 47).

57. *Saint Moulin, L. de*, La construction et la propriété des maisons. Expressions des structures sociales Seraing depuis le debut du XIXe siècle, Brussels, 1969.

58. *Santbergen, R. van*, Un bourrasque sociale: Liège 1886, Liège, 1969.

59. *Schepper, L. de*, Henniksen, invloed van de nijverheid op het bevolkingscijfer, in Tijdschrift voor Folklore. Prov. d'Anvers, Vol. XI (1948), pp. 20–44 (=Henniksen, the impact of handicraft and industry on the population).

60. *Scholliers, E.*, De Gentse textielarbeiders in de 19de en 20ste eeuw. Reactie, in Tijdschrift voor Geschiedenis, Vol. 93 (1980), pp. 261–265 (=Gent textile workers in the 19th and 20th centuries).

61. *Stephany, P.*, Cent cinquante ans de vie quotidienne, Brussels, 1979.

62. *Weert, D. de*, Les ouvriers de l'industrie textile gantoise et leur mouvement entre 1866 et 1881. Étude sociale, Louvain and Paris, 1959.

63. *Wollast-Theret, E.*, Etude socio-économique de la population indigente de la ville de Bruxelles, in Revue de l'Institut de Sociologie, 1968.

(d)   Town Planning, Housing

64. *Bruxelles 1890–1971*, Guide d'architecture, pub. by Ministre de la Cul-

ture Française, Brussels, 1972.

65. *Cabus, P.*, De stedelijke ontwikkelingen in Vlaanderen 1947–1976. Vaststellingen en indicaties voor een stedelijk beleid, n.p. 1980 (GERV reports) (=Urban developments in Flanders 1947–1976. Findings and indications for an urban policy).

66. *Farlier, J.*, and *Alphwanten*, Géographie et histoire des communes Belges, Brussels, 1963.

67. *Monteyne, A., et al.*, De architectuur en de stedelijke ontwikkeling van Brussel van 1780 to 1914, Brussels, 1979 (=The architecture and urban development of Brussels: 1780 to 1914).

68. *Rottier, H. L. E. M.*, Stedelijke strukturen in historisch perspektief, Hulst, 1974 (=Urban structures in historical perspective).

(e)   Economy and Transport

69. *Avondts, G.*, and *P. Scholliers*, Geentse prijzen, huishuren en budgetonderzoeken in de 19e und 20e eeuw, Brussels, 1977 (=Gent prices, rents and budget studies in the 19th and 20th centuries).

70. *Delbeke, J.*, and *S. Greefs*, A Quantitative Economic History of Antwerp in the 19th and 20th Century, in Economisch en Sociaal- Historisch Jaarboek, Vol. 48 (1985), pp. 212–232.

71. *Donnay, J.* and *J. Jour*, Liège en flanant. La Batte et les quais, Brussels, 1978.

72. *Eeckhout, P. van den*, Lonen van Brusselse arbeiders en openbare instellingen (1809–1934). Bouwvakarbeiders, ziekenhuis- en stadtspersoneel, Brussels, 1979 (=The wages of workers in Brussels and public institutions (1809–1934). Skilled construction workers, hospital workers and civil servants).

73. *Gand*, Ville et port: 1904–1979. Gent havenstad 1904–1979, n.p. 1980.

74. *Kint, P.* and *R. C. W. van der Voort*, Stedelijke industriele arbeidsmarkten in 1819: Een modern kwantitatief economisch-historisch onderzoek, in Economisch en Sociaal- Historisch Jaarboek, Vol. 46 (1983), pp. 113–127 (=Urban industrial labour market in 1819: A modern, quantitative, economic-historical study).

75. *Mokyr, J.*, Industrialization in Lower Countries 1795–1850, New Haven, 1976.

76. *Neyens, J.*, De buurtspoorwegen in de provincie Oost-Vlaanderen. 1885–1968, Mechelen, 1978 (=Local railways in the province of East Flanders).

77. *Soete, J. -L.*, L'industrie textile à Mouscron des origines à 1930, Vol. I, n.p. 1979 (Société d'Histoire de Mouscron et de la Région).

78. *Vanduffel, F.*, Industrialisatie en verandering. Lommel tussen 1890 en 1914, Assen, 1979 (Maaslandse monografieen, Vol. 42) (=Industrialisation and change. Lommel between 1890 and 1914).

(f)   Arts and Sciences, Churches

79. *Boon, H.*, Enseignement primaire et alphabétisation dans l'agglomération bruxelloise de 1830 à 1879, Louvain, 1969.

80. *Capouillez, M.*, Industries et charbonnages de Boussu, Boussu, 1981.

81. *Daele, H. van*, Histoire de l'enseignement primair communal à Anvers de 1830 à 1872, Brussels, 1972.

82. *Vliegher, L. de*, Patrimoine artistique de la Flandre occidentale, Vol. 2–3: Les Maisons à Bruges, 2 vols., Tielt and The Hague, 1968, 2nd ed. Tielt and Amsterdam 1975; Vol. 5: Damme, Tielt and Utrecht, 1971.

E.   Local Studies (a representative selection)

● Antwerp

83. *Prims, F.*, Geschiedenis van Antwerpen. Nederlandsche en eerste Belgische periode 1814–1914, Antwerp, 1948 (=History of Antwerp. Dutch and first Belgian periods 1814–1914).

84. *Prims, F.*, Histoire d'Anvers, des origines à 1914, 10 vols., Antwerp, 1927–1949.

● Aywaille

85. *Xhignesse, A.*, Aywaille, ma commune, Aywaille, 1980.

● Breendonk

86. *Vivys, S.*, Brede Dunc, een bijdrage tot de geschiedenis van Breendonk, Dendermonde, 1981 (Brede Dunc, a contribution to its history).

● Bruges

87. *Houtte, J. A. van*, Bruges. Essai d'histoire urbaine, Brussels, 1967.

● Brussels

88. *Bogaert-Damin, A. M.*, and *L. Mareschal*, Bruxelles, développement de l'ensemble urbain 1846–1961. Analyse historique et statistique des recencements, Namur, 1978.

89. *Bruxelles.* Construire et reconstruire. Architecture et aménagement urbain 1780–1914, Brussels, 1979.

90. *Dons, R.*, Histoire de Bruxelles, 2 vols., n.p. 1947.

91. *Hannes, J.,* and *M. Despontin,* Brussel omstreeks 1830. Enkele sociale aspekten, in Vrije Univesiteit Brussel, Vol. IV (1981), pp. 199–218 (=Brussels around 1830. Some social aspects).

92. *Henne, A.* and *A. Wauters,* Histoire de la ville de Bruxelles, 4 vols., Brussels, 1845 (reprinted 1969).

93. *Histoire de Bruxelles,* ed., M. Martens in conjunction with V.-G. Martigny *et al.,* Toulouse, 1976.

94. *Verniers, L.,* Bruxelles et son agglomération de 1830 à nos jours, Brussels, 1976.

95. *Verniers, L.,* Un millénaire d'histoire de Bruxelles, depuis les origines jusqu'en 1830, Brussels, 1965.

● Chapelle-lez-Herlaimont

96. *Darquemal, R.,* Chapelle-lez-Herlaimont, son histoire, ses gens, Chapelle-lez-Herlaimont, 1891.

● Charleroi

97. *Alexandre, A.,* and *M. Depelsenaire,* Charleroi hier . . . aujourd'hui, Brussels, n.d.

● Comines

98. *Duvosquel, J.-H.,* Comines, ville de frontières, ou comment trouver les sources de son passé, in Athénée royale de Comines 1945–1970, n.p. n.d.

● Deinze

99. *Cassiman, A.,* Histoire de la ville de Deinze, Deinze, n.p., n.d.

● Gand (Gent)

100. *Fris, V.,* Histoire de Gand, Brussels, 1913, 2nd ed., Gent, 1930.

101. *Saint-Nicolas,* La ville de Gand du passé vers l'avenir, Gent, 1971.

● Gembloux

102. *Nameche, L.,* La ville et le comté de Gembloux. L'histoire et les institutions, Gembloux, 1922.

● Kortrijk

103. *Huysentruyt, J.*, Herinneringen aan Kortrijk 1900–1940, Kortrijk 1981 (=Memories of Kortrijk 1900–1940).

104. *Peel, A.*, Kortrijk 70 jaar terug. Courtrai il y a 70 ans, Kortrijk 1946–1948 (=Kortrijk 70 years ago).

● Liège

105. *Lejeune, J.*, Liège, de la principauté à la métropole, Antwerp, 1967.

● Namur

106. *Rousseau, F.*, Namur ville mosane, Brussels, 1948.

● Ninove

107. *Vangassen, H.*, Histoire de Ninove, 2 vols., Ninove, 1959–1960.

● Renaix

108. *Delghust*, Renaix à travers les âges, Renaix, 1936.

● Tirlemont

109. *Wauters, J.*, Contributions à l'histoire de Tirlemont, Tirlemont, 1962.

● Ypres

110. *Prisme de l'Histoire d'Ypres*, Ypres, 1974.

LILIANE SHANDANOVA

Bulgaria

A. Urban History Institutions

—

B. Aids to Research

(a)   Urban History Journals

1. *Arhiv za poselištni proučvanija Sofia*, 1938–1914 (=Scientific journal featuring historical, geographical, and economic studies on settlements in Bulgaria; published quarterly).
2. *Izvestija na Instituta za gradoustrojstvo i arhitektura*, Sofia, Vols. 1–25, 1951–1973 (=Material on town planning, history and modern-day life; published annually).

(b)   Bibliographies

3. *Mihov, N.*, Naselenieto na Turcija i Bălgarija prez XVIII i XIX v. Bibliografski izdirvanija săs statističeski i etnografski danni, Vols. 1–5, Sofia, 1915–1967 (=The population of Turkey and Bulgaria during the 18th and 19th centuries. Bibliographical studies with statistics and ethnographical material).
4. *Stopanska i socijalna knižnina v Bălgarija*. Bibliografija za bălgarski knigi i statii. 1858–1945, Svištov, 1948 (=Economic and sociological literature in Bulgaria. Bibliography of Bulgarian books and articles from 1858 to 1945).
5. *Šandanova, L.*, and *S. Angelova*, Sozialno-ikonomicčsko razvitie na grada XV–XIX v. Bibliografski obzor na bălgarskata literatura 1878–1973, Sofia, 1974 (=The socio-economic evolution of the town in the 15th to 19th centuries; bibliographic review of Bulgarian literature from 1878–1973).

(c)   *Handbooks on Urban History*

—

(d)   *Atlases on Urban History and Urban Development*

—

(e)   *Urban History Sources*

6. *Jireček, K.*, Pătuvanija po Bălgarija, Sofia, 1974 (=Travelling in Bulgaria).
7. *Kanitz, F.*, Donau-Bulgarien und der Balkan: Historisch-geographisch-ethnographische Reisestudien aus den Jahren 1860–1879, Leipzig, 1882.

C.   Research Reports

(a)   *General Surveys*

8. *Problemi na urbanizacijata i poselištnata mreža.* Materiali na simpoziuma, săstojal se na 15–18 mai 1973 v Plovdiv i Smoljan, Sofia, 1974 (=Reports on the socio-economic problems of increased urbanisation in Bulgaria after the Second World War).

(b)   *Surveys of Individual Fields of Urban Research*

—

D.   Literature on Individual Areas of Urban History Research

(a)   *Concept and Definition of Town and Town Types*

9. *Devedžiev, M.*, Kratka istorija na selištnoto razvitie po bălgarskite zemi, Sofia, 1979 (=Brief history of the settling of Bulgaria).
10. *Georgiev, G.*, Preustrojstvo na tradicionnata selištna sistema v rezultat ot Osvoboždenieto, in Istoričeski pregled, 1977, Nos. 5–6, pp. 111–126 (=Re-establishing the traditional settlement system after the War of Liberation in 1877–1878).
11. *Iširkov, A.*, Harakterni čerti na gradovete v carstvo Bălgarija, Sofia, 1925 (=Characteristic features of towns in the Kingdom of Bulgaria).
12. *Velčev, I.*, Narastvane, količestvena kvalifikacija i geografsko razpredele-

nie na gradovete v Bălgarija, in Sbornik v čest na Jordan Zahariev, Sofia, 1964, pp. 107–123 (=Growth, quality classification and geographical distribution of towns in Bulgaria).

(b) Politics, Law and Statutes

13. *Simeonov, S.*, Administrativno-teritorijalno ustrojstvo i mestno upravlenie na Iztočna Rumelija, in Izvestija na Dăržavnite arhivi, Vol. 33 (1977), pp. 23–37 (=Administrative and territorial structure, and local government in Eastern Roumalia).

14. *Zlatev, T.*, Bălgarskijat grad prez epohata na Văzraždaneto, Sofia, 1955 (Bălgarska nacionalna arhitektura, Vol. 1) (=The Bulgarian town during the Bulgarian National Revival Period).

15. *Zlatev, T.*, Bălgarskite gradove po r. Dunav prez epohata na Văzraždaneto, Sofia, 1962 (Bălgarska nacionalna arhitektura, Vol. 4) (=Bulgarian towns along the River Danube during the Bulgarian National Revival).

(c) Population and Social Structure

16. *Atanasov, M.*, Narastvane na gradskoto naselenie u nas, in Ikonomičeska mišal, No. 3 (1963), pp. 68–81 (=The growth of Bulgaria's urban population).

17. *Bojadžieva, P.*, Urbanizacija na naselenieto v NR Bălgarija, in Problemi na geografijata na naselenieto i selistata, Sofia, 1973, pp. 133–137 (= Urbanising the population in the People's Republic of Bulgaria).

18. *Danailov, G.*, Izsledvanija vărhu demografijata na Bălgaria, Sofia, 1931 (=Demographic studies of Bulgaria).

19. *Jurdanov, J.*, Našite gradove. Naselenie i pominak, in Spisanie na Bălgarskoto ikonomičesko družestvo, 1936, No. 1, pp. 3–19 (=Bulgarian towns: population and town life).

20. *Matov, G.*, Materiali za izučavaneto na razpredelenieto na naselenieto v Bălgarija po naseleni mesta, in Sbornik Za narodni umotvorenia, nauka i knižnina, Vols. 22–23 (1906/1907), pp. 1–48 (=Material on the distribution of the population in towns and villages).

21. *Todorov, N.*, Balkanskijat grad XV–XIX v. Socialno-ikonomičesko i demografsko razvitie, Sofia, 1972 (=The Balkan City 1400–1900, Seattle and London, 1983.)

22. *Vasilev, G.*, Njakolko beležki po našeto gradsko naselenie, in Spisanie na Bălgarskoto ikonomičesko družestvo, 1902, No. 7, pp. 467–479 (=Notes on Bulgaria's urban population).

23. *Vasileva, B.*, Organizacionnoto nabirane na rabotnata răka za stroitelstvoto i promišlenostta i migracionnite procesi v Bălgarija, in Istoričeski pregled, 1979, No. 4–5, pp. 143–155 (=Organisational recruit of builders and industrial workers, and migration to the towns in Bul-

garia).

24. *Vasileva, B.*, Problemi na urbanizacijata i migracionnite procesi v Bălgarija prez prehodnija period, in Iz istorijata na stopanskija i socialnija život v bălgarskite zemi, Sofia, 1984, pp. 85–122 (=Problems of urbanisation and migration processes in Bulgaria during the period of transition).

25. *Velčev, I.*, Paraškeva Oreškova. Osobenosti v promenite na broja i teritorialnoto razpoloženie na gradskoto naselenie v NR Bălgarija ot 1946–1970 g., in Problemi na geografijata na naselenieto i selištata, Sofia, 1973, pp. 59–67 (=Some surprising changes in population numbers and the settlement of the urban population in the People's Republic of Bulgaria from 1946–1970).

(d)   Town Planning, Housing

26. *Avramov, I.*, Planiraneto na naselenite mesta v Bălgarija ot Osvoboždenieto do 9.ix.1944. Istoričesko-gradoustrojstven očerk, in Isvestija na Instituta po gradoustrojstvo i arhitektura, Vols. 10–11 (1957), pp. 389–454 (=Planning of towns and villages in Bulgaria from the Liberation in 1878 to the Uprising on 9 September 1944).

27. *Konjarska, E.*, Arhitekturno-gradoustrojstvenija oblik na vazroždenskite gradove ot Sredna Stara-planina, in Arhitekturata na bălgarskoto văzraždane, Sofia, 1975, pp. 27–55 (=Architectural appearance of towns in the central part of the Balkan range during the Bulgarian National Revival).

28. *Kratka istorija na bălgarskata arhitektura*, Sofia, 1965 (=Brief history of Bulgaria's architecture).

29. *Penkov, I.*, Novite gradove v N.R. Bălgarija, Sofia, 1977 (=New towns in the People's Republic of Bulgaria).

30. *Stanišev, H.*, Istorija na stroežite i săobštenijata v Bălgarija ot Osvoboždenieto do kraja na 1939, Sofia, 1947 (=History of architecture and communications in Bulgaria from the War of Liberation to the end of 1939).

31. *Tonev, L.*, Gradoustrojstveni planove (1878–1944), in Arhitekturata Bălgarija. 1878–1944, Sofia, 1978, pp. 18–30 (=Town planning 1878–1944).

(e)   Economy and Transport

32. *Beškov, A. S.*, Stopanskoto vlijanie na železopătnata linija Sofia-Varna za izmenjane obštija oblik na njakoi selišta, Sofia, 1940 (=Economic impact of the Sofia-Varna railway line on the overall appearance of some towns and villages).

33. *Stopanska istorija na Bălgarija 681–1981*, Sofia, 1981 (=An economic

history of Bulgaria from 681–1981).

(f)   Arts and Sciences, Churches

—

E.   Local studies (a representative selection)

● Gabrovo

34. *Končev, P.*, Iz stopanskoto minalo na Gabrovo. Monograficni izsledvanija, Sofia, 1929 (=The economic past of the town of Gabrovo).

● Plovdiv

35. *Šiškov, S. N.*, Plovdiv v svoete minalo i nastojašte: Istoriko-etnografski i političeski pregled, Plovdiv, 1926 (=Plovdiv's past and present: historical, ethnographic and political review).

● Ruse

36. *Dojkov, V.*, Ruse. Ikonomo-geografska harakteristika, Sofia, 1926 (=Ruse: economic and geographic features).

● Sliven

37. *Tabakov, S.*, Opit za istorija na grad Sliven, Vol. II, Sofia, 1929 (=Attempt at a history of Sliven).

JAN HAVRÁNEK

Czechoslovakia

A. Urban History Institutions

Chair of regional history at the *Palacký-University* in Olomouc.
Slezský ústav ČSAV, Opava (= Silesian Institute of the Czechoslovak Academy of Sciences) in Opava. Reports from the institute are published in *Zpravodaj Slezského ústavu ČSAV Opava*. Research reports are published in *Průmyslové oblasti*, Vols. 1–7 (1973–1981) (= Industrial regions) and in the journal *Slezský sborník*.
A list of publications is published in *Zpravodaj Slezského ústavu*, Parts I–II (1984), No. 17.

B.   Aids to Research

(a)   Urban History Journals

1. *Brno v minulosti a dnes*, Vols. 1–9, Brno (1959–1970) (= Brno in the past and today).
2. *Brno mezi městy střední Evropy*, Brno, 1983 (= Brno among the cities of Central Europe).
3. *Sborník příspěvků k dějinám a výstavbě města*, Ostrava, Vols. 1–10 (1962–1979) (= Collection of articles on urban history and development, Ostrava).
4. *Minulost západočeského kraje*, Plzeň, No. 2 (1981) and No. 19 (1983) (= West Bohemia's past).
5. *Sborník příspěvků k dějinám hlavního města Prahy*, 8 vols., Prague (1907–1938) (= Collection of articles on the history of the capital, Prague).
6. *Pražský sborník historicky*, Prague, 1965 ff. (= Historical collection, Prague).
7. *Documenta Pragensia*, Prague, 1980 ff. (= Journal of the city archives of Prague; published annually).

(b)   Bibliographies

8. *Jiřík, K.*,   Historicko-vlastivědná bibliografie Ostravy v letech 1945–1961, in Ostrava, No. 1 (1962), pp. 343–374 (= Historical – local historical and geographical bibliography of Ostrava in the years 1945–1961).

9. *Jiřík, K.*, Literatura o Ostravě z let 1962–1970, in Ostrava, No. 12 (1983), pp. 411–466 (= Literature on Ostrava in the years 1962–1970).

10. *Kubíček, J.*, Literatura o Brně. 1801–1949. Soupis publikací a článků, Brno, 1980 (= Literature on Brno. A list of publications and articles).

11. *Mihóková, M.*, Politický život v Košiciach v rokoch 1901–1918. 1.–3. Tématická bibliografia novín a časopisov, Košice, 1979 (= Political life in Košice in the years 1901–1918).

● Prague

Literature since 1945

12. 1945–1956: *Čarek, J.*, in Časopis společnosti přátel starožitností českých, Vol. 66 (1958), pp. 168–190.
1959–1960: *Holec, F.*, in Československý časopis historický (ČSČH), Vol. 9 (1961), pp. 284–285.
1961–1962: *Holec, F.*, in ČSČH, Vol. 11 (1963), pp. 536–537.
1963:   *Holec, F.*, in Pražský sborník historický (PSH), 1965, pp. 175–180.
1964–1965: *Jarolímková, M.*, in PSH, 1969/70, pp. 236–249.
1966–1967: *Jarolímková, M.*, in PSH, No. 6 (1971), pp. 213–224.
1968:   *Jarolímková, M.*, in PSH, No. 7 (1972), pp. 196–204.
1969–1972: *Jarolímková, M.*, in PSH, No. 9 (1975), pp. 238–270.
1973–1975: *Jarolímková, M.*, in PSH, No. 11 (1979), pp. 222–258.
1976–1978: *Jarolímková, M.*, in PSH, No. 14 (1981), pp. 162–201.
1979–1981: *Korbelová, H., V. Ledvinka* and *J. Mendelová*, in PSH, No. 16 (1983), pp. 152–186.
1982–1984: *Ledvinka, V., J. Mendelová* and *B. Zilynskij*, in PSH, No. 19 (1986), pp. 163–209.

Unpublished Dissertations:

13. 1966–1967: *Pelikánová-Nová, Z.*, in PSH, 1969/70, pp. 249–250.
1968–1980: *Pešek, J.*, in PSH, No. 15 (1982), pp. 168–173.

14. *Novodobé dějiny v československé historiografii*. Bibliography, ed. A. Ježek and K. Gavalierová, Prague, 1964 ff. (= Bibliography published yearly on the history of the labour movement, later on entire contemporary history).

15. *Muneles, O.*, Bibliografický přehled židovské Prahy, Prague, 1952 (= Bibliographical overview of Jewish Prague).

16. *Podzimek, J.*, Literatura o Praze 1945–1961, in Kniha o Praze, Prague, 1962, pp. 274–297 (= Literature on Prague).

(c)   Handbooks on Urban History

Historical-topographical monography of various towns and districts in Moravia published in more than 30 volumes of *Moravská vlastivěda* which appeared between 1897 and 1939. For modern history this series is being continued in a more sophisticated form in *Historický místopis Moravy a Slezska 1848–1860* (10 vols. published since 1967).

17. *Československá historická města*, eds., O. Dostál *et al.*, Prague, 1954 (= Historic towns of Czechoslovakia).

(d)   Atlases on Urban History and Urban Development

18. *Hlavsa, V.*, Plány města Prahy a okolí 1801–1918, in Sborník archívních prací, Vol. 24 (1974), pp. 135–259 (= The maps of Prague and surroundings 1801–1918).

(e)   Urban History Sources

19. *Architektura v českém národním dědictví*, eds., Z. Wirth and A. Müllerová, Prague, 1961 (= Architecture in the Czech national tradition).

20. *Hlavsa, V.*, Statistické materiály k vývoji hlavního města Prahy v letech 1945–1965, in Pražský sborník historický, 1965, pp. 29–50 (= Statistical material on the development of the capital Prague 1945–1965).

21. *Scheufler, P.*, Praha 1848–1914. Čteni nad dobovými fotografiemi, Prague, 1984, 2nd edition Prague, 1986 (= Prague 1848–1914. Comments on contemporary photographs).

22. *Wirth, Z.*, Praha v obraze pěti století, Prague 1932, 2nd ed., Prague, 1939 (= Prague in pictures of five centuries).

23. *Wirth, Z.*, Stará Praha, Prague, 1937, 2nd ed., Prague, 1942 (= Old Prague – pictures from the 19th century).

C.   Research Reports

(a)   General Surveys

24. *Bartoš, J.*, Jak psát dějiny, Prague, 1984 (= How to write history).
25. *Hrůza, J.*, Slovník soudobého urbanizmu, Prague, 1977 (= Encyclopaedia of contemporary urbanism).
26. *Klusáková, L.*, Evropská města na prahu kapitalismu, Prague, 1986

(= European towns on the threshold of capitalism).

27. *Kobylková, L.*, and *V. Kubišová*, Západoevropská historiografie o sociálně ekonomickém vyvoji měst. Období přechodu od feudalismu ke kapitalismu, in Československý časopis historický, Vol. 29 (1981), pp. 570–599 (= West European historiography on the social and economic development of towns. The period of transition from feudalism to capitalism).

28. *Musil, J.*, Urbanizace v socialistikých zemích, Brno, 1977 (= Urbanisation in the socialist countries).

29. *Otázy urbanizace. Sborník*, ed. J. Musil, Prague, 1976 (= Problems of urbanisation. A collection).

(b)   Surveys of Individual Fields of Urban Research

30. *Musil, J.*, Sociologie soudobého města, Prague, 1967 (= Sociology of the contemporary town).

31. *Purš, J.*, Průmyslová revoluce, Prague, 1975 (= The industrial revolution).

D.   Literature on Individual Areas of Urban History Research

(a)   Concept and Definition of Town and Town Types

32. *Hapák, P.*, Priemyselná revolúcia a vývin miest za kapitalizmu, in Historický časopis, Vol. 21 (1973), pp. 161–187 (= The industrial revolution and the development of towns in capitalism).

33. *Holotíková, Z.*, Mestá na Slovensku v medzivojnovom období, in Historický časopis, Vol. 21 (1973), pp. 189–204 (= Towns in Slovakia between the wars).

34. *Horská, P.*, On the Problem of Urbanisation in the Czech Lands at the Turn of the 19th and 20th Centuries, in Hospodářské dějiny, Vol. 2 (1978), pp. 259–294.

35. *Horská-Vrbová, P.*, Kapitalistická industrializace a středoevropská společnost, Prague, 1970 (= Capitalist industrialisation and society in central Europe).

36. *Hrůza, J.*, Hledání soudobého města, Prague, 1973 (= In search of the contemporary town).

37. *Hrůza, J.*, Města utopistů, Prague, 1967 (= Towns of the utopists).

38. *Hrůza, J.*, Teorie města, Prague 1965 (= Theory of the city).

39. *Kobylková, L.*, Proměna středověkého města v "historické jádro" v období průmyslové revoluce, in Sborník historický, Vol. 26 (1979), pp. 61–108 (= The change of the medieval town into the "historical

nucleus" of the city in the period of the industrial revolution).
40. *Myška, M.*, Město v proměnách průmylsové revoluce, in Slezský sborník, Vol. 68 (1970), pp. 142–200 (= The town in the industrial revolution).
41. *Nový, O.*, Konec velkoměsta, Prague 1964 (= The end of the metropolis).
42. *Tatják, L.*, Východoslovenská mestá v období priemyslnej revolúcie, in Historický časopis, Vol. 21 (1973) pp. 231–241, (= Towns in eastern Slovakia in the period of the industrial revolution).

(b)   Politics, Law and Statutes

43. *Bianchi, L.*, The subordinate position of self-government in relation to state government in bourgeois Czechoslovakia, in Entwicklungsfragen der Verwaltung in Mitteleuropa, Pécs, 1972, pp. 17–32.
44. *Bouček, M.*, Praha v únoru 1948, Prague, 1963 (= Prague in February 1948).
45. *Havránek, J.*, Pražští voliči roku 1907. Jejich třídní složení a politicke smýšlení, in Pražský sborník historický, Vol. 12 (1980), pp. 170–212 (= Prague electorate in 1907, its class structure and political orientation).
46. *Havránek, J.*, Soziale Struktur und politisches Verhalten der großstädtischen Wählerschaft im Mai 1907 – Wien und Prag im Vergleich, in Politik und Gesellschaft im alten und neuen Österreich. Commemorative publication by Rudolf Neck, Vienna, 1981, pp. 150–166.
47. *Holec, F.*, Zápas o Velkou Prahu, in Pražský sborník historický, 1969/70, pp. 117–136 (= The struggle for Great Prague).
48. *Klabouch, J.*, Geschichte der Gemeindeselbstverwaltung in Österreich 1848–1918, Vienna, 1968.
49. *Klabouch, J.*, Die Lokalverwaltung in Cisleithanien, in Die Habsburgmonarchie 1848–1918, Vol. 2: Verwaltung und Rechtswesen, Vienna, 1975, pp. 270–305.
50. *Kratochvíl, M. V.*, O vývoji městské správy pražské od r. 1848, Prague, 1936, (= Development of the Prague city administration since 1848).
51. *Ledvinka, V.*, Zastoupení KSČ v obecní samosprávě města Prahy v období 1923–1939, in Documenta Pragensia, Vol. 2 (1981), pp. 5–51 (= The representation of the Communist Party in Prague city self-government 1923–1939).
52. *Malý, K.*, Die Selbstverwaltung in der Politik des tschechischen Bürgertums in der 2. Hälfte des 19. Jahrhunderts, in Entwicklungsfragen der Verwaltung in Mitteleuropa, Pécs, 1972, pp. 161–174.
53. *Malý, K.*, Zu den Tendenzen der Entwicklung der örtlichen Verwaltung in den Böhmischen Ländern 1848–1945, in Entwicklung der städtischen und regionalen Verwaltung in den letzten hundert Jahren

in Mittel- und Osteuropa, Vol. 1, Budapest, 1978/79, pp. 207–240.

54. *Maňák, J., et al.*, Komunisté a Praha. Nástin dějin městské organizace KSČ v Praze, Prague, 1983 (= Communists and Prague. An outline of the urban organisation of the Communist Party in Prague. Vol. 1 (up to 1948).

55. *Merta, A.*, Pražské národní výbory a jejich úloha v uplynulých dvaceti letech, in Pražský sborník historický, 1965, pp. 5–28 (= The City of Prague government 1945–1965).

56. *Merta, A.*, Vývoj pražské městské správy od roku 1922 do roku 1945, in Pražský sborník historický, Vol. 9 (1975), pp. 147–195 (= The development of Prague city administration 1922–1945).

57. *Městské právo v 16.–18. století v Evropě*, ed., K. Malý, Prague, 1982 (= Communal law in the 16th–18th century in Europe).

58. *Novotný, J.*, Dějiny pražského dělnického hnutí do založení KSČ v datech, Prague 1981 (Acta musei pragensis) (= History of the Prague labour movement until the foundation of the Communist Party in Czechoslovakia in dates).

59. *Příručka k dějinám pražské stranické organizace*, 5 vols., Prague 1981–1982 (= Manual on the history of the Prague organisation of the communist party).
– Vols. 1 and 2: 1849–1921, eds. R. Wohlgemuthová *et al.*,
– Vol. 3: 1921–1929, ed., V. Dubský,
– Vol. 4: 1929–1939, ed., R. Hlušicková,
– Vol. 5: 1939–1945, ed., A. Hájková.

60. *Šolle, Z., V. Mencl and Z. Richtová*, Praha hrdinská, Prague, 1961 (= Heroic Prague, its revolutionary socialistic working class 1844–1960).

61. *Urfus, V.*, Die Auffassung der Stadt in der Rechtsentwicklung der böhmischen Länder um die Wende des 19. Jahrhunderts und an der Schwelle zur Gegenwart, in Entwicklung der städtischen und regionalen Verwaltung in den letzten hundert Jahren in Mittel- und Osteuropa, Vol. 2, Budapest, 1978/79, pp. 349–372.

62. *Urfus, V.*, Josefinský osvícenský absolutismus, jeho reformy a regulace magistrátů, in Documenta Pragensia, Vol. 4 (1984), pp. 322–328 (= The enlightened absolutism of Joseph II, his reforms and the regulation of the magistrates).

(c)   Population and Social Structure

63. *Babincová, M., and D. Gawrecki*, Politická orientace obyvatelstva v průmyslových oblastech českých zemí 1920–1935, in Slezský sborník, Vol. 83 (1985), pp. 81–138 (= Political orientation of the population of the industrial regions of the Bohemian provinces 1920–1935).

64. *Bělohlávek, M.*, Příspěvek k poznání populačních a bytových poměrů v první polovici 19. století ve Starém Plzenci, in Historická demografie,

Vol. 4 (1970), pp. 59–75 (= Contribution to the population and living conditions in Starý Plzenec in the first half of the 19th century).

65. *Bílová M., L. Dokoupil* and *I. Krulikovská,* Obyvatelstvo dělnické kolonie Krasnovec v Moravské Ostravě, in Ostrava, Vol. 11 (1981), pp. 285–298 (= The inhabitants of the workers' settlement Krasnovec in Moravská Ostrava).

66. *Čtrnáct, P.,* Vývoj rozmístěni obyvatelstva v ČSR v letech 1961–1980, in Demografie, Vol. 24 (1982), pp. 110–121 (= Population movement in Czechoslovakia in the years 1961–1980).

67. *Demografická příručka,* pub. by Federální statistický úřad, Prague, 1982 (= Demographic manual).

68. *Dokoupil, L.,* Příspěvek k demografickému vývoji Vítkovic v letech 1820–1879, in Slezský sborník, 1966, pp. 179–189 (= A contribution to the demographic development of Vítkovice in the years 1820–1879).

69. *Dokoupil, L.,* Struktury populace ostravské aglomerace před první světovou válkou, in Sborník prací pedagogické fakulty Ostrava, 1977, pp. 21–54 (= Population structures of the Ostrava agglomeration before the First World War).

70. *Dokoupil, L.,* Teritoriální a sociální mobilita populace ostravské průmyslové oblasti, in Československý časopis historický, Vol. 21 (1973), pp. 355–368 (= Territorial and social mobility of the population of the industrial region of Ostrava).

71. *Dušek, L.,* Obyvatelstvo města Ústí nad Labem do konce 18. století, Ústí n.L. 1974 (= The population of the Usti n.L. up to the end of the 18th century).

72. *Fojtík, K.,* Tři typy dělnickych obydlí v Brně / od nejstarši kolonie k nouzovým sídlištím, in Brno v minulosti a dnes, Vol. 1 (1959), pp. 23–40 (= Three types of workers' living conditions in Brno; from the oldest settlements to the poverty slums).

73. *Fojtík, K.,* Dům na předměstí. Etnografická studie o životě obyvatel činžovního domu v Brně, in Brno v minulosti, Vol. 5 (1963), pp. 45–68 (= A house in the suburbs. Ethnographical study on the inhabitants of a block of rented flats in Brno).

74. *Gawrecki, D., J. Bakala* and *A. Grobelný,* Průmyslové oblasti Slovenska za kapitalismu 1780–1945, Opava, 1983 (= The industrial regions in Slovakia in the epoch of capitalism, 1780–1945).

75. *Häufler, V.,* Changes in the Geographical Distribution of Population in Czechoslovakia, Prague, 1966.

76. *Hampl, M.,* Vývoj hlavních prostorů koncentrace obyvatelstva v ČSR v letech 1869–1970, in Demografie, No. 23 (1981), pp. 317–325 (= The development of the most densely populated centres of Czechoslovakia).

77. *Havránek, J.,* Češi v severočeských a západočeských městech v letech 1880–1930, in Ústecký sborník historický, 1979, pp. 227–254 (= Czechs in the towns of Northern and Western Bohemia,

1880–1930).

78. *Havránek, J.*, Demografický vývoj Prahy v druhé polovině 19. století, in Pražský sborník historický, 1969/70, pp. 70–105 (= Demographic development of Prague in the second half of the 19th century).

79. *Havránek, J.*, Social Classes, Nationality Ratios and Demographic Trends in Prague 1880–1900, in Historica, Vol. 13 (1966), pp. 171–208.

80. *Havránek, J.*, Životní podmínky dělnických rodin roku 1900 ve světě demografické statistiky, in Etnografie dělnictva, No. 9 (1977), pp. 55–124 (= Living conditions of working-class families in 1900 according to demographic statistics).

81. *Horská, P.*, and *L. Fialová*, eds. Dlouhodobé populační trendy na území ČSR – předstatistické období, Prague, 1981 (Acta demographica, IV) (= Long-term trends in the development of population on the territory of the ČSR – the period before the introduction of modern statistics).

82. *Janák, J.*, Snahy o zabránění další koncentrace dělnictva v polovině 19. století na příkladu Brna, in Časopis matice moravské, No. 96 (1977), pp. 129–153 (= Attempts to prevent further concentration of workers in the middle of the 19th century using Brno as an example).

83. *Janák, P.*, Sto let obytného domu nájemného v Praze, Prague 1933 (= A hundred years of blocks of rented flats in Prague).

84. *Jírový, K.*, and *J. Formánek*, Vývoj obyvatelstva hlavního města Prahy v letech 1920–1965, Prague, 1967 (= Development of the population of Prague 1920–1965).

85. *Kárníková, L.*, Vývoj obyvatelstva v českých zemích 1754–1914, Prague, 1965 (= The development of the population in the Bohemian provinces).

86. *Kučera, M.*, and *V. Srb*, Atlas obyvatelstva ČSSR, Prague, 1962 (= Atlas of the ČSSR population).

87. *Matějček, J.*, Formování hornictva sokolovského uhelného revíru, Opava, 1978 (= The development of the miner's population of the Sokolov coal mining region).

88. *Matějček, J.*, Rozhovory s mlčenlivými svědky, Ústí n.L. 1982 (= Conversations with taciturn witnesses. Social history of the coal mining region of northern Bohemia).

89. *Míka, Z.*, Příspěvek ke vzniku a formování pražského dělnictva v 1. polovině 19. století, in Etnografie dělnictva, No. 11 (1978), pp. 7–29 (= A contribution about the origins of the Prague working class in the first half of the 19th century).

90. *Musil, J.*, Sociologie bydlení, Prague, 1971 (= The sociology of housing conditions).

91. *Myška, M.*, Historicko-demografická charakteristika západní části ostravské průmyslové oblasti na konci 19. století, in Ostrava, No. 5 (1968), pp. 81–112 (= Historical demographic characteristics of the western part of the Ostrav industrial region until the end of the 19th century).

92. *Myška, M.*, Migranti z Haliče a jejich podíl na vytváření dělnicke třídy v uhelném průmyslu Moravské Ostravy v 2. polovině 19. stol., in Ostrava, No. 4 (1967), pp. 147–181 (= The immigrants from Galicia and their participation in the creation of the working class in the coal industry of Mŏravská Ostrava in the second half of the 20th century).

93. *Myška, M.*, Počátky vytváření dělnicke třídy na Ostravsku, Ostrava, 1962 (= The first phase of the establishment of the working class around Ostrava).

94. *Myška, M.*, and *C. Nečas*, Nástin kolonizace Ostravskokarvínského kamenouhelného revíru do r. 1945, Ostrava, 1969 (= A survey of the colonisation of Ostrava-Karviná pitcoal-basin up to 1945).

95. *Pelikánová-Nová, Z.*, Lidnatost Prahy v 18. a první čtvrti 19. století, in Pražský sborník historický, 1967/68, pp. 5–43 (= The population of Prague in the 18th and in the first quarter of the 19th century).

96. *Pešek, J.*, Chudina z Benešova a Sedlčanska mezi nejnižšími vrstvami proletariátu Královských Vinohrad, in Sborník vlastivědných prací z Podblanicka (Benešov), No. 23 (1982), pp. 273–289. (= Poverty in the regions of Berešov and Sedlčany among the lowest strata of the proletariat of Královské Virohrady).

97. *Pitronová, B.*, Podíl migrací na demografickém vývoji ostravské oblasti, in Slezský sborník, No. 76 (1978), pp. 26–43 (= The role of migration in the demographic development of the region of Ostrava).

98. *Placht, O.*, Lidnatost a společenská skladba českého státu v 16.–18. století, Prague, 1975 (= Population density and social structure in the Bohemian state in the 16th–18th century).

99. *Robek, A., et al.*, Stará dělnická Praha. Život a kultura pražských dělníků 1848–1939, Prague, 1981 (= The old workers' Prague. Life and culture of Prague workers 1848–1939).

100. *Sommer, K., et al.*, Materiály k dějinám průmyslových oblastí v období výstavby socialismu, Opava, 1983 (= Documents about the history of the industrial regions during the period of the establishment of social-ism).

101. *Steiner, J.*, Průmyslové oblasti v českých zemích v roce 1930. Charak-teristika podle ekonomicky aktivního obyvatelstva, in Slezský sborník, No. 82 (1984), pp. 161–180, and No. 83 (1985), pp. 129–160 (= The industrial areas in the Bohemian provinces in 1930. Characteristics of the working population).

102. *Štěpánek, L.*, Vývoj pražských nouzových kolonií a život jejich oby-vatel, in Pražský sborník historický, No. 11 (1979) pp. 139–153 (= The development of Prague temporary housing settlements and the life of their inhabitants).

103. *Šubrtová, A.*, Kojenecká úmrtnost v Praze na přelomu 18. a 19. století, in Statistika a demografie, No. 9 (1972), pp. 133–165 (= Infant mortality in Prague at the turn of the 18th to the 19th century).

104. *Teige, K.,* and *J. Kroha,* Avantgardní architektura, Prague, 1969 (= Architecture of the avant-garde in the 1930s).

105. *Vančík, F.,* Proletářský Žižkov, Prague, 1978 (= Žižkov of the proletariat).

106. *Vytiska, J., et al.,* K otázce charakteru brněnské průmyslové oblasti a jejího teritoriálního vymezení v letech 1945–1960, in Slezský sborník, No. 78 (1980), pp. 161–201 (= The question of territorial separation in the Brno industrial region in the years from 1945–1960).

(d)   Town Planning, Housing

107. *Andrle, A.,* and *Z. Kiesewetter,* Rozvoj měst a obcí v Československé socialistické republice, Prague, 1982 (= The development of towns and communities in the ČSSR).

108. *Bartušek, O.,* Long-term Radial Extension of the Growth Pole Effect in the Prague Suburban Area, in Hospodářské dějiny – Economic History, No. 2 (1968), pp. 295–311.

109. *Borovička, B.,* and *J. Hrůza,* Praha – 1000 let stavby města, Prague, 1984 (= Prague – 1000 years of urban development).

110. *Čarek, J., et al.,* Ulicemi města Prahy od 14. století do dneška, Prague, 1958 (= Through the streets of Prague from the 14th century up to today).

111. *Fuchs, B.,* Nové zónování, Prague, 1967 (= The new regulation of zones).

112. *Hlavsa, V.,* Pražské teritorium v druhé polovině 19. století (Rozvoj zástavby), in Pražský sborník historický, 1969/70, pp. 5–51 (= The territory of Prague in the second half of the 19th century, the development of house building).

113. *Hruška, E.,* Stavba miest, jej história, prítomnosť a budúcnosť, Bratislava, 1970 (= Urban development, its past, present and future).

114. *Hrůza, J.,* Budoucnost měst, Prague, 1962 (= The future of towns).

115. *Janák, P., B. Hübschmann* and *Z. Wirh,* Jak rostla Praha, Prague, 1939 (= How did Prague grow?).

116. *Matějů, P.,* Vývoj sociálně prostorové struktury Prahy v letech 1930–1970 ve světle faktorové analýzy, in Sociologický časopis, No. 16 (1980), pp. 572–592 (= The development of the territorial structure of Prague, its factor analysis).

117. *Míka, Z.,* Průmyslové předměstí Karlín v 19. století a jeho význam pro Prahu, in Pražský sborník historický, No. 9 (1975), pp. 78–146 (= The industrial suburb Karlín in the 19th century and its importance for Prague).

118. *Švácha, R.,* Od moderny k funkcionalismu. Proměny pražské architektury 1. poloviny 20. století, Prague, 1985 (= From the modern age to functionalism. Changes in Prague architecture in the first half of the

20th century).

119. *Vondrová, A.*, Český funkcionalismus 1920–1940, architektura, Prague, 1978 (= Czech functionalism in town planning and architecture 1920–1940).

120. *Zelinka, T. C.*, Pražská předměstí, Prague, 1955 (= Prague suburbs).

(e) Economy and Transport

121. *Bělina, P.*, Česká města v 18. století a osvícenské reformy, Prague, 1985 (= Bohemian towns in the 18th century and enlightenment reforms).

122. *Bělina, P.*, Příspěvek k ekonomické stratifikaci měst v Čechách koncem 18. století, in Hospodářské dějiny, No. 1 (1978), pp. 231–262 (= The economic stratification of towns in Bohemia at the end of the 18th century).

123. *Buchtík, J.*, Pražský vodovod. Historie a současnost, výstavba a výhled, Prague, 1973 (= Prague water supply. History and present-day, construction and perspectives).

124. *Cvik, J.*, 70 let městské dopravy na Ostravsku 1894–1964 Ostrava, 1964 (= 70 years of local transport in the region of Ostrava).

125. *Dudek, F.*, Vývoj cukrovarnického průmyslu na území Velké Prahy v období průmyslové revoluce, in Historická geografie, No. 12–15 (1978), pp. 329–365 (= The development of the sugar industry in the territory of Great Prague in the period of industrial revolution).

126. *Frohmann, J.*, O pražské zastavárně, době a lidech kolem ní, Prague, 1947 (= The Prague pawnshop, its times and people).

127. *Horská-Vrbová, P.*, Pražský průmysl v druhé polovině 19. století, in Pražský sborník historický, 1969/70, pp. 52–69 (= Industry in Prague in the second half of the 19th century).

128. *Janková, Y.*, Pražská tržnice, in Staletá Praha, No. 13 (1983), pp. 59–70 (= Prague market hall).

129. *Kopačka, L.*, Vývoj průmyslu v Praze v období 1945–1975, in Historická geografie, No. 14/15 (1978), pp. 265–306 (= The development of industry in Prague 1945–1975).

130. *Losos, L.*, Dějiny městské dopravy, Prague, 1984 (= The history of city transport).

131. *Loubal, F.*, Sto let veterinární služby hlavního města Prahy, Prague, 1968 (= One hundred years of veterinary service in the capital city of Prague).

132. *Míka, A.*, Řemesla a obchod v českých městech ve světle tereziánského katastru, in Pražský sborník historický, No. 11 (1979), pp. 104–138 (= Craft and trade in Bohemian towns in the 18th century).

133. *Míka, Z.*, Počátky průmyslové výroby v Praze, in Pražský sborník historický, No. 12 (1980), pp. 83–169 (= The beginnings of industry

in Prague).

134. *Pošusta, S., et al.,* Od koňky k metru, Prague, 1975 (= From horse tramway to underground).

135. *Průmyslové oblasti Slovenska za kapitalismu 1780–1945,* Opava, 1983 (= Industrial regions of Slovakia within the epoch of capitalism 1780–1945).

136. *Roubal, J.,* Problémy hospodaření měst České Budějovice a Písek v období od r. 1923 do r. 1958, in Jihočeský sborník historický, No. 34 (1965), pp. 155–179, and No. 35 (1966), pp. 41–57 (= Problems of the communal economy of České Budějovice and Písek 1923–1958).

137. *Roubík, F.,* Od nosítek k trolejbusu, Prague 1956 (= From sedan-chair to trolleybus).

138. *Rys, J.,* and *J. Vlček,* Všeobecná nemocnice v Praze 1790–1950, Prague, 1956 (= The public hospital in Prague).

139. *Smrček, O.,* Počátky strojírenského průmyslu v Praze (do r. 1873), in Historická geografie, No. 14/15 (1978), pp. 307–328 (= The beginning of the machine-building industry in Prague up to 1873).

140. *Sto let boje proti požárům 1864–1964,* Prague, 1964 (= One hundred years of fire-fighting).

141. *Vytiska, J.,* Ostravská průmyslová oblast v letech 1945–1969, Opava, 1980 (= The industrial region of Ostrava 1945–1969).

(f)   Arts and Sciences, Churches

142. *Honzík, K.,* Tvorba životního prostředí, Prague, 1946 (= Creating a Milieu for living).

143. *Honzík, K.,* Tvorba životního slohu, Prague, 1965 (= Creating a style of living).

144. *Honzík, K.,* Ze života avantgardy, Prague, 1963 (= From the life of the avant garde – recollections).

145. *Koula, J. E.,* Nová česká architektura, Prague, 1940 (= New Czech architecture).

146. *Melniková-Papoušková, N.,* Praha před sto lety, Prague, 1935 (= Prague one hundred years ago).

147. *Město v české kultuře 19. století,* Prague, 1983 (= The town in 19th century Czech culture).

148. *Nejedlý, Z.,* Bedřich Smetana. III. Praha 1839–40, Prague, 1929, 2nd ed., Prague, 1954.

149. *Novotný, A.,* Praha "Temna" (1719–1729), Prague, 1946 (= "Dark" Prague).

150. *Novotný, A.,* Z Praha doznívajícího baroka 1730–1740, Prague, 1947 (= Prague at the end of the Baroque period).

151. *Novotný, A.,* O Praze mládí F. L. Věka (1757–1792), Prague, 1940 (= Prague of the young Vek).

152. *Novotný, A.*, Naposledy o Praze F. L. Věka (1792–1815), Prague, 1948 (= For the last time: The Prague of the young Vek).

153. *Praha našeho věku*, ed., E. Poche, Prague, 1978 (= Prague in our century).

154. *Pražské památky obdobi 1860–1960 a jejich ochrana*, in Staletá Praha, No. 7 (1975), and No. 9 (1981) (= Prague monuments 1860–1960 and their protection).

155. *Pražské památky pokrokových tradic*, in Staletá Praha, No. 13 (1983) (= Prague monuments of the progressive tradition).

156. *Technika a památky*, n.p. n.d. (The protection of technical monuments).

E. Local Studies (a representative selection)

● Bratislava

157. *Butvin, J.*, Bratislava v slovenskom národnom obrodení a otázka slovenského národného strediska v rokoch 1780–1848, in Historický časopis, No. 21 (1973), pp. 531–574 (= Bratislava and the question of the national centre in the years 1780–1848).

158. *Horváth, V., D. Lehotská* and *J. Pleva*, Dejiny Bratislavy, Bratislava 1978 (= The history of Bratislava).

159. *Horváth, V., S. Rákoš* and *J. Watzka*, Bratislava hlavné mesto Slovenska. Pripojenie Bratislavy k Československej republike roku 1918. Dokumenty, Bratislava, 1977 (= Bratislava, the capital of Slovakia. The connection with the Czechoslovak Republic in 1918. Documents).

160. *Lehotská, D.*, and *V. Horváth*, Dejiny Bratislavy, Bratislava, 1982 (= The history of Bratislava).

161. *Lehotská, D.*, and *V. Lehotský*, Sociální zápasy bratislavského robotnictva. Dokumenty, Bratislava, 1979 (= Social struggles amongst the working class of Bratislava. Documents).

162. *Provazník, D.*, Robotnicke hnutie v Bratislave, Bratislava, 1970 (= The working class movement in Bratislava 1918–1929).

163. *Provazník, D.*, Sociálno-ekonomická charakteristika Bratislavy v 20. rokoch predmníchovskej ČSR, in Sborník filozofickej fakulty UK., marx.-len., Vol. 20 (1960), pp. 201–218 (Social economic characteristics of Bratislava in the twenties before the Munich agreement).

● Brno

164. *Dřímal, J.*, and *V. Peša*, Dějiny města Brna II. 1848–, Brno, 1973 (= History of the city of Brno since 1848).

165. *Zřidkaveselý, F., et al.*, Brno mezi městy střední Evropy, Brno, 1983 (= Brno among the cities of Central Europe).

● Česká Lípa

166. *Vojtíškova, M.*, and *J. Panáček*, Česká Lípa, Ústi, n.L., 1976.

● Havlíčkův Brod

167. *Sochr, J.*, Havlíčkův Brod a staletí, Havlíčkův Brod, 1971 (= Havlíčkův Brod through the centuries).

● Towns and cities in the region of Ostrava

— Bílovec

168. *650 let města Bílovce*, Bilovec, 1971 (= 650 years of Bílovec).

— Bohumín

169. *Bohumín.* Studie a materiály k dějinam a výstavbě města, eds., A. Grobelný and B. Čepelák, Ostrava, 1976 (= Bohumin. Studies and material on the history and construction of the town).

— Brušperk

170. *Brušperk, město nikolív nejmenší*, ed., L. Dokoupil, Ostrava, 1969 (= Brušperk, not the smallest of towns).

— Český Těšín

171. *Český Těšín, 50 let městem*, eds., A. Grobelný and B. Čepelák, Ostrava, 1973 (= 50 years of Český Těšín).

— Orlová

172. *Plaček, V., et al.*, Orlová, 1223–1973, Ostrava, 1973.

— Ostrava

173. *Jiřík, P., et al.*, Dějiny Ostravy, Ostrava, 1967 (= History of Ostrava).
174. *Ostravská průmyslová oblast v 1. polovině 20. století*, Opava-Ostrava, 1973 (= The industrial regions of Ostrava in the 1st half of the 19th century).

● Pelhřimov

175. *Dobiáš, J.*, Dějiny Pelhřimova, Vol. I.–VI, Prague, 1927–1970 (= History of Pelhřimov).

● Plzeň

176. *Čepelák, V., et al.*, Dějiny Plzně, II. (1788–1948), Plzeň, 1981

(= History of Plzeň).

177. *Laštovka, V., et al.*, Dějiny Plzně, III. (1918–1948), Plzeň, 1981. (= History of Plzeň).

● Prague

178. *Dějiny Prahy*, ed. J. Janáček, Prague, 1964 (= History of Prague).

179. *Historická geografie*, No. 14/15 (1976): Příspěvky k dějinám pražské aglomerace, 2 vols. and a volume of maps (= Contributions to the history of Prague agglomeration).

180. *Honzík, M.*, and *J. Galandauer*, Praha 1921, Prague, 1981 (= Prague 1921).

181. *Král, J.*, Zeměpisný průvodce Velkou Prahou a její kulturní oblastí, Prague, 1946 (= Geographic guide through Great Prague and its cultural sphere).

182. *Ledvinka, V., et al.*, Vývoj Prahy v moderní velkoměsto v období 1784–1984, in Documenta Pragensia, Vol. 5/1 and 5/2, Prague 1985 (= The Development of Prague into a modern city 1784–1984).

183. *Lehovec, O.*, Prague. Town geography and local history. Prague, 1944.

184. *Novotný, J.*, K národnostnímu složení pražského obyvatelstva na sklonku 18. století, in Documenta Pragensia, Vol. 4, (1984), pp. 335–341 (= On the national structure of the Prague population at the end of the 18th century).

185. *Praha národního probuzení*, ed. E. Poche, Prague, 1980 (= Prague in the time of national revival).

186. *Tomek, V. V.*, Dějepis města Prahy, Vol. I. –XII Prague 1855–1901 (= History of the city of Prague).

187. *Zmizelá Praha*, 6 vols. Prague 1945–1948 (= The Prague that has disappeared).

● Moravian towns and cities

— Prečova

188. *Hosák, L., et al.*, Dějiny města Přerova, Přerov, 1971 (= History of Přerov).

— Třebíč

189. *Janák, J.*, Třebíč. Dějiny města, Vol. 2, Brno, 1981 (= Třebíč. A history).

— Uherský Brod

190. *Zemek, M.*, Uherský Brod. Minulost i současnost slováckého města, Brno, 1972 (= Past and present of the Moravian-Slovakian town Uherský Brod).

— Uherský Hradiš

191. *Verbík, A.*, and *M. Zemek*, Dějiny Uherského Hradiště, Brno, 1972 (= History of Uherský Hradiš).

— Žďár

192. *Zemek, M., et al.*, Dějiny Žďáru nad Sázavou, Brno, 1974 (= History of Žďár).

● Slovak Towns and Cities

— Bardejov

193. *Kokula, A., A. Lukác* and *L. Tajták*, Dejiny Bardejova, Košice, 1975 (= The history of Bardejov).

— Levoča

194. *Suchý, M.*, and *I. Chalupecký*, Dejiny Levoče, Part 2: 1848–súčasnosť), Košice, 1975 (= The history of Levoča).

— Prešov

195. *Sedlák, I., et al.*, Dejiny prešova, Košice, 1965 (= The history of Prešov).

— Rožňava

196. *Tajták, L.*, Dejiny Rožňavy, Košice, 1978 (= The history of Rožňava).

— Trebišov

197. *Tatják, L.*, Dejiny Trebišova, Košice, 1982 (= The history of Trebišov).

— Trstená

198. *Langer, J.*, Trstená 600-ročná, Martin, 1973 (= 600-year-old Trstená).

— Žiar

199. *Ratkoš, P., et al.*, Dejiny Žiaru nad Hronom, Martin, 1978 (= The history of Žiar nad Hronom).

THOMAS RIIS AND SØREN FEDERSPIEL

Denmark

Denmark was urbanised relatively early; most of its present cities can trace their beginnings back to the Middle Ages. Town dwellers made up 20% of the population in 1769 (1870: 25%; 1890: 33%). In spite of this, urban history research had still not made much progress by 1960. There was a mere handful of comparative town histories concentrating on the sphere of urban constitutional history. A few source publications were added to these, and a general town chronicle, often written by enthusiasts, could be found for almost every urban centre.

This situation has changed since 1960. Nowadays there is scarcely a town without its own general history written, or at least in the process of being written, by an historian, and a number of works has been published dealing, in particular, with the history of industrialisation and the workers' movement. It is likely that this interest in the 19th and early 20th centuries has partly to do with the establishment of the "Society for the History of the Workers' Movement" and partly with the two projects that the Danish Research Council for the Humanities is conducting on the industrialisation of Denmark from 1840 to 1940 and on the town-like settlements sprouting up at new rail stations. A corresponding interest in the topography of towns in the Middle Ages was cultivated by a third project of the Research Council on the Middle Ages' topography of ten selected townships.

Despite this most welcome overall increase in urban history research activity, many areas have been given no more than a cursory glance to date. While there are studies on urban demography and on the relationship between towns and their environs, surveys on the size of households and families, and on urban water and food supplies have been neglected so far. Other subjects which have received little research attention — despite the existence of relevant sources — is the extent of urban property in the hands of the church and aristocracy, for example, and the economic ties between towns in the south of Denmark and German towns on the Baltic coast.

There is still much to be done in the field of urban history. However, it is encouraging to see increased interest in this subject, which might be the result of migration from the country to the towns, a characteristic feature of the last few decades.

A. Urban History Institutions

Aarhus Byhistoriske Udvalg, Århus (= Committee for history of the city of Århus).

Arbejderbevægelsens Bibliotek og Arkiv, Copenhagen (= Library and archives of the workers' movement).

Dansk Komité for Byhistorie, Frederiksberg (= Danish Committee for urban history).

Erhvervsarkivet, Århus (= Archives for employer and industrial history).

Københavns Stadsarkiv, Copenhagen (= Copenhagen's State Archives).

Købstadmuseet Den gamle By, Århus (= Open-air museum "The Old City").

Lokalhistorisk Afdeling, Copenhagen (= University of Copenhagen, Institute of History, Department of Local History).

Nationalmuseets Købstadundersøgelser, Lyngby (= Danish National Museum, Dept. III: Section for Urban History and Urban Culture).

Planstyrelsen, Copenhagen (= Government Department of Planning including preservation of monuments and historically valuable buildings).

B. Aids to Research

(a) Urban History Journals

1. *Aalborgbogen,* Ålborg (= Monographs on the history of the city of Ålborg; published annually).
2. *Aarbog for Arbejderbevægelsens Historie* (= Yearbook on history of the workers' movement).
3. *Erhvervshistorisk Aarbog* (= Yearbook on employer and industrial history).
4. *Fabrik og bolig,* 1975 ff. (= Factory and housing); up to 1978 under the title "Industrialismens byginger og boliger" (= Buildings and housing in the industrial era).
5. *Historiske Meddelelser om København. Aarbog* (= Yearbook on the history of Copenhagen).
6. *Nyt fra Stationsbyen,* 1982 ff. (= News from railway settlements).

(b) Bibliographies

Regularly published bibliographies on urban history are found in the journals *Aarbog for Arbejderbevægelsens Historie* (= Yearbook on history of the workers' movement), *Fortid og Nutid* (= History and the present. Regular review of the contents of local history journals), and the *Scandinavian Economic History Review*.

7. *International Bibliography of Urban History. Denmark, Finland, Norway, Sweden*, Stockholm, 1960.
8. *Jansen, H. M., K. Hannestad* and *T. Riis*, A Select Bibliography of Danish Works on the History of Towns published 1960–1976, Odense, 1977 (Dansk Komité for Byhistorie: Byhistoriske Hjælpemidler II).
9. *Jansen, H. M., T. Riis* and *P. Strømstad*, A Select Bibliography of Danish Works on the History of Towns published 1979–1982, Copenhagen, 1983 (Dansk Komité for Byhistorie: Byhistoriske Hjælpemidler VI).
10. *Jansen, H. M., T. Riis* and *P. Strømstad*, Denmark, in Guide International d'Histoire Urbaine, Vol. 1, ed. P. Wolff, Paris, 1977, pp. 146–155.
11. *Lunding, F.*, and *M. Ø. Jensen*, Bibliografi over arbejderboliger å socialt boligbyggeri i Danmark 1850–1981, Copenhagen, 1983 (= Bibliography on the history of working-class housing and publicly assisted housing).

(c)   Handbooks on Urban History

12. *Trap, J. P.*, Danmark, Tl. I–XXXI, 5th ed., Copenhagen 1953–1972 (= Topographical description of Denmark).

(d)   Atlases on Urban History and Urban Development

13. *Scandinavian Atlas of Historic Towns*
    – Vol. 3, Degn, O., *Ribe*, Odense, 1983.
    – Vol. 5, Tuxen, P., *Stege*, Odense, 1987.
    – *Køge, Randers* and *Svendborg*, in preparation.
14. *Adriansen, I.*, Sønderborg byhistorisk atlas, Sønderborg, 1982 (= Town atlas of Sønderborg).
15. *Dencker, H.* and *H. Fangel*, Åbenrå: Byhistorisk Atlas, Åbenrå, 1985 (= Town atlas of Åbenrå).
16. *Viborg Købstads Historie*, Vol. IV, Copenhagen, 1940 (= History of Viborg).

(e)   Urban History Sources

17. *Hyldtoft, O., H. Askgaard* and *N. F. Christiansen*, Det industrielle Danmark 1840–1914, Herning, 1981 (= Sources related to the industrialisation of Denmark 1840–1914).

- Åbenrå

18. *Kamphövener, M.*, ed., Borgerskaber i Åbenrå 1686–1867, Vols. I–II, Åbenrå, 1974 (= Åbenrå citizens' deeds 1686–1867).

Bibliographies

- Århus

19. *Hübertz, J. R.*, ed., Aktstykker vedkommende Staden og Stiftet Århus, Vols. I–III, Copenhagen 1845–1846 (= Records on the history of the city and bishopric of Århus).

20. *Enemark, P.*, ed., Erhverv i Århus 1735: Indberetninger om byens økonomiske tilstand, Århus, 1963 (= Reports on the economy of Århus in 1735).

- Assens

21. *Jonasen, O.*, ed., Gamle huse i Assens: Jænføringsregister over ejendomsnumre samt grundejerfortegnelse for Assens Købstads Bygrunde 1682–1863, Svendborg, 1981 (Byhistoriske Hjælpemidler IV. Skrifter for Svendborg og Omegns Museum. 5) (= Comparative register containing the cadastral numbers and the names of landowners in the urban district of Assens 1682–1863).

- Copenhagen

22. *Grove, G. L.*, Københavns Huse og Indvaaner efter Branden 1728, Copenhagen, 1906 (= Copenhagen's houses and inhabitants after the fire of 1728).

23. *Holbergtidens Københavns skildret af malerne Rach og Eegberg*. En billedrække kommenteret af P. Strømstad, Copenhagen, 1977 (= 72 pictures of Copenhagen around the mid-18th century).

- Hadersleben

24. *Achelis, T. O.*, Bürgerbuch der Stadt Hadersleben bis zum Jahre 1864, Vol. I, Flensburg, 1940.

- Helsingør

25. *Pedersen, K.*, ed., Jævnføringsregister over Helsingør Købstads Bygrunde matrikelnumre 1682–1975, Helsingør, 1979, (Byhistoriske Hjælpemidler III) (= Comparative register of the cadastral numbers in the urban district of Helsingør 1682–1975).

- Køge

26. *Witt, T.*, Jænføringsregister for Køge købstads bygrunde 1682–1963, Copenhagen, 1964 (= Comparative register of the cadastral numbers in the urban district of Køge 1682–1963).

296

• Svaneke

27. *Andersen, P. A., et al.*, eds., Kilder til Svanekes bygningshistorie, Copenhagen, 1969 (= Sources on the architectural history of Svaneke).

• Svendborg

28. *Jonasen, O.*, ed., Gamle huse i Svendborg: Jævnføringsregister over ejendomsnumre samt grundejerfortegnelse for Svendborg Købstads Bygrunde 1682–1867, Svendborg, 1983 (Byhistoriske Hjælpemidler VII. Skrifter for Svendborg og Omegns Museum. 8) (= Comparative register of the cadastral numbers and names of landowners in the urban district of Svendborg 1682–1867).

• Tønder

29. *Andresen, L.*, ed., Bürger- und Einwohnerbuch der Stadt Tondern, Kiel, 1937.

• Viborg

30. *la Cour Dragsbo, J. P.*, and *G. Rung*, Jævnføringsregister over Viborg Købstads Bygrundes matrikelnumre 1682–1974, Copenhagen, 1976 (Byhistoriske Hjælpemidler I) (= Comparative register of the cadastral numbers in the urban district of Viborg 1682–1974).

31. *Spreckelsen, O. von*, ed., Viborg Bys Borgerbog 1713–1860, Viborg, 1955 (= Record book of Viborg citizens 1713–1860).

C. Research Reports

(a) General Surveys

32. *Authén Blom, G.*, ed., Urbaniseringsprosessen i Norden I–III, Oslo et al., 1977 (= Urbanisation in Scandinavia, Vol. I: Denmark in the Middle Ages; Vol. II: Denmark 1600–1800; Vol. III: Denmark 1800–1920).

33. *Danske byers udvikling*: En registrering udarbejdet af Arkitektskolen i København, Copenhagen, 1972 (= Development of urbanisation in Denmark).

34. *Jansen, H. M.*, Early Urbanization in Denmark, in H. B. Clarke and A. Simms, eds., The Comparative History of Urban Origins in Non-Roman Europe, Oxford, 1985, pp. 183–216.

35. *Lebech, M.*, Danske købstæder for tohundrede år siden og idag, Vols.

I–II, Copenhagen, 1961 (= Danish towns 200 years ago and today).

36. *Olsen, G.*, De danske Købstæder gennem Tiderne, Copenhagen, 1943 (= Danish towns and their history).

37. *Steensberg, A.*, ed., Dagligliv i Danmark, I–IV, Copenhagen 1963–1969 (= Everyday life in Denmark, Vol. I: on towns 1620–1720; Vol. II: 1720–1790; Vol. III/IV: 19th–20th centuries).

38. *Svensson, O.*, Danish Town Planning Guide, Copenhagen, 1981.

(b)   Surveys on Individual Fields of Urban Research

39. *Callesen, G.*, Zur Geschichte der dänischen Arbeiterbewegung, in Archiv für Sozialgeschichte, Vol. XII, (1972), pp. 628–648.

40. *Degn, O.*, Urbanisering og industrialisering. En forskningsoversigt, Copenhagen, 1978 (= Urbanisation and industrialisation; a research report).

41. *Grelle, H.*, Under de røde faner: En historie om arbejderbevægelsen, Copenhagen, 1984 (= History of the workers' movement).

42. *Kayser, K.* and *P. Strømstad*, Vejledning i undersøgelse af købstadbygninger, in Fortid og Nutid, 1968, pp. 355–382 (= An introduction to the study of town houses).

43. *Strømstad P.*, Slum Clearance and the Investigation of Town Buildings, in E. Rasmussen, ed., Dansk Folkemuseum, Copenhagen, 1966, pp. 77–104.

D.   Literature on Individual Areas of Urban History Research

(a)   Concept and Definition of Town and Town Types

44. *Balle-Petersen, P.*, De nye byer, in Arv og Eje, 1976, pp. 69–92 (= New towns).

45. *Hansen, V.*, Den rurale by: De bymæssige bebyggelsers opståen og geografiske udbredelse, in Geografisk Tidsskrift, 1965, pp. 54–69 (= The country town).

46. *Illeris, S.*, The Functions of Danish Towns, in Geografisk Tidsskrift, 1964, pp. 203–236.

47. *Illeris, S.*, Research on Changes in the Structure of the Urban Network, Copenhagen, 1980.

48. *Jansen, C. R.*, ed., Stationsbyen: Rapport fra et seminar om Stationsbyens historie 1840–1940, Århus, 1980 (= Reports from a symposium on the history of railway settlements 1840–1940).

49. *Rasmussen, V. D.*, Nørrejyske jernbanebyer: udvalgte problemer omkring placeringen og befolkningsudviklingen 1850–1901, Århus, 1981 (= Railway settlements in North Jutland 1850–1901: settlement problems and demographic growth).

50. *Riis, T.*, Les villes et les campagnes au Danemark ca. 1350–1800, in Storia della Città, Vol. 36 (1986), pp. 25–36.

51. *Stilling, N. P.*, De nye byer. Stationsbyernes befolkningsforhold og funktion 1840–1940, Copenhagen 1987 (= Demography and functions of railway settlements).

(b)   Politics, Law and Statutes

52. *Dybdahl, V.*, Partier og erhverv. Studier i partiorganisation og byerhvervenes politiske aktivitet ca. 1880–1913, Vols. I–II, Århus, 1969 (= Party organisation and political activity in the urban economy).

53. *Henningsen, Lars N.*, Fattigvæsenet i de sønderjyske købstæder 1736–1841, Åbenrå, 1978 (= Public assistance to the poor in North Schleswig towns 1736–1841).

54. *Jørgensen, J.*, Patriciat og Enevælde, in Historiske Meddelelser om København, 1963, pp. 11–62, and 1964, pp. 7–89 (= Patricians and absolutism).

55. *Linde, H.*, Magistrat og Borger: Købstadstyret på Sjælland omkring 1750 med særlig hensyntagen til forholdene i Helsingør, Roskilde, Næstved og Holbæk, Århus, 1978 (= Town councils in Zealand around 1750: examples from Helsingør, Roskilde, Næstved and Holbæk).

56. *Munch, P.*, Købstadstyrelsen i Danmark fra Christian IV til Enevældens Ophor 1619–1848, Vols. I–II Copenhagen, 1900 (rpt. 1977) (= The Danish town constitution 1619–1848).

57. *Riis, T.*, Le pouvoir central et les villes du Danemark. XVe–XVIIIe siècles, in T. Riis and P. Strømstad, eds., Le pouvoir central et les villes en Europe (du Nord) du XVe siècle aux débuts de la révolution industrielle, Copenhagen, 1978, pp. 51–60 (Byhistoriske Skrifter I).

(c)   Population and Social Structure

58. *Burchardt, J.*, Arbejdsmandens Historie i 100 år, Vol. I: Fabrik, Copenhagen, 1982 (= History of factory workers since the end of the 19th century).

59. *Jensen J. H., E. Hansen* and *L. Voss*, Sociale studier. Kriminalitet, Prostitution og Fattigom i Århus ca. 1870–1906, Århus, 1975 (= Crime, prostitution and poverty in Århus 1870–1906).

60. *Møller Hornemann, I.*, Klassekamp og sociallovgivning 1850–1970, Copenhagen, 1981 (= Class struggle and social legislation 1850–1970).

61. *Olsen, A.*, Bybefolkningen i Danmark på Merkantilismens Tid, Århus and Copenhagen, 1932 (rpt. 1975) (= The urban population in Denmark at the time of mercantilism).

62. *Vammem, T.*, Rent og urent: Hovedstadens piger og fruer 1880–1920, Copenhagen, 1986 (= Women and housemaids in Copenhagen 1880–1920).

63. *Wichmann Matthiessen, C.*, Danske byers folketal 1801–1981, Copenhagen, 1985 (= Demographic development in Danish towns 1801–1981).

(d)   Town Planning, Housing

64. *Arbejderen og boligen*, Copenhagen, 1984 (Årbog for Arbejderbevægelsens Historie, Vol. XIV) (= Workers and their dwellings).

65. *Danmarks Arkitektur*, Vols. I–II, Copenhagen, 1979 (= Denmark's Architecture).
   – Vol. I: *Jørgensen, L. B.*, Enfamilienhuset (= One-family dwelling).
   – Vol. II: *Sestoft, J.*, Arbejdets Bygninger (= Factories).

66. *la Cour Dragsbo, P.*, Mennesker og huse i Aabenraa. Et etnologisk studie af kvarterudvikling i en nordslesvigsk købstad 1850–1920, Esbjerg, 1978 (= The evolution of districts in Åbenrå 1850–1920).

67. *Dehn-Nielsen, H.*, Danske byer set fra luften, Copenhagen, 1986 (= Aerial view of Denmark's towns).

68. *Dybdahl, L.*, Byplan og boligmiljø efter 1800, Copenhagen, 1973 (= Town planning and living quality after 1800).

69. *Lorenzen, V.*, Vore Byer: Studier i Bybygning, Vols. I–V, Copenhagen, 1947–1958 (= Our towns: studies in town planning).

70. *Strømstad, P.*, ed., Ildebrandshuse: En bygningshistorisk og etnologisk undersøgelse af 24 ejendomme i gaderne Åbenrå og Landemærket, Copenhagen, 1966 (= Architectural, historical and ethnological study of a group of Copenhagen buildings constructed directly after the fire of 1728).

71. *Strømstad, P.*, ed., Rapport fra Nordisk Forskersymposium om bevaring og dokumentation af industrimiljøer, København og Horsens 3.–7. Okt. 1983, Copenhagen, 1984 (= A collection of reports from a Scandinavian symposium on the preservation and documentation of industrial milieu).

72. *Toft Jensen, H.*, and *P. Axelsen*, Fabriksboliger i Danmark: Lolland — Falster, Maribo Amt, Copenhagen, 1982 (= Factory dwellings on Lolland and Falster).

73. *Vasström, A.*, Holmens by. Nyboder og dets beboere - især i nyere tid, Copenhagen, 1985 (Orlogsmuseets Skriftrække 1) (= The residential district of members of the navy in the 20th century in particular).

74. *Wichmann Matthiessen, C.*, Danske Byers Vækst, Copenhagen, 1985 (= The growth of Danish towns 1801–1918).

75. *Willerslev, R.*, Sådan boede vi. Arbejdernes boligforhold i København omkring 1880, Copenhagen, 1979 (Industrialismens Bygninger og Boliger, Publikation 15) (= Living conditions of Copenhagen workers around 1880).

(e)   Economy and Transport

76. *Becker-Christensen, H.*, De danske købstæders økonomiske udvikling og regeringens erhvervspolitik 1660–1750, in Erhvervshistorisk Årbog, Vol. XXIX (1979), pp. 41–97 (= Danish cities' economic development and the government's economic policy 1660–1750).

77. *Bjørn, H.*, Staten, kræmmerne og forlagssystemet 1620–1735, in Erhvervshistorisk Årbog, Vol. XXVII (1976/77), pp. 7–34 (= The state, small retailers and cottage industry 1620–1735).

78. *Boje, P.*, Danske provinskøbmænds vareomsætning og kapitalforhold 1815–1847, Århus, 1977 (= Turnover of merchandise and merchants' capital in the provinces 1815–1847).

79. *Christensen, A. E., J. O. Bro-Jørgensen and A. Nielsen*, Industriens Historie i Danmark, Vols. I–IV, Copenhagen, 1943–1944 (= Industrial history in Denmark).

80. *Dybdahl, V., et al.*, eds., Handværkets Kulturhistorie, Vols. I–IV, Copenhagen, 1982–1984 (= A cultural history of the craftsmen's trade).

— Vol. III: *Dybdahl, V.* and *I. Dübeck*, Handværket og statsmagten 1700–1862 (= The craftsmen's trade and the power of the State 1700–1682)

— Vol. IV: *Fode, H., et al.*, Kapløbet med industrien. Perioden 1862–1890 (= Race against industry)

81. *Fink, J.*, Træk af den industrielle udvikling 1897–1914 in Erhvervshistorisk Årbog, Vol. XXXI (1981), pp. 159–182 (= Guidelines to industrial development 1897–1914).

82. *Hansen, G.*, Købmændene i Sakskøbing og Maribo i 1700-arene — deres økonomiske og sociale placering, in Fortid og Nutid, Vol. XXV (1972), pp. 20–62 (= Merchants in Sakskøbing and Maribo in the 18th century – their economic and social role).

83. *Hansen, S. A.*, Early Industrialization in Denmark, Copenhagen, 1970.

84. *Hastrup, B.*, Håndværkets økonomiske Historie 1879–1979, Copenhagen, 1979 (= Economic history of handicraft and small industry 1879–1979).

85. *Jørgensen, J.*, The Economic Condition of Zealand Provincial Towns in the 18th century, in Scandinavian Economic History Review, Vol. XIX (1971), pp. 1–11.

86. *Jørgensen, J.*, Denmark's Relations with Lübeck and Hamburg in the 17th century, in Scandinavian Economic History Review, Vol. XI (1963), p. 73–116.

87. *Meier, P. U.*, Omkring de fire species: dansk merkantilistisk stabel- og navigationspolitik i 1720'erne. Copenhagen, 1981 (= Mercantile

storage and shipping policy in the 1720s).

88. *Nicolaisen, S.*, Dansk industri i 1800-tallet: produktion og mennesker, Copenhagen, 1982 (= Danish industry in the 19th century).

89. *Rasmussen, E.*, Mester og Svend: Studier over københavnske tømrer- og murersvendes lønproblemer og sociale forhold 1756–1800, Århus, 1985 (= Master craftsman and journeyman: studies on the wages and social conditions of Copenhagen journeymen-carpenters and -masons 1756–1800).

90. *Thestrup, P.*, The Standard of Living in Copenhagen 1730–1800, Copenhagen, 1971.

91. *Vang Hansen, J., et al.*, Industrisabotagen under besættelsen i tal og komentarer, Copenhagen, 1914 (= Industrial sabotage under the German occupation 1940–1945).

(f)   Arts and Sciences, Churches

92. *Andersen, S. A.*, Dansk arbejderkultur: Grundtræk af dansk arbejderkultur og arbejderlitteratur i perioden fra 1870 til 1930, Vols. I–II, Århus, 1982 (= Features of Danish working-class culture and literature 1870–1930).

93. *Arbejderliv.* Knejpe — kirke — kino, Copenhagen, 1985 (Årbog for Arbejderbevægelsens Historie, Vol. XV) (= Life of the workers: pub–church–cinema).

94. *Danmarks Kirker*, Vol. I, Copenhagen, 1933 (= Denmark's churches: archaeological – art historical description).

95. *Linde, H., et al.*, eds., Københavns kommunes biblioteker 1885–1985, in Historiske Meddelelser om København, 1985, pp. 7–199 (= Copenhagen's municipal libraries 1885–1985).

E.   Local Studies (a representative selection)

● Århus

96. *Andersen, D.*, Århus under storlockouten, Århus, 1970 (= Århus during the lockout in 1899).

97. *Andersen, H. H., P. J. Crabb* and *H. J. Madsen*, Århus Søndervold. En byarkælogisk undersøgelse, Århus, 1971 (Jysk Arkæologisk Selskabs Skrifter. 9) (= Århus Søndervold – a study of a city centre).

● Copenhagen

98. *Cedergreen Bech, S., E. Kjersgaard* and *J. Danielsen*, eds., Københavns Historie, Vols. I–VI, Copenhagen, 1980–1983 (= History of Copenhagen).

99. *Møller, A. M.*, Københavns Handelsflåde 1814–1832: en historisk statistisk detailundersøgelse, Copenhagen, 1974 (Københavns Universitet, Institut for Økonomisk Historie, Publikation 7) (= Copenhagen's merchant fleet 1814–1832).

● Haderslev

100. *Fangel, H.*, Haderslev Bys Historie 1800–1945, Vol. I, Haderslev, 1975 (= History of Haderslev).

● Holbæk

101. *Hertz, M.*, Holbæk i hundred år o. 1880–1980: fra kornhandelsby til storkommune, Holbæk, 1986 (= Holbæk 1880–1980: from corntrading village to large municipality).

● Kalundborg

102. *Nyberg, T.*, and *T. Riis*, eds., Kalundborgs Historie, Vols. I–IV, Kalundborg, 1983 (= History of the city of Kalundborg; Vols. I and III published to date).

● Køge

103. *Nielsen, H.*, ed., Køge Bys Historie 1288–1988, Vol. I: 1288–1850, Køge, 1985 (= History of the city of Køge).

● Nibe

104. *Christensen, H.*, Ni tværsnit af Nibes historie, Nibe, 1977 (= Nine studies on the history of Nibe).

● Nykøbing

105. *Nørregaard, G.*, Nykøbing på Falster gennem tiderne, Vols. I–II, Nykøbing Falster, 1978–1982 (= History of the city of Nykøbing on Falster).

● Odense

106. *Johansen, H. C., P. Boje* and *A. M. Møller*, Fabrik og bolig. Det industrielle miljø i Odense 1840–1940, Odense, 1983 (= Factories and housing: the industrial milieu of Odense 1840–1940).

107. *Kaarsted, T., et al.*, eds., Odense Bys Historie, Vols. I–XII, Odense, 1979 ff. (= History of the city of Odense, Vols. I–V, VII, IX published to date).

- Ribe

108. *Bencard, M.*, ed., Ribe Excavations 1970–1976, Vols. I–II, Esjerg, 1981.

- Svendborg

109. *Jansen, H. M.*, ed., The Archaelogy of Svendborg, Denmark, Vols. I–IV, Odense, 1978–1986. (A further ten volumes are intended to complete the series.)

JÜRGEN REULECKE

Federal Republic of Germany

A. Urban History Institutions

Arbeitsgemeinschaft Die alte Stadt e.V.L (previously "Arbeitsgemeinschaft für reichsstädtische Geschichtsforschung, Denkmalpflege und bürgerschaftliche Bildung", since 1974 "Arbeitsgemeinschaft für Stadtgeschichtsforschung, Stadtsoziologie und städtische Denkmalpflege"), founded in 1960; based in Esslingen am Neckar.

Arbeitskreis für genetische Siedlingsforschung in Mitteleuropa, founded in 1974; based in Bonn.

Arbeitskreis für südwestdeutsche Stadtgeschichtsforschung, founded in 1960; based in Esslingen am Neckar.

Arbeitskreis Geschichtliche Entwicklung des Stadtraumes (previously "Forschungsausschuß Historische Raumforschung" of the Akademie für Raumforschung und Landesplanung), founded in 1959; based in Hanover.

Deutsches Institut für Urbanistik (Difu), founded in 1973; based in Berlin (West).

Institut für vergleichende Städtegeschichte, founded in 1970; based in Münster Westphalia.

B. Aids to Research

(a)   Urban History Journals

See the *Landesgeschichtliche Zeitschriftenschau*, published in the annals of "Blätter für deutsche Landesgeschichte" (latest edition Year 122, 1986, pp. 229–254) for the numerous urban and regional history journals of individual towns and areas featuring articles on urban history.

1. *Archiv für Kommunalwissenschaften (AfK)*, 1962 ff., ed. U.K.-H. Hansmeyer, W. Haus *et al.*, Stuttgart; published biannually.
2. *Die alte Stadt*: Quarterly journal on urban history, town sociology and the preservation of monuments, 1974 ff. (until 1977 under the name "Zeit-

schrift für Stadtgeschichte, Stadtsoziologie und Denkmalpflege), ed. O. Borst in conjunction with H. P. Bahrdt *et al.*, Esslingen am Neckar.

3. *Informationen zur modernen Stadtgeschichte (IMS)*, 1970 ff., ed. C. Engeli *et al.*, Berlin (West); appears biannually.

(b)   Bibliographies

Regular bibliographies on the subject are contained in the journals, *Archiv für Kommunalwissenschaften* and *Informationen zur modernen Stadtgeschichte.*

4. *Bibliographie zur Deutschen Historischen Städteforschung*, ed. B. Schröder and H. Stoob, Part 1, Cologne and Vienna, 1986 (Part 2 due to appear in 1989).
5. *Kommunalwissenschaftliche Dissertationen*, 1974 ff., ed. Deutsches Institut für Urbanistik, Berlin (West), published annually.
6. *Schmidt, R. D.* and *H. P. Kosack*, Bibliographie der Landesbeschreibungen und Regionalatlanten Deutschlands, Bonn, Bad Godesberg, 1972.
7. *Schöller, P., et al.*, Bibliographie zur Stadtgeographie. Deutschsprachige Literatur 1952–1970, Paderborn, 1973.
8. *Neue Veröffentlichungen zur vergleichenden Städtegeschichte*, in Blätter für deutsche Landesgeschichte, ed. W. Ehbrecht *et al.*, 1953 ff.

(c)   Handbooks on Urban History

9. *Deutsches Städtebuch*. Handbuch städtischer Geschichte, ed. E. Keyser (from vol. 5 with H. Stoob), 5 Vols., Berlin and Stuttgart, 1939–1974.
10. *Handbuch der Historischen Stätten Deutschlands*, Stuttgart 1958 ff. (most recent: Vol. 12; Schlesien, Stuttgart, 1977).
11. *Das Lexikon der deutschen Städte und Gemeinden*, ed. F. Siefert, Munich, 1973.

(d)   Atlases on Urban History and Urban Development

12. *Deutscher Städteatlas*, ed. H. Stoob *et al.*, Dortmund, 1973, 1979 and 1984 (3 instalments published to date with 25 Vols.).
13. *Pläne und Grundrisse von Städten sozialistischer Länder Europas. 1574–1850*, ed. W. Klaus, Berlin (DDR), 1976.
14. *Rheinischer Städteatlas*, ed. E. Ennen *et al.*, Bonn, 1972–1982, (7 instalments published to date).
15. *Stadtkernatlas Schleswig-Holstein*, ed. J. Habich *et al.*, Neumünster, 1976.
16. *Westfälischer Städteatlas*, ed. H. Stoob, Dortmund, 1975 and 1981 (2 instalments published to date).

(e)   Urban History Sources

17. *Quellen zum modernen Gemeindeverfassungsrecht in Deutschland*, ed. Ch. Engeli and W. Haus, Stuttgart *et al.*, 1975. Publications of the Deutsches Institut für Urbanistik, Vol. 45.
18. *Silbergleit, H.*, Preußens Städte, Berlin, 1908.

C. Research Reports

(a)   General Surveys

19. *Bog, I.*, Die Stadt als Problem interdisziplinärer Forschung, in Zeitschrift für Stadtgeschichte, Stadtsoziologie und Denkmalpflege, Vol. 3 (1976), pp. 173–180.
20. *Croon, H.*, Forschungsprobleme der neueren Städtegeschichte, in Blätter für deutsche Landesgeschichte, Year 105 (1969), pp. 14–26.
21. *Croon, H.*, Methoden zur Erforschung der gemeindlichen Sozialgeschichte des 19. und 20. Jahrhunderts, in Westfälische Forschungen, Vol. 8 (1955), pp. 139–149.
22. *Ehbrecht, W.*, Thesen zur Stadtgeschichtsschreibung heute, in Westfälische Forschungen, Vol. 34 (1984), pp. 29–48.
23. *Engeli, Ch., W. Hofmann* and *H. Matzerath*, eds., Probleme der Stadtgeschichtsschreibung, Berlin, 1981 (= IMS. Beiheft 1).
24. *Heineberg, H.*, Geographische Aspekte der Urbanisierung: Forschungsstand und Probleme, in H. J. Teuteberg, ed., Urbanisierung im 19. und 20. Jahrundert, Cologne and Vienna, 1983, pp. 35–63.
25. *Herzfeld, H.*, Aufgaben der Geschichtswissenschaft im Bereich der Kommunalwissenschaften, in Archiv für Kommunalwissenschaften Year 1 (1962), pp. 27–40.
26. *Herzfeld, H.*, and *Ch. Engeli*, Neue Forschungsansätze in der modernen Stadtgeschichte, in AfK, Year 12 (1975), pp. 1–21.
27. *Huppertz, M.*, Überlegungen zu einem Konzept historisch orientierter sozialwissenschaftlicher Stadtforschung, in Die alte Stadt, Year 11 (1984), pp. 292–312.
28. *Köllmann, W.*, Zur Bedeutung der Regionalgeschichte im Rahmen struktur- und sozialgeschichtlicher Konzeptionen, in Archiv für Sozialgeschichte, Vol. XV (1975), pp. 43–50.
29. *Lubenow, H.*, Neue Aspekte der Stadtgeschichtsforschung, in Geschichte in Wissenschaft und Unterricht, Year 28 (1977), pp. 86–102.
30. *Reulecke, J.*, Stadtgeschichtsschreibung zwischen Ideologie und Kommerz: Ein Überblick, in Geschichtsdidaktik, Year 7 (1982), pp. 1–18.
31. *Reulecke, J.*, and *G. Huck*, Urban History Research in Germany: Its Development and Present Condition, in Urban History Yearbook, 1981, pp. 39–54.

32. *Reuter H. -G.*, Stadtgeschichtsschreibung im Wandel, in Archiv für Kommunalwissenschaften, Year 17 (1978), pp. 68–81.

33. *Teuteberg, H. J.*, Historische Aspekte der Urbanisierung: Forschungsstand und Probleme, in H. J. Teuteberg, Urbanisierung im 19. und 20. Jahrhundert, Cologne and Vienna, 1983, pp. 2–34.

(b)   Surveys of Individual Fields

34. *Denecke, D.*, Historisch-geographische Stadtforschung: Problemstellungen – Betrachtungsweisen – Perspektiven, in Tagungsbericht und wissenschaftliche Abhandlungen des 44. Deutschen Geographentags, Stuttgart, 1984, pp. 136–144.

35. *Denkmalschutz im Städtebau.* Eine Literaturdokumentation 1965–1975, Cologne, 1975.

36. *Ehbrecht, W.*, ed., Voraussetzungen und Methoden geschichtlicher Städteforschung, Cologne and Vienna, 1979.

37. *Först, W.*, Stadtgeschichtsschreibung und Geschichtsbewußtsein in einer Stadtlandschaft, in Archiv für Kommunalwissenschaften, Year 8 (1969), pp. 91–108.

38. *Haus, W.*, Zur Entwicklung der Kommunalwissenschaften in Deutschland, in the same editor, Kommunalwissenschaftliche Forschung, Stuttgart *et al.*, 1966, pp. 31–58 (Schriftenreihe des Vereins für Kommunalwissenschaften, Vol. 12).

39. *Herlyn, U.*, Notizen zur stadtsoziologischen Literatur der 60er Jahren in H. P. Bahrdt, Die moderne Großstadt, Hamburg, 1969, pp. 153–182.

40. *Herzfeld, H.*, Leistung und Aufgaben der Kommunalgeschichte, in W. Haus, (ed.), Kommunalwissenschaftliche Forschung, Stuttgart *et al.*, 1966, pp. 65–88 (Schriftenreihe des Vereins für Kommunalwissenschaften, Vol. 12).

41. *Hofmann, W.*, Erkenntnisprobleme moderner Verwaltungsgeschichte: Geschichtsschreibung in pragmatischer Absicht, in Die Verwaltung, Vol. 8 (1975), pp. 47–68.

42. *Korte, H.*, Zum Weg und gegenwärtigen Stand der Stadtsoziologie, in Die alte Stadt, Year 11 (1984), pp. 281–291.

43. *Lichtenberger, E.*, Perspektiven der Stadtgeographie, in Tagungsbericht und wissenschaftliche Abhandlungen des 42. Deutschen Geographentags, Wiesbaden, 1980, pp. 103–128.

44. *Mitterauer, M.*, Das Problem der zentralen Orte als sozial- und wirtschaftshistorische Forschungsaufgabe, in Vierteljahrsschrift für Wirtschafts- und Sozialgeschichte, Vol. 58 (1971), pp. 433–467.

45. *Niethammer, L.*, Die deutsche Stadt im Umbruch 1945 als Forschungsproblem, in Die alte Stadt, Year 5 (1978), pp. 138–154.

46. *Schäfer, H.*, Neuere stadtgeographische Arbeitsmethoden zur Untersuchung der inneren Struktur von Städten, in Berichte zur deutschen Landeskunde, Vol. 43 (1969), pp. 261–297.

47. *Städtestatistik und Stadtforschung*. Leistungen, Aufgaben, Ziele. 100 Jahre Verband Deutscher Städtestatistiker 1879–1979, Hamburg, 1979.

48. *Steinbach, P.*, Zur Diskussion über den Begriff der "Region" – Eine Grundfrage der modernen Landesgeschichte, in Hessisches Jahrbuch für Landesgeschichte, Vol. 31 (1981), pp. 185–210.

49. *Steinbach, P.*, Oral History und moderne Stadtgeschichte – Mündliche Stadtgeschichte?, in Informationen zur modernen Stadtgeschichte, 1981, pp. 1–6.

50. *Steinbach, P.*, Territorial- und Regionalgeschichte: Wege der modernen Landesgeschichte: Ein Vergleich der "Blätter für deutsche Landesgeschichte" und des "Jahrbuchs für Regionalgeschichte", in Geschichte und Gesellschaft, Year 11 (1985), pp. 528–540.

51. *Zang, G.*, Die unaufhaltsame Annäherung an das Einzelne: Reflexionen über den theoretischen und praktischen Nutzen der Regional- und Alltagsgeschichte, Constance, 1985.

D. Literature on Individual Areas

(a) Concept and Definition of Town and Town Types

52. *Arnold, U.*, ed., Die Stadt in Preußen. Beiträge zur Entwicklung vom frühen Mittelalter bis zur Gegenwart, Lüneburg, 1983.

53. *Besch, W., et al.*, eds., Die Stadt in der europäischen Geschichte: Festschrift für Edith Ennen, Bonn, 1972.

54. *Borst, O.*, Babel oder Jerusalem? Sechs Kapitel Stadtgeschichte, Stuttgart, 1984.

55. *Christaller, W.*, Die zentralen Orte Süddeutschlands. Eine ökonomisch-geographische Untersuchung über die Gesetzmäßigkeit der Verteilung und Entwicklung der Siedlungen mit städtischen Funktionen, Jena 1933 (Rpt. Darmstadt, 1968).

56. *Dietrich, R.*, Probleme stadtgeschichtlicher Untersuchungen im Zeitalter der Industrialisierung am Beispiel Berlins, in Jahrbuch für die Geschichte Mittel- und Ostdeutschlands, Vol. 16/17 (1968), pp. 169–209.

57. *Ennen, E.*, Die Stadt zwischen Mittelalter und Gegenwart, in Rheinische Vierteljahresblätter, No. 30 (1965), pp. 118–131 (rpt. in *C. Haase*, ed., Die Stadt des Mittelalters, Vol. 1, 3rd ed., Darmstadt, 1978, pp. 423–442).

58. *Glaser, H.*, ed., Urbanistik: Neue Aspekte der Stadtentwicklung, Munich, 1974.

59. *Habermann, K., et al.*, Historische, politische und ökonomische Bedingungen der Stadtentwicklung, Hanover, 1978.

60. *Heide, U.*, Städtetypen und Städtevergesellschaftungen im rheinisch-westfälischen Raum, Cologne, 1977.

61. *Hofmeister, B.*, Der Stadtbegriff des 20. Jahrhunderts aus der Sicht der Geographie, in Die alte Stadt, Year 11 (1984), pp. 197–213.

62. *Ipsen, G.*, Art. "Stadt (IV) Neuzeit", in: Handwörterbuch der Sozialwissenschaften, Vol. 9, Stuttgart, et al., 1956, pp. 786–800.

63. *Jäger, H.*, ed., Probleme des Städtewesens im industriellen Zeitalter, Cologne and Vienna, 1978.

64. *Jäger, H.*, *et al.*, eds., Civitatum Communitas: Studien zum europäischen Städtewesen. Festschrift Heinz Stoob, 2 Parts, Cologne and Vienna, 1984.

65. *Jasper, K.*, Der Urbanisierungsprozeß – dargestellt am Beispiel der Stadt Köln, Cologne, 1977.

66. *Klemmer, P.*, Ursachen des Verstädterungsprozesses. Der Beitrag der Ökonomie, in B. Külp *et al.*, eds., Soziale Probleme der modernen Industriegesellschaft, Berlin, 1977, pp. 265–288.

67. *Maschke, E.*, Städte und Menschen: Beiträge zur Geschichte der Stadt, der Wirtschaft und Gesellschaft 1959–1977, Wiesbaden, 1980.

68. *Matzerath, H.*, Urbanisierung in Preußen 1815–1914, 2 Parts Stuttgart *et al.*, 1985 (Schriften des Deutschen Instituts für Urbanistik, Vol. 72).

69. *Matzerath, H.*, ed., Städtewachstum und innerstädtische Strukturveränderungen. Probleme des Urbanisierungsprozesses im 19. und 20. Jahrhundert, Stuttgart *et al.*, 1985.

70. *Matzerath, H.* and *K. Ogura*, Moderne Verstädterung in Deutschland und Japan, in Zeitschrift für Stadtgeschichte, Stadtsoziologie und Denkmalpflege, Year 2 (1975), pp. 228–253.

71. *Pfeil, E.*, Großstadtforschung: Entwicklung und gegenwärtiger Stand, 2nd ed., Hanover, 1972.

72. *Rausch, W.*, ed., Die Städte Mitteleuropas im 19. Jahrhundert, Linz, 1983.

73. *Rausch, W.*, ed., Die Städte Mitteleuropas im 20. Jahrhundert, Linz, 1984.

74. *Reulecke, J.*, Geschichte der Urbanisierung in Deutschland, Frankfurt/M., 1985.

75. *Reulecke J.*, ed., Die deutsche Stadt im Industriezeitalter, 2nd ed., Wuppertal, 1980.

76. *Schäfers, B.*, Phasen der Stadtbildung und Verstädterung, in: Zeitschrift für Stadtgeschichte, Stadtsoziologie und Denkmalpflege, Year 4 (1977), pp. 243–268.

77. *Schöller, P.*, Die deutschen Städte, 2nd ed., Wiesbaden, 1980.

78. *Schöller, P.*, ed., Zentralitätsforschung, Darmstadt, 1972.

79. *Schröder, H. W.*, ed., Moderne Stadtgeschichte, Stuttgart, 1979.

80. *Teuteberg, H.-J.*, ed., Stadtwachstum, Industrialisierung, sozialer Wandel: Beiträge zur Erforschung der Urbanisierung im 19. und 20. Jahrhundert, Berlin and Munich, 1986.

81. *Teuteberg, H.-J.*, ed., Urbanisierung im 19. und 20. Jahrhundert: Historische und geographische Aspekte, Cologne and Vienna, 1983.

82. *Thienel, I.*, Städtewachstum im Industrialisierungsprozeß des 19. Jahrhunderts: Das Berliner Beispiel, Berlin, 1973.

(b)   *Politics, Law and Statutes*

Publications on self-government are included under this heading.

83. *Bey-Heard, F.*, Hauptstadt und Staatsumwälzung Berlin, 1919, Stuttgart *et al.*, 1969 (Schriftenreihe des Vereins für Kommunalwissenschaften, Vol. 27).

84. *Croon, H.*, Die gesellschaftlichen Auswirkungen des Gemeindewahlrechts in den Gemeinden und Kreisen des Rheinlands und Westfalens im 19. Jahrhundert, Cologne and Opladen, 1960.

85. *Croon, H., W. Hofmann* and *G.-Ch. von Unruh*, Kommunale Selbstverwaltung im Zeitalter der Industrialisierung, Stuttgart *et al.*, 1971 (Schriftenreihe des Vereins für Kommunalwissenschaften, Vol. 33).

86. *Dann, O.*, ed., Köln nach dem Nationalsozialismus. Der Beginn des gesellschaftlichen und politischen Lebens in den Jahren 1945/46, Wuppertal, 1981.

87. *Deutscher Städtetag*, Im Dienst deutscher Städte. 1905–1980, Stuttgart, 1980.

88. *Engeli, Ch.*, Gustav Böß. Oberbürgermeister von Berlin 1921–1930, Stuttgart *et al.*, 1971 (Schriftenreihe des Vereins für Kommunalwissenschaften, Vol. 31).

89. *Engeli, Ch.*, Zur Geschichte der regionalen Städtetage, in Archiv für Kommunalwissenschaften, Year 19 (1980), pp. 173–199.

90. *Faber, K.-G.*, Die kommunale Selbstverwaltung in der Rheinprovinz im 19. Jahrhundert, in Rheinische Vierteljahrsblätter, Year 30 (1965), pp. 132–151.

91. *Fülberth, G.*, Konzeption und Praxis sozialdemokratischer Kommunalpolitik 1918–1933: Ein Anfang, Marburg, 1984.

92. *Heffter, H.*, Die deutsche Selbstverwaltung im 19. Jahrhundert, 2nd ed., Stuttgart, 1969.

93. *Herlemann, B.*, Kommunalpolitik der KPD im Ruhrgebiet 1924–1933, Wuppertal, 1977.

94. *Herzfeld, H.*, Demokratie und Selbstverwaltung in der Weimarer Epoche, Stuttgart, 1957.

95. *Hofmann, W.*, Aufgaben und Struktur der kommunalen Selbstverwaltung in der Zeit der Hochindustrialisierung, in Deutsche Verwaltungsgeschichte, Vol. III, Stuttgart, 1984, pp. 578–644.

96. *Hofmann, W.*, Die Bielefelder Stadtverordneten: Ein Beitrag zu bürgerlicher Selbstverwaltung und sozialem Wandel. 1850–1914,

Lübeck and Hamburg, 1964.

97. *Hofmann, W.*, Die Entwicklung der kommunalen Selbstverwaltung von 1848 bis 1918, in G. Püttner, ed., Handbuch der kommunalen Wissenschaft und Praxis, Vol. 1, Berlin, *et al.*, 1981, pp. 71–85.

98. *Hofmann, W.*, Zwischen Rathaus und Reichskanzlei: Die Oberbürgermeister in der Kommunal- und Staatspolitik des Deutschen Reiches von 1890 bis 1933, Stuttgart *et al.*, 1974 (Schriften des Deutschen Instituts für Urbanistik, Vol. 46).

99. *Hofmann, W.*, Städtetag und Verfassungsordnung: Position und Politik der Hauptgeschäftsführer eines kommunalen Spitzenverbandes, Stuttgart *et al.*, 1966 (Schriftenreihe des Vereins für Kommunalwissenschaften, Vol. 13).

100. *Jeserich, K., H. Pohl* and *G. Ch. von Unruh*, eds., Deutsche Verwaltungsgeschichte, 5 vols., Stuttgart, 1983–1987.

101. *Kirchgässner, B.*, and *J. Schadt*, eds., Kommunale Selbstverwaltung - Idee und Wirklichkeit, Sigmaringen, 1983.

102. *Koch, R.*, Staat oder Gemeinde? Zu einem politischen Zielkonflikt in der bürgerlichen Bewegung des 19. Jahrhunderts, in Historische Zeitschrift, Vol. 236 (1983), pp. 74–96.

103. *Krabbe, Wolfgang R.*, Die lokale Polizeiverwaltung in der preußischen Provinz Westfalen (1815–1914), in Blätter für deutsche Landesgeschichte, Year 119 (1983), pp. 141–157.

104. *Luntowski, G.*, Die kommunale Selbstverwaltung: Geschichte Dortmunds im 19. und 20. Jahrhundert, Vol. 1, Dortmund, 1977.

105. *Marssolek, I.*, and *R. Ott*, Bremen im Dritten Reich. Anpassung - Widerstand - Verfolgung, Bremen, 1986.

106. *Matthias, E.*, and *H. Weber*, eds., Widerstand gegen den Nationalsozialismus in Mannheim, Mannheim, 1984.

107. *Matzerath, H.*, Nationalsozialismus und kommunale Selbstverwaltung, Stuttgart *et al.*, 1970 (Schriftenreihe des Vereins für Kommunalwissenschaften, Vol. 29).

108. *Matzerath, H.*, Von der Stadt zur Gemeinde: Zur Entwicklung des rechtlichen Stadtbegriffs im 19. und 20. Jahrhundert, in Archiv für Kommunalwissenschaften, Year 13 (1974), pp. 17–46.

109. *Mutius, A. von*, ed., Selbstverwaltung im Staat der Industriegesellschaft: Festschrift für Georg Christoph von Unruh, Heidelberg, 1984.

110. *Naunin, H.*, ed., Städteordnungen des 19. Jahrhunderts, Cologne and Vienna, 1984.

111. *Nürnberger, R.*, Städtische Selbstverwaltung und sozialer Wandel im Königreich und in der Provinz Hannover während des 19. Jahrhunderts, in Niedersächsisches Jahrbuch für Landesgeschichte, Vol. 48, (1976), pp. 1–16.

112. *Nürnberger, R.*, Städtische Selbstverwaltung und sozialer Wandel in der Provinz Sachsen während des 19. Jahrhunderts, in Blätter für deutsche Landesgeschichte, Year 112 (1976), pp. 229–243.

113. *Pietsch, H.*, Militärregierung, Bürokratie und Sozialisierung: Zur Entwicklung des politischen Systems in der Städten des Ruhrgebiets 1945–1948, Duisburg, 1978.

114. *Poll, B.*, Die neuere kommunale Selbstverwaltung Aachens: Ein Beitrag zur Rheinischen Städteordnung 1856–1918, in Veröffentlichungen des Kölner Geschichtsvereins, Vol. 25, (1960), pp. 259–284.

115. *Püttner, G.*, ed., Handbuch der kommunalen Wissenschaft und Praxis, 3 Vols., Berlin *et al.*, 1981–1983.

116. *Rebentisch, D.*, Ludwig Landmann: Frankfurter Oberbürgermeister der Weimarer Republik, Wiesbaden, 1975.

117. *Rebentisch, D.*, Programmatik und Praxis sozialdemokratischer Kommunalpolitik in der Weimarer Republik, in Die alte Stadt, Year 12 (1985), pp. 33–56.

118. *Rebentisch, D.*, Die Selbstverwaltung in der Weimarer Zeit, in G. Püttner, ed., Handbuch der kommunalen Wissenschaft und Praxis, Vol. 1, Berlin *et al.*, pp. 86–100.

119. *Rebentisch, D.*, Die deutsche Sozialdemokratie und die kommunale Selbstverwaltung: Ein Überblick über Programmdiskussion und Organisationsproblematik 1890–1975, in Archiv für Sozialgeschichte, Year 25 (1985), pp. 1–78.

120. *Rebentisch, D.*, and *A. Raab*, Neu-Isenburg zwischen Anpassung und Widerstand (1933–1945), Neu-Isenburg, 1978.

121. *Ribhegge, W.*, Die Systemfunktion der Gemeinden: Zur deutschen Kommunalgeschichte seit 1918, in Aus Politik und Zeitgeschichte, B 47, (1973).

122. *Rodenstein, M.* Thesen zum Wandel der kommunalen Selbstverwaltung in Deutschland, in R. Emenlauer *et al.*, eds., Die Kommune in der Staatsorganisation, Frankfurt/M., 1974, pp. 35–71.

123. *Saldern, A. von*, Die Gemeinde in Theorie und Praxis der deutschen Arbeiterorganisationen 1863–1920: Ein Überblick, in Internationale Wissenschaftliche Korrespondenz, Year 12 (1976), pp. 295–352.

124. *Saldern, A. von*, Sozialdemokratische Kommunalpolitik in Wilhelminischer Zeit, in K.-H. Naßmacher, ed., Kommunalpolitik und Sozialdemokratie, Bonn-Bad Godesberg, 1977, pp. 18–62.

125. *Schloßmacher, N.*, Düsseldorf im Bismarckreich. Politik und Wahlen, Parteien und Vereine, Düsseldorf, 1985.

126. *Schwabe, K.*, ed., Oberbürgermeister, Boppard, 1981.

127. *Schwarz, K.-D.*, Weltkrieg und Revolution in Nürnberg, Stuttgart, 1971.

128. *Stehkämper, H.*, ed., Konrad Adenauer: Oberbürgermeister von Köln, Cologne, 1976.

129. *Steinborn, P.*, Grundlagen und Grundzüge Münchener Kommunalpolitik in den Jahren der Weimarer Republik, Munich, 1968.

130. *Unruh, G. Ch. von*, Die historischen Grundlagen der kommunalen Selbstverwaltung nach dem Grundgesetz für die Bundesrepublik Deutschland in Geschichte in Wissenschaft und Unterricht, Year 26 (1975), pp. 290–312.

131. *Wünderich, V.*, Arbeiterbewegung und Selbstverwaltung: KPD und Kommunalpolitik in der Weimarer Republik. Mit dem Beispiel Solingen, Wuppertal, 1980.

132. *Wünderich, V.*, Von der bürgerlichen zur proletarischen Kommunalpolitik, in G. Zang, ed., Provinzialisierung einer Region, Frankfurt/M., 1978.

133. *Ziebill, O.*, Geschichte des Deutschen Städtetages, 2nd ed., Stuttgart, 1956.

134. *Ziebill, O.*, Politische Parteien und kommunale Selbstverwaltung, 2nd ed., Stuttgart *et al.*, 1972 (Schriftenreihe des Vereins für Kommunalwissenschaften, Vol. 7).

(c) Population and Social Structure

Publications on communal social provisions and administration of services are included under this heading.

135. *Angermann, G.*, Land-Stadt-Beziehungen. Bielefeld und sein Umland 1760–1860. Münster, 1982.

136. *Artelt, W., et al.*, eds., Städte-, Wohnungs- und Kleiderhygiene des 19. Jahrhunderts in Deutschland, Stuttgart, 1969.

137. *Aycoberry, P.*, Der Strukturwandel im Kölner Mittelstand 1820–1850, in Geschichte und Gesellschaft, Year 1 (1975), pp. 78–98.

138. *Baumann, R.*, ed., Sozialer Wandel. Ansätze zur Gesellschaftsveränderung am Beispiel der Entwicklung von Stadt und Land, Cologne, 1983.

139. *Blaich, F.*, Der private Wohnungsbau in den deutschen Großstädten während der Krisenjahre 1929–1933, in Jahrbücher für Nationalökonomie und Statistik, Vol. 183 (1969), pp. 435–447.

140. *Borscheid, P.*, Schranken sozialer Mobilität und Binnenwanderung im 19. Jahrhundert, in W. Conze and U. Engelhardt, eds., Arbeiter im Industrialisierungsprozeß, Stuttgart, 1979, pp. 31–50.

141. *Breitling, P.*, Die großstädtische Entwicklung Münchens im 19. Jahrhundert, in H. Jäger, ed., Probleme des Städtewesens im industriellen Zeitalter, Cologne and Vienna 1975, pp. 178–196.

142. *Bulst, N., et al.*, eds., Bevölkerung, Wirtschaft und Gesellschaft: Stadt-Land-Beziehungen in Deutschland und Frankreich, Trier, 1983.

143. *Ditt, K.*, Industrialisierung, Arbeiterschaft und Arbeiterbewegung in Bielefeld, Dortmund, 1962.

144. *Fischer, I.*, Industrialisierung, sozialer Konflikt und politische Willensbildung in der Stadtgemeinde: Ein Beitrag zur Sozialgeschichte Augsburgs 1840–1914, Augsburg, 1977.

145. *Flade, R.,* Juden in Würzburg 1918–1933, Würzburg 1985 (Mainfränkische Studien, Vol. 34).

146. *Fritzsche, B.,* Das Quartier als Lebensraum, in W. Conze and U. Engelhardt, eds., Arbeiterexistenz im 19. Jahrhundert, Stuttgart, 1981, pp. 92–113.

147. *Glaser, H., et al.,* eds., Industriekultur in Nürnberg. Eine deutsche Stadt im Maschinenzeitalter, Munich, 1980.

148. *Hamm, B.,* ed., Lebensraum Stadt. Beiträge zur Sozialökologie deutscher Städte, Frankfurt/M. *et al.,* 1979.

149. *Haseloff, O. W.,* ed., Die Stadt als Lebensform, Berlin, 1970.

150. *Haumann, H.,* ed., Arbeiteralltag in Stadt und Land, Berlin, 1982.

151. *Herzig, A., et al.,* eds., Arbeiter in Hamburg: Unterschichten, Arbeiter und Arbeiterbewegung seit dem ausgehenden 18. Jahrhundert, Hamburg, 1983.

152. *Hildenbrand, H.,* ed., Die strukturelle Entwicklung von Wirtschaft und Bevölkerung im Stadtkreis Hagen von 1945 bis 1967, Hagen, 1970.

153. *Hippel, W. von,* Regionale und soziale Herkunft der Bevölkerung einer Industriestadt: Untersuchungen zu Ludwigshafen 1867–1914, in W. Conze and U. Engelhardt, eds., Arbeiter im Industrialisierungsprozeß, Stuttgart, 1979, pp. 51–69.

154. *Höroldt, D.,* and *M. Rey,* eds., Bonn in der Kaiserzeit 1871–1914: Festschrift zum 100jährigen Jubiläum des Bonner Heimat- und Geschichtsvereins, Bonn, 1986.

155. *Köllmann, W.,* Bevölkerung in der industriellen Revolution, Göttingen, 1974.

156. *Krabbe, W. R.,* Die Anfänge des sozialen Wohnungsbaus vor dem Ersten Weltkrieg, in Vierteljahrsschrift für Wirtschafts- und Sozialgeschichte, Vol. 71 (1984), pp. 30–57.

157. *Krabbe, W. R.,* Die Gründung städtischer Arbeiterschutz-Anstalten in Deutschland: Arbeitsnachweise, Arbeitslosenfürsorge, Gewerbegericht und Rechtsauskunftstelle, in W. Conze and U. Engelhardt, eds., Arbeiterexistenz im 19. Jahrhundert, Stuttgart, 1981, pp. 425–445.

158. *Kraus, A.,* Die Unterschichten Hamburgs in der ersten Hälfte des 19. Jahrhunderts: Entstehung, Struktur und Lebensverhältnisse, Stuttgart, 1965.

159. *Kromer, W.,* Propagandisten der Großstadt: Die Bedeutung von Informationsströmen zwischen Stadt und Land bei der Auslösung neuzeitlicher Land-Stadt-Wanderungen, illustriert an Beispielen aus dem Hohenloher Land, Baden-Württemberg und den benachbarten Zentren Frankfurt am Main, Mannheim, Nürnberg und Stuttgart, Frankfurt/M. *et al.,* 1985.

160. *Langewiesche, D.,* Mobilität in deutschen Mittel- und Großstädten: Aspekte der Binnenwanderung im 19. und 20. Jahrhundert, in W. Conze and U. Engelhardt, eds.,, Arbeiter im Industrialisierungsprozeß, Stuttgart, 1979, pp. 70–93.

161. *Langewiesche, D.*, Wanderungsbewegungen in der Hochindustrialisierungsperiode: Regionale, interstädtische und innerstädtische Mobilität in Deutschland 1880–1914, in Vierteljahrsschrift für Wirtschafts- und Sozialgeschichte, Vol. 64 (1977), pp. 1–40.

162. *Matzerath, H.*, Industrialisierung, Mobilität und sozialer Wandel am Beispiel der Städte Rheydt und Rheindahlen, in H. Kaelble *et al.*, eds., Probleme der Modernisierung in Deutschland, Opladen, 1978, pp. 13–79.

163. *Nahrstedt, W.*, Die Entstehung der Freizeit, dargestellt am Beispiel Hamburgs, Göttingen, 1972.

164. *Niethammer, L.*, ed., Wohnen im Wandel, Wuppertal, 1979.

165. *Niethammer, L.*, and *F. Brüggemeier*, Wie wohnten Arbeiter im Kaiserreich?, in Archiv für Sozialgeschichte, Vol. XVI (1976), pp. 61–134.

166. *Reulecke, J.*, Sozioökonomische Bedingungen und Folgen der Verstädterung in Deutschland, in Zeitschrift für Stadtgeschichte, Stadtsoziologie und Denkmalpflege, Year 4 (1977), pp. 269–287.

167. *Reulecke, J.*, and *W. Weber*, eds., Fabrik–Familie–Feierabend: Beiträge zur Sozialgeschichte des Alltags im Industriezeitalter, 2nd ed., Wuppertal, 1978.

168. *Saalfeld, D.*, Methodische Darlegungen zur Einkommensentwicklung und Sozialstruktur 1760–1860 am Beispiel einiger deutscher Städte, in H. Winkel, ed., Vom Kleingewerbe zur Großindustrie, Berlin, 1975, pp. 227–259.

169. *Sack, F.*, Stadtgeschichte und Kriminalsoziologie, in P. Ch. Ludz, ed., Soziologie und Sozialgeschichte, Opladen 1972, pp. 357–385.

170. *Saldern, A. von*, Vom Einwohner zum Bürger: Zur Emanzipation der städtischen Unterschicht Göttingens 1890 bis 1920, Berlin and Munich, 1973.

171. *Tenfelde, K.*, Großstadtjugend in Deutschland vor 1914. Eine historisch-demographische Annäherung, in Vierteljahrsschrift für Wirtschafts- und Sozialgeschichte, Vol. 69 (1982), pp. 182–218.

172. *Teuteberg, H. J.*, ed., Homo habitans. Zur Sozialgeschichte des ländlichen und städtischen Wohnens in Europa in der Neuzeit, Münster, 1985.

(d)   Town Planning, Housing

173. *Atteslander, P.*, and *B. Hamm*, eds., Materialien zur Siedlungssoziologie, Cologne, 1974.

174. *Bahrdt, H. P.*, Die moderne Großstadt: Soziologische Überlegungen zum Städtebau, Hamburg, 1969.

175. *Bauer, E.*, Zur Entstehung und Entfaltung der Stadt: Eine Kritik der baugeschichtlichen und stadtgeschichtlichen Ansätze zur Erklärung der Stadtentwicklung in Mitteleuropa, Diss., Berlin, 1975.

176. *Birker, O.*, Die Bedeutung der Bauordnung im Städtebau des 19. Jahrhunderts, in Zeitschrift für Stadtgeschichte, Stadtsoziologie und Denkmalpflege, Year 3, (1976), pp. 26–37.

177. *Boberg, J., et al.*, eds., Exerzierfeld der Moderne: Industriekultur in Berlin im 19. Jahrhundert, Munich, 1984.

178. *Boberg, J., et al.*, eds., Die Metropole: Industriekultur in Berlin im 20. Jahrhundert, Munich, 1986.

179. *Böhm, H.*, Bodenmobilität und Bodenpreisgefüge in ihrer Bedeutung für die Siedlungsentwicklung, Bonn, 1980.

180. *Böhm, H.*, Rechtsordnungen und Bodenpreise als Faktoren städtischer Entwicklungen im Deutschen Reich zwitschen 1870 und 1937, in H.-J. Teuteberg, ed., Urbanisierung im 19. und 20. Jahrhundert, Cologne and Vienna, 1983, pp. 214–240.

181. *Brake, K.*, ed., Stadtentwicklungsggeschichte und Stadtplanung, Oldenburg, 1985 (Beiträge der Universität Oldenburg zur Stadt- und Regionalplanung, Vol. 2).

182. *Dülffer, J.*, and *J. Thies*, Hitlers Städte: Baupolitik im Dritten Reich, Cologne, 1978.

183. *Engeli, C.*, Landesplanung in Berlin-Brandenburg: Eine Untersuchung zur Geschichte des Landesplanungsverbandes Brandenburg-Mitte 1929–1936, Stuttgart et al., 1986 (Schriften des Deutschen Instituts für Urbanistik, Vol. 75).

184. *Engeli, Ch.*, Siedlungsstruktur und Verwaltungsgrenzen der Stadt im Verstädterungsprozeß, in Zeitschrift für Stadtgeschichte, Stadtsoziologie und Denkmalpflege, Year 4 (1977), pp. 288–307.

185. *Fehl, G.*, and *J. Rodriguez-Lores*, eds., Stadterweiterungen 1800–1875: Von den Anfängen des modernen Städtebaues in Deutschland, Hamburg, 1983.

186. *Fehl, G.*, and *J. Rodriguez-Lores*, eds., Städtebau um die Jahrhundertwende, Cologne, 1980.

187. *Fritzsche, B.*, Grundstückspreise als Determinanten städtischer Strukturen, in Zeitschrift für Stadtgeschichte, Stadtsoziologie und Denkmalpflege, Year 4 (1977), pp. 36–54.

188. *Grote, L.*, ed., Die deutsche Stadt im 19. Jahrhundert. Bauplanung und Baugestaltung im industriellen Zeitalter, Munich, 1974.

189. *Hahn, E.*, ed., Siedlungsökologie. Ökologische Aspekte der neuen Stadt- und Siedlungspolitik, Karlsruhe, 1982.

190. *Hamm, B.*, ed., Einführung in die Siedlungssoziologie, Munich, 1982.

191. *Hartog, R.*, Stadterweiterungen im 19. Jahrhundert, Stuttgart et al., 1962 (Schriftenreihe des Vereins für Kommunalwissenschaften, Vol. 6).

192. *Kantzow, W.*, Sozialgeschichte der deutschen Städte und ihres Bau- und Bodenrechts bis 1918, Frankfurt/M. and New York, 1980.

193. *Krabbe, W. R.*, Eingemeindungsprobleme vor dem Ersten Weltkrieg:

Motive, Widerstände und Verfahrensweisen, in Die alte Stadt, Year 7 (1980), pp. 368–387.

194. *Mattausch, R.*, Siedlungsbau und Stadtgründungen im deutschen Faschismus, Frankfurt/M., 1981.

195. *Matzerath, H.*, Städtewachstum und Eingemeindungen im 19. Jahrhundert, in J. Reulecke, ed., Die deutsche Stadt im Industriezeitalter, 2nd ed., Wuppertal, 1980, pp. 67–89.

196. *Matzerath, H.* and *I. Thienel*, Stadtentwicklung, Stadtplanung, Stadtentwicklungsplanung: Probleme im 19. und 20. Jahrhundert am Beispiel der Stadt Berlin, in Die Verwaltung, Year 10 (1977), pp. 173–196.

197. *Meckseper, C.*, Stadtgeschichte und Stadtentwicklung, in Zeitschrift für Stadtgeschichte, Stadtsoziologie und Denkmalpflege, Year 1 (1974), pp. 242–260.

198. *Niethammer, L.*, Umständliche Erläuterung der seelischen Störung eines Communalbaumeisters in Preußens größtem Industriedorf oder: Die Unfähigkeit zur Stadtentwicklung, Frankfurt/M., 1979.

199. *Panerai, P., et al.*, Vom Block zur Zelle: Wandlungen der Stadtstruktur, Brunswick, 1984.

200. *Peltz-Dreckmann, U.*, Nationalsozialistischer Siedlungsbau. Versuch einer Analyse der die Siedlungspolitik bestimmenden Faktoren am Beispiel des Nationalsozialismus, Munich, 1978.

201. *Petsch, J.*, Baukunst und Stadtplanung im Dritten Reich, Munich and Vienna, 1976.

202. *Petsch, J.*, ed., Architektur und Städtebau im 20. Jahrhundert, 2 Parts, Berlin, 1974.

203. *Piccinato, G.*, Städtebau in Deutschland 1871–1914, Brunswick, 1983.

204. *Rebentisch, D.*, Die Anfänge der Raumordnung und Regionalplanung im Rhein-Main-Gebiet, in Hessisches Jahrbuch für Landesgeschichte, Vol. 25, (1975), pp. 307–339.

205. *Recker, M.-L.*, Die Großstadt als Wohn- und Lebensbereich im Nationalsozialismus: Zur Gründung der "Stadt des KdF-Wagens", Frankfurt/M. and New York, 1981.

206. *Reulecke, J.*, Metropolis Ruhr? Regionalgeschichtliche Aspekte der Ruhrgebietsentwicklung im 20. Jahrhundert, in Die alte Stadt, Year 8 (1981), pp. 13–30.

207. *Rodriguez-Lores, J.*, and *G. Fehl*, eds., Städtebaureform 1865–1900: Von Licht, Luft und Ordnung in der Stadt der Gründerzeit, 2 vols., Hamburg, 1985.

208. *Rödel, V.*, Ingenieurbaukunst in Frankfurt am Main 1806–1914, Frankfurt/M., 1983.

209. *Rublack, H.-Ch.*, Von der Stadtbaukunst zur Stadt der neuen Gesellschaft: Städtebau in Deutschland in den ersten drei Jahrzehnten des 20. Jahrhunderts, in Stadtverfassung - Verfassungsstaat - Pressepolitik: Festschrift für Eberhard Naujoks, Sigmaringen 1980, pp. 169–187.

210. *Die europäische Stadt.* Beiträge zur Stadtbaugeschichte und Stadtgestaltung, Stuttgart, 1984.

211. *Teuteberg, H. J.*, and *C. Wischermann*, eds., Wohnalltag in Deutschland 1850–1914: Bilder, Daten, Dokumente, Münster, 1985.

212. *Thienel, I.*, Verstädterung, städtische Infrastruktur und Stadtplanung, in Zeitschrift für Stadtgeschichte, Stadtsoziologie und Denkmalpflege, Year 4 (1977), pp. 55–84.

213. *Walz, M.*, Wohnungsbau- und Industrieansiedlungspolitik in Deutschland 1933–1939, Frankfurt/M., 1979.

214. *Wenzel, S.*, Jüdische Bürger und kommunale Selbstverwaltung in preußischen Städten 1808–1848, Berlin, 1967.

215. *Wischermann, C.*, Wohnen in Hamburg vor dem Ersten Weltkrieg, Münster, 1983.

216. *Wischermann, C.*, Wohnungsnot und Städtewachstum: Standards und soziale Indikatoren städtischer Wohnungsversorgung im späten 19. Jahrhundert, in W. Conze and U. Engelhardt, eds., Arbeiter im Industrialisierungsprozeß, Stuttgart, 1979, pp. 201–226.

217. *Zang, G.*, ed., Provinzialisierung einer Region: Zur Entstehung der bürgerlichen Gesellschaft in der Provinz, Frankfurt/M., 1978.

(e)   Economy and Transport

218. *Ahrens, G.*, Das Staatsschuldenwesen der freien Hansestädte im frühen 19. Jahrhundert, in Vierteljahrsschrift für Wirtschafts- und Sozialgeschichte, Vol. 68 (1981), pp. 22–51.

219. *Ambrosius, G.*, Aspekte kommunaler Unternehmenspolitik in der Weimarer Republik, in Archiv für Kommunalwissenschaften, Year 19, (1980), pp. 239–261.

220. *Blaich, F.*, Möglichkeiten und Grenzen kommunaler Wirtschaftspolitik während der Weltwirtschaftskrise 1929 bis 1932, in Archiv für Kommunalwissenschaften, Year 9 (1970), pp. 92–108.

221. *Bodenschatz, H.*, Moderne Infrastruktur und die Produktion städtischer Lage: Das Beispiel des Eisenbahnbaues bis 1875, in G. Fehl and J. Rodriguez-Lores, eds., Stadterweiterungen 1800–1875, Hamburg, 1983, pp. 81–100.

222. *Bolenz, J.*, Wachstum und Strukturwandlungen der kommunalen Ausgaben in Deutschland 1849–1913, Freiburg, 1965.

223. *Brunckhorst, H. -D.*, Kommunalisierung im 19. Jahrhundert am Beispiel der Gaswirtschaft in Deutschland, Munich, 1978.

224. *Büsch, O.*, Geschichte der Berliner Kommunalwirtschaft in der Weimarer Republik, Berlin, 1960.

225. *Büsch, O.*, Industrialisierung und Gewerbe im Raume Berlin/

Brandenburg 1800–1850, Berlin, 1971.

226. *Czada, P.*, Die Berliner Elektroindustrie in der Weimarer Zeit, Berlin, 1969.

227. *Elsner, H.*, Das Gemeindefinanzsystem: Geschichte, Ideen, Grundlagen, Stuttgart *et al.*, 1979.

228. *Fremdling, R.*, and *R. Tilly*, eds., Industrialisierung und Raum: Studien zur regionalen Differenzierung im Deutschland des 19. Jahrhunderts, Stuttgart, 1979.

229. *Freudenberger, H.*, and *G. Mensch*, Von der Provinzstadt zur Industrieregion, Göttingen, 1975.

230. *Führbaum, H.*, Die Entwicklung der Gemeindesteuern in Deutschland (Preußen) bis zum Beginn des 1. Weltkriegs, Diss. Münster, 1971.

231. *Gröttrup, H.*, Die kommunale Leistungsverwaltung: Grundlagen der gemeindlichen Daseinsvorsorge, Stuttgart *et al.*, 1973 (Schriftenreihe des Vereins für Kommunalwissenschaften, Vol. 37).

232. *Hansmeyer, K.- H.*, ed., Kommunale Finanzpolitik in der Weimarer Republik, Stuttgart *et al.*, 1973 (Schriftenreihe des Vereins für Kommunalwissenschaften, Vol. 36).

233. *Heindl, W.*, Die Haushalte von Reich, Ländern und Gemeinden in Deutschland von 1925 bis 1933: Öffentliche Haushalte und Krisenverschärfung, Frankfurt/M., 1984.

234. *Hoff, H.-V. von*, Die Entwicklung der Wirtschafts- und Bevölkerungsstruktur in der kreisfreien Stadt Herne von 1950 bis 1970, Bern and Frankfurt/M., 1974.

235. *Hofmann, W.*, Kommunale Daseinsvorsorge, Mittelstand und Städtebau 1871–1918, in E. Mai *et al.*, eds., Kunstpolitik und Kunstförderung im Kaiserreich, Berlin, 1982, pp. 167–196.

236. *Hoth, W.*, Die Industrialisierung einer rheinischen Gewerbestadt - dargestellt am Beispiel Wuppertal, Cologne, 1975.

237. *Krabbe, W. R.*, Die Entfaltung der modernen Leistungsverwaltung in den deutschen Städten des späten 19. Jahrhunderts, in H. J. Teuteberg, ed., Urbanisierung im 19. und 20. Jahrhundert, Cologne and Vienna, 1983, pp. 373–391.

238. *Krabbe, W. R.*, Kommunalpolitik und Industrialisierung: Die Entfaltung der städtischen Leistungsverwaltung im 19. und frühen 20. Jahrhundert, Stuttgart *et al.*, 1985 (Schriften des Deutschen Instituts für Urbanistik, Vol. 74).

239. *Krabbe, W. R.*, Munizipalsozialismus und Interventionsstaat: Die Ausbildung der städtischen Leistungsverwaltung im Kaiserreich, in Geschichte in Wissenschaft und Unterricht, Year 30 (1979), pp. 265–283.

240. *Lange, M. G.*, Die Funktionen der Stadt in der ersten industriellen Revolution, in O.W. Haseloff, ed., Die Stadt als Lebensform, Berlin, 1970, pp. 84–94.

241. *Marschalck, P.*, Die Rolle der Stadt für den Industrialisierungsprozeß in Deutschland in der 2. Hälfte des 19. Jahrhunderts, in J. Reulecke, ed., Die deutsche Stadt im Industriezeitalter, Wuppertal, 1978, pp. 57–66.

242. *Maschke, E.*, and *J. Sydow*, eds., Zur Geschichte der Industrialisierung in den süddeutschen Städten, Sigmaringen, 1977.

243. *Mauersberg, H.*, Wirtschafts- und Sozialgeschichte zentraleuropäischer Städte in neuerer Zeit, Göttingen, 1960.

244. *Pollard, S.*, ed., Region und Industrialisierung: Studien zur Rolle der Region in der Wirtschaftsgeschichte der letzten zwei Jahrhunderte, Göttingen, 1980.

245. *Radicke, D.*, Öffentlicher Nahverkehr und Stadterweiterung: Die Anfänge einer Entwicklung, in G. Fehl and J. Rodriguez-Lores, eds., Stadterweiterungen 1800–1875, Hamburg, 1983, pp. 343–357.

246. *Rebentisch, D.*, Kommunalpolitik, Konjunktur und Arbeitsmarkt in der Endphase der Weimarer Republik, in R. Morsey, ed., Verwaltungsgeschichte: Aufgaben, Zielsetzungen, Beispiele, Bern 1977, pp. 107–157.

247. *Rebentisch, D.*, Städte und Monopol. Privatwirtschaftliches Ferngas oder kommunale Verbundwirtschaft in der Weimarer Republik, in Zeitschrift für Stadtgeschichte, Stadtsoziologie und Denkmalpflege, Year 3 (1976), pp. 38–80.

248. *Reulecke, J.*, Auswirkungen der Inflation auf die städtischen Finanzen, in G. D. Feldman, ed., Die Nachwirkungen der Inflation auf die deutsche Geschichte: 1924–1933, Munich, 1985, pp. 97–116.

249. *Reulecke, J.*, Die wirtschaftliche Entwicklung der Stadt Barmen von 1910 bis 1925, Neustadt/Aisch, 1973.

250. *Reulecke, J.*, Zur städtischen Finanzlage in den Anfangsjahren der Weimarer Republik, in Archiv für Kommunalwissenschaften, Year 21, (1982), pp. 199–219.

251. *Reulecke, J.*, Städtische Finanzprobleme und Kriegswohlfahrtspflege im Ersten Weltkrieg, in Zeitschrift für Stadtgeschichte, Stadtsoziologie und Denkmalpflege, Year 2 (1975), pp. 48–79.

252. *Reulecke, J.*, ed., Die deutsche Stadt im Industriezeitalter, 2nd ed., Wuppertal, 1980.

253. *Schivelbusch, W.*, Disenchanted Night: The Industrialisation of Light in the Nineteenth Century, Oxford and Berkeley, Cal., 1988.

254. *Simson, J. von*, Kanalisation und Städtehygiene im 19. Jahrhundert, Munich and Vienna, 1983.

255. *Steitz, W.*, Kommunale Infrastruktur und Gemeindefinanzen in der Zeit der deutschen Hochindustrialisierung, in K. Düwell and W. Köllman, eds., Rheinland-Westfalen im Industriezeitalter, Vol. 2, Wuppertal, 1984, pp. 412–443.

256. *Sydow, J.*, ed., Städtische Versorgung und Entsorgung im Wandel der Geschichte, Sigmaringen, 1981.

257. *Teppe, K.*, Die kommunale Energiewirtschaft der Provinzen Rheinland und Westfalen 1900–1945, in K. Düwell and W. Köllmann, eds., Rheinland-Westfalen im Industriezeitalter, Vol. 2, Wuppertal, 1984, pp. 444–455.

258. *Tilly, R. H.*, Gemeindefinanzen und Sparkassen in Westfalen in der Inflation: 1918–1923, in K. Düwell and W. Köllmann, eds., Rheinland-Westfalen im Industriezeitalter, Vol. 2, Wuppertal, 1984, pp. 398–411.

259. *Witt, P.-Ch.*, Inflation, Wohnungszwangswirtschaft und Hauszinssteuer, in L. Niethammer, ed., Wohnen im Wandel, Wuppertal, 1979, pp. 385–407.

260. *Yago, G.*, The Decline of Transit: Urban Transportation in German and U.S. Cities 1900–1970, Cambridge, 1984.

(f) Arts and Sciences, Churches

Publications dealing with criticism of big cities are included under this heading.

261. *Bergmann, K.*, Agrarromantik und Großstadtfeindschaft, Meisenheim/Glan, 1970.

262. *Freisfeld, A.*, Das Leiden an der Stadt: Spuren der Verstädterung in deutschen Romanen des 20. Jahrhunderts, Cologne and Vienna, 1982.

263. *Hartmann, K.*, Deutsche Gartenstadtbewegung: Kulturpolitik und Geselleschaftsreform, Munich, 1976.

264. *Hartwich, B.*, Vom Stadt-Land-Gegensatz zum Stadt-Umlandproblem: Soziologische Theorien zum Verhältnis von Stadt und Land, Diss, Göttingen, 1976.

265. *Klotz, V.*, Die erzählte Stadt: Ein Sujet als Herausforderung des Romans von Lesage bis Döblin, Munich, 1969.

266. *Mai, E., et al.*, eds., Das Rathaus im Kaiserreich: Kunstpolitische Aspekte einer Bauaufgabe des 19. Jahrhunderts, Berlin, 1982.

267. *Maschke, E.*, and *J. Sydow*, eds., Stadt und Hochschule im 19. und 20. Jahrhundert, Sigmaringen, 1983.

268. *Meckseper, C.*, and *E. Schraut*, eds., Die Stadt in der Literatur, Göttingen, 1983.

269. *Mitscherlich, A.*, Die Unwirtlichkeit unserer Städte. Anstiftung zum Unfrieden, Frankfurt/M., 1965.

270. *Quandt, S.*, and *J. Calließ*, eds., Die Regionalisierung der historisch-politischen Kultur, Gießen, 1984.

271. *Rebentisch, D.*, Stadtverwaltung und Hochschulgründungen, in Archiv für Frankfurts Geschichte und Kunst, No. 55, (1976), pp. 203–233.

272. *Riha, K.*, Die Beschreibung der "Großen Stadt": Zur Entstehung des Großstadtmotivs in der deutschen Literatur, Bad Homburg *et al.*, 1970.

273. *Rohe, K.*, Regionalkultur, regionale Identität und Regionalismus im Ruhrgebiet, in W. Lipp, ed., Industriegesellschaft und Regionalkultur, Munich, 1984, pp. 123–153.

274. *Rothe, W.*, ed., Großstadtlyrik vom Naturalismus bis zur Gegenwart, Stuttgart, 1973.

275. *Walter, H.*, ed., Region und Sozialisation, 2 vols., Stuttgart and Bad Cannstatt, 1981.

276. *Wiegelmann, G.*, ed., Kulturelle Stadt-Land-Beziehungen in der Neuzeit, Münster, 1978.

E. Local Studies (a representative selection)

● Augsburg

277. *Gottlieb, G., et al.*, eds., Geschichte der Stadt Augsburg von der Römerzeit bis zur Gegenwart, Stuttgart, 1985.

278. *Zorn, W.*, Augsburg: Geschichte einer deutschen Stadt, 2nd ed., Augsburg, 1972.

● Barmen

279. *Köllmann, W.*, Sozialgeschichte der Stadt Barmen im 19. Jahrhundert, Tübingen, 1960.

● Berlin

280. *Herzfeld, H.*, ed., Berlin und die Provinz Brandenburg im 19. und 20. Jahrhundert, Berlin 1968.

281. *Ribbe, W.*, ed., Geschichte Berlins, 2 vols., Munich, 1987.

● Bielefeld

282. *Vogelsang, E.*, Geschichte der Stadt Bielefeld, Bielefeld, 1980.

● Bochum

283. *Crew, D.*, Bochum: Sozialgeschichte einer Industriestadt. 1860–1914, Frankfurt/M., 1980.

● Bonn

284. *Ennen, E.*, and *D. Höroldt*, Vom Römerkastell zur Bundeshauptstadt: Kleine Geschichte der Stadt Bonn, 3rd ed., Bonn, 1976.

● Bremen

285. *Schwarzwälder, H.*, Geschichte der Freien Hansestadt Bremen, 3 vols., Bremen, 1975–1983.

● Bremerhaven

286. *Scheper, B.*, Die jüngere Geschichte der Stadt Bremerhaven, Bremerhaven, 1977.

● Cologne

287. *Ayçoberry, P.*, Cologne entre Napoléon et Bismarck: La croissance d'une ville rhénane, Paris, 1981.
288. *Kellenbenz, H.*, ed., Zwei Jahrtausende Kölner Wirtschaft, 2 vols., Cologne, 1975.

● Dortmund

289. *Luntowski, G.*, and *N. Reimann*, eds., 1100 Jahre Stadtgeschichte Dortmund, Dortmund, 1982.

● Düsseldorf

290. *Henning, F.-W.*, Düsseldorf und seine Wirtschaft, 2 vols., Düsseldorf, 1981.

● Duisburg

291. *Roden, G. von*, Geschichte der Stadt Duisburg, 2 vols., Duisburg, 1974/75.

● Esslingen

292. *Borst, O.*, Geschichte der Stadt Esslingen am Neckar, 2nd ed., Esslingen, 1977.

● Frankfurt

293. *Böhme, H.*, Frankfurt und Hamburg, Frankfurt/M., 1968.

● Fürth

294. *Mauersberg, H.*, Wirtschaft und Gesellschaft Fürths in neuerer und neuester Zeit, Göttingen, 1974.

- Fulda

295. *Mauersberg, H.*, Wirtschaft und Gesselschaft Fuldas in neuerer Zeit, Göttingen, 1969.

- Hamburg

296. *Jochmann, W.*, and *H.-D. Loose*, eds., Hamburg: Geschichte der Stadt und ihrer Bewohner, 2 vols., Hamburg, 1982 and 1986.

297. *Schramm, P. E.*, Hamburg, Deutschland und die Welt: Leistung und Grenzen hanseatischen Bürgertums zwischen Napoleon I. und Bismarck, 2nd ed., Hamburg, 1952.

- Langenberg

298. *Quandt, S.*, Sozialgeschichte der Stadt Langenberg und der Landgemeinde Hardenberg-Neviges unter besonderer Berücksichtigung der Periode 1850–1914, Neustadt/Aisch, 1971.

- Linden

299. *Buschmann, W.*, Linden. Geschichte einer Industriestadt im 19. Jahrhundert, Hildesheim, 1981.

- Lippstadt

300. *Ehbrecht, W.*, ed., Lippstadt – Beiträge zur Stadtgeschichte, 2 vols., Lippstadt, 1985.

- Lüdenscheid

301. *Herbig, W.*, Wirtschaft und Bevölkerung der Stadt Lüdenscheid im 19. Jahrhundert, Dortmund, 1977.

- Marburg

302. *Brocke, B. von*, Marburg im, Kaiserreich 1866–1918, Marburg, 1980.

- Neuss

303. *Engels, W.*, Geschichte der Stadt Neuss. Part 3: Die Preußische Zeit (1814/15 bis 1945), Neuss, 1986.

- Nordhorn

304. *Looz-Corswarem, C. von*, and *M. Schmidt*, eds., Nordhorn: Beiträge zur 600 jährigen Stadtgeschichte, Nordhorn, 1979.

● Remscheid

305. *Stursberg, E.*, Remscheid und seine Gemeiden: Geschichte, Wirtschaft, Kultur, Remscheid, 1969.

● Solingen

306. *Rosenthal, H.*, Solingen. Geschichte einer Stadt, 3 vols., Duisburg, 1969–1975 (Vol. 3 ed. by R. Schneider- Berrenberg).

● Stuttgart

307. *Borst, O.*, Stuttgart: Die Geschichte der Stadt, 2nd ed., Stuttgart, 1973.

● Trier

308. *Zenz, E.*, Geschichte der Stadt Trier im 19. Jahrhundert, 2 vols., Trier, 1979/80.
309. *Zenz, E.*, Geschichte der Stadt Trier im 20. Jahrhundert, Trier, 1981.

● Ulm

310. *Specker, H. E.*, Ulm. Stadtgeschichte, Ulm, 1977.

MARJATTA HIETALA

Finland

In Finland urbanisation is a very young phenomenon. In the Middle Ages
there were only a few towns along the south and south-western coasts. The
most important town was Turku (Åbo), the medieval episcopal, see and
administration centre. The towns remained very small. The total urban
population in the late 18th century was only 5% to 6% of the overall
population, but this proportion began to increase by about the turn of the
century. After the Second World War there was a drastic change in the
industrial structure of the country leading to increased urban settlement
and now more than 60% of the population lives in urban areas.

Local history has a long tradition in Finland as well as in some other
nordic countries. Urban history has mainly taken the form of monographs
on individual towns. Some scholars have pointed out that the intention
behind this interest was to strengthen national identity first under Czarist
Russia, and then after independence was declared in late 1917.

In recent years interest has been growing in demographic and social
history — especially since the wealth of statistical material dating from the
mid-18th century was rediscovered by urban historians. Nowadays there is
a great number of comparative studies on births, deaths, marriages and
inter-town migration.

The History of Civic Administration in Finland, edited by Päiviö Tommila, is
the best evidence of this increasing interest in urban history. These four
volumes, which were published from 1981 to 1985, consist of articles from
various sectors of urban history: history of the development of towns from
the Middle Ages to modern times, town planning, administration and
economy, cultural policies, health care in cities and international contacts
between towns.

In the course of the last century, Finnish towns established various
contacts with European cities; civil servants participated in congresses and
visited continental institutions. Some new research projects on the diffusion
of innovations to institutions in the nordic countries (Hietala, Kuusanmäki)
are being conducted at present.

The research on the history of town and regional planning has a long tradition in Finland, especially at the Institutes of Geography in Turku and Helsinki. Sven Erik Åström's work about town planning in Helsinki can be cited as a classic example. The centre for urban and regional studies (Helsinki University of Technology) has conducted some projects on planning and housing in Finland. Finnish wooden town architecture has interested several researchers, too. Micro-historical studies are as popular in Finland nowadays as they are elsewhere.

A. Urban History Institutions

Centre for Urban and Regional Studies, Helsinki University of Technology

B. Aids to Research

(a) Urban History Journals

1. *Suomen kunnallislehti*, 1916 ff., Helsinki, Suomen Kunnallisliitto (= The Finnish municipal journal).
2. *Fennia*, 1899 ff., Helsinki, Societas Geographica Fenniae.
3. *Yhteiskuntasuunnittelu*, 1971 ff., Helsinki, The Finnish Society for Housing and Planning (= Community planning).
4. *Kunnallistieteellinen aikakauskirja*, 1977 ff., Helsinki, Kunnallistieteellinen yhdistys (= Municipal science journal).

(b) Bibliographies

5. *International Bibliography of Urban History*, Denmark, Finland, Norway, Sweden, Stockholm, 1960.
6. *Cahiers Bruxellois*, Vol. XIV (1969), No. II, pp. 135–136.
7. *Jutikkala, E.*, Finland, in Guide international d'histoire urbaine, Paris 1977, pp. 188–191.
8. *Paikallishistoriallinen bibliografia* (= The Bibliography of Local History), published by Y. S. Koskimies and P. Virrankoski, Parts 1–6, Helsinki, 1965–1967.

(c) Handbooks on Urban History

9. *Hammarström, I.*, Urban History in Scandinavia. A Survey of Recent Trends, in Urban History Yearbook, 1978, pp. 46–55.
10. *Kaupunkihistoria ja sen tutkimus*, eds. P. Tommila and R. Ranta, Turku, 1972 (Turun yliopisto, Suomen historian laitos monistesarja A.

Käsikirjoja 8) (= Urban history and its research).

11. *Kaupunki- ja aluetutkimus Suomessa 1981–1983. Tutkimuskyselyn tulokset.* Ympäristöministeriö, Helsinki, 1984 (= Urban and regional research in Finland).

12. *Synpunkter på lokal historia,* in Historisk Tidskrift för Finland, 1981, pp. 35–60 (= Aspects of local history).

(d) Atlases on Urban History and Urban Development

13. *Jutikkala, E.,* Finland: Turku – Åbo, Odense, 1977 (Scandinavian Atlas of Historic Towns, Vol. 1).

14. *Jutikkala, E.,* Finland: Borgå – Porvoo, Odense, 1977 (Scandinavian Atlas of Historic Towns, Vol. 2).

15. *Plans for the Towns in Finland to Scales 1: 3200–1: 10.000 published by C. W. Gylden during the Years 1837–1843,* Facsimile Editions, published by Maanmittaushallitus, Helsinki, 1983–1985 (The collection includes plans of the following cities: Hamina, Heinola, Helsinki, Jyväskylä, Kajaani, Kaskinen, Kokkola, Kristiinankaupunki, Kuopio, Käkisalmi, Lappeenranta, Loviisa, Mikkeli, Naantali, Oulu, Pietarsaari, Pori, Porvoo, Raahe, Rauma, Savonlinna, Sortavala, Tampere, Tornio, Turku, Uusikaupunki, Uusikaarlepyy, Vaasa, Viipuri).

(e) Urban History Sources

16. *Gylden, C. W.,* Historiska och statistiska anteckningar om städerna i Finland, Helsingfors, 1845 (= Historical and statistical facts about Finnish towns).

17. *Kallenautio, J.,* ed., Suomen kaupunkilaitoksen historia: Tilasto-osa, Helsinki, 1985 (= The history of civic administration in Finnish towns, municipal statistics).

18. *Laaksonen, H.,* Turun latinankieliset piirtokirjoitukset - Latinska inskrifter i Åbo, Åbo, 1984 (Åbo Landskapsmuseum, Rapporter 7) (= Latin epigraphs in Turku).

19. *Suomen taloushistoria 3.* Historiallinen tilasto, Helsinki, 1983 (= The economic history of Finland 3, historical statistics).

C. Research Reports

(a) General Surveys

20. *Alestalo, J.,* The Concentration of Population in Finland between 1880 and 1980, in Fennia, Vol. 161 (1983), No. 2, pp. 263–288.

21. *Jutikkala, E.,* Städernas tillväxt och näringsstruktur, in Urbaniserings-

prosessen i Norden 3. Industrialiseringens förste fase: Det XVII historikermöte Trondheim 1977, ed. by G. Authén Blom, Oslo, 1977, pp. 95–125 (= The impact of industrialism on urbanisation).

22. *Jutikkala, E.*, Urbaniseringen i Finland efter andra världskriget, in Historica IV. Föredrag vid det XVIII Nordiska historikermötet Jyväskylä 1981, ed. by M. Jokipii and I. Nummela, Jyväskylä, 1983, pp. 171–176 (= Urbanisation in Finland after the Second World War).

23. *Niitemaa, V.*, Die frühen Städte Finlands, in Acta Visbyensia, Vol. I (1965), pp. 190–205.

24. *Peltonen, A.*, Suomen kaupunkijärjestelmän kasvu 1815–1970: Teollistumisen vaikutuksista periferisen maan kaupungistumiseen, geogr. Diss. Helsinki, 1982 (Bidrag till kännedom av Finlands natur och folk; H. 128), (= Size-growth process of the Finnish town system, 1815–1970).

25. *Salo, U.*, Soumen kaupunkilaitoksen syntymäjuuria ja varhaisvaiheita, in Historiallinen arkisto, Vol. 78, Helsinki, 1982, pp. 7–98 (= Birth and early stages of the Finnish city).

26. *Suomen kaupunkilaitoksen historia 1.* Keskiajalta 1870-luvulle, ed. by P. Tommila, Vantaa, 1981 (= The history of civic administration in Finland, 1: from the Middle Ages to the 1870s).

27. *Suomen kaupunkilaitoksen historia 2.* 1870-luvulta autonomian ajan loppun, ed. by P. Tommila, Vantaa, 1983 (= The history of civic administration in Finland, 2: from the 1870s till the end of the period of autonomy).

28. *Suomen kaupunkilaitoksen historia 3.* Itsenäisyyden aika, ed. by Suomen Kaupunkiliitto, Vantaa, 1984 (= The history of civic administration in Finland, 3: the time of independence).

29. *Urbaniseringsprosessen i Norden*, Parts 1–3, Det XVII nordiske historikermöte Trondheim 1977, ed. by G. Authén Blom, Oslo, 1977 (= Urbanisation in the Nordic countries).

(b)   Surveys of Individual Fields of Urban Research

—

D. Literature on Individual Areas of Urban History Research

(a)   Concept and Definition of Town and Town Types

30. *Gardberg, C. J.*, Kaupunkilaitos keskiajalla ja uuden ajan alussa, in Suomen kaupunkilaitoksen historia 1, ed. by P. Tommila, Vantaa, 1981, pp. 9–49 (= Development of towns in the Middle Ages and at the beginning of the Modern Age).

31. *Jutikkala, E.*, Urbanisoituminen, in Suomen kaupunkilaitoksen historia 1, ed. by P. Tommila, Vantaa, 1981, pp. 9–25, and Part 2, pp. 9–37 (= Urbanisation).

32. *Leinonen, P.*, Kaupungistuminen ja elinkeinorakenteen muutos: Tampereen yliopiston tutkimuslaitos, Tutkimuksia A No 40, Tampere 1971 (= Urbanisation and the change in trade structure).

33. *Nikula, O.*, Kaupunkilaitos 1721–1875, in Suomen kaupunkilaitoksen historia 1, ed. by P. Tommila, Vantaa, 1981, pp. 135–301 (= The history of the development of towns between 1721 and 1875).

34. *Ranta, R.*, Suurvalta-ajan kaupunkilaitos, in Suomen kaupunkilaitoksen 1, ed. by P. Tommila, Vantaa, 1981, pp. 51–133 (= The development of towns in the 1600s).

35. *Tommila, P.*, Suomen kaupunkilaitoksen kehityslinjat, in Suomen kaupunkilaitoksen historia 3, ed. by Suomen Kaupunkiliitto, Vantaa, 1984, pp. 547–597 (= The main trends in the development of towns in Finland).

36. *Turpeinen, O.*, De finländska städernas folkmängd 1727–1810, in Historisk Tidskrift för Finland, 1977, pp. 109–127 (= The number of inhabitants in Finnish towns 1727–1810).

(b) Politics, Law and Statutes

37. *Åström, S. E.*, Anlagda städer och centralortssystemet i Finland 1550–1785, in Urbaniseringsprosessen i Norden 2. De anlagte steder på 1600–1700 tallet. Det XVII. nordiske historikermöte Trondheim 1977, ed. by G. Authén Blom, Oslo, 1977, pp. 134–181 (= Towns and network of cities in Finland 1550–1785).

38. *Hakalehto, I.*, Kunnallisen kansanvallan kehitys, kunnallisvaalit ja -valtuustot 1917–1970, in Suomen kaupunkilaitoksen historia 3, ed. by Suomen Kaupunkiliitto, Vantaa, 1984, pp. 107–211 (= Development of municipal democracy, elections and city councils).

39. *Holopainen, T.*, Kunnan asema valtiossa, Vammala, 1969 (Suomalaisen Lakimiesyhdistyksen julkaisuja A, No. 81) (= The municipality and the state).

40. *Johanson, L. O.*, and *V. Tattari*, Kaupunkien yhteistoiminta: Kaupungit ja valtiovalta, in Suomen kaupunkilaitoksen historia 2, ed. by P. Tommila, Vantaa, 1983, pp. 411–429, and Part 3, pp. 509–545 (= Cooperation between towns; towns and the state).

41. *Kallenautio, J.*, Kaupunkien keskushallinto ja henkilöstöpolitiikka, in Suomen kaupunkilaitoksen historia 3, ed. by Suomen Kaupunkiliitto, Vantaa, 1984, pp. 215–265 (= Local administration of towns and personnel policy).

42. *Kuujo, E.*, Finlands medeltida städer, in Urbaniseringsprosessen i Norden 1: Middelaldersteder. Det XVII nordiske historikermöte Trond-

heim 1977, ed. by G. Authén Blom, Oslo, 1977, pp. 147–160 (= Towns in the Middle Ages in Finland).

43. *Kuusanmäki, J.*, Kunnallisen kansanvallan kehitys ja kunnallishallinnon organisaatio 1875–1917, in Suomen kaupunkilaitoksen historia 2, ed. by P. Tommila, Vantaa, 1983, pp. 51–125 (= Municipal democracy and local government 1875–1917).

44. *Piilonen, J.*, Punainen kunnallishallinto 1918, in Suomen kaupunkilaitoksen historia 3, ed. by Suomen Kaupunkiliitto, Vantaa, 1984, pp. 87–104 (= Municipal administration of the Reds during the Civil War in 1918).

45. *Tommila, P.*, Städernas kommunalförvaltning, in Urbaniseringsprosessen i Norden 3: Industrialiseringen förste fase. Det XVII nordiske historikermöte Trondheim, 1977, ed. by G. Authén Blom, Oslo 1977, pp. 126–142 (= The local administration of towns).

(c) Population and Social Structure

46. *Engman, M.*, St. Petersburg och Finland. Migration och influens 1703–1917, Helsingfors, 1983 (Bidrag till kännedom av Finlands natur och folk 130) (= St. Petersburg and Finland: migration and influence 1703–1917).

47. *Hakkarainen, H.*, Pitkänsillan pohjoispuolen teollisuusalueiden syntyvaiheista ja rakentamisesta, in Narinkka, 1982/1983, pp. 7–67 (= The birth and growth of industrial areas north of Pitkäsilta Bridge in Helsinki).

48. *Hietala, K.*, Internal Migration and Technological Development, in Yearbook of Population Research in Finland, Vol. XIX, 1981, pp. 28–46.

49. *Hietala, M.*, Servicefaktorn i Helsingfors och Stockholm. En komparativ analys av utvecklingen kring sekelskiftet, in Städer i utveckling. Tolv studier kring stadsförändringar tillägnade Ingrid Hammarström, ed. by T. Hall, Stockholm 1984, pp. 147–165 (= Services in Helsinki and Stockholm: A comparative analysis at the turn of the century).

50. *Hietala, M.*, The Diffusion of Innovations: Some Examples of Finnish Civil Servants' Professional Tours in Europe, in Scandinavian Journal of History, 1983, pp. 23–36.

51. *Hietala, M.*, Urbanisation: Contradictory Views. Finnish Reactions to the Continental Discussion at the beginning of the 20th Century, in Studia historica 12: Miscellanea, ed. by A. Tammisto, Helsinki, 1983, pp. 7–20.

52. *Knapas, M. T.*, Korkeasaari ja Seurasaari: Helsinki-läisten ensimmäiset kansanpuistot, Karkkila, 1980 (= The first public parks for the people of Helsinki).

53. *Lento, R.*, Maassamuutto ja siihen vaikuttavat tekijät Suomessa

1878–1939, Helsinki, 1951 (= Internal Migration in Finland 1878–1939).

54. *Lindgren, J.*, Towards Smaller Families in the Changing Society: Fertility Transition during the First Phase of Industrialisation in Three Finnish Municipalities, Helsinki, 1984 (Publications of the Population Research Institute, D 11).

55. *Lindgrén, S.*, Äktenskap, föräktenskapliga förbindelser och sammanboends: Sociala mönster i den tidiga industrialismens Helsingfors, in Historisk Tidskrift för Finland, 1984, pp. 281–300 (= Marriage, premarital relations and cohabitation: social patterns in early industrial Helsinki).

56. *Lindgrén, S.*, Äktenskapsbildning och nativitet i sekelskiftets Helsingfors, in Svenskt i Finland 2. Demografiska och sosialhistoriska studier, ed. by M. Engman and H. Stenius, Helsingfors, 1984, pp. 77–100 (Skrifter utgivna av Svenska Litteratursällskapet i Finland, Vol. 519) (= Marriages and birth rate in Helsinki around 1900).

57. *Lindgrén, S.*, Utomäktenskaplig fertilitet i Helsingfors under 1800-talets senare del, in Historiallinen Arkisto 76. När samhället förändras Kun yhteiskunta muuttuu, Helsinki, 1981, pp. 301–320 (= Illegitimate fertility in later 19th century Helsinki).

58. *Manninen, M.*, Pigornas levnadslopp i Uleåborg på 1700-talet, in Historisk Tidskrift för Finland, 1984, pp. 207–231 (= The life of a housemaid in Uleåborg in the 18th century).

59. *Manninen, M.*, The Opportunities of Independent Life for Women in an 18th-century Finnish Provincial Town, in Scandinavian Journal of History, 1984, pp. 149–168.

60. *Pitkänen, K.*, Stad och influensområde. Flyttningsrörelse och social förändring före industrialiseringsperioden (ca. 1720–1850), in By och bygd. Stad og omland: Nordisk lokalhistorie-seminarraport, No. 3, Oslo, 1981, pp. 7–16 (= City and regional influence, migration and social change before industrialisation, ca. 1720–1850).

61. *Rasila, V.*, Teollistumiskauden muuttoliikkeet: Mikrohistoriallinen tutkimus Tampereen seudulta, Tampere, 1983 (Tempereen yliopisto Historiatieteen laitoksen julkaisuja 7) (= Migration in Finland during the period of industrialisation: a microhistorical study).

62. *Rasila, V.*, Sosiaalitoimi ja terveyshuolto, in Suomen kaupunkilaitoksen historia 2, ed. by P. Tommila, Vantaa, 1983, pp. 333–376; and Part 3, pp. 407–460 (= Social work and health services in towns).

63. *Turpeinen, O.*, Befolknings förhållanden i Viborgs finska, svenska och tyska församlingar åren 1816–1865, in Svenskt i Finland 2. Demografiska och sosialhistoriska studier, ed. by M. Engman and H. Stenius, Helsingfors, 1984, pp. 37–51 (Skrifter utgivna av Svenska Litteratursällskapet i Finland, Vol. 519) (= The structure of the population in Viborg's Finnish, Swedish and German parishes in 1816–1865).

64. *Waris, H.*, Työläisyhteiskunnan syntyminen Pitkänsillan pohjoispuolelle, 2nd ed., Tapiola, 1973 (= The establishment of the working-class community north of the Pitkäsilta Bridge in Helsinki).

(d) Town Planning

65. *Andersson, H.*, Urban Structural Dynamics in the City of Turku, Finland, in Fennia, Vol. 161 (1983), No. 2, pp. 145–261.

66. *Åström, S.-E.*, Samhällsplanering och regionsbildning i kejserlig Helsingfors: Studier i stadens differentierung 1810–1910, Helsingfors, 1957 (= Town planning in Helsinki in the 19th century: Studies in social differentiation in 19th-century Helsinki).

67. *Hertzen, H. von,* and *P. D. Speiregen,* Building a New Town: Finland's New Garden City Tapiola, Cambridge, Mass., and London, 1971.

68. *Jumppanen, S.*, Die innere Differenzierung der Stadt Rauma, Vammala, 1973 (Turun yliopiston Maantieteen laitoksen julkaisuja 65 = Fennia, Vol. 126).

69. *Jutikkala, E.*, Town Planning in Sweden and Finland until the Middle of the 19th Century, in Scandinavian Economic History Review, Vol. XVI (1968).

70. *Kuoppamäki-Kalkkinen,* Kaupunkisuunnittelu ja rakentaminen Helsingin Kalliossa 1880–1980, Helsinki, 1984 (Yhdyskuntasuunnittelun laitos, Teknillisen korkeakoulun arkkitehtiosasto, julk. A 30) (= Town planning and construction in Kallio 1880–1980).

71. *Lilius, H.*, Kaupunkirakentaminen 1617–1856, in Suomen kaupunkilaitoksen historia 3, ed. by P. Tommila, Vantaa, 1981, pp. 303–388 (= Town construction 1617–1856).

72. *Lilius, H.*, Suomalainen puukaupunki – Trästaden, Rungsted Kyst, 1985 (= Trästaden – Finnish wooden town).

73. *Lilius, H., R. Nikula* and *R. Wäre,* Kaupunkirakentaminen 1856–1917, in Suomen kaupunkilaitoksen historia 2, ed. by P. Tommila, Vantaa, 1983, pp. 127–269 (= Construction of cities 1856–1917).

74. *Perälä, T.*, Kaupunkien aluepolitiikka ja esikaupunkiliitokset 1875–1918, in Suomen kaupunkilaitoksen historia 2, ed. by P. Tommila, Vantaa, 1983, pp. 29–48; and Part 3, pp. 39–85 (= Municipal land policy and incorporation of suburbs 1875–1918).

75. *Ranta, R.*, Städernas handelsomland och gränsens inverkan i Gamla Finland, in Historisk Tidskrift för Finland, 1982, pp. 48–77 (= Trading area of towns in the Carelian Isthmus 1743–1812).

76. *Salokorpi, A.*, Kaupunkirakentaminen, in Suomen kaupunkilaitoksen historia 3, ed. by Suomen Kaupunkiliitto, Vantaa, 1984, pp. 269–329 (= Urban construction in independent Finland).

(e)   Economy and Transport

77. *Kallenautio, J.*, Kunnallistalous, yhdyskuntatekniikka, kunnalliset liikelaitokset ja joukkoliikenne, in Suomen kaupunkilaitoksen historia 2, ed. by P. Tommila, Vantaa, 1983, pp. 271–330; and Part 3, pp. 331–404 (= Economy, infrastructure, municipal enterprises and public transport services in Finnish towns).

78. *Keskumäki, O.*, Kaupunkien menotalous ja urbanisoituminen, Tampere, 1971 (Tampereen yliopiston tutkimuslaitos, Tutkimuksia A No. 39) (= Urbanisation and municipal expenditure).

79. *Roslin, B.*, Kommunal lånepolitik i långtidsperspektuv. En Studie i idéutveckling och ekonomiskpolitisk diskussion, Åbo, 1970 (Meddelanden från institutet för samhällsforskning, upprätthallet av statsvetenskaplig fakultäten vid Åbo Akademin No 52) (= Question of the debts of cities: a study of political discussion).

(f)   Arts and Sciences, Churches

80. *Halila, A.*, Kaupunkien kunnallinen kulttuuripolitiikka, in: Suomen kaupunkilaitoksen historia 2, ed. by P. Tommila, Vantaa, 1983, pp. 377–408, and Part 3, pp. 463–506 (= Cultural policies in cities).

81. *Viljo E. M.*, Theodor Höjer: En arkitekt under den moderna stadsarkitekturens genombrottstid i Finland fran 1870 till sekelskiftet, Helsinki, 1985 (Suomen Muinaismuistoyhdistyksen aikakauskirja 88) (= Theodor Höjer: an architect from the first period of modern urban building in Finland from around 1870 to the turn of the century).

E.   Local Studies (a representative selection)

● Hämeenlinna

82. *Koskimies, Y. S.*, Hämeenlinnan kaupungin historia 1875–1944, Hämeenlinna, 1966 (= History of Hämeenlinna 1875–1944).

● Helsinki

83. *Helsingin kaupungin historia*, 9 vols., Helsinki, 1950–1967 (= History of Helsinki).

● Jyväskylä

84. *Tommila, P.*, Jyväskylän kaupungin historia 1837–1965, 2 vols., Jyväskylä, 1970–1972 (= History of Jyväskylä 1837–1965).

- Kemi

85. *Hedman, O.*, Kemin kaupungin historia sekä katsaus Kemin seudun ja Kemin Lapin varhaisempiin vaiheisiin, 2 vols., Tampere, 1969 / Kemi 1976 (= History of Kemi).

- Oulu

86. *Hautala, K.*, Oulun kaupungin historia, Vols. 3–5, Oulu, 1975–1983 (= History of Oulu).

- Savonlinna

87. *Vehviläinen, O.*, Savonlinnan kaupungin historia 3. Savonlinnan kaupunki 1876–1976, Savonlinna, 1978 (= History of Savonlinna 1876–1976).

- Tampere

88. *Jutikkala, E.*, Tampereen historia 3. Vuodesta 1905 vuoten 1945, Tampere, 1979 (= History of Tampere in the years 1905–1945).
89. *Rasila, V.*, Tampereen historia 2. 1840-luvulta vuoten 1905, Tampere, 1984 (= History of Tampere in the years 1840–1905).

- Turku

90. *Turku.* Turun kaupungin historia. Kivikaudesta vuoteen 1970, 8 vols., Turku, 1957–1981 (= History of Turku: from the Stone Age to the year 1970).

FRANÇOIS BÉDARIDA AND GILLES JEANNOT

France

A. Urban History Institutions

The situation of urban history in France is characterised by an abundance of works in the field and the absence of organisation and centralisation: there are few institutions, and no journals which could review the works in progress and serve as a place of confrontation between specialists. In 1975 an international urban history group was created at the "Maison des Sciences de l'Homme". This group, which is very informal in structure, was first directed by D. Roche and then by B. Lepetit. It sets up meetings and organises colloquiums: Urban Skeletons in Western Europe (Paris, 1977); Urban Space (London, 1979); Migrations (Göttingen, 1982); The Dissemination of Innovation (Paris, 1984). The group has concentrated on a period ranging from the pre-industrial town to the industrial town, that is to say, the time span is from the 16th to the 19th century (the group rarely ventures into the 20th century).

No specific course of studies in urban history exists at university level. However, several works have been undertaken in conjunction with the seminar taught by L. Bergeron and M. Roncayolo at "l'Ecole des Hautes Etudes en Sciences Sociales". Many university centres conduct studies in urban history, often in laboratories associated with the "Centre National de la Recherche Scientifique" (CNRS): for example, the Centre for Economic and Social History in the Lyon Region (Lyon University II), the Centre for the Study of Urban Spaces (Bordeaux University III), the Centre for Research in Quantitative History (Caen University), the University of Paris X-Nanterre, Lille University III and, on the history of labour in suburbs, the GRECO 55. The CNRS's own laboratory, the "Institut d'Histoire du Temps Présent", co-ordinates research on the contemporary period.

B. Aids to Research

(a) Urban History Journals

1. *Annales ESC (Economies, Sociétés, Civilisations)*, Paris, 1929 ff.
2. *Annales de la recherche urbaine*, Paris, 1978 ff.
3. *Bulldoc*, Paris, 1967–1979.
4. *Cahiers de la recherche architecturale*, Paris, 1977 ff.
5. *Espaces et Sociétés*, Paris, 1970 ff.
6. *Ethnologie française*, Nancy, 1953 ff.
7. *Le Mouvement social*, Paris, 1960 ff.
8. *Population*, Paris, 1946 ff.
9. *Urbi: Arts, histoire, ethnologie des villes*, Paris, 1979 ff.
10. *La vie urbaine*, Paris, 1919–1939, new editions, 1950–1971, 1975–1978.

(b) Bibliographies

11. *Dezès, M.-G.*, Politique urbaine et recherche urbaine 1945–1980: Eléments de bibliographie, in Bulletin de l'Institut d'Histoire du Temps Présent, No. 8 (1982), pp. 24–53.
12. *Dollinger, P., P. Wolff* and *S. Guenée*, Bibliographie d'histoire des villes de France, Paris, 1967.
13. *Histoire de la France urbaine*, Paris, 1983–1985 (The bibliographies are included in Volumes IV and V).

(c) Handbooks on Urban History

—

(d) Atlases on Urban History and Urban Development

14. *Couperie, P.*, Paris au fil du temps: Atlas historique et d'architecture, Paris, 1968.
15. *Dupeux, G.*, Atlas historique de l'urbanisation de la France 1811–1975, Paris, 1981 (geographical-historical synthesis).
16. *Fortier, B.*, A partir du cadastre parisien, Paris (Institut Français d'Architecture) (unpublished at time of printing).

(e) Urban History Sources

—

C. Research Reports

(a) General Surveys

17. *Analyse et évaluation de la recherche en sciences sociales au Ministère de l'Equipement*, in Le Progrès Scientifique, No. 173 (1974), pp. 43–66.

18. *Bédarida, F.*, The French Approach to Urban History, in D. Fraser and A. Sutcliffe, eds., The pursuit of Urban History, London, 1983, pp. 395–406.

19. Bédarida, F., The Growth of Urban History in France, in H. J. Dyos, ed., The Study of Urban History, London, 1968, pp. 47–60.

20. *Bergeron, L.* and *M. Roncayolo*, De la ville pré-industrielle à la ville industrielle: Essai sur l'historiographie française, in Quaderni Storici, 1974, pp. 826–876.

21. *Centre de Documentation de l'Urbanisme*, pub. Fiches analytiques de la recherche urbaine en France, 1975 ff. (= Trilingual reports on research projects sponsored by the various ministries, published annually).

22. *Centre de Documentation de l'Urbanisme*, pub., Urban Research in France: Trends and Results (1971–1975), Paris, 1976.

23. *Conan, M.* and *L. Le Floch*, La recherche urbaine, Essai de rapport de conjoncture, in Bulldoc, No. 50 (1975).

24. *MSH Informations* (Bulletin de la Maison des Sciences de l'Homme), Paris, 1973 ff.

25. *Roche, D.*, Urban History in France, in Urban History Yearbook, 1980, pp. 12–22.

26. *Roche, D.*, Villes, in J. Le Goff *et al.*, La nouvelle histoire, Paris, 1978.

27. *Roche, D.*, and *M.-G. Dezès*, in F. Ascher *et al.*, eds., Les thèmes émergents de la recherche urbaine, Paris, 1985 (Ministère de l'Urbanisme, Ministère de l'Education nationale, CNRS).

(b)   Surveys of Individual Fields of Urban Research

● Architecture

28. *Boudon, F.*, L'architecture à Paris de 1850 à 1940: Revue des publications récentes, in Revue de l'Art, No. 29 (1975), pp. 107–114.

29. *Le Brenn, F.*, Présence de l'histoire contemporaine dans la recherche en architecture, and *M. Morel*, L'histoire de la contemporaine dans les diplômes d'architecture et d'urbanisme, in Bulletin de l'Institut d'Histoire du Temps Présent, No. 13 (1983), pp. 25–59.

30. *Recherche Architecturale* (= Special issue of the journal Les Cahiers de la Recherche Architecturale, No. 13 (1983)).

● Ethnology

31. *Morel A.*, Ethnologie dans la ville: Une bibliographie indicative, in Terrain, No. 3 (1984), pp. 43–54.

● Geography

32. *Dalmasso, E.*, Le thème de la croissance urbaine dans les recherches françaises, in Norois, 1977, pp. 431–443.

● Politics

33. *Loinger, G.*, Esquisse d'analyse de l'évolution de la politique urbaine en France depuis la Libération, in Espaces et Sociétés, 1981.
34. *Les politiques urbaines françaises depuis 1945* (= Supplément No. 5 (1984) of the Bulletin de l'Institut d'Histoire du Temps Présent).

● Sociology

35. *Aballea, F.*, Y-a-t-il crise de la sociologie urbaine?, in Recherche Sociale, No. 86 (1983).
36. *Crise de la sociologie urbaine*, in Economie et Urbanisme, No. 252 (1980).

● Urban Studies

37. *Recherche scientifique et prospective urbaine*, in Urbanisme, No. 156–157 (1977).
38. *La recherche urbaine: Quel avenir?*, in Métropolis, No. 57 (1983).

● Economics

39. *Derycke, P.-H.*, Situation et perspectives de la recherche urbaine, in idem, Economie et planification urbaine, Vol. 1, Paris, 1979, pp. 48–70, as well as idem, Vers une conception de la ville tant qu'agent économique, in the same, Vol. 2, Paris, 1982, pp. 140–146.

D. Literature on Individual Areas of Urban History Research

(a) Concept and Definition of Town and Town Types

40. *L'analyse interdisciplinaire de la croissance urbaine*, Paris, 1972.
41. *Bauer, G.* and *J. M. Roux*, La Rurbanisation, Paris, 1976.
42. *Borde, J., P. Barrère* and *M. Cassou-Mounat*, Les villes françaises, Paris, 1980.
43. *Bruyelle, P.*, L'organisation urbaine de la région Nord-Pas-de-Calais, Cergy, 1981.
44. *Castells, M.*, La question urbaine, Paris, 1972.

45. *Castex, J., J. -C. Depaule* and *P. Panerai*, Formes urbaines: De l'îlot à la barre, Paris, 1977.

46. *Claval, P.*, La logique des villes, Paris, 1981.

47. *Dagnaud, M.*, Le mythe de la qualité de la vie et la politique urbaine en France 1945–1973, Paris and La Haye, 1978.

48. *Histoire de la France urbaine*, Vol. IV: *M. Agulhon et al.*, La ville de l'âge industriel: Le cycle haussmannien, Paris, 1983; Vol. V: *M. Roncayolo et al.*, La ville aujourd'hui: Croissance urbaine et crise du citadin, Paris, 1985.

49. *Merriman, J.*, ed., French Cities in the Nineteenth Century, London, 1982.

50. *Pumain, D.*, Contribution à l'étude de la croissance urbaine dans le système urbain français, Diss. Paris, 1980.

51. *Pumain, D.*, and *T. Saint-Julien*, Les dimensions du changement urbain: Evolution des structures socio-économiques du système urbain français de 1954 à 1975, Paris, 1978.

52. *Prendre la ville*: Esquisse d'une histoire de l'urbanisme d'Etat, Paris, 1977.

53. *Saint-Julien, T.*, Croissance industrielle et système urbain, Paris, 1982.

54. *Vant, André*, Imagerie et urbanisation, Diss. Lyon, 1982.

55. *Villes et campagnes XVème-XXème siècles*, Lyon, 1977.

(b) Politics, Law and Statutes

56. *Brunet, J.-P.*, Un demi-siècle d'action municipale à Saint-Denis la Rouge 1890–1939, Paris, 1981.

57. *Bruston, A.*, La régénération de Lyon 1853–1865, in Espaces et Sociétés, No. 15 (1975), pp. 81–104.

58. *Chaline, J.-P.*, Les bourgeois de Rouen: Une élite urbaine au XIXème siècle, Paris, 1982.

59. *Dreyfus, J.*, La ville disciplinaire, Paris, 1976.

60. *Duriez, B.*, and *D. Cornoel*, La naissance de la politique urbaine: Le cas de Roubaix, in Annales de la recherche urbaine, 1979, pp. 22–84.

61. *Joly J.*, Aspects de la politique urbaine à Grenoble, in Revue de Géographie Alpine, Vol. 70 (1982).

62. *Pinol, J. -L.*, Espace social et espace politique: Lyon à l'époque du Front Populaire, Lyon, 1980.

63. *Topalov, C.*, Expropriation et préemption publique en France 1950–1973, Paris, 1974.

64. *Voilliard, O.*, Nancy au XIXème siècle 1815–1871: Une bourgeoisie urbaine, Paris, 1978.

(c) Population and Social Structure

65. *Agulhon, M.*, Une ville ouvrière au temps du socialisme utopique:

Toulon de 1815 à 1851, Paris, 1970.

66. *Ariès P.*, La famille et la ville, in Esprit, 1978, pp. 3–12.

67. *Bonneville, M.*, Villeurbanne: Naissance et métamorphose d'une banlieue ouvrière, Lyon, 1978.

68. *Chatelain, A.*, Les migrants temporaires en France de 1800 à 1914, Lille, 1977.

69. *Chombart de Lauwe, P. H.*, Des hommes et des villes, Paris, 1965.

70. *Codaccioni, F. P.*, De l'inégalité sociale dans une grande ville industrielle: Le drame de Lille, n.p. 1976.

71. *Courgeau, D.* and *M. Lefebvre*, Les migrations internes en France de 1954 à 1975: Migrations et urbanisation, in Population, Vol. 37 (1982), pp. 341–369.

72. *Démographie urbaine XVème-XXème siècle*, Lyon 1977 (Université de Lyon).

73. *Désert, G.*, Centres urbains et courants migratoires en Basse Normandie 1846–1911, in Annales de démographie historique, 1976, pp. 261–277.

74. *Dupeux, G.*, La croissance urbaine en Aquitaine 1811–1968, Bordeaux, 1976.

75. *Dupeux, G.*, La croissance urbaine en France au XIXème siècle, in Revue d'histoire économique et sociale, 1973, pp. 173–189.

76. *Frey, J. P.*, Le Creusot: urbanistique patronale, in Annales de la recherche urbaine, No. 22 (1984), pp. 3–46.

77. *Garden, M.*, Le bilan démographique des villes: Un système complexe, in Annales de démographie historique, 1982, pp. 267–276.

78. *Gérard, A. -L.*, Quartier et unité de voisinage dans la pratique urbanistique française 1919–1973, Strasbourg, 1980.

79. *Guillaume, P.*, La population de Bordeaux au XIXème siècle, Paris, 1972.

80. *Guerrand, R.*, Les origines du logement social en France, Paris, 1967.

81. *Guerrand, R.*, and *E. Canfora-Argandona*, La répartition de la population: Les conditions de logement des classes ouvrières au XIXème siècle, Paris, 1976.

82. *Hanagan, M.*, The Logic of Solidarity: Artisans and Industrial Workers in three French Towns 1871–1914, Urbana, Ill., 1980.

83. *Lefebvre, M.*, Evolution démographique des villes de plus de 50.000 habitants hormis Paris de 1954 à 1975, in Population, Vol. 36 (1981), pp. 295–315.

84. *Lepetit, B.* and *J. -F. Royer*, Croissance et taille des villes: Contribution à l'étude de l'urbanisation au début du XIXème siècle, in Annales ESC, Vol. 35 (1980), pp. 987–1010.

85. *Lequin, Y.*, Les ouvriers de la région lyonnaise 1848–1914, Lyon 1977.

86. *Merlin, P.*, L'exode rural, Paris, 1971.

87. *Moch, L. P.*, Marriage, Migration and Urban Demographic Structure: A Case from France in the Belle Epoque, in Journal of Family History, Vol. 6 (1981), pp. 70–88.

88. *Perrot, M.*, La ménagère dans l'espace parisien au XIXème siècle, in Annales de la recherche urbaine, 1980, pp. 3–22.

89. *Prost, A.*, Mariage, jeunesse et société à Orléans en 1911, in Annales ESC, Vol. 36 (1981), pp. 672–701.

90. *Raison-Jourde, F.*, La colonie auvergnate de Paris, Paris, 1976.

91. *Rougerie, J.*, Espace populaire et espace révolutionnaire, in Recherches et Travaux de l'Institut d'Histoire économique et sociale, Diss., Paris, 1981.

92. *Tugault, Y.*, Fécondité et urbanisation, Paris, 1975.

93. *Verret, M.*, L'espace ouvrier, Paris, 1979.

(d)   Town Planning, Housing

94. *Aydalot, P., L. Bergeron* and *M. Roncayolo*, Industrialisation et croissance urbaine dans la France du XIXème siècle, Paris, 1981.

95. *Bertrand, M.-J.*, Architecture de l'habitat urbain: La maison, le quartier, la ville, Paris, 1980.

96. *Boudon, F.*, Tissu urbain et architecture: L'analyse parcellaire comme base de l'histoire architecturale, in Annales ESC, Vol. 30 (1975), pp. 773–818.

97. *Boudon, F., et al.*, Système de l'architecture urbaine: Le quartier des Halles à Paris, 2 Vols., Paris, 1977.

98. *Chaline, J.-P.*, Les grands travaux d'urbanisme à Rouen au XIXème siècle, in Bulletin des amis des monuments rouennais, 1975, pp. 33–46.

99. *Cottereau, A.*, L'apparition de l'urbanisme comme action collective: De Haussmann à la construction du métropolitain, in Sociologie du Travail, 1969, pp. 342–365.

100. *Cottereau, A.*, Les débuts de la planification urbaine dans l'agglomération parisienne, in Sociologie du Travail, 1970, pp. 362–392.

101. *Daumard, A.*, Maisons de Paris et propriétaires parisiens au XIXème siècle, Paris, 1956.

102. *Dion, R. -M.*, Effets des processus volontaristes dans la formation d'une région urbaine: Nancy et les plans d'aménagement et d'extension de la première moitié du XXème siècle, in Bulletin de géographie de l'Est, (1974), pp. 245–311.

103. *Dupuy, G.*, Assainir la ville hier et aujourd'hui, Paris, 1982.

104. *Garden, M.*, and *Y. Lequin*, eds., Construire la ville, Lyon, 1983.

105. *Garden, M.*, and *Y. Lequin*, eds., Habiter la ville, Lyon, 1985.

106. *Gaudin, J. -R.*, L'avenir en plan: Technique, et politique dans la prévision urbaine 1900–1930, Paris and Seyssel 1985.

107. *Gloton, J. J.*, Architecture et urbanisme à Marseille au XIXème siècle, in Marseille, No. 112 (1978).

108. *Haumont, N., et. al.*, Les pavillonnaires, Paris, 1966.

109. *Jacquemet, G.*, Belleville, Diss., Paris, 1979.

110. *Jacquemet, G.*, Belleville au XIXéme et XXème siècle: Une méthode d'analyse de la croissance urbaine à Paris, in Annales ESC, Vol. 30 (1975), pp. 819–843.

111. *Kopp, A., F. Boucher* and *D. Pauly*, L'architecture de la reconstruction 1945–1953, Paris, 1982.

112. *Lacave, M.*, Stratégies d'expropriation et haussmannisation: L'exemple de Montpellier, in Annales ESC, Vol. 35 (1980), pp. 1011–1025.

113. *Larroque, D.*, Industrialisation et équipements urbains à Paris 1830–1914, in Annales de la recherche urbaine, No. 8 (1980), pp. 49–86.

114. *Lescure, M.*, Les sociétés immobilières en France au XIXème siècle, Paris, 1980.

115. *Moulin, R., et. al.*, Les architectes: Métamorphose d'une profession libérale, Paris, 1974.

116. *Pincon, M.* and *E. Préteceille*, Introduction à l'étude de la planification urbaine en région parisienne: Histoire des plans et éléments de méthode, Paris, 1973.

117. *Préteceille, E.*, La production des grands ensembles, Paris, 1973.

118. *Préteceille, E.* and *T. Regazzola*, L'appareil juridique de la planification urbaine: Les plans d'urbanisme de 1958 à 1970, Paris, 1974.

119. *Réveil de l'architecture?* (Special issue of the journal, Esprit. (1985)).

120. *Rouleau, B.*, L'espace urbain parisien à travers ses cartes, Diss., Paris, 1982.

121. *Rouleau, B.*, Le tracé des rues de Paris: Formation, typologie, fonctions, 2nd edition, Paris, 1978.

122. *Stratégies sur la ville*: Construire en quartier ancien (= Special issue Cahiers de la recherche architecturale (1980)).

123. *Sutcliffe, A.*, Towards the Planned City: Germany, Britain, the United States and France 1780–1914, Oxford, 1981.

124. *Thoenig, J. -C.*, L'ère des technocrates: Le cas des Ponts et Chaussées, Paris, 1973.

125. *Urbanisme et architecture en Lorraine 1830–1930*, Metz, 1982.

126. *Veillard, J. -Y.*, Rennes au XIXème siècle: Urbanisme et architecture, Rennes, 1978.

(e)   Economy and Transport

127. *Bairoch, P.*, De Jérusalem à Mexico: villes et économie dans l'histoire, Paris, 1985.

128. *Bairoch, P.*, Taille des villes, conditions de vie et développement économique, Paris, 1978.

129. *Bardet, J. -P.* and *G. Désert*, Le bâtiment. Enquête d'histoire économique XIVème-XIXème siècle, Paris, 1971.

130. *Bleitrach, D.* and *A. Chenu,* L'usine et la vie, Paris, 1982.
131. *Derycke, P. -H.,* Economie et planification urbaine, Paris. 1979.
132. *Derycke, P. -H.,* L'économie urbaine, Paris, 1970.
133. *Dupuy, G.,* Urbanisme et technique: Chronique d'un mariage de raison, Paris, 1978.
134. *Larroque, D.,* Enjeux politiques et financiers autour d'une technique urbaine: Paris et ses transports 1855–1939, in Annales de la recherche urbaine, No. 14 (1982), pp. 70–98.
135. *Lescure, M.,* Les banques, l'Etat et le marché immobilier en France 1820–1940, Paris, 1982.
136. *Pumain, D.,* Chemin de fer et croissance urbaine en France au XIXème siècle, in Annales de géographie, 1982, pp. 529–550.
137. *Rémy, J.,* La ville phénomène économique, Brussels, 1966.
138. Les reseaux techniques urbains, in Annales de la rechere architecturale, Nos. 23–24 (1984).

(f) Arts and Sciences, Churches

139. *Castells, M.,* The City and the Grassroots: A Cross-Cultural Theory of Urban Movements, Berkeley, Cal., 1983.
140. *Cauquelin, A.,* Essai de philosophie urbaine, Paris, 1982.

E. Local Studies (a representative selection)

141. Refer in particular to the collection, *Univers de la France* with reports on *Angers* (F. Lebrun), *Bordeaux* (C. Higounet), *Brest* (Y. Le Gallo), *Le Mans* (F. Dornic), *Lyon* (A. Latreille), *Marseille* (E. Baratier), *Nancy* (R. Tavernaux), *Nantes* (P. Bois), *Nizza* (M. Bordes), *Reims* (P. Desportes), *Rennes* (J. Meyer), *Rouen* (M. Mollat), *Toulon* (M. Agulhon), *Toulouse* (P. Wolff), *Tourcoing* (L. Trénard).

● Cherbourg

142. *Demangeon, A.,* and *B. Fortier,* Les vaissaux et les villes: L'arsenal de Cherbourg, Liège, 1978.

● Decazeville

143. *Wolff, J.,* Decazeville: Expansion et déclin d'un pôle de croissance, in Revue du Rouergue, Vol. 31 (1977), pp. 223–238.

● Grenoble

144. *Parent, J. -F.*, Grenoble: Deux siècles d'urbanisation. Projets d'urbanisme et réalisations architecturales 1815–1965, Grenoble, 1982.

- Le Creusot

145. *Devillers, C.* and *B. Huet*, Le Creusot: Naissance et développement d'une ville industrielle 1782–1914, Seyssel, 1981.

- Lyon

146. *Léon, P.*, Géographie de la fortune et structures sociales à Lyon au XIXème siècle 1815–1914, Lyon, 1974.

- Marseille

147. *Roncayolo, M.*, Croissance et division sociale de l'espace urbain. Essai sur la genèse des structures urbaines. Diss. Paris, 1981.

- Montceau-les-Mines

148. *Satet, M.*, Montceau-les-Mines: Essor d'une mine, naissance d'une ville, Roanne, 1981.

- Paris (and its suburbs)

149. ·*Bertier de Sauvigny, D. de*, La Restauration, in Nouvelle histoire de Paris, Paris.
150. *Brunet, J. -P.*, Saint-Denis, la ville rouge, Paris, 1980.
151. *Carmona, M.*, Le Grand Paris: L'évolution de l'idée d'aménagement de la région parisienne, 2 vols., Paris, 1980.
152. *Gaillard, J.*, Paris, la ville (1852–1870), Paris, 1976.
153. *Girard, L.*, La Deuxiéne République et le Second Empire, in Nouvelle histoire de Paris, Paris, Part. 9 (1981).
154. *Hénon, P.* and *A. Thiébout*, Levallois, histoire d'une banlieue, Liege, 1981.
155. *Lavedan, P.*, Histoire de l'urbanisme à Paris, Paris, 1975.

- Reims

156. *Développement du capitalisme, politique urbaine et habitat ouvrier*: L'exemple de l'agglomération de Reims, de la première moitié du XIXème siècle à nos jours, Paris, 1977.

- Rennes

157. *Denis, M.*, Rennes au XIXème siècle: Ville parasitaire?, in: Annales de Bretagne, Vol. 80 (1973), pp. 403–439.

- St. Etienne

158. *Fournial, E., et al.*, St. Etienne: Histoire de la ville et de ses habitants, Roanne, 1976.
159. *Martourey, A.*, St. Etienne, Diss. Lyon, 1984.

- Vittel

160. *Contal, M.-H..*, Vittel 1854–1936. Création d'une ville thermale. Paris, 1982.

GÜNTER BRAUN, MAGDALENA HEIDER AND
HERMAN SCHWENGER

German Democratic Republic

In the systematics of Marxist-Leninist historical science in the GDR,
research into urban history is assigned to the sub-discipline of regional
history, both with respect to its contents and institutionally, in the organisation of research. The stages of development, the organisational forms, the
functions, achievements and methods of urban history research in the GDR
are thus closely connected with regional history. At the same time, they also
follow the general ideological-political framework and directives set by the
Socialist Unity Party (SED) that govern this sub-discipline.

In general, regional history is defined in the GDR as "a comprehensive
term for all forms of a geographically limited historical approach below the
level of national history".[1] It is usually divided into the history of industrial
enterprises, history of towns, and territorial history, and sometimes it is
typologically characterised by the concept of "Heimatgeschichte" (local
history). Only since the mid-1970s has it become possible to develop a
differentiated approach to the organisation and practice of research in these
areas, and to define with any degree of success the meaning and aim of
Marxist-Leninist regional history and its institutional guidelines.[2]

Up until the end of the 1950s when "socialist historical science" was
establishing itself in the GDR[3] little attention was paid initially to history on
either the regional level or, consequently, on an urban level. The main
reason for this was that Marxist historians, in their critical confrontation
with the still prevalent bourgeois historiography, were striving for a new
appraisal of fundamental historical events and processes. Studies in regional
history "had been carried out for decades as reactionary bourgeois areal
studies (Landeskunde), transfigured into romanticising local history or
abused by 'blood and soil' phraseology".[4] This was reflected in the conceptual system: whereas, until then, a distinction had been made between the
history of defined local areas (Landesgeschichte), local history (Heimat-
sgeschichte), and history of towns (Ortsgeschichte), the concept of regional
history (Regionalgeschichte), was now introduced to demonstrate a con-

scious rejection of the bourgeois system.[5]

Not until more attention was given to hitherto neglected areas of research, such as the history of the labour movement, in conjunction with reflection on revolutionary traditions and the gradual assertion of a materialist view of history, did regional and local history approaches gain more recognition. This became apparent once the leadership of the Socialist Unity Party emphasised the potential of this discipline of history in raising consciousness in its resolution of 5 July 1955, on "improving research and teaching in historical science in the GDR".[6]

The Politburo directive was realised in organisational terms above all through the creation of research commissions on the history of the local labour movement, which were affiliated to the SED at the district and regional administrative levels, and through extending the institutional basis of local history in the Cultural Association (Kulturbund) of the GDR. The Central Committee of Experts on Local History and Preservation of Monuments of the Central Commission on Nature and Homeland (Zentraler Fachausschuß Heimatgeschichte-Denkmalpflege der Zentralen Kommission Natur und Heimat) was founded in 1956. One year earlier, the first "instruction on keeping local chronicles" had been published in the Legal Gazette of the GDR.[7] In 1957 the first volume in the series "Values of our Homeland: Taking Stock of Local History and Geography in the GDR" (*Werte unserer Heimat: heimatkundliche Bestandsaufnahme in der DDR*) was published. This volume was followed by others portraying a number of towns. An "Introduction to Local History" was finally published in 1959,[8] defining the tasks, methods and aims of local history for the first time from a Marxist viewpoint. This work had a strong influence on later research.

Despite these clear signs of progress at the end of the 1950s, research into regional history was still "largely fragmented, its theoretical tools little developed, its place within historical science in the GDR not precisely defined," according to the chronicler, P. Köppen.[9]

This description of the state of regional history also applies largely to the 1960s. As a result, intensive discussions on the functions and possibilities of regional historiography were held while compiling a national history of the GDR,[10] and at the same time an attempt was made to improve research practice through new publications (including the trail-blazing Yearbook of Regional History) and through the further development of institutions.

The founding of the study group on local history and the history of specific geographical areas of the German Society of Historians ("Arbeitsgemeinschaft Heimat- und Landesgeschichte der Deutschen Historikergesellschaft") in 1961 is generally regarded as a turning point in regional historiography in the GDR. The task of this study group has been to offer guidance and to contribute to more intensive co-ordination of the scattered research into local history, and — in a critical confrontation with bourgeois West German history of specific areas — it was given the job of developing a concept for regional history.

In a first comprehensive assessment of research work, K. Czok observed in 1970 that "despite some faults and weaknesses" there had been "a remarkable upswing . . . and considerable success."[11] The main areas of interest were publications focusing on the history of the local labour movement and, to an increasing extent, the history of industrial enterprises, as well as descriptions of the socialist transformation in towns, villages and administrative districts of the GDR.

However, not until the 1970s does Köppen perceive clear "progress in the clarification of methodological questions, and above all in the quantity and quality of works on regional history."[12] Important impulses were provided first by various directives and plan targets of the SED,[13] then by the formation of new research institutions. In 1974, the Commission of Experts on Urban History of the Society of Historians ("Fachkommission Stadtgeschichte der Historikergesellschaft") was founded, followed in 1979 by the Society for Local History of the Cultural Association of the GDR ("Gesellschaft für Heimatgeschichte im Kulturbund der DDR"). These, together with the relevant departments of the Institute for Marxism-Leninism of the Central Committee of the SED and the Research Department for regional history of the Academy of Sciences of the GDR ("Forschungsstelle für Regionalgeschichte der Akademie der Wissenschaften der DDR"), founded in 1981 (the latter concentrating on urban history), would make it seem likely that an organisational structure has now been found that permits "substantiated guidance and integration of all researchers into regional history."[14] At the local and regional levels, the reins are still held by the Research Commissions on the local labour movement, affiliated to the SED at the district and regional administrative levels.

Within this network, the society for local history ("Gesellschaft für Heimatgeschichte") constitutes a meeting ground for amateur and professional historians. The voluntary work of its members is concentrated on producing local chronicles, something all towns and communities are required to do by law.[15] A further task of the society is the distribution of research directives and research results.[16]

In the GDR, too, regional historiography is on the rise; its requirements, both in terms of function and content, its tasks and its problems, have appeared more frequently in print and have been more widely discussed in recent times. Central to the definition of its meanings and aims are its potential for raising consciousness and creating a sense of identity, its understanding of legacy and tradition, and the role local history plays in the ideological conflict with the class enemy. W. Gutsche has commented on this, using research and propagation of urban history to illustrate his argument. The following quotations from his essay "Urban history — important source for the formation of socialist consciousness"[17] might well serve as an exemplary clarification of the tasks and aims of regional history and its resulting significance as viewed by historians in the GDR.

W. Gutsche calls for use to be made of urban history's role in shaping tradition, in order to "impart convincingly and with mass effectiveness the knowledge, realisations and experiences that form a socialist historical awareness and socialist values". This is because on the one hand, urban history reflects "to a special degree the rich progressive legacy and the various traditions that are part of our national identity and of our people's progressive humanistic history". And on the other hand, the special immediacy of their daily contact with the testimony of its traditions, gives citizens a particularly close and familiar relationship with the history of their home towns, and that of their immediate spheres of work and life. Thus, urban histories can greatly contribute to developing and deepening a love of the socialist homeland, the socialist fatherland and "furthermore, they make an important contribution to the combative dispute with bourgeois regional history of the FRG . . ."[18]

W. Gutsche sees the main task for the future to be the integration of separately researched aspects of local history into comprehensive urban history studies. He feels that "comprehensive urban history studies are the prerequisite for more effective use of the various segments of research work conducted in the field of urban history. Integrated into an overall local framework, they permit a complex analysis of the development of all aspects of life in society and thus provide a conceptual orientation for further specialised studies." Furthermore, for science, politics and society they represent the necessary basis for "the effective, historically founded propagation of our politics as well as for perspective planning, permitting as they do insight into development trends in the various areas of life in society, and into general and specific local conditions, that can make an essential contribution to our awareness of the historical greatness of the success and achievements of our socialist structure."

According to W. Gutsche, the fulfilment of this function requires "the collective co-operation of all forces in the town working in the area of regional history: professional and amateur historians, historical commissions, archives, museums and libraries, the Cultural Association and the Society of Historians."[19] In this connection, he refers to a number of published comprehensive urban history studies[20] that have set the standard for following projects. They, as well as the numerous publications of towns and museums, are an expression of the Marxist urban historiography that has become far more prevalent since the mid-1970s.

Notes on Introduction

(1) *H. Schultz*, Zum Inhalt und Begriff marxistischer Regionalgeschichts-forschung, in Zeitschrift für Geschichtswissenschaft (ZfG), 1985, p. 885.

(2) See the most recent outline by *P. Köppen*, Zur Entwicklung der Regio-nalgeschichtschreibung in der Deutschen Demokratischen Republik (unter besonderer Berücksichtigung des Bezirkes Rostock), in Wis-senschaftliche Zeitschrift der Universität Rostock. Gesellschaftswis-senschaftliche Reihe, Year 33 (1984), No. 8, pp. 20–26, with additional literature.

(3) See *W. Schmidt*, Die Geschichtswissenschaft der DDR in den fünfziger Jahren, in ZfG, 1983, p. 291 ff.

(4) *Köppen*, p. 20

(5) The (non-Marxist) GDR historian K. Blaschke recently spoke out critically with regard to the conceptual debate. He pleads for the traditional distinction between history of defined local areas (Landes-geschichte), local history (Heimatgeschichte) and history of towns (Ortsgeschichte); he sees "no need to throw over this time-tested system of spatially defined historiography and to blur the subject through new terminology (to be explicit: regional history)"; see *K. Blaschke*, Probleme und Begriffe – Beobachtungen aus der Deutschen Demokratischen Republik zum Thema "Regionalgeschichte", in In-formationen zur modernen Stadtgeschichte (IMS), 1986, No. 1, pp. 10–15 (see p. 11).

(6) *Dokumente der SED*, Vol V, Berlin (GDR), 1956, p. 365.

(7) Gesetzblatt der DDR, Part II, No. 17 (1955), p. 117 f.

(8) *H. Mohr* and *E. Hühns*, Einführung in die Heimatgeschichte, Berlin (GDR), 1959.

(9) *Köppen*, p. 21.

(10) Such as the essay by *M. Steinmetz*, Die Aufgaben der Regionalge-schichtsschreibung in der DDR bei der Ausarbeitung eines nationalen Geschichtsbildes, in ZfG, 1961, p. 1734.

(11) *Forschungen zur Regionalgeschichte*, in ZfG, 1970, Special edition, p. 247.

(12) *Köppen*, p. 21.

(13) Richtlinien für die Kommission zur Erforschung der örtlichen Ar-beiterbewegung vom 19. Juni 1973; Richtlinien zur Erforschung und Propagierung der Betriebsgeschichte vom 7. Juni 1977; Perspektivplan zur regionalen Geschichte der Arbeiterbewegung 1967.

(14) *Köppen*, p. 22. Membership figures and lists of members in the indivi-dual organisations can be found here, too. See also *Aufgaben und Probleme der regional-geschichtlichen Forschung und Propaganda in der DDR*. Reports of the conference of the same name of the Präsidium des Kulturbund der DDR and the Fachkommission Regionalgeschichte der Historikergesellschaft held in Berlstedt from 9–11 April, 1978,

Berlin (GDR), 1979 (Working material for the working groups Heimatgeschichte/Ortschronik des Kulturbundes der DDR, No. 6.)

(15) The current legislation was passed in November, 1981. See Gesetzblatt der DDR, Part I, No. 1 (1982), p. 11 f.

(16) See publications listed in the bibliography, *"$ächsische Heimatblätter"*, *"Eichsfelder Heimathefte"*, *"Schweriner Blätter"*, which are often published in conjunction with other corporate bodies.

(17) *Stadtgeschichte - wichtige Quelle sozialistischer Bewußtseinsbildung*, in Einheit, 1982, pp. 789–795.

(18) ibid., p. 789 f; see also *H. Moritz* and *H. Suhr*, Zum Beitrag regionaler Geschichte in der ideologischen Auseinandersetzung unserer Zeit, in BfG, 1983, p. 427 ff; see *R. Badstübner*, Die Geschichte der DDR unter dem Aspekt von Erbe und Tradition, in ZfG, 1985, p. 338 ff., and *M. Bensing*, Erbe und Tradition in der Geschichte der Deutschen Demokratischen Republik, in ibid., 1984, p. 883 ff. for articles on problems of inheritance and tradition among other things; see also *H. Hanke* and *T. Koch*, Kulturelle Identität, in Weimarer Beiträge, 1985, p. 1237 ff., and *K. Hager*, Geschichte und Gegenwart, in Einheit, 1983, p. 161 ff.

(19) *Stadtgeschichte*, p. 792 ff.

(20) See publications listed in section E of the bibliography on Berlin, Halle, Erfurt, Leipzig, Magdeburg, Potsdam, Rostock, Schwerin, Stralsund and Weimar.

A.   Urban History Institutions

Akademie der Wissenschaften der DDR / Zentralinstitut für Geschichte / Forschungsstelle für Regionalgeschichte, founded in 1981; based in Berlin (GDR).

Historikergessellschaft der DDR / Fachkommission Regionalgeschichte, founded in 1979; *Fachkommission Stadtgeschichte*, founded in 1974; *Hansische Arbeitsgemeinschaft*, based in Berlin (GDR).

Institut für Denkmalpflege; based in Berlin (GDR).

Institut für Marxismus-Leninismus beim ZK der SED / Problemrat für regionale Geschichte, Fachgruppe Lokalund Regionalgeschichte; based in Berlin (GDR).

Kulturbund der DDR / Gesellschaft für Denkalpflege, founded in 1977 (Zentrale Delegiertenkonferenz 1981 ff.); *Gesellschaft für Heimatgeschichte*, founded in 1979 (Precursor: Zentraler Fachausschuß Heimatgeschichte-/Ortschronik der Zentralen Kommission Natur und Heimat des Präsidialrates des Kulturbundes der DDR (Zentrale Delegiertenkonferenz 1981 ff.)); based in Berlin (GDR).

Pädagogische Hochschule "Erich Weinert" / Forschungsgruppe Stadtgeschichte; based in Magdeburg.

Universität Berlin / Sektion Geschichte, Arbeitsgruppe Territorialgeschichte Berlin-Brandenburg, founded in 1981; based in Berlin (GDR).

Wissenschaftlicher Rat für Soziologische Forschung in der DDR / Problemräte "Sozialstruktur"; "Genossenschaftsbauern / Stadt – Land"; "Lebensweise und Territorium", "Kulturbedürfnisse und Stadtgestaltung"; based in Berlin (GDR).

B. Aids to Research

(a) Urban History Journals

Regular publications on urban history are included under this heading.

1. *Arbeitsberichte zur Geschichte der Stadt Leipzig*, 1963 ff., ed. P. Beyer *et al.*, Leipzig.

2. *Archivmitteilungen: Zeitschrift für Theorie und Praxis des Archivwesens*, 1949 ff., pub. by the Staatliche Archivverwaltung der DDR, Berlin (GDR).

3. *Beiträge zur Geschichte der Arbeiterbewegung*, 1959 ff., pub. by the Institut für Marxismus-Leninismus beim ZK der SED, Berlin (GDR).

4. *Beiträge zur Geschichte der Stadt Erfurt*, 1955 ff., pub. by F. Weigand *et al.*, Erfurt.

5. *Beiträge zur Geschichte der Stadt Rostock*, up-dated 1981 ff., pub. by the Stadtarchiv Rostock and the Kulturhistorisches Museum der Stadt Rostock, Rostock.

6. *Beiträge zur Geschichte der Stadt und des Bezirkes Magdeburg*, 1969 ff., pub. by the Kommission zur Erforschung der Geschichte der örtlichen Arbeiterbewegung bei der Bezirksleitung der SED, Magdeburg.

7. *Beiträge zur Heimatgeschichte von Karl-Marx-Stadt*, 1953 ff. (1952 under the title. "Beiträge zur Heimatgeschichte von Chemnitz"), pub. by the Rat der Stadt und Stadtarchiv, Karl-Marx-Stadt.

8. *Berliner Geschichte: Dokumente, Beiträge, Informationen*, 1980 ff. (1964–1977 under the title "Schriftenreihe des Stadtarchivs Berlin"; 25 issues altogether), pub. by the Stadtarchiv der Hauptstadt der DDR, Berlin (GDR).

9. *Blätter für Heimatgeschichte*, 1983 ff., pub. by the Zentralvorstand der Gesellschaft für Heimatgeschichte im Kulturbund der DDR, Berlin (GDR).

10. *Dresdner Hefte: Beiträge zur Kulturgeschichte*, 1984 ff., pub. by the Rat des Bezirkes Dresden, Abt. Kultur *et al.*, Dresden.

11. *Eichsfelder Heimathefte*, 1961 ff., pub. by the Pädagogisches Kreiskabinett Worbis, Worbis.

12. *Frankfurter Beiträge zur Geschichte*, 1975 ff., pub. by Frankfurt Information *et al.*, Frankfurt/Oder.

13. *Geographische Berichte: Mitteilungen der Geographischen Gesellschaft der DDR*, Gotha, 1956 ff.

14. *Geschichte und Gegenwart des Bezirkes Cottbus*, 1971 ff. (from 1967–1970 under the title. "Niederlausitzer Studien"), pub. by the Niederlausitzer

Arbeitskreis für regionale Forschung beim Rat des Bezirkes Cottbus in conjunction with the Bezirkskommission zur Erforschung der Geschichte der örtlichen Arbeiterbewegung bei der Bezirksleitung der SED, Cottbus.

15. *Greifswald-Stralsunder Jahrbuch*, 1961–1982, pub. by the Kulturhistorisches Museum Stralsund *et al.*, Schwerin.

16. *Heimatgeschichte: Arbeitsmaterial für die Fachgruppen Heimatgeschichte/Ortschronik der Gesellschaft für Heimatgeschichte im Kulturbund der DDR*, 1980 ff., (from 1975–1979 under the title "Arbeitsmaterial für die Fachgruppen Heimatgeschichte/Ortschronik des Kulturbundes der DDR" (= Beiträge zur Heimatgeschichte und Ortschronik)), Berlin (GDR).

17. *Historische Beiträge*, 1982 ff., pub. by the Geschichtsmuseum der Stadt Halle.

18. *Jahrbuch des Märkischen Museums: Kulturhistorisches Museum der Hauptstadt der Deutschen Demokratischen Republik*, 1975 ff., pub. by H. Hampe et al., Berlin (GDR).

19. *Jahrbuch für Regionalgeschichte*, 1965 ff., pub. by the Historische Kommission bei der Sächsischen Akademie der Wissenschaften, Weimar (previously Dresden), eds., K. Czok, *et al.*

20. *Jahrbuch für Volkskunde und Kulturgeschichte*, new ed., 1973 ff. (previously under the title "Deutsches Jahrbuch für Volkskunde"), pub. by the Akademie der Wissenschaften der DDR, Wissenschaftsbereich Kulturgeschichte/Volkskunde, Berlin (GDR).

21. *Jahrbuch für Wirtschaftsgeschichte*, 1960 ff., pub. by the Institut für Wirtschaftsgeschichte, Berlin (GDR).

22. *Jahrbuch zur Geschichte Dresdens* (= *Informationsdienst des Museums für Geschichte der Stadt Dresden*), Dresden, 1972 ff.

23. *Leipzig: Aus Vergangenheit und Gegenwart. Beiträge zur Stadtgeschichte*, 1981 ff. (from 1975–1980 under the title "Jahrbuch zur Geschichte der Stadt Leipzig"), pub. by the Museum für Geschichte der Stadt Leipzig *et al.*, Leipzig.

24. *Leipziger Stadtgeschichtliche Forschungen*, Leipzig, 1952–1969.

25. *Magdeburger Beiträge zur Stadtgeschichte*, 1977 ff., pub. by the Arbeitskreis Stadtgeschichte des Kulturbundes der DDR *et al.*, Magdeburg.

26. *Magdeburger Blätter: Jahresschrift für Heimat- und Kulturgeschichte im Bezirk Magdeburg*, 1982 ff., pub. by the Pädagogische Hochschule "Erich Weinert", Magdeburg.

27. *Museum für Geschichte: Schriftenreihe des Museums für Geschichte der Stadt Leipzig*, Leipzig, 1958–1974.

28. *Petermanns Geographische Mitteilungen*, 1948 ff., pub. by the Geographische Gesellschaft der DDR, Gotha *et al.*

29. *Regionalgeschichtliche Beiträge aus dem Bezirk Karl-Marx-Stadt*, 1979 ff., pub. by the Rat des Bezirkes Karl-Marx-Stadt *et al.*, Karl-Marx-Stadt.

30. *Rostocker Beiträge: Regionalgeschichtliches Jahrbuch der mecklenburgischen*

Seestädte, Rostock, Vol. 1 (1966/1967) (no further volumes published).

31. *Rudolstädter Heimathefte*, 1955 ff., pub. by the Rat des Kreises Rudolstadt, Abt. Kultur *et al.*, Rudolstadt.

32. *Sächsische Heimatblätter: Wissenschaftliche Zeitschrift der Bezirksvorstände Dresden, Karl-Marx-Stadt und Leipzig der Gesellschaften für Heimatgeschichte, für Denkmalpflege und Natur und Umwelt*, 1955 ff., pub. by the Kulturbund der DDR, Dresden.

33. *Schriftenreihe des Ratsarchivs der Stadt Görlitz*, 1963 ff., pub. by the Rat der Stadt, Görlitz.

34. *Schweriner Blätter: Beiträge zur Heimatgeschichte des Bezirkes Schwerin*, 1981 ff., pub. by the Bezirksvorstand der Gesellschaft für Heimatgeschichte beim Kulturbund der DDR et al., Schwerin.

35. *Sozialistisches Rostock: Information und Dokumentation aus dem Stadtarchiv* (= Kleine Schriftenreihe des Stadtarchivs Rostock), Rostock, 1972–1979.

36. *Tradition und Gegenwart: Weimarer Schriften*, 1981 ff., (1953–1984 under the title "Weimarer Schriften zur Heimatgeschichte und Naturkunde" and 1966–1981 under the title "Weimar: Tradition und Gegenwart"), pub. by the Ständige Kommissionen Kultur und Stadtverordnetenversammlung Weimar *et al.*, Weimar.

37. *Aus der Vergangenheit der Stadt Erfurt*, new ed. 1985 ff. (old ed. 1955–1967), pub. by the Rat der Stadt, Erfurt.

38. *Zeitschrift für den Erdkundeunterricht*, 1949 ff., pub. by the Ministerium für Volksbildung der DDR, Berlin (GDR).

(b) Bibliographies

39. *Auswahlbibliographie zur Entwicklung der Stadt Suhl*, pub. by the Wissenschaftliche Allgemeinbibliothek des Bezirks Suhl, Suhl, 1977 (Blickpunkt Bibliothek, Vol. 13).

40. *Auswahlbibliographie zur Industriegeschichte von Chemnitz/Karl-Marx-Stadt*, ed. E. Barth, Karl-Marx-Stadt, 1983.

41. *Auswahlbibliographie der Jahre 1945 bis 1967 zur Geschichte von Karl-Marx-Stadt*, ed. E. Barth, Karl-Marx-Stadt, 1968 (Beiträge zur Heimatgeschichte von Karl-Marx-Stadt, Vol. 16).

42. *Auswahlbibliographie zur Methodik und zur Methodologie der marxistischen Regionalgeschichtsforschung in der DDR. Veröffentlichungen der Jahre 1945–1970/71*, ed. H. Maur, in Letopis, Series B, No. 1, (1972).

43. *Auswahlbibliographie zur Regional- und Betriebsgeschichte*, ed. G. Pretsch, Berlin (GDR), 1976 (Beiträge zur Heimatgeschichte und Ortschronik, No. 3).

44. *Berlin, Hauptstadt der DDR, in Buch und Zeitschrift*, pub. by the Berliner Stadtbibliothek, Berlin (GDR), 1956 ff.

45. *Bibliographie zur Geschichte der mark Brandenburg und der Stadt Berlin.* 1941–1956, pub. by the Arbeitsgruppe Bibliographie im Institut für

Geschichte an der Deutschen Akademie der Wissenschaften zu Berlin, Berlin (GDR), 1961.

46. *Bibliografie zur Geschichte der Stadt Cottbus.* Gedrucktes Schrifttum vom 17. Jahrhundert bis zum Jahre 1968, ed. W. Drangosch, Cottbus, 1974 (Geschichte und Gegenwart des Bezirkes Cottbus; Special issue).

47. *Bibliographie zur Geschichte der Stadt Dresden,* pub. by the Historische Kommission der Sächsischen Akademie der Wissenschaften in Zusammenarbeit mit der Sächsischen Landesbibliothek, Dresden, 1981 ff.

48. *Bibliographie zur Geschichte der Stadt Halle und des Saalkreises,* ed. H. Höhne, Halle, 1974 ff.

49. *Bibliographie zur Geschichte der Stadt Leipzig,* ed. H. Heilemann, Weimar, 1971 ff.

50. *Bibliographie zur Geschichte der Stadt Weimar,* ed. G. Günther *et al.,* Weimar, 1982.

51. *Bibliographie selbständiger Publikationen zur Geschichte der örtlichen Arbeiterbewegung und Betriebsgeschichte,* pub. by Institut für Marxismus-Leninismus beim ZK der SED, Part 1: 1971–1979, eds. W. Dick *et al.,* Berlin (GDR) 1980; Part 2: 1980–1982, ed. M. Beck, Berlin (GDR), 1984.

52. *Bibliographie selbständiger Schriften des Kulturbundes der DDR zur Heimatgeschichte 1945–1978,* ed. G. Pretsch, Berlin (GDR), 1979 (Beiträge zur Heimatgeschichte und Ortschronik, No. 8).

53. *Bibliographie stadtgeschichtlicher Veröffentlichungen in der DDR 1974–1976.* Auswahl, ed. K. Czok *et al.,* Berlin and Leipzig, 1977 (Manuscript).

54. *Bibliographien und Nachschlagewerke zur Geschichte Berlins.* Eine annotierte Auswahlbibliographie, ed. R. Straubel, Berlin (GDR), 1978.

55. *Brandenburgische Literatur.* Regionalbibliographie für die Bezirke Cottbus, Frankfurt (Oder) und Potsdam, pub. by the Wissenschaftliche Allgemeinbibliothek des Bezirkes Potsdam, Potsdam, 1945 ff.

56. *Gera: Auswahlbibliographie zur Entwicklung der Stadt,* eds. J. Kloss and C. Scurla, Gera 1983 (Territorialkundliches Auswahlverzeichnis, Vol. 10).

57. *Literatur über die Stadt und den Bezirk Gera.* Regionalkundliches Auswahlverzeichnis, pub. by the Wissenschaftliche Allgemeinbibliothek Gera, Gera, 1977.

58. *Mecklenburgische Bibliographie.* Regionalbibliographie für die Bezirke Neubrandenburg, Rostock und Schwerin, pub. by the Wissenschaftliche Allgemeinbibliothek des Bezirkes Schwerin, Schwerin 1945–1964, 1979/80 ff.

59. *Neubrandenburg 1248–1977.* Bibliographie zur Geschichte der Stadt Neubrandenburg, ed. J. Grambow, 2nd ed., Neubrandenburg, 1977.

60. *Sachsen-Anhalt.* Landeskundliche Regionalbibliographie für die Bezirke Halle und Magdeburg, pub. by the Landes- und Universitätsbibliothek Halle, Halle, 1965–1966, 1969 ff.

61. *Sächsische Bibliographie.* Regionalbibliographie für die Bezirke Dresden,

Karl-Marx-Stadt und Leipzig, pub. by the Sächsische Landesbibliothek Dresden, Dresden, 1961/1962 ff.

62. *Thüringen-Bibliographie*, pub. by the Nationale Forschungs- und Gedenkstätten der klassischen deutschen Literatur in Weimar, Berlin (GDR) et al., 1961–1963, 1972 ff.

(c) Handbooks on Urban History (and Dictionaries)

63. *Die Bezirke der Deutschen Demokratischen Republik*, Gotha et al., 1974.
64. *Eichler, E.*, and *H. Walter*, Städtenamenbuch der DDR, Leipzig, 1986.
65. *Grimm, F.*, Die Kreisstädte der DDR, in Geographische Berichte, Year 19 (1974), No. 4, p. 229 ff.
66. *Lexikon der Städte und Wappen der DDR*, ed. H. Göschel, 3rd ed. Leipzig, 1985.
67. *Ortslexikon der Deutschen Demokratischen Republik*, ed. W. Christ and K. Balkow, Berlin (GDR), 1986.

(d) Atlases on Urban History and Urban Development

68. *Deutscher Städteatlas*, pub. by H. Stoob, No. 1: Colditz (Sachsen), ed. K. Blaschke, Altenbecken, 1984.
69. *Pläne, und Grundrisse von Städten sozialistischer Länder Europas*. 1574–1850, ed. W. Klaus, Berlin (GDR), 1976 (Kartographische Bestandsverzeichnisse Deutsche Staatsbibliothek).
70. *Die Städte im Kartenbild*. Part 1: Pläne und Grundrisse von 1550–1850, ed. W. Klaus, Berlin (GDR), 1983; Part 2: Pläne und Grundrisse von 1851–1945, ed. W. Klaus, Berlin (GDR), 1976 (Kartographische Bestandsverzeichnisse / Deutsche Staatsbibliothek).
71. *Stams, W.*, Die Stadtkarte von Dresden: Inhalt und Gestaltung komplexer thematischer Stadtkarten, in Petermanns Geographische Mitteilungen, Vol. 111 (1967), p. 67 ff.

(e) Urban History Sources

Lists of the contents of town archives are included under this heading.
72. *Archivwesen der Deutschen Demokratischen Republik*. Theorie und Praxis, edited by a group of authors directed by B. Brachmann, Berlin (GDR), 1984.
73. *Beyer, P.*, and *M. Unges*, Übersicht über die Bestände der Stadtarchive des Bezirks Leipzig, Leipzig, 1967.
74. *Biederstedt, R.*, Übersicht über die Bestände des Stadtarchivs Greifswald und archivalische Quellennachweise zur Geschichte der örtlichen Arbeiterbewegung, Greifswald, 1966.
75. *Bräuer, H.*, Probleme der marxistisch-leninistischen Archivgeschichts-

schreibung, dargestellt am Beispiel der Geschichte von Stadtarchiven in den Bezirken Leipzig, Dresden und Karl-Marx-Stadt seit 1945, Diss. Berlin (GDR), 1974.

76. *Förster, R.*, Das Museum für Geschichte der Stadt Dresden, 2nd ed., Dresden, 1972.

77. *Kretschmar, H.*, Archive und Heimatforschung, in Archivarbeit und Geschichtsforschung, pub. by the Hauptabteilung Archivwesen im Ministerium des Innern der Regierung der Deutschen Demokratischen Republik, Berlin (GDR), 1952, p. 55 ff. (Schriftenreihe des Instituts für Archivwissenschaft, No. 2).

78. *Leopoldi, H. H.*, Stadtarchive, Stadtgeschichte und Ortschronik, in Archivarbeit und Geschichtsforschung, pub. by the Hauptabteilung Archivwesen im Ministerium des Innern der Regierung der Deutschen Demokratischen Republik, Berlin (GDR), 1952, p. 196 ff. (Schriftenreihe des Instituts für Archivwissenschaft, No. 2).

79. *Das Stadtarchiv Berlin*, edited by a group of authors directed by R. Leining, Berlin (GDR), 1973.

80. *Das Stadtarchiv Erfurt und seine Bestände*, ed. F. Wiegand, Potsdam, 1962.

81. *Das Stadtarchiv Frankfurt (Oder) und seine Bestände*, ed. E. Schirrmacher, Frankfurt/Oder, 1972.

82. *Das Stadtarchiv Mühlhausen und seine Bestände*, ed. D. Lösche and G. Günther, Mühlhausen, 1965.

83. *Das Stadtarchiv Rostock*, pub. by the Stadtarchiv Rostock, Rostock, 1976 (Kleine Schriftenreihe des Stadtarchivs Rostock; Special series No. 1).

84. *Das Stadtarchiv Weimar und seine Bestände*, ed. G. Günther and L. Wallraf, Weimar, 1967.

85. *Das Stadtarchiv Wismar und seine Bestände*, ed. A. Düsing, Wismar, 1970.

C. Research Reports

(a) General Surveys

86. *Blaschke, K.*, Probleme um Begriffe – Beobachtungen aus der Deutschen Demokratischen Republik zum Thema "Regionalgeschichte", in Informationen zur modernen Stadtgeschichte (IMS), No. 1 (1986), p. 10 ff.

87. *Blaschke, K.*, Qualität, Quantität und Raumfunktion als Wesensmerkmal der Stadt vom Mittelalter bis zur Gegenwart, in Jahrbuch für Regionalgeschichte, Vol. 3 (1968), p. 34 ff.

88. *Czok, K.*, Zu den Entwicklungsetappen der marxistischen Regionalgeschichtsforschung in der DDR, in Jahrbuch für Regionalgeschichte, Vol. 1 (1965), p. 9 ff.

89. *Czok, K.*, Zum Erscheinen neuer Stadtgeschichten in der DDR, in

Jahrbuch für Regionalgeschichte, Vol. 6 (1978), p. 167 ff.

90. *Czok, K.*, Forschungen zur Regionalgeschichte, in Zeitschrift für Geschichtswissenschaft, Special issue 1970, p. 234 ff., and ibid., Special issue 1980, p. 720 ff.

91. *Czok, K.*, Über Forschungen zur Regionalgeschichte 1970–1980, in Jahrbuch für Regionalgeschichte, Vol. 8 (1981), p. 194 ff.

92. *Fritze, K. et al.*, Forschungen zur Stadt- und Hansegeschichte in der DDR, in Zeitschrift für Geschichtswissenschaft, Special issue 1960, p. 74 ff.

93. *Hajna, K.-H., H. Mehls* and *V. Weiß*, Neue Forschungen zur Stadtgeschichte in der DDR, in Zeitschrift für Geschichtswissenschaft, 1986, pp. 928 ff.

94. *Heitzer, H.*, Ortsgeschichtsschreibung über die neueste Zeit. 1945 bis zur Gegenwart, in Arbeitsmaterial der Zentralen Kommission Natur und Heimat des Präsidialrates des Deutschen Kulturbundes, 1963, p. 20 ff.

95. *Köppen, P.*, Zur Erforschung, Darstellung und Propagierung der Regionalgeschichte der neuesten Zeit in der DDR, Diss. Rostock, 1984.

96. *Wick, P.*, Die Regionalgeschichte der DDR im System der geschichtswissenschaftlichen Information und Dokumentation, in Jahrbuch für Regionalgeschichte, Vol. 4 (1972), p. 259 ff.

(b)   Surveys of Individual Fields of Urban Research

97. *Hahn, T.*, and *L. Niederländer*, Zur großstädtischen Lebensweise: Theoretisch-methodologische Probleme ihrer Erforschung, in Deutsche Zeitschrift für Philosophie, Year 30 (1982), No. 6, p. 754 ff.

98. *Jacob, F.-D.*, Prolegomena zu einer quellenkundlichen Betrachtung historischer Stadtansichten, in Jahrbuch für Regionalgeschichte, Vol. 6 (1978), p. 129 ff.

99. *Küttler, W.*, Theoretische und methodologische Probleme der Diskussion über das soziale Wesen des Städtebürgertums, in Wissenschaftliche Mitteilungen der Historiker-Gesellschaft der DDR, 1980, Parts 1/2, p. 27 ff.

100. *Voigt, P.*, Soziologie und Stadtentwicklung – Gedanken zur soziologischen Analyse der Stadt, Diss. Rostock, 1977.

101. *Zühlke, D.*, Aspekte der Entwicklung sächsischer Städte im 19. Jahrhundert aus historisch-geographischer Sicht, in Jahrbuch für Regionalgeschichte, Vol. 8 (1981), p. 107 ff.

102. *Zühlke, D.*, Historisch-geographische Untersuchungen zur Stadtgeschichte der sächsischen Bezirke, in Wissenschaftliche Abhandlungen der Geographischen Gesellschaft der DDR, Vol. 8 (1970), p. 87 ff.

103. *Zwahr, H.*, Das deutsche Stadtadreßbuch als orts- und sozialgeschichtliche Quelle, in Jahrbuch für Regionalgeschichte, Vol. 3 (1968), p. 204 ff.

D. Literature on Individual Areas of Urban History Research

(a)   Concept and Definition of Town and Town Types

Publications on town development in general as well as comprehensive collections are included under this heading.

104. *Blaschke, K.*, Altstadt – Neustadt – Vorstadt: Zur Typologie genetischer und topographischer Stadtgeschichtsforschung, in Vierteljahrschrift für Sozial- und Wirtschaftsgeschichte, Vol. 57 (1970), p. 350 ff.

105. *Böcker, H.*, Zur Rolle der bürgerlichen Stadttypologie und der Widerspiegelung der Theorien Max Webers in der modernen bürgerlichen Stadtgeschichtsschreibung, in Haupttendenzen der europäischen Stadtgeschichte im 14. und 15. Jahrhundert, Part 1, Magdeburg, 1974, p. 51 ff.

106. *Burg und Stadt in Geschichte und Gegenwart*, in Wissenschaftliche Zeitschrift der Friedrich-Schiller-Universität Jena. Gesellschafts wissenschaftliche und sprachwissenschaftliche Reihe, No. 3 (1979), p. 305 ff.

107. *Czok, K.*, Die Stadt, Jena et al., 1969.

108. *Czok, K.*, Zur Stellung der Stadt in der deutschen Geschichte, in Jahrbuch für Regionalgeschichte, Vol. 3 (1968), p. 9 ff.

109. *Götze, D.*, Der soziale Gegensatz von Stadt und Land und seine Lösung im revolutionären Prozeß des Übergangs vom Kapitalismus zum Sozialismus, Diss. Leipzig, 1980.

110. *Grundmann, S.*, Die Stadt: Gedanken über Geschichte und Funktion, Berlin (GDR), 1984.

111. *Reinisch, U.*, Sozialökonomische Aspekte von Verstädterungs- und Urbanisierungsprozessen unter den Bedingungen kapitalistischer Produktionsverhältnisse: Zu den politökonomischen Grundlagen einer marxistischen Theorie der Stadt, Diss. Berlin (GDR), 1976.

112. *Röhr, F.*, and *L. Röhr*, Die Urbanisierung als gesellschaftlicher Prozeß: Ein Beitrag zur marxistisch-leninistischen Theorie der Urbanisierung, Diss. Berlin (GDR), 1983.

113. *Röseler, B.*, and *K. Scharf*, Sozialökonomische Aspekte der Urbanisierung, in Petermanns Geographische Mitteilungen, 1976, No. 2, p. 85 ff.

114. *Rudolph, W.*, Die Hafenstadt; Eine maritime Kulturgeschichte, Leipzig, 1979.

115. *Schmidt-Renner, G.*, Ursachen der Städtebildung, in Petermanns Geographische Mitteilungen, 1965, No. 1, p. 23 ff.

116. *Stadt und Land in der DDR*. Entwicklung – Bilanz – Perspektiven, pub. by the Akademie für Gesellschaftswissenschaften beim ZK der SED, Berlin (GDR), 1984.

117. *Stadt und Umland in der Deutschen Demokratischen Republik*, Gotha et al., 1979.

118. *Windelband, U.*, Typologisierung städtischer Siedlungen: Erkenntnistheoretische Probleme in der ökonomischen Geographie, Gotha et al., 1973.

119. *Zühlke, D.*, Erscheinungsformen und Strukturelemente in den Städten der Bezirke Dresden, Leipzig und Karl-Marx-Stadt in historischer Betrachtung, Diss. Halle-Wittenberg, 1981.

(b) Politics, Law and Statutes

120. *Arndt, H.*, Zu einigen Aspekten sozialdemokratischer Kommunalpolitik in der Weimarer Republik, in Jahrbuch für Regionalgeschichte, Vol. 9 (1982), p. 105 ff.

121. *Baudis, K.*, Elementare Arbeiterbewegung und städtische Arbeitervereine in Mecklenburg während und nach der Revolution von 1848/1849, Diss. Rostock, 1973.

122. *Böl, H.*, Zur Entwicklung der kommunalpolitischen Konzeption der KPD von 1929 bis 1932, Diss. Halle, 1975.

123. *Czok, K.*, Ausgangspositionen und Anfänge revolutionärer Kommunalpolitik in der zweiten Hälfte des 19. Jahrhunderts, in Evolution und Revolution in der Weltgeschichte, Vol. 2, Berlin (GDR), 1976, p. 595 ff.

124. *Czok, K.*, Zur Kommunalpolitik in der deutschen Arbeiterbewegung während der neunziger Jahre des 19. Jahrhunderts, in Jahrbuch für Regionalgeschichte, Vol. 7 (1979), p. 67 ff.

125. *Emmerich, J.*, Die Entwicklung demokratischer Selbstverwaltungsorgane und ihr Kampf um die antifaschistisch-demokratische Ordnung in Chemnitz vom 8. Mai 1945 bis Mitte 1948, Diss. Leipzig, 1974.

126. *Die Entwicklung der Arbeiterbewegung in Chemnitz zwischen 1862 und 1866.* Eine Studie zu Triebkräften, Handlungsmotiven und Erfahrungen im Prozeß der politisch-ideologischen Konstituierung des Proletariats, pub. by the Stadtarchiv Karl-Marx-Stadt, Karl-Marx-Stadt 1982 (Beiträge zur Heimatgeschichte von Karl-Marx-Stadt, Vol. 25).

127. *Grossert, W.*, Die Arbeiterbewegung in Dessau nach der bürgerlich-demokratischen Revolution von 1848/49 bis 1871. Part 1: bis 1868; Part 2: 1867–1871, Dessau 1983/1985 (Zwischen Wörlitz und Mosigkau, No. 25 and No. 26).

128. *Hermann, R.*, Zur Entwicklung der kommunalpolitischen Konzeption der KPD (1919–1929), phil. Diss. Halle, 1975.

129. *Hofmann, E.*, Die Chemnitzer Arbeiterbewegung 1862 bis 1867: Eine Regionalstudie zu Triebkräften (. . .), phil. Diss. Dresden, 1984.

130. *Hüschner, F.*, Veränderungen der Sozialstruktur, innerstädtische Volksbewegung und Verfassungskämpfe in der Stadt Wismar vom

Ende des 18. bis zur Mitte des 19. Jahrhunderts, phil. Diss. Rostock, 1972.

131. *John, M.*, Karl Liebknechts Tätigkeit in Ausschüssen der Berliner Stadtverordnetenversammlung: Ein Beispiel revolutionärer Kommunalpolitik der deutschen Linken, in Jahrbuch für Regionalgeschichte, Vol. 7 (1979), p. 92 ff.

132. *Kluge, G.*, Die Rolle des Deutschen Städtetages in der Zeit der Weimarer Republik von 1919 bis 1933, dargestellt an seiner Verhaltensweise in wirtschaftspolitischen Fragen und zum Abbau der Selbstverwaltung durch den imperialistschen Staat, Diss. Leipzig, 1970.

133. *Pontow, K.*, Bourgeoise Kommunalpolitik und Eingemeindungsfrage in Leipzig im letzten Viertel des 19. Jahrhunderts, in Jahrbuch für Regionalgeschichte, Vol. 8 (1981), p. 84 ff.

134. *Rackow, H.-G.*, Zum Kampf um die Veränderung der Machtverhältnisse in der Stadt Rostock im ersten Jahr der antifaschistisch-demokratischen Umwälzung (Mai 1945 bis Herbst 1946), phil. Diss. Rostock, 1968.

135. *Richter, G.*, Zur Herausbildung und Ausprägung der kommunistischen Kommunalpolitik der Kommunistischen Partei Deutschlands in Chemnitz von 1918/19 bis 1929, Diss. Leipzig, 1981.

136. *Rosonsky, B.*, Die Entwicklung der Arbeiterbewegung in Leipzig vom Sturz des Sozialistengesetzes bis zur Jahrhundertwende, Diss. Leipzig, 1981.

137. *Rüdiger, B.*, Revolutionäre Kommunalpolitik in der Revolution. Zur Rolle der Arbeiter- und Soldatenräte in den Städten Sachsens während der Novemberrevolution bis zum 1. Reichsrätekongreß, in Jahrbuch für Regionalgeschichte, Vol. 7 (1979), p. 121 ff.

138. *Ruhland, V.*, Die Rolle der Volksmassen, der Bourgeoisie und der herrschenden Klasse in den revolutionären Ereignissen der Jahre 1830/31 in Dresden: Die revolutionären Unruhen im Lichte der archivalischen Quellen, phil. Diss. Dresden, 1982.

139. *Schroeder, H.-D.*, Zur Geschichte des Greifswalder Stadtparlaments: Vom Ausgang des Mittelalters (. . .) bis zur Gegenwart. Parts 1–3, in Greifswald-Stralsunder Jahrbuch, Vol. 1 (1961)-Vol. 3 (1973).

140. *Schultz, H.*, Soziale und politische Auseinandersetzungen in Rostock im 18. Jahrhundert, Weimar, 1974.

141. *Ziegs, D.*, Die Haltung der Leipziger Parteiorganisation der SPD zur Politik des sozialdemokratischen Parteivorstandes in den Jahren 1919 bis 1933, Diss. Leipzig, 1978.

142. *Zwahr, H.*, Vom feudalen Stadtregiment zur bürgerlichen Kommunalpolitik. Eine historisch-soziologische Studie zum Beginn der bürgerlichen Umwälzung in Sachsen 1830/31, in Jahrbuch für Regionalgeschichte, Vol. 7 (1979), p. 7 ff.

(c) Population and Social Structure

143. *Baar, L.*, Zur Industrialisierung, Urbanisierung und zu Veränderungen der städtischen Sozialstruktur während der industriellen Revolution in Deutschland, in Proceedings of the Seventh International Economic History Congress, Edinburgh, 1978.

144. *Böhmer, W.*, and *R. Kabus*, Zur Geschichte des Wittenberger Gesundheits- und Sozialwesens, 2 parts, Wittenberg 1981 and 1983 (Schriftenreihe des Stadtgeschichtsmuseums Wittenberg).

145. *Burkhardt-Osadnik, L.* and *C. Otto*, Tendenzen der Urbanisierung und der Bevölkerungsagglomeration in der DDR in den Jahren 1950 bis 1973, in Jahrbuch für Wirtschaftsgeschichte, Part 1 (1976), p. 211 ff.

146. *Eisermann, H.*, Die städtischen Mittelschichten in der revolutionären Umwälzung von 1945–1949/50, die Entwicklung ihrer Struktur und ihrer Stellung in der Gesellschaft, insbesondere zur Arbeiterklasse, dargestellt am Beispiel des ehemaligen Landes Sachsen-Anhalt, phil. Diss. Leipzig, 1973.

147. *Zur Entwicklung des Proletariats.* Untersuchung zu den Vorformen, der Entwicklung, der Lage und der Struktur der Arbeiterklasse bis zum 19. Jahrhundert: Protokoll der 2. Tagung der Fachkommission Stadtgeschichte der Historiker-Gesellschaft der DDR vom 5.-7. April 1977 in Karl-Marx-Stadt "Die Genesis des städtischen Proletariats'', Magdeburg, 1980.

148. *Frau, Ehe und Familie in der europäischen Sicht vom Mittelalter bis zur neuesten Zeit. 5.* Konferenz der Fachkommission Stadtgeschichte der Historiker-Gesellschaft der DDR vom 25.-27. Oktober 1982 in Halberstadt, in Wissenschaftliche Mitteilungen der Historiker-Gesellschaft der DDR, Part 3 (1983), p. 90 ff.

149. *Grammdorf, G.*, Zur dynamischen Veränderung der sozialen Struktur in der Stadt Rostock im Prozeß des Aufbaus des Sozialismus in den Jahren 1945–1970, Diss. Rostock, 1972.

150. *Haack, H.*, Einige Bemerkungen zur Entwicklung der Stadtbevölkerung in Mecklenburg-Schwerin, in Wissenschaftliche Zeitschrift der Universität Rostock. Gesellschaftswissenschaftliche und sprachwissenschaftliche Reihe, 1979, No. 10, p. 625 ff.

151. *Hoppe, H.-J.*, Probleme der Wirtschafts- und Sozialstruktur der Stadt Drebkau zwischen 1780 und 1880, in Gesellschaft und Gegenwart des Bezirkes Cottbus, Vol. 15 (1981), p. 63 ff.

152. *Kabus, R.*, Die Konstituierung des Görlitzer Proletariats im Verlauf der industriellen Revolution. Ein Beitrag zur Geschichte der ökonomischen, sozialen und politisch-ideologischen Formierung der Deutschen Arbeiterklasse, Diss. Leipzig, 1975.

153. *Kahl, A.*, and *S. Riedel*, Wohnverhältnisse, Wohnweise und Wohnverhalten in der sozialistischen Großstadt, in Jahrbuch für Soziologie und Sozialpolitik, 1985, p. 136 ff.

154. *Karasek, E.*, Großstadtproletariat: Zur Lebensweise einer Klasse, Berlin (GDR), 1983.

155. *Lehmann, E.*, Der sozialgeographische Faktor in den landeskundlichen Darstellungen Sachsens, Leipzig, 1952 (Wissenschaftliche Veröffentlichungen des Deutschen Zentralinstituts für Länderkunde, new ed. Vol. 11).

156. *Leipoldt, J.*, Soziale Umschichtungen vor und während der industriellen Revolution in Reichenbach im Vogtland, in Jahrbuch für Regionalgeschichte, Vol. 3 (1968), p. 230 ff.

157. *Mohs, G.*, Urbanisierung – Geographische Aspekte ihrer weltweiten Entwicklung, in Geographische Berichte, Vol. 23 (1978), No. 4, p. 270 ff.

158. *Röhr, F.*, and *L. Röhr*, Thesen zu einigen Grundfragen der Urbanisierung, Berlin (GDR), 1979.

159. *Schoetz, S.*, Städtische Mittelschichten in Leipzig während der bürgerlichen Umwälzung (1830–1870), untersucht auf der Grundlage biographischer Massenquellen, phil. Diss. Leipzig 1985.

160. *Schug, W.*, Binnenwanderung des Stadtkreises Erfurt unter besonderer Berücksichtigung der Alters-, Geschlechts- und Berufsgliederung, Diss. Halle, 1974.

161. *Schultz, H.*, Zur Herausbildung der Arbeiterklasse am Beispiel der mittleren ostelbischen Handelsstadt Rostock (1876 bis 1870), in Jahrbuch für Geschichte, Vol. 13 (1975), p. 153 ff.

162. *Siedlungsstruktur und Urbanisierung*, Gotha *et al.*, 1981.

163. *Skoda, R.*, Wohnhäuser und Wohnverhältnisse der Stadtarmut (ca. 1750 bis 1850), erläutert anhand von Beispielen aus Quedlinburg, Halle, Hamburg und Berlin, in Jahrbuch für Volkskunde und Kulturgeschichte, new ed. Vol. 2 (1974).

164. *Strauss, R.*, Die Lage und die Bewegung der Chemnitzer Arbeiter in der ersten Hälfte des 19. Jahrhunderts, Berlin (GDR), 1960.

165. *Strenz, W.*, Entwicklungstendenzen der regionalen Verteilung der Bevölkerung im Prozeß der Industriellen Revolution des Kapitalismus auf dem heutigen Territorium der DDR: Eine Materialstudie unter historischgeographischem Aspekt, in Jahrbuch für Wirtschaftsgeschichte, Part 1 (1976), p. 163 ff.

166. *Vogeley, D.*, Demographische Auswirkungen des Urbanisierungsprozesses in Ballungsgebieten und Ballungsrandgebieten mit Beispielen aus dem Ballungsgebiet Karl-Marx-Stadt/Zwickau, Berlin (GDR), 1972.

167. *Weigt, H.*, Die Entwicklung von Morbidität und Mortalität in der Stadt Magdeburg in den Jahren 1900 bis 1914 unter Berücksichtigung der sozialen Lage der Arbeiterklasse, phil. Diss. Dresden, 1980.

168. *Großstädtische Wohn- und Siedlungsbedingungen sowie Wohn- und Siedlungsweise des Industrieproletariats.* Der Beginn der Kommunalpolitik der

Arbeiterklasse, Berlin (GDR), 1981 (Institut für Weiterbildung des Ministeriums für Kultur. Kulturhistorische Studientexte, Series 1).

169. *Zastrow, H. von*, Zur historischen Entwicklung der Lebensbereiche Arbeiten und Wohnen in Berlin, Berlin (GDR), 1981, (Diploma thesis).

170. *Zwahr, H.*, Die Bevölkerungsbewegung in der Stadt Leipzig, ihren Grenz-, Vorstadt- und Außendörfern im Verlauf der Industriellen Revolution in Deutschland, in Sächsische Heimatblätter, Vol. 19 (1973), No. 4, p. 156 ff.

171. *Zwahr, H.*, Zur Konstituierung des Proletariats als Klasse: Strukturuntersuchung über das Leipziger Proletariat während der industriellen Revolution, Berlin (GDR), 1978 (Schriften des Zentralinstituts für Geschichte, Vol. 56).

(d)   Town Planning

172. *Benedict, E.*, Traditionelle und moderne Züge im Funktionsgefüge und Stadtbild von Delitzsch, in Wissenschaftliche Veröffentlichungen des Deutschen Instituts für Länderkunde, new ed. Vols. 21/22 (1964), p. 467 ff.

173. *Bierschenk, E.*, Der planmäßige Städtebau in der Hauptstadt der DDR 1951–1966, Berlin (GDR), 1967.

174. *Blaschke, K.*, Die Umlandbeziehungen Dresdens als Residenzstadt, in Veröffentlichungen der Akademie für Raumforschung und Landesplanung, Vol. 88 (1974), p. 139 ff.

175. *Brause, G.*, Entwicklungsprobleme von Großstadtzentren unter besonderer Berücksichtigung von Leipzig, in Jahrbuch für Regionalgeschichte, Vol. 3 (1968), p. 184 ff.

176. *Chronik Bauwesen der Deutschen Demokratischen Republik*, pub. by the Ministerium für Bauwesen, Bauakademie der DDR, Part 1: 1945–1971; Part 2: 1971–1976, Berlin (GDR), 1971 and 1979.

177. *Czok, K.*, Zur Entwicklung der Vorstädte und Vororte in Leipzig im 19. Jahrhundert, in Jahrbuch für Regionalgeschichte, Vol. 9 (1982), p. 121 ff.

178. *Deiters, L.*, Denkmalpflege in der Deutschen Demokratischen Republik, Dresden, 1983.

179. *Technische Denkmale in der Deutschen Demokratischen Republik*, ed. O. Wagenbreth *et al.*, Leipzig 1983.

180. *Deutsche Bauakademie et al.*, Geschichte und Gegenwart. Materialien der Konferenz Erfurt 1956 im Auftrag der Arbeitsgruppe "Geschichte des Städtebaus und Aufbau in historischen Städten", ed. G. Strauss, Berlin (GDR) 1959.

181. *Emmerich, C.*, and *P. Emmerich*, Die Beziehungen zwischen den Wohn- und Arbeitsstätten in der Strukturentwicklung der Großstädte, Diss.

Dresden, 1978.

182. *Die städtebauliche Entwicklung der Stadt Rostock von ihrer Gründung bis zur Gegenwart*, Rostock, 1968.

183. *Fromm, G.*, Eine neue Stadt entsteht: Zur Entwicklung der Wohnstadt des Eisenhüttenkombinats Ost bis 1952, in Heimatkalender für den Stadt- und Landkreis Eisenhüttenstadt 1983, Frankfurt/O. 1983, pp. 22 ff.

184. *Gattos, B.*, and *E. Kristen*, Charakterisierung des Massenwohnbaus 1870–1918 und Leitbilder für seine Umgestaltung, dargestellt an einem Teilgebiet in Erfurt-Ost, Diss. Weimar, 1977.

185. *Grundsätze der Planung und Gestaltung sozialistischer Stadtzentren*, in Deutsche Architektur, 1960, No. 8, special supplement.

186. *Junghans, K.*, Über einige Auswirkungen der verschärften sozialen und politischen Gegensätze im Deutschen Reich auf die Architektur 1898–1917/18, in Jahrbuch für Geschichte, Vol. 15 (1977), pp. 329 ff.

187. *Junghans, K.*, Der deutsche Städtebau von 1848 bis 1945 im Überblick, in Jahrbuch der Deutschen Bauakademie 1961, Berlin (GDR) 1961, pp. 75 ff.

188. *Junghans, K.*, Die deutsche Städtebautheorie unter dem Einfluß der Novemberrevolution, in Jahrbuch für Regionalgeschichte, Vol. 3 (1968), pp. 154 ff.

189. *Leipziger Bautradition*, in Leipziger Stadtgeschichtliche Forschungen, 1955, No. 4.

190. *Reinisch, U.*, Zur räumlichen Dimension und Struktur sozialer Prozesse: Studien zur deutschen Städtebau- und Stadtplanungsgeschichte zwischen dem hohen Mittelalter und dem ausgehenden 19. Jahrhundert, kunstwiss. Diss. Berlin (GDR), 1984.

191. *Topfstedt, T.*, Abriß der Städtebaugeschichte der DDR von der Mitte der 1950er bis zum Beginn der 1970er Jahre, Diss. Leipzig, 1984.

192. *Topfstedt, T.*, Grundlinien der Entwicklung von Städtebau und Architektur in der Deutschen Demokratischen Republik 1949 bis 1955, phil. Diss. Leipzig, 1980.

(e) Economy and Transport

193. *Asmus, H.*, Die ökonomischen Kämpfe der Magdeburger Arbeiter 1899–1906, phil. Diss. Berlin (GDR), 1968.

194. *Beck, F.*, Die wirtschaftliche Entwicklung der Stadt Greiz während des 19. Jahrhunderts: Ein Beitrag zur Geschichte der Industrialisierung in Deutschland, Berlin (GDR), 1955.

195. *Beyer, P.*, Leipzig und die Anfänge des deutschen Eisenbahnbaus: Die Strecke nach Magdeburg als zweitälteste deutsche Fernverbindung und das Ringen der Kaufleute um ihr Entstehen 1829–1840, Weimar, 1978 (Abhandlungen zur Handels- und Sozialgeschichte, Vol. 17).

Bibliographies

196. *Bürger, K.*, Die Entwicklung der Stadt Gera zum Industriestandort der Gegenwart, Diss. Potsdam 1959.

197. *Technische Denkmale in Großstädten.* Tagung vom 9./10. Juni 1983 in Leipzig, in Jahrbuch für Wirtschaftsgeschichte, Part 4 (1984), p. 275 ff.

198. *75 Jahre Cottbusser Straßenbahn*, pub. by VEB Cottbusverkehr, Cottbus 1978.

199. *Gutsche, W.*, Die Veränderungen in der Wirtschaftsstruktur und der Differenzierungsprozeß innerhalb des Bürgertums der Stadt Erfurt in den ersten Jahren der Herrschaft des Imperialismus (Ende des 19. Jahrhunderts bis 1914), in Jahrbuch für Geschichte, Vol. 10 (1974), pp. 343 ff.

200. *Jagdmann, E.*, Das Elektrizitätswerk und die Straßenbahn in Stralsund. Ein Beitrag zur Wirtschaftsgeschichte der Stadt, in Greifswald-Stralsunder Jahrbuch, Vol. 6 (1966), pp. 53 ff.

201. *Kleinpeter, O.*, Zur Dynamik der sozialökonomischen Struktur der Stadt Rostock in den Jahren 1945–1966, Diss. Rostock, 1969.

202. *Köhler, D.*, Die historisch-geographische Entwicklung der Industrie des Kreises Greiz, unter besonderer Berücksichtigung der Entwicklung der Stadt Greiz, phil. Diss. Potsdam, 1969.

203. *Kramm, H.-J.*, Wirtschaft und Siedlung des Bezirkes Frankfurt/Oder unter besonderer Berücksichtigung der historisch-geographischen Entwicklung, Habil.-Schrift Potsdam, 1958.

204. *Lange, S.*, Armenschulwesen und Kinderausbeutung in Pirna 1770–1870, Diss. Dresden, 1972.

205. *Mühlberg, D.*, Arbeiterleben um 1900, Berlin (GDR), 1983.

206. *Niederländer, L.*, Vergesellschaftung von Arbeit und Produktion in der sozialistischen Stadt, Diss. Berlin (GDR), 1979.

207. *Von der Pferdebahn zum Gelenkzug.* Betriebsgeschichte des VEB(K) Verkehrsbetriebe der Stadt Leipzig (VBL), Leipzig, 1966.

208. *Schmidt, U.*, Die Industrie als stadtbildender Faktor für Halle an der Saale, phil. Diss. Halle, 1960.

209. *Schröder, W.*, Wirtschaftsorganismus und Bevölkerungsstruktur Berlins in den "Gründerjahren", in Jahrbuch des Märkischen Museums, Vol. 6/7 (1980/81), p. 32 ff.

210. *Schulze, G.*, Entwicklung der Industrie Leipzigs von 1800–1945: Eine industriegeographische Untersuchung, phil. Diss. Halle, 1959.

211. *Schumann, E.*, Die Herausbildung der Fabriken in Leipzig von 1830 bis 1971, phil. Diss. Leipzig, 1971.

212. *Thamm, R.*, Ökonomisch-geographische Studien über die Entwicklung und gegenwärtigen Funktionen der Doppelstadt Ribnitz-Damgarten Diss. Greifswald, 1971.

213. *Viehrig, H.*, Ökonomisch-georgaphische Strukturwandlungen der Stadt Potsdam von 1860 bis zur Gegenwart, Diss. Potsdam, 1965.

214. *Wallosek, W.*, Die Entwicklung der Standortverteilung der Industrieflächen der Stadt Halle (Saale) von 1945 bis 1975 und Probleme ihrer zukünftigen Planung, in Hallesches Jahrbuch für Geowissenschaften, Vol. 6 (1981), p. 75 ff.

215. *Weigel, W.*, Verkehr in der modernen Stadt, Berlin (GDR), 1962.

216. *Wießner, J.*, and *S. Zeidler*, Beiträge zur Durchsetzung des Kapitalismus in Dresden im Zeitraum von 1830 bis 1890, Dresden, 1978.

(f)   Arts and Sciences, Churches

217. *Dehne, H.*, Die Beiträge der Klassiker des Marxismus-Leninismus zum kulturtheoretischen Verständnis der großstädtischen Lebensweise der Arbeiterklasse, gesellschaftswiss. Diss. Berlin (GDR), 1976.

218. *Ebert, D.*, Städtische Kultur und Wege zu ihrer Erforschung, gesellschaftswiss. Diss. Jena, 1985.

219. *Emmerich, I.*, Das Bild der Stadt in der Malerei und seine strukturellen Veränderungen, in Wissenschaftliche Zeitschrift der Friedrich-Schiller-Universität Jena. Gesellschaftswissenschaftliche und sprachwissenschaftliche Reihe, Vol. 30 (1981), Nos. 3/4, p. 461 ff.

220. *Groschopp, H.* Zwischen Bierabend und Bildungsverein. Zur Kulturarbeit in der deutschen Arbeiterbewegung vor 1914, Berlin (GDR), 1985.

221. *Kunst und Stadt.* 3. Jahrestagung des Jenaer Arbeitskreises für Ikonographie und Ikonologie, in Wissenschaftliche Zeitschrift der Friedrich-Schiller-Universität Jena. Gesellschaftswissenschaftliche und sprachwissenschaftliche Reihe, Vol. 30 (1981), Nos. 3/4.

222. *Proletariat.* Kultur und Lebensweise im 19. Jahrhundert, ed. D. Mühlberg, Leipzig, 1986.

223. *Richter, G.*, Zur Rolle und Bedeutung von örtlichen Geschichtsvereinen für die Erforschung und Darstellung der bürgerlichen Heimatgeschichte, dargestellt durch eine vergleichende Untersuchung am Beispiel der Geschichtsvereine von Freiberg, Leipzig, Dresden und Chemnitz, Diss. Leipzig, 1971.

224. *Rohls, H.*, Theoretiker der Arbeiterbewegung zu den großstädtischen Wohn- und Siedlungsbedingungen des Proletariats, zu Kommunalpolitik und Stadtentwicklung: Ein Beitrag zur Kulturauffassung der deutschen Arbeiterklasse 1860–1914, Diss. Berlin (GDR), 1979.

225. *Schellhas, W.*, Die Vorläufer der "Volksbibliothek für die Stadt Freiberg". Die Literaturvermittlung in Freiberg (Sachsen) von der Mitte des 18. Jahrhunderts bis 1875, Freiberg, 1984 (Veröffentlichungen des wissenschaftlichen Informationszentrums der Bergakademie Freiberg, Vol. 104).

226. *Seydewitz, M.*, Dresden, Museen und Menschen: Ein Beitrag zur Geschichte der Stadt, ihrer Kunst und Kultur, Berlin (GDR), 1971.

227. *Wächter, B.*, Tendenzen der Stadtdarstellung in der Malerei der DDR,

in Wissenschaftliche Zeitschrift der Friedrich-Schiller-Universität Jena. Gesellschaftswissenschaftliche und sprachwissenschaftliche Reihe, Vol. 30 (1981), Nos. 3/4, p. 487 ff.

228. *Zänsler, A.*, Die Stadtmusik von Pirna: Von den Anfängen der Stadtpfeiferei bis zum Zerfall der Stadtkapelle im Jahre 1907, phil. Diss. Halle-Wittenberg, 1983.

E. Local Studies (a representative selection)

● Arnstadt

229. *Arnstadt.* Ältester urkundlich erwähnter Ort der DDR, pub. by the Rat der Stadt, Arnstadt, 1978.

● Berlin (GDR)

230. *Berlin.* 800 Jahre Geschichte in Wort und Bild, edited by a group of authors directed by R. Bauer et al, Berlin (GDR), 1980.

231. *Geschichte Berlins von den Anfängen bis 1945,* ed. L. Demps *et al.*, Berlin (GDR), 1987.

232. *Keiderling, G.*, Berlin 1945–1986. Geschichte der Hauptstadt der DDR, Berlin (GDR), 1987.

233. *750 Jahre Berlin.* Thesen, pub. by Komitee der Deutschen Demokratischen Republik zum 750jährigen Bestehen von Berlin directed by E. Diehl, Berlin (GDR), 1986.

● Dresden

234. *Dresden.* Geschichte der Stadt in Wort und Bild, ed. R. Förster *et al.*, Berlin (GDR), 1985.

● Eberswalde

235. *Nerlich, B.P.*, Die politische und wirtschaftliche Entwicklung der Stadt Eberswalde in der Zeit der Herausbildung und Festigung einer antifaschistisch-demokratischen Ordnung bis zur Gründung der DDR, Diss. Berlin (GDR), 1966.

● Erfurt

236. *Geschichte der Stadt Erfurt*, pub. by W. Gutsche, Berlin (GDR), 1986.
237. *Wiegand, F.*, Erfurt: Eine Monographie, Rudolstadt, 1964.

● Forst

238. *Scholz, W.,* and *W. Ihlo,* Geschichte der Stadt Forst. Part 1: Die Stadt von ihren Anfängen bis zum Ende des 1. Weltkrieges; Part 2: Die Stadt während der Novemberrevolution 1918 und ihre Entwicklung in der revolutionären Nachkriegszeit bis Ende 1923, Bautzen, 1969 and 1984.

● Freiberg

239. *Geschichte der Bergstadt Freiberg,* ed. H.-H. Kasper and E. Wächter, Weimar, 1986.

● Fürstenwalde

240. *Fürstenwalde/Spree.* Vom Werden und Wachsen einer Märkischen Stadt. 1285–1985, pub. by the Rat der Stadt, Fürstenwalde 1985.

● Gera

241. *Gera.* Geschichte der Stadt in Wort und Bild, edited by a group of authors directed by H. Embersmann, Berlin (GDR), 1987.

● Geringswalde

242. *Geringswalde.* Zur Geschichte der Stadt, pub. by the Rat der Stadt, Geringswalde, 1983.

● Gotha

243. *Gotha.* Zur Geschichte der Stadt, pub. by H. Leuthold, Gotha et al., 1979.

● Greifswald

244. *Greifswald,* edited by a group of authors directed by K. Fritze, Rostock, 1973.

● Halberstadt

245. *Scholke, H.,* Halberstadt, Leipzig, 1974.

- Halle

246. *Halle.* Geschichte der Stadt in Wort und Bild, ed. E. Könnemann et al., 2nd ed., Berlin (GDR), 1983.

- Jena

247. *Schultz, H. J.*, Jena – Werden, Wachsen und Entwicklungsmöglichkeiten der Universitäts- und Industriestadt, Jena, 1955.
248. *750 Jahre Jena*, ed. W. Mägdefrau, Jena, 1985 (Wissenschaftliche Zeitschrift der Friedrich-Schiller-Universität Jena, Vol. 34 (1985), Nos. 5/6).

- Karl-Marx-Stadt

249. *Ergebnisse der heimatkundlichen Bestandsaufnahme im Gebiet von Karl-Marx-Stadt*, ed. E. Barth, Berlin (GDR), 1979 (Werte unserer Heimat, Vol. 33).

- Leipzig

250. *Arndt, H., et al.*, Leipzig in acht Jahrhunderten, Leipzig, 1965 (Leipziger Stadtgeschichtliche Forschungen, Vol. 7).
251. *Czok, K., et al.*, Leipzig: Geschichte der Stadt in Wort und Bild, Berlin (GDR), 1978.

- Magdeburg

252. *Geschichte der Stadt Magdeburg*, edited by a group of authors directed by H. Asmus, 2nd ed. Berlin (GDR), 1977.

- Meißen

253. *Mrusek, H.-J.*, Meißen, 2nd ed. Leipzig, 1978.

- Nordhausen

254. *1050 Jahre Nordhausen.* Beiträge zur Geschichte der Stadt Nordhausen, pub. by the Rat der Stadt im Auftrag der Kommission zur Erforschung der Geschichte der örtlichen Arbeiterbewegung bei der Kreisleitung der SED Nordhausen, Nordhausen 1977.

● Potsdam

255. *Müller, H.*, Zur Geschichte der Stadt Potsdam von 1789 bis 1871, Potsdam 1968 (Veröffentlichung des Bezirksmuseums Potsdam, No. 15.)

256. *Müller, H.*, Zur Geschichte der Stadt Potsdam von 1918 bis 1933, Potsdam, 1970.

257. *Potsdam* – Erbe, Tradition und sozialistische Gegenwart. Konferenz zur Geschichte der Stadt Potsdam am 15./16. Mai 1984, Protokollband, pub. by the Rektor der Pädagogischen Hochschule "Karl Liebknecht" Potsdam, Potsdam, 1984.

258. *Potsdam*. Geschichte der Stadt in Wort und Bild, eds. M. Uhlemann *et al.*, Berlin (GDR), 1986.

259. *Schulte, D.*, and *H. Knitter*, Potsdam im Bild der Geschichte. Part 1: Von den Anfängen bis zum Jahre 1945, 3rd ed., Potsdam, 1985.

● Rostock

260. *Bernitt, H.*, Zur Geschichte der Stadt Rostock, Rostock, 1956.

261. *Geschichte der Universität Rostock 1419–1969*. Festschrift zur Fünfhundertfünfzig-Jahr-Feier der Universität, pub. by the Forschungsgruppe Universitätsgeschichte directed by G. Heidorn *et al.*, 2 vols. Berlin (GDR), 1969.

262. *Olechnowitz, K.F.*, Rostock von der Stadtrechtsbestätigung im Jahre 1218 bis zur frühbürgerlich-demokratischen Revolution 1848/49, Rostock, 1968.

263. *Polzin, M.*, and *H. Witt*, Rostock von der bürgerlich-demokratischen Revolution 1848/49 bis 1945, Rostock, 1974, (Beiträge zur Geschichte der Stadt Rostock).

264. *Rackow, G., M. Heyne*, and *O. Kleinpeter*, Rostock 1945 bis zur Gegenwart, Rostock, 1969.

265. *Rostock*. Geschichte der Stadt in Wort und Bild, edited by a group of authors directed by L. Elsner, Berlin (GDR), 1980.

● Schwerin

266. *Schwerin*. Geschichte der Stadt in Wort und Bild, eds. M. Krieck et al., Berlin (GDR), 1985.

● Stralsund

267. *Geschichte der Stadt Stralsund*, pub. by H. Ewe, Weimar, 1984 (Veröffentlichungen des Stadtarchivs Stralsund).

● Waren

268. *Frank, J.*, Waren. Geschichte einer kleinen Stadt und ihrer Einwohner von den Anfängen bis 1914, Waren, 1983.

● Weimar

269. *Geschichte der Stadt Weimar*, ed. G. Günther *et al.*, 2nd ed., Weimar, 1976.

● Wismar

270. *Wismar 1229–1979*. Beiträge zur Geschichte einer Stadt, pub. by the Rat der Stadt Wismar, Wismar, 1979.

● Wittenberg

271. *Festausgabe zum 750jährigen Bestehen der Stadt Wittenberg*: Beiträge zur Chronik, pub. by the Rat der Stadt, Wittenberg, 1976.

ANTHONY SUTCLIFFE

Great Britain

A. Urban History Institutions

Urban History Group, School of Education, University of Leicester.
Planning History Group, Centre for Urban and Regional Studies, University of Birmingham.
Centre for Urban History, Department of Economic and Social History, University of Leicester.
Constructions History Group, The Chartered Institute of Building, Ascot.
Historical Geography Research Group, Department of Geography, University of Exeter.
Pre-Modern Towns Group, Royal Holloway and Bedford New College, University of London.

B. Aids to Research

(a) Urban History Journals

1. *Journal of Historical Geography*, London, 1975 ff., ed. H. Prince.
2. *Planning History Bulletin*, 1979 ff., ed. D. Hardy.
3. *Planning Perspectives*, London, 1986 ff., ed. G. Cherry and A. Sutcliffe.
4. *Urban History Newsletter*, Leicester, 1963–1974, 1986 ff., ed. P. Clark.
5. *Urban History Yearbook*, Leicester, 1974 ff., ed. D. Reeder.

(b) Bibliographies

6. *Dixon, D., et al.*, Current Bibliography of Urban History, in Urban History Yearbook, 1974 ff.
7. *Martin, G. H.*, and *S. C. McIntyre*, A Bibliography of British and Irish Municipal History. Vol. 1: General Works, Leicester, 1972.
8. *Mullins, E. L. C.*, A Guide to the Historical and Archeological

cations of Societies in England and Wales. 1901–1933, London, 1968.

9. *Sutcliffe, A.*, The History of Urban and Regional Planning: A Bibliographic Guide, London, 1981.

(c)   Handbooks on Urban History

10. *Riden, P.*, Local History: A Practical Handbook for Beginners, London, 1983.

11. *Rogers, A.*, Approaches to Local History, London, 1977.

(d)   Atlases on Urban History and Urban Development

12. *Lobel, M. D.*, ed., Historic Towns: Maps and Plans of Towns and Cities in the British Isles, Oxford, 1969.

(e)   Urban History Sources

13. *Blakiston, H. N.*, Maps and Plans in the Public Record Office, Vol. 1, British Isles: 1410–1860, London, 1967.

14. *Bond, M. F.*, Guide to the Records of Parliament, London, 1971.

15. *Emmison, F. G.*, Archives and Local History, Chichester, 1974.

16. *Mullins, E. L. C.*, Texts and Calendars: An Analytical Guide to Serial Publications, London, 1958.

17. *Public Record Office*, Guide to the Contents of the Public Record Office, London, 1963–1968.

18. *Ranger, F.*, Record Repositories in Great Britain, London, 1956.

19. *Stephens, W. B.*, Sources for English Local History, Manchester, 1973.

20. *West, J.*, Town Records, Chichester, 1983.

C.   Research Reports

(a)   General Surveys

21. *Clark, P.*, ed., The Transformation of English Provincial Towns, London 1984.

22. *Dyos, H. J.*, ed., The Study of Urban History, London, 1968.

23. *Dyos, H. J.*, and *M. Wolff*, eds., The Victorian City, London, 1973.

24. *Fraser, D.*, and *A. Sutcliffe*, eds., The Pursuit of Urban History, London, 1983.

25. *Girouard, M.*, Cities and People: A Social and Architectural History, New Haven and London, 1985.

26. *Gordon, G.*, ed., Perspectives of the Scottish City, Aberdeen, 1985.

27. *Gordon, G.*, and *B. Dicks*, eds., Scottish Urban History, Aberdeen, 1983.

28. *Hepburn, A. C.*, Teaching Urban History. A Survey of Courses Offered in British Universities and Polytechnics, in Urban History Yearbook, 1976, pp. 35–36.
29. *Martin, G. H.*, Royaume-Uni, in P. Wolff, ed., Guide international d'histoire urbaine, Vol. 1: Europe, Paris, 1977, pp. 395–427.

(b)   Surveys of Individual Fields of Urban History Research

30. *Carter, H.*, An Introduction to Urban Historical Geography, London, 1983.
31. *Darby, H. C.*, ed., A New Historical Geography of England after 1600, Cambridge, 1976.
32. *Dodgshon, R. A.*, and *R. A. Butlin*, eds., An Historical Geography of England and Wales, London, 1978.

D. Literature on Individual Areas of Urban History Research

(a)   Concept and Definition of Town and Town Types

33. *Adams, I. H.*, The Making of Urban Scotland, London, 1978.
34. *Briggs, A.*, Victorian Cities, London, 1963.
35. *Corfield, P. J.*, The Impact of English Towns. 1700–1800, Oxford, 1982.
36. *Daunton, M. J.*, Towns and Economic Growth in 18th-Century England, in P. Abrams and E.A. Wrigley, eds., Towns in Societies: Essays in Economic History and Historical Sociology, London, 1978, pp. 245–278.
37. *Donnison, D.*, and *P. Soto*, The Good City: A Study of Urban Development and Policy in Britain, London, 1980.
38. *Fraser, D.*, The Edwardian City, in D. Read, ed., Edwardian England, London, 1982, pp. 56–74.
39. *Lawton, R.*, An Age of Great Cities, in Town Planning Review, Vol. 43 (172), pp. 200–224.
40. *McInnes, A.*, The English Town, 1660–1760, London, 1981.
41. *Read, D.*, England 1868–1914: The Age of Urban Democracy, London, 1979.
42. *Reynolds, S.*, An Introduction to the History of English Medieval Towns, Oxford, 1977.
43. *Robson, B. T.*, Urban Growth: An Approach, London, 1973.
44. *Waller, P. J.*, Town, City and Nation: England, 1850–1914, Oxford, 1963.
45. *Walton, J. K.*, The English Seaside Resort: A Social History, 1750–1914, Leincester, 1983.

46. *Wrigley, E. A.*, Parasite or Stimulus: The Town in a Pre-Industrial Economy, in P. Abrams and E. A. Wrigley, eds., Towns in Societies: Essays in Economic History and Historical Sociology, London, 1978, pp. 295–310.

(b)   Politics, Law and Statutes

47. *Fraser, D.*, Urban Politics in Victorian England. The Structure of Politics in Victorian Cities, Leicester, 1976.
48. *Fraser, D.*, Power and Authority in the Victorian City. Oxford, 1979.
49. *Gibbon, I. G.*, and *R. W. Bell*, History of the London City Council, 1889–1939, London, 1939.
50. *Hart, T.*, Urban Growth and Municipal Government: Glasgow in a Comparative Context: 1846–1914, in A. Slaven and D. H. Aldcroft, eds., Business, Banking and Urban History: Essays in Honour of S. G. Checkland, Edinburgh, 1982, pp. 193–219.
51. *Hennock, E. P.*, Fit and Proper Persons: Ideal and Reality in Nineteenth-Century Urban Government, London, 1973.
52. *Keith-Lucas, B.*, English Local Government in the Nineteenth and Twentieth Centuries, London, 1977.
53. *Kellet, J.R.*, Municipal Socialism, Enterprise and Trading in the Victorian City, in Urban History Yearbook, 1978, pp. 36–45.
54. *Offer, A.*, Property and Politics, 1870–1914: Landownership, Law Ideology and Urban Development in England, Cambridge, 1981.
55. *Owen, D.*, The Government of London, 1855–1889: The Metropolitan Board of Works, the Vestries, and the City Corporation, Cambridge, Mass., 1982.
56. *Robson, W. A.*, The Government and Misgovernment of London, London, 1939.
57. *Smellie, K. B.*, A History of Local Government, London, 1968.
58. *Webb, S.*, and *B. Webb*, English Local Government from the Revolution to the Municipal Corporations Act, 9 Vols., London, 1906–1929.
59. *Wohl, A. S.*, Endangered Lives: Public Health in Victorian Britain, London, 1983.
60. *Young, K.*, and *P. L. Garside*, Metropolitan London: Politics and Urban Change, 1837–1981, London 1982.

(c)   Population and Social Structure

61. *Anderson, M.*, Family Structure in Nineteenth-Century Lancashire, London, 1971.
62. *Armstrong, W. A.*, Stability and Change in an English Country Town: A Social Study of York, 1801–1851, Cambridge, 1974.
63. *Bailey, P.*, Leisure and Class in Victorian England: Rational Recreation

and the Context for Control, 1830–1885, London, 1978.

64. *Borsay, P.*, The English Urban Renaissance: The Development of Provincial Urban Culture, c.1680–c.1760, in Social History, Vol. 5 (1977), pp. 581–603.

65. *Carter, H.*, and *S. Wheatley*, Residential Segregation in Nineteenth-Century Cities, in Area, Vol. 12 (1980), pp. 57–62.

66. *Carter, H.*, and *S. Wheatley*, Merthyr Tydfil in 1851: A Study of the Spatial Structure of a Welsh Industrial Town, Cardiff, 1982.

67. *Crossick, G.*, An Artisan Elite in Victorian Society: Kentish London, 1840–1880, London, 1978.

68. *Crossick, G.*, Urban Society and the Petty Bourgeoisie in Nineteenth-Century Britain, in D. Fraser and A. Sutcliffe, eds., The Pursuit of Urban History, London, 1983, pp. 306–325.

69. *Crossick, G.*, and *H. G. Haupt*, eds., Shopkeepers and Master Artisans in Nineteenth-Century Europe, London, 1984.

70. *Cunningham, H.*, Leisure in the Industrial Revolution, c.1780–1880, London, 1980.

71. *Dennis, R.*, and *S. Daniels*, "Community" and the Social Geography of Victorian Cities, in Urban History Yearbook, 1981, pp. 7–23.

72. *Dyos, H. J.*, The Slums of Victorian London, in Victorian Studies, Vol. 11 (1968), pp. 5–40.

73. *Englander, D.*, Landlord and Tenant in Urban Britain, Oxford, 1983.

74. *Foster, J.*, Class Struggle in the Industrial Revolution, London, 1970.

75. *George, M. D.*, London Life in the Eighteenth Century, London, 1925.

76. *Gray, R. Q.*, The Labour Aristocracy in Victorian Edinburgh, Oxford, 1976.

77. *Jones, G. S.*, Outcast London: A Study in the Relationship between Classes in Victorian Society, Oxford, 1971.

78. *Joyce, P.*, Work Society and Politics: The Culture of the Factory in Later Victorian England, Brighton, 1980.

79. *Lees, L.*, Exiles of Erin. Irish Migrants in Victorian London, Manchester, 1979.

80. *Melling, J.*, Rent Strikes: People's Struggle for Housing in West Scotland, 1890–1916, Edinburgh, 1983.

81. *Morris, R. J.*, Voluntary Societies and British Urban Elites. 1780–1850, in Historical Journal, Vol. 26 (1983), pp. 95–118.

82. *Morris, R. J.*, The Middle Class and British Towns and Cities of the Industrial Revolution, 1780–1870, in D. Fraser and A. Sutcliffe, eds., The Pursuit of Urban History, London, 1983, pp. 286–305.

83. *Pooley, C. G.*, Residential Mobility in the Victorian City, in Institute of British Geographers Transactions, Vol. 4 (1979), pp. 258–277.

84. *Pooley, C. G.*, The Residential Segregation of Migrant Communities in Mid-Victorian Liverpool, in Institute of British Geographers Transactions, Vol. 2 (1977), pp. 364–382.

85. *Reeder, D.*, Suburbanity and the Victorian City, Leicester, 1980.
86. *Roberts, E.*, Working-Class Standards of Living in Barrow and Lancaster, 1890–1914, in Economic History Review, Vol. 30 (1977), pp. 306–321.
87. *Roberts, R.*, The Classic Slum: Salford Life in the First Quarter of the Century, Manchester, 1971.
88. *Rubinstein, W. D.*, Men of Property. The Very Wealthy in Britain since the Industrial Revolution, London, 1981.
89. *Rubinstein, W. D.*, The Victorian Middle Class: Wealth, Occupation and Geography, in Economic History Review, Vol. 30 (1977), pp. 602–623.
90. *Samuel, R.*, East End Underworld. Chapters in the Life of Arthur Harding, London, 1981.
91. *Seaman, L. C. B.*, Life in Victorian London, London, 1973.
92. *Walvin, J.*, English Urban Life, 1776–1851, London, 1984.
93. *Walvin, J.*, Passage to Britain: Immigration in British History and Politics, Harmondsworth, 1984.

(d)   Town Planning, Housing

94. *Aldridge, M.*, The British New Towns: A Programme Without a Policy, London, 1979.
95. *Ashworth, W.*, The Genesis of Modern British Town Planning: A Study in Economic and Social History of the Nineteenth and Twentieth Centuries, London, 1954.
96. *Aspinall, P. J.*, Building Applications and the Building Industry in Nineteenth-Century Towns: The Scope for Statistical Analysis, Birmingham, 1978 (Centre for Urban and Regional Studies, Birmingham University).
97. *Bell, C.*, and *R. Bell*, City Fathers. The Early History of Town Planning in Britain, London, 1969.
98. *Beresford, M. D.*, The Back-to-Back House in Leeds. 1787–1937, in S. D. Chapman, ed., The History of Working–Class Housing, Newton Abbot, 1971, pp. 93–132.
99. *Beresford, M. D.*, The Making of a Townscape: Richard Paley in the East End of Leeds, 1777–1803, in C. W. Chalklin and M. A. Havinden, eds., Rural Change and Urban Growth, London, 1974, 281–320.
100. *Borsay, P.*, Culture, Status and the English Urban Landscape, in History, Vol. 67 (1982), pp. 1–12.
101. *Bowley, M.*, Housing and the State, 1919–1944, London, 1945.
102. *Burke, G.*, Towns in the Making, London, 1971.
103. *Burnett, J.*, A Social History of Housing, 1815–1970, Newton Abbot, 1978.
104. *Calabi, D.*, Architettura domestica in Gran Bretagna. 1890–1939, Milan, 1982 (= Housing Architecture in Britain).

105. *Cannadine, D.*, Lords and Landlords: The Aristocracy and the Towns: 1774–1967, Leicester, 1980.
106. *Cannadine, D.*, ed., Patricians, Power and Politics in Nineteenth-Century Towns, Leicester, 1982.
107. *Chalklin, C. W.*, The Provincial Towns of Georgian England: A Study of the Building Process, 1740–1820, London, 1974.
108. *Chapman, S. D.*, ed., The History of Working-Class Housing. A Symposium, Newton Abbot, 1971.
109. *Cherry, G. E.*, Urban Change and Planning: A History of Urban Development in Britain since 1750, Henley-on-Thames, 1972.
110. *Cherry, G. E.*, The Evolution of British Town Planning, Heath and Reach, 1974.
111. *Cherry, G. E.*, ed., Pioneers in British Planning, London, 1981.
112. *Clark, K.*, The Gothic Revival: An Essay in the History of Taste, London, 1928.
113. *Creese, W.*, The Search for Environment: The Garden City Before and After, New Haven, 1966.
114. *Cunningham, C.*, Victorian and Edwardian Town Halls, London, 1981.
115. *Daunton, M. J.*, House and Home in the Victorian City: Working-Class Housing. 1850–1914, London, 1983.
116. *Daunton, M. J.*, ed., Councillors and Tenants: Local Authority Housing in English Cities, 1919–1939, Leicester, 1984.
117. *Dellheim, C.*, The Face of the Past: The Preservation of the Medieval Inheritance in Victorian England, Cambridge, 1982.
118. *Dennis, R. J.*, English Industrial Cities of the Nineteenth Century: A Social Geography, Cambridge, 1984.
119. *Dixon, R.*, and *S. Muthesius*, Victorian Architecture, London, 1978.
120. *Doughty, M.*, ed., Building the Industrial City, Leicester, 1986.
121. *Dunleavy, P.*, The Politics of Mass Housing in Britain. 1945–1975, Oxford, 1981.
122. *Dyos, H. J.*, The Speculative Builders and Developers of Victorian London, in Victorian Studies, Vol. 11 (1968) Supplement, pp. 641–690.
123. *Dyos, H. J.*, Victorian Suburb. A Study of the Growth of Camberwell, Leicester, 1961.
124. *Dyos, H. J.*, and *D. A. Reeder*, Slums and Suburbs, in H. J. Dyos and P. Wolff, eds., The Victorian City, London, 1973, 359–386.
125. *Edwards, A. M.*, The Design of Suburbia: A Critical Study in Environmental History, London, 1981.
126. *Esher, L.*, A Broken Wave. The Rebuilding of England. 1940–1980, London, 1981.
127. *Forster, C. A.*, Court Housing in Kingston-upon-Hull, Hull, 1972.
128. *Gaskell, S. M.*, Building Control: National Legislation and the Introduction of Local By-Laws in Victorian England, London, 1983.

129. *Hall, P.*, The Containment of Urban England, 2 vols., London, 1973.
130. *Hall, P.*, Great Planning Disasters, London, 1980.
131. *Harper, R. H.*, Victorian Building Regulations: Summary Tables of the Principal English Building Acts and Model By-Laws, 1840–1914, London, 1985.
132. *Hebbert, M.*, The Inner City Problem in Historical Context, London, 1980.
133. *Hickman, D.*, Birmingham, London, 1970.
134. *Hobhouse, H.*, Lost London: A Century of Demolition and Decay, London, 1971.
135. *Hughes, Q.*, Liverpool, London, 1969.
136. *Jackson, A. A.*, Semi-Detached London: Suburban Development, Life and Transport, 1900–1939, London, 1973.
137. *Jordan, R. F.*, Victorian Architecture, Harmondsworth, 1966.
138. *Lloyd, D. W.*, The Making of English Towns: 2000 Years of Evolution, London, 1984.
139. *Melling, J.*, ed., Housing, Social Policy and the State, London, 1980.
140. *Merrett, S.*, State Housing in Britain, London, 1979.
141. *Muthesius, S.*, The English Terraced House, New Haven and London, 1982.
142. *Olsen, D. J.*, The Growth of Victorian London, London, 1978.
143. *Olsen, D. J.*, Town Planning in London: The Eighteenth and Nineteenth Centuries, New Haven and London, 1964.
144. *Prince, H. C.*, North-West London 1864–1914, in J. T. Coppock and H. C. Prince, eds., Greater London, London, 1964, pp. 120–141.
145. *Rasmussen, S. E.*, London: The Unique City, London, 1937.
146. *Ravetz, A.*, Model Estate: Planned Housing at Quarry Hill, Leeds, London, 1974.
147. *Ravetz, A.*, Remaking Cities: Contradictions of the Recent Urban Environment, London, 1980.
148. *Rodger, R. G.*, The Invisible Hand: Market Forces, Housing and the Urban Form in Victorian Cities, in D. Fraser and A. Sutcliffe, eds., The Pursuit of Urban History, London, 1983, pp. 190–211.
149. *Service, A.*, Edwardian Architecture: A Handbook to Building Design in England, 1890–1914, London, 1977.
150. *Sharp, D.*, Manchester, London, 1969.
151. *Simpson, M. A.*, Thomas Adams and the Modern Planning Movement, London, 1985.
152. *Simpson, M. A.*, and *T. H. Lloyd*, eds., Middle-Class Housing in Britain, Newton Abbot, 1977.
153. *Stevens, D. F.*, The Central Area, in J. T. Coppock and H. C. Prince, eds., Greater London, London, 1964, pp. 167–201.
154. *Summerson, J.*, Georgian London, London, 1945.
155. *Sutcliffe, A.*, Towards the Planned City: Germany, Britain, the United

States and France, 1780–1914, Oxford, 1981.

156. *Sutcliffe, A.*, ed., Multi-Storey Living: The British Working-Class Experience, London, 1974.

157. *Sutcliffe, A.*, ed., Metropolis 1890–1940, London 1984.

158. *Swenarton, M.*, Homes Fit for Heroes: The Politics and Architecture of Early State Housing in Britain, London, 1981.

159. *Tarn, J. N.*, Five per cent Philanthropy: An Account of Housing in Urban Areas between 1840 and 1914, Cambridge, 1973.

160. *Taylor, I. C.*, The Court and Cellar Dwelling: The Eighteenth-Century Origin of the Liverpool Slum, in Transactions of the Historic Society of Lancashire and Cheshire, Vol. 122 (1970), pp. 67–90.

161. *Thompson, F. M. L.*, ed., The Rise of Suburbia, Leicester, 1982.

162. *Ward, D.*, Victorian Cities: How Modern?, in Journal of Historical Georgraphy, Vol. 1 (1975), pp. 135–151.

163. *Wohl, A. S.*, The Eternal Slum: Housing and Social Policy in Victorian London, 1977.

164. *Worsdall, F.*, Victorian City: A Selection of Glasgow's Architecture, Glasgow, 1982.

165. *Youngson, A. J.*, The Making of Classical Edinburgh, 1750–1840, Edinburgh 1966.

(e)   Economy and Transport

166. *Abrams, P.*, Towns and Economic Growth: Some Theories and Problems, in P. Abrams and E. A. Wrigley, eds., Towns in Societies: Essays in Economical History and Historical Sociology, London 1978, pp. 9–34.

167. *Barker, T. C.*, and *M. Robbins*, A History of London Transport Development Since the Later Eighteenth Century, in Journal of Transport History, 3rd Series, Vol. 1 (1980), pp. 75–90.

168. *Hunt, E. H.*, Regional Wage Variations in Britain 1850–1914, Oxford, 1973.

169. *Kellett, J. R.*, The Impact of Railways on Victorian Cities, London, 1969.

170. *Lee, C. H.*, British Regional Employment Statistics 1841–1971, Cambridge, 1979.

171. *McKay, J. P.*, Tramways and Trolleys: The Rise of Urban Mass Transport in Europe, Princeton, 1976.

172. *Perkin, H.*, The Age of the Automobile, London, 1976.

173. *Pollard, S.*, A History of Labour in Sheffield, Liverpool, 1959.

174. *Powell, C. G.*, An Economic History of the British Building Industry, 1815–1979, London, 1980.

175. *Pred, A.*, The External Relations of Cities During 'Industrial Revolution', Chicago, 1962.

176. *Simpson, M. A.*, Urban Transport and the Development of Glasgow's West End, 1830–1914, in Journal of Transport History, N.S., Vol. 1 (1972), pp. 146–160.

177. *Trinder, B.*, The Making of the Industrial Landscape, London, 1982.

(f)   Arts and Sciences, Churches

178. *Coleman, B. I.*, The Church of England in the Mid-Nineteenth Century, London, 1980.

179. *MacLaren, A. A.*, Religion and Social Class: The Disruption Years in Aberdeen, London, 1974.

180. *McLeod, H.*, Class and Religion in the Late Victorian City, London, 1974.

181. *Wickham, E. R.*, Church and People in an Industrial City, London, 1957.

E.   Local Studies (a representative selection)

- Birmingham

182. *Briggs, A.*, History of Birmingham. Vol. 2: Borough and City, 1865–1938, London, 1952.

183. *Gill, C.*, History of Birmingham. Vol. 1: Manor and Borough to 1865, London, 1952.

184. *Sutcliffe, A.*, and *R. Smith*, Birmingham 1939–1970, London, 1974.

- Bradford

185. *Reynolds, J.*, The Great Paternalist. Titus Salt and the Growth of Nineteenth-Century Bradford, London, 1983.

- Cardiff

186. *Daunton, M. J.*, Coal Metropolis: Cardiff, 1870–1914, Leicester, 1977.

- Coventry

187. *Richardson, K.*, Twentieth-Century Coventry, London, 1972.

- Crewe

188. *Chaloner, W. H.*, The Social and Economic Development of Crewe, 1780–1923, Manchester, 1950.

- Glasgow

189. *Checkland, S. G.*, The Upas Tree: Glasgow 1875–1975 . . . and After, 1975–1980, Glasgow, 1981.
190. *Gibb, A.*, Glasgow: The Making of a City, London, 1983.

- Hampstead

191. *Thompson, F. M. L.*, Hampstead: Building a Borough, 1650–1964, London, 1974.

- Hull

192. *Jackson, G.*, Hull in the Eighteenth Century: A Study in Economic and Social History, Oxford, 1972.

- Leeds

193. *Fraser, D.*, ed., A History of Modern Leeds, Manchester, 1980.

- Leicester

194. *Simmons, J.*, Leicester: Past and Present, 3 vols., London, 1974.

- Lincoln

195. *Hill, F.*, Victorian Lincoln, Cambridge, 1974.

- London

196. *Garside, P. L.*, West End, East End: London 1890–1940, in A. Sutcliffe, ed., Metropolis 1890–1940, London, 1984, 221–258.
197. *Sheppard, F.*, London 1808–1870: The Infernal Wen, London, 1971.
198. *Weightman, G.*, and *S. Humphries*, The Making of Modern London, London, 1984.

- St. Helens

199. *Barker, T. C.*, and *J. R. Harris*, A Merseyside Town in the Industrial Revolution: St. Helens 1750–1900, Liverpool, 1954.

- Southampton

200. *Temple Patterson, A.*, A History of Southampton 3 Vols., Southampton, 1966–1975.

ELENA KALAFATI

Greece

A. **Urban History Institutions**

—

B. **Aids to Research**

(a)   *Urban History Journals*

1. Πόλη και Περιφέρεια (= Town and Surrounding Area).
2. Αρχιτεκτονικά θέματα (= Architecture in Greece).

(b)   *Bibliographies*

3. *Chrabanis, P.*, Χρονολογικός κατάλογος πολεοδομικών μελετών και άρθρων περιόδου 1900–1940, in Αθήνα *1900–1940 (1985)*, Athens, 1985, pp. 55–57 (= Chronological catalogue of treatises and essays of the period 1900–1940).

(c)   *Handbooks on Urban History*

(d)   *Atlases on Urban History and Urban Development*

4. *Kayser, B., C. Thompson* and *B. Coukis*, Οικονομικός και κοινωνικός Ατλας της Ελλάδος (τριγλωδδοδ), EKKE, Athens, 1964. (= Economic and social atlas of Greece – in three languages).
5. *Traylos, J.*, Athènes au fil du temps. Atlas historique d'urbanisme et d' architecture, Boulogne, 1972.

(e)   Urban History Sources

—

C.   Research Reports

(Collections which include a large number of the titles listed below)

6. Νεοκλασσική Πόλη (1983) = *Πρακτικά Α' Πανελληνίου Συνεδρίου: Νεοκλασσική πόλη και Αρχιτεκτονική*, Θεσσαλονίκη 2–4 Δεκ. 1983, Α.Π.Θ. / Σπουδαστήριο Ιστορίας Αρχιτεκτονικής, Athens, 1983 (= The Neoclassic town. Files of the 1st Panhellenist Congress: The Neoclassic town and architecture).

7. Νεοελληνική πόλη (1985) = Εταιρεία Μελέτης Νέου Ελληνισμού, *Πρακτικα του Διεθνούς Συμποσίου Ιστορίας: Νεοελληνική πόλη. Οθωμανικές κληρονομίες και Ελληνικό Κράτος*, Αθήνα 26–28 Σεπτεμβρίου 1984, Ερμούπολη 29–30 Σεπτεμβρίου 1984, τ.Α΄, Β, Athens, 1985. (= The modern Greek town. Files of the International Symposium for history: The modern Greek town, the Osman heritage and the Greek state).

8. Αθήνα Πρωτεύουσα Πόλη (1985) = Υπουργείο Πολιτισμού – Ταμείο Αρχαιολογικών Πόρων και Απαλλοτριώσεων (ΤΑΠ), *Αθήνα Πρωτεύουσα Πόλη*, Athens, 1985 (= Athens, the capital).

9. Αθήνα 1900–1940 (1985) = Υπουργείο Πολιτισμού, *Η Αθήνα στον 20ο αιώνα, 1900–1940: Αθήνα Ελληνική Πρωτεύουσα*, Athens 1985 (= Athens in the 20th century, 1900–1940: Athens as the Greek capital).

10. Η Αθήνα όπως (δεν) φαίνεται = Υπουργείο Πολιτισμού – Σύλλογος Αρχιτεκτόνων Δ.Α.Σ., *Η Αθήνα στον 20ο αιώνα – Η Αθήνα όπως (δεν) φαίνεται 1940–1985*, Athens, 1985 (= Athens in the 20th century. 1940–1985: Athens as it (does not) appear(s)).

D.   Literature on Individual Areas of Urban History Research

(a)   Concept and Definition of Town and Town Types

11. *Agriantoni, C.*, Πόλεις και εκβιομηχάνηση στην Ελλάδα ή η εκβιομηχάνηση σε μια μόνη πόλη, in Αθήνα Πρωτεύουσα Πόλη, Athens, 1985, pp. 103–109 (= Towns and industrialisation in Greece – industrialisation in a single town).

12. *Burgel, G.*, Trois méthodes pour l'étude d'une agglomération millionaire, in L' espace géographique, No. 3 (1972), pp. 183–191.

13. *Demathas, Z.*, and *G. Tsouyiopoulos*, Η νεοελληνική πόλη: η διαδικασία

ανάπτυξής της. Ενα πλαίσιο θεωρητικής προσέγγισης, in Νεοελληνική πόλη (1985), τ.Β΄, Athens, 1985, pp. 505–510 (= The modern Greek town: The process of its development).

14. *Dimitrakopoulos, A.*, Σχέδια πόλεων. Πολεοδομία εν Ελλάδι, in Τεχνική Επετηρίς της Ελλάδος, τ.ΑΙΙ, εκσ. ΤΕΕ, Athens, 1937, 359–449 (= Town plans. Urbanisation in Greece).

15. *Kalafati, E.*, Η κατασκευή μιας νέας πόλης: Προδιαγραφές και προγραμματισμός, in Αθήνα Πρωτεύουσα Πόλη (1985), Athens, 1985, pp. 100–102 (= The construction of a new town; guidelines and programmes).

16. *Karadimou-Gerolympou, A.*, et al., Πόλη και πολεοδομία στή Βόρειο Ελλάδα μετά το 1912, in Νεοελληνική πόλη (1985), τ.Β΄, Athens, 1985, pp. 397–421 (= Towns and urbanisation in northern Greece after 1912).

17. *Loukakis, P.*, Αθήνα 1830–1940: Ιστορικές φάσεις παγίωσης του υπερσυγκεντρωτισμού της, in Νεοελληνική πόλη (1985). τ.Α΄, Athens, 1985, pp. 85–96 (= Athens 1830–1940: Historical phases in the consolidation of its over-centralisation).

18. *Mantouvalou, M.*, and *I. Polyzos*, Αστικοποίηση και οργάνωση του χώρου στήν προπολεμική Ελλάδα, ΕΜΠ, Athens, 1984 (= Urban development and spatial organisation in Greece prior to the war).

19. *Michael, J.*, Η Πολεοδομική εξέλιξις των αστικών κέντρων της χερσονήσου του Αίμου, μετά την αρχαιότητα, in Τεχνικά Χρονικά, 3 (1968) (= The development of urban centres on the Haemus peninsula since antique times).

20. *Michael, J.*, Από τη συνέχεια της ελληνικής πόλης: η περίπτωση της Πλάκας, in Νεοελληνική πόλη (1985), τ.Α΄, Athens, 1985, pp. 129–132 (= On the continuity of the Greek town: the case of Plaka).

21. *Philippides, D.*, Urbanisme colonial en Grèce, in Urbi, Vol. VI (1982), pp. 115–120.

22. *Polyzos, I.*, Processus d' urbanisation en Grèce, 1920–1940, Toulouse, 1978.

23. *Sariyannis, G.*, Το δίκτυο των αστικών κέντρων στην Ελλάδα τον 19ο αι., in Νεοκλασσική πόλη (1983), Athens, 1983, pp. 27–34 (= The catchment area of urban centres in Greece in the 19th century).

24. *Sivignon, M.*, L' organisation urbaine de la Théssalie depuis la fin de la domination ottomane jusqu' à l' arrivée des réfugiés d' asie mineure, in Νεοελληνική πόλη (1985), τ.Β΄, Athens, 1985, pp. 511–517.

25. *Tsiomis, Y.*, Athènes a soi-même étrangère, éléments de formation et de réception du modèle urbain en Europe et en Grèce au XIXème siècle, Diss: Paris, 1983.

(b) Politics, Law and Statutes

26. *Bakounakis, N.*, Οι Αστικές όψεις της πολιτικής συμπεριφοράς. Το ανώτερο κοινωνικό στρώμα της Πάτρας και οι σχέσεις του με τους μηχανισμούς εξουσίας (1828–1900), in Νεοελληνική πόλη (1985), τ.Β΄, Athens, 1985, pp. 341–357 (= Urban forms of political behaviour. The upper social class of Patras and its relations to control mechanisms 1828–1900).

27. *Fiandra, E.*, Atene, Nascità di una capitale, in Urbanistica, Vol. 41 (1964) (= Birth of a capital).

28. *Kalafati, E.*, Κράτος, δημοτική διοίκηση και οργάνωση του χώρου τον 19ο αιώνα, in Νεοελληνική πόλη (1985), τ.Β΄, Athens, 1985, pp. 367–373 (= State, local administration and spatial organisation in the 19th century).

29. *Kalafati, E.*, Η πολεοδομία της Επανάστασης, Ναύπλιο 1822–1830, in Τα Ιστορικά. 2/Δεκ. 1984, pp. 265–282 (= Urban development during the revolution: Nauplia 1822–1830).

30. *Katifori, D.*, Ενδιαφέρον ομογενών για την ίδρυση πόλεων στην ελληνική επικράτεια επί Καποδίστρια, in Νεοελληνική πόλη (1985), τ.Α΄, Athens, 1985, pp. 273–285 (= The interest of expatriate Greeks in the founding of towns in the Greek administrative area under Kapodistrias).

31. *Kleiosis, C.*, Ιστορία της Τοπικής Αυτοδιοικήσεως, Athens, 1977 (= The history of local self-administration).

32. *Loukatos, S.*, Η θεμελίωσις της ελευθέρας Τριπόλεως επί Ιω. Καποδιστρίου, Πρακτικά Α' Συνεδρίου Αρκαδικών Σπουδών, in Πελοποννησιακά, τ.ΙΒ'/1976–77 (= The founding of the free town of Tripolis under Kapodistrias).

33. *Loukos, C.*, Μια ελληνική πόλη σε παρακμή: η Ερμούπολη το δεύτερο μισό του 19ου αιώνα, in Νεοελληνική πόλη (1985), Athens, 1985, pp. 591–601 (= A Greek town in decline: Ermoupolis in the second half of the 19th century).

34. *Metallinou, A.*, Η Θεσσαλονίκη επί Τουρκοκρατίας κατά τον 19ον αιώνα, Thessaloniki, 1952 (= Thessaloniki during the Turkish rule in the 19th century).

35. *Moutsopoulos, N.*, Τρίπολις, Το Ρυθμιστικόν σχέδιον. Ιστορική εισαγωγή, τ.Α΄, Thessaloniki, 1974 (= Tripolis. Regulative plan. Historical introduction).

36. *Panayiotopoulos, B.*, Κωνσταντινούπολη-Αθήνα. Από την Οικουμενική πόλη στην Εθνική πρωτεύουσα, in Αθήνα Πρωτεύουσα Πόλη (1985), Athens, 1985, pp. 93–94 (= Constantinople-Athens. From the eucumenical city to national capital).

37. *Paraskevopoulos, G.*, Οι δήμαρχοι των Αθηνών (1835–1907), Athens, 1907 (= The mayors of Athens [1835–1907]).

38. *Romas, D.*, Η πόλη της Ζακύνθου ηριν και μετά την ένωση, in

Χρονικά Ζακύνθου, τ.Α΄, 1964, pp. 153–175 (= The town of Zakynthos before and after the alliance).

39. *Simaiophoridis, G.*, Αθήνα, μια πόλη πρωτεύουσα του 19ου αιώνα, in Νεοκλασσική πόλη (1983), Athens, 1983, pp. 97–109 (= Athens, a capital in the 19th century).

40. *Tataki, A.*, The Capital of Greece, in Ekistics, Vol. 20 (1965), No. 117 pp. 53–82.

(c)   Population and Social Structure

41. *Bafounis, Y.*, Ο σχηματισμός του εργατικού δυναμικού στον Πειραιά, in Νεοελληνική πόλη (1985), τ.Β΄, Athens, 1985, pp. 561–564 (= The development of worker potential in Piraeus).

42. *Bafounis, Y.*, Γάμοι στην Ερμούπολη (1845–1853). Δημογραφικά φαινόμενα μιας μοντέρνας πόλης του 19ου αιώνα, in Μνήμων, τ.9 (1983–1984) (= Marriages in Ermoupolis 1845–1853. Demographic phenomena of a modern town in the 19th century).

43. *Bouerman, A.*, Τρίπολις, η ζωή μιας ελληνικής πόλης, Athens, 1957 (= Tripolis. Life in a Greek town).

44. *Chamoudopoulos, A.*, Οι Ισραηλίται της Θεσσαλονίκης, Athens, 1935 (= The Jews of Thessaloniki).

45. *Demathas, Z.* und *S. Tzilenis*, Πληθυσμός και απασχόληση στην Αθήνα την περίοδο 1950–1981, in Η Αθήνα όπως (δεν) φαίνεται, Athens, 1985, pp. 46–63 (= The development of population and employment in Athens 1950–1981).

46. *Gizeli, B.*, Επικαιρότητα, in Κοινωνικοί μετασχηματισμοί και προέλευση της κοινωνικής κατοικίας στην Ελλάδα (1920–1930), Athens, 1984 (= Social classes and the origin of public housing in Greece).

47. *Gizeli, B.*, Μετασχηματισμοί του περιβάλλοντος και 'κοινωνική δυναμική' στή νεοελληνική πόλη, in Νεοελληνική πόλη (1985), τ.Α΄, Athens, 1985, pp. 119–128 (= Transformation of the surroundings and social dynamics in the modern Greek town).

48. *Kairophyllas, G.*, Η Αθήνα και οι Αθηναίοι, 1834–1934, τ.1ος, 2ος, Athens, 1978, 1982 (= Athens and Athenians).

49. *Kalogirou, N.*, Salonique: Aspects sociogéographiques de l'urbanisation, Diss. Paris, 1978.

50. *Kaloyiannis, B.*, Η ιστορία της ισραηλιτικής κοινότητος Λαρίσσης, Larissa, 1959 (= History of the Jewish community of Larissa).

51. *Karadimas, P.*, Δημογραφία. Πειραιάς, εκδ. Καραμπελόπουλος, Χ.Χ. (= Demography of Piraeus).

52. *Kardassis, V.*, Ερμούπολη: αστικές λειτουργίες και συμπεριφορές, in Νεοελληνική πόλη (1985), τ.Β΄, Athens, 1985, pp. 585–589 (= Ermoupolis: Town functions and urban life).

53. *Kayser, B., P. Pechoux* and *M. Sivignon*, Exode rural et attraction urbaine

en Grèce, Athens, 1971.

54. *Leontidou, L.*, Industrial Restructuring and the Relocation of Manufacturing Employment in Postwar Athens, in Πόλη και Περιφέρεια, τχ. 7/Μάϊος-Αύγ., 1983, pp. 79–109.

55. *Leontidou, L.*, Πολεοδομική οργάνωση και κοινωνικοί μετασχηματισμοί στην Αθήνα 1914–1984, in Η Αθήνα όπως (δεν) φαίνεται. pp. 78–83 (= Urban development and social change in Athens 1914–1984).

56. *Leontidou-Emmanuel, L.*, Working Class and Land Allocation: The Urban History of Athens, 1880–1890, phil. Diss. London, 1981.

57. *Loukas-Phanopoulos, G.*, Θήβα και Λειβαδιά, χωραϊται και χωρικοί το '21, Athens, 1975 (= Thebes and Levadheia, town dwellers and farmers in '21).

58. *Maratou-Aliprandi, L.*, Γυναικεία αποσχόληση και νεοελληνική πόλη στο ά μισό του 20ου αιώνα, in Νεοελληνική πόλη (1985), τ.Β', Athens, 1985, pp. 533–551 (= Female employment and the modern Greek town in the first half of the 20th century).

59. *Mauridou, M.*, Εγκατάσταση στην Αθήνα, σε περιοχή αυθαιρέτων, in Η Αθήνα όπως (δεν) φαίνεται, Athens, 1985, pp. 42–45 (= Immigration into the illegal living areas of Athens).

60. *Moschonas, E.*, Διαδικασίες αφομοίωσης και άπωσης του εσωτερικού μετανάστη, in Αλληλογραφία, 'Οδυσσέας' στο Α. Παπαδιαμάντης, Athens, 1981 (= Internal migration processes).

61. *Panayiotopoulos, B.*, Αγροτική έξοδος και σχηματισμός της εργατικής δύναμης στην ελληνική πόλη, in Νεοελληνική πόλη (1985), τ.Β', Athens, 1985, pp. 521–531 (= Rural exodus and origin of the working class in the Greek town).

62. *Papaioannou, I., G. Papageorgiou* and *D. Simeon*, Growth Indicators for Athens over the Century 1870–1970, in Ekistics, Vol. 30 (1970), No. 176, pp. 3–7.

63. *Philippides, D.*, A Tale of two Suburbs in Athens, in Aarp, Vol. 14 (1979), pp. 46–53.

64. *Polyzos, I.*, Η εγκατάσταση των προσφύγων του 1922: μια οριακή περίπτωση αστικοποίησης, ΕΜΠ, Athens, 1984 (= The settlement of refugees of 1922: a border case of urbanisation).

65. *Riginos, M.*, Ενεργός πληθυσμός και διάρθρωση των οικονομικών δομών, 1909–1936, in Τα Ιστορικά, τχ.2 (Δεκ. 1984), pp. 371–388 (= The employed population and economic structures 1909–1936).

66. *Shapiro, R.*, Mariage et urbanité, in Νεοελληνική πόλη (1985), τ.Β', Athens, 1985, pp. 445–467.

67. *Sideris, N.*, Η αρρώστια ως συμβάν και λόγος στον αστικό χώρο, Η περίπτωση της Λευκάδας (α' μισό 19ου αι.), in Νεοελληνική πόλη (1985), τ.Α', Athens, 1985, pp. 251–254 (= Illness in the urban setting. The case of Levkas in the first half of the 19th century).

68. *Skaltsa, M.*, Κοινωνική ζωή και δημόσιοι χώροι κοινωνικών συναθροίσεων στην Αθήνα του 19ου αι., Thessaloniki, 1983 (= For a social cartography of Athens in the 19th century).

69. *Sorocos, E.*, La morphologie sociale du Pirée à travers son evolution, Athens, 1985.

70. *Stalidis, K.*, Οι συντεχνίες και τα επαγγέλματα στην Εδεσσα την περίοδο της Τουρκοκρατίας, Edessa, 1974 (= The guilds and the professions in Edhessa during the Turkish rule).

71. *Stavropoulos, A.*, Η νοσοκομειακή και νοσηλευτική πολιτική στην Αθήνα τα πρώτα ογδόντα χρόνια της ως πρωτεύουσας, in Αθηνα Πρωτεύουσα Πόλη (1985), Athens, 1985, pp. 128–134 (= Hospitals and public health care in Athens during its first 80 years as a capital).

72. *Tomara-Sideri, M.*, Η διαφοροποίηση του αστικού χώρου στο πεδίο των δημογραφικών συμπεριφορών. Η περίπτωση της Λευκάδας τον 19ο αι., in Νεοελληνική πόλη (1985), τομ.Β΄, Athens, 1985, pp. 483–486 (= Demographic differentiation in the urban setting. The case of Levkas in the 19th century).

73. *Tryphonidis, M.*, Πόλη και κοινωνικοί αγώνες, in Η Αθήνα όπως (δεν) φαίνεται, Athens, 1985, pp. 148–155 (= The town and social conflicts).

(d)   Town Planning, Housing

74. *Angellidis, M.*, Το κέντρο της Αθήνας και οι μετασχηματισμοί του, in Η Αθήνα όπως (δεν) φαίνεται. Athens, 1985, pp. 102–108 (= The centre of Athens and its changes 1950–1978).

75. *Biris, K.*, Τα πρώτα σχέδιο των Αθηνών. Athens, 1933 (= The first plans of Athens).

76. *Biris, M.*, Das athenische Bürger-Haus 1885–1905, phil. Diss. Munich, 1982.

77. *Cholevas, N.*, Εκλεκτικισμός: Μια ,,μεταβατική" μορφολογία στην κατάκτηση της νέας ελληνικής μεσοπολεμικής αρχιτεκτονικής, in Νεοκλασσική Πόλη (1983), Athens, 1983, pp. 304–312 (= Eclecticism: Morphology of the transition to modern Greek architecture).

78. *Chrabanis, P.*, Η αυθαίρετη δόμηση, in Αθήνα 1900–1940 (1985), Athens, 1985, pp. 143–149 (= Illegal settlements).

79. *Dimakopoulos, I.*, Ανθολογία της ελληνικής αρχιτεκτονικής. Η κατοικία στην Ελλάδα από τον 15ο στον 20ο αιώνα. Υπουργείο Πολιτισμού, Athens, 1981 (= Anthology of Greek architecture. Housing in Greece from the 15th to the 20th century).

80. *Dimitriadis, B.*, Τοπογραφία της Θεσσαλονίκης κατά την εποχή της Τουρκοκρατίας, 1430–1912, in Εταιρία Μακεδονικών Σπουδών, Thessaloniki 1983 (= Topography of Thessaloniki during the Turkish rule, 1430–1912).

81. *Dorovinis, B.*, Capodistrias et la planification d' argos, in Bulletin de correspondence hellénique, Supplément VI, 1980.

82. *Dorovinis, B.*, Ο σχεδιασμός του Ναυπλίου κατά την Καποδιστριακή περίοδο (1823–33). Η ειδική περίπτωση και τα γενικότερα προβλήματα, in Νεοελληνική πόλη (1985), τ.Α΄, Athens, 1985, pp. 287–296 (= The planning of Nauplion during the Kapodistrian era [1823–1833]. Special and general problems).

83. *Emmanuel, D.*, The Growth of Speculative Building in Greece: Modes of Housing Production and Socioeconomic Change, 1950–1974, phil. Diss. London, 1981.

84. *Kalafatis, T.*, Επαγγελματικός καταμερισμός και χωροταξικές όψεις στο Αίγιο τον 19ο αιώνα, in Νεοελληνική πόλη (1985), τ.Β΄, Athens, 1985, pp. 469–481 (= Division of labour and spacial aspects in Aiyion in the 19th century).

85. *Kalogirou, N.*, Η ανοικοδόμηση της Θεσσαλονίκης από τον Ernest Hebrard. Μια επέμβαση στον αστικό χώρο και την αρχιτεκτονική της πόλης, in Νεοκλασσική πόλη (1983), Athens 1983, pp. 84–96 (= The reconstruction of Thessaloniki by Ernest Hebrard. An intervention in the space and architecture of the town).

86. *Karadimou-Gerolymbou, A.*, Εκσυγχρονισμός και πολεοδομία στη Θεσσαλονίκη του 19ου αι., in Νεοκλασσική πόλη (1983), Athens, 1983, pp. 54–67 (= Modernisation and urbanisation in Thessaloniki in the 19th century).

87. *Karadimou-Gerolympou, A.*, Θεσσαλονίκη 1917: Συνιστώσες και εμβέλεια μιας πολεοδομικής παρέμβασης, in Πόλη και Περιφέρεια, 8/ Σεπτ.–Δεκ. 1983, pp. 73–95 (= Saloniki 1917: The history of a reconstruction).

88. *Karadimou-Gerolymbou, A.*, Σχεδιασμός και ανάκτηση του χώρου της πόλης. Χαρακτήρας της πολεοδομικής παρέμβασης του κράτους κατά της μετάβαση από την οθωμανική στην Νεοελληνική πόλη, in Νεοελληνική πόλη (1985), τ.Β΄, Athens, 1985, pp. 381–395 (= Planning and reconstitution of the urban area. On the character of state measures during the transition from the Osman to the Modern Greek town).

89. *Kokkou, A.*, Σχέδια αθηναϊκών κτιρίων που δεν εφαρμόστηκαν, in Νεοκλασσική Πόλη (1983), Athens, 1983, pp. 134–144 (= Plans for buildings in Athens which were never realised).

90. *Kokkou, A.*, Η πολεοδομική ανασυγκρότηση στην περίοδο 1828–1843. Κρατική πολιτική και πραγματικότητα, in Νεοελληνική πόλη (1985), τ.Β΄, Athens, 1985, pp. 359–366 (= Urban reconstruction in the period 1828–1843. State policy and reality).

91. *Kolonas, B.*, Αρχιτεκτονικές μορφές και ιδεολογία στη Θεσσαλονίκη του 19ου αιώνα. Ένα παράδειγμα τα κτίρια της ελληνικής κοινότητας, in Νεοελληνική πόλη (1985), τ.Α΄, Athens, 1985, pp.

215–233 (= Architectonic forms and ideology in Thessaloniki in the 19th century. An example for the building of houses in Greek communities).

92. *Lavedan, P.*, L' oeuvre d' Ernest Hebrard en Grèce, in Urbanisme, May 1933.

93. *Lavvas, G.*, Αρχιτεκτονική και πολεοδομία (1830–1981), in Ελλάδα, Ιστορία, Πολιτισμός, τ.9ος, Θεσσαλονίκη, εκδ. Μάλλιαρης, pp. 184–230 (= Architecture and urban construction [1830–1981]).

94. *Lianos, I.*, Ιστορία της συνοικίας Αηλυσίων, ήδη ενορία αγίου Χαραλάμπους, Athens, 1970 (= History of the suburb of Aelysia, now the parish of Agios Charalampos).

95. *Loukatos, S.*, Η ανοικοδόμηση των ερειπωμένων πόλεων στην ελεύθερη Ελλάδα επί Ιω. Καποδίστρια, in Ετος Καποδίστρια, ΥΠΕΠΘ, Εθνικό Τυπογραφείο, Athens, 1978, pp. 79–207 (= The reconstruction of destroyed towns in free Greece under Kapodistrias).

96. *Mantouvalou, M.*, Η οικοδομή στην Αθήνα: οικονομικές και κοινωνικές απόψεις μιας ευκαιριακής ανάπτυξης, in Η Αθήνα όπως (δεν) φαίνεται, Athens, 1985, pp. 36–41 (= Buildings in Athens: Social and economic aspects of speculative growth).

97. *Marmaras, E.*, Η ,,γένεση" και η πρώτη εμπορευματική ανάπτυξη της πολυκατοικίας, in Αθήνα 1900–1940 (1985) Athens, 1985, pp. 124–133 (= Origin and early economic development of apartment blocks).

98. *Matton, L.*, and *R. Matton*, Athènes et ses monuments du XVIIème siècle à nos jours, Athens, 1963 (Institut Français d'Athènes).

99. *Meletopoulos, I.*, Η δημιουργία του Πειραιώς και το πρώτον σχέδιον της πόλεως, Piraeus, 1969 (= The origins of Piraeus and the first plan of the town of Piraika).

100. *Michael, J.*, Entwicklungsüberlegungen und Initiativen zum Stadtplan von Athen nach der Erheburg zur Hauptstadt Griechenlands, Diss. Aachen, 1969.

101. *Papastathi, C.*, Ενα υπόμνημα για την πυρκαγιά της Θεσσαλονίκης στα 1917 και την περίθαλψη των θυμάτων, in Μακεδονικά, ΙΗ´/1978, pp. 143–170 (= A memorandum on the fire of Thessaloniki 1917 and the care of its victims).

102. *Philipides, D.*, Ο αυτόνομος συνοικισμός του Ιλισσού στην Αθήνα, in Οικισμοί στην Ελλάδα, Athens, 1974, pp. 159–171 (= The autonomous municipality of Ilissios in Athens).

103. *Philippides, D.*, Early Suburban Architecture in Athens, Greece, 1840–1920, in Lotus, March 1980.

104. *Photopoulou-Lagopoulou, I.*, Πολεοδομική εξέλιξη του κέντρου της Αθήνας, in Διδακτορική Διατριβή, ΑΠΘ, 1978 (= Urban development in the centre of Athens).

105. *Polyzos, I.*, Η πολεοδομική οργάνωση μετά την πλημμύρα των προσφύγων, in Οικονομικός Ταχυδρόμος, τχ. 922, 1973. (= The urban organisation after the influx of refugees).

106. *Polyzos, G.*, Μεταρρυθμιστικά όνειρα και πολεοδομικές ρυθμίσεις, in Αθήνα 1900–1940 (1985), Athens, 1985, pp. 36–46 (= Ideas on reform and planning measures).

107. *Sariyannis, G.*, Η εξέλιξη της εμπορευματοποίησης της κατοικίας και η επίδρασή της στη μορφή της κατοικίας και της πόλεως, in Αρχιτεκτονικά Θέματα, No. 12 (1978), pp. 108–116 (= Commercialisation of housing. Its impact on the form of housing and the appearance of towns).

108. *Schmidt, H.*, Η ,,Βιλελμίνεια Αθήνα". Το πολεοδομικό σχέδιο του Ludwig Hoffmann για την Αθήνα, in Θέματα χώρου + τεχνών, Η. 11 (1980), pp. 50–56 (= Ludwig Hoffmann's general building plan of Athens).

109. *Skouzes, G., and D. Gerontas*, Το χρονικό της υδρεύσεως των Αθηνών, Athens, 1963 (= Chronicle of Athens' water supply).

110. *Tournikiotis, P.*, Βασιλέως Κωνσταντίνου versus Ιλισός Περί γενεαλογίας της αστικής μορφής, in Η Αθήνα όπως (δεν) φαίνεται., Athens, 1985, pp. 91–97 (= Vassileos Konstantinoy Avenue versus Ilissos in the geneology of urban planning design).

111. *Traylos, J., and A. Kokkou*, Πολεοδομία και αρχιτεκτονική (1833–1881), in Ιστορία του Ελληνικού Εθνους, τ. ΙΓ΄, Αθήνα, Εκδοτική Αθηνών, 1977, pp. 515–528 (= Town planning and architecture 1833–1881).

112. *Tsilalis, C.*, Βενιζέλος, Παπαναστασίου και η χάραξη της νεώτερης Θεσσαλονίκης, in Το Βήμα, 2/11/1975 (= Venizelos, Papanastasiou and the design of more modern Thessaloniki).

113. *Vlachos, G., G. Yiannitzaris and E. Chatzikosta*, Η στέγαση των προσφύγων στην Αθήνα και στον Πειραιά στην περίοδο 1920–1940. Προσφυγικές πολυκατοικίες, in Αρχιτεκτονικά Θέματα No. 12 (1978), pp. 117–125 (= Living conditions of refugees from Asia Minor in Athens and Piraeus 1920 to 1940).

114. *Voivonda, A., et al.*, Ρύθμιση του χώρου στην Ελλάδα. Μια σύντομη ιστορική επισκόπιση, in Αρχιτεκτονικά Θέματα No. 11 (1977), pp. 130–151 (= Town and regional planning in Greece. An historical overview).

(e) Economy and Transport

115. *Agriantoni, C.*, Η θέση της Ερμούπολης στην ελληνική οικονομία τον 19ο αιώνα: οι παγίδες των πηγών, in Ιστορικά, τχ.1, Σεπτ. 1983 (= The position of Ermoupolis in the Greek economy of the 19th century).

116. *Agriantoni, C.*, Οι μετασχηματισμοί της βιομηχανικής δομής της Ερμούπολης τον 19ο αιώνα, in: Πρακτικά του Διεθνούς Συμποσίου Ιστορίας: Νεοελληνική πολη . . ., τ.Β΄, Athens, 1985, pp. 603–608 (= Change in the industrial structure of Ermoupolis in the 20th century).

117. *Angeloudi, S.P.*, Η Καβάλα ως καπνούπολη, in Αρχαιολογία, τχ. 18, φεβρ, 1986, pp. 48–53 (= Kavalla as a tobacco city).

118. *Baxevanis, J.*, The Port of Thessaloniki, Thessaloniki, 1963.

119. *Burgel, G.*, La condition industrielle à Athènes, Vol. I, II, Athens, 1970, 1973.

120. *Hoffman, G.*, Thessaloniki: The Impact of a Changing Hinterland, in East European Quarterly, March 1968, pp. 1–27.

121. *Kalogri, P.* and *B. Tsokopoulos*, Βιομηχανία και πόλεις στην Ελλάδα το δεύτερο ήμισυ του 19ου αιώνα, in Νεοελληνική πόλη (1985), τ.Β΄, Athens, 1985, pp. 431–438 (= Industry and towns in Greece in the second half of the 19th century).

122. *Koumelis, N.*, Recherches sur l'économie de Volos, 1880–1940, Paris, 1984.

123. *Labrianidis, L.*, Κατανομή της καπνοβιομηχανίας και του καπνεμπορίου στον Ελλαδικό χώρο: πορεία αυξανόμενης συγκέντρωσης, in Πόλη και Περιφέρεια, τχ.7/ Μάιος–Αυγ. 1983, pp. 11–40 (= Distribution of tobacco production and trade centres in Greece. A process of increasing spatial concentration).

124. *Tountas, M.*, Πόλη και Βιομηχανία. Η περίπτωση της Ερμούπολης, in Νεοελληνική πόλη (1985), τ.Β΄, Athens, 1985, pp. 609–634 (= Town and industry. The case of Ermoupolis).

125. *Traganou, O.*, Η απαρχή της Βιομηχανικής ανάπτυξης στην Θεσσαλονίκη, in Αρχαιολογία, τχ. 7, 1983, pp. 97–102 (= The beginnings of industrial development in Thessaloniki).

126. *Vakounakis, N.*, Patras et le commerce du raisin sec au XIX siècle, 1828–1904, Paris.

127. *Zarkada-Pistioli, C.*, Εργοστάσια κλωστοϋφαντουργίας στην 'Εδεσσα, in Αρχαιολογία, τχ. 18, φεβρ. 1986, pp. 37–47 (= Textile factories in Edhessa).

128. *Zoumpoulidis, K.*, Ιστορία και εξέλιξις του λιμένος Πειραιώς. Piraeus, 1932 (= The history and development of the port of Piraeus).

(f) *Arts and Sciences, Churches*

129. *Biris, K.*, Αι τοπωνυμίαι της πόλεως και των περιχώρων των Αθηνών, Athens, 1971 (= Names of the city and the suburbs of Athens).

130. *Bousoulas, N.*, Ιστορία της Εκκλησίας των Αθηνών, Athens, 1948 (= History of the Athenian church).

131. *Boutzouvi-Mania, A.*, Το Ναύπλιο στα χρόνια 1828–1833. Σκιαγράφηση της κοινωνικής, πολιτισμικής και πνευματικής ζωής, in Ο Ερανιστής, ΙΗ΄/1982. (= Nauplia in the years 1828–1833. Sketch of the social, cultural and spiritual life).

132. *Chatzipantazis, T.*, Αθηναϊκή Επιθεώρηση, 3τ., in Ερμής, Athens, 1977 (= Athenian review).

133. *Chionidis, G.*, Τά σχολείο της Βεροίας κατά τα έτη 1849–1912, in Ανάτυπο από τα Μακεδονικά, Thessaloniki, 1971 (= The schools of Beroia during the years 1849–1912).

134. *Dimakopoulos, I.*, Ο Ιω. Λαζάριμος και το δημοτικό θέατρο του Πειραιά, in Νεοκλασσική πόλη (1983), pp. 110–127 (= Lazarismos and the town theatre of Piraeus).

135. *Evangelatos, S.*, Η ιστορία του θεάτρου εν Κεφαλληνία (1600–1900), Athens, 1970 (= History of the theatre in Kefallenia [1600–1900]).

136. *Iakovidis, C.*, Δωδώνη, in Νεοελληνική αρχιτεκτονική και αστική ιδεολογία, Athens, 1982 (= Modern Greek architecture and bourgeois ideology).

137. *Kalogirou, N.*, Η ταυτότητα της νεοελληνικής πόλης. Εκσυγχρονισμός και μεταλλάξεις της αστικότητας (1800–1923), in Πόλη και Περιφέρεια, No. 12 (1986), pp. 103–132 (= The identity of the Neohellenist town. Modernisation and change of urban awareness).

138. *Kolonas, B.*, Η αρχιτεκτονική του Art-Deco στη μεσοπολεμική Θεσσαλονίκη, in Νεοκλασσική Πόλη (1983) Athens, 1983, pp. 249–258 (= Art-Deco architecture in Saloniki in the inter-war years).

139. *Kolyba, B.*, Ο αστικός χώρος στα μυθιστορήματα των Γ. Θεοτοκά, Α. Τερζάκη και Κ. Πολίτη, της δεκαετίας 1930–1940, in Νεοελληνική πόλη (1985), τ.Α΄, Athens, 1985, pp. 197–201 (= Urban area in the novels of G. Theotokas, A. Terzakis and K. Politis in the years 1930–1940).

140. *Kremos, P.*, and *G. Simaiogoridis*, Αθήνα. Η πρωτεύουσα, η μητρόπολη. Πολεοδομικοί σχηματισμοί και κουλτούρα της πόλης, in Θέματα χώρου + τεχνών, 12/1981, pp. 68–76 (= Athens. Capital, metropolis, urban change and culture of the city).

141. *Margariti, P.*, Η Αθήνα των λέξεων – ένα πρώτο σχεδίασμα αναπαράστασης της μέσα από την νεοελληνική λογοτεχνία, in Η Αθήνα όπως (δεν) φαίνεται, Athens, 1985, pp. 182–194 (= Athens in Greek literature – an attempt).

142. *Metsolis, G.*, Το θέατρο στην Αθήνα (1836–1967). Συνοπτική ιστορία., in Ανάτυπο από τη Νέα Ελληνική Εγκυκλοπαίδεια, 1969 (= The theatre in Athens, 1836–1967. A short history).

143. *Nehama, J.*, Histoire des Israélites de Salonique, T. VI–VII, Salonique, 1978.

144. *Oreopoulos, P.*, L' histoire de la pensée sur la ville et l' architecture en Grèce du XVème au XIXème siècle, première approche métho-

dologique, Paris, 1983 (Institut Neohellénique Sorbonne).

145. *Protopapa-Bouboulidi, G.*, Το θέατρον εν Ζακύνθω από του ΙΖ΄ μέχρι του ΙΘ΄ αιώνος, Athens, 1958 (= The theatre in Zakinthos from the 17th to the 19th century).

146. *Sariyannis, G.*, Η έννοια της αστικοποίησης μέσα από την λογοτεχνία, in Τεχνικά Χρονικά, Vol. 3 (1978) (= The definition of urbanisation in literature).

147. *Spathis, D.*, Οι πρωτες θεατρικές προσπάθειες στην Αθήνα το 1836 και 1837, in Ο διαφωτισμός και το νεοελληνικό θέατρο, Thessaloniki, 1985 (= The beginnings of modern theatre in Athens 1836 and 1837).

148. *Triantaphyllou, K.*, Ο Τύπος των Πατρών τον ΙΘ΄ αιώνα., in Ανάτυπο από το Λειμωνάριον, 1973 (= The press of Patras).

149. *Tsirimokou, L.*, Γραμματολογία της πόλης. Λογοτεχνία της πόλης/ πόλεις της λογοτεχνίας, in Νεοελληνική πόλη (1985), τ.Α΄, Athens, 1985, pp. 167–196 (= Town grammatology. Literature on the town, towns in literature).

150. *Tsokopoulos, B.*, Τα σταδια της τοπικής συνείδησης. Ο Πειραιάς, 1835–1935, in Νεοελληνική πόλη (1985), τ.Α΄, Athens, 1985, pp. 245–249 (= The stages of local awareness. Piraeus, 1835–1935).

151. *Vakalopoulos, K.*, Χριστιανικές συνοικίες της Θεσσαλονίκης στα μέσα του 19ου αι, in Μακεδονικά, 18, 1978, pp. 103–142 (= The Christian area of Thessaloniki in the middle of the 19th century).

E. Local Studies (a representative selection)

● Aiyion

152. *Stavropoulos, A.*, Ιστορίο της πόλεως του Αιγίου, Patras, 1966 (= History of the town of Aiyion).

● Athens

153. *Biris, K.*, Αθηναϊκαί μελέται, Vol. I–III, Athens, 1938–1940 (= Athenian Studies).

154. *Biris, K.*, Αι Αθήναι από του 19ου εις τον 20ον αι., Athens, 1966 (= Athens from the 19th to the 20th century).

155. *Burgel, G.*, Αθήνα: Η ανάπτυξη μιας μεσογειακής πρωτεύουσας, Μετ. Πέτρος Πυλμόν, Athens, 1978 (= Athens. The development of a capital on the Mediterranean).

156. *Kairophyllas, G.*, Η Αθήνα της Μπελ Επόχ, Athens, 1983 (= Athens in the Belle Epoque).

157. *Lampikis, D.*, Τα εκατό χρόνια του Δήμου Αθηναίων, Athens, 1938

(= One hundred years of the city of Athens).
158. *Lampros, S.*, Ιστορία της πόλεως των Αθηνών, Athens, 1904 (= History of the city of Athens).

● Ermoupolis

159. *Kolodny, E.*, Hermiopolis-Syra. Naissance et évolution d' une ville insulaire grècque, in Méditerranée, No. 2 (1969).
160. *Traylos, J.* and *A. Kokkou,* Ερμούπολη, in εκδ. Εμπορικής Τράπεζας, Athens, 1980 (= Ermoupolis).

● Kavalla

161. *Chionis, K.*, Ιστορία της Καβάλας, Kavalla, 1968 (= History of Kavalla).

● Larisa

162. *Asteriadis, A.*, Λάρισσα, Athens, 1978 (= Larisa).

● Messini

163. *Tserpes, T.*, Ιστορία της πόλεως Μεσσήνης, Kalamata, 1973 (= The history of the town of Messini).

● Patras

164. *Maraslis, A.*, Πάτρα 1900, Patras, 1978 (= Patras around 1900).
165. *Thomopoulos, S.*, Ιστορία της πόλεως Πατρών, 1888 (2nd ed., *K. Triantaphyllou*, Patras, 1950) (= History of the town of Patras).
166. *Triantaphyllou, K.*, Ιστορικόν Λεξικόν των Πατρών, 2nd ed., Patras, 1980 (= Historical Lexicon of Patras).

● Piraeus

167. *Bafounis, Y.*, La formation d'une ville nouvelle, le pirée au XIXème siècle (1835–1879), Diss. Paris, 1985.
168. *Tsokopoulos, B.*, Πειραιάς 1835–1870: Εισαγωγή στην ιστορία του ελληνικού Μαντσεστερ, in Καστανιώτης, Athens, 1984 (= Piraeus 1835–1870: Introduction to the history of the Greek Manchester).

● Serrai

169. *Kaftanzis, G.*, Ιστορία της πόλεως Σερρών και της περιφερείας της,

Vol. I–II, Athens, 1967, 1972 (= History of Serrai and its environs).

170. *Pennas, P.*, Ιστορία των Σερρών από της αλώσεως αυτών υπό των Τούρκων μέχρι της απελευθερωσεως των υπό των Ελλήνων (1383–1913), Athens, 1938, 2nd ed., Athens, 1966 (= History of Serrai and its conquest by the Turks up until its liberation by the Greeks [1383–1913]).

● Thessaloniki

171. *Enepekidis, P.*, Η Θεσσαλονίκη στα χρόνια 1875–1912, Thessaloniki, 1981 (= Thessaloniki in the years 1875–1912).

172. *Letsas, A.*, Ιστορία της Θεσσαλονίκης, I–II, Thessaloniki, 1961–1963 (= History of Thessaloniki).

173. *Papayannopoulos, A.*, Ιστορία της Θεσσαλονίκης, Thessaloniki, 1982 (= History of Thessaloniki).

174. *Moutsopoulos, N.*, Θεσσαλονίκη 1900–1917, in εκδ.Μόλχος, Thessaloniki, 1981 (= Thessaloniki 1900–1917).

175. *Vakalopoulos, A.*, History of Thessaloniki, Thessaloniki, 1972 (Institute of Balkan Studies).

● Tripolis

176. *Tsakopoulos, P.*, Τρίπολη: Πολεοδομική, μορφολογική μελέτη της μετάβασης από την Οθωμανική στη νεοελληνική πόλη, in Νεοελληνική πόλη (1985), τ.Α΄, Athens, 1985, pp. 297–325 (= Tripolis: From the Osman to the Modern Greek town).

SÁNDOR GYIMESI

Hungary

A. Urban History Institutions

Fővárosi Levéltar Budapest (= Archives of the capital, Budapest).

Fővárosi "Szabó Ervin" Könyvtár (= "Szabó Ervin" Library – bibliographic works).

Budapesti Müszake Egyetem, Városépitési Tanzsék (= Technical University, Department of Town Planning, Budapest).

Városépitési Tudományos és Tervező Intézet (= Scientific Planning Institute for town planning).

Magyar Urbanisztikai Társaság (= Hungarian urban society with its focus on architecture – town planning).

A Magyar Tudományos Akadémia Regionális Kutatóintézete (= Institute for Regional Research of the Hungarian Academy of Sciences).

Közep-és Kelet-Európai Akadémiai Kutatási Központ (= Working group for comparative urban history research of the 19th and 20th centuries in the Research Centre for Central and Eastern Europe of the Hungarian Academy of Sciences).

Kossuth Lajos Tudományegyetem Történeti Intézete (= Working group for market area research in the Institute for History and the University Lajos Kossuth in Debrecen).

A Magyar Tudományos Akadémia Várostörténeti Albizottsága és Településtudományi Albizottsága (= Subcommittee of urban history and subcommittee of Settlement Sciences of the Hungarian Academy of Sciences).

B. Aids to Research

(a) Urban History Journals

– Journals with Articles on Urban History

1. *Településtudományi Közlemények*, Budapest, 1952 ff. (= Settlement-

scientific information).

2. *Városépítés*, Budapest, 1964 ff. (= Town planning).
3. *Budapest*, Budapest, 1945–1947, 1966 ff.
4. *Területi Statisztika*, Budapest, 1968 ff. (= Town Statistics). 1951–1956: Statisztikai Értesítő (= Statistic reports); 1957–1967: Megyei és Városi Statisztikai Értesítő (= Statistic comitia and town reports).
5. *Földrajzi Értesítő*, Budapest, 1952 ff. (= Geographical report).
6. *Földrajzi Közlemények*, Budapest, 1863 ff.; New ed. 1951 ff. (= Geographical information).
7. *Századok*, Budapest, 1867 ff. (= Centuries).
8. *Történeti Szemle*, Budapest, 1958 ff. (Historical observer).
9. *Arrabona (Győr)*, 1959.
10. *Soproni Szemle*, 1937–1944, Sopron, 1956 ff. (= Sopron observer).

(b)   Bibliographies

Regular bibliographical reviews of new historical works can be found in the journal "Századok".

11. *Bodor, A.* and *I. Gazda*, Magyarország honismereti irodalma 1527–1944, Budapest, 1984 (= Local historical and geographical literature of Hungary for the period 1527–1944).
12. *Budapest bibliográfiája*, Vol. 1–7, Budapest, 1963–1974 (= Bibliography of Budapest).
13. *Magyar történeti bibliográfia 1828–1867* (ed., Z. Tóth), Vols. 1–4, Budapest, 1828–1867 (= Bibliography of Hungarian history).
14. *A magyar történettudomány válogatott bibliográfiája* 1945–1966, Budapest, 1971 (= Selected bibliography of Hungarian history 1945–1966).

(c)   Handbooks on Urban History

—

(d)   Atlases on Urban History and Urban Development

—

(e)   Urban History Sources

15. *Acsády, I.*, Magyarország népessége a Pragmatica Sanctio korában, Budapest 1986 (= The population of Hungary at the time of the Pragmatic Sanction 1715–1720).

16. *Az elsö magyarországi népszámlálás,* Budapest, 1960 (= Published material on the census at the time of Joseph II 1784–1787).

17. *Budapest Statisztikai Évkönyve,* pub., Budapest Székesfőváros Statisztikai Hivatala, Budapest, 1874 ff. (= Statistical yearbook of Budapest).

18. *Magyar Városok Statisztikai Évkönyve,* 7 vols., Budapest, 1912 (= Annal of Hungarian towns).

19. *Statisztikai Közlemények,* pub., Budapest Székesfőváros Statisztikai, Hivatala, Budapest, 1873 ff. (= Statistical information).

C. Research Reports

(a)   General Surveys

20. A magyar *városépités-történet kutatásának helyzete és problemai,* in Településtudományi Közlemények, Vol. 17 (1965), pp. 5–13 (= State and problems facing Hungarian urban history research).

21. *Vörös, K.,* A magyarországi várostörténet problémái a dualizmus korában, in Történelem, Budapest, 1966, pp. 114–138 (= Problems of Hungarian urban history at the time of Dualism).

(b)   Surveys of Individual Fields of Urban Research

22. *Gransztói, P.,* A magyar városközpontkutatás eddigi munkálatairól, in Településtudományi Közlemények, 15 (1963), pp. 56–70 (= Works to date on urban-centre research).

23. *Hánto, Z.,* and *Z. Kárpáti,* Az agglomeráció kutatás szociológiai módszereiről, in Vonzáskörzetek – Agglomerációk, Budapest, 1982, pp. 139–186 (= Sociological methods of agglomeration research).

24. *Lettrich, E.,* Helyzetkép a szociálgeográfia mai állásáról, in Földrajzi Értesitő, Vol. 21 (1972), pp. 359–366 (= On the current state of social geography).

25. *Wallner, E.,* A hazai településföldrajzi kutatás időszerü kérdéseiről, in Földrajzi Közlemények, Vol. 24 (1976), pp. 45–80 (= Current questions facing settlement-geographic research in Hungary).

D.   Literature on Individual Areas of Urban History Research

(a)   Concept and Definition of Town and Town Types

26. *Bácskai, V.,* and *L. Nagy,* Piackörzetek, piackőzpontok és városok Magyarországon 1828–ban, Budapest, 1984 (= Market areas, market centres and towns in Hungary in the year 1828).

27. *Bácskai, V.*, ed., Bürgertum und bürgerliche Entwicklung in Mittel- und Osteuropa, Budapest, 1986.

28. *Bartke, I.*, and *M. Tomcsányi*, Városaink fejlődése és, in Valóság, Vol. 7 (1964), pp. 47–49 (= Development and structural redesigning of our towns).

29. *Beluszky, P.*, Néhány megjegyzés Horváth Géza hozzászólásához, in Földrajzi Értesitő, Vol. 24 (1975), pp. 489–493 (= Some remarks on the lecture of Géza Horváth. See No. 40).

30. *Beluszky, P.*, A településosztályozás néhány elvi-módszertani szempontjai, in Földrajzi Értesitő, Vol. 22 (1973) (= Some theoretical, methodical aspects on classifying settlements).

31. *Berend T., I.*, Fordulópont és ellentmodáok az urbanizációban, in I. Berend T. and G. Ránki, Gazdaság és Társadalom, Budapest, 1974, pp. 504–521 (= Turning point and contradictions in urbanisation).

32. *Dávid, Z.*, A városi népesség nagysága Magyarországon 1785–ben és 1828–ban, in Történeti Statisztikai Evkönyv, Budapest 1965, pp. 110–127 (= Urban population in Hungary 1785 and 1828).

33. *Erdei, F.*, Magyar Város, Budapest 1939 (reprinted 1974) (= The Hungarian town).

34. *Erdei, F.*, Településpolitika, közigazgatás, urbanizáció, Budapest, 1977 (= Settlement policy, administration, urbanisation).

35. *Fórizs, M.*, and *J. Orlicsek*, Vidéki városaink funkcionális tipusai, in Földrajzi Értesitő, Vol. 20 (1963), pp. 167–196 (= Functional types of rural towns in Hungary).

36. *Gyimesi, S.*, Die Städte Ungarns in der ersten Hälfte des 19. Jahrhunderts, in Österreichische Osthefte, Vol. 20 (1978), pp. 383–392.

37. *Gyimesi, S.*, Városok a feudalizmusból a kapitalizmusba való átmenet időszakában, Budapest, 1975 (= Towns in the period of transition from feudalism to capitalism).

38. *Hajdu, Z.*, Dél-Dunántúl 1925. évi vonzáskörzeti rendszere. Történeti Statisztikai Tanulmányok 5. Budapest, 1984 (= The system of conurbation in the Southern Transdanube in 1925).

39. *Hegedüs, M.*, ed., Gazdasági fejlödés és Urbanizáció, Budapest 1973 (= Economic development and urbanisation).

40. *Horváth, G.*, Hozzászólás Belunszky Pál: A települések osztályozásának elvi-módszertani szempontjai c. tanulmányához, in Földrajzi Értesitő, Vol. 24 (1975), pp. 79–80 (= Contribution to the discussion on the study of P. Beluszky. See No. 30).

41. *Ivancsis, I.*, A kialakuló agglomerációk igazgatási rendszerének problemai, in Vonzáskörzetek – Agglomerációk I, Budapest, 1982, pp. 201–228 (= Problems of administration in developing agglomerations).

42. *Kovácz, T.*, A településhálózat statisztikai vizsgálatának alapjai, in V.

Kulcsár, ed., A regionális elemzés módszerei, Budapest, 1976, pp. 66–84 (= The methods of regional analysis).

43. *Kóródi, J.*, and *G. Köszegfalvi*, Városfejlesztés Magyarországon, Budapest, 1971 (= Town planning in Hungary).

44. *Lettrich, E.*, Urbanizálódás Magyarországón, Budapest, 1965 (= Urbanisation in Hungary).

45. *Lettrich, E.*, Városiasodásunk mai sajátosságai, in Földrajzi Értesitő, Vol. 27 (1978), pp. 54–64 (= Characteristic features of urbanisation in Hungary).

46. *Madárasz, T.*, Városigazgatás és urbanizáció. A városigazgatási tevékenység elmeleti modellje, Budapest, 1971 (= Urban administration and urbanisation. The theoretical model of town administration activity).

47. *Mendöl, T.*, Általános településföldrajz, Budapest, 1963 (= General settlement geography).

48. *Mendöl, T.*, Néhány szempont a hazai településhálózat vizsgálata, településeink osztályozása és elhatárolódása kérdéseiben, in Földrajzi Értesitő, Vol. 16 (1967), pp. 107–118 (= Some aspects on the question of studying the Hungarian settlement network and on the classification and delineation of settlements).

49. *Perényi, I.*, Településtervezés, Budapest, 1963 (= Settlement planning).

50. *Ruzsás, L.*, A városi fejlődés a Dunántulon a XVIII-XIX. században, Budapest, 1963 (Különnyomat a Magyar Tudományos Akadémia Dunántuli Tudományos Intézete, Ertekezések 1961–62 c. kötetből) (= Urban development in Trans-Danube in the 18th and 19th centuries).

51. *Ruzsás, L.*, A városi fejlődés a XVIII-XIX. századi Dél-Magyarországon, Budapest, 1966 (Különnyomat a Magyar Tudományos Akadémia Dunántuli Tudományoyos Intézete Értekezések. 1964–65. c. kötetből) (= Urban development in southern Hungary in the 18th and 19th centuries).

(b) Politics, Law and Statutes

52. *Bácskai, V.*, A pesti Belváros háztulajdonosainak mobilitása 1733–1820, in Történeti Statisztikai Evkönyv, Budapest, 1968, pp. 143–174 (= The mobility of house owners in the Pest inner city 1733–1820).

53. *Baranyai, B.*, Gondolatok az uralkodó elitről, valamint a helyi elit történetéről a debreceni virilizmus kapcsán 1870–1930, in Acta Universitatis Debrecensiensis. Series Historica. Magyar Történeti Tanulmányok V, Vol. 14 (1972), pp. 4–67 (= Some thoughts on the ruling elite and on their history in conjunction with the Debrecen Virilism 1870–1930).

54. *Bónis, G.*, Pest-budai hivatali utasitások a XVIII. században, Budapest, 1974 (= Public institutions of Pest-Buda in the 18th century).

55. *Both, Ö.*, Szeged város büntetőbiraskodása 1848–ban, Szeged 1958 (Acta juridica et politica, Vol. 10) (= The criminal jurisdiction of Szeged in 1848).

56. *Budapest gazdaságának és társadalmának száz éve*, Budapest, 1972 (= 100 years of society and economy in Budapest).

57. *Csizmadia, A.*, Az egyházi mezővarosok jogi helyzete és küzdelmük a felszabadulásért a XVIII. szazadban, Budapest, 1962 (= The parishes and their struggle for liberation in the 18th century).

58. *Gyáni, G.*, Hódmezővásárhely legnagyobb adófizetői 1788–1941, in Történelmi Szemle XX, Vol. 3–4 (1977), pp. 626–640 (= Hódmezővásárhely's highest taxpayers 1788–1941).

59. *Hársfalvi, P.*, Az önkormányzat Nyiregyházán a XVIII.- XIX. században, Budapest, 1982 (= Local government in Nyiregyháza in the 18th and 19th century).

60. *Komoróczy, G.*, Városigazgatás Debrecenben 1848-ig, Debrecen, 1969 (= Local government in Debrecen up to 1848).

61. *Magyar városok*, Budapest, 1966 (= Hungarian towns).

62. *Magyarország megyéi és városai*, Budapest, 1975 (= Comitia and Hungarian towns).

63. *Orosz, I.*, Földesúri támadások a hegyaljai mezővárosok ellen a XVIII. század második felében, in Agrartörténeti Szemle, Vol. 17 (1975), pp. 21–45 (= Manorial offences against the market-towns in the wine district of Tokai in the 18th century).

64. *Szabady, E.*, Társadalmi fejlődés és átrétegződés Budapesten és a vidéki városokban, in Valóság, Vol. 9 (1966), pp. 19–28 (= Social development and restructuring in Budapest and rural towns).

65. *A társadalmi átrétegződés demográfiai hatásai*, Budapest, 1965 (= The demographic effect of the first social restructuring in Budapest and in rural towns).

66. *Tóth, Z.*, A szekszárdi mezővárosi blokk felbomlása a századfordulón, in Agrártörténeti Szemle, Vol. 22 (1980), pp. 349–433 (= The break-up of the Szekszárder agrarian block around the turn of the century).

67. *Vidéki városaink*, Budapest, 1961 (= Hungary's rural towns).

68. *Vörös, K.*, Budapest legnagyobb adófizetői 1873–1917, Budapest, 1979 (= Budapest's highest tax payers 1873–1917).

(d)   Town Planning Development, Housing

69. *Gerő, L.*, Történelmi városrészek, Budapest, 1961 (= Historical town centres).

(e)   Economy and Transport

70. *Benda, K.* and *K. Irinyi*, A 400 éves debreceni nyomda Budapest, 1961 (= The 400-year-old Debrecen printers).

71. *Dóka, K.*, A pesti céhrendszer válságának kibontakozása az 1840–es években, Budapest, 1970 (= The crisis of the guild system in Pest in the 1840s).

72. *Eperjessy, G.*, Mezővárosi és falusi céhek az Alföldön és a Dunántulon, Budapest, 1967 (= The guilds in the market towns and in the country in the Great Lower Hungarian Plain and in the Trans-Danube 1686–1848).

73. *Gyömrei, S.*, A kereskedelmi tőke kialakulása és szerepe Pest-Budán 1848–ig, in Tanulmányok Budapest multjabóból XII., Budapest, 1957, pp. 197–278 (= The formation and the role of trading capital in Pest-Buda up to 1848).

74. *A magyarországi céhes kézmüvesipar forrásanyagának katasztere*, Vol. I–II, Budapest, 1975–1976 (= A catalogue of sources on the history of handicraft guilds in Hungary).

75. *Nagy, I.*, A manufakturaipar kialakulása Pest-Budán, in Tanulmányok Budapest multjából XIV., Budapest, 1961, pp. 285–342 (= The formation of the manufacturing industry in Pest-Buda).

76. *Ránki, G.*, ed., Debrecen iparának története a kapitalizmus kialakulásától napjainkig, Debrecen, 1976 (= A history of Debrecen industry from the time of the development of capitalism up to the present).

77. *Sándor, V.*, A budapesti nagymalomipar kialakulása 1839–1880, in Tanulmányok Budapest multjából XIII, Budapest, 1959, pp. 315–422 (= The formation of Budapest's agrar-industrial centres 1839–1880).

E.   Local Studies (a representative selection)

● Budapest

78. *Budapest Története*, Vol. I–V, Budapest, 1975–1980 (The history of Budapest).

● Debrecen

79. *Debrecen története*, Part 1: up to 1693, Debrecen 1984; Part 2: 1693–1849, Debrecen 1981; Part 4: 1919–1944, Debrecen, 1986 (= The history of Debrecen).

Bibliographies

● Győr

80. *Balász, P.*, Győr a feudalizmus bomlása és a polgári forradalom idején, Budapest, 1978 (= Győr at the time of the decline of feudalism and the bourgeois revolution).

81. *Borbiró, V.* and *I. Valló*, Győr városepitéstörténete, Budapest, 1956 (= The history of town planning in Győr).

● Hajdunánás

82. *Rácz, I.*, ed., Hajdunánás története, Hajdunánás, 1973 (= The history of Hajdunánás).

● Kecskemét

83. *Lettrich, E.*, Kecskemét és tanyavilága, in Földrajzi Tanulmányok IX, Budapest, 1968 (= Kecskemét and its isolated farms).

● Nyiregyháza

84. *Beluszky, P.*, Nyiregyháza vonzáskörzete, Budapest, 1974 (= The catchment area of Nyiregyháza).

● Pécs

85. *Dercsényi, D.* and *F. Pogány*, Pécs, Budapest, 1956.

● Sopron

86. *Csatkai, E.*, Sopron. Magyar Müemlékek, Budapest, 1956 (= Sopron. Hungarian art monuments).

● Szeged

87. *Szeged története*, Part 1: up to 1686, Szeged 1983; Part 2: 1686–1849, Szeged, 1985 (= The history of Szeged).

● Vác

88. *Dercsényi, D.* and *P. Granasztói*, Vác, Budapest, 1960.

LESLIE A. CLARKSON

Ireland

A. Urban History Institutions

B. Aids to Research

(a) Urban History Journals

1. *Irish Economic and Social History*, Dublin, 1974 ff., published annually.
2. *Irish Historical Studies*, Dublin, 1938/1939 ff., published quarterly.
3. *Saothar*, Dublin, 1974 ff., published annually.

(b) Bibliographies

4. *Eager, A. R.*, A Guide to Irish Bibliographical Material, 2nd ed. London, 1980.
5. *Gross, C.*, Bibliography of British Municipal History, London, 1897.
6. *Hayes, R. J.*, ed., Manuscript Sources for the History of Irish Civilisation, 11 vols., Boston, Mass., 1966.
7. *Lee, J. J.*, ed., Irish Historiography 1970–79, Cork, 1981.
8. *Martin, G. H.*, and *S. C. McIntyre*, Bibliography of British and Irish Municipal History, Vol. 1: General Works, Leicester, 1972.
9. *Moody, T. W.*, ed., Irish Historiography 1936–70, Dublin, 1936.
10. *Shannon, M. O.*, Modern Ireland. A Bibliography on Politics, Planning, Research and Development, London, 1981.
11. *Writings on Irish History*, Dublin, 1979 (The Irish Committee of Historical Sciences) (Microfiche).

(c) Handbooks on Urban History

—

(d)   Atlases on Urban History and Urban Development

12. *Atlas of Ireland*, Dublin, 1979 (The Irish National Committee for Geography / Royal Irish Academy); of these particularly Map 43: Towns: Origins of Principal Towns; Map 44: Urban Morphology; Map 49: Population Change 1926–1966; Map 50: Population Change 1966–1971; Map 51: Urban and Rural Population Change 1966–1971; Map 54: Towns: Population Change 1961–1971.

13. *Hamilton, G.*, Northern Ireland Town Plans. 1828–1966: A Catalogue of Large Scale Town Plans, 2nd ed. Belfast, 1981 (P.R.O.N.I.).

14. *Irish Historic Town Atlases*. Royal Irish Academy.
   – No. 1: Kildare, ed., K. H. Andrews, Dublin, 1985.
   – No. 2: Carrickfergus, ed., P. Robinson, Dublin, 1986.

(e)   Urban History Sources

15. *Gilbert, J.*, ed., Calendar of the Ancient Records of the City of Dublin, 19 vols. Dublin, 1899–1944.

16. *Lewis, S.*, A Topographical Dictionary of Ireland, 2 vols., London, 1837.

17. *Municipal Corporations.* Commissioners on Municipal Corporations in Ireland, 3 vols. and extra vol., London, 1835–1836 (British Parliamentary Papers, Vols. 27, 28 (1835) and Vol. 29 (1836)).

18. *Report of Commission on Fairs and Markets.* British Parliamentary Papers, 1952–1953, Vol. 41, 1854–1855, Vol. 19.

19. *Vaughan, W. E.*, and *A. J. Fitzpatrick*, eds., Irish Historical Statistics: Population, Dublin 1978 (Royal Irish Academy); of these, particularly Table 9: Population of Towns as a Percentage of the Total Population 1841–1971; Table 10: Population of Towns 1813–1911; Table 11: Population of Towns in the Republic of Ireland 1926–1971; Table 12: Population of Towns in Northern Ireland 1926–1971.

20. *Young, R. M.*, ed., The Town Book of the Corporation of Belfast 1613–1816, Belfast, 1892.

C.   Research Reports

(a)   General Surveys

21. *Butlin, R. A.*, The Urban History of Ireland: An Introduction Survey, in Urban History Newsletter, No. 6 (1966), pp. 4–6.

22. *Camblin, G.*, The Town in Ulster, Belfast, 1951.

23. *Cullen, L. M.*, Townlife (Insights into Irish History), Dublin, 1973.

24. *Cullen, L. M.*, Irish Towns and Villages, Dublin, 1979.

25. *Duncan, G. A.*, The Decline of the Country Town, in Journal of the Statistical and Social Inquiry Society of Ireland, 1931/32, pp. 21–33.

26. *Freeman, T. W.*, Irish Towns in the Eighteenth and Nineteenth Centuries, in R. A. Bultin, ed., The Development of the Irish Town, London, 1977.

27. *Freeman, T. W.*, Pre-Famine Ireland: A Study in Historical Geography, Manchester, 1957.

28. *Gannon, P.*, The Country Towns of Ireland and their Future, Dublin, 1929.

29. *Green, E. R. R.*, Some Agenda for Irish Urban History, in Urban History Newsletter, No. 9 (1967), p. 7.

30. *Harkness, D.*, and *M. O'Dowd*, eds., The Town in Ireland, Belfast, 1981 (Historical Studies, Vol. XIII).

31. *Horner, A. A.*, Stability and Change in the Towns and Villages West of Dublin, in Irish Economic and Social History, Vol. III, 1976, pp. 78–80.

32. *Shaffery, P.*, The Irish Town: An Approach to Survival, Dublin, 1975.

(b)   Surveys of Individual Fields of Urban Research

33. *National Heritage Inventory.* Architectural Heritage Series. An Foras Forbartha, Dublin (in preparation).

34. *Ulster Architectural Heritage Society*, Historic Buildings, Groups of Buildings, Areas of Architectural Importance, Belfast (in preparation).

D.   Literature on Individual Areas of Urban History Research

(a)   Concept and Definition of Town and Town Types

35. *Crawford, W. H.*, The Evolution of Ulster Towns, in P. Roebuck, ed., Plantation to Partition: Essays in Ulster History in Honour of J. L. McCracken, Belfast, 1981, pp. 140–156.

36. *Hughes, T. J.*, Village and Town in Mid-19th Century Ireland, in Irish Geography, Vol. XIV (1981), pp. 99–106.

(b) Politics, Law and Statutes

37. *Bew, P.*, Politics and the Rise of the Working Man, in J. C. Beckett *et al.*, Belfast: The Making of the City, Belfast, 1983, pp. 143–152.

38. *Hill, J.*, The Politics of Privilege: Dublin Corporation and the Catholic Question. 1792–1823, in Maynooth Review, Vol. VII (1982), pp. 17–36.

39. *Hill, J.*, Religion, Trade and Politics in Dublin, 1798–1848, in P. Butel and L. M. Cullen, eds., Cities and Merchants: French and Irish

Perspectives on Urban Development, 1500–1900, Dublin, 1986, pp. 247–259.

40. *Instructions (. . .) on (. . .) Boundaries of Cities, Boroughs and Towns*, London, 1837 (British Parliamentary Papers, Vol. 29).

41. *Jupp, P.*, Urban Politics in Ireland. 1801–1831, in D. Harkness and M. O'Dowd, eds., The Town in Ireland, Belfast, 1981, pp. 103–124 (Historical Studies, Vol. XIII).

42. *O'Leary, C.*, Belfast Urban Government in the Age of Reform, in D. Harkness and M. O'Dowd, eds., The Town in Ireland, Belfast, 1981, pp. 187–202 (Historical Studies, Vol. XIII).

43. *Lucas, B. K.*, Municipal Corporations, in ibid., Aspects of Government, Dublin, 1978.

44. *Partridge, P.*, Crime in the Dublin Metropolitan Police District. 1894–1914, in Retrospect, New edition, Vol. II (1982), pp. 36–43.

45. *Report of Select Committee on Local Government and Taxation of Towns*, London, 1878 (British Parliamentary Papers, Vol. 16).

46. *Walker, B. M.*, ed., Parliamentary Election Results in Ireland. 1801–1922, Dublin, 1978 (Royal Irish Academy).

47. *Webb, J. J.*, Municipal Government in Ireland, Dublin, 1918.

(c)   Population and Social Structure

48. *Clarkson, L. A.*, The Demography of Carrick-on-Suir, in Proceedings of the Royal Irish Academy, Section C Vol. 87, No. 3 (1987), pp. 13–36.

49. *Clarkson, L. A.*, Population Change and Urbanisation 1821–1911, in L. Kennedy and P. Ollerenshaw, eds., An Economic History of Ulster 1820–1940, Manchester, 1985, pp. 137–157.

50. *Curtin, D., et al.*, Population Growth and other Statistics of Middle-sized Irish Towns, Dublin, 1976 (The Economic and Social Research Institute, Paper No. 85).

51. *Daly, M. E.*, The Social Structure of the Dublin Working Class, 1871–1911, in Irish Historical Studies, Vol. XXIII (1982), No. 90, pp. 121–133.

52. *Froggatt, P.*, Industrialisation and Health in Belfast in the Early Nineteenth Century, in D. Harkness and M. O'Dowd, eds., The Town in Ireland, Belfast, 1981, pp. 155–186 (Historical Studies, Vol. XIII).

53. *Gribbon, S.*, Edwardian Belfast: A Social Profile, Belfast, 1982.

54. *Heatley, F.*, Community Relations and the Religious Geography, in J. C. Beckett *et al.*, Belfast: The Making of the City, Belfast, 1983, pp. 129–142.

55. *Hepburn, A. C.*, Employment and Religion in Belfast 1901–1971, Belfast, 1982 (Fair Employment Agency for Northern Ireland).

56. *Hepburn, A. C.*, Industrial Society: The Structure of Belfast. 1901, in P. Roebuck, ed., Plantation to Partition: Essays in Ulster History in

Honour of J. L. McCracken, Belfast, 1981.

57. *Hepburn, A. C.*, Work Class and Religion in Belfast. 1871–1911, in Irish Economic and Social History, Vol. X (1983), pp. 33–50.

58. *Horner, A. A.*, Potential Hinterland Populations and their Regional Variations in Ireland in 1971, in Proceedings of the Royal Irish Academy, Section C, Vol. 82 (1982), No. 2.

59. *Hourihan, K.*, Urban Population Density Patterns and Change in Ireland. 1901–1979, in Economic and Social Review, Vol. XIII (1982), No. 2, pp. 125–147.

60. *Morgan, V.*, A Case Study of Population Changes over Two Centuries: Blaris, Lisburn 1661–1848, in Irish Economic and Social History, Vol. III (1976), pp. 5–16.

(d)   Town Planning, Housing

61. *Cleary, P. C.*, Spatial Expansion and Urban Ecological Change in Belfast 1861–1917, in Irish Economic and Social History, Vol. VIII (1981), pp. 107–109.

62. *Dickson, D.*, Large-scale Developers and the Growth of Eighteenth-Century Irish Cities, in P. Butel and L. M. Cullen, eds., Cities and Merchants: French and Irish Perspectives on Urban Development, 1500–1900, Dublin, 1986, pp. 109–123.

63. *Maguire, W. A.*, Lord Donegall and the Sale of Belfast: A Case Study from the Encumbered Estates Court, in Economic History Review, 2nd Series, Vol. XXIX (1976), pp. 570–584.

64. *Maguire, W. A.*, Lords and Landlords – the Donegall Family, in J. C. Beckett *et al.*, Belfast: The Making of the City, Belfast, 1983, p. 240.

65. *McParland, E.*, Strategy in the Planning of Dublin, 1750–1800, in P. Butel and L. M. Cullen, eds., Cities and Merchants: French and Irish Perspectives on Urban Development, 1500–1900, Dublin, 1986, pp. 97–108.

66. *Reports on Sanitary Conditions of Individual Towns*, London, 1902 (British Parliamentary Papers, Vol. 37).

67. *Roebuck, P.*, The Donegall Family and the Development of Belfast, 1600–1850, in P. Butel and L. M. Cullen, eds., Cities and Merchants: French and Irish Perspectives on Urban Development, 1500–1900, Dublin, 1986, pp. 125–138.

(e)   Economy and Transport

68. *Boyle, E.*, "Linenopolis": The Rise of the Textile Industry, in J. C. Beckett *et al.*, Belfast: The Making of the City, Belfast, 1983, pp. 41–56.

69. *Clarkson, L. A.*, The City and the Country, in J. C. Beckett *et al.*, Belfast: The Making of the City, Belfast, 1983, pp. 153–166.

70. *Clarkson, L. A.*, and *B. Collins*, Proto-Industrialization in a Northern Irish Town: Lisburn 1820–1821, in Proceedings of International Economic History Conference, A Theme on Proto-Industrialization, Budapest, 1982, pp. 1–20 (Report No. 8).

71. *Cullen, L. M.*, Princes and Pirates: The Dublin Chamber of Commerce 1783–1983, Dublin, 1983.

72. *Daly, M.*, Dublin in the Nineteenth Century, in P. Butel and L. M. Cullen, eds., Cities and Merchants: French and Irish Perspectives on Urban Development, 1500–1900, Dublin, 1986, pp. 53–66.

73. *Davies, A. C.*, Roofing Belfast and Dublin 1896–8: American Penetration of the Irish Market for Welsh Slate, in Irish Economic and Social History, Vol. IV (1977), pp. 26–35.

74. *Maybin, J. M.*, Belfast Corporation Tramways. 1905–1954, Broxbourne, 1981.

75. *Murphy, M.*, The Economic and Social Structure of Nineteenth Century Cork, in D. Harkness and M. O'Dowd, eds., The Town in Ireland, Belfast 1981, pp. 125–154 (Historical Studies, Vol. XIII).

76. *Sweetnam, R.*, The Development of the Port, in J. C. Beckett *et al.*, Belfast: The Making of the City, Belfast, 1983, pp. 57–70.

(f) Arts and Sciences, Churches

77. *Adams, J. R. R.*, Popular Art in Belfast. 1824–1836, in Ulster Folklife, Vol. XXXIX (1983), pp. 43–54.

78. *Black, E.*, Of Arts and Artists, in J. C. Beckett, Belfast: The Making of the City, Belfast, 1983, pp. 83–98.

79. *Brooke, P.*, Religion and Secular Thought 1850–75, in J. C. Beckett *et al.*, Belfast: The Making of the City, Belfast, 1983, pp. 111–128.

80. *Butler, H.*, The Kilkenny Theatre 1801–1819, in Journal of the Butler Society, Vol. II (1981), No. 1, pp. 37–44.

81. *Davies, A. C.*, The First Irish Industrial Exhibition: Cork 1852, in Irish Economic and Social History, Vol. II (1975), pp. 46–59.

82. *Davies, A. C.*, Ireland's Crystal Palace 1853, in J. M. Goldstrom and L. A. Clarkson, eds., Irish Population, Economy and Society: Essays in Honour of the Late K. H. Connell, Oxford, 1981.

83. *Flannery, J. W.*, High Ideals and the Reality of the Market Place: A Financial Record of the Early Abbey Theatre (Dublin), in Studies, Vol. LXXI (1982), No. 283, pp. 246–269.

84. *Gray, J.*, Popular Entertainment, in J. C. Beckett *et al.*, Belfast: The Making of the City, Belfast, 1983, pp. 99–110.

85. *Hewitt, J.*, "The Northern Athens" and After, in J. C. Beckett *et al.*, Belfast: The Making of the City, Belfast, 1983, pp. 71–82.

86. *Meenan, J.*, and *D. Clarke*, eds., The Royal Dublin Society. 1731–1981, Dublin, 1981.

87. *Nesbitt, N.*, A Museum in Belfast: A History of the Ulster Museum and its Predecessors, Belfast, 1979.

E. Local Studies (a representative selection)

● Belfast

88. *Bardon, J.*, Belfast: An Illustrated History, Belfast, 1982.
89. *Beckett, J. C.*, and *R. E. Glasscock*, eds., Belfast: The Origin and Growth of an Industrial City, London, 1967.
90. *Beckett, J. C., et al.*, Belfast: The Making of the City, Belfast, 1983.
91. *Butt, J.*, Belfast and Glasgow: Connections and Comparisons. 1790–1850, in T. T. Devine and D. Dickson, eds., Ireland and Scotland. 1600–1850: Parallels and Contrasts in Economic and Social Development, Edinburgh, 1983.
92. *Collins, B.*, The Edwardian City, in J. C. Beckett *et al.*, Belfast: The Making of the City, Belfast, 1983, pp. 167–182.
93. *Gribbon, S.*, An Irish City: Belfast, in D. Harkness and M. O'Dowd, eds., The Town in Ireland, Belfast, 1981, pp. 203–220 (Historical Studies, Vol. XIII).
94. *Public Record Office of Northern Ireland*, Problems of a Growing City: Belfast 1780–1870, Belfast, 1973.
95. *Walker, B. M.*, and *H. Dixon*, No Mean City. Belfast 1880–1914, Belfast, 1983.

● Carrick-on-Suir

96. *Power, P. C.*, Carrick-on-Suir and its People, Dun Laoghaire, 1981.

● Cork

97. *Coughlan, C.*, Old Cork: Historical, Theatrical, Commercial, Cork, 1975.
98. *Fahy, A.*, Residence Workplace and Patterns of Change. Cork 1787–1863, in P. Butel and L. M. Cullen, eds., Cities and Merchants: French and Irish Perspectives on Urban Development, 1500–1900, Dublin, 1986, pp. 41–52.
99. *O'Brien, J.*, Merchants in Cork before the Famine, in P. Butel and L. M. Cullen, eds., Cities and Merchants: French and Irish Perspectives on Urban Development, 1500–1900, Dublin, 1986, pp. 221–232.

- Dublin

100. *Daly, M. E.*, Late Nineteenth and Early Twentieth Century Dublin, in D. Harkness and M. O'Dowd, eds., The Town in Ireland, Belfast, 1981, pp. 221–252 (Historical Studies, Vol. XIII).
101. *Daly, M. E.*, Dublin – The Deposed Capital: A Social and Economic History 1860–1914, Cork, 1984.
102. *O'Brien, J. V.*, Dear Dirty Dublin: A City in Distress 1899–1916, Berkeley, Cal., 1982.

- Londonderry

103. *Murphy, D.*, Derry, Donegal and Modern Ulster 1790–1921, Londonderry, 1981.

ALBERTO CARACCIOLO

Italy

A. Urban History Institutions

Italy has no institutions solely devoted to urban history research. The various bodies of the national association for historical research ("Giunta centrale per gli studi storici") follow a period approach, not a thematic one. Modest activity in the field of Middle Ages urban history research, in particular, was forthcoming for some time from the Italian section of the International Commission for Urban History. However, there is no evidence of any current work.

In contrast to this, recent years have witnessed the development of focal aspects of urban history at universities, partly due to the establishment of full professorships. These have been allocated to different faculties: architecture, philosophy, social sciences. The University of Perugia, in conjunction with other universities, has been conducting a doctorate colloquium ("corso di dottorato") on urban and rural history ("storia urbana e rurale") since 1983/84. The Universities of Florence, Turin and Venice are preparing comparable doctorate courses on the history of architecture and urbanism ("storia dell'architettura e urbanistica").

B. Aids to Research

(a) Urban History Journals

1. *Storia della città*, Milan, 1976 ff., ed. E. Guidoni; published quarterly (= Urban history).
2. *Storia Urbana*, Milan, 1977 ff., ed. C. Carozzi *et al.*, published biannually (= Urban history).
3. *Storia dell'architettura*, 1974 ff., ed. P. Portoghesi *et al.*; three issues per year (= History of architecture).
4. *Storia dell'urbanistica*, Milan, 1981–1982, ed. E. Guidoni (= History of

town planning).

5. *Erodote/Herodote*, Paris, 1979 ff., ed. M. Quaini; three issues per year (= Herodot).

6. *Archeologia industriale*, 1983 ff., ed. F. Battisti *et al.*, three issues per year (= Industrial archeology).

7. *Quaderni* pub. by Centro per la storie delle cerchia urbane (CISCU), Lucca (A series of issues related to urban history).

(b)   Bibliographies

8. *La storiografia urbanistica*, pub. by Centro per la storie delle cerchia urbane, Lucca, 1976 (= Writing urban history).
Bibliographic summaries are included in the following books:

9. *Bortolotti, L.*, Storia città e territorio, Milan, 1979 (= Urban and territorial history).

10. *Caracciolo, A.*, La città moderna e contemporana, Naples, 1982 (= The modern and present-day city).

11. *Gambi, L.*, L'evoluzione storica della città italiane, in SIDES. La demografia storica della città italiane, Bologna, 1982, pp. 42–44 (= The historical development of the Italian town).

12. *Pierotti, P.*, Introduzione all'eccostoria, Milan, 1982 (= Introduction to economic history).

13. *Senn, L.*, La crisi della città, in Vita e pensiero, 1973, pp. 83–90 (= The urban crisis).

14. *Storia Urbana*, 1977 and 1979.

(c)   Handbooks on Urban History

15. *Mioni, A.*, and *C. Carozzi*, L'Italia in formazione, 2nd ed., Bari, 1980 (= Italy undergoing development).

16. *Petraccone, C.*, Le città italiane del 1860 ad oggi, Turin, 1979 (= Italian towns from 1860 to the present day).

(d)   Atlases on Urban History and Urban Development

17. *Morini, M.*, Atlante di storia dell'urbanistica, 2nd ed., Milan, 1979 (= Atlas on urban history).

18. *Storia d'Italia Einaudi*, Vol. 9: Atlas, Turin, 1979 (= History of Italy).

(e)   Urban History Sources

—

C. Research Reports

(a) General Surveys

19. *Benevolo, L.*, Storia della città, 3rd ed., Bari, 1982 (= Urban history).
20. *Caracciolo, A.*, ed., Dalla città tradizionale alla città del capitalismo, 2nd ed., Bologna, 1980 (= From the traditional to the capitalist city).
21. *Gambi, L.*, Capire l'Italia. Le città, Milan, 1978 (= Understanding Italy).
22. *Giuntella, V. E.*, La città dell'illuminismo, Rome, 1982 (= The town during the Age of Enlightenment).
23. *Olmo, C.*, La città industriale, Turin, 1950 (= The town in the industrial age).
24. *Portoghesi, P.*, La città barocca, 2nd ed., Bari, 1982 (= The Baroque town).
25. *Sica, P.*, Storia dell'urbanistica. Il Settecento. L'ottocento. Il Novecento, 2nd edition, Bari, 1980 (= Urban history, 18th century. 19th century. 20th century).
26. *Simoncini, G.*, Città e società nel Rinascimento, 2 vols., Turin, 1976 (= Town and society during the Renaissance).
27. *Violante, G.*, ed., La storia locale. Temi, fonti e metodi per la ricerca, Bologna, 1983 (= Local history. Subjects, sources and methods).

(b) Surveys of Individual Fields of Urban Research

28. *Aquarone, A.*, Grandi città e aree metropolitane in Italia, Bologna, 1970 (= Big cities and conurbations in Italy).
29. *Guidoni, E.*, and *A. Marino*, Storia dell'urbanistica. Il XVI secolo. Il XVII secolo, 2 vols., 2nd ed., Bari, 1980 (= The history of town planning. 17th century. 18th century).
30. *Insolera, I.*, L'urbanistica, in Storia d'Italia Einaudi, Vol. 5, Turin, 1973 (= Town planning).
31. *Mainardi, R.*, ed., Le grandi città italiane: saggi geografici e urbanistici, Milan, 1971 (= The large Italian cities: geographical and town planning essays).
32. *Pavia, R.*, L'idea di città: XV–XVIII secolo, Milan, 1982 (= The idea of the town: 16th to 19th centuries).
33. *Pizzorno, A.*, Sviluppo economico e urbanizzazione, in Quaderni di sociologia, 1962, No. 1 (= Economic development and urbanisation).
34. *Tafuri, M.*, L'architettura dell'umanesimo, 2 vols., Turin, 1964 (= The Architecture of Humanism).

D. Literature on Individual Areas of Urban History Research

(a) Concept and Definition of Town and Town Types

35. *Assunto, R.*, La città di Anfione e la città di prometeo, Milan, 1984 (= The city of Anfione and the promised city).

36. *Aymonino, C.*, Origini e sviluppo della città moderna, Padua, 1971 (= Origin and development of the modern city).

37. *Belli, A.*, La città come sistema, Naples, 1972 (= The city as a system).

38. *Benevolo, L.*, La città e l'architetto, 3rd ed., Bari, 1984 (= The city and architecture).

39. *Cacciari, M.*, ed., Metropolis: saggi sulla grande città, Rome 1973 (= Metropolis: attempts at a large city).

40. *Caracciolo, A.*, Città come modernità, città come male, in Quaderni Storici, No. 47 (1981) (= Town as progress, town as evil).

41. *Castelnovi, P.*, La città: istruzioni per l'uso, Turin, 1980 (= The town: instructions for use).

42. *Cattaneo, C.*, La città considerata come principio ideale delle istorie italiane, n.p. 1858 (reprinted in Opere scelte, Vol. V, Scritti 1852–1864, Turin 1972) (= The town as a motif of Italian history).

43. *Insolera, I. et al.*, La città e la crisi del capitalismo, Bari, 1978 (= The town and the crisis of capitalism).

44. *Samonà, G.*, L'urbanistica e l'avvenire della città, Bari, 1950 and 5th ed., Bari, 1980 (= Town planning and the future of the town).

45. *Sica, P.*, L'immagine della città da Sparta a Las Vegas, Bari, 1975 (= The image of the town from Sparta to Las Vegas).

46. *Tafuri, M.*, Progetto e utopia. Architettura e sviluppo capitalistico, 3rd ed., Bari, 1977 (= Plan and Utopia. Architecture and the development of capitalism).

(b) Politics, Law and Statutes

47. *Calandra, P.*, Storia dell'amministrazione publica in Italia, Bologna, 1978 (= The history of public administration in Italy).

48. *Cassese, S.*, L'amministrazione dello Stato in Italia, Milan, 1976 (= State administration in Italy).

49. *Compagna, F.*, La politica della città, Bari, 1977 (= The political system of the town).

50. *De Cesare, G.*, L'ordinamento proviniciale e communale in Italia 1861–1942, Milan, 1977 (= Provincial and communal administration in Italy 1861–1942).

51. *Falco, L.*, Storia dello sviluppo industriale e della legislazione urbanistica 1861–1977, Turin, 1978 (= The history of industrial development

and urban legislation 1861–1977).
52. *Rossi, P.*, ed., La città come instituzione politica, Milan, 1985 (= The town as a political institution).
53. *Rotelli, E.*, Costituzione e amministrazione dell'Italia unita, Bologna, 1981 (= Constitution and administration of United Italia).
54. *La storiografia amministrativa italiana contemporanea*, in Archivio Isap, Milan, 1985 (= The history of present-day Italian administration).

● Rome

55. *Amministrazione provinciale di Roma*. Studi in occasione del centenario, 2nd ed., Rome, 1971 (= Roman provincial administration. Studies on the occasion of its 100th anniversary).
56. *Caracciolo, A.*, Roma capitale dal Risorgimento alla crisi liberale, 3rd ed., Rome, 1984 (= Rome as the capital of Risorgimento. From the time of national unity up to the Liberal era).
57. *Istituto Gramsci*, ed., Le città capitali in Europa, Rome, 1985 (= The capitals of Europe).
58. *Roma capitale*. Documenti, 2nd ed., Rome, 1971 (= Capital city, Rome. Documents).

(c)   Population and Social Structure

59. *Assante, F., et al.*, La popolazione del Mezzogiorno d'Italia, Naples, 1975 (= The population of Mezzogiorno).
60. *Bellettini, A.*, La popolazione italiana d'all inizio dell'era volgare ai nostri giorni, in Storia d'Italia Einaudi, Turin, 1973 (= The population of Italy from the Middle Ages to the present day).
61. *Beltrami, D.*, Storia della popolazione di Venezia dal secolo XVI alla caduta della Repubblica, Padua, 1954 (= The demographic history of Venice from the 16th century to the downfall of the Republic).
62. *Del Panta, L.*, Una traccia di storia demografica della Toscana nei secoli XVI–XVIII, Florence 1974 (= Draft of the demographic history of Tuscany from the 17th to 19th century).
63. *Petraccone, C.*, Napoli dal '500 all '800. Problemi di storia demografica e sociale, Naples, 1974 (= Naples from the 16th to 19th century. Problems of a demographic and social history).
64. *Pizzorno, A.*, Comunità e razionalizzazione: Rescaldina, Turin, 1960 (= Community and rationalisation: Rescaldina).
65. *SIDES*, La demografia storica delle città italiane, Bologna, 1981 (= Demographic history of Italian towns).
66. *Sori, E.*, ed., Città e controllo sociale in Italia fra XVIII e XIX secolo, Milan, 1982 (= Town and social control in Italy in the 19th and 20th centuries).

67. *Ugolini, P.*, Un paese della campagna romana: Formello, Rome, 1957 (= A village in the countryside: Formello).

(d)   Town Planning, Housing

Books and articles related to *town and regional planning* are included under this heading.

68. *AISS*, Città e campagna, 2nd ed., Milan, 1959 (= Town and country).
69. *Archibugi, F.*, Città e regione in Italie, Rome, 1967 (= Towns and regions in Italy).
70. *Aymonino, C.*, La città territorio, Bari, 1964 (= Town and urban area).
71. *Carozzi, C.*, and *R. Rozzi*, Suolo urbano e popolazione: l'urbanizzazione nelle città nord-orientali 1881–1971, Milan, 1982 (= Urban area and population: urbanisation in the north-east Italian towns 1881–1971).
72. *Cederna, A.*, Mussolini urbanista, Bari 1979 (= Mussolini as town planner).
73. *Compagna, F.*, La politica della città, Bari, 1967 (= Town politics).
74. *Ferrarotti, F.*, Roma da capitale a periferia, Rome, 1970 (= Rome between centre and periphery).
75. *Mariani, R.*, Fascismo e "città nuove", Milan, 1976 (= Fascism and "new towns").
76. *Nuti, L.*, and *R. Martinelli*, Le città di strapaese: la politica di "fondazione" nel ventennio, Milan, 1982 (= The flogged towns: the politics of "foundation" in the 1920s).
77. *Tintori, S.*, Piano e pianificatori dall'età napoleonica al fascismo nella città italiana contemporanea, Milan, 1985 (= Planning and planners of the modern Italian town from the time of Napoleon up to Fascism).

(e)   Economy and Transport

78. *Bonelli, F.*, Evoluzione demografica e ambiente nelle Marche e nell'Umbria, Turin, 1967 (= Demographic and spatial development in Marches and Umbria).
79. *Felloni, G.*, Popolazione e sviluppo economico della Liguria nel sec. XIX, Turin, 1961 (= Population and economic development in Liguria in the 20th century).
80. *Fuà, G.*, ed., Lo sviluppo economico italiano, 3rd ed., Milan, 1970 (= The economic development of Italy).
81. *Treves, A.*, Le migrazioni interne nell'Italia fascista, Turin, 1980 (= Internal migration in fascist Italy).
82. *Vitali, O.*, L'evoluzione rurale-urbana in Italia, Milan, 1983 (= Rural and urban development in Italy).

(f)   Arts and Sciences, Churches

83. *Guidicini, P.*, Sviluppo urbano e immagine della città, Milan, 1971 (= Urban development and the picture of the town).
84. *Lugli, P.*, Storia e cultura della città italiana, Bari, 1967 (= History and culture of the Italian town).
85. *Argan, G. C.*, and *M. Fagiolo*, Premessa all'arte italiana: storia della città, storia dell'arte, in Storia d'Italia Einaudi, Vol. 1, Turin, 1972 (= Prerequisites of Italian art: History, urban history and art history).
86. *Previtali, G.*, and *F. Zeri*, Storia dell'arte italiana Einaudi, Vol. 1: Materiali e problemi; Vol. 3: Inchieste sui centri minori, Turin, 1979 and 1980 (= Italian art history, Vol. 1: Material and problems; Vol. 3: Studies on minor centres).

E.   Local Studies (a representative selection)

In this respect, compare especially *Le città nella storia d'Italia* (= Towns in the history of Italy) with documentation, pictures and maps on *Bari* (M. Petrignani and F. Porsia, 1980), *Bologna* (G. Ricci, 1980), *Cagliari* (I. Principe, 1981), *Capua* (I. Di Reste, 1985), *Florence* (G. Fanelli, 1980), *Genoa* (E. Poleggi and P. Cevini, 1981), *La Spezia* (A. Fara, 1983), *Lecce* (V. Cazzato and M. Fagiolo, 1983), *Livorno* (D. Matteoni, 1985), *Milan* (L. Gambi and M. C. Gozzoli, 1982), *Messina* (A. Iolo Gigante, 1980), *Naples* (C. de Seta, 1981), *Padua* (L. Puppi and M. Universo, 1982), *Palermo* (C. de Seta and L. Di Mauro, 1980), *Perugia* (A. Grohmann, 1981), *Ravenna* (G. Giovannini and G. Ricci, 1985), *Rimini* (G. Gobbi and P. Sica, 1982), *Rome* (I. Insolera, 1980), *Sassari e Alghero* (I. Principe, 1983), *Siena* (L. Bortolotti, 1983), *Trient* (R. Bocchi and C. Oradini, 1983), *Trieste* (E. Godoh, 1984), *Turin* (V. Comoli Mandracci, 1983), *Venice* (G. Bellavitis and G. Romanelli, 1985). In addition, the new series *Storia delle città italiane* (= History of Italian towns). To date, volumes on *Bologna* (R. Zangheri, 1986), *Catania* (G. Giarrizzo, 1986), *Florence* (G. Spini and A. Casali, 1986), *Turin* (V. Castronovo, 1987), *Venice* (E. Franzina, 1986).

• Ancona

87. *Salinari, M.*, Ancona, Rome, 1955.

• Bari

88. *Di Ciommo, E.*, Bari, 1806–1940: Evoluzione del territorio e sviluppo urbanistico, Milan, 1984 (= Bari 1806–1940: Spatial and urban development).

- Bologna

89. *D'Attorre, P.*, ed., Bologna. Città e territorio tra Ottocento e Novecento, Milan, 1983 (= Bologna. Town and territory in the 19th and 20th centuries).

- Catania

90. *Petino, A.*, Catania contemporanea. Cento anni di vita economica, Catania, 1976 (= Contemporary Catania. One hundred years of economic development).

- Ferrara

91. *Zevi, B.*, Ferrara di Biagio Rossetti: La prica città moderna europea, Turin, 1971 (= Ferrara of the architect Biagio Rossetti: The first modern European city).

- Florence

92. *Fei, S.*, Nascita e sviluppo di Firenze città borghese, Florence, 1971 (= Birth and development of Florence, the town of citizens).

- Livorno

93. *Bortolotti, L.*, Livorno dal 1748 al 1958, Florence, 1970.

- Milan

94. *Reggiore, F.*, Milano 1800–1943, Milan, 1956.

- Naples

95. *De Seta, C.*, Storia della città di Napoli dalle origini al Settecento, Bari, 1973 (= History of Naples from its origins up to the 18th century).

- Padua

96. *Aymonino, C.*, and *A. Rossi*, La città di Padova, Rome, 1970.

- Parma

97. *Banzola, V., et al*, Parma, la città storica, Parma, 1978 (= Parma, the historic town).

● Pisa

98. *Masetti, A. R.*, Pisa: Storia urbana, Pisa, 1964 (= Pisa: urban history).

● Prato

99. *Prato.* Storia di una città, Florence, 1987 (= Prato. History of a town).

● Rome

100. *Insolera, I.*, Roma moderna: Un secolo di storia urbanistica, 7th ed., Bari, 1977 (= Modern Rome: One hundred years of town planning history).

101. *Quaroni, L.*, Immagine di Roma, Rome, 1960 (= The image of Rome).

102. *Roma nell'età giolittinia*, Rome, 1986 (= Rome in the era of Giolitti – president of the council 1903–1912).

103. *Seronde Baboneaux, A. -M.*, Rome della città alla metropoli, Rome 1983 (= Rome: from town to metropolis).

● San Remo

104. *Scattareggia, M.*, Sanremo 1815–1915, Milan, 1986.

● Trieste

105. *Semerani, L.*, Gli elementi della città e lo sviluppo di Trieste nel XIX e XX secolo, Trieste, 1965 (= The elements of the town. Trieste's evolution in the 19th and 20th centuries).

● Turin

106. *Bagnasco, A.*, Torino: un profilo sociologico, Turin, 1986 (= Turin: a sociological profile).

107. *Falco, L.* and *G. Morbelli*, Torino, un secolo di sviluppo urbano, Turin, 1976 (= Turin: One century of urban development).

● Urbino

108. De Carlo, G., Urbino, la storia della città, Padua, 1966 (= Urbino: The town's history).

● Venice

109. *Romanelli, G.*, Venezia Ottocento, Rome, 1977 (= Venice in the 19th century).

- Verona

110. *Marchi, G., et al.*, Ritratto di Verona: Lineamenti di storia urbanistica, Verona, 1978 (= The picture of Verona: An introduction to its urban development).

RYUICHI NARITA, KINICHI OGURA AND AKIO
YOSHIE

Japan

A. Urban History Institutions

Not only historians and other specialists in universities are concerned with
modern urban history; there are also practitioners among the general public
as well as in administration, working in the field of urban history. This
becomes obvious in the many publications of interested citizens as well as in
anniversary papers published by provinces or communities to mark centennial celebrations. This bibliography restricts itself to research institutes and
organisations dealing in general with urban history.

The *Tokyo-Study-Group in Comparative Urban History* of the Department of
Economics at St. Paul's University in Tokyo is the only study group
working nationwide. Since its foundation in 1971 it has been concerned
mainly with urban development in various civilisations before modern
industrialisation.

The *Hokuriki Toshishi Gakkai* in the Seminar of Japanese History at
Kanazawa University is the urban history society of the provinces of
Toyama, Kanazawa and Fukui on the coast of the Sea of Japan. It was
founded in 1978 through an initiative of the medievalist Prof. Dr. Takeshi
Toyoda, in order to encourage interdisciplinary research in certain areas.

The *Center for Urban Studies* of the Tokyo Metropolitan University is the
university institute for urban history founded in 1977. One of their research
projects deals with the urban history of Tokyo.

The *National Museum of Japanese History*, founded in 1981, is concerned
with the development of urban life in Japan from antiquity to the present.

B. Aids to Research (all in Japanese)

(a) Urban History Journals

Most of the studies on *modern* urban history are found in periodicals about general and local history and in university publications. The following three periodicals, however, concentrate on research about urban history and urban problems in general.

1. *The Comparative Urban History Review*, 1982 ff., pub. by the Tokyo-Study-Group in Comparative Urban History; published biannually.
2. *Comprehensive Urban Studies*, 1977 ff., pub. by Center for Urban Studies, Tokyo Metropolitan University; published three times a year.
3. *Hokuriku Toshishi Gakkaiho*, 1971 ff., ed. Hokuriku Toshishi Gakkai; published annually.

(b) Bibliographies

The monthly periodical *Shigaku Zasshi* regularly contains a list of new publications; especially important is the May issue with research reports.

4. *Azusaka, R.*, ed., General Bibliography on Local History, 3 vols., n.p., 1970–1975.
5. *Inoue, M.* and *K. Nagahara*, eds., Nihonshi Kenkyu Nyumon, 5th ed., Tokyo, 1982 (= Introduction to Japanese history).
6. *Kindainihon Shakaijigyoshi Bunkenmokuroku Henshuiinkai*, ed., Bibliography on the History of Social Security in Modern Japan, Tokyo, 1971.
7. *Kurabayashi, Y.*, ed., A Select Bibliography about the Kanto-Earthquake (1923), Tokyo, 1982.
8. *Namase, K.*, ed., List of Literature About the Slum in Modern Japan, in Momoyama Daigaku Sogokenkyujoho, Vol. 7, No. 1 (1981), pp. 49–67.
9. *The National Committee of Japanese Historians*, ed., Historical Studies in Japan 1973–1977. A Bibliography. Japan at the 15th International Congress of Historical Sciences in Bucharest, Tokyo, 1980.
10. *Sasaki, J.*, (1968), and *S. Ishii*, eds., New Introduction to Japanese History, Tokyo, 1982.
11. *Tada, H.*, ed., A Selected Bibliography on the Socio-economic Development of Japan, Part 1: 1600–1940, Tokyo, 1980.
12. *Tashiro, K.*, ed., Bibliography about the Slum, in Nihon Jyutaku Kyokai, ed., Jyutaku, Vol. 15 (1966), No. 5–Vol. 17 (1968) No. 1.

(c) Handbooks on Urban History

13. *Murai, Y.*, ed., Kyoto-Jiten, Tokyo, 1979 (Kyoto-reference book).
14. *Nihon Toshinenkan*, Vol. 1–12 pub. by Tokyo Shisei Chosakai), Tokyo 1931–1943; Vol. 13–16 pub. by Nihon Toshirenmei), Tokyo 1948–1952; Vol. 17 ff. pub. by Zenkoku Shichokai), Tokyo 1955 ff. (= Japanese City Yearbook).
15. *Shimonaka, K.*, ed., Outline of Historical Place Names in Japan, 50 vols., n.p. 1979 ff.

16. *Takeuchi, R., et al.*, eds., Kadokawa's Comprehensive Reference Book of Place Names in Japan, 48 vols., Tokyo, 1978 ff.

(d)   Atlases on Urban History and Urban Development (all in Japanese)

17. *Kensetsusho Kokudo Chriin*, ed., The National Atlas of Japan, Tokyo, 1977.
18. *Kochizu Kenkyukai*, ed., Collection of Japanese Atlases of the Meiji and Taisho Periods, 4 vols., Tokyo, 1984.
19. *Nihon Chizusenshu Kankoiinkai*, ed., Collection of Town Maps of Modern Tokyo During the Meiji, Taisho and Showa Periods, Tokyo, 1981.
20. *Nihon Chizu Senta*, ed., The Development of Tokyo as Recorded by its Town Maps, Tokyo, 1984.
21. *Yamaguchi, K., et al.*, eds., 12 vols. Outline of Japanese Topography, Tokyo, 1976 ff.

(e)   Urban History Sources

22. *Iijma, N.*, ed., Revised Chronological Table of Pollution of the Environment, Industrial Accidents and Occupational Diseases, Osaka, 1979.
23. *Kamioka, N.*, ed., Sources about Pollution of the Environment in Modern Japan, Tokyo, 1973.
24. *Koyama, H.*, ed., Sources about Pollution Problems of Osaka since the Showa Period Until the End of the War, Kyoto, 1973.

C.   Research Reports

D.   Literature on Individual Areas of Urban History Research

1.   Publications in European Languages

25. *Dore, R. P.*, City Life in Japan. A Story of a Tokyo Ward, London, 1958.
26. *Fujioka, K.*, The Changing Face of Japanese Jokamachi (Castle Towns) since the Meiji-Period, in The Association of Japanese Geographers pub., Geography of Japan, Tokyo, 1980.
27. *Hall, J. W.*, The Castle Town and Japan's Modern Urbanization, in Far Eastern Quarterly, Vol. 15 (1955), No. 1, pp. 35–56.
28. *Hashimoto, T.*, The Lower Socio-Economic Classes and Mass Riots in Provincial City, Tokyo, 1981.
29. *Ishida, T.*, Urbanisation and its Impact on Japanese Politics: A Case of a Late and Rapidly Developed Country, in Annals of the Institute of Social Science, Tokyo University, No. 8 (1967), pp. 1–11.

30. *Ishizuka, H.*, Methodological Introduction to the History of the City of Tokyo, Tokyo, 1981.

31. *Ishizuka, H.*, The Early History of the Control of Water borne Diseases in Tokyo, Tokyo, 1983.

32. *Kiuchi, S.*, Tokyo als Weltstadt, in J. Schultze, ed., Zum Problem der Weltstadt, Berlin, 1959.

33. *Kobori, I.*, ed., Urban Growth in Japan and France, Tokyo, 1978.

34. *Matzerath, H.*, and *K. Ogura*, Moderne Verstädterung in Deutschland und Japan, in Zeitschrift für Stadtgeschichte, Stadtsoziologie und Denkmalpflege 2, Year 2 (1975), No. 2, pp. 228–253.

35. *Nakamura, H.*, Town Organization in Pre-War Tokyo, Tokyo, 1980.

36. *Ogura, K.*, Anfänge und Entwicklung Tokios bis zur Modernisierung Japans, in Archiv für Kulturgeschichte, Vol. 57 (1975), No. 2, pp. 465–474.

37. *Schöller, P.*, Japan, in Fischer Länderkunde, Vol. 10, Chapter 7: Ostasien, Frankfurt/M., 1978, pp. 325–440.

38. *Schöller, P.*, Wachstum und Wandlung japanischer Stadtregionen, in Die Erde, No. 93 (1963), pp. 202–234.

39. *Seidensticker, E.*, Low City, High City, Tokyo from Edo to the Earthquake: How the Shoguns' Ancient Capital Became a Great Modern City. 1867–1923, Rutland-Bermont and Tokyo, 1984.

40. *Smith, H. D.*, Tokyo as an Idea: An Exploration of Japanese Urban Thought up to 1945, in Journal of Japanese Studies, Vol. 4 (1978), No. 1, pp. 45–80.

41. *Smith, T. C.*, ed., City and Village in Japan, Chicago, 1960.

42. *Willkinson, T. O.*, The Urbanization of Japanese Labour 1868–1955, Amherst, 1965.

43. *Yasaki, T.*, Social Change and the City in Japan from Earliest Times through the Industrial Revolution, Tokyo, 1968.

2. Publications in Japanese

(a) Concept and Definition of Town and Town Types

44. *Fujioka, K.*, The Japanese Town, Tokyo, 1968.

45. *Furushima, T.*, City Trends During the Meiji Period, in Chihoshikenkyu Kyogikai, ed., Bakumatsu Meijiki niokeru Toshi to Noson, Nihon no Machi III, Tokyo, 1961, pp. 23–48.

46. *Hashimoto, T.*, Urban Development During the Period of the Taisho Democracy, in Kanazawa Daigaku Hobungakubu Ronshu Keizaigakubuhen, No. 22 (1975), pp. 25–52.

47. *Shibata, T.*, Studies of the City Today, 1st ed., Tokyo, 1967; 2nd ed. Tokyo, 1976.

48. *Unno, F.*, Research Problems in Urban History at the Beginning of the Meiji-Period, in Chihoshikenkyu Kyogikai, ed., Bakumatsu Meijiki niokeru Toshi to Noson, Nihon no Machi III, Tokyo, 1961, pp. 271–310.
49. *Yamada, M.*, Constitution of Town and Geography, in Nihonshikenkyu, No. 200 (1979), pp. 101–124.

(b)   Politics, Law and Statutes

50. *Akagi, S.*, Studies on the Constitution of the Imperial Capital, Tokyo, Tokyo, 1977.
51. *Akimoto, R.*, The War and the People. City Life During the Second World War, Tokyo, 1974.
52. *Eguchi, K.*, History of the Urban Petty Bourgeois Movement, Tokyo, 1976.
53. *Fukuoka, S.*, Urban Politics During the Taisho Period, in Tokyo Toritsu Daigaku Hogakukai Zasshi, Vol. 11, No. 2; Vol. 12, No. 1; Vol. 13, No. 1 (1971–1972).
54. *Hamaguchi, H.*, The Organisation of Society, Contrasting Ideas in the Modernisation of Japan, Tokyo, 1980.
55. *Harada, K.*, The Structure of Urban Government, in Rekishi Hyoron, No. 393 (1983), pp. 64–96.
56. *Harada, K.*, Reorganisation of Urban Government, in Historia, No. 101 (1983), pp. 66–86.
57. *Hashimoto, T.*, Urbanisation and Mobility, in Iwanamikoza Nihonrekishi, Vol. 17 (1976), pp. 305–349.
58. *Kikegawa, H.*, The Establishment of Local Government During the Meiji period, Tokyo, 1967.
59. *Kojita, Y.*, The Basic Structure of Party Politics. Problems of Urban Property Taxing, in Nihonshikenkyu, No. 235 (1982), pp. 122–146.
60. *Kojita, Y.*, Urban Politics During the Establishment of Japanese Imperialism, in Rekishi Hyoron, No. 393 (1983), pp. 27, 87–110.
61. *Mikuriya, T.*, The Foundation of the Meiji State and Urban Planning, in Tokyo Toritsudaigaku Hogakukai Zasshi, Vol. 23 (1982), No. 1, pp. 1–88.
62. *Miyaji, M.*, Political History after the Russo-Japanese War, Tokyo, 1973.
63. *Mizobe, H.*, Goto Shimpei, Parts I and II, in Hogaku Ronso, Vol. 100 (1976), No. 2, pp. 62–96; Vol. 101 (1977), No. 2, pp. 36–59.
64. *Nakamura, A.*, Another Study of the Laws of Urban Planning in the 8th Year of the Taisho Period, in T. Okita *et al.*, eds., Chihojichi to Toshiseisaku, Tokyo, 1981, pp. 99–134.
65. *Nakayama, G.*, The Town District Association, Tokyo, 1980.
66. *Narita, R.*, The City People's Movement of the Taisho Democracy, in Chihoshi Kenkyu, No. 165 (1980), pp. 33–42.

67. *Narita, R.*, Daikichiro Tagawa's Idea of the Town, in Rekishi Hyoron, No. 330 (1977), pp. 11–28.

68. *Noda, M.*, Co-operatives of White-Collar Workers Before the Second World War, I-XIV, in Ginko Rodo Chosa Jiho, Nos. 111–113, 115–120, 122, 125, 128–129 (1960–1961).

69. *Okuda, S.*, Citizens' Struggles During the Economic Crisis of the Showa Period, in Ritsumeikan Daigaku Jimmonkagaku Kenkyujo Kiyo, No. 10 (1980), pp. 64–114.

70. *Oshima, T.*, State Bureaucracy and the Autonomy of Local Government, Tokyo, 1981.

71. *Shibamura, A.*, The Historical Significance of Seki Hajime's Urban Politics, in Osaka Rekishi Gakkai, ed., Kindai Osaka no Rekishiteki Tenkai, Tokyo, 1976, pp. 397–456.

72. *Shibamura, A.*, The City Administration of Osaka at the Beginning of the Twenties, in Historia, No. 100 (1983), pp. 75–92.

73. *Suzuki, R.*, The Laws Concerning Leasehold Property and Blocks of Rented Flats, in N. Ugai et al., eds., Koza Nihon Kindaiho Hattatsushi, Vol. 11 (1967), pp. 55–132.

74. *Takagi, S.*, Urban Planning Laws, in N. Ugai et al., eds., Koza Nihon Kindaiho Hattatsushi, Vol. 9 (1960), pp. 128–160.

75. *Watanabe, S.*, and *Y. Sadayuki*, Biography of Hiroshi Ikeda. An Attempt, in Tochi Jyutaku Mondai, Nos. 56–60, 62–67 (1979–1980).

76. *Watanabe, Y.*, Laws Concerning Land and Buildings, Parts I and II, Tokyo, 1960–1962.

(c) Population and Social Structure

77. *Yokoyama, G.*, Collected Works, Vol. 1 and 3, Tokyo 1972–1974 (Vols. 2 and 4 have not been released).

78. *Hashimoto, T.*, Urbanisation and Workers' Mobility after the Russo-Japanese War, in Nihonshikenkyu, No. 200 (1979), pp. 76–100.

79. *Ishizuka, H.*, Urban Lower Classes and Housing Problems of the Poor, Tokyo, 1980.

80. *Kagawa, T.*, Studies on the Psychology of the Poor, Tokyo, 1915.

81. *Kyotoshi, S.*, ed., Reports, 10 Vols., Kyoto, 1978.

82. *Naimusho-Chihokyoku – Shakaikyoku*, ed., Statistical Tables of the Census of the Poor, 1912–1914, with commentary by M. Tsuda, Tokyo, 1971 (reprinted).

83. *Nakagawa, K.*, The Urban Lower Classes Exemplified by Tokyo before the Second World War, I and II, in Mita Gakkai Zasshi, Vol. 71 (1978), No. 3, pp. 58–104 and No. 4, pp. 73–119.

84. *Nishida, C.*, The Genesis of Gennosuke Yokoyama's "The Society of the lower classes in Japan", in Rekishigaku Kenkyu, No. 161 (1953), pp. 36–46.

85. *Nishida, C.*, The Society of the Urban Lower Classes, Tokyo, 1949.
86. *Nishida, C.*, ed., The Society of the Urban Lower Classes During the First Half of the Meiji Period, Tokyo, 1970.
87. *Osaka – Shiyakusho*, Report about Work, 14 vols. Osaka, 1975–1981.
88. *Sumiya, M.*, A History of Labour in Japan, Tokyo, 1955.
89. *Tachibana, Y.*, A Biography of Gennosuke Yokoyama, Tokyo, 1979.
90. *Tsuda, M.*, The Society of the Urban Lower Classes in Japan, Kyoto, 1972.
91. *Yamada, M.*, A History of Urban Problems in the Keihin Area, Tokyo, 1974.

(d) Town Planning, Housing

92. *Fujimori, T.*, Urban Planning in Tokyo in the Meiji Period, Tokyo, 1982.
93. *Fujimori, T. et al.*, Symposium on Urban Planning in Tokyo in the Meiji Period, in Tokyo Metropolitan University, Comprehensive Urban Studies, No. 19 (1983), pp. 133–168.
94. *Harada, R.*, The Air Attack on Japan, Parts I and II, Tokyo, 1973–1980.
95. *Hatsuda, T.*, "Meiji" in the City, Tokyo, 1981.
96. *Imai, S.*, The Big Attack of 29th May. The Second World War and Yokohama, Yokohama, 1981.
97. *Inagaki, E.*, Modern Architecture in Japan, Tokyo, 1959 (reprinted 1979).
98. *Iwami, R.*, Study about Urban Development, Tokyo, 1978.
99. *Narita, R.*, Changing Ideas of the City and the Reconstruction of the Capital, in Tokyo Rekisikagaku Kenkyukai, ed., Tenkanki no Rekishigaku, Tokyo 1979, pp. 199–234.
100. *Nihonno Kushu Henshu Iinkai*, ed., Air Attacks on Japan, 10 vols., Tokyo, 1980–1981.
101. *Saotome, K.*, The Air Attack on Tokyo. A Document of 10 March 1945, Tokyo, 1971.

(e) Economy and Transport

102. *Ishizuka, H.*, Social and Economic History of Tokyo. Capitalism and Urban Problems, Tokyo, 1977.
103. *Ishizuka, H.*, Studies about the Genesis of Japanese Capitalism, the Meiji State and its Support of Industry, Tokyo, 1973.
104. *Kodama, T.*, The Reconstruction of Tokyo after the Big Earthquake and the Subsidised Society, in Nihonshikenkyu, No. 245 (1983), pp. 33–63.
105. *Miyamoto, K.*, Studies on Urban Economics, Tokyo, 1980.
106. *Mochida, N.*, The Reconstruction Project of Goto Shimpei after the Big

Earthquake, in Tokyo Daigaku Shakaikagaku Kenkyu, Vol. 35 (1983), No. 2 pp. 1–60.

107. *Narita, R.*, Tokijiro Kato, Tokyo, 1983.

108. *Oda, Y.*, Pollution Problems in Modern Japan, Kyoto, 1983.

109. *Omori, M.*, The Middle Classes and "Mimpon"-ism at the Beginning of Urban Social Security, in Historia, No. 97 (1982), pp. 58–74.

110. *Yoshida K.*, Studies on Contemporary Social Security, Tokyo, 1979.

(f)   Arts and Sciences, Churches

111. *Isoda, K.*, The City of Tokyo and its Idea, Tokyo, 1978.

112. *Kawazoe, N.*, Urban Landscape in its Archetype and Tokyo, Tokyo, 1979.

113. *Kawazoe, N.*, et al., eds., Collected Works of Wajiro Kon, 9 vols. Tokyo, 1971–1972.

114. *Maeda, A.*, Literature in the Sphere of the Town, Tokyo, 1982.

115. *Minami, H.*, Taisho Culture, Tokyo, 1965.

116. *Miyata, N.*, The Task of City Folklore, Tokyo, 1982.

117. *Ogi, S.*, Studies on How People Lived During the Tokei Period, Tokyo, 1979.

118. *Ogi, S.*, The Tokei Period Between Edo and Tokyo, Tokyo, 1980.

119. *Urban Folklore*, in Rekishikoron, No. 92 (1983) (special edition).

120. *Yamamoto, T.*, Studies on the History of Conversion in Modern Urban Japan, Tokyo, 1972.

E.   Local Studies (a representative selection)

● Abiko

121. *Tagaki, S.*, Description of the Urban History of Abiko by its Citizens, in Chihoshi Kenkyu, No. 167 (1980), pp. 87–99.

● Amagasaki

122. *The Urban History of Amagasaki*, 12 vols., Amagasaki, 1966–1983.

● Hachioji

123. *Hachioji Kushu o Kirokusuru Kai*, ed., Flames in the Valley; Documents about the Big Air Attack on Hachioji, 3 vols., n.p., 1980–1983.

● Kawasaki

124. *Kawasaki-si*, ed., Air Attacks and Bomb Damage in Kawasaki, 3 vols., Kawasaki, 1974–1975.

● Kobe

125. *Modern History of Kobe*, in Rekishikoron, No. 90 (1983).

● Osaka

126. *Osaka Rekishi Gakkai*, ed., The Historical Development of Modern Osaka, Tokyo, 1976.

● Tokyo

127. *History of the Town District of Tokyo-Nakano during the Showa Period*, 3 vols. and 3 vols. of sources, Tokyo, 1971–1978.
128. *A Hundred Years in the History of Tokyo*, 7 vols., Tokyo, 1972–1979.
129. *Power and the People During the Time of the Foundation of the Imperial Capital*, Rekishihyoron, No. 405 (1984) (special edition).
130. *Ishizuka, H.* and *R. Narita*, A Century of Tokyo, 1853–1980, Tokyo, 1986.
131. *The Taisho Period in Tokyo.* Reflections about Culture, in Rekishitecho, Vol. 5 (1977), No. 1 (special edition).
132. *Tokyo Kushu o Kirokusuru Kai*, ed., Air Attacks on Tokyo. Documentary of the Bomb Damage, Tokyo, 1973–1974.

● Yokohama

133. *Urban History of Yokohama*, 9 vols. and 18 vols. of sources, Yokohama, 1958–1982.
134. *Yokohama no Kusho o Kirokusuru Kai*, ed., Air Attacks and Bomb Damage in Yokohama, 6 vols., Yokohama, 1975–1977.

MARCEL ENGEL AND JOSEPH GOEDERT

Luxemburg

A. Urban History Institutions

B. Aids to Research

(a) Urban History Journals

—

(b) Bibliographies

1. *Bibliographie luxembourgeoise*, pub. by the Bibliothèque Nationale, Luxemburg, 1945 ff.

(c) Handbooks on Urban History

(d) Atlases on Urban History and Urban Development

2. *Mirguet, F.*, Le Duché de Luxembourg à la fin de l'Ancien Régime. Atlas de géographie historique, Fasc. III, Louvain-la-Neuve, 1983.

(e) Urban History Sources

3. *Emmel, F.*, Das Stadtarchiv Luxemburg, in Les Amis de l'Histoire, No. 13 (1983), pp. 131–139.
4. *Klees, H.*, Materialien zur Sozial- und Wirtschaftsgeschichte der Gemeinden des Kantons Esch, in Galerie. Revue culturelle et pédagogique, No. 1 (1982/83), pp. 384–400, 667–675.
5. *Thein, J.*, Les archives communales de la ville de Wiltz, Luxemburg, 1961.
6. *Wurth-Paquet, F. X. et al.*, Cartulaire ou recueil de documents politiques et administratifs de la ville de Luxembourg de 1244–1795, Luxemburg, 1881.

C. Research Reports

(a) *General Surveys*

—

(b) *Surveys of Individual Fields of Urban Research*

—

D. Literature on Individual Areas of Urban History Research

(a) *Concept and Definition of Town and Town Types*

(b) *Politics, Law and Statutes*

7. *Glaesener, J. P.*, Verfassung und innere Verwaltung der freien Stadt Diekirch in den Jahren 1747 bis 1785, in Publications de la Section Historique de l'Institut Grand-Ducale, No. 51, 2 (1903).
8. *Herr, J.*, Administration de la ville de Diekirch 1795–1960, in Diekirch 700, published on the occasion of the 700th centenary of the city of Diekirch.
9. *Trausch, G.*, Aspects et problèmes de la vie municipale à Luxembourg sous la République (1795–1799), in Hémecht, 1963, pp. 449–498.

(c) *Population and Social Structure*

10. *Herr, J.*, Bevölkerung und Verwaltung der Stadt Diekirch, Diekirch, 1960.
11. *Hurt, J.*, Aus dem Bürgerbuch der Stadt Grevenmaches, in Hémecht, 1959, pp. 97–133.

(d) *Town Planning*

12. *Koltz, J. P.*, Baugeschichte der Stadt und Festung Luxemburg, 3 vols., Luxemburg, 1944–1951 (Vol. 1 in 2nd ed., Luxemburg, 1970).
13. *Koltz, J. P.*, Die Hofburg Vianden, in Burgen und Schlösser. Zeitschrift für Burgenkunde und Burgenpflege, 1977, pp. 13–28.
14. *Pauly, J.*, Luxembourg. La forteresse éclatée, Paris and Luxemburg, 1981.
15. *Pauly, J.*, and *P. Spang*, Luxembourg. Von der Festung zur offenen Stadt, Luxemburg, 1983.

437

16. *Ulveling, J.*, Notice historique sur l'ancienne forteresse de Luxembourg, in Publications de la Section Historique de l'Institut Grand-Ducale, No. 23 (1868), pp. 73–114.

(e)   Economy and Transport

—

(f)   Arts and Sciences, Churches

—

E. Local Studies (a representative selection)

● Diekirch

17. *Herr, J.*, Diekirch hier et aujourd'hui. Histoire et population, Luxemburg, 1980.
18. *Livre du 7ᵉ centenaire de l'affranchissement de la ville de Diekirch*, Diekirch, 1960.
19. *Olinger, P.*, Diekirch im Wandel der Zeiten. Bilder aus der Diekircher Geschichte, 2nd ed., Luxemburg, 1941.

● Echternach

20. *Schritz, P.*, and *A. Hoffmann*, Abteistadt Echternach, Luxemburg, 1981.
21. *Schroeder, J.*, Echternach in Forschung und Literatur, in Hémecht, No. 3 (1983), pp. 459–481.
22. *Spang, P.*, Echternach. Geschichte einer Stadt, Luxemburg, 1983.

● Esch-sur-Alzette

23. *Flies, J.*, Das andere Esch-sur-Alzette. Ein Gang durch seine Geschichte, Luxemburg, 1979.
24. *Flies, J.*, 1200 Jahre Esch-sur-Alzette 773–1973, in Annuaire de la Ville d'Esch-sur-Alzette, 1973, pp. 5–38.
25. *Livre du Cinquantenaire de la Ville d'Esch-sur-Alzette 1906–1956*, Esch-sur-Alzette, 1956.
26. *Roeltgen, F.*, Esch-sur-Alzette au jour le jour. Recueil chronologique de 773 à 1976, Esch-sur-Alzette, 1977.

● Grevenmacher

27. *Berens, A.*, Die Anfänge der Stadt und Festung Grevenmacher. Zur 700. Jahrfeier der Verleihung des Freiheitsbriefes 1252–1952, Grevenmacher, 1952.

● Luxemburg

28. *Biermann, J. P.*, Abrégé historique de la ville et de la forteresse de Luxembourg, 1976 (reprinted).

29. *Engelhardt, F. W.*, Geschichte der Stadt und Festung Luxemburg seit ihrer ersten Entstehung bis auf unsere Tage, Luxemburg, 1853 (reprinted 1979).

30. *Koltz, J. P.*, Europazentrum Luxemburg, in R. Jätzold, ed., Der Trierer Raum und seine Nachbargebiete, Trier, 1984, pp. 323–329.

31. *Margue, N.*, and *P. Margue*, Histoire sommaire de la ville de Luxembourg, Luxemburg, 1963.

● Remich

32. *Remich et le carrefour lorrain*, Luxembourg, 1932 (Cahiers luxembourgeois).

● Vianden

33. *Neyen, A.*, Histoire de la ville de Vianden et de ses comtes, Luxemburg, 1851.

HERMAN A. DIEDERIKS

The Netherlands

A. Urban History Institutions

—

B. Aids to Research

(a) Urban History Journals

—

(b) Bibliographies

1. *Bibliografie van Doetinchem*, ed. W. G. Voltman and A. Schouten, Doetinchem, 1978 (= Bibliography of Doetinchem).
2. *Bibliografie van de Stedengeschiedenis van Nederland*, compiled by G. van Herwijnen, Leiden, 1978 (Acta collegii Historiae Urbanae Societatis Historicum Internationalis) (= Bibliography of urban history of the Netherlands).
3. *Diederiks, H. A.*, and *P. H. J. van der Laan*, Urban History in the Netherlands, in Urban History Yearbook, Leicester, 1976, pp. 28–35.
4. *Hooff, G. van*, Een nuttig hulpmiddel om de mechanisatie van stad tot stad te volgen in een voorlopig rapport tot stand gekomen aan de Technische Hogeschool Eindhoven. Machinefabrieken in Nederland tot 1914, overzicht en bibliografie, Eindhoven, 1985 (= A useful aid to follow mechanisation from town to town. An interim report of the "Technische Hogeschool Eindhoven". Machine factories in the Netherlands up to 1914. Overview and bibliography).
5. *Vooys, A. C. de*, and *J. M. G. Kleinpenning*, Bronnen voor het regionale onderzoek in Nederland, Groningen, 1963 (= Sources for regional research in the Netherlands).

(c)   Handbooks on Urban History

—

(d)   Atlases on Urban History and Urban Development

6. *Gids voor Kaartenverzamelingen in Nederland*, compiled by A. van Slobbe, n.p., 1980 (= Guide to map collections in the Netherlands).
7. *Kuyper, J.*, Gemeenteatlas van Nederland naar officiele bronnen verwerkt, 11 vols., Leeuwarden, 1865–1871 (= Communities' Atlas of the Netherlands, updated using official sources).

(e)   Urban History Sources

8. *Overzichten van de archieven en verzamelingen in de openbare archiefbewaarplaatsen in Nederland*, published under the supervision of the Vereniging van Archivarissen in Nederland, eds., L.M.T.L. Hustinx *et al.*, Alphen/Rh., 1979 ff. (= Summary of archives and collections).

C.   Research Reports

—

D.   Literature on Individual Areas of Urban History Research

(a)   Concept and Definition of Town and Town Types

9. *Diederiks, H.*, The Role of Amsterdam during the 19th Century in the Process of Urbanization. Some Observations, in Urbanisierung im 19. und 20. Jahrhundert. Historische und geographische Aspekte, ed., H. J. Teuteberg, Cologne and Vienna, 1983, pp. 130–141.
10. *Diederiks, H.*, Verstädterung in den Niederlanden 1795–1870. Ein Überblick, in Städtewachstum und innerstädtische Strukturveränderungen. Probleme des Urbanisierungsprozesses, ed. H. Matzerath, Stuttgart, 1984, pp. 29–43.
11. *Engelsdorp Gastelaars, R. van* and *M. Wagenaar*, The Rise of the "randstad". 1815–1930, in Patterns of European Urbanization since 1500, ed., H. Schmal, London, 1981, pp. 231–246.
12. *Kooy, P.*, Stad en Platteland, in De Nederlandse Samenleving sinds 1815. Wording en samenhang, ed. F. L. van Holthoon, Assen and Maastricht, 1985, pp. 93–115 (= Town and country).

Bibliographies

13. *Thurkow, A. J.*, Verstedelijkingsaspecten in de 19e en begin 20e eeuw in Nederland buiten Holland en Utrecht, in Historisch Geografisch Tijdschrift, Year 1 (1983), No. 2, pp. 43–49 (= Aspects of urbanisation in the 19th century and early 20th century in the Netherlands, excluding Holland and Utrecht).

(b) Politics, Law and Statutes

14. *Bakker, J. H. M.*, and *E. Nijhof*, Het Jordaanoproer verzet tegen de steunverlaging in juli 1934, in Tijdschrift voor Sociale Geschiedenis, Vol. 3 (1978), pp. 35–69 (= The Jordaan uprising: resistance to the drop in unemployment benefits in July 1934).

15. *Blok, L.*, Van een wettelijke fictie tot eene waarheid. Beschouwingen over kiesstelsel en kiesrecht in Nederland in de eerste helft van de negentiende eeuw, in Tijdschrift voor Geschiedenis, Vol. 92 (1979), pp. 391–412 (= From legal fiction to truth: observations on the election system and laws in the Netherlands in the first half of the 19th century).

16. *Borrie, G. W. B.*, Pieter Lodewijk Tak (1848–1907). Journalist en politicus, Assen, 1973 (= Pieter Lodewijk Tak (1848–1907): Journalist and politician).

17. *Faber, S.*, De politie in en sinds de achttiende eeuw in het bijzonder te Amsterdam, in Redenen van wetenschap, opstellen over de politie veertig jaar na het politiebesluit 1945, Arnhem, 1985, pp. 33–44 (= The police in and since the 18th century, particularly in Amsterdam).

18. *Horssen, P.*, and *D. Rietveld*, Der Sociaal-Democratische Bond. Een onderzoek naar het ontstaan van haar afdelingen en haar sociale structuur, in Tijdschrift voor Sociale Geschiedenis, Vol. 1 (1975), pp. 5–69 (= The "Sociaal-Democratische Bond". A study on the emergence of its sub-groups and its social structure).

19. *Kempen, A.F.J. van*, Ijvorst und Ijverzucht, ambities en rivaliteit in stadsbestuur en gouvernement rondom het belastingoproer van 1835, in Jaarboek Amstelodamum, Vol. 77 (1985). pp. 122–169 (= Zealous and jealous, ambition and rivalry in the city council and in the government at the time of the tax uprising of 1830).

20. *Meyer, W., J. W. B. van Overhagen* and *P. Wolff*, De financien van de Nederlandse provincien en gemeenten in de periode 1850–1914, in Economisch en Sociaal-Historisch Jaarboek, Vol. 33 (1971), pp. 27–66 (= The finances of provinces and communities in the Netherlands from 1850–1914).

21. *Perry, J.*, Socialisme in Maastricht 1884–1894, in Tijdschrift voor Sociale Geschiedenis, Vol. 1 (1975), pp. 72–146 (= Socialism in Maastricht 1884–1894).

(c) Population and Social Structure

22. *Binnenveld, J. M. W.*, and *F. S. Gaastra*, Organisatie en conflict van een vergeten groep, in Economisch en Sociaal-Historisch Jaarboek, Vol. 35 (1972), pp. 303–323 (= Organisation and conflict of a forgotten group).

23. *Blok, L.*, and *J. M. M. de Meere*, Welstand, ongelijkheid in welstand en censuskiesrecht in Nederland omstreeks het midden van de 19de eeuw, in Economisch en Sociaal-Historisch Jaarboek, Vol. 41 (1978), pp. 175–293 (= Affluence, inequality in affluence and the right to vote in the Netherlands in the mid–19th century).

24. *Boltendal, R.*, De Heeren en de anderen. Heerenveen 1934–1984, Leeuwarden, 1984 (= The men and the others. Heerenveen 1934–1984).

25. *Bovenkerk, F.*, and *L. Brunt*, eds., De rafelrand van Amsterdam. Jordaners, pinda-chinezen, ateliermeisjes en venters in de jaren dertig. Vier sociografische schetsen, Meppel and Amsterdam, 1977 (= The frayed edge of Amsterdam: Jordanese, Pinda-Chinese, seamstresses and peddlars in the thirties. Four sociographical sketches).

26. *Bos, N.*, De "deftige lui". Elites in Maastricht tussen 1850 en 1890, in Tijdschrift voor Sociale Geschiedenis, Vol. 12 (1986), pp. 53–89 (= The "nobs". The elite of Maastricht between 1850 and 1890).

27. *Bruin, K.*, and *H. Schuif*, De eerste bewoners in een deftige straat, in Van stadskern tot stadsgewest. Stedebouwkundige geschiedenis van Amsterdam, ed. M. Jonker, L. Noordegraaf and M. Wagenaar, Amsterdam, 1984, pp. 133–156 (Amsterdamse Historische Reeks. Grote Serie Deel 1) (= The first inhabitants of a genteel street).

28. *Deurloo, M. C.*, and *G. A. Hoekveld*, The Population Growth of the Urban Municipalities in the Netherlands between 1849 and 1970 with Particular Reference to the Period 1899–1930, in Patterns of European Urbanisation since 1950, ed. H. Schmal, London, 1981, pp. 247–283.

29. *Diederiks, H.*, Le choléra aux Pays-Bas en 1832 en particulier: Diffusion de mesures pour combattre l'épidémie, in Annales de Démographie Historique. Bulletin d'Information, No. 45 (1985), pp. 23–33.

30. *Diederiks, H.*, Sociale Geleding van Amsterdam omstreeks 1800, in Van stadskern tot stadsgewest. Stedebouwkundige geschiedenis van Amsterdam, ed. M. Jonker, L. Noordegraaf and M. Wagenaar, Amsterdam, 1984, pp. 113–131 (Amsterdamse Historische Reeks. Grote Serie Deel 1) (= Social classes in Amsterdam around 1800).

31. *Diederiks, H.*, Migration und soziale Eingliederung. Amsterdam am Anfang des 19. Jahrhunderts, in Bevölkerung, Wirtschaft und Gesellschaft. Stadt-Land-Beziehungen in Deutschland und Frankreich. 14. bis 19. Jahrhundert, ed. N. Bulst, J. Hoock and F. Irsigler, Trier, 1983, pp. 93–113.

32. *Diederiks, H.*, Partnerkeuze te Amsterdam in het begin van de 19e eeuw, in Holland en Historische Demografie, Dordrecht 1985, pp. 123–129

(Hollandse Studiën, Vol. 16) (= Partner selection in Amsterdam at the beginning of the 19th century).

33. *Diederiks, H.*, Een stad in verval. Amsterdam omstreeks 1800. Demografisch, economisch, ruimtelijk, Amsterdam, 1982 (Amsterdamse Historische Reeks, Vol. 2) (= A city in decline. Amsterdam in 1800. A demographic, economic and spatial study).

34. *Diederiks, H.*, Structures ethniques et espace social. Amsterdam à la fin du XVIIIe siècle, in Habiter la ville XVe-XXe siècles, eds., M. Garden and Y. Lequin, Lyon, 1984. pp. 107–126.

35. *Diederiks, H.*, and *R. C. van Eyck*, Twee leidse volksbuurten in de dertiger jaren. Een vergelijkend onderzoek met behulp van de "oral history", in Holland, regionaal-historisch tijdschrift, Year 11 (1979), No. 5, pp. 274–297 (= Two Leiden municipalities in the thirties. A comparative study aided by "oral history").

36. *Diederiks, H.*, and *H. D. Tjalsma*, Wonen en weggaan. Aspecten van migratie in verband met een aantal binnenstadswijken van Leiden op het einde van de 19e eeuw en in de dertiger jaren van de 20ste, in De jaren dertig. Aspecten van crisis en werkloosheid, edited by P. W. Klein and G. J. Borger, Amsterdam, 1979, pp. 166–175 (= Living and leaving. Aspects of migration in conjunction with a few inner-city suburbs of Leiden at the end of the 19th century and in the 1930s).

37. *Dijk, H. van*, Rotterdam 1810–1880. Aspecten van een stedelijke samenleving, Schiedam, 1976 (= Rotterdam 1810–1880. Aspects of an urban society).

38. *Doremalen, H. van*, Sociale onrust. Aktie en vroege organisatievormen onder de arbeidende bevolking in Tilburg 1825–1875, in Jaarboek De Lindeboom, Vol. VI (1982), pp. 115–134 (= Social unrest. Action and early organisational forms among the working population in Tilburg in 1825–1875).

39. *Engelen, T.*, and *H. Hillebrand*, Vruchtbaarheid in verandering. Een gezinsreconstructie in Breda. 1850–1940, in Tijdschrift voor Sociale Geschiedenis, Vol. 11 (1985), No. 3, p. 248 ff. (= Fertility in change. A reconstruction of family in Breda. 1850–1940).

40. *Eyl, C. E. A. van*, Het vergeten voetvolk. Een onderzoek naar de leefwereld van SDAP'ers in de Utrechtse wijk Ondiep 1920–1940, in Tijdschrift voor Sociale Geschiedenis, Vol. 11 (1985), pp. 1–29 (= The forgotten infantry. A study on the lives led by SDAPs in the Utrecht district of Ondiep 1920–1940).

41. *Franssen, J. J. M.*, De Bossche arbeider in zijn werk- en leefmilieu in de tweede helft van de negentiende eeuw, 2 Vols., Tilburg, 1976 (Bijdragen tot de geschiedenis van het Zuiden van Nederland, Vol. XXXIII) (= The worker in 's Hertogenbosch in his working and living environment in the second half of the 19th century).

42. *Giele, J.*, and *G.-J. van Oenen*, Theorie en praktijk van het onderzoek naar de sociale structuur, in Tijdschrift voor Sociale Geschiedenis, Vol. 2 (1976), pp. 167–186 (= Theory and practice of the study of social structures).

43. *'t Hart, P. D.*, De stad Utrecht en haar inwoners. Een onderzoek naar samenhangen tussen sociaal-economische ontwikkelingen en de demografische geschiedenis van de stad Utrecht 1771–1825, Enschede, 1983 (= The city of Utrecht and its inhabitants. A study on the connections between social-economic developments and the demographic history of the city of Utrecht from 1771–1825).

44. *Heinemeyer, W. F.*, Het levendige getal. De amsterdamse bevolking 1877–1977, in Spiegel van Onroerend Goed, Deventer, 1877, pp. 333–349 (= The living number. Amsterdam's population 1877–1977).

45. *Hofman, J., W. Terwisscha van Scheltinga* and *F. van Vree*, Plan Oost. Van grasland tot renovatiebuurt. Een geschiedenis van de Oosterparkwijk te Groningen van 1917 tot 1977, Groningen, 1977 (= Plan Oost. From meadow to modernisation. A history of the Oosterpark district in Groningen from 1917 to 1977).

46. *Holthoon, F. L. van*, Beggars and Social Control. Government Policy and Beggars, particularly in the Province of Groningen between 1823 and 1870, in Economisch en Sociaal-Historisch Jaarboek, Vol. 43 (1980), pp. 154–193.

47. *Jansen, P. C.*, and *J. M. M. de Meere*, Het sterftepatroon in Amsterdam 1774–1930. Een analyse van de doodsoorzaken, in Tijdschrift voor Sociale Geschiedenis, No. 26 (1982), pp. 180–223 (= Dying in Amsterdam 1774–1830. An analysis of the causes of death).

48. *Kam, B. J.*, Meretrix en Medicus. Een onderzoek naar de invloed van de geneeskundige visitatie op handel en wandel van Zwolse publiek vrouwen tussen 1876 en 1900, Zwolle, 1983 (= Meretrix and Medicus. A study on the influence of medical visits on the commercial activities of prostitutes in Zwolle between 1876 and 1900).

49. *Kielich, W.*, Jordaners op de barricaden. Het oproer van 1934, Zutphen, 1984 (= Jordanese take up arms. The uprising of 1934).

50. *Kok, P. T.*, Het Elberfelder stelsel te Leeuwarden 1893–1913, in Economisch en Sociaal-Historisch Jaarboek, Vol. 46 (1983), pp. 265–312 (= The Elberfeld system in Leeuwarden 1893–1913).

51. *Kooy, P.*, Gezondheitszorg in Groningen 1870–1914, in Tijdschrift voor Sociale Geschiedenis, Vol. 26 (1982), pp. 112–155 (= Public health services in Groningen 1870–1914).

52. *Kramers, H., J. Slangen* and *M. Vroegin de Wey*, Het Leidse volkshuis 1890–1980. Geschiedenis van een stichting sociaal-kultureel werk, Leiden, 1982 (= The Leiden people's home 1890–1980. History of a foundation for social and cultural work).

53. *Meere, J. M. M. de*, Inkomensgroei en ongelijkheid te Amsterdam 1877–1940. Een schets, in Tijdschrift voor Sociale Geschiedenis, No.

13 (1979), pp. 3–37 (= Income growth and inequality in Amsterdam 1877–1940. A short survey).

54. *Meere, J. M. M. de*, and *L. Noordegraf*, De sociale gelaagdheid van Amsterdam in de franse tijd. Het beeld van een tijdgenoot, in Jaarboek Amstelodamum, Vol. 69 (1977), pp. 156–175 (= Social conditions in Amsterdam in the French era).

55. *Meeter, H.*, and *H. Wijffes*, Bouwen en wonen in twee Leidse arbeiders-wijken. Noorderkwartier en de Kooi in (sociaal)historisch perspectief, in Holland, regionaal-historisch tijdschrift, Year 16 (1984), No. 5, pp. 238–267 (= Building and living in two Leiden workers' districts. "Noorderkwartier" and "de Kooi" from a (social) historical perspective).

56. *Moulin, D. de, I. H. van Eeghen* and *R. Meischke*, Vier eeuwen Amsterdams Binnengasthuis, Amsterdam, 1980 (= Four centuries of Amsterdam's Binnengasthuis).

57. *Nijhof, E., P. Schrage* and *M. Sturkenboom*, De geesel van onze tijd. Een onderzoek naar werklozenbeleid en werkloosheidsbeleving in de jaren dertig te Utrecht, Leiden, 1983 (Cahiers 3 Sociale Geschiedenis) (= The hostages of our time. A study on employment policy and experiencing unemployment in the 1930s in Utrecht).

58. *Nusteling, H.*, Welvaart en werkgelegenheid in Amsterdam. Een relaas over demografie, economie en sociale politiek van een wereldstad, Amsterdam and Diemen, 1985 (= Affluence and jobs in Amsterdam. A report on the demography, economy and social policy of a metropolis).

59. *Olvers, J. A. S. M.*, Cholera en gemeentebeleid in Dordrecht in de negentiende eeuw, Dordrecht, 1982 (= Cholera and communal policy in Dordrecht in the 19th century).

60. *Perry, J.*, Roomsche kinine tegen de roode koorts. Arbeiderbeweging en katholieke kerk in Maastricht 1880–1920, Amsterdam, 1983 (= Roman quinine for red fever. The workers' movement and the Catholic Church in Maastricht, 1880–1920).

61. *Poppel, F. van*, Sociale ongelijkheid voor de dood. Het verband tussen sociaal-economische positie en zuigelingen- en kindersterfte in Nederland in de periode 1850–1940, in Tijdschrift voor Sociale Geschiedenis, No. 27 (1982), pp. 231–281 (= Social inequality in the face of death. The connection between social-economic position and infant and child mortality in the Netherlands from 1850–1940).

62. *Simonse, J.*, Belemmerde kansen. Sociologie van de volksbuurt, Alphen/Rh., 1977 (= Hindered opportunities. Sociology of people's districts).

63. *Siraa, H. T.*, Schiedam in 1807. Bestudering van een stedelijke samenleving vanuit demografisch, economisch en sociaal oogpunt, in Holland, regionaal-historisch tijdschrift, Year 13 (1981), pp. 22–45 (= Schiedam in 1807. View of an urban society including demographic, economic and social aspects).

64. *Sterk, H.*, Rondom de Galekopsteeg. 1858–1885. Enige aspecten van de prostitutie te Utrecht, in Tijdschrift voor Sociale Geschiedenis, No. 30 (1983), pp. 79–107 (= Around Galekopsteeg. 1858–1885. Some aspects of prostitution in Utrecht).

65. *Timp, W.*, De invoering van de huisnummering, in Jaarboek Amstelodamum, Vol. 71 (1979), pp. 79–92 (= The introduction of house numbers).

66. *Vandenbroek, C., F. van Poppel* and *A. M. van der Woude*, De zuigelingen- en kindersterfte in België en Nederland in seculair perspectief, in Tijdschrift voor Geschiedenis, Vol. 94 (1981), pp. 461–491 (= Infant and child mortality in Belgium and the Netherlands from a secular perspective).

67. *Verdoorn, J. A.*, Volksgezondheid en sociale ontwikkeling. Beschouwingen over het gezondheidswezen te Amsterdam in de 19e eeuw, Utrecht and Amsterdam, 1965 (= Public health and social development. Some views on health matters in Amsterdam in the 19th century).

68. *Vries, B. de*, Electoraat en elite. Social structuur en sociale mobiliteit in Amsterdam 1850–1895, Amsterdam, 1986 (= The voting population and the elite. Social structure and mobility in Amsterdam 1850–1895).

69. *Wagenaar, M.*, Van "gemengde" naar "gelede" wijken. Amsterdamse stadsuitbreidingen in het laatste kwart van de negentiende eeuw, in Van stadskern tot stadsgewest. Stedebouwkundige geschiedenis van Amsterdam, eds., M. Jonker, L. Noordegraaf and M. Wagenaar, Amsterdam, 1984, pp. 157–182 (Amsterdamse Historische Reeks. Grote Serie Deel 1) (= Of "mixed" and "linked" municipalities. Amsterdam's urban expansion in the last 25 years of the 19th century).

(d) Town Planning, Housing

70. *Amsterdamse School.* Nederlandse architectuur 1910–1930. Catalogus bij tentoonstelling in Stedelijk Museum te Amsterdam 13/9 t/m 9/11 1975, ed. E. Bergveld et al., n.p. n.d. (= The Amsterdamse School. Architecture in the Netherlands 1910–1930).

71. *Ancona, H. D', et al.*, Nederlandse architectuur en stedebouw. '45–80, Amsterdam, 1984 (= Architecture and town planning in the Netherlands 1945–1980).

72. *Architectuur en volkshuisvesting.* Nederland 1870–1940, ed. M. Casciato, F. Panzini, S. Polano, n.p., 1980 (Sunschrift, Vol. 173) (= Architecture and social housing. The Netherlands 1870–1940).

73. *Beekman, P.*, Eindhoven. Stadsontwikkeling 1900–1960, Mierlo, 1982 (= Eindhoven. Urban development 1900–1960).

74. *Dijksterhuis, R.*, Spoorwegtracering en stedebouw in Nederland. Een historische analyse van een wisselwerking, de eerste eeuw 1840–1940, 2 vols. Diss. Delft, 1985 (= Railroad planning and town planning in the Netherlands. An historical analysis of a reciprocal relationship, the first century 1840–1940).

75. *Engelsdorp Gastelaars, R. van*, De stad als ideaal. Het stadsgewest als realiteit. Bouwen aan Amsterdam tussen 1900 en 1970, in Van stadskern tot stadsgewest. Stedebouwkundige geschiedenis van Amsterdam, eds. M. Jonker, L. Noordegraaf and M. Wagenaar, Amsterdam, 1984, pp. 183–206 (Amsterdamse Historische Reeks. Grote Serie Deel 1) (= The city as an ideal. The urban province as reality. Construction in Amsterdam between 1900 and 1970).

76. *Havenarchitectuur.* Een inventarisatie van industriële gebouwen in het Rotterdamse havengebied, Rotterdam, 1982 (= Harbour architecture. An inventory of industrial buildings in Rotterdam's harbour area).

77. *Heinemeyer, W. F.*, Sociografie en gemeentelijk ruimtelijk beleid, in Jaarboek Amstelodamum, Vol. 74 (1982), pp. 131–145 (= Sociography and communal ordering of space).

78. *Hoogewoud, G., J. J. Kuyt* and *A. Oxenaar*, P. J. H. Cuypers en Amsterdam. Gebouwen en ontwerpen 1860–1898, n.p., 1985 (Cahiers van het Nederlands Documentatiecentrum voor de Bouwkunst) (= P. J. H. Cuypers and Amsterdam. Buildings and designs 1860–1898).

79. *Maanen, R. C. J.*, and *B. N. Leverland*, Leiden buiten de veste, in Leids Jaarboekje, Vol. 73 (1981), pp. 157–204 (= Leiden beyond the fortress).

80. *Meischke, R.*, Amsterdam Burgerweeshuis, Den Haag, 1975 (= Amsterdam's "Burgerweeshuis").

81. *Mens, R.*, Stadsuitbreiding van Haarlem rond 1900, in Haarlems Jaarboek, 1981, pp. 9–42 (= Urban expansion of Haarlem around 1900).

82. *Oud Werk.* Overzicht van industrieel erfgoed in Rotterdam, compiled by C. Asch *et al.*, Rotterdam, 1983 (= Old workshops. Overview of the industrial heritage of Rotterdam).

83. *Reynarts, J.*, Prijstekeningen uit het Amsterdamse bouwkundig onderwijs 1820–1844, in Bulletin Kon. Ned. Oudheidkundige Bond, Year 84 (1985), No. 5, pp. 248–269 (= Prize drawings from the Amsterdam architecture class 1820–1844).

84. *Roy van Zuydewijn, H. J. F. de*, Amsterdamse Bouwkunst 1815–1940, n.p. n.d. (= Amsterdam's Architecture 1815–1940).

85. *Smook, R. A. F.*, Binnensteden veranderen. Atlas van het ruimtelijk veranderingsproces van Nederlandse binnensteden in de laatste anderhalve eeuw, Zutphen, 1985 (= Changing inner cities. Atlas on the spatial process of change of inner cities in the Netherlands in the last one and a half centuries).

86. *Voorden, F. W. van*, Schakels en stedebouw. Een model voor de analyse van de ruimtelijke kwaliteiten van de 19de eeuwse stadsuitbreidingen op grond van een onderzoek in Gelderse steden, Zutphen, 1983 (= Links in town planning. A model for the analysis of spatial qualities of urban expansion in the 19th century on the basis of a study of

Gelderland towns).

87. *Vries, A. de,* De Amsterdamse Beurs 1825–1840. Prijsvraag en polemiek, in Jaarboek Amstelodamum, Vol. 76 (1984), pp. 140–159 (= The Amsterdam stock exchange 1825–1840. Price issues and polemic).

88. *Vries, W. de Wzn., J. C.* van Marken en het Agnetapark te Delft, in Tijdschrift voor Sociale Geschiedenis, No. 10 (1978), pp. 3–35 (= J. C. van Marken and the Agneta Park in Delft).

(e) Economy and Transport

89. *Akker, H. J. M. van den,* Een eeuw Bredase Gasfabriek 1858–1958, in Economisch en Sociaal-Historisch Jaarboek, Vol. 36 (1973), pp. 277–344 (= One century of the Breda Gas Works 1858–1958).

90. *Bergh, G. A. van den,* De NV Sleephelling Sociëteit te Rotterdam 1840–1895, in Economisch en Sociaal-Historisch Jaarboek, Vol. 35 (1972), pp. 187–208 (= The "NV Sleephelling Sociëteit" in Rotterdam 1840–1895).

91. *Beyer, H.,* Honderd jaar telefonie in Haarlem, in Haarlems Jaarboek, 1981, pp. 72–90 (= One hundred years of the telephone in Haarlem).

92. *Blauw, M. J. E.,* De zeevaart op Groningen en de betekenis van het Eemskanaal, in Tijdschrift voor Zeegeschiedenis, Vol. 4 (1985), pp. 117–128 (= The sea voyage to Groningen and the significance of the Ems Canal).

93. *Boomgard, P.,* De havenstaking van 1946 in Amsterdam en Rotterdam. Confrontatie met conflict- en stakingstheorieën, in Economisch en Sociaal-Historisch Jaarboek, Vol. 40 (1977), pp. 242–312 (= The harbour strike of 1946 in Amsterdam and Rotterdam. Confrontation with conflict and strike theories).

94. *Den Haag energiek.* Hoofdstukken uit de geschiedenis van de energievoorziening in Den Haag, 's Gravenhage 1981 (= Den Haag energy. Some chapters from the history of the supply of energy to Den Haag).

95. *Diederiks, H. A.,* Die Wirtschaftsstruktur von Amsterdam um 1800, in Festschrift für Prof. Zwanowetz, Innsbruck, 1984, pp. 63–70.

96. *Diederiks, H. A.,* and *H. D. Tjalsma,* Negentiende en twintigste eeuwse fabrieksgebouwen in de Leidse binnenstad, in Industriële Archeologie, Year 2 (1982), No. 5, pp. 116–138 (= Factory buildings from the 19th and 20th centuries in the Leiden inner city).

97. *Dijk, K. F. van,* Productie van gas en electriciteit te Rotterdam, in Rotterdamse Jaarboek, Vol. X (1982), pp. 208–237 (= The production of gas and electricity in Rotterdam).

98. *Engberts, G. E.,* De Nederlandse en Amsterdamse bouwactiviteiten 1850–1914. Een poging tot raming van de omvang met behulp van technische en economische samenhangen, Amsterdam, 1977 (= Building activity in the Netherlands and Amsterdam 1850–1914).

99. *Gaastra, F. S.*, Werknemers en werkgevers in de Rotterdamse haven 1900–1920, in Tijdschrift voor Sociale Geschiedenis, No. 2 (1975), pp. 219–238 (= Employees and employers in the Rotterdam harbour 1900–1920).

100. *Groen, J. A. jr.*, Een cent per emmer. Het amsterdamer drinkwater door de eeuwen heen, Amsterdam, 1978 (= A cent a bucket. Amsterdam's drinking water through the centuries).

101. *Havelaar, J. J.*, L. I. Enthoven en Co. Fabriekanten te 's Hage: Een schets van haar "Haagse jaren", in Industriële Archeologie, Year 4 (1984) No. 13, pp. 181–193 (= L. I. Enthoven and Co., factory owners in Den Haag. A sketch of their "Haag years").

102. *Hoek Ostende, J. H. van den*, Rosmolens in Amsterdam 1519–1919, in Jaarboek Amstelodamum, Vol. 73 (1981), pp. 10–24 (= Horsedriven mills in Amsterdam 1519–1919).

103. *Kistemaker, R., M. Wagenaar* and *J. Assendelft*, Amsterdam markstad, Amsterdam, 1984 (= Market town Amsterdam).

104. *Knoppers, J. V. T.*, and *F. Snapper*, De nederlandse scheepvaart op te oostzee vanaf het eind van de 17e eeuw tot het begin van de 19e eeuw, in Economisch en Sociaal-Historisch Jaarboek, Vol. 41 (1978), pp. 115–153 (= Dutch navigation in the direction of the Baltic from the end of the 17th century to the beginning of the 19th century).

105. *Knotter, A.*, De Amsterdamse bouwnijverheid in de 19e eeuw tot ca. 1870. Loonstarheid en trekarbeid op een dubbele arbeidsmarkt, in Tijdschrift voor Sociale Geschiedenis, No. 34 (1984), pp. 123–154 (= The Amsterdam building industry in the 19th century up to about 1870. Wage halt and itinerant work on a double work market).

106. *Koopmans, B.*, De Koninklijke Nederlandsche Lood- en Zinkpletterij voorheen A. D. Hamburger te Utrecht, in Industriële Archeologie, Year 3 (1983) No. 8, pp. 117–127 (= The Royal Dutch Lead and Zinc Rolling Mill, formerly A. D. Hamburger in Utrecht).

107. *Kooy, P.*, De gasvoorziening in Nederland rond 1880, in Gas. Maandblad van de Stichting Tijdschrift Openbare Gasvoorziening, Year 100 (1980), pp. 266–277 (= The gas supply in the Netherlands around 1880).

108. *Kooy, P.*, De eerste verbruikers van electriciteit in de gemeente Groningen (1895–1912), in Economisch en Sociaal-Historisch Jaarboek, Vol. 35 (1972), pp. 274–302 (= The first electricity consumers in the Groningen community 1895–1912).

109. *Kouwenberg, L. J. N.*, Alkmaar verlicht. Van pijpgaz tot aardgas. De geschiedenis van de gasvoorziening in Alkmaar en omstreken sinds 1853, Schoorl, 1982 (= Alkmaar illuminated. From city gas to natural gas. The history of the gas supply in Alkmaar and its environs since 1853).

110. *Krouwel, E. J.*, Herwaardering van de textielindustrie in Hengelo, in Textielhistorische Bijdragen, Vol. XXIII (1982), pp. 12–49 (= A

changed appraisal of the textile industry in Hengelo).

111. *Meyer, J. L.*, Industriële ontwikkelingen op Oostenburg na 1800, in Industriële Archeologie, Year 5 (1985), No. 16, pp. 97–126 (= Industrial development on Oostenburg – i.e. an island in the old part of the city in Amsterdam – after 1800).

112. *Middelhoven, P. J.*, De amsterdamse veilingen van Noord-Europees naaldhout 1717–1808. Een bijdrage tot de Nederlandse Prijsgeschiedenis, in Economisch en Sociaal-Historisch Jaarboek, Vol. 41 (1978), pp. 86–114 (= Amsterdam auctions of North European softwood 1717–1808. A contribution to Dutch history of prices).

113. *Muller, H.*, Muller. Een Rotterdams zeehandelaer Hendrik Muller Szn (1819–1898), Schiedam, 1977 (= Muller. A overseas trader from Rotterdam. Hendrik Muller Szn. 1819–1898).

114. *Nieuwmeyer G.G.*, and *M. Kuipers*, Overzicht van de gasvoorziening van Amsterdam sinds 1825 en de aanleg van de westergasfabriek in opdracht van de Imperial Continental Gas Association in 1885 in gebruik gesteld, in Industriële Archeologie, Year 3 (1983), No. 9. pp. 155–168, and Year 4 (1984), No. 10, pp. 4–25 (= An outline of Amsterdam's gas supply since 1825 and the construction in 1885 "westergasfabriek" as contracted by the Imperial Continental Gas Association).

115. *Schmal, H.*, Knellende banden geslaakt? Railvervoer en het wonen tot aan de eerste wereldoorlog, in het bijzonder in en rond Amsterdam, in Economisch- en Sociaal-Historisch Jaarboek, Vol. 46 (1983), pp. 93–112 (= Cutting chains released? Rail transport and living up to the First World War, particularly in and around Amsterdam).

116. *Schouten, J.*, De honderdjarige Goudse Waterleiding Maatschappij n.v. 1883–1983, Gouda, 1983 (= The 100-year-old "Goudse Waterleiding Maatschappij n.v." 1883–1983).

117. *Stolp, A.*, De oprichting van de stedelijke gasfabriek te Leiden, in Holland, regionaal-historisch tijdschrift, Year 15 (1984), pp. 6–23 (= The erection of the city gas works in Leiden).

118. *Tijn, T. van*, Geschiedenis van de Amsterdamse diamanthandel en nijverheid 1845–1897, in Tijdschrift voor Geschiedenis, Vol. 87 (1974), pp. 16–70, and 160–201 (= History of Amsterdam's diamond trade and diamond industry 1845–1897).

119. *Wagemakers, T.*, Een moderne textielfabriek omstreeks 1830. Een industriëel-archeologische reconstructie, in Jaarboek De Lindeboom, Vol. VI (1982), pp. 91–114 (= A modern textile factory around 1830. An industrial-archeological reconstruction).

120. *Zanden, J. L. van*, Lonen en arbeidsmarkt in Amsterdam 1800–1865, in Tijdschrift voor Sociale Geschiedenis, No. 29 (1983), pp. 3–27 (= Wages and the work market in Amsterdam 1800–1865).

(f) Arts and Sciences, Churches

121. *Boon-de Gouw, A.*, Feuilletons in de Rotterdamse pres in de jaren 1880–1920, in Tijdschrift voor Sociale Geschiedenis, No. 35 (1984), pp. 291–314 (= Feuilletons in the Rotterdam press in the years 1880–1920).

122. *Kaajan, H. J. P.*, Zestig jaars kerksplitsing te 's Gravenhage, in Holland, regionaal-historisch tijdschrift, Year 17 (1985), No. 5, pp. 269–283 (= Sixty years of division in the church in 's Gravenhage).

E. Local Studies (a representative selection)

● Delft

123. *Jonge, J. A. de*, Delft in de negentiende eeuw. Van een "stille nette" plaats tot een centrum van industrie. Enkele facetten van de omslag in een totale sociaal-economische evolutie, in Economisch en Sociaal-Historisch Jaarboek, Vol. 37 (1974), pp. 145–147 (= Delft in the 19th century: from a "quiet, clean" place to an industrial centre. Some aspects of the turnabout in a local social-economic evolution).

● Eindhoven

124. *Dorschot, J. M. P.*, Eindhoven. Een samenleving in verandering, 2 vols. Eindhoven, 1982 (= Eindhoven. A city in transition).

● Enkhuizen

125. *Vries, R. J. de*, Enkhuizen. Opkomst en verval van een zuiderzeestad, in Historisch Geografisch Tijdschrift, Year 1 (1983), No. 2, pp. 26–32 (= Enkhuizen. Rise and fall of a city on the Zuidersee).

● Groningen

126. *Kooy, P.*, Groningen 1870–1914. Sociale verandering en economische ontwikkeling in een regionaal centrum, Diss. Groningen, 1986 (= Groningen 1870–1914. Social change and economic development in a regional centre).

● Leeuwarden

127. *Collecteur, G., T. Dankert* and *W. Terwisscha van Scheltinga*, Patentbelasting en economische structuur van Leeuwarden 1870–1890, in

Economisch- en Sociaal-Historisch Jaarboek, Vol. 45 (1982), pp. 114–153 (= Patent tax and economic structure of Leeuwarden 1870–1890).

128. *Schroor, M.*, Woningbouw en stadsuitbreiding in 't 19e eeuwse Leeuwarden, in Historisch Geografisch Tijdschrift, Year 2 (1984), No. 3, pp. 72–82 (= Housing and urban expansion in Leeuwarden of the 19th century).

• Maastricht

129. *Philips, R.*, Meestrechts Aagt. Geschiedenis van de Maastrichtse brouwers en hun bier, Maastricht, 1982 (Stichting Historische Reeks) (= "Meestrechts Aagt". The history of the Maastricht brewery and its beer).

130. *Philips, R.*, Stroombierbrouwerij De Keizer v/h fa. N.A. Bosch Maastricht, in Industriële Archeologie, Year 2 (1982), No. 3, pp. 40–54 (= Steam beer brewery "De Keizer v/h fa. N. A. Bosch Maastricht").

• Middelburg

131. *Stol, T.*, Middelburg ontstaan, bloei en achteruitgang, in Historisch Geografisch Tijdschrift, Year 1 (1983), No. 3, pp. 65–72 (= Middelburg. Birth, peak and decline).

• Rotterdam

132. *Oosterwijk, B.*, Vlucht na victorie. Lodewijk Pincoffs (1827–1911), Rotterdam, 1979 (= Flight and victory. Lodewijk Pincoffs. 1827–1911).

JAN EIVIND MYHRE

Norway

Research on urban history in Norway has been pursued along two lines, corresponding to two different approaches to history.

First, urban history has been written as local history, as biographies of individual towns and cities, or parts thereof. This branch of history has a very long tradition in Norway among amateur as well as professional historians. The latter have dominated the scene for the past few decades, and nearly all the local studies in the bibliography have been written by historically trained scholars.

Secondly, we find urban history as studies of the process of urbanisation in Norway. In spite of the rapid urbanisation experienced by Norwegian society from the mid-19th century onwards, historical or historically oriented social scientific studies on urbanisation have been relatively scarce until recently (the percentage of people living in urban areas was 15% in 1946 and 71% in 1980).

Relatively few comprehensive studies encompassing many aspects of the urbanisation process exist for the period prior to the Second World War. Myhre (1977 and 1983) are examples of an historian's approach, while Torstenson et al. exemplifies the approach of social scientists, where planning aspects are particularly focused upon.

In the field of urban historical studies there has been a division of labour between historians and social scientists. Not surprisingly, historians have concentrated on more distant periods. Less obvious, there is also a division in the choice of themes and problems.

Historians have been especially interested in placing urban themes and individual towns in a wider historical perspective. They have also taken a particular interest in the study of social mobility and the development of social structure.

Social researchers, on the other hand, have dedicated themselves to investigating settlement patterns or urban politics (Baldersheim, Gulbrandsen). Historically interested geographers have been among the most industrious contributors to Norwegian historical urban research. Myklebost is mostly concerned with the settlement aspect of urbanisation, Rasmussen and Hansen concentrate on metropolitan growth and commuting. There are relatively few studies on urban planning; considerably more energy has been devoted to regional development and policies. Centre-periphery relations — political, social and economic — have been potent issues in modern Norwegian history. Nationalism and rural life have often been associated with each other; rural life has been idealised and urban culture frowned upon. The inherent values of regional balance and a well-distributed settlement pattern are, politically, almost sacred. This is also reflected in the status of urban and regional research (Torstenson *et al.*, 1985).

Relations between towns and their surroundings are, in accordance with this, quite well taken care of in most town histories. They are also the subject of many specialised studies (Fladby and Winge, Sund).

Many lacunae in the field of Norwegian urban historical research need to be filled. Other fields need more extensive scholarly treatment. Among them are urban planning, the foundation of new towns, internal urban politics, urban housing and urban demography.

A. Urban History Institutions

Norsk lokalhistorisk institutt, Oslo (= Norwegian Institute of Local History).
Norsk Institutt for By- og Regionforskning, Oslo (= Norwegian Institute of Urban and Regional Research).

B. Aids to Research

(a) Urban History Journals

1. *Byminner,* 1955 ff. (= City monuments. Published by the Oslo city museum).
2. *Gamle Bergen.* Årbok, Bergen, 1951 ff. (= Old Bergen. Yearbook).
3. *Heimen,* Oslo, 1920 ff. (= Journal of local and regional history).
4. *St. Hallvard,* Oslo, 1915 ff. (= Local history in Oslo).
5. *Trondhjemske samlinger. Årsskrift,* Trondheim, 1901 ff. (Yearbook, published by Trondheim's Historical Association).

(b) Bibliographies

6. *International Bibliography of Urban History.* Denmark, Finland, Norway, Sweden, Stockholm, 1960.
7. *Langholm, S.,* The Christiania Project: Historians Investigate the Making of Urban Society, in Research in Norway, 1976, pp. 49–57.

8. *Myhre, J. E.*, Historien om Oslo-historiene, in Byminner, No. 3 (1986), pp. 2–14 (= The history of Oslo's histories).
9. *Ropeid, A.*, Byhistorie og byhistorisk forskning, in Lokal historie, Oslo, 1970, pp. 113–136 (= Urban history and urban historical research).

(c)   Handbooks on Urban History

10. *Hammarström, I.*, Urban History in Scandinavia: A Survey of Recent Trends, in Urban History Yearbook, 1978, pp. 46–55.
11. *Marthinsen, L*, ed., Om Byhistorie. Problemstillinger og metode, Oslo, 1986 (= On urban history. Problems and methods).

(d)   Atlases on Urban History and Urban Development

12. *Myklebost H.*, and *J. Sandal*, Kart over pendleromland, Oslo, 1977 (= Maps of commuting hinterlands).

(e)   Urban History Sources

13. *Myklebost, H.*, Norges tettsteder. Folketall og næringsstruktur, Oslo, 1979 (= Norway's urban settlements: population and occupational structure 1900–1970).

C.   Research Reports

(a)   General Surveys

14. *Bjørnland, D.*, ed., Innenlands samferdsel i Norge siden 1800. Part 1: Demring (1800–1850-tallet) (= Internal communications in Norway c. 1800–1850), Oslo, 1977.
15. *Gjesdal Christensen, A.L.*, Byeksplosjonen, in Norsk kulturhistorie, Vol. 5 (1980), pp. 19–36 (= The urban explosion).
16. *Moren, S.*, By og land, hand i hand?, in Norsk kulturhistorie, Vol. 6 (1980), pp. 69–90 (= City and country, hand in hand?).
17. *Myhre, J. E.*, Urbaniseringen i Norge i industrialiseringens første fase ca. 1850–1914, in I. Authén Blom, ed., Urbaniseringsprosessen i Norden, Vol. 3, Oslo, 1977, pp. 13–93 (= The process of urbanisation in the north in the first phase of industrialization).
18. *Myhre, J. E.*, Urbaniseringen i Norge etter første verdenskrig, Jyväskyla 1983, pp. 157–170 (Historica IV. Studia Historica Jyväskyländsia, Vol. 27) (= The urbanisation of Norway after the First World War).
19. *Myklebost, H.*, Bosetningsutviklingen i Norge 1950–1975, Oslo, 1978 (= Norway's settlement structure 1950–1975).

20. *Myklebost, H.*, Norges tettbygde steder 1875–1950, Oslo, 1960 (= The urban places of Norway 1875–1950).
21. *Rasmussen, T. F.*, Byregioner i Norge. Den regional konsentrasjon i bosettingsmønstret, Oslo, 1969 (= Urban regions of Norway: The regional concentration of the settlement pattern).
22. *Rasmussen, T. F.*, Urbanisering og næringsutvikling i Norge i dette århundret, Oslo, 1979 (NOU 1975, Vol. 5: Bypolitikk) (= Urbanisation and economic development in Norway in the 20th century in Norwegian Official Reports, 1975, Vol. 5).
23. *Torstenson, J. S., M. F. Metcalf* and *T.F. Rasmussen*, Urbanization and Community Building in Norway, Oslo, 1985.

(b)   Surveys of Individual Fields of Urban Research

24. *Hansen, J. C.*, Administrative grenser og tettstedsvekst, Bergen, 1970 (= Administrative boundaries and urban growth).
25. *Isachsen, F.*, Bidrag til Oslos geografi, in Svensk geografisk årsbok, 1928, pp. 166–167 (= Contribution to the geography of Oslo).
26. *Lorange, E.* and *J. E. Myhre*, Urban Planning in Norway, in T. Hall, ed., Urban Planning in Scandinavia, London, 1986.

D.   Literature on Individual Areas of Urban History Research

(a)   Concept and Definition of Town and Town Types

27. *Gamborg, J.*, Om Byerne og Landet i deres indbyrdes Forhold med Hensyn til Befolkning og Produktion, Christiania (Oslo), 1877 (= About cities and rural areas and their relationships concerning population and production).
28. *Hansen, J. C.*, Urbaniseringen av landsbygden, in R. Fladby and S. Imsen, eds., Lokalhistorie fra gard til tettsted, Oslo, 1974, pp. 9–40 (= The urbanisation of the countryside).
29. *Juhasz, L.*, Byhistorie, in Heimen, 1967, pp. 177–187 (= Urban history).
30. *Myhre, J. E.*, "By", "Tettsted", "Urbanisering" – En innledning, in G. Authén Blom, ed., Urbaniseringsprosessen i Norden, Vol. 3, Oslo, 1977, pp. 9–12 (= The process of urbanisation in Norden).

(b)   Politics, Law and Statutes

31. *Baldersheim, H.*, ed., Bypolitikk i Norge, Oslo, 1983 (= Urban politics in Norway).

32. *Guldbrandsen, L.*, Boligmarked og boligpolitikk. Eksemplet Oslo, Oslo, 1983 (= Housing market and housing politics: the Oslo example).

33. *Mykland, K.*, Hovedstadsfunksjonen. Christiania som eksempel, in T. Hall, ed., Städer i utveckling. Tolv studier kring stadsföränderingar tillägnade Ingrid Hammarstrøm, Stockholm, 1984, pp. 49–58 (= The functions of capital cities. Example Christiania).

(c)   Population and Social Structure

34. *Bull, E.*, Grünerløkka – beste østkant, in St. Hallvard, 1961, pp. 201–301 (= Grünerløkka – "Best East End").

35. *Bull, E.*, Håndverkssvenner og arbeiderklasse i Kristiania. Sosialhistoriske problemer, in Historisk Tidsskrift, 1966, pp. 89–114 (= Journeymen and working class in Christiania).

36. *Gjesdal Christensen, A. L.*, Vålerenga. Treby i murbyen, Oslo, 1972 (= Vålerenga: Wooden town in a stone city).

37. *Langholm, S.*, "Noget at fare med" - Angående handverksmestrene i Christiania, in Vandringer. Festskrift til Ingrid Semmingsen, Oslo, 1980, pp. 141–162. (= The origins of master artisans in Christiania).

38. *Langholm, S.*, Frå Holmestrand til hovudstaden. Litt om røtene til handelsborgerskapet i Christiania på 1800-talet, in B. Gjerdåker, ed., På flyttefot. Innanlands vandring på 1800-talet, Oslo, 1981, pp. 90–124 (= The roots of the commercial bourgeoisie in Christiania in the 19th century).

39. *Myhre, J. E.*, "Det livligste vexel-forhold" – flyttingene til Kristiania på annen halvdel av 1800-tallet, in B. Gjerdåker, ed., På flyttefot. Innanlands vandring på 1800-talet, Oslo, 1981, pp. 125–145 (= Migration to Christiania in the second half of the 19th century).

40. *Myhre, J. E.*, Sagene – en arbeiderforstad befolkes 1801–1875, Oslo, 1978 (= Sagene – the peopling of a working-class suburb 1801–1875).

41. *Myhre, J. E.*, Fra småby til storby. Kristianias vekst i det nittende århundret in T. Hall, ed., Städer i utveckling. Tolv studier kring stadsförändringar tillägnade Ingrid Hammarstrøm, Stockholm 1984, pp. 78–94 (= From small town to big city. The growth of Christiania in the 19th century).

42. *Myhre, J. E.*, and *J. S. Østberg*, eds., Mennesker i Kristiania. Sosialhistorisk søkelys på 1800-tallet, Oslo, 1979 (= People of Christiania: Social historical searchlight on the 19th century).

43. *Sundt, E.*, Om fattigforholdene i Christiania, Oslo, 1870 (reprinted 1978) (= About the conditions of the poor in Christiania).

44. *Sundt, E.*, Om Piperviken og Ruseløkbakken. Undersøgelser om arbeiderklassens kår og sæder i Christiania, Oslo, 1858 (reprinted 1968) (= About Piperviken and Ruseløkbakken: Inquiries into the conditions of working-class people in Christiania).

(d) Town Planning

45. *Aslaksby, T.*, Grønland og Nedre Tøyens bebyggelses historie, Oslo, 1986 (= The building history of Grønland and Nedre Tøyens).

46. *Hall, T.*, Planung europäischer Hauptstädte, Stockholm, 1986 (Christiania, pp. 156–163).

47. *Jensen, R.*, Moderne norsk byplanlegging blir til, Trondheim, 1980 (= The formation of modern Norwegian town planning).

48. *Pedersen, B. S.*, Oslo i byplanhistorisk perspektiv, in St. Hallvard, 1965, pp. 190–208 (= Oslo in a town-planning perspective).

(e) Economy and Transport

49. *Ahlmann, H. W.*, De norske städernas geografiska forutsättningar, in Ymer, 1917, pp. 249–299 (= The geographic foundations of Norwegian towns).

50. *Fladby, R.*, and *H. Winge*, eds., By og bygd. Stad og omland, Oslo, 1981 (= Town and country: City and hinterland).

51. *Hansen, J. C.*, Industriell utvikling og tettstedsvekst, in Norsk geografisk tidsskrift, 1965/66, pp. 181–265 (= Industrial development and urban growth).

52. *Rasmussen, T. F.*, Storbyutvikling og arbeidsreiser, Oslo, 1966 (= Urban development change and urbanisation in the Oslo region).

53. *Sund, T.*, Bergens byområde og dets geografiske utstrekning 1900–1940, Bergen, 1947 (= The Bergen city region and its geographical extension 1900–1940).

54. *Sund, T.*, and *F. Isachsen*, Bosteder og arbeidssteder i Oslo, Oslo, 1942 (= Places of residence and places of work in Oslo).

(f) Arts and Sciences, Churches

55. *Nordhagen, P. J.*, Trebyen faller. Bergen 1870–1970, Oslo, 1975 (= The fall of the wooden city).

E. Local Studies (a representative selection)

● Arendal

56. *Dannevig, B.*, Arendal gjennom skiftende tider. 1528–1723–1973, Arendal, 1973 (= Arendal through changing times).

● Asker

57. *Thue, L.*, Asker 1840–1980, Oslo, 1984 (= Suburban history).

● Bærum

58. *Myhre, J. E.*, Bærum 1810–1980, Oslo, 1982 (= Suburban history).

● Bergen

59. *Helle, K., et al.*, Bergen bys historie, I–IV, Bergen, 1979–1985 (= The history of Bergen).
60. *Steen, S.*, Bergen – byen mellom fjellene, Bergen, 1969 (= Bergen – the city amidst the mountains).

● Bodø

61. *Coldevin, A.*, Bodø By 1816–1966, Bodø, 1966 (= The city of Bodø 1816–1966).

● Drammen

62. *Pedersen, T., O. W. Thorson* and *B. Nøkleby*, Drammen. En norsk østlandsbys utviklingshistorie I–IV, Drammen, 1961–1981 (= The history of Drammen, a city of south-east Norway).

● Fredrikstad

63. *Dehli, M.*, Fredrikstad bys historie, I–III, Fredrikstad, 1960–1973 (= The history of Fredrikstad).

● Hammerfest

64. *Sivertsen, J.*, Hammerfest 1789–1914, Hammerfest, 1973 (= Hammerfest 1789–1914).

● Haugesund

65. *Østensjø, R.*, Haugesund 1835–1895, Haugesund, 1958 (= Haugesund 1835–1895).

● Hønefoss

66. *Ropeid, A.*, Hønefoss, I–III (1600–1963), Hønefoss, 1952–1968 (= Hønefoss 1600–1963).

● Kristiansand

67. *Steen, S.* and *J. N. Tønnessen*, Kristiansands historie 1641–1945, I–II, Kristiansand, 1941–1974 (= The history of Kristiansand).

● Lillehammer

68. *Buggeland, T.*, and *J. E. Ågotnes*, eds., Lillehammer. By og bygd, gate og grend, Lillehammer, 1977 (= Lillehammer, town and country).

● Lillestrøm

69. *Hals, H.*, Lillestrøms historie, I–II, Skedsmo, 1978 (= The History of Lillestrøm).

● Moss

70. *Andressen, L. T.*, Moss bys historie, I, Oslo, 1984 (= The history of Moss).

● Notodden

71. *Hansen, J. C.*, Notodden, Notodden, 1963.

● Oslo (Christiania)

72. *Bull, E., V. Sønstevold* and *S. C. Hammer*, Kristianias historie I–V, Oslo, 1922–1936 (= The history of Oslo).

● Porsgrunn

73. *Tønnessen, J. N.*, Porsgrunns historie 1576–1920, I–II, Porsgrunn, 1956–1957 (= The history of Porsgrunn).

● Rjukan

74. *Dahl, H.*, Rjukan, I–II, Tinn, 1983–1985.
75. *Kjeldstadli, S.*, Rjukan – en moderne eventyr, Oslo, 1943 (= Rjukan – a modern fairytale).

- Sarpsborg

76. *Dehli, M., E. Johansen* and *L. Opstad,* Sarpsborg før 1839, Sarpsborg, 1976 (= Sarpsborg before 1839).

- Skien

77. *Seierstad, I.* and *E. Østvedt,* Skiens historie (1184–1925), I–III, Skien, 1958–1959 (= The history of Skien).

- Stavanger

78. *Egeland, K.,* ed., Stavanger på 1800-tallet, Stavanger, 1975 (= Stavanger in the 19th century).

- Strinda

79. *Sjøholt, P.,* . . . og bygda ble by. Strindas historie 1945–1963, Trondheim, 1971 (= Suburban history: Strinda's history 1945–1963).

- Tønsberg

80. *Johnsen, A. O.,* Tønsberg gjennom tidene, Oslo, 1971 (= Tønsberg through the ages).
81. *Johnsen, O. A.,* Tønsberg historie I–III, Oslo, 1929–1954 (= The history of Tønsberg).

- Tromsø

82. *Ytreberg, N. A.,* Tromsø bys historie I–III, Tromsø, 1946–1971 (= The history of Tromsø).

- Trondheim

83. *Blom, G. et al.,* Trondheim bys historie I–V, Trondheim, 1955–1973 (= The history of Trondheim).

- Vadsø

84. *Niemi, E.,* Vadsøs historie I, Vadsø, 1983 (= The history of Vadsø).

ADELHEID SIMSCH

Poland

A. Urban History Institutions

Instytut Historii Polskiej Akademii Nauk, Warszawa (= Historical Institute of the Polish Academy of Sciences, Warsaw).

Instytut Historii Kultury Materialnej Polskiej Akademii Nauk, Warszawa, (= Institute for History of Material Culture of the Polish Academy of Sciences, Warsaw).

Komitet Architektury i Urbanistyki Polskiej Akademii Nauk, Warszawa, (= Committee of Architecture and Urbanism of the Polish Academy of Sciences, Warsaw).

B. Aids to Research

(a) Urban History Journals

1. *Kwartalnik Architektury i Urbanistyki. Teorie i Historia*, 1956 ff., pub. by Komitet Architektury i Urbanistyki PAN (= Quarterly journal on architecture and urban studies. Theory and history).
2. *Kwartalnik Historii Kultury Materialnej*, 1953 ff., pub. by Instytut Historii Kultury Materialnej PAN (= Quarterly journal on history of material culture).
3. *Roczniki dziejów społecznych i gospodarczych*, 1932 ff., pub. by Poznánskie Towarzystwo Przyjaciół Nauk, Poznań (= Annals on social and economic history).
4. *Studia Historiae Oeconomicae*, 1965 ff., pub. by der Uniwersytet Adama Mickiewicza, Poznań.

(b) Bibliographies

5. *Bibliografia historii Elbląga i regionu za lata 1962–1963 wraz z uzupełnieniami od*

roku 1945, ed., Z. Baranowska, in Rocznik Elbląski, No. 3 (1965/66), pp. 337–344 (= Bibliography on the history of Elblag and its environs for the years 1962–1963 with supplements from 1945 onwards).
6. *Bibliografia Warszawy 1864–1903*, eds., C. Bezegowa *et al.*, Wrocław, 1971 (= Bibliography of Warsaw 1864–1903).
7. *Bibliografia Warszawy 1904–1918*, eds., C. Bezegowa *et al.*, Wrocław, 1973 (= Bibliography of Warsaw 1904–1918).
8. *Dzieje Poznania i województwa poznańskiego*: informator o materiałach archiwalnych, ed., C. Skopowski, Poznań, 1982 (= History of Poznań and the Wojewodschaft of Poznań. Catalogue of archive material).
9. *Szymańska, M.*, Bibliografia historii Poznania, Poznań, 1960 (Materiały Sekoji Historii Poznania przy PTH Oddział Poznań) (= Bibliography on the history of Poznań).

(c)   Handbooks on Urban History

—

(d)   Atlases on Urban History and Urban Development

10. *Domański, J.*, Katalog planów miast i osiedli śląskich z XVI–XIX w. w zbiorach Archiwum Państwowego we Wrocławiu, Warsaw, 1973 (= Catalogue of Slask town and village plans from the 16th to 19th centuries).

(e)   Urban History Sources

11. *Chmiel, A.*, Dom nr 12 na ulicy Św. Jana w Krakowie. Z opisem ulicy Św. Jana, Kraków, 1927 (= House No. 12 in St. John Street in Kraków, with a description of the street).
12. *Chmiel, A.*, Domy krakowskie. Ulica Floriańska, Kraków, 1917–1920 (Bibl. Krakowska, Nr. 54, 57/58) (= Kraków houses. Florian Street).
13. *Chmiel, A.*, Domy krakowskie. Ulica Grodzka, Kraków, 1934–1935 (Bibl. Krakowska 85, Nr. 81) (= Kraków houses. Fortress Street).
14. *Chmiel, A.*, Domy krakowskie. Ulica Sławska, Kraków, 1931–1932 (Bibl. Krakowska, Nr. 73, 75) (= Kraków houses. Sława Street).
15. *Chmiel, A.*, Domy krakowskie. Ulica św. Jana, Kraków, 1924 (Bibl. Krakowska, Nr. 61/62) (= Kraków houses. St. John's Street).
16. *Grochowska, I.*, Źródła archiwalne do dziejów miasta Białegostoku w latach 1795–1915/1918, in Rocznik Białost., No. 11 (1972), pp. 317–337 (= Archive sources on the history of the city of Białystok in the years 1795–1915/1918).
17. *Kazimierski, J.*, Źródła do dziejów Warszawy w latach 1939–1944, in Warszawa lat wojny i okupacji 1939–1944, Warsaw, 1973, pp. 43–53

(Studia Warszawskie Vol. 17) (= Sources on the history of the city of Warsaw in the years 1939–1944).

18. *Materiały do historii miast, przemysłu i klasy robotniczej w okręgu łódzkim.* – Vol. 1 Źródła do dziejów rewolucji 1905–1907 w okręgu łódzkim, ed., N. Gąsiorowska, Warsaw, 1957 (= Material on the history of the city, industry and the working class in the area of Łódź. Part 1: Sources on the history of the revolution in the years 1905–1907 in the area of Łódź). – Vol. 2 Źródła do dziejów rewolucji 1905–1907 w okręgu łódzkim, ed., N. Gąsiorowska, Warsaw, 1964 (= Sources on the history of the revolution 1905–1907 in the area of Łódź). – Vol. 3 Źródla do historii przemysłu włókienniczego okręgu łódzkiego w XIX w., ed., N. Gąsiorowska, Warsaw, 1966 (= Sources on the history of the cloth industry in the Łódź area in the 19th century).

19. *Perlińska, A.*, Materiały do dziejów Bydgoszczy z lat 1945–1950 w Wojewódzkim Archiwum Pánistwowym w Bydgoszczy, in Prace Komisji Historycznej Bydgoszcz, No. 11 (1975), pp. 219–243 (= Material on the history of Bydgoszcz from the years 1945–1950 in the state waywordship archive in Bydgoszcz).

20. *Warszawa w pamiętnikach pierwszej wojny światowej*, ed., K. Dunin-Wąsowicz, Warsaw, 1971 (= Warsaw in memoirs from the First World War).

21. *Zbiór statutów miejskich.* Statuty miejscowe, wazniejsze uchwały gminne i regulaminy miejskie oraz najważniejsze rozporządzenia miejsscowej władzy policyjnej, obowiązujace na obszarze gminy stoł. m. Poznania, Poznań 1926 (= Collection of urban statutes. Town statutes, important community resolutions and town service regulations as well as the most important decrees of the town police authorities in force in this area.

22. *Zgierz: źródła do dziejów miasta w XIX i XX w.*, ed., M. Bandurka, Łódź, 1976 (= Zgierz (near Łódź) (= Sources on the history of the city in the 19th and 20th centuries).

C. Research Reports

(a) General Surveys

23. *Jelonek, A.*, Struktura płci i wieku ludności Krakowa w latach 1946–1960, in Folia Geographica Seria Geographica-Oeconomica, Vol. 2 (1969), pp. 5–55 (= Sex and age structure of the Kraków population in the years 1946–1960).

24. *Kołodziejczyk, R.*, Miasta, mieszczaństwo, burżuazja w Polsce w XIX w.: Szkice i rozprawy historyczne, Warsaw, 1979 (= Towns, urban population, the middle classes in Poland in the 19th century: Outlines

and historical treatises.

25. *Kraków*. Rozwój miasta w Polsce Ludowej, ed., J. Jasieński, Kraków, 1971 (= Kraków. The development of the city in the People's Republic of Poland).

26. *Nietyksza, M.*, Les recherches polonaises de la ville de l'époque du capitalisme jusqu'à 1939, in Acta Poloniae Historica, Vol. 41 (1980), pp. 259–281.

(b) Surveys of Individual Fields of Urban Research

27. *Wyrobisz, A.*, Stan badań i główne problemy rozwoju przestrzenego miast polskich w latach 1815–1914, in Prace historyczne, Vol. 6 (1982), pp. 41–86 (= State of research and the main problems of the spatial development of Polish towns in the years 1815–1914).

D. Literature on Individual Areas of Urban History Research

(a) Concept and Definition of Town and Town Types

28. *Ćwik, W.*, Miasta rządowe małopolskiej części Królestwa Polskiego 1815–1866, in Rocznik Lubelski, Vol. 10 (1967/69), pp. 229–247 (= Government towns in the Little Poland section of the Kingdom of Poland 1815–1866).

29. *Huba, W.* Własność nieruchoma w miastach rządowych w okresie Królestwa Kongresowego (1815–1866): na przykładzie województwa płockiego, Warsaw and Poznań, 1978 (Bibliogr. Bydgoskie Towarzystwo Naukowe, Prace Wydziału Nauk Humanistycznych. Series E, No. 12) (= Realty in the government towns in Congress Poland (1815–1866): the example of waywodship in Plock).

30. *Madurowicz-Urbańska, H.*, Struktura wielkości miast i osiedli typu miejskiego w Wielkim Księstwie Poznańskim, Królestwie Polskim i Galicji w drugiej połowie XIX wieku (do 1910 r.). Z historycznych procesów urbanizacji – próba analizy, in Badania nad historią gosp.-społ. w w Polsce, Warsaw, 1978, pp. 171–185 (= The structure of the size of towns and settlements of urban nature in the Grand Duchy of Poznán, the Kingdom of Poland and Galicia in the second half of the 19th century (up to 1910). An attempt at an analysis of the historical process of urbanisation).

31. *Tłoczek, J.*, Miasteczka rolnicze w Wielkopolsce, Warsaw, 1955 (= Agricultural settlements in Great Poland).

32. *Topolski, J.*, Badania nad dziejami miast w Polsce, in Studia i Materiały do Dziejów Wielkopolski i Pomorza, VI (1961), No. 2, pp. 5–43 (= Research on urban history in Poland).

(b)   Politics, Law and Statutes

33. *Biegeleisen, L. W.*, Stan i tendencje rozwoju polskich urżadzeń miejskich (1919–1928), Warsaw, 1930 (= State and development trends of urban authorities (1919–1928).

34. *Dunin-Wasowicz, K.*, Warszawa w czasie pierwszej wojny światowej, Warsaw, 1974 (= Warsaw during the First World War).

35. *Gajewski, M.*, Odbudowa warszawskich urżadseń komunalnych w latach 1944–1951, in Warszawa stolica Polski Ludowej, Warsaw, 1972, pp. 95–122 (Studia Warszawskie, Vol. 11) (= Setting up of Warsaw local authorities in the years 1944–1951).

36. *Gajewski, M.*, Urządzenia komunalne miasta stołecznego Warszawy w latach 1939–1944, in Warszawa lat wojny i okupacji. 1939–1945, Warsaw, 1975, pp. 61–98 (Studia Warszawskie, Vol. 23) (= Local authorities in the capital Warsaw in the years 1939–1944).

37. *Gajewski, M.*, Urządzenia komunalne w Warszawie. Zarys historyczny, Warsaw, 1979 (= Local bodies in Warsaw. An historical outline).

38. *Lipiec, J.*, Ekonomiczno-społeczna i prawna degradacja miast regionu częstochowskiego w XIX wieku, in Ziemia Częstochowska, Vols. 6/7 (1967), pp. 83–125. (= Economic, social and legal degradation of towns in the Częstochowa region in the 19th century).

39. *Marczuk, J.*, Budowa i rozwój urządzeń komunalnych w Lublinie w latach 1925–1939, in Kwartalnik Historii Kultury Materialnej, Series 26 (1978), No. 4, pp. 505–519 (= Construction and development of communal authorities in Lublin in the years 1925–1939).

40. *Marczuk, J.*, Samorząd miasta Lublina 1915–1918, in Kwartalnik Historyczny, Series 86 (1979), No. 2, pp. 181–196 (= Self-government in the city of Lublin 1915–1918).

41. *Moraczewski, A.*, Samorząd w dobie powstania listopadowego, Warsaw, 1934 (Biblioteka Historyczna im Tadeusza Korzona, No. 23) (= Self-government in the time of the November uprising).

42. *Pawłowicz, H.*, Okupacyjne dzieje samorządu Warszawy, ed., Z. Ogrodzki, Warsaw, 1974 (= Governing Warsaw during the occupation).

43. *Warszawa popowstaniowa 1864–1918*, eds., S. Kalabiński and R. Kołodziejczyk, Warsaw 1968 (= Warsaw after the uprising 1864–1918).

44. *Wasiak, J.*, Organizacja samorządu miejskiego w Łódzi w latach 1915–1939, in Rocznik Łódzki, Vol. 23 (1978), pp. 183–206 (= The organisation of urban administration in Łódź in the years 1915–1939).

45. *Wojciechowski, M.*, Toruń w latach I wojny światowej 1914–1918, in Rocznik Toruński, Vol. 2 (1967), pp. 131–150 (= Toruń during the First World War 1914–1918).

(c)   Population and Social Structure

46. *Archacki, J.*, Ludność miasta Bogatyni w latach 1945–1950, in Śląski Kwartalnik Historyczny Sobótka, Series 24 (1969), No. 2, pp. 237–255 (= The population of the town of Bogatynia in the years 1945–1950).

47. *Bender, R.*, Ludność miasta lubelskiego w akcji przedpowstaniowej w latach 1861–1862, Lublin, 1961 (= The academic society of the Catholic University of Lublin).

48. *Białecki, T.*, Przemiany w strukturze ludnościowej miast powiatu chojeńskiego w latach 1945–1962, Szczecin, 1966 (= Changes in the population structure in the towns of Chojnice in the years 1945–1962).

49. *Bonusiak, W.*, Rozwój demograficzny Rzeszowa w latach 1867–1939, in Rozprawy Politechniki Rzeszowskiej. Prace Nauk Społecznych, No. 1 (1977), pp. 5–23 (= The demographic development of Rzeszów 1867–1939).

50. *Borowski, S.*, Ewolucja reprodukcji ludności w Poznaniu w świetle badań nad rodzinami z przełomu XIX i XX w. oraz z bieżącego stulecia, in Przeszł. Demogr. Pol., Vol. 4 (1971), pp. 215–239 (= The development in population reproduction in Poznán in the light of family research at the turn of the 19th to the 20th centuries and in the 20th century).

51. *Brzeziński, B.*, Klasa robotnicza Warszawy 1944–1949, Warsaw, 1975 (= Warsaw's working class 1966–1949).

52. *Chramiec, A.*, Dynamika rozwoju i przemiany strukturalne ludności w kształtowaniu aglomeracji miejskiej w Polsce, Warsaw, 1966 (= Dynamics of demographic and structural changes in the population in urban conurbations in Poland).

53. *Cynalewska, U.*, Sytuacja społeczno-ekonomiczna miast wielkopolskich 1918–1939, Warsaw and Poznań, 1977 (= The socio-economic situation of towns in Great Poland 1918–1939).

54. *Drozdowski, M. M.*, Klasa robotnicza Warszawy (1918–1972), in Kronika Warszawy, 1973, No. 1, pp. 17–28 (= Warsaw's working class 1918–1972).

55. *Drozdowski, M. M.*, The Urbanisation in Poland in the Years 1870–1970, in Studia Historiae Oeconomicae, Vol. 9 (1974), pp. 223–244.

56. *Drozdowski, M. M.*, Uwagi o strukturze społeczno-gospodarczej Warszawy lat 1918–1939, in Rocznik Warszawy, Vol. 7 (1966), pp. 328–388 (= Comments on the socio-economic structure of Warsaw in the years 1918–1939).

57. *Grześ, B.*, Ludność niemiecka w mieście Inowrocławiu i powiecie na przełomie XIX i XX w., in Ziemia Kuj, Vol. 3 (1971), p. 47 (= The German population in the town and district of Inowroclaw at the turn of the 19th to the 20th century).

58. *Hensel, J.*, Burżuazja warszawska drugiej połowy XIX w. w świetle akt notarialnych, Warsaw, 1979 (= Warsaw's middle classes in the second half of the 19th century in the light of notarial files).

59. *Jastrzębski, W.*, Przeobrażenia ludnościowe i narodowościowe Bydgoszczy w okresie okupacji hitlerowskiej (1939–1945), in Prace Komisji Historii, Vol. 3 (1966), No. 1, pp. 3–32 (= Restructuring of the population and its nationality in Bydgoszczy during the Hitler occupation 1939–1945).

60. *Kaczkowski, S.*, Niektóre zagadnienia stosunków ludnościowych Szczecina w latach 1945–1955, in Materiały i Studia z Najnowszej Historii Polski, Vol. 2 (1965), pp. 81–103 (= Some problems of Sczcecin's population relationships in the years 1945–1955).

61. *Kolendo, J. J.*, Transfer ludności niemieckiej z miasta Elbląga i powiatu w latach 1945–1947, in Rocznik Elbląski, Vol. 4 (1969), pp. 169–203 (= The resettlement of the German population from the town and area of Elblag in the years 1945–1947).

62. *Kościk, E.*, Struktura demograficzna, zawodowa i społeczna ludności Oławy w świetle spisu z 1846 r., in Historia, Vol. 30 (1978), pp. 139–160 (= The demographic, occupational and social structure of the population of Olawy in the light of residents' registers from the year 1846).

63. *Krzeczkowski, K.*, Kwestia mieszkaniowa w miastach polskich, Warsaw, 1939 (= The housing issue in Polish towns).

64. *Mazurkiewicz, J.*, Własność i zmiany w stosunkach własnościowych w Lublinie w latach sześćdziesiątych XIX stulecia, in Rocznik Lubelski, Vol. 6 (1963/67), pp. 169–184 (= Property and changes in ownership conditions in Lublin in the 1860s).

65. *Mienicki, H.*, Struktura płci, wieku i stanu cywilnego ludności Torunia w I połowie XIX wieku, in Zap. Hist., Vol. 36 (1971), No. 2, pp. 67–88 (= Structure specific to sex, age and state of civil rights of the Torun population in the years 1782–1961).

66. *Musiał, W.*, Ludność Piotrkowa Trybunalskiego w latach 1782–1961, in Zeszyty Naukowe Uniwersytetu Łódzkiego, Series 3 (1964/65), No. 8, pp. 99–125 (= The population of Piotrków Trybunalski in the years 1782–1961).

67. *Nietyksza, M.*, Ludność Warszawy na przełomie XIX i XX wieku, Warsaw, 1971 (= The population of Warsaw at the turn of the 19th to the 20th century).

68. *Nietyksza, M.*, Struktura zatrudnienia młodzieży Warszawy w świetle spisów ludności z lat 1882 i 1897, in Pokolenia, Series 4 (1966), No. 3, pp. 40–56 (= The employment structure of youth in Warsaw in the light of residents' registers from the years 1882 and 1897).

69. *Piątkowski, A.*, Zadłużenie ludności miejskiej i mniejszych miast Prus Zachodnich w początkach XIX wieku, in Zap. Hist., Series 45 (1980), No. 3, pp. 51–78 (= Debts of the urban population and small West

Prussian towns at the beginning of the 19th century).

70. *Poznańska, B.*, Dzieje burżuazij w Polsce w XIX i XX w. Zarys problematyki badawczej, in Dzieje Najnowsze, Vol. 9 (1977), No. 1, pp. 121–135 (= History of the middle classes in Poland in the 19th and 20th centuries. An outline of a problematic research area).

71. *Rachwał, A.*, Eksterminacja Ludności w Przemyślu i powiecie przemyskim w latach 1939–1944, in Studia Okup. Hitler, Vol. 1 (1976), pp. 45–63 / Rocznik Muz. Rol. Szreniawa, Vol. 9 (1976), pp. 189–276 (= The extermination of the Przemyśl population and area in the years 1939–1944).

72. *Rum, M.*, Przemiany społeczno-gospodarcze Poznania w latach 1918–1928, in Roczniki Historyczne, Series 35 (1969), pp. 57–82 (= The socio-economic changes in Poznań in the years 1918–1928).

73. *Sobczak, I.*, Dynamika przemian demograficznych w Gdyni, in Nautologia, Series 12 (1977), No. 4, pp. 3–15 (= The dynamics of demographic changes in Gdynia).

74. *Sobociński, A. W.*, Przemiany społeczeństwa Gdyni w latach 1945–1970, Gdansk, 1977 (= Societal changes in Gdynia in the years 1945–1970).

75. *Szaniawska, W.*, Mieszkańcy Warszawy w latach 1525–1655, in Rocznik Warszawski, Vol. 7 (1966), pp. 118–135 (= The inhabitants of Warsaw 1525–1655).

76. *Szczygielski, Z.*, Niektóre problemy sytuacji warszawskiej klasy robotniczej w latach trzydziestych, in Polska klasa robotnicza. Studia historyczne, ed., S. Kalabiński, Warsaw, 1970, pp. 325–354 (= Some problems of Warsaw's working class in the 1930s).

77. *Szczypiorski, A.*, Structura ludności Warszawy w latach 1810–1974, in Studia Demograficzne, 1979, No. 55, pp. 57–91 (= The structure of the population of Warsaw 1810–1974).

78. *Taust, W.*, Dżuma w mieście Breslau (dotyczy eksterminacji ludności żydowskiej przez hitlerowców), Warsaw, 1973 (= The plague in Breslau [dealing with the extermination of the Jews by Hitler]).

79. *Tymbarski, K.*, Zarys dziejów gospordarczo-społecznych Muszyny w czasach galicyjskich (1770–1918), in Rocznik Sądecki, Vol. 17 (1982), pp. 47–70 (= Outline of the economic and social history of Muszyny in Galician times 1770–1918).

80. *Zajac, K.*, Studium nad ruchem naturalnym miasta Rymanowa w świetle ksiąg parafialnych z lat 1850–1950, in Przeszłość Demograficzna Polski, Vol. 3 (1970), pp. 143–177 (= Studies on natural demographic development (births, deaths, marriages) in Rymanow in the light of church registers from the years 1850 to 1950).

81. *Żarnowska, A.*, Klasa robotnicza Królestwa Polskiego 1870–1914, Warsaw, 1974 (= The working class in the Kingdom of Poland 1870–1914).

82. *Znaniecki, F.*, Miasto w świadomości jego obywateli. Z badań Pol. Inst. Socjologicznego nad miastem Poznaniem, Poznań, 1931 (= The town in the consciousness of its inhabitants. From research by the Polytechnical Institute of Sociology on the city of Poznań).

(d)　Town Planning

83. *Bartkowski, T.*, Transurbacje miast Wielkopolski i niektóre zagadnienia przestrzennoplastyczne ich rozwoju oraz zastosowanie do nich niektórych metod fizjografii urbanistycznej, Poznań, 1981 (= Urbanisation of Great Poland's towns and some spatial–planning problems of its development and the application of some physiographical–urbanistic methods).

84. *Chruściel, A.*, Zniszczenia wojenne gospodarki Torunia i jej odbudowa w latach 1945–1950, in Rocznik Toruński, Series 15 (1980), pp. 71–88 (= War damage to Toruń's economy and its reconstruction in the years 1945–1950).

85. *Dangel, J.*, Przekształcenia sieci miejskiej w okresie 1946–1965, in Studia Demograficzne, 1969, No. 19, pp. 63–77 (= The restructuring of the urban network [in Poland] in the period 1946–1965).

86. *Dangel, J.*, Przekształcenia sieci miejskiej w Polsce pod wpływem rozwoju ludności i uprzemysłowienia kraju w okresie 1946–1960, Warsaw, 1968 (= The restructuring of the urban network in Poland under the influence of the demographic development and industrialisation of the country in the period 1946–1960).

87. *Dąbrowa Górnicza: zarys rozwoju miasta*, Katowice, 1976 (= Dąbrowa Górnicza: Outline of a city's development).

88. *Dumała, K.*, Przemiany przestrzenne miast i rozwój osiedli przemysłowych w Królestwie Polskim w latach 1831–1869, Wrocław 1974 (= Spatial changes in towns and the development of industrial settlements in the Kingdom of Poland in the years 1831–1869).

89. *Jasieński, J.*, Problemy mieszkalnictwa w rozwoju Krakowa 1945–1975, Kraków 1974 (Prace Monograficzne WSP w Krakowie, Vol. 11) (= Housing problems in the evolution of Kraków 1945–1975).

90. *Kachniarz, T.*, Zmiany struktury przestrzennej miast w Polsce w latach 1950–1965, Warsaw, 1973 (Instytut Urbanistyki Architektury. Seria Prac Własnych, No. 195) (= Changes in the spatial structure of towns in Poland in the years 1950–1965).

91. *Procesy urbanizacji kraju w okresie XXX-lecia Polskiej Rzeczpospolitej Ludowej*, ed., J. Turowski, Wrocław 1978 (= The country's urbanisation processes in the three decades of the Polish People's Republic).

92. *Przekształcenia miast na tle przemian urbanizacyjnych*, Warsaw, 1982 (Komitet Przestrzennego Zagospodarowania Kraju. Polska Akademia Nauk. Biuletyn Zeszyt 121) (= The restructuring of towns against the back-

drop of urbanisation changes).

93. *Sekuła, B.*, Odbudowa i rozbudowa miast i osiedli Pomorza Zachodniego w latach 1945–1965, in Przegląd Zachodnio-Pomorski, 1965, No. 3, pp. 5–91 (= Construction and expansion of towns and settlements in Pomorze in the years 1945–1965).

94. *Strategie uprzemysłowienia a proces urbanizacji*, Warsaw, 1982 (Komitet Przestrzennego Zagospodarowania Kraju. Polska Akademia Nauk. Biuletyn Zeszyt 119) (= Industrialisation strategy and urbanisation processes).

95. *Stryczyński, M.*, Gdańsk w latach 1945–1948: odbudowa organizmumiejskiego, Wrocław 1981 (Studia i Materiały do Dziejów Gdańska 9. Seria Monografii) (= Danzig in the years 1945–1948: construction of the urban organism).

96. *Szkurłatowski, Z.*, Budownictwo i gospodarka mieszkaniowa Legnicy w latach 1945–1970, in Acta Universitatis Wratislaviensis, No. 279 Hist. 1976, Vol. 27, pp. 239–254 (= Building and housing in Legnica in the years 1945–1970).

97. *Teodorowicz-Czerpińska, J.*, Kazimierz Dolny: monografia historycznourbanizacyjna, Kazimierz, 1981 (= Kazimierz Dolny: monography on the history of urbanisation).

98. *Wein, A.*, Nabywanie i budowa nieruchomości przez Żydów w Warszawie, in Biuletyn Żydowskiego Instytut Hist., No. 64 (1967), pp. 33–53 (= Acquisition and building of property by Jews in Warsaw).

99. *Wędzki, A.*, Przemiany przestrzenne Konina w czasach nowożytnych, in Rocznik Koniński, Vol. 9 (1981), pp. 41–80 (= Spatial changes in Konin in modern times).

100. *Wielkomiejski rozwój Warszawy do 1918 r.*, ed., I. Pietrzak-Pawłowska, Warsaw, 1973 (= Warsaw's big-city development up to 1918).

101. *Zawiercie. Zarys rozwoju powiatu i miasta*, ed., M. Grabania et al., Katowice 1969 (= Zawiercie. Outline of the history of the district and the town).

102. *Zejer, W.*, Rozwój przestrzenny Katowic w latach międzywojennych (1922–1939) in Rocznik Katowicki, Vol. 1 (1973/74), pp. 115–130 (= Spatial development of Katowice in the years between the World Wars 1922–1939).

(e) Economy and Transport

103. *Bartnik, J.*, Gospodarstwa domowe miasta Krakowa w latach 1910–1970, in Zeszyty Naukowe Akademii Ekonomicznej Kraków, No. 70 (1975), pp. 223–240 (= Households in Kraków in the years 1910–1970).

104. *Biegeleisen, L. W.*, Polityka gospodarczo-aprowizacyjna miast polskich. Warszawy i Lwowa, Warsaw, 1935 (= Economic and provisions policies in Polish towns).

105. *Czyżewski, A.*, Miasta wielkopolskie w Polsce Ludowej: ekonomiczno-demograficzne podstawy rozwoju w okresie 1946–1970, Poznań, 1976 (Wydział Historii Nauk Społecznych. Badania z Dziejów Społecznych i Gospodarczych, No. 52) (= Great Polish towns in the Polish People's Republic: Economic–demographic basis of development in the years 1946–1970).

106. *Eberhardt, P.*, Rola wielkich miast w strukturze regionalnej powiązań przestrzennych w Polsce, Warsaw, 1970 (Komitet Przestrzennego Zagospodarowania Kraju. Polska Akademia Nauk. Biuletyn Zeszyt 58) (= The role of big cities in the regional structure of spatial connections in Poland).

107. *Hoszowski, S.*, Ekonomiczny rozwój Lwowa w l. 1772–1914, Lwów, 1935 (= Economic development of Lwów in the years 1772–1914).

108. *Jelonek, A.*, Niektóre problemy sieci miejskiej na ziemiach Polski na początku XIX wieku, in Zeszyty Naukowe Uniwersytetu Jagiellońskiego 1967. No. 165. Prace Etnograficzne, No. 15, pp. 95–112 (= Some problems of the urban network in Polish areas at the beginning of the 20th century).

109. *Kotula, F.*, Obrona przeciwpożarowa Rzeszowa od XVI do XIX w., in Rocznik Województwa Rzeszowskiego, Series 6 (1966/67), pp. 107–123 (= The fire brigade of Rzeszów from the 16th to the 18th centuries).

110. *Krzymień, E.*, Gospodarka i działalność Zarządu Miejskiego m. Poznania w latach 1919–1939 w świetle sprawozdań budżetowych, Poznań, 1967 (= Economy and activities of the town administration of Poznán in the years 1919–1939 in the light of budgetary matters).

111. *Łuczak, C.*, Życie gospodarczo-społeczne w Poznaniu 1815–1918, Poznań, 1965 (= The economic and social life of Poznán 1815–1918).

112. *Lutman, T.*, Studia nad dziejami handlu Brodów w r. 1773–1880, Lwów, 1937 (= Studies on the history of trade in Brody in the years 1773–1880).

113. *Przybyszewski, K.*, Przedsiębiorstwa miejskie Torunia w międzywojennym dwudziestoleciu, in Rocznik Tor., Series 15 (1980), pp. 117-146 (= Urban businesses in Toruń between the two World Wars).

114. *Purol, M.*, Aktywizacja gospodarcza powiatu kaliskiego i miasta Kalisza w latach 1945–1960, in Rocznik Kaliski, Vol. 1 (1968), pp. 10–158 (= Economic activities of the district and town of Kalisz in the years 1945–1960).

115. *Rozwój gospodarczy Poznania w dwudziestoleciu Polski Ludowej 1945–1964*, eds., Z. Zakrzewski and A. Przestalski, Poznań, 1966 (= The economic development of Poznań in the 20 years after the existence of the Polish People's Republic).

116. *Secomski, K.*, Rola Warszawy w organizmie gospodarczym Polski

Ludowej, in Rocznik Warszawski, Vol. 7 (1966), pp. 465–483 (= The role of Warsaw in the economic organisation of the Polish People's Republic).

117. *Szkurłatowski, Z.*, Akcja osiedleńcza i problemy demograficzne Legnicy w latach 1945–1970, in Śląski Kwartalnik Historyczny Sobótka, Series 29 (1974), No. 4, pp. 549–567 (= Settlement actions and demographic problems of Legnica in the years 1945–1970).

118. *Widernik, M.*, Głowne problemy gospodarczo-społeczne miasta Gdyni w latach 1926–1939, Gdańsk, 1970 (= The most important economic and socio-historical problems of Gdynia in the years 1926–1939).

119. *Wrzosek, A., et al.*, Powiązania ekonomiczne większych miast w świetle przewozów towarowych, Warsaw, 1967 (Komitet Przestrzennego Zagospodarowania Kraju. Polska Akademia Nauk. Biuletyn Zeszyt 44) (= Economic links of large cities in the light of transportation of goods).

120. *Zejer, W.*, Gospodarka mieszkaniowa miasta Katowic w latach 1922–1939, in Sprawy Mieszkaniowe, Series 10 (1972), No. 1, pp. 73–86 (= Housing in Katowice in the years 1922–1939).

(f) Arts and Sciences, Churches

121. *Gdańsk, jego dzieje i kultura*, Warsaw, 1969 (Danzig, its history and culture).

122. *Gdynia a sylwetki ludzi, oświata i nauka, literatura i kultura*, ed., A. Bukowski, Gdańsk, 1979 (= Gdynia and the silhouette of its people, education and science, literature and culture).

123. *Gumowski, M.*, Herby miast polskich, Warsaw, 1960 (= The coats of arms of Polish towns).

124. *Homola, I.*, Kuria inteligencji w krakowskiej Radzie Miejskiej (1866–1914), in Inteligencja polska pod zaborami. Studia, ed., R. Czepulis-Rastenis, Warsaw, 1978, pp. 107–157 (= The curia of intelligence in the Kraków city council 1866–1914).

125. *Trzeciakowska, M. and L. Trzeciakowski*, W dziewiętnastowiecznym Poznaniu: życie codzienne miasta 1815–1914, Poznań, 1982 (= In 19th century Poznań; daily life in the city 1815–1914).

126. *Warszawa, jej dzieje i kultura*, eds., A. Gieysztor and J. Durko, Warsaw, 1980 (= Warsaw, its history and culture).

E. Local Studies (a representative selection)

- Brzeg

127. *Brzeg*. Dzieje, gospodarka, kultura, ed., W. Dziewulski, Opole, 1975

(Instytut Śląski w Opolu) (= Brzeg. History, economy, culture).

● Bydgoszcz

128. *Kabaciński R., W. Kotowski* and *J. Wojaciak*, Bydgoszcz zarys dziejów, Bydgoszcz, 1980 (= Bydgoszcz, an outline of its history).

● Bytom

129. *Bytom*: zarys rozwoju miasta, ed., W. Długoborski, Warsaw, 1979 (= Bytom: outline of its urban history).

● Chorzów

130. *Chorzów*: zarys rozwoju miasta, ed., J. Kantyka, Katowice, 1977 (= Chorzów: Outline of its urban history).

● Gdańsk (Danzig)

131. *Cieślak, E.* and *C. Biernat*, Dzieje Gdańska, Gdańsk, 1975 (= History of Danzig).

● Gdynia

132. *Dzieje Gdyni*, ed., R. Wapiński, Warsaw and Gdańsk, 1980 (= History of Gdynia).

● Gniezno

133. *Dzieje Gniezna*, ed., J. Topolski, Warsaw, 1965 (= History of Gniezno).

● Inowroclaw

134. *Dzieje Inowrocławia*, ed., M. Biskup, Warsaw and Poznań, 1978 (= History of Inowroclaw).

● Kalisz

135. *Dzieje Kalisza*, ed., W. Rusiński, Poznań, 1977 (= History of Kalisz).

● Katowice

136. *Katowice, ich dzieje i kultura na tle regionu,* Warsaw, 1976 (= Katowice: its history and culture against a regional backdrop).

137. *Katowice 1865–1945:* zarys rozwoju miasta, ed., von J. Szaflarski, Katowice, 1978 (= Katowice, 1865–1945: outline of urban history).

- Koszalin

138. *Gasztold, T., A. Muszyński* and *H. Rybicki,* Koszalin, zarys dziejów, Poznań, 1974 (= Koszalin. Historic outline).

- Kraków

139. *Dzieje Krakowa,* eds., J. Bieniarzówna, J. Małecki and J. Mitkowski, Part 3: Kraków w latach 1796–1918, Kraków, 1979 (= The history of Kraków Part 3: Kraków in the years 1796–1918).

- Krosno

140. *Krosno.* Studia z dziejów miasta i regionu, ed., J. Garbacik, Part 1: Do roku 1918, Kraków, 1972 (= Krosno. Studies on the history of the city and the region).

141. *Muszyński, J.,* Krosno Odrzańskie. Przeszłość i teraźniejszość, Warsaw, 1972 (= Krosno on the Oder. Past and present).

- Legnica

142. *Legnica:* monografia historyczna miasta, Wrocław, 1977 (= Legnica: historical monography of the city).

- Łódź

143. *Łódź, dzieje miasta,* ed., R. Rosin, Warsaw and Łódź, 1980 (= Łódź, history of the city).

- Lublin

144. *Dzieje Lublina,* Part 2, ed., S. Krzykała, Lublin 1975/76 (= History of Lublin).

- Malbork

145. *Górski, K.,* Dzieje Malborka, Gdańsk, 1973 (= History of Malbork).

- Olecko

146. *Olecko.* Z dziejów miasta i powiatu, ed., A. Chilecki *et al.*, n.p. n.d. (= Olecko, History of the city and the region).

● Olsztyn

147. *Olsztyn.* Part 1: 1353–1945, ed., M. Lossman, Olsztyn, 1971; Part 2: 1945–1950, ed., C. Berwiński, Olsztyn, 1974 (= Olsztyn. An anthology).

● Racibórz

148. *Racibórz.* Zarys rozwoju miasta, ed., J. Kantyka, Katowice, 1981 (= Racibórz. An outline of the city's development).

● Słupsk

149. *Historia Słupska*, ed., S. Gierszewski, Poznań, 1981 (= History of Słupsk).

● Śrem

150. *Dzieje Śremu*, ed., S. Chmielewski, Poznań, 1972 (= The history of Śrem).

● Szczecin

151. *Białecki, T.*, Szczecin: rozwój miasta w Polsce Ludowej, Poznań, 1977 (= Szczecin: the evolution of the city in the People's Republic of Poland).

● Toruń

152. *Cieślak, T.*, Etapy rozwoju miasta Torunia w XIX i XX wieku, in Rocznik Toruński, Series 15 (1980), pp. 241–252 (= The stages of Toruń's development in the 19th and 20th centuries).

● Warsaw

153. *Warszawa.* Rozwój miasta w Polsce Ludowej, ed., R. Kołodziejczyk, Warsaw, 1970 (= Warsaw. Evolution of the city in the People's Republic of Poland).

154. *Dzieje Warszawy*, Part 3: Warszawa w latach 1795–1914, ed., S. Kieniwicza, Warsaw, 1976 (= The history of Warsaw. Part 3: Warsaw in the years 1795–1914).

155. *Warszawa II Rzeczypospolitej* (1918–1939), Part 1, ed., M. M. Drozdowski, Warsaw, 1968 (= Warsaw of the 2nd Republic. 1918–1939).

- Zabrze

156. *Zabrze.* Zarys rozwoju miasta, published by H. Rechowicz, Katowice 1967 (= Zabrze. An outline of its evolution).

MARIA ALEXANDRE LOUSADA AND
BERNARDO VASCONCELOS E SOUSA

Portugal

The collected bibliography coincides with the period between the mid-18th and mid-20th centuries. Although this is not the place for even a brief historical introduction to urbanism in Portugal, it is necessary to explain briefly the selected chronological limits. Although urbanisation resulting from industrialisation is very recent in Portugal (late 19th century, accentuated after 1945), it can be said that it was in the second half of the 18th century that a historical turning point was observed in Portugal's cities. This was linked either to the first signs of industrialisation, which then established itself, or to the consequences of urban reconstruction in Lisbon and Vila Real de Santo António after the big earthquake of 1755. That is why we have commenced with this period. The other significant time — the 1960s — marks the decade in which phenomena emerged or intensified, profoundly changing the country's settlement process. The migratory current abroad and the rural exodus to major cities and their industrial peripheries (Porto's metropolitan area, and especially Lisbon's), gave quantitative and qualitative expression to new urban forms, framed in urban schemes of official or illegal nature. Thus, in answer to this situation, the 1960s witnessed the first attempts at systematic planning aimed at reorganising the urban network.

The unbalanced economic development in Portugal with its concentration of population along the coastal areas, and the features of urban development peculiar to the country (the low degree of urbanisation allows the 'network' of the cities to be polarised into more or less two centres, Lisbon and Porto, the absence of medium-sized urban centres, the high number of small urban centres) led to a concentration of studies on the two principal Portuguese cities, Lisbon and Porto. This is reflected in the literature. On the other hand, the almost total lack of historical studies on the urban phenomenon in Portugal, explains the relative importance of work on urbanism in the geographical and economic spheres, especially since the 1960s. What might be an excessive number of studies in this sphere, tends to compensate for the shortage in specific studies on urbanism.

A. Urban History Institutions

—

B. Aids to Research

(a) Urban History Journals

1. *Reportório das Publicações Periódicas Portuguesas*, pub. by Biblioteca Nacional Lisboa, Lisbon.
2. *Anais da Academia Portuguesa de História*, Lisbon, 1946 ff.
3. *Boletim da Academia Portuguesa de História*, Lisbon, 1937 ff.
4. *Finisterra*, Lisbon, 1966 ff., pub. by Centro de Estudos Geográficos (C.E.G.) Universidade de Lisboa.
5. *Ler História*, Lisbon, 1983 ff.
6. *Revista de História Económica e Social*, Lisbon, 1978 ff.
7. *Revista Municipal*, Lisbon, 1939 ff., pub. by La Câmara Municipal de Lisboa.
8. *Revista Portuguesa de História*, Lisbon, 1941 ff., pub. by Faculdade de Letras, Universidade de Coimbra.

(b) Bibliographies

9. *Bibliografia Corográfica de Portugal*, Lisbon, 1962–1975 (= Chorographic bibliography of Portugal).
10. *Catálogo dos Mapas de Portugal Continental existentes na Mapoteca do C.E.G.*, Lisbon, 1974 (= Catalogue of existing maps of continental Portugal from the collection of ancient maps of the C.E.G.).
11. *Cunha, A. P. da*, Achegas para uma bibliografia do distrito, in O Distrito de Braga, Vol. I, 2nd edition, Series V, Braga, 1975 (= Aids to a district bibliography).
12. *Garcez, C.*, Subsídios para uma bibliografia geral de Lisboa, in Revista Municipal, Vol. 100 (1964), pp. 69–76; Vol. 101/102 (1964), pp. 101–116; Vol. 103 (1965), pp. 55–86; Vol. 104/105 (1965), pp. 107–130; Vol. 106/107 (1965), pp. 99–110 (= Support for a general Lisbon bibliography).
13. *Gaspar, J.*, Portugal, in Guide International d'Histoire Urbaine, Vol. I: Europe, Paris, 1977.
14. *Gomes, J. P.*, Subsídios para a bibliografia do distrito da Guarda, Lisbon, 1970 (= Aids to the Guarda district bibliography).
15. *Guerreiro, A. D.*, ed., Bibliografia sobre a Economia Portuguesa, Lisbon, 1958 (= Bibliography on the Portuguese economy).
16. *Lautensach, H.*, and *M. Feio*, Bibliografia Geográfica de Portugal, Lisbon, 1948 (= Geographic bibliography of Portugal).

17. *Loureiro, J.* P., Bibliografia Coimbrã, Coimbra, 1964 (= Bibliography of Coimbra).

18. *Marques, A. H. de Oliveira,* Guia de História da 1ª. República Portuguesa, Lisbon, 1981 (= Guide to the history of the first Portuguese Republic).

19. *Matos, J. V. M. de,* Apontamentos para uma Bibliografia da Beira Baixa, in Estudos de Castelo Branco, Vol. 4 (1978), pp. 51–97 (= Notes for a bibliography of Beira Baixa).

20. *Roseira, M. J. Q.,* Bibliografia Geográfica de Portugal Continental: 1977 e 1978, in Finisterra, Vol. XII. 24 (1977); XIII. 26 (1978); XIV. 28 (1979); XV. 30 (1980) (= Geographic bibliography of continental Portugal).

21. *Subsídios para a Bibliografia da História Local Portuguesa,* Lisbon, 1933 (= Aids to the bibliography on Portuguese local history).

(c)   Handbooks on Urban History

22. *Guia de Portugal,* 5 vols., 2nd ed., Lisbon, 1983–1985 (= Guide to Portugal).

(d)   Atlases on Urban History and Urban Development

23. *Alegria, M. F.,* Cartografia antiga de Portugal Continental, in Finisterra, Vol. XII. 24 (1977), pp. 169–210 (= Ancient cartography of continental Portugal).

24. *Bolama, M. d'Avila e,* A nova carta chorographica de Portugal, 3 vols. Lisbon, 1909, 1912 and 1914 (= Portugal's new chorographic map).

25. *Carta Concelhia de Portugal.* Mapas indicativos das contribuições e impostos por concelho de 1883 a 1889. Escala 1:2 250 000 (= Portugal's municipal map. Maps indicating contributions and taxes per council from 1883 to 1889. Scale: 1:2 250 000).

26. *Carta Corográfica de Portugal,* Lisbon, 1948–1949 (Escala 1:400 000) (= Chorographic map of Portugal. Scale: 1:400 000).

27. *Carte du Royaume de Portugal Divisé en ses Six Provences avec les Routes,* n.p. 1831.

28. *Cunha, J. C. da,* Da região Centro do País – Caracterização da rede urbana, Coimbra, 1967 (= On the Central region of the country – characterisation of urban network).

29. *Fernandez, F.,* El más antigo Mapa de Poblacion de la Peninsula Ibérica, in Estudios Geograficos, Vol. 17.65 (1956), pp. 704–706 (= The oldest demographic map of the Iberian Peninsula).

(e)   Urban History Sources

30. *Anuário Estatístico de Portugal,* Lisbon, 1875, 1884, 1885, 1886, 1892,

1900, 1901/1903, 1904/1905, 1906/1907 (= Portugal's statistic annual).

31. *Balbi, A.*, Essai Statistique du Royaume de Portugal et d'Algarve, 2 vols. Paris, 1822.

32. *Balbi, A.*, Variétés Politico-Statistiques sur la Monarchie Portugaise, Paris, 1822.

33. *Boletim de Minas*, Lisbon, 1915 (= Minas bulletin).

34. *Boletim do Trabalho Industrial*, Lisbon, 1906–1926 (= Industrial work bulletin).

35. *Cabido, A. G. F.*, Corografia industrial do concelho de Viseu. Monografia estatística, Lisbon, 1912 (= Viseu Council's industrial chorography: statistic monography).

36. *Censo eleitoral da cidade de Lisboa.* Eleições de Deputados, de Câmaras Municipais e de Juntas de Paróquia desde 1878 até hoje, Lisbon, 1916 (= Parish elections from 1878 to the present day).

37. *A cidade do Porto.* Súmula estatística (1864–1968), Lisbon, 1971 (= Porto City. Statistic summary. (1864–1968).

38. *Consumo em Lisboa*: 1891–1902, Lisbon, 1903 (= Consumption of goods in Lisbon).

39. *Inquérito Industrial*, Lisbon, 1959 (= Industrial inquiry).

40. *Neves, J. A. das*, Memórias sobre os meios de melhorar a indústria portuguesa, considerada nos seus diferentes ramos, Lisbon, 1820; 2nd ed., Lisbon, 1983 (= Thoughts on ways of improving Portuguese industry, presented in its different sectors).

41. *Neves, J. A. das*, Noções históricas, económicas e administrativas sobre a produção e manufactura das sedas em Portugal, particularmente sobre a Real Fábrica do subúrbio do Rato e suas anexas, Lisbon, 1827 (= Historical, economical and administrative views of silk production and manufacture in Portugal, particularly of the Royal Factory and its associated factories in the suburb of Rato).

42. *Oliveira, E. F. de*, Elementos para a história do município de Lisboa, 17 vols. Lisbon, 1812–1911 (Publicaram-se ainda 2 vols. de indice temático) (= An introduction to the history of the Municipality of Lisbon).

43. *Pereira, D. J.*, Memoria historica da villa de Barcelos, Barcelinhos e Villa Nova de Famalição, Viana, 1867 (= Historical memories of the towns of Barcelos, Barcelinhos and Villa Nova de Famalicao).

44. *Sá, J. A. de*, Cadastro do Reino (1801–1812). I: Instruções gerais e plano; II; Tábuas topográficas e estatísticas – 1801, Lisbon, 1945 and 1948 (= Record of the kingdom (1801–1812). I: General instructions and plan II: Topographical and statistical tables – 1801).

45. *Serrão, J.*, Fontes de Demografia Portuguesa, Lisbon, 1973 (= Portuguese demography sources).

46. *Serrão, J.*, ed., Roteiro de Fontes da História Portuguesa Contemporânea. Arquivo Nacional da Torre do Tombo, 2 vols., Lisbon, 1984 (= Guide to contemporary Portuguese history sources).

C. Research Reports

—

D. Literature on Individual Areas of Urban History Research

(a) Concept and Definition of Town and Town Types

47. *Colóquio sobre Urbanismo.* 8 a 21 da Março de 1961, Lisbon, n.d. (= Colloquy on urbanism – 8–21 March, 1961).

48. *Correa, J. A.*, Cidades de Portugal, Lisbon, 1907 (= Cities of Portugal).

49. *Ferro, G.*, Per uno studio della cittá portoghesi, in Annali di Ricerche e Studi di Geografia, Vol. 14 (1958), No. 2, pp. 73–90 (= For a study of the Portuguese town).

50. *Gaspar, J.*, Estudo geográfico das aglomerações urbanas em Portugal Continental – Projecto de Investigação, in Finisterra, Vol. X. 19 (1975), pp. 107–152 (= Geographic study on urban agglomerations in continental Portugal – research project).

51. *Gaspar, J.*, and *J. Ferrão*, As Cidades Portuguesas e a Geografia Urbana na Universidade de Lisboa, in Quatro Ensaios sobre a Geografia em Portugal, Lisbon, 1980, pp. 15–42 (= Portuguese cities and urban geography at the University of Lisbon).

52. *Girão, A. de Amorim*, Origens e evolução do urbanismo em Portugal, in Revista do Centro de Estudos Demográficos, No. 1 (1945), pp. 39–77 (= Origins and development of urbanism in Portugal).

53. *Girão, A. de Amorim*, A população rural e população urbana em Portugal, in Boletim do Centro de Estudos Geográficos, Vol. 12/13 (1956), pp. 67–76 (= Rural and urban population in Portugal).

54. *Godinho, V. M.*, A estrutura da antiga sociedade portuguesa, 2nd ed., Lisbon, 1975 (= The structure of ancient Portuguese society).

55. *Ribeiro, O.*, Cidade, in Dicionário de História de Portugal, Vol. I, Lisbon, n.d. (= City).

56. *Ribeiro, O.*, Proémio metodológico ao estudo das pequenas cidades portuguesas, in Finisterra, Vol. IV. 7 (1969), pp. 64–73 (= Methodological proem to the study of Portuguese towns).

57. *Saraiva, J. H.*, Evolução Histórica dos Municípios Portuguesas, Lisbon, 1956 (= Historical evolution of Portuguese municipalities).

58. *Serrão J. V.*, A concessão do foro de cidade em Portugal nos séculos XII a XIX, in Portugaliae Historica, Vol. 1 (1973), pp. 13–80 (= City-category concession in Portugal from 12th – 19th century).

59. *Silva, J. G. da*, Vida Urbana e Desenvolvimento: Portugal, país sem cidades, in Arquivo do Centro Cultural Português, Vol. V, Part II, Paris, 1972, pp. 734–746 (= Urban life and development: Portugal, country without cities).

60. *Vieira, A. L.*, Noções operatórias sobre cidade, populaçao urbana e populaçao rural, in Revista de História Económica e Social, No. 1 (1978), pp. 105–129 (= Operative ideas on towns and urban and rural populations).

(b)   Politics, Law and Statutes

61. *Administração Regional*, 2 vols., Lisbon, 1976 (= Regional administration).

62. *Almeida, F. de*, História das Instituições em Portugal, 2nd ed., Porto, 1903 (= History of Portuguese institutions).

63. *Caetano, M.*, A Codificação Administrativa em Portugal. Um Século de Experiência: 1836–1935, in Revista da Faculdade de Direito, Lisbon, 1935 (= Administrative codification in Portugal: one century of experience: 1836–1935).

64. *Caldas, E. de Castro*, and *M. de Santos Loureiro*, Regiões Homogénas no Continente Português. Primeiro Ensaio de Delemitação, Lisbon, 1966 (= Homogeneous regons on the Portuguese continent. First attempt at demarcation).

65. *Lapa, A.*, História da Polícia de Lisboa, 1964 (= Lisbon's police history).

66. *Noronha, E. de*, Pina Manique, o Intendente de antes quebrar . . . Costumes, banditismo e polícia no fim do século XVIII, princípios do século XIX, 2nd ed., Porto, 1940 (= Pina Manique, o Intendente de antes quebrar . . . . morals, banditry and police from the end of 18th to beginning of 19th century).

(c)   Population and Social Structure

67. *Alarcão, A. de*, Mobilidade Geográfica da População de Portugal. Continente e Ilhas Adjacentes. Migrações internas 1921–1960, Lisbon, 1969 (= Geographic mobility of the Portuguese population [continent and adjacent islands]. Internal Migration 1921–1960).

68. *Campos, E.*, O Enquadramento Geo-Económico da População Portuguesa através dos séculos, 2nd ed., 1943 (= Geographic–economic classification of the Portuguese population through the centuries).

69. *Evangelista, J.*, Um século de População Portuguesa (1864–1960), Lisbon, 1971 (= A century of Portuguese population. 1864–1960).

70. *Girão, A. de Amorim*, Densidade da População por Freguesias 1940, Coimbra, 1948 (= Population density in individual communities, 1940).

71. *Narciso, M. A. de Sousa*, Evolução da cidade de Lisboa e desenvolvimento da sua população de 1890 a 1940, Diss. Lisbon, 1947 (= Evolution of Lisbon and development of its population from 1890 to 1940).

72. *Pereira, M. H.*, Níveis de consumo e níveis de vida em Portugal (1874–1922), in Política e Economia. Portugal nos séculos XIX e XX, Lisbon 1979, pp. 73–110 (= Consumption and standards of living in Portugal (1874–1922)).

73. *Ribeiro, O.*, Une nouvelle carte de la répartition de la population au Portugal, in Comptes Rendus du Congrès International de Géographie de Lisbonne, Vol. 1, Part 1, n.p. 1949, pp. 276–280.

74. *Roque, J. L.*, Alguns aspectos da criminalidade no distrito de Coimbra nos anos de 1841 a 1844, in Boletim do Arquivo da Universidade de Coimbra, Vol. III (1978), pp. 120–160 (= Aspects of criminality in the district of Coimbra from 1841 to 1844).

75. *Santos, C. dos*, A população do Porto de 1700 a 1820. Contribuição para o estudo da demografia urbana, in Revista de História, Vol. I (1978), pp. 281–349 (= Population of Porto from 1700 to 1820).

76. *Schwarz, S.*, História da moderna comunidade israelita de Lisboa, Coimbra, 1959 (= History of the modern Israelite community in Lisbon).

77. *Serrão, J.*, Emigração Portuguesa. Sondagem Histórica, Lisbon, n.d. (= Portuguese emigration. Historical examination).

78. *Serrão, J., et al.*, População activa e população na vida religiosa em Trás-os-Montes nos finais do século XVIII, in Análise Social, Vol. XII. 47 (1976), pp. 748–762 (= The population at work and in the religious life in Trás-os-Montes at the end of 18th century).

79. *Silva, F. M. da*, O povoamento da Metrópole através dos Censos, Lisbon, 1970 (= Population of the metropolis on the basis of the census).

80. *Silva, L. A. R. da*, Memoria sobre a População e a Agricultura de Portugal desde a Fundação da Monarquia até 1865, Lisbon, 1868 (= Report on Portugal's population and agriculture from the foundation of the monarchy until 1865).

81. *Sousa, F. A. P. de*, A população portuguesa nos inícios do século XIX, 2 vols. Diss. Porto, 1979 (= The Portuguese population at the beginning of the 19th century).

(d)   Town Planning, Housing

82. *Araújo, A.*, O Desenvolvimento Urbano da Póvoa de Varzim na Segunda Metade do Século XVIII, in Póvoa de Varzim. Boletim Cultural, Vol. XVII. 2 (1978), pp. 257–294 (= Urban development in Póvoa de Varzim in the second half of the 19th century).

83. *Betoun, J.*, La Baixa – Centre traditionnel des affaires de Lisbonne,

Nanterre, 1971 (Mémoire de Maitrise de Géographie Urbaine).

84. *Brito, R. S. de*, Lisboa. Esboço geográfico, in Boletim Cultural da Junta Distrital de Lisboa, Lisbon, 1976 (= Lisbon. Geographic sketch).

85. *Câmara Municipal de Lisboa*, Exposição iconográfica e bibliográfica comemorativa da reconstrução da cidade depois do Terramoto de 1755. Lisbon, 1955 (= Iconographic and bibliographic exhibition celebrating the city's reconstruction after the earthquake of 1755).

86. *Casas e Ruas na História de Setúbal*, Setúbal, 1977–1978 (= Houses and streets in the history of Setúbal).

87. *Costa, E.*, O terramoto de 1755 no distrito de Aveiro, Coimbra, 1956 (= The earthquake of 1755 in the district of Aveiro).

88. *Ferreira, J. A. P.*, O urbanismo do Porto no século XVIII e seus reflexos no plano económico-social. Simples achega para o seu estudo, Porto 1966 (= Urbanism in Porto in 18th century and its impact on the socio-economic level).

89. *Garrett, A. de Almeida*, História da evolução dos planos gerais de urbanização da cidade do Porto, in Boletim-Secção de Planeamento Urbanístico – Centro de Estudos de Engenharia Civil, Vol. 14 (1974) (= History of the development of general urbanisation plans in the city of Porto).

90. *Gaspar, J.*, A dinâmica Funcional do centro de Lisboa, in Finisterra, Vol. XI. 21 (1976), pp. 37–150 (= The functional dynamics of Lisbon's city centre).

91. *Iria, A.*, Vila Real de Santo António reedificada pelo Marquês de Pombal (1773–1776). Subsídios para a sua monografia e elementos para a história da administração pombalina, in Ethnos, Vol. III (1948), pp. 5–76 (= Vila Real de Santo António rebuilt by the Marquis of Pombal (1773–1775): Aids for its monography and an introduction to the history of Pombal's administration).

92. *Loureiro, J. P.*, Toponímia de Coimbra, 2 vols. Coimbra, 1964 (= Toponymy of Coimbra).

93. *Macedo, L. P. de*, Lisboa de lés a lés. Subsídios para a história das vias públicas da cidade, 5 vols, Lisbon, 1940–1943 (= Lisbon from one end to the other. Aids to the history of its streets).

94. *Marques, M. da Conceição Oliveira*, Introdução ao estudo do desenvolvimento urbano de Lisboa. 1879–1938, in Arquitectura, Vol. 113 (1970), pp. 5–7; Vol. 114 (1971), pp. 74–78 (= Introduction to the study of urban development in Lisbon).

95. *Oliveira, E. V. de*, and *F. Galhano*, Casas do Porto, in Douro Litoral, No. 8 (7–8) (1958), pp. 637–687 (= Houses of Porto).

96. *Problemas de Urbanização*. Conferências realizadas no salão nobre dos paços do concelho de Novembro de 1934 a Janeiro de 1935, Lisbon, 1936 (Câmara Municipal de Lisboa) (= Problems of urbanisation).

97. *Ribeiro, O.*, A Rua Direita de Viseu, in Geographica, Year 4 (1968), No. 16, pp. 49–63 (= The street 'Rua Direita' of Viseu).

98. *Rodrigues, M. J. M.*, Tradição, Transição e Mudança. A produção do Espaço Urbano na Lisboa Oitocentista, in Boletim Cultural da Assembleia Distrital de Lisboa, Vol. 84 (1979), pp. 3–96 (= Tradition, transition and change: creation of urban space in 18th century Lisbon).

99. *Santana, F.*, ed., Lisboa na 2ª. metade do século XVIII. Plantas e Descrições das suas freguesias, Lisbon, n.d. (= Lisbon in the second half of 18th century. Plans and descriptions of its parishes).

(e) Economy and Transport

100. *Alegria, M. F.*, O desenvolvimento da rede ferroviária portuguesa e as relações com Espanha no século XIX, Lisbon, 1983 (Centro de Estudos Geográficos) (= The development of the Portuguese railway and relations with Spain in the 19th century).

101. *Amaral, J. M. B. Ferreira do*, A industrialização em Portugal, Lisbon, 1966 (= Industrialisation in Portugal).

102. *Bebiano, J. B.*, O Porto de Lisboa. Estudo de história económica, Lisbon, 1960 (= The harbour of Lisbon. Study in economic history).

103. *Cabreira, T.*, O Algarve económico, Lisbon, 1918 (= The Algarve economy).

104. *Capela, J.*, A Burguesia mercantil do Porto e as Colónias (1834–1900), Porto, 1973 (= Mercantile bourgeoisie of Porto and the colonies, 1834–1900).

105. *Castelo-Branco, F.*, Do tráfico fluvial e da sua importância na economia portuguesa, in Boletim da Sociedade de Geografia de Lisboa, 1958, pp. 39–66 (= Fluvial traffic and its importance for the Portuguese economy).

106. *Costa, M. Pereira da*, Subsídios para a história da indústria vidreira no concelho de Oliveira de Azemeis, Coimbra, 1955 (= Aids to the history of the glass industry in the municipality of Oliveira de Azemeis).

107. *Cruz, A.*, Geografia e Economia da Província do Minho nos fins do século XVIII, Porto, 1970 (= Geography and economy of the province of Minho at the end of the 18th century).

108. *Dias, L. F. de Carvalho*, História dos lanifícios (1750–1834), Vols. 1 and 2, Lisbon, 1958–1965 (= History of woollen goods).

109. *Ferreira, J. A. P.*, Preços dos géneros alimentícios comerciados nos mercados do Porto, no séc. XIX (1844–1899), in Boletim Cultural da Câmara Municipal do Porto, Vol. XXXIII (1970), pp. 575–889 (= The price of provisions at the markets of Porto in the 19th century (1844–1899)).

110. *Gaspar, J.*, Os Portos Fluviais do Tejo, in Finisterra, Vol. V. 10 (1970), pp. 153–204 (= The river ports of Tejo).

111. *Geraldes, M. de Melo Nunes*, Monografia sobre a indústria do linho no distrito de Braga, Coimbra, 1913 (= Monography on the linen industry in the Braga district).

112. *Godinho, V. M.*, Prix et Monnaie au Portugal 1750–1850, Paris, 1955.

113. *Gomes, M.*, A Vista Alegre – Memória Histórica, Aveiro, 1924 (= Vista Alegre – historical review).

114. *Gonçalves, M. de Lourdes J.*, Tomar na origem do movimento industrial portugês, Diss., Lisbon, 1968 (= Tomar at the beginning of the Portuguese industrial movement).

115. *Indice ponderado do custo da alimentação e de alguns artigos de consumo domestico na cidade de Lisboa.* Memória justificativa, Lisbon, 1940 (= Weighted index of the cost of victuals and some domestic consumer goods in the city of Lisbon).

116. *Indices de salários por profissões para a cidade do Porto*, Lisbon, 1959 (= Index of wages for the different professions in the city of Porto).

117. *Inquérito ao custo de vida na cidade do Porto.* 1950–1951, n.p. 1955 (= Inquiry into the cost of living in the city of Porto).

118. *Lopes, M. M.*, O Entroncamento – o caminho de ferro, factor de povoamento e de urbanização, in Boletim do Centro de Estudos Geográficos, Vol. 4–5 (1952), pp. 17–53 (= The railway as a factor in settlement and urbanisation).

119. *Macedo, J. B. de*, Problemas da História da Indústria Portuguesa no século XVIII, Lisbon, 1963 (= Problems of Portuguese industrial history in the 18th century).

120. *Moura, F. P. de*, Localização das indústrias e desenvolvimento económico, Lisbon, 1960 (= Localisation of industries and economic development).

121. *Oliveira, A. de*, Elementos para a história dos preços na região bracarense (1680–1830), Braga, 1973 (= An introduction to the history of prices in the region of Braga (1680–1830)).

122. *Paixão, V. M. de Braga*, Cem anos do Banco Nacional Ultramarino na vida portuguesa, 1864–1964, 3 vols. Lisbon, 1964 (= One hundred years of the National Overseas Bank in Portuguese life).

123. *Pereira, E.*, and *C. Fonseca*, Subsídios para a história da indústria portuguesa, Lisbon, 1979 (= Aids to the history of Portuguese industry).

124. *Pereira, M. H.*, Assimetrias de crescimento e dependêcias externa, in Política e Economia. Portugal nos séculos XIX e XX, Lisbon, 1979, pp. 16–49 (= Irregularities in growth and external dependence).

125. *Pereira, M. J.*, Subsídios para a história da Fábrica Nacional de Cordoaria, Lisbon, 1971–1973 (= Aids to the history of the national rope-yard factory).

126. *Pereira, M. de Lourdes Santos*, Abastecimento de produtos hortícolas a Lisboa, Lisbon, 1949 (= The supply of horticultural products to Lisbon).

127. *Pinheiro, M. de Avelar*, Investimentos estrangeiros, política financeira e caminhos-de-ferro em Portugal na segunda metade do século XIX, in

Análise Social, Vol. XV. 58 (1979), pp. 265–286 (= Foreign investment, financial policies and railways in Portugal in the second half of the 19th century).

128. *O Porto de Lisboa.* Estudo de história económica seguido de um catálogo bibliográfico e iconográfico, Lisbon, 1960 (= The harbour of Lisbon: A study of economic history followed by a bibliographic and iconographic catalogue).

129. *Schwalbach, L.*, A geografia da circulação e os agregados humanos – o Entroncamento, in Revista de Faculdade de Letras, 2nd series, Vol. 12 (1946), pp. 46–58 (= Circulation geography and human aggregates).

130. *Serrão, J.*, and *G. Martins*, Da indústria portuguesa. Do Antigo Regime ao Capitalismo. Antologia, Lisbon, 1978 (= On Portuguese industry: From the ancient regime to capitalism. An anthology).

131. *Sousa, F. de*, A Indústria das Sedas em Trás-os-Montes (1790–1813), in Revista de História Económica e Social, No. 2 (1978), pp. 59–73 (= The silk industry in Trás-os-Montes).

132. *Tenreiro, A. G.*, Douro – Esboços de História Económica, 3 vols. Porto 1942–1944 (= Douro – sketches on economic history).

133. *Torres, C. M.*, O Caminho de Ferro em Portugal – Apontamento Cronológíco Relativo ao Periodo 1845–1930, Lisbon, 1931 (= The railway in Portugal – chronological note referring to the period 1845–1930).

134. *Vieira, A. L.*, Investimentos britânicos nos transportes urbanos e suburbanos em Portugal na segunda metade do século XIX – Fracasso e sucesso, in Revista de História Económica e Social. Vol. 7 (1981), pp. 80–92 (= British investment in urban and suburban transport in Portugal in the second half of the 19th century – failure and success).

135. *Vieira, A. L.*, Os transportes públicos de Lisboa entre 1830 e 1910, Lisbon, 1982 (= Public transport in Lisbon between 1830 and 1910).

136. *Vieira, A. L.*, Os transportes rodoviários em Portugal. 1900–1940, in Revista de História Económica e Social, Vol. 5 (1980), pp. 57–94 (= Road transport in Portugal. 1900–1940).

(f)   Arts and Sciences, Churches

137. *Azevedo, D. J. de*, História eclesiástica da cidade e bispado de Lamego, Porto, 1878 (= Ecclesiastical history of the town and bishopric of Lamego).

138. *Carvalho, P. de*, História do Fado, 2nd ed., Lisbon, 1983 (= History of Fado).

139. *Costa, A. F. da*, and *M. das Dores Guerreiro*, O Trágico e o Contraste. O Fado no bairro de Alfama, Lisbon, 1984 (= The tragedy and the

contrast. Fado in the Alfama quarter).

140. *Lima, D. P. de*, História dos Mosteiros, Conventos e Casas Religiosas de Lisboa, Lisbon, 1950 (= History of Lisbon's monasteries, convents and religious houses).

141. *Paixão, V. M. de Braga*, Institutos de ensino e cultura na cidade de Lisboa, depois da instalação definitiva do Regima Liberal na mesma cidade (1833), in: Papel das Areas Regionais na formação histórica de Portugal – Actas do Colóquio, Lisbon, 1975, pp. 487–498 (= Educational and cultural institutions in Lisbon after the definite instalment of the Liberal regime).

142. *Ramalho, R. de Sousa Lobo*, Guia de Portugal Artístico, Lisbon, 1935 (= Art guide to Portugal).

143. *Salvado, A.*, Elementos para um inventário artístico do distrito de Castelo Branco, in Estudos de Castelo Branco, Vol. I (1976), pp. 3–40 (= Introduction to an artistic inventory of the Castelo Branco district).

144. *Zoquete, A.*, Leiria. Subsídios para a história da sua diocese, Leiria, 1943 (= Leiria. Aids to the history of its diocese).

E. Local Studies (a representative selection)

• Alentejo

145. *Gaspar, J.*, A área de inflûência de Evora. Sistema de funções e lugares centrais, Lisbon, 1972 (= The sphere of influence of Evora: System of functions and central places).

146. *Viana, A.*, Origem e evolução histórica de Beja, Beja 1944 (= Origin and historical evolution of Beja).

• Algarve

147. *Anacleto, J. J.*, and *J. A. Quaresma*, Portimão em 1810. Esboço de análise sócio-economica, in História e Sociedade, Vol. 4–5 (1979), pp. 41–51 (= Portimão in the year 1810. Short socio-economic analysis).

148. *Neves, J.*, A evolução histórico-geográfica da cidade de Faro. Ensaio de Geografia Urbana, Faro, 1974 (= Historical geographical evolution of Faro city. Urban geography essay).

• Beiras

149. *Aguiar, C. A. de*, Causas que presidiram á urbanização da cidade da Guarda, Coimbra, 1940 (= Background to the urbanisation of the city of Guarda).

150. *Aragão, M.*, Viseu. Subsídios para a sua história desde os fins do século XV, 2 vols., Porto, 1928 (= Viseu. Aids to its history since the end of the 15th century).

151. *Arroteia, J. C.*, Figueira da Foz. Contribuição para o seu conhecimento geográfico, Diss. Lisbon, 1972 (= Figueira da Foz. Contribution to its geographic knowledge).

152. *Cardoso, J. R.*, Saibam quantos . . . Subsídios para o estudo das classes do distrito de Castelo Branco, Castelo Branco n.d. (= That many know . . . Aids to the study of classes in the district of Castelo Branco).

153. *Cardoso, J. R.*, Subsídios para a história regional da Beira Baixa, Lisbon, 1940 (= Aids to the regional history of the Beira Baixa).

154. *Correia, V.*, and *A. N. Gonçalves*, Distrito de Coimbra, Lisbon, 1952 (= The district of Coimbra).

155. *Costa, E. da*, A Covilhã no trabalho, Covilhã 1928 (= Covilhã at work).

156. *Gomes, M.*, O Distrito de Aveiro, Coimbra, 1877 (= The District of Aveiro).

157. *Lamy, A. S.*, Monografia de Ovar, 2 vols., Ovar, 1977 (= Monography on Ovar).

158. *Loureiro, J. P.*, Coimbra no passado, 2 vols., Coimbra, 1964 (= Coimbra in the past).

159. *Oliveira, C. A. de*, Apontamentos para a monografia da Guarda, Guarda, 1940 (= Notes on the Monography of Guarda).

160. *Quintella, A. de Moura*, Subsídios para a monografia da Covilhã, Covilhã, 1889 (= Aids to the Monography on Covilhã).

161. *Silva, J. A. da*, História da Covilhã, Lisbon, 1970 (= History of Covilhã).

162. *Vale, L. e.*, Viseu Antigo, in Beira Alta, Vol. I, Facs. I, Viseu 1942, pp. 27–35 (= Old Viseu).

● Estremadura and Ribatejo

163. *Ferreira, M. F. G.*, Caldas da Rainha. Elementos para a história do aglomerado urbano, 2 vols. Diss. Lisbon, 1972 (= Caldas da Rainha. Introduction to the history of urban conurbations).

164. *Gonçalves, A.*, Memórias de Torres Novas. Novos Subsídios para a sua História, Barcelos, 1937 (= Review of Torres Novas: Aids to its history).

165. *Gonçalves, A.*, Torres Novas. Subsídios para a sua história, Barcelos, 1935 (= Torres Novas. Aids to its history).

166. *Henriques, G. da Carnota*, Alenquer e o seu concelho, 2nd ed., Lisbon, 1902 (= Alenquer and its municipality).

167. *Paviani, A.* Alenquer, aspectos geográficos de uma vila portuguesa, in

Finisterra. Vol. III. 5 (1968), pp. 32–78 (= Alenquer. Geographic aspects of a Portuguese town).

168. *Reis, D.*, and *M. L. Fonseca*, Caldas da Rainha. Estrutura funcional e áreas sociais, Lisbon, 1981 (= Caldas da Rainha. Functional structure and social areas).

169. *Salguaro, T. B.*, Torres Vedras. A vila na região, 2 vols., Diss. Lisbon, 1970 (= Torres Vedras. The town in the region).

● Lisbon and its Metropolitan Area

170. *Almeida, M. de*, Lisboa do Romantismo. Lisboa antes da Regeneração, Lisbon, 1916 (= Lisbon in the romantic period. Lisbon before the regeneration).

171. *Andrade, M. V. F. de*, Monografia de Cascais, Lisbon, 1969 (= Monography on Cascais).

172. *Araújo, N. de*, and *D. P. de Lima*, Inventário de Lisboa, 12 Vols., Lisbon, 1944–1956 (= Lisbon's register).

173. *Barros, M. A. de S. N. de*, O desenvolvimento de Lisboa de 1890 a 1940. Contribuição para o seu estudo geográfico, in Revista Municipal, Vol. 71 (1956), pp. 26–37; Vol. 72 (1956), pp. 43–56; Vol. 73 (1957), pp. 41–60; Vol. 74 (1957), pp. 29–57 (= Lisbon's development from 1890–1940. Contribution to its geographic study).

174. *Becken, U.*, Die Entwicklung des Stadtbildes von Lissabon, Diss. Hamburg, 1937.

175. *Câncio, F.*, Lisboa no século XIX, Lisbon, 1939 (= Lisbon in the 19th century).

176. *Câncio, F.*, Lisboa – Tempos idos, 2 vols. Lisbon 1957–1958 (= Lisbon – Past times).

177. *Duas cidades ao serviço de Portugal*. Subsídios para o estudio das relações de Lisboa e Porto durante oito séculos, 2 vols., Porto, 1947 (= Two cities of service to Portugal. Aids to the study of the relations between Lisbon and Porto throughout eight centuries).

178. *Dantas, J.*, Lisboa dos nossos avós, Lisbon, 1966 (= Lisbon of our grandparents).

179. *Ferreira, M. D. de Freitas*, O abastecimento de água à Cidade de Lisboa nos séculos XVIII e XIX, in Finisterra, Vol. XVI. 31 (1981), pp. 122–138 (= The water supply to the city of Lisbon in the 18th and 19th centuries).

180. *Floridi, V.*, Setúbal: Il porto, la pesca et le industrie, in Boletim de la Società de Geografia Italiana, Serie IX, Vol. 4–5 (1968), pp. 173–225 (= Setúbal: the harbour, fishing and industries).

181. *França, J. A.*, A reestruturação de Lisboa e a arquitectura pombalina, Lisbon, 1978 (= The reconstruction of Lisbon and architecture under Pombal).

182. *França, J. A.*, Une ville de lumières: La Lisbonne de Pombal, Paris, 1965.

183. *Freire, J. P.*, Lisboa do meu tempo e do passado. Do Rocio à Rotunda, 2 vols., Lisbon, 1931–1932 (= Lisbon of my time and of the past. From Rocio to Rotunda).

184. *Gaspar, J.*, A Dinâmica Funcional do Centro de Lisboa, in Finisterra, Vol. XI.21 (1976), pp. 37–150 (= The functional dynamics of Lisbon's city centre).

185. *Gaspar, J.*, Zentrum und Peripherie im Ballungsraum Lissabon, Kassel, 1979.

186. *Lima, M. A. F. F. de*, Alcântara. Evolução dum bairro de Lisboa, Lisbon, 1971 (= Alcântara. Evolution of a Lisbon quarter).

187. *Lisboa – Oito séculos de História*, 2 vols., Lisbon, 1947 (= Lisbon – Eight centuries of history).

188. *Marques, I. C. P.*, Almada e Barreiro – Contrastes e semelhanças da sua evolução, Diss. Coimbra, 1956 (= Almada and Barreiro – contrasts and similarities of their evolution).

189. *Pais, A. da Silva*, O Barreiro antigo e moderno. As outras terras do concelho, Barreiro, 1963 (= Ancient and Modern Barreiro. The other lands of the municipality).

190. *Pereira, J. C.*, Lisboa, 5 vols., Lisbon, 1973 (= Lisbon).

191. *Pinto, M.*, Setúbal cidade centennária. 1860–1960, Sétubal, 1966 (= Setúbal – centenarian city).

192. *Portugal, F.*, and *A. de Matos*, Lisboa em 1758, Lisbon, 1973 (= Lisbon in the year 1758).

193. *Ribeiro, O.*, Evolução e Perspectivas dos Estudos Olisiponenses, in Revista Municipal, No. 27 (1945), pp. 3–12 (= Evolution and perspectives of Lisbon studies).

194. *Rodrigues, F.*, O porto de Lisboa no país e na cidade. Lisbon, 1979 (Centro de Estudos Geográficos da Universidade de Lisboa) (= Lisbon's harbour in the country and in the city).

195. *Sequeira, G. de Matos*, O Carmo e a Trindade. Subsídios para a história de Lisboa, 3 vols., Lisbon 1939–1941 (= Carmo and Trindade. Aids to the history of Lisbon).

196. *Sequeira, G. de Matos*, Depois do Terramoto, 4 vols. Coimbra, 1916–1933 (= After the earthquake).

197. *Sequeira, G. de Matos*, and *L. P. de Macedo*, A nossa Lisboa, Lisbon, n.d. (= Our Lisbon).

198. *Silva, A. V. da*, Dispersos, Vol. I–III 2nd ed., Lisbon 1960–1968 (= Several themes).

199. *Silva, A. V. da*, Os limites de Lisboa, Lisbon, 1891 (= The borders of Lisbon).

200. *Silva, A. V. da*, A população de Lisboa. Estudo Histórico, Lisbon, 1919 (= The population of Lisbon, Historical study).

201. *Simões, A. M.*, Concelho de Oeiras e Freguesia da Amadora. Apontamentos a sua história, Lisbon, 1969 (= The municipality of Oeiras and the parish of Amadora. Notes on their history).

202. *Sousa, A. A.*, Le Port de Lisbonne, Lisbon, 1926.

203. *Vasconcellos, J. L. de*, Páginas olisiponenses, Lisbon, 1959 (= Lisbon pages).

● Minho

204. *Araújo, M.*, Industriais de Braga. Notas de um journalista, Braga, 1923 (= Braga industrialists. Notes of a journalist).

205. *Caldas, P. A. J. F.*, Guimarães. Apontamentos para a sua história, 2 vols. Porto, 1881 (= Guimarães. Notes on its history).

206. *Flores, A. de Quadros*, Guimarães na última quadra do Romantismo. 1898–1918. Memórias, Guimarães 1967 (= Guimarães in the last period of Romanticism. 1898–1918).

207. *Lemos, M. R. dos Reys*, Anais Municipais de Ponte de Lima, 2nd ed. Ponte de Lima 1977 (= Ponte de Lima – municipal annals).

208. *Martins, A.*, Braga antiga, Porto 1971 (= Ancient Braga).

209. *Medeiros, I. M.*, Arcos de Valdevez. Estudo de Geografia Urbana de uma Vila do Alto Minho, in Finisterra, Vol. V. 10 (1970), pp. 205–244 (= Arcos de Valdevez. Urban-geographical study of an Alto Minho town).

210. *Oliveira, A. L. de*, Valença do Minho, Póvoa do Varzim 1978 (= Valenca do Minho).

211. *Soares, A. F. S. N.*, O Distrito de Viana do Castelo nos Inquéritos Paroquiais de 1775, 1825 e 1845, in Arquivo do Alto Minho, Vol. 21 (1975), pp. 1–27 (= The district of Viana do Castelo in the parish inquiry of 1775, 1825 and 1845).

● Porto and Metropolitan Area

212. *Azevedo, F. P. de*, História da Prostituição e Polícia Sanitária no Porto, Porto, 1864 (= The history of prostitution and sanitary police in Porto).

213. *Basto, A. de Magalhães*, Estudos portuenses, Porto, 1962 (= Porto studies).

214. *Basto, A. De Magalhães*, O Porto do Romantismo, Coimbra, 1932 (= Porto of the Romantic period).

215. *Basto, A. de Magalhães, D. Peres* and *A. Cruz*, História da cidade do Porto, 3 vols., Barcelos, 1962–1965 (= History of the city of Porto).

216. *Guichard, F.*, Amarante: Structures socio-économiques et liens de dépendance dans un "concelho" du nord-ouest portugais, Lisbon, 1980.

217. *Jorge, R.*, Origem e desenvolvimento da cidade de Porto, Porto, 1897 (= Origin and development of the city of Porto).

218. *Lima, M. A.*, Matosinhos, Coimbra, 1963 (= Matosinhos).

219. *Monterey, G. de*, O Porto, origem, evolução e transportes, Porto, 1971 (= Porto, origin, evolution and transport).

220. *Oliveira, C. M. de*, O Concelho de Gondomar. Apontamentos monográficos, 4 vols. Porto, 1931–1938 (= The municipality of Gondomar. Monographic notes).

221. *Oliveira, J. M. Pereira de*, O Espaço urbano do Porto – Condições naturais e desenvolvimento, Coimbra, 1973 (= Porto's urban space. Natural conditions and development).

222. *Santos, M. T. da Costa*, Matosinhos – Aspectos históricos, económicos e humanos, Diss. Coimbra, 1964 (= Matosinhos – Historical, economical and human aspects).

● Trás-os-Montes and Alto Douro

223. *Carvalho, A. C. R. de*, Chaves antiga, Lisbon, 1929 (= Ancient Chaves).

224. *Costa, J. G. da*, Montalegre e as Terras de Barroso, Braga, 1968 (= Montalegre and the lands of Barroso).

225. *Queiroz, M. J. V.*, Lamego. Um passado, um presente, Lisbon, 1970 (= Lamego. A past, a present).

226. *Ribeiro, O.*, Localização e destino dos centros urbanos de Trás-os-Montes, in Finisterra, Vol. 7. 13 (1972), pp. 46–70 (= Localisation and destiny of the urban centres of Trás-os-Montes).

227. *Sales, P. E. A. P. de*, Mirandela. Apontamentos Históricos, Bragança, 1978 (= Mirandela. Historical notes).

228. *Silva, J. L. R. da*, Histórias . . . para a História. Vila Real do meu tempo. Período decorrido entre 1890, aproximedamente e 1904, Barcelos, 1959 (= Stories about a history. My old Vila Real. The period between 1890 and approximately 1904).

FERNANDO DE TERÁN AND MARTIN BASSOLS

Spain

A. Urban History Institutions

Centro de Estudios de Ordenación del Territorio y Medio Ambiente – Ministerio de Obras Públicas y Urbanismo (M.O.P.U.), Madrid.

Comisión de Estudios Históricos de Obras Públicas y Urbanismo – Ministerio de Obras Públicas y Urbanismo (M.O.P.U.), Madrid.

Instituto de Estudios de Administración Local, Madrid.

Instituto de Estudios Madrileños – Consejo Superior de Investigaciones Científicas (C.S.I.C.), Madrid.

Instituto Geográfico Vasco Andrés de Urdaneta, San Sebastián.

Instituto Gonzalo Fernández de Oviedo – Consejo Superior de Investigaciones Científicas (C.S.I.C.), Madrid.

Instituto Juan Sebastián Elcano – Consejo Superior de Investigaciones Científicas (C.S.I.C.), Madrid.

Instituto Provincial d'Urbanisme, Barcelona.

Real Academia de la Historia, Madrid.

Real Sociedad Geográfica, Madrid.

Societat Catalana de Geografia, Barcelona.

B. Aids to Research

(a) Urban History Journals

1. *Anales del Instituto de Estudios Madrileños*, Madrid, 1966 ff., pub. by Consejo Superior de Investigaciones Científicas.

2. *Arquitectura. Organo del Colegio Oficial de Arquitectos de Madrid*, Madrid, 1959 ff., (from 1918–1936 under the title "Arquitectura", 1941–1958 under the title "Revista Nacional de Arquitectura").

3. *Ciudad y Territorio. Revista de Cienca Urbana*, Madrid, 1969 ff., pub. by Instituto de Estudios de Administración Local. Centro de Estudios

Urbanos.

4. *Cuadernos de Geografía,* Valencia 1964 ff., pub. by Universidad de Valencia.

5. *Eria. Revista Geográfica,* Oviedo, Vol. 7 (1984), pub. by Universidad de Oviedo, Sección de Geografía.

6. *Estudios Geográficos,* Madrid, 1940 ff., pub. by Consejo Superior de Investigaciones Científicas.

7. *Lurralde. Investigación y espacio,* San Sebastian, 1978 ff., pub. by Instituto Geográfico Vasco.

8. *Quaderns d'Arquitectura i Urbanisme,* Barcelona, 1981 ff., pub. by Collegio Official d'Arquitectes de Catalunya (1944–1970 under the title "Cuadernos de Arquitectura", from 1971–1981 under the title "Cuadernos de Arquitectura y Urbanismo").

9. *Papeles de Geografía / Papeles del Departamento de Geografía,* 1968 ff., pub. by Universidad de Murcia.

10. *Paralelo 37. Revista de Estudios Geográficos,* Almeria, 1977 ff., pub. by Departamento de Geografia. Colegio Universitario de Almería, 1977 ff.

11. *Revista Catalana de Geografía / Revista de Geografía,* Barcelona, 1967 ff., pub. by Departamento de Geografía de la Universidad de Barcelona.

12. *Revista de Derecho Urbanístico,* Madrid, 1967 ff.

13. *Revista de Geografía,* Barcelona, 1967 ff., pub. by Departamento de Geografía de la Universidad de Barcelona.

(b) Bibliographies

(c) Handbooks on Urban History

14. *Banco Hipotecario de España,* Vivienda y urbanismo en España, Barcelona, 1982.

15. *Capel, H.,* Capitalismo y morfología urbana, Barcelona, 1975.

16. *Chueca Goitia, F.,* Breve historia del urbanismo, Madrid, 1977 (= A short history of urban planning).

17. *Instituto de Estudios de Administración Local* pub., Resumen histórico del urbanismo en Espana, Madrid, 1963 (= An outline of the history of town planning in Spain).

18. *Terán, F. de,* Planeamiento urbano en la España contemporánea, Barcelona, 1978 (= Contemporary town planning in Spain).

19. *Vara Ortiz, E. de la,* El urbanismo en sus aspectos histórico y doctrinal, Madrid, 1929 (= Town planning, its historical aspects and teachings).

(d) Atlases on Urban History and Urban Development

20. *Ayuntamento de Madrid,* Cartografía Madrileña: 1635–1982, Madrid, 1986.

21. *Coello, F.,* Atlas de España y sus posesiones de ultramar, Madrid, 1850

(= Atlas of Spain and its overseas possessions).

22. *Colegio de Arquitectos de Madrid* pub., Planos de Madrid, Madrid, 1983 (= Town plans of Madrid).

23. *Comisión de Planeamiento y Coordinación del Area Metropolitana de Madrid* pub., Atlas básico del Area Metropolitana de Madrid, Madrid, 1979 (= Basic atlas of the metropolitan area of Madrid).

24. *Galera, M. et al.*, Atlas de Barcelona, Siglos XVI–XX, Barcelona, 1982 (= Atlas of Barcelona. 16th–20th century.

25. *Rocafort, C. et al.*, La España regional, Barcelona, 1935 (= Regional Spain).

(e)   Urban History Sources

—

C. **Research Reports**

—

D. **Literature on Individual Areas of Urban History Research**

(a)   Concept and Definition of Town and Town Types

26. *Bosque Maurel, J.*, El medio fisico, el capital humano y el sector agrario, in Banco de Bilbao, La España de las Autonomías, Madrid, 1981 pp. 207–295 (= The agrarian sector, physical fundamentals, population resources).

27. *Calvo Palacios, J. L.*, Lo industrial y lo urbano en la España moderna, in Geographica, Madrid, 1973 (= Industry and urbanism in modern Spain).

28. *Capel, H.*, Estudios sobre el sistema urbano, in Ch. Beringuier *et al.*, Urbanismo y practica política, Barcelona, 1974, Introduction (= Studies on the urban system).

29. *Capel, H.*, La red urbana española. 1950–1961, in Revista de la Universidad de Barcelona, 1973 (= Spain's urban network 1950–1961).

30. *Capel Saez, H.*, La red urbana española y la nueva demarcación judicial in Revista de Geografía, Vol. 2 (1968), No. 1, pp. 56–65. (= Spain's urban network and the new judicial districts).

31. *Díez Nicolás, J.*, Especialización funcional y dominación en la España urbana, Guadarrama, 1972 (= Functional specialisation and control in urban Spain).

32. *Díez Nicolás, F.*, Influencia de la definiciones adminstratives en el análisis de conceptos sociológigos. El municipio como unidad de análisis en el estudio del grado de urbanización, in Revista Internacional de Sociología, Vol. 25 (1967), No. 97/98, pp. 75–87 (= Analysis of the influence of administrative definitions on sociological concepts. The commune as a unit of analysis to study the degree of urbanisation).

33. *Ferrer Regales, M.*, El sistema de Localización urbano e industrial, in Banco de Bilbao, La España de las Autonomías, Madrid, 1981 pp. 299–365 (= The system of urban and industrial settlement).

34. *Gavira, J.*, La geografía de la ciudad, in Estudios Geográficos, Vol. 1 (1940), No. 1, pp. 119–168 (= Urban geography).

35. *Juaristi Linacero, J. M. de*, El proceso de urbanización en España y las distribuciones de tamanos de los asentamientos, in Geographica, Vol. 19 (1977), No. 1, p. 161–169 (= The urbanisation process in Spain and the distribution of settlements).

36. *Perpiña Grau, R.*, Corologia. Teoria estructural y estructurante de la población de España. 1900–1950, Madrid, 1954 (= Study of areas. Structure and structurising theories of the Spanish population).

37. *Perpiña Grau, R.*, De Economia Hispana. Infrastructura, Historia, Madrid, 1974 (= The Spanish economy. Infrastructure, history).

38. *Plan Nacional de Desarrollo Económico y Social*, Madrid, 1971 (= National plan for social and economic development).

39. *Plan Nacional de Desarrollo Económico y Social*. Ponencia sobre Desarrollo Regional, Madrid, 1972 (= National plan for social and economic development. Report on regional development).

40. *Racionero, L.*, Sistemas de ciudades y ordenación del territorio, Madrid, 1981 (= Town systems and ordering of space).

41. *Ribas Piera, M., et al.*, Estudios de economía urbana, Madrid, 1974 (= Studies on urban economy).

42. *Uña Juárez, O.*, Las tipologías históricas de la ciudad y la sociología urbana, in La Ciudad de Dios, Vol. 191 (1978), No. 3, pp. 93–106 (= Historical town – typologies and urban sociology).

43. *Vila, J.*, and *H. Capel*, Campo y ciudad en la geografía española, Barcelona, 1970 (= Town and country in Spanish geography).

(b)   Politics, Law and Statutes

44. *Arnanz Delgado, R.*, Notas para una historia de legislación urbanística española, in Municipalía, No. 239 (1974) (= Notes for a history of Spanish urban legislation).

45. *Artola, M.*, La burguesía revolucionaria. Historia de España Alfaguara V., Madrid, 1973 (= The bourgeois revolution. A history of 'España Alfaguara V').

46. *Baena del Alcázar, M.*, La organización adminstrativa local (1852–1977), in El Consultor, Vol. 125 (1978) (= The organisation of local administration).

47. *Bassols, M.*, Génesis y evolución del derecho urbanístico español (1812–1956), Madrid, 1973 (= Origin and development of Spanish town planning rights).

48. *Beneyto Pérez J.*, Historia de la Administración española e hispanoamericana, Madrid, 1958 (= The history of Spanish and Hispano-American administration).

49. *Coloma Marti, G.*, Contadores, presupuesto y cuentas en la Administración local española en el s. XIX, Madrid, 1975 (= Inspectors. Levies and their requirements in Local Spanish administration in the 19th century).

50. *Cosculluela Montaner, L.*, and *E. Orduna Rebollo*, Legislación de Adminstración Local 1900–1975, Madrid, 1981 (= Legislation and local administration).

51. *Flores, J. M.*, and *J. García Murillo*, La acción municipal socialista en Madrid. Bienio republicano 1931–1933, in Documentos y Estudios, No. 7 (1977) (= Socialist municipal activity in Madrid. The two republican years 1931–1933).

52. *Fontana Lázaro, J.*, Cambio económico y actitudes políticas en la España del siglo XIX., Barcelona, 1973 (= Economic change and political attitudes in Spain in the 19th century).

53. *Gonzáles Navarro, F.*, Bibliografía sobre derecho urbanistico, Madrid, 1981 (= Bibliography on urban legislation).

54. *Instituto de Estudios de Administración Local*, Derecho urbanistico español, Madrid, 1950 (= Spanish town planning rights).

55. *Jordana de Pozas, L.*, Significación del estatuto en la historia del municipalismo español, Madrid, 1975 (= The significance of town statutes in the history of Spanish communities).

56. *Larrainzar Yoldi, R.*, Breve historia de la Administración Local española, Madrid, 1969 (= A short history of local Spanish administration).

57. *Linz, J. J., et al.*, Informe sociológico sobre el cambio político en España. 1975–1981, Madrid, 1981 (= A sociological report on the political change in Spain 1975–1981).

58. *Martinez Cuadrado, M.*, El sistema político español (1975–1979) y el compartamiento electoral regional en el Sur de Europa, Madrid, 1984 (= The Spanish political system (1975–1979) and the regional electoral behaviour in Southern Europe).

59. *Moral Ruiz, J.*, Hacienda central y haciendas locales en España. 1845–1905, Madrid, 1984 (= Central and communal finance matters in Spain).

60. *Morell Ocana, L.*, La articulación entre la Administración del Estado y las entidades locales, Madrid, 1972 (= The relations between state administration and the local units.

61. *Orduña Rebollo, E.*, Bibliografía iberoamericana de Administración Local, Madrid, 1983 (= Iberoamerican bibliography of local administration).

62. *Parejo, L.*, La ordenación urbanística. El periodo 1956–1975, Madrid, 1979 (= Town planning regulations. The period 1956–1975).

63. *Posada, A.*, Evolución legislativa del Régimen Local en España. 1812–1909, Madrid, 1910 (= The development of legislation of the municipal regulations in Spain).

64. *Posada, A.* Régimen municipal de la ciudad moderna, Madrid, 1936 (= The municipal regulations of the modern town).

65. *Rodríguez Moniño, R.*, Pasado y presente de la hacienda municipal espanola, Palma de Mallorca, 1979 (= Past and present of Spanish communal finance matters).

66. *Tezanos Tortajada, J. F.*, El espacio político y sociológico del socialismo español, Madrid, 1979 (= The scope for political and sociological activity in Spanish socialism).

67. *Valenzuela, M.*, Ciudad y acción municipal. La política de vivienda del Ayuntamiento de Madrid (1868–1976), in Anales del Instituto de Estudios Madridleños, Vol. 15 (1978), pp. 327–362 (= Town and municipal activity. Housing policy of town authorities in Madrid).

(c)   Population and Social Structure

68. *Abascal Garayoa, A.*, La evolución de la población urbana española en la primera mitad del siglo XX, in Geographica, Vol. 3 (1956), no. 9–12, pp. 47–58 (= The development of the Spanish urban population in the first half of the 20th century).

69. *Capel, H.*, Estructura funcional de las ciudades españales en 1950, in Revista de Geografía de la Universidad de Barcelona, Vol. 2 (1968), No. 2, pp. 93–129 (= The functional structure of Spanish towns in 1950).

70. *Capel, H.*, Estudios acerca de la migraciones interiores en España, Barcelona, 1967 (= Studies on internal migration in Spain).

71. *Díez, Nicolás, J.*, Componentes del crecimiento de la población en España. 1900–1960, in Revista Internacional de Sociología, Vol. 29 (1971), No. 116, pp. 87–113 (= Growth components of the Spanish population 1900–1960).

72. *Díez Nicolás, J.*, Concentración de la población en capitales de provinicias españolas. 1940–1960, in La Provincia, 1966 (= Concentration of population in Spanish provincial capitals. 1940–1960).

73. *Díez Nicolás, J.*, Determinación de la población urbana en España en 1960, in Boletín del Centro de Estudios Sociales, Vol. 8 (1968), No. 3, pp. 5–17 (= Determination of the urban population in Spain in 1960).

74. *Díez Nicolás, J.*, Tamaño, densidad y crecimiento de la población en España. 1900–1960, Madrid, 1971 (= Extent, density and growth of the Spanish population. 1900–1960).

75. *Estébanez Alvarez, J.*, and R. Puyol Antolín, Los movimientos migratorios españoles durante el decenio 1961–1970, in Geographica, Vol. 15 (1973), No. 2, pp. 105–142 (= Spanish migration in the period 1961–1970).

76. *Ferrer, M.*, La población española, Barcelona, 1976 (= The Spanish population).

77. *Ferrer, M.*, and A. Precedo Lede, La estructura interna de la ciudades españolas, in Geographica, Vol. 19 (1977), No. 1, pp. 105–142 (= Internal structure of Spanish towns).

78. *Garcia Barbancho, A.*, Las migraciones interiores españolas. Estudio cuantitativo desde 1900, Madrid, 1975 (= Internal Spanish migration. Quantitative studies since 1900).

79. *García Barbancho, A.*, Las migraciones interiores españolas en 1961–1970, Madrid, 1975 (= Internal Spanish migration in the period 1961–1970).

80. *Gavira, J.*, El crecimiento de la población urbana española, in Estudios Geográficos, Vol. 8 (1947), No. 27, pp. 411–417 (= Growth of the Spanish urban population).

81. *Hoyos Sainz, L.*, Análisis por partidos judiciales del acrecentamiento de la población en España, in Revista Internacional de Sociología, Vol. 8 (1950), No. 29, pp. 99–128 (= Study on the growth of the population in Spain according to municipal areas).

82. *Majoral, R.*, Estructura funcional de las ciudades españolas de 10 000 a 20 000 habitantes en 1950, in Estudios Geográficos, Vol. 31 (1970), No. 118, pp. 77–106 (= The functional structure of Spanish towns with a population between 10 000 and 20 000 inhabitants in the year 1950).

83. *Martín, J.*, and A. de Miguel, La estructura social de las ciudades españolas, Madrid, 1978 (= The social structure of Spanish towns).

84. *Melón y Ruiz de Gordejuela, A.*, El crecimiento de las ciudades españolas, in Geographica, Vol. 1 (1954), No. 2–4, pp. 96–106 (= Growth of Spanish towns).

85. *Ministerio de Trabajo y Previsión. Dirección General de Acción Social y Emigración*, Despobalción y repoblación de España (1482–1920), Madrid, 1929 (= Depopulation and repopulation of Spain (1482–1920)).

86. *Nadal Oller, J.*, El fracaso de la Revolución Industrial en España. 1814–1913, Barcelona, 1975 (= The failure of the industrial revolution in Spain. 1814–1913).

87. *Nadal Oller, J.*, La población española. Siglos XVI a XX, Barcelona, 1973 (= The population of Spain. 16th and 20th centuries).

88. *Perpiña Grau, R.*, Problemas de los movimientos de población en España, in Anales de Moral Social y Económia, 1965 (= Problems of population movement in Spain).

89. *Ruiz Almansa, J.*, Crecimiento y repartición de la población en España, in Revista Internacional de Sociología, Vol. 4 (1944), No. 5, pp.

77–106 (= Growth and distribution of population in Spain).

90. *Villar Salinas, J.*, Demografía urbana y rural de España, in Revista Internacional de Sociología, Vol. 3 (1943), No. 4, pp. 73–114 (= Urban and rural demography of Spain).

(d) Town Planning, Housing

91. *Alarcón Alvarez, E. de*, Los urbanistas del ochocientos español, in Revista de obras publicas, No. 3085 (1972) (= Town planners of 19th century Spain).

92. *Ayuntamiento de Madrid*, Madrid, urbanismo y gestión municipal 1920–1940, Madrid, 1984 (= Madrid, town planning and municipal administration 1920–1940).

93. *Barreiro, P.*, Desarrollos urbanos de vivienda unifamiliar en Madrid de los años veinte-treinta, in Storia della città, No. 23 (1983) pp. 41–46 (= Urban developments of one-family houses in Madrid in the 1920s and 1930s).

94. *Bidagor Lasarte, P.*, El siglo XIX. El urbanimso en España durante, in Resumen histórico del urbanismo en España, Madrid 1954 pp. 191–214 (Publicaciones del Instituto de Estudios de Administración Local – IEAL) (= Urban planning in Spain during the 19th century).

95. *Bidagor Lasarte, P.*, Situación general del urbanismo en España (1939–1967), in Revista de derecho urbanistico, Vol. 1 (1967), No. 4, pp. 23–70) (= General situation of urban planning in Spain).

96. *Blein Zarazaga, G.*, Resumen urbanístico del último bienio (antecedentes de la Ley del Suelo), in Crónica de la VI Reunión de Técnicos Urbanistas, Madrid 1955 (Publicaciones del Instituto de Estudios de Adminstración Local – IEAL) (= An outline of urban development in the last two years before the Land Act).

97. *Bohigas, O.*, Arquitectura española de la 2ª República, Barcelona, 1970 (= Spanish architecture in the Second Republic).

98. *Bonet, A.*, Los "ensanches" y el urbanismo burgués del siglo XIX en España, in Storia della città, No. 23 (1983), pp. 27–34 (= The "ensanches" (= urban expansion) and bourgeois town planning in the 19th century in Spain).

99. *Collins, G. R., et al.*, Arturo Soria y la Ciudad Lineal, Madrid 1968 (= Arturo and the "Ciudad Lineal" (= geometric town)).

100. *Fernández Balbuena, G.*, Trazado de ciudades, Madrid, 1932 (= Plans of towns).

101. *Fernández Ordoñez, J. A.*, Ildefonso Cerdá, padre del urbanismo, in Batik, No. 22 (1976) (= Ildefonso Cerdá, the father of town planning).

102. *Larrodera López, E.*, Evolución del planeamiento en España, in Ciudad y Territorio, No. 4 (1972) pp. 6–13 (= The development planning in Spain).

103. *Larrodera López, E.*, La evolución del planeamiento urbanístico en España, in Problemas . . ., Vol. XIII (1973) (= Development of town planning in Spain).

104. *Martínez Diez, R.*, Pasado, presente y futuro de la ordenación del territorio en España, in Ciudad y Territorio, Vol. 1 (1983) pp. 55–75 (= Past, present and future of spatial planning in Spain).

105. *Martínez Sarandeses, J., et al.*, La ordenación urbana en España. Balance de dieciseis ãnos de aplicación de la Ley del Suelo, in Ciudad y Territorio, No. 2 (1974) pp. 37–56 (= Urban spatial planning in Spain. Balance of sixteen years implementation of the Land Act).

106. *Martorell Otzet, V., et al.*, Historia del urbanismo en Barcelona, Barcelona, 1970 (= The history of town planning in Barcelona).

107. *Monclus, J. F., and J. L. Oyón*, Colonización agraria y urbanismo rural en el siglo XX, in Ciudad y Territorio, No. 3–4 (1983) pp. 67–84 (= Agra–colonisation and rural town planning in the 20th century).

108. *Ribas Piera, M.*, La planificación urbanística en España, in Zodiac, 1965 pp. 144–164 (= Spatial town planning in Spain).

109. *Richardson, H. W.*, Política y planificación del desarrollo regional en España, Madrid, 1975 (= Politics and planning of regional development in Spain).

110. *Roca, F.*, El GATCPAC y la crisis urbana de los años 30, in Cuadernos Arquitectura Urbanismo, No. 30 (1972) (= GATCPAC and the urban crisis of the 30s).

111. *Sáenz Ridruejo, F.*, Ildefonso Cerdá y la evolución urbana de Barcelona, in Revista de obras públicas, No. 3085 (1972) (= Ildefonso Cerdá and town planning development of Barcelona).

112. *Serratosa, A.*, Del Plan Comarcal de Barcelona al Plan Director de Cataluña, in Ciudad y Territorio, No. 2 (1977) pp. 109–112 (= From the local plan of Barcelona to the master plan of Catalonia).

113. *Tarrago, S.*, El "Plan Maciá" o "La Nova Barcelona" (1931–1938), in Cuadernos Arquitectura y Urbanismo. No. 90 (1972) (= The "Plan Macia" or "La Nova Barcelona").

114. *Terán, F. de*, Diez ãnos de urbanismo en España, in Ciudad y Territorio, No. 1 (1980) pp. 7–15 (= Ten years of urban planning in Spain).

115. *Terán, F. de*, Algunos aspectos de la relaciones entre planificación fisica y planificación económica en la experiencia española, in Ciudad y Territorio, No. 2 (1973) pp. 7–38 (= Some aspects of the relations between material and economic planning – the Spanish experience).

116. *Terán, F. de*, La Ciudad Lineal, antecedente de un urbanismo actual, Madrid, 1968 (= The geometric town, precursor of a contemporary urban planning).

117. *Terán, F. de*, Evolución del planeamiento de núcleos urbanos nuevos, in Ciudad y Territorio, No. 1 (1969) (= The development and

planning of new city centres).
118. *Terán, F. de*, Notas para la historia del planeamiento de Madrid, in Ciudad y Territorio, No. 2/3 (1976) pp. 9–26 (= Notes on the history of the planning of Madrid).
119. *Terán, F. de*, Planeamiento urbano en la España contemporánea, Barcelona, 1978 (= Urban planning in contemporary Spain).
120. *Terán, F. de*, La situación actual del planeamiento urbano y sus antecedentes, in Ciudad y Territorio, No. 2 (1971) pp. 13–26 (= The present–day state of town planning and its precursors).
121. *Ureña, R.*, Arquitectura y urbanística civil y militar en el período de la Autarquia (1936–1945), Madrid, 1979 (= Architecture, civil and military town planning in the period of Autarky (1936–1945)).
122. *Valenzuela Rubio, M.*, Notas sobre el desarrollo histórico del planeamiento en España, in Cuadernos de Investigación.Geografia e Historia, Vol. 4 (1978), No. 2 (= Notes on the historic development of planning in Spain).

(e)   Economy and Transport

123. *Aguilar, I., et al.*, Las estaciones ferroviarias de Madrid, Madrid, 1980 (= The railway stations of Madrid).
124. *Alzola, P.*, Historia de las Obras Públicas en España, Madrid, 1900 (= History of public building in Spain).
125. *Artola, M.*, Los ferrocarriles en España. 1844–1943, Madrid, 1978 (= Railways in Spain).
126. *Banco de Bilbao*, La España de las Autonomías, Madrid, 1981 (= Self-administration in Spain).
127. *Banco de España*, Ensayos sobre la economía española a mediados del siglo XIX, Madrid, 1970 (= Contributions to the economy of Spain in the middle of the 19th century).
128. *Brandis, D.*, El paisaje residencial de Madrid, Madrid, 1983 (= Madrid's residential landscape).
129. *Cabezas, J. A.*, Cien años de teléfono en España, Madrid, 1974 (= One hundred years of telephone in Spain).
130. *Capel, H.*, Capitalismo y morfología urbana in España, Barcelona, 1975 (= Capitalism and urban morphology in Spain).
131. *Carreras, J. M., and J. Margalef*, La evolución de las ciudades catalanas entre 1857 y 1975, in Ciudad y Territorio, No. 2 (1977) pp. 32–45 (= The development of Catalonian towns from 1857–1975).
132. *Casares Alonso, A.*, Estudio histórico económico de las construcciones ferroviarias españolas en el siglo XIX, Madrid, 1973 (= Historical and economic study of Spanish railway construction in the 19th century).
133. *Clavera, J., et al.*, Capitalismo espanol (1939–1959), Madrid, 1973

(= Spanish capitalism).

134. *Fernández Durán, R.*, El sistema de transportes en Madrid. Evolución, situación actual y perspectivas futuras, in Revista Internacional de Sociología, Vol. 43 (1982), No. 43, pp. 277–325 (= The transport system in Madrid. Development, current state and future perspectives).

135. *Galvarriato, J. A.*, El correo y la telecommunicación en España, Madrid, 1920 (= Post and telecommunications in Spain).

136. *González Yanci, P.*, Los accesos ferroviarios a Madrid, Madrid, 1977 (= The rail transfer into Madrid).

137. *Herrero, A.*, El desarrollo de nuestras ciudades después de la Ley del Suelo, in Ciudad y Territorio, No. 4 (1972), pp. 15–31 (= The development of our towns since the Land Act).

138. *Izquierdo, R.*, El modelo de transporte, in Banco de Bilbao, ed., La España de las Autonomías, Madrid, 1981, pp. 639–679 (= The transport model).

139. *López Gómez, A.*, Los transportes urbanos de Madrid, Madrid, 1983 (= Urban transport in Madrid).

140. *Mas, R.*, El barrio de Salamanca, Madrid, 1982 (= The suburb of Salamanca).

141. *Menéndez Pidal, G.*, Los caminos en la historia de España, Madrid, 1951 (= Roads in the history of Spain).

142. *Molina Negro, F.*, Las telecommunicaciones en España, Madrid, 1970 (= Telecommunications in Spain).

143. *Moneo, R.*, El urbanismo contemporáneo. 1950–1980, in: Banco Hipotecario de España, Vivienda y urbanismo en España, Barcelona, 1982 pp. 201–214 (= Contemporary town planning 1950–1980).

144. *Moya González, L.*, Barrios de promoción oficial. Madrid 1939–1976, Madrid, 1983 (= Publicly financed suburbs. Madrid 1939–1976).

145. *Muñoz Muñoz, J.*, El abastecimiento de aguas a Madrid, Diss. Madrid, 1983 (= Madrid's water supply).

146. *Rodríguez Maroto, E.*, Pequeña historia de las telecommunicaciones españolas, Diss. Madrid, 1955 (= A short history of Spanish telecommunications).

147. *Sambricio, C.*, La política urbana de Primo de Rivera, in Ciudad y Territorio, No. 4 (1982), pp. 33–54 (= Urban politics in Primo de Rivera).

148. *Sánchez Albornoz, N.*, España hace un siglo: una economía dual, Barcelona, 1968 (= A century of Spain: a dual economy).

149. *Solá-Morales, I. de*, Urbanismo en España, 1900–1950, in Banco Hipotecario de España, Vivienda y urbanismo en España, Barcelona, 1982, pp. 183–196 (= Urban planning in Spain).

150. *Solá-Morales, M. de*, Siglo XIX. Ensanche y saneamiento de las ciudades, in Banco Hipotecario de España, Vivienda y urbanismo en España, Barcelona, 1982, pp. 161–178 (= The 19th century. Urban expansion and restoration of towns).

151. *Terán, F. de*, Crecimiento urbano y planeamiento en Madrid, in Revista de Occidente, Vol. 27 (1983), pp. 151–167 (Extraord. VII. Madrid. Villa y Communidad) (= Urban growth and planning in Madrid).

152. *Tortella, G.*, Los orígenes del capitalismo en España. Banca, industria y ferrocarriles en el siglo XIX, Madrid, 1973 (= The origins of capitalism in Spain. Banks, industry and railways in the 19th century).

153. *Vicens Vives, J.*, Historia económica de España, Barcelona, 1955 (= Economic history of Spain).

154. *Vicens Vives, J.*, Historia social y económica de España, y América, Vol. IV: Burguesía, industrialización, obrerismo, Barcelona, 1959 (= A social and economic history of Spain and Latin America, Vol. IV: The bourgeois, industrialisation, workers' movement).

155. *Wais San Martín, F.*, Origen de los ferrocarriles españoles, Madrid, 1943 (= The origin of the Spanish railway).

E. Local Studies (a representative selection)

• Albacete

156. *Lles, C., et al.*, Albacete. Una aproximación a su realidad urbana, Albacete 1982 (= Albacete. An approach to its urban reality).

• Barcelona (and its surroundings)

157. *Banco Urquijo*, ed., Barcelona. Génesis y problemática del Area Metropolitana, Barcelona, 1972 (= Barcelona. Its birth and the problems of the metropolitan area).

158. *Esteban Noguera, J.*, Los ensanches menores de la región de Barcelona, Barcelona, 1976 (= Small urban expansion in the region of Barcelona).

159. *Solá-Morales, M. de, et al.*, Barcelona. Remodelación capitalista o desarrollo urbano en el sector de la Ribera Oriental, Barcelona, 1974 (= Barcelona. Capitalist reforming or urban development in the region of Ribera Oriental).

• Bilbao

160. *Losada, R.*, Historia urbanística de Bilbao, Bilbao, 1981 (= Urban history of Bilbao).

- Burgos

161. *Iglesias Rouco, L. S.*, Burgos en el siglo XIX. 1813–1900, Valladolid, 1979 (= Burgos in the 19th century).

- Cáceres

162. *Lozano Bartolozzi, M. del M.*, El desarrollo urbanístico de Cáceres (siglos XVI–XIX), Cáceres, 1980 (= Urban development of Cáceres, 16th–19th century).

- Calatyud

163. *Terán, M. de*, Calatayud, Daroca y Albarracin, in Estudios Geográficos, 1942, pp. 163–202.

- Cuenca

164. *Troitiño, M. A.*, Cuenca, evolución y crisis de una vieja ciudad castellana, Madrid, 1984 (= Cuenca, development and crisis of an old Castilian town).

- Gijón

165. *Alvargonzález, R. M.*, Gijón. Industrialización y crecimiento urbano, Oviedo 1977 (= Gijón. Industrialisation and urban growth).
166. *Llordén Minambres, M.*, La producción del suelo urbano en Gijón. 1860–1975, Oviedo, 1978 (= The yield of urban soil in Gijón 1860–1975).

- Guadalajara

167. *García Ballesteros, A.*, Geografía urbana de Guadalajara, Madrid, 1978 (= Urban geography of Guadalajara).

- La Coruña

168. *Batanero Díaz, M.*, Morfología urbana de La Coruña, in Revista del Instituto José Cornide, No. 8/9 (1972/73) (= The urban appearance of La Coruña).
169. *Gonzáles Cebrián, J.*, La ciudad a través de su plano: La Coruña, La Coruña, 1984 (= The town as reflected in its town planning: La Coruña).

Spain

- Madrid

170. *Brandis García, D.* and *R. Mas Hernández*, La Ciudad Lineal y la práctica inmobiliaria de la Companía Madrileña de Urbanización (1894–1931), in Ciudad y Territorio, No. 3 (1981) (= The "Ciudad Lineal" (= geometric town) and real estate politics of the Madrid Society for Town Planning).
171. *Ruiz Palomeque, E.*, Ordenación y transformación urbanas del casco antiguo madrileño durante los siglos XIX y XX, Madrid, 1976 (= Urban planning and transformation of the old part of Madrid during the 19th and 20th centuries).
172. *Terán, M. de*, Dos calles madrileñas. Las de Alcalá y Toledo, in Estudios Geográficos, Vol. 22 (1961), No. 84/85, pp. 375–476 (= Two streets of Madrid, Alcalá and Toledo streets).
173. *Terán, F. de*, La Paloma, in Madrid. Espasa Calpe, Vol. 1 (1979), pp. 241–260 (= La Paloma (suburb of Madrid)).

- Murcia

174. *Roselló, V. M.* and *C. M. Cano*, Evolución urbana de Murcia. 1831–1973, Murcia, 1975 (= Urban development of Murcia. 1831–1973).

- Oviedo

175. *Morales Saro, Ma. C.*, Oviedo, arquitectura y desarrollo urbano, Oviedo 1981 (= Oviedo, architecture and urban development).

- San Sebastián

176. *Calvo Sánchez, M. J.*, Crecimiento y estructura urbana de San Sebastián, San Sebastián, 1983 (= Growth and urban structure of San Sebastián).
177. *Font, J. M., et al.*, La comarca de San Sebastián: Crónica de una formación (= The region of San Sebastián. Chronicle of its formation).

- Santa Cruz de Tenerife

178. *García, L. M.*, Santa Cruz de Tenerife: La formación de una ciudad marginal, Santa Cruz de Tenerife, 1981 (= Santa Cruz, Tenerife: The formation of a marginal town).

509

● Segovia

179. *Mártinez de Pisón, E.*, Segovia. Evolución de un paisaje urbano, Madrid, 1976 (= Segovia. Development of an urban landscape).

● Sigüenza

180. *Terán, M. de*, Sigüenza. Estudio de geografía urbana, in Estudios Geográficos, Vol. 7 (1946), No. 25, pp. 633–666 (= Sigüenza. Study on urban geography).

● Valladolid

181. *Font Arellano, et al.*, Valladolid. Procesos y formas del crecimiento urbano, Valladolid, 1976 (= Valladolid. Processes and forms of urban growth).
182. *Garcia Fernández, J.*, Crecimiento y estructura urbana de Valladolid, Valladolid, 1972 (= Growth and urban structure of Valladolid).
183. *Virgili Blanquet, M. A.*, Desarrollo urbanistico y arquitectónico de Valladolid (1851–1936), Ayuntamiento de Valladolid, 1979 (= Town planning and architectonic development of Valladolid).

● Vigo

184. *Pereiro Alonso, J. L.*, El desarrollo urbano de Vigo, Madrid, 1977 (= Town planning of Vigo).

● Zaragoza

185. *García Lasaosa, J.*, Desarrollo urbano de Zaragoza. 1885–1908, Zaragoza, 1979 (Institución "Fernando el Católico") (= Urban development of Zaragoza. 1885–1908).

EVA SJÖDÉN

Sweden

A. Urban History Institutions

Stadshistoriska institutet, founded 1919, based in Stockholm.

B. Aids to Research

(a) Urban History Journals

1. *Bebyggelsehistorisk tidskrift*, Stockholm, 1981 ff., ed. by A. K. Atmer, I. Sjöström and B. Sundin (= Journal of settlement history).

(b) Bibliographies

2. *International Bibliography of Urban History*. Denmark, Finland, Norway, Sweden, Stockholm, 1960.
3. *Lindberg, F.*, and *R. Hagstedt*, Suède, in Guide International d'Histoire Urbaine, Vol. 1: Europe, Paris 1977, pp. 453–464.
4. *Register över Stadshistorisk litteratur behandlad i de stadshistoriska revyerna*, pub. by Stadshistoriska institutet, Part 1: 1920–1944, Stockholm 1946; Part 2: 1945–1963, Stockholm, 1972 (= Index of literature on urban history dealt with in the urban history reviews).
5. *Revy över stads- och kommunhistoria*, Stockholm, 1976 ff., pub. by Stadshistoriska institutet; appears 5-yearly (= Review of urban and communal history). (Previously "Stadshistorsk Revy": from 1922–1964 "Svenska stadsförbundets tidskrift", 1970–1976 'Kommunal tidskrift').
6. *Svensk lokalhistorisk bibliografi*, in Historielärarnas förenings årsskrift, 1972, pp. 43–82 (= Swedish bibliography of local history).

511

(c)   Handbooks on Urban History

7. *Andersson, H. O.*, Tätorternas bebyggelsestruktur och föranderung. En översikt över Sverige och övriga Norden, Lund, 1977 (= Settlement structure and change in built-up areas. A survey of the Nordic countries).

(d)   Atlases on Urban History and Urban Development

8. *Ahlberg, N.*, and *T. Hall*, Uppsala, Sweden. Scandinavian Atlas of Historic Towns, No. 4, Odense, 1983.

(e)   Urban History Sources

9. *Améen, L.*, Stadsplaner som källa, in Bebyggelsehistorisk tidskrift, 1984, pp. 44–56 (= Town plans as historical sources).
10. *Historisk statistik för Sverige*, 3 vols., Stockholm, 1955–1960 (= Historical statistics of Sweden.)
11. *Norborg, L.-A.*, Källor till Sveriges historia, Lund, 1968 (= Sources for the history of Sweden.)

C.   Research Reports

(a)   General Surveys

12. *Ahnlund, N.*, Svenska stadshistorier och svensk stadshistoria, in Svenska Stadsförbundets tidskrift, 1917 (= Swedish town histories and Swedish urban history).
13. *Growth and Transformation of the Modern City.* The Stockholm Conference, Sept. 1978, ed. I. Hammarström and T. Hall, Stockholm, 1978.
14. *Hammarström, I.*, Urban History in Scandinavia. A Survey of Recent Trends, in Urban History Yearbook, Leicester, 1978, pp. 46–55.
15. *Hammarström, I., R. Hagstedt* and *L. Nilsson*, Projektet jämförande stadshistoria (PJÄS), in Historisk Tidskrift, 1975, pp. 472–481.
16. *Herlitz, N.*, Några ord om den stadshistoriska forskningens närmaste uppgifter, in Svenska Stadsförbundets tidskrift, 1919 (= Future tasks of urban history research).
17. *Johannesson, G.*, Fran köpstad till storkommun, Lund, 1978 (= From market town to big municipal district).
18. *Lindberg, F.*, Svensk stadshistoria. En blick på forskningsläget och de väntande uppgifterna, in Svensk Stadsförbundets tidskrift, 1951 (= Sweden's urban history. A summary of the state of research and a list of tasks).

19. *Öhngren, B.*, Urbaniseringen i Sverige 1840–1920, in Urbaniserings-prosessen i Norden, Vol. 3: Industrialiseringens förste fase, ed. by G. Authén Blom, Oslo, 1977, pp. 261–356 (= The process of urbanisation in the Scandinavian countries).

20. *Paulsson, G.*, Svensk stad 1–2, 2nd ed., Lund, 1974 (= Swedish towns).

21. *Städer i utveckling*: Tolv studier kring stadsförändringar tillägnade Ingrid Hammarström, ed. by T. Hall, Stockholm, 1984 (= Towns in transition: Twelve studies on urban change dedicated to Ingrid Hammarström).

(b)   *Surveys of Individual Fields of Urban Research*

22. *Andrae, C.-G.*, Sveriges lokalhistoria. Inledning till en diskussion, in Historisk tidskrift, 1979 pp. 1–5 (= Sweden's local history. Introduction to a debate).

23. *Gaunt, D.*, Börje Hanssens betydelse för Svensk stad, in Perspektiv på Svensk stad. Staden som forskningsobjekt 1950–1980, ed. by I. Hammarström and T. Hall, Stockholm, 1981 (= Börje Hanssens significance for Swedish towns).

24. *Kleineisel, J.*, Stadens form. Samhällsmönsters och teknikens betydelse för städernas utveckling, Stockholm, 1971 (= Urban form: The importance of societal patterns and technology for urban development).

25. *Nordisk lokalhistoria. Mötesrapporter 1–4* (= Nordic local history. Conference reports 1–4).

1. *Nordens naere fortid*. Lokalsamfundene i de seneste 100 år. Foredrag och diskussioner på det første nordiske seminar i lokalhistorie Sostrup slot, August 1973, Sostrup, 1973 (= Local communities during the last hundred years. Report from the first nordic local history conference).

2. *Den andra nordiska lokalhistoriska konferensen i Viitasaari 1976*. Föredrag och diskussioner, Viitasaari, 1976 (= Report from the second nordic local history conference).

3. *By och bygd, stad och omland*. Nordisk lokalhistorie. Seminarrapport No. 3, Oslo, 1981 (= Town and Countryside. The City and the urban district).

4. *Lokal Praxis på det sociala området i de nordiska länderna 1800–1920*, Stockholm, 1986 (= Social policy and local practice in the Nordic countries 1800–1920).

D. Literature on Individual Areas of Urban History Research

(a) Concept and Definition of Town and Town Types

26. *Hägerstrand, T.*, Urbaniseringen. Stadsutveckling och regionala olikheter, Stockholm , 1971 (= Urbanisation. Urban development and regional differences).

27. *Perspektiv på svensk stad.* Staden som forskningsobjekt 1950–1980. En skrift från Projektet Svensk stadsmiljö: byggande och boende under de senaste hundrå åren, eds. I. Hammarström and T. Hall, Stockholm, 1981 (= Perspectives on Swedish towns. The town as a research object 1950–1980. A book from the research project "Swedish urban environment building and housing during the past hundred years").

(b) Politics, Law and Statutes

28. *Årberg, I.*, Förening och politik. Folkrörelsernas politiska aktivitet i Gävle under 1880-talet, Diss. Uppsala, 1975 (Studia Historica Upsaliensia, Vol. 69 (= Association and politics. The political activity of people's movements in Gävle in the 1880s).

29. *Attman, A.*, and *M. Fahl*, Göteborgs stadsfullmäktige 1863–1962, Parts 1–3, Gothenburg, 1963–1971 (= The town council of Gothenburg 1863–1962).

30. *Bringmark, G.*, Från dagaträl till medborgare. Malmö stadsfullmäktige 100 år. En krönika i ord och bild om stadens utveckling 1863–1962, Malmö, 1962 (= From serf to citizen. Malmö Town Council 100 years. A chronicle in words and pictures concerning the development of the town 1863–1962).

31. *Forssell, H.*, Anteckningar om Sveriges handel och om städernas förhållanden under de första femtio åren av Vasahusets regering. Del 2 av Sveriges inre historia från Gustaf I med särskilt afseende på förvaltning och ekonomi, Stockholm, 1875 (= Comments on Swedish internal trade and on urban relations during the first 50 years of the House of Vasa. Part 2 of Swedish national history since Gustav I with special reference to administration and economics).

32. *Heckscher, E.*, Städernas plats i Sveriges samhällshistoria, in Ekonomisk tidskrift, 1938 (= The role of the town in Swedish national history).

33. *Herlitz, N.*, Svensk stadsförvaltning på 1830-talet, Stockholm, 1924 (= Swedish town administration in the 1830s).

34. *Hundra år under kommunalförfattningarna 1862–1962.* Minnesskrift, ed. U.S. Palme, Stockholm, 1962 (= A century under the municipal laws 1862–1962).

35. *De hundra åren.* Stadsfullmäktige i Hälsingborg 1862–1962, ed. K.

Gierow, Helsingborg, 1965 (= The hundred years. The town council of Hälsingborg 1862–1962).

36. *Johansson, B.*, Social differentiering och kommunalpolitik. Enköping 1863–1919, Diss. Uppsala, 1974 (Studia Historica Upsaliensia, Vol. 59) (= Social differentiation and municipal politics. Enköping 1863–1919).

37. *Kommunal självstyrelse i Lund.* Minnesskrift med anledning av stadsfullmäktiges 100-årsjubileum, ed., K. Gierow, Lund, 1964 (= Municipal self-government in Lund. Memorial publication in connection with the centenary of the town council).

38. *Larsson, Y.*, På marsch mot demokratin. Från hundragradig skala till allmän rösträtt, 1900–1920, Stockholm, 1967 (= Monografier utgivna av Stockholms kommunalförvaltning, Vol. 22. IV 2) (= On march towards democracy. From the centigrade scale [suffrage based on wealth] to universal suffrage).

39. *Lindberg, F.*, Växande stad. Stockholms stadsfullmäktige 1862–1900, Stockholm, 1980 (Monografier utgivna au Stockholms kommunalförvaltning, Vol. 22. IV 1) (= Growing city. The town council of Stockholm 1862–1900).

40. *Norrlid, I.*, Demokrati, skatterättvisa och ideologisk förändring: den kommunala självstyrelsen och demokratins genombrott i Sverige, Lund, 1983 (Bibliotheca historica Lundensis, Vol. 57) (= Democracy, tax distribution and ideological change. Local self-government and the democratic breakthrough in Sweden).

41. *Odhner, C. T.*, Bidrag till den svenska stadsförfattningens historia, Stockholm, 1861 (= Contribution to the history of Swedish municipal administration).

42. *Schück, A.*, Studier rörande det svenska stadsväsendets uppkomst och tidigare utveckling, Uppsala, 1926 (= Studies on the creation and early development of Swedish town matters).

43. *Stadsfullmäktige i Kalmar 1863–1962.* Minneskrift, Kalmar, 1962 (= The town council of Kalmar 1863–1962. Memorial publication).

44. *Strömberg, T.*, Kommunalsocialismen inför verkligheten, Diss. Malmö 1984 (Örebro Studies, 2) (= Communal socialism and reality).

45. *Tomson, R.*, Etik och politik. Etiskt-kulturellt-socialt initiativ i Stockholms stadsfullmäktige åren 1900–1960, Parts 1–4, Stockholm, 1962–1966 (= Ethics and politics. Ethical-cultural-social initiatives in the town council of Stockholm 1900–1960).

46. *Westerlund, U.*, Borgarsamhällets upplösning och självstyrelsens utveckling i Nyköping 1810–1880, Diss. Uppsala, 1973 (Studia Historica Upsaliensia, Vol. 48) (= The dissolution of the burgess society and the growth of self-government in Nyköping 1810–1880).

(c)   Population and Social Structure

47. *Ahlberg, G.*, Befolkningsutvecklingen och urbaniseringen i Sverige 1911–1950, Stockholm, 1953 (Monografier utgivna av Stockholms kommunalförvaltning, Vol. 13) (= Population growth and urbanisation in Sweden 1911–1950).

48. *Åkerman, S.*, Internal Migration. Industrialisation and Urbanisation (1895–1930): A Summary of the Västmanland Study, in: The Scandinavian Economic History Review, 1975, pp. 149–158.

49. *Cederqvist, J.*, Arbetare i streijk. Studier rörande arbeternas politiska mobilisering under industrialismens genombrott. Stockholm, 1850–1909, Diss. Stockholm, 1980 (Monografier utgivna av Stockholms kommun, Vol. 41) (= Workers on strike: the political mobilisation of the working class in Stockholm 1850–1909).

50. *Ek, S. B.*, Nöden i Lund. En etnologisk stadsstudie, Lund, 1971 (= A slum area in Lund. An ethnological city study).

51. *Elison, I.*, Arbetarrörelse och samhälle i Göteborg 1910–1922, Diss. Gothenburg, 1970 (Meddelanden från ekonomisk-historiska institutionen vid Göteborgs universitet, Vol. 16) (= The labour movement and society in Gothenburg, 1910–1922).

52. *Eriksson, M.*, and *S. Åkerman*, Geografisk och social rörlighet. Resultat från trestads-studien, in Scandia, 1974 (= Migration, social mobility and social change).

53. *Falk, T.*, Urban Sweden. Changes in the Distribution of Populations — The 1960s in Focus, Diss. Stockholm, 1976 (The Economic Research Institute at the Stockholm School of Economics).

54. *Fürth, T.*, De arbetslösa och 1930-talskrisen. En kollektivbiografi över hjälpsökande arbetslösa i Stockholm 1928–1936, Diss. Stockholm, 1979 (Monografier utgivna av Stockholms kommun. Vol. 40) (= The unemployed and the crisis of the 1930s. A collective biography of applicants for unemployment relief in Stockholm 1928–1936).

55. *Gejvall, B.*, 1800-talets stockholmsbostad. En studie över den borgerliga bostadens planlösning i hyreshusen, Stockholm, 1954 (Monografier utgivna av Stockholms kommunalförvaltning) (= The Stockholm dwelling of the 19th Century. A study of the planning of the upper class dwelling in blocks of flats).

56. *Grip, R.*, Konstförvanter och bokbindare i Stockholm 1850–1914. Studier av härkomst och social rörlighet hos arbetare inom boktryckar- och bokbinderiyrkena. En kollektivbiografi, Stockholm, 1981 (Monografier utgivna av Stockholms kommun, Vol. 44) (= Printers and bookbinders in Stockholm 1850–1914. A collective biography).

57. *Gustafson, U.*, Industrialismens storstad. Studier rörande Stockholms sociala, ekonomiska och demografiska struktur 1860–1910, Diss. Stockholm, 1976 (Monografier utgivna av Stockholms kommunalförvaltning, Vol. 37) (= Industrialism's metropolis. Study of the economic and demographic structure of Stockholm 1860–1910).

58. *Hanssen, B.*, Samhällsklasser i de svenska småstäderna under 1850- och 1860-talen, in Historisk tidskrift, 1978 (= Economic and social classes in Swedish provincial towns by the mid-19th century. Context and material).

59. *Hanssen, B.*, Urban Activity, Urban People and Urban Environment in Scandinavian History, in International Journal of Comparative Sociology, 1963, pp. 243–258.

60. *Hedenskog, S.*, Folkrörelserna i Nyköping 1880–1915. Uppkomst, social struktur och politisk aktivitet, Diss. Uppsala, 1973 (Studia Historica Upsaliensia, Vol. 49) (= The popular movements in Nyköping 1880–1915. Rise, social structure and political activity).

61. *Hellspong, M.*, and *O. Löfgren*, Land och stad. Svenska samhällstyper och livsformer från medeltid till nutid, Lund, 1972 (= Town and country. Swedish community types and modes of the life from medieval to present times).

62. *Hörsell, A.*, Borgare, smeder och änkor. Ekonomi och befolkning i Eskilstuna gamla stad och fristad 1750–1850. Uppsala, 1983 (= Burghers, smiths and widows: economy and population in Eskilstuna old town and the free city 1750–1850).

63. *Horgby, B.*, Den disciplinerade arbetaren. Brottslighet och social förändering i Norrköping 1850–1910, Stockholm, 1986 (= The disciplined worker. Crime and social change in Norrköping 1850–1910).

64. *Jansson, S.*, Förening och gemenskap. En etnologisk studie av föreningslivet i en svensk småstadt. Enköping 1880–1970, Diss. Stockholm, 1981/Malmo 1981 (= Association and Community. An ethnological of associational life in a small Swedish town: Enköping 1880–1970).

65. *Jansson, U.*, Mortality Patterns in 19th Century Stockholm. Research Report No. 2. The Project "Stagnating Metropolis: Growth Problems and Social Inequality in Stockholm 1760–1850", Stockholm, 1984.

66. *Johansson, I.*, Strejken som vapen. Fackföreningar och strejker i Norrköpping 1870–1910, Diss. Stockholm, 1982 (= Unions and strikes in Norrköping 1870–1910).

67. *Jungen, R.*, Vävarstad i uppror. Arbetarrörelsen i Borås 1880–1920, Stockholm, 1978 (Arkivs avhandlingsserie, Vol. 7) (= Textile town in revolt. The workers' movement in Borås, 1880–1920).

68. *Kronborg, R.*, and *T. Nilsson*, Stadsflyttare. Industrialisering, migration och social mobilitet med utgångspunkt från Halmstad, 1870–1910, Diss. Uppsala, 1975 (Studia Historica Upsaliensia, Vol. 65) (= Urban grants. Industrialisation, migration and social mobility on the basis of Halmstad, 1870–1910).

69. *Kuuse, J.*, Inkomstutveckling och förmögenhetsbildning. En undersökning av vissa yrkesgrupper 1924–1959, Diss. Gothenburg, 1970 (Meddelanden

från ekonomisk-historiska institutionen vid Göteborgs universitet, Vol. 23) (= Income and property formation. A study of three occupational groups, 1924–1959).

70. *Lindberg, F.*, Stockholm vid tiden för den stora kommunreformen. En socialhistorisk skiss, in Sankt Eriks årsbok, Stockholm, 1963, pp. 105–124 (= Stockholm at the time of the great municipal reform. A social-historical sketch).

71. *Lundequist, K.*, Socialhjälpstagande. Utveckling och orsaker 1945–1965. Med en intensivundersökning av hjälptagandet i Uppsala, Uppsala, 1976 (Uppsala Studies in Economic History, Vol. 13) (= Social assistance. Development and causes 1945–1965. With a intensive investigation of social assistance in Uppsala).

72. *Matovic, M.*, Stockholmsäktenskap. Familjebildning och partnerval i Stockholm, 1850–1890, Diss. Stockholm, 1984 (Stockholmsmonografier, Vol. 57) (= The "Stockholm marriage": Family formation and choice of partners in Stockholm, 1850–1890).

73. *Nilsson, F.*, Emigrationen från Stockholm till Nordamerika 1880–1893. En studie i urban utvandring, Stockholm, 1970 (Studia Historica Upsaliensia, Vol. 31) (= The emigration from Stockholm to North America. A study in urban emigration).

74. *Norman, H.*, Från Bergslagen till Nordamerika. Studier i migrationsmönster, social rörlighet och demografisk struktur med utgångspunkt från örebro län 1851–1915, Uppsala, 1974 (= From Bergslagen to North America. Studies in migration pattern, social mobility and demographic structure on the basis of örebro country).

75. *Öhngren, B.*, Folk i rörelse. Samhällsutveckling flyttningsmönster och folkrörelser i Eskilstuna 1870–1900, Diss., Uppsala, 1974 (Studia Historica Upsaliensia, Vol. 55) (= People on the move. Social development, migration patterns and popular movements in Eskilstuna, 1870–1900).

76. *Ohlsson, R.*, Invandrarna på arbetsmarknaden. En undersökning av invandrare i Malmö under perioden 1945–1967, Lund, 1975 (Skrifter utgivna av ekonomiskhistoriska föreningen i Lund, Vol. 16) (= Immigrants and the labour market. An investigation of immigrants in Malmö during the period 1945–1967).

77. *Olsson, K.*, Hushållsinkomst, inkomstfördelning och försörjningsbörda. En undersökning av vissa yrkesgrupper i Göteborg 1919–1960, Diss. Gothenburg, 1972 (Meddelanden från ekonomisk-historiska institutionen vid Göteborgs universitet, Vol. 25) (= Household income. Income distribution and maintenance liability. An investigation of nine occupational groups in Gothenburg 1919–1960).

78. *Olsson, S.-O.*, Husqvarna arbetare 1850–1900. Med jämförande studier av arbetare vid. Carl Gustafs stads gevärsfaktori i Eskilstuna, Jönköping, 1983 (= The workers of Huskvarna 1850–1900. With comparative

studies of workers at the rifle factory in Eskilstuna).

79. *Söderberg, J.*, Poverty and Social Structure in Stockholm in 1850. Research Report No. 1: The Project "Stagnating Metropolis: Growth Problems and Social Inequality in Stockholm 1760–1850", Stockholm, 1982.

80. *Söderberg, J.*, Teorier om klass i stadshistoria, in Scandia, 1984, pp. 19–38 (= Theories on class in urban history).

81. *Söderberg, T.*, Hantverkarna i genombrottsskedet 1870–1920, Stockholm, 1965 (= The artisans in the breakthrough period 1870–1920).

82. *Stenkula, C. G.*, Gammal i Lund — Utvecklingstendenser inom den kommunala, kyrkliga och enskilda åldringsvården i Lund 1900–1918, Diss. Lund, 1983 (Bibliotheca Historica Lundensis, Vol. LVI) (= Old in Lund — development tendencies within the communal, church and private care of the elderly in Lund, 1900–1918).

83. *Wallentin, H.*, Arbetslöshet och levnadsförhållanden i Göteborg under 1920-talet, Diss. Gothenburg, 1978 (Meddelanden från ekonomisk-historiska institutionen vid Göteborgs universitet, Vol. 42) (= Unemployment and living conditions in Gothenburg in the 1920s).

84. *Zacke, B.*, Koleraepidemin i Stockholm 1834 En socialhistorisk studie, Stockholm, 1971 (Monografier utgivna av Stockholms kommunalförvaltning, Vol. 32) (= The cholera epidemic in Stockholm, 1834. A social-historical study).

(d) Town Planning, Housing

85. *Åström, K.*, Svensk stadsplanering, Stockholm, 1967 (= Swedish town planning).

86. *Bedoire, F.*, and *L. Petersens*, Från Klara till City. Stockholms innerstad i förvandling, Stockholm, 1985 (Monografier utgivna av Stockholms kommun, Vol. 67) (= From Klara to city. The transformation of the centre of Stockholm).

87. *Björk, C., P. Kallstenius* and *L. Repper*, Så byggdes husen 1880–1980: Arkitektur, konstruktion och material i vara flerbostadshus under 100 år, Stockholm, 1983 (= House building 1880–1980: Architects, construction and material during 100 years).

88. *Bjur, H.*, Stadsplanering kring 1900: Med exempel från Göteborg och Albert Lilienbergs verksamhet, Gothenburg, 1984 (Doktorsavhandling vid Chalmers tekniska högskola. Ny serie, Vol. 490) (= Town planning ca. 1900: with examples from Gothenburg and the work of Albert Lilienberg).

89. *Citybildning och cityarkitektur*, Special issue of the journal "Bebyggelsehistorisk Tidskrift", 1983 (= City building and city architecture).

90. *Dufwa, A.*, Trafik, broar, tunnelbanor, gator. Stockholms tekniska historia 1, Stockholm, 1985 (Monografier utgivna av Stockholms kom-

mun, Vol. 62 (= Traffic, bridges, underground, streets. The technical history of Stockholm Vol. 1).

91. *Egerö, B.*, En mönsterstad granskas. Bostadsplanering i Örebro 1945–1975, Stockholm, 1979 (Byggforskningsradet, Vol. 26) (= A model town examined. Housing planning in Örebro 1945–1975).

92. *Eriksson, K.*, Studier i Umeå stads byggnadshistoria. Från 1621 till omkring 1895, Diss. Umeå, 1975 (Umeå Studies in the Humanities, Vol. 3) (= Studies in the history of architecture of the town of Umeå. From 1621 to about 1895).

93. *Franzén, M.*, and *E. Sandstedt*, Grannskap och stadsplanering. Om stat och byggande i efterkrigstidens Sverige, Uppsala, 1981 (Studia Sociologica Upsaliensia, Vol. 17) (= Neighbourhood and town planning. On the State and the building process in Sweden since the Second World War).

94. *Gelotte, G.*, Stadsplaner och bebyggelsetyper i Södertälje intill år 1910, Diss. Södertälje, 1980 (= Town plans and building types in Södertälje up to the year 1910).

95. *Godlund, S.*, and *K. Godlund*, Tätortsarea och markanvändning. En studie av sambandet mellan bebyggelseutbredning och strukturförskjutning – särskilt inom industri och partihandel – i Norrköping under perioden 1900–1968, Gothenburg, 1972 (Meddelanden från Göteborgs universitets geografiska institutioner, Ser. B, Vol. 27) (= Built-up area and land-use. A study of the relation between settlement and structural change – specially within industry and wholesale trade – in Norrköping, 1900–1968).

96. *Hall, T.*, 'i nationell skala . . .' Studier kring cityplaneringen i Stockholm, Stockholm, 1985 (= 'on a national scale. . . .' Studies on the redevelopment of Stockholm's city centre).

97. *Hall, T.*, Planung europäischer Hauptstädte. Zur Entwicklung des Städtebaus im 19. Jahrhundert, Stockholm, 1986.

98. *Hus i Helsingborg 1850–1920*: Stadsväxt och förnyelse, ed., E. Morting, Stockholm, 1983 (= Buildings in Helsingborg 1850–1920: City growth and renewal).

99. *Johansson, I.*, Den stadslösa storstaden. Förortsbildning och bebyggelseutveckling kring Stockholm 1870–1970, Diss. Stockholm, 1974 (Byggforskningen. Rapport, Vol. 26) (= The townless city. Suburban development and spatial change around Stockholm, 1870–1970).

100. *Karlström, T.*, Gävle stadsbild. Bebyggelsehistoria och samhällsutveckling till 1900-talets början, Diss. Gävle, 1974 (= The town scene of Gävle. The history of construction and social development up to the beginning of the 20th century).

101. *Larsson, L.-I.*, Förändringar i Visby innerstad. En studia i stadsbildens omvandling efter 1945, Stockholm, 1973 (= Changes in the town centre of Visby. A study in the development of the town scene after

1945).

102. *Martin, E.*, and *F. Wulz*, Bostadsområden i Stockholm 1930–1980, Stockholm, 1980 (= Residential areas in Stockholm, 1930–1980).

103. *Rödemölle, K.*, Från Brännkyrka till Söderort, åren 1870–1950. En förortsgeografisk studie, Uppsala, 1968 (Geografica. Skrifter från Uppsala universitets geografiska institution) (= From the parish of Brännkyrka to a southern borough, Söderort, 1870–1950. A geographical study of suburban development).

104. *Scharp, B.*, Stockholm och kranskommunerna. Huvudstadens markförvärv, markanvändning och inkorporeringar 1880–1920, Stockholm, 1986 (= Stockholm and it's municipal neighbours. Landownership, land-use and incorporated areas in Stockholm 1880–1920).

105. *Selling, G.*, Esplanadsystemet och Albert Lindhagen. Stadsplanering i Stockholm åren 1857–1887, Stockholm, 1970 (Monografier utgivna av Stockholms kommunalförvaltning, Vol. 1) (= The Esplanade system and Albert Lindhagen. Town planning in Stockholm 1857–1887).

106. *Sidenbladh, G.*, Norrmalm förnyat 1951–1981, Stockholm, 1985 (Monografier utgivna av Stockholms kommun, Vol. 66) (= The renewal of Norrmalm 1951–1981).

107. *Sidenbladh, G.*, Planering för Stockholm 1923–1958, Stockholm, 1981 (Stockholmsmonografier Vol. 22.5.3.) (= Planning for Stockholm 1923–1958).

108. *Thunwall, C.*, Stadsbilden i Kalmar. Förändringar i innerstaden 1945–1972, Diss. Stockholm, 1977 (= The urban scene of Kalmar: Changes in the town centre 1945–1972).

109. *William-Olsson, W.*, Stockholms framtida utveckling. Huvuddragen av Stockholms geografiska utveckling 1850–1930, Stockholm, 1937; new ed., Stockholm, 1984 (Stockholmsmonografier, Vol. 1) (= The future development of Stockholm. Central aspects of the geographic development of Stockholm, 1850–1930).

(e)   Economy and Transport

110. *Book, T.*, Stadsplan och järnväg i Norden, Diss. Lund, 1974 (Meddelanden från Lunds universitets geografiska institution) (= Town planning and railway in Scandinavia).

111. *Hammarström, I.*, Stockholm i svensk ekonomi 1850–1914, Stockholm, 1970 (Monografier utgivna av Stockholms kommunalförvaltning, Vol. 22. II) (= Stockholm in the Swedish economy, 1850–1914).

112. *Heckscher, E.*, Den ekonomiska innebörden av 1500- och 1600-talens svenska stadsgrundningar, in Historisk tidskrift, 1923 (= The economic significance of the founding of towns in Sweden in the 16th and 17th centuries).

113. *Järnek, M.*, Studier i hushållens inkomstförhållanden 1925–1964. En undersökning av Malmö mot bakgrund av den svenska inkomstdebatten, Diss. Lund, 1971 (Skrifter utgivna av ekonomisk-historiska föreningen i Lund, Vol. 10) (= A case-study of the income conditions of the households in Malmö, 1925–1964. An investigation of Malmö related to the Swedish income debate).

114. *Layton, I.*, The Evolution of Upper Norrland's Ports and Loading Places 1750–1976, Diss. Umeå, 1981 (University of Umeå. Department of Geography. Geographical Reports, No. 6).

115. *Nilsson, L.*, Näringsliv och befolkning i Kalmar 1910–1975, Diss. Karlshamn, 1980 (= Economy and population in Kalmar 1910–1975).

116. *Ohlsson, R.*, Ekonomisk strukturförändring och invandring. En undersökning av invandrare i Malmö under perioden 1945–1967, Kristianstad, 1978 (Skrifter utgivna av ekonomisk-historiska föreningen i Lund, Vol. 25) (= Changes in the economic structure and immigration. An investigation of immigrants in Malmö during the period 1945–1967).

117. *Olsson, U.*, Lönepolitik och lönestruktur. Göteborgs verkstadsarbetare 1920–1949, Gothenburg, 1970 (Meddelanden från ekonomisk-historiska institutionen vid Göteborgs universitet, Vol. 19) (= Wage policy and wage structure. The workers in the mechanical engineering industry of Gothenburg, 1920–1949).

118. *Söderberg, J.*, and *N. G. Lundgren*, Ekonomisk och geografisk koncentration 1850–1980, Lund, 1982 (= Economic and geographical concentration 1850–1980).

119. *Ström-Billing, I.*, Stockholms hamn 1909–1939: Näringsliv och politik i samverkan, Stockholm, 1984 (Stockholmsmonografier Vol. 59) (= Business, politics and the port of Stockholm 1909–1939).

(f) Arts and Sciences, Churches

120. *Sandberg, K.*, Carl Theodor Malm 1815–1890. En stadsarkitekt och storbyggmästare i landsorten Diss., Norrköping, 1980 (Föreningen Gamla Norrköping, Vol. 15) (= Carl Theodor Malm 1815–1890. A town architect and building contractor in the provinces).

121. *Stenstadens arkitekter*: sju studier över arkitekternas verksamhet och betydelse vid utbyggnaden av Stockholms innerstad 1850–1930, ed. T. Hall, Stockholm, 1981 (= Seven studies on the activities and importance of architects during the building of the centre of Stockholm 1850–1930).

E. Local Studies (a representative selection)

● Enköping

122. *Enköpings stads historia*, 1–2, ed., S. Dahlgren, Lund, 1963, and Uppsala, 1979 (= A history of Enköping).

● Eskilstuna

123. *Eskilstuna fristad*. Fristadsinrättningen i Eskilstuna före sammanslagningen med gamla staden 1771–1833, Diss. Eskilstuna, 1971 (= The free town of Eskilstuna. Its history from its foundation to its amalgamation with the old town, 1771–1833).

● Gothenburg

124. *Almquist, H.*, Göteborgs historia. Del. I.1: Grundläggningen och de första hundra åren, Gothenburg, 1929 (= History of Gothenburg. Part I: Foundation and the first 100 years).
125. *Göteborg förr och nu*, ed. Göteborgs hembygdförbund, Gothenburg, 1960 ff. (= Gothenburg in earlier times and today).
126. *Historia kring Göteborg*, ed. H. Andersson, Stockholm, 1967 (= History concerning Gothenburg).

● Härnösand

127. *Wik, H.*, Härnösands historia 1810–1920, Härnösand, 1981 (Härnösands historia, Part 3) (= A history of Härnösand).

● Hälsingborg

128. *Hälsingborgs historia*, Vol. 1–6, ed. L. M. Bååth and G. Johannesson, Hälsingborg, 1925–1979 (= A history of Hälsingborg).

● Hudiksvall

129. *Lundbäck, B.-M.*, En industri kommer till stad: Hudiksvall och trävaruindustrin 1855–1876, Stockholm, 1982 (Studia Historica Upsaliensia, Vol. 123) (= An industry comes to town. Hudiksvall and the timber and lumber industry 1855–1876).

● Jönköping

130. *Jönköpings stads historia*, Vol. 1–4, Jönköping and Värnamo, 1963–1984

(= A history of Jönköping).

● Kalmar

131. *Kalmar stads historia*, Vol. 1–3, ed. I. Hammarström, Kalmar, 1979–1984 (= A history of Kalmar).

● Karlshamn

132. *Karlshamn historia*, Vol. 1–3, 5, ed. H. Rosenoren, Vol. 1–3, 2nd ed. Karlshamn, 1979–1980 (= A history of Karlshamn).

● Karlstad

133. *Moberg, O.*, Karlstad under fyra sekler. Sammanfattning av delarna 1–3. Utvecklingen efter 1950. Karlstads historia, Vol. 4, Karlstadt, 1983 (= A history of Karlstad, Vol. 4. Karlstad during four centuries. Summary of Vol. 1–3. The development after 1950).

● Kiruna

134. *Brunnström, L.*, Kiruna – ett samhällsbygge i sekelskiftets Sverige, Vol. 1–2, Diss. Umeå, 1981 (Norrländska städer och kulturmiljöer. Forskningsrapport, No. 3) (= Kiruna – a Swedish mining city from the turn of the century).

● Linköping

135. *Linköpings historia*, 5 Vols., Vol. 1–3, 2nd ed., F. Lindberg and S. Kraft, Vol. 4–5, ed. S. Hellström, Linköping, 1975–1981 (= A history of Linköping).

● Lund

136. *Blomqvist, R.*, Lunds historia, Vol. 1–2, Lund, 1951 and 1978 (= A history of Lund).

● Malmö

137. *Malmö stads historia*, Vol. 1–4, ed. O. Bjurling, Malmö, 1981 (= A history of Malmö).

● Norrköping

138. *Norrköpings historia*, Vol. 1–6, ed. B. Helmfried and S. Kraft, Stockholm, 1965–1976 (= A history of Norrköping).

● Nyköping

139. *Nyköpings stads historia*, Vol. 1–2, ed. S. Dahlgren, Nyköping, 1973 (= A history of Nyköping).

● Skellefteå

140. *Lundkvist, G.*, Den industriella utvecklingen 1900–1975. Basindustrin Boliden. Skelleftebygdens historia, Part 2, Stockholm, 1980 (= A history of Skelleftebygden. The industrial development 1900–1975).

● Södertälje

141. *Södertälje stads historia*, Vol. 1–2, Stockholm, 1968 (= A history of Södertälje).

● Stockholm

142. *Högberg, S.*, Stockholms historia, Vol. 1–2, Stockholm, 1981 (= A history of Stockholm).
143. *Historia kring Stockholm*, Vol. 1–3, ed. H. Ahnlund and I. Hammarström, Stockholm, 1965–1967 (= A history of Stockholm).
144. *Studier och handlingar rörande Stockholms historia*, Vol. 1–5, pub. by Stockholms Stadsarkiv, Stockholm, 1953–1986 (= Studies and sources concerning the history of Stockholm).

● Sundsvall

145. *Ahnlund, N.*, Sundsvalls historia, Uppsala, 1921 (= History of Sundsvall).

● Umeå

146. *Olofsson, S. I.*, Umeå stads historia 1888–1972, Umeå, 1972 (= A history of Umeå)
147. *Steckzén, B.*, Umeå stads historia 1588–1888, Umeå, 1981 (Norrländska skrifter, Vol. 6) (= A history of Umeå).

Bibliographies

● Uppsala

148. *Uppsala stads historia*, Vol. 1–7, Uppsala, 1953–1986 (= A history of Uppsala).

● Västerås

149. *Västerås genom tiderna*, Vol. 1–12, Västerås, 1956–1971 (= Västerås through the centuries).

● Vindeln

150. *Bunte, R., S. Gaunitz* and *L.-E. Borgegård*, Vindeln. En norrländsk kommuns utveckling 1800–1980, Lund, 1982 (= Vindeln. A regional history 1800–1980).

BRUNO FRITZSCHE

Switzerland

A. Urban History Institutions

Lehrstuhl fur Geschichte des Städtebaus an der Abteilung Architektur der Eidgenössischen Technischen Hochschule (ETH) Zürich.

B. Aids to Research

(a) Urban History Journals

—

(b) Bibliographies

1. Guyer, P., Bibliographie der Städtegeschichte der Schweiz, Schweizerische Zeitschrift für Geschichte, Text 11 (1968).
2. *Handbuch der Schweizer Geschichte*, Vol. 2, Zürich, 1977.

(c) Handbooks on Urban History

—

(d) Atlases on Urban History and Urban Development

—

(e) Urban History Sources

—

C.   Research Reports

(a)   General Surveys

3. *Weber, A. F.*, The Growth of Cities in the Nineteenth Century, New York, 1899.

(b)   Surveys of Individual Fields of Urban Research

4. *Birkner, O.*, Bauen und Wohnen in der Schweiz. 1850–1928, Zürich, 1975.
5. *Gyr, U.*, Volkskunde und Stadt – Volkskundler in der Stadt? Zur Situation städtischer Kulturforschung in der Schweiz, in Großstadt. Aspekte empirischer Kulturforschung. 24. Deutscher Volkskunde-Kongreß in Berlin vom 26–30. September 1983, eds T. Kohlmann and H. Bausinger, Berlin, 1985, pp. 157–165 (Schriften des Museums für Deutsche Volkskunde, Vol. 13).

D. Literature on Individual Areas of Urban History Research

(a)   Concept and Definition of Town and Town Types

6. *Fritzsche, B.*, Schweizer Städte im 19. Jahrhundert. Moderne Stadtgeschichte als Aufgabe der historischen Forschung, in Schweizerische Zeitschrift für Geschichte, Year 26 (1976), pp. 434–447.
7. *Garnier, A.*, Les nouvelles cités dortoirs, Lausanne, 1984.
8. *Schuler, M.*, Délimitation des agglomérations suisses en 1980. Contributions á la statistique suisse, No. 105, Bern, 1984.

(b)   Politics, Law and Statutes

9. *Fritzsche, B.*, Städtisches Wachstum und soziale Konflikte, in Schweizerische Zeitschrift für Volkswirtschaft und Statistik, No. 4 (1977), pp. 447–472.
10. *Haefliger, M.*, Christliche Obrigkeit, Nachtwächterstaat, Staatsunternehmen, Basel, 1982 (unpublished).
11. *Müller, C.*, Arbeiterbewegung und Unternehmerpolitik in der aufstrebenden Industriestadt Baden nach der Gründung der Firma Brown-Boveri 1891–1914, Diss. Zürich, Aarau, 1974.

(c) Population and Social Structure

12. *Atteslander, P.*, Probleme der sozialen Anpassung. Eine soziologische Untersuchung über den Zuzug nach der Stadt Zürich, Diss. Zürich, Cologne, 1956.

13. *Birkner, O.*, Bauen und Wohnen in Basel. 1850–1900, Basel, 1981 (New Year's publication of the Gesellschaft des Guten und Gemeinnützigen, 159).

14. *Bruderer, E.*, Die sozialstatistischen Ergebnisse der Baseler Wohnungserhebung vom 12. Dez. 1910, Diss., Basel, Liestal, 1918.

15. *Brunner, H.*, Luzerns Gesellschaft im Wandel, Diss. Zürich, Luzern, 1981.

16. *Bücher, K.*, Die Wohnungsenquête in der Stadt Basel vom 1–19. Februar 1889, Basel, 1891.

17. *Burri, H.-R.*, Die Bevölkerung Luzerns im 18. und frühen 19. Jahrhundert, Diss. Basel, Lucerne, 1975.

18. *Cattani, A.*, Die Aktienhäuser in Aussersihl, Zürich, 1961.

19. *Frey, R. L.*, Von der Land- zur Stadtflucht. Bestimmungsfaktoren der Bevölkerungswanderungen in der Region Basel, Bern, 1981.

20. *Fritzsche, B.*, Die Einwohner Zürichs im 19. Jahrhundert – ein EDV-Projekt, in Neue Zürcher Zeitung, 8.10.1980.

21. *Fritzsche, B.*, Das Quartier als Lebensraum, in W. Conze, ed., Arbeiterexistenz im 19. Jahrhundert, Stuttgart, 1981, 92–113 (Industrielle Welt, Vol. 33).

22. *Hamm, B.*, Die Organisation der städtischen Umwelt. Ein Beitrag zur sozialökologischen Theorie der Stadt, Frauenfeld, 1972.

23. *Heller, G.*, "Propre en ordre". Habitation et vie domestique 1850–1930: L'exemple vaudois, Lausanne, 1979.

24. *Horat, E.*, Die Wanderung der Innenschweizer nach Zürich. 1865–1898, Zürich, 1983 (unpublished).

25. *Hugger, P.*, Kleinhüningen: Von der Dorfidylle zum Alltag eines Basler Industriequartiers, Basel, 1984.

26. *Kreis, K.*, Städtische soziale Segregation und Arbeiterwohnungsfrage. Die soziale und bauliche Entwicklung einer Arbeitervorstadt, am Beispiel von Zürich-Aussersihl. 1860–1980, Zürich, 1981 (unpublished).

27. *Landolt, C.*, Die Wohnungsenquête in der Stadt Bern 1896, Bern, 1899.

28. *Landolt, C.*, Die Wohnungsenquête in der Stadt St. Gallen 1897, St. Gallen, 1901.

29. *Landolt, C.*, Die Wohnungsenquête in der Stadt Winterthur 1896, Winterthur, 1901.

30. *Looser, H.*, Der Italienerkrawall von 1896. Widerstände gegen die Einführung bürgerlicher Verhältnisse in der Großstadt, Zürich, n.d (unpublished).

31. *Ruf, W.*, Das gemeinnützige Baugenossenschaftswesen in der Schweiz, Diss. Basel, 1930.

32. *Schaffner, M.*, Die Basler Arbeiterbevölkerung im 19. Jahrhundert, Diss. Basel, 1973.

33. *Schnetzler, A.*, Ville de Lausanne. Enquête sur les conditions du logement. Année 1894, Lausanne, 1896.

34. *Schüpbach, W.*, Die Bevölkerung der Stadt Luzern. 1850–1914, Diss. Zürich, Lucerne, 1983.

35. *Stadt Zürich – Statistisches Amt*, Mitteilungen über die Wohnungs- und Grundstückserhebung in der Stadt Zürich, 7 vols., Zürich, 1898–1987.

36. *Suter, E.*, Wasser und Brunnen im alten Zürich, vom Mittelalter bis ins 19. Jahrhundert, Diss. Zürich, 1981.

37. *Ulrich, A.*, Bordelle, Straßendirnen und bürgerliche Sittlichkeit in der Belle Epoque, Diss. Zürich, 1985.

38. *Walser, E.*, Wohnlage und Sozialprestige, in Berner Zeitschrift für Geschichte und Heimatkunde, Year 38 (1976), pp. 99–108.

39. *Wolfensberger, H.*, Die Zuwanderung in die Stadt Zürich seit 1893, Diss. Zürich, 1952.

(d) Town Planning, Housing

40. *Archithese*, 1972 ff., pub. by Verband freierwerbender Schweizer Architekten.

41. *Schriftenreihe zur Orts-, Regional- und Landesplanung*, pub. by ORL-Institut der Eidgenössischen Technischen Hochschule in Zürich.

42. *Werk*. Schweizer Monatsschrift für Architektur, Kunst und Künstlerisches Gewerbe (in 1977 joined with "Archithese" to form "Werk-Archithese"; in 1980 again separated, "Werk" absorbed in "Werk Bauen, Wohnen").

43. *Bärtschi, H.-P.*, Industrialisierung, Eisenbahnschlachten und Städtebau. Die Entwicklung des Züricher Industrie- und Arbeiterstadtteils Aussersihl, Diss. Zürich, Basel, 1983.

44. *Fritzsche, B.*, Grundstückspreise als Determinanten städtischer Strukturen, in Zeitschrift für Stadtgeschichte, Stadtsoziologie und Denkmalpflege, Year 4 (1977), pp. 36–54.

45. *Geographische Gesellschaft Bern*, ed., Bern – von der Naturlandschaft zur Stadtregion, Bern, 1973.

46. *Guyer, P.*, Die Geschichte der Enge, Zürich, 1980.

47. *Hebeisen, A.*, Die Lorraine in Bern. Ursprung, Werden und ihr heutiges Sein, Bern, 1952.

48. *Hebeisen, K.*, Die Grundstückspreise in der Stadt Bern von 1858 bis 1917, Diss. Bern, 1920.

49. *Röllin, P.*, St. Gallen. Stadtveränderung und Stadterlebnis im 19. Jahrhundert, Diss. Zürich, St. Gallen, 1981.

50. *Rupp, M.*, Der bauliche Umwandlungsprozeß in der Länggasse (Bern). Eine Quartieranalyse, Bern, 1983 (Geographica Bernensia, p 10).

51. *Schenkel, Ch.*, Die erste Züricher Stadtvereinigung von 1893, Diss. Zürich, Andelfingen, 1980.

52. *Schweizer, A.*, Die modernen Baubeschränkungen, Diss. Bern, Zürich, 1896.

53. *Steinmann, M.*, CIAM. Dokumente 1928–1939, Zürich, 1979.

54. *Stolz, P.*, Stadtwirtschaft und Stadtentwicklung. Basel in den Jahrzehnten nach der Kantonstrennung, in Basel im 19. Jahrhundert, Basel, 1980.

55. *Vieli, M.*, Ein Regressionsindex der Bodenpreisänderung, Diss. Zürich, 1967.

56. *Zweifel, P.*, Aspekte von Stadtentwicklung und Stadtplanung in Zürich. 1860–1890, Zürich, 1981 (unpublished).

(e)   Economy and Transport

57. *Abt, R.*, Agglomerationseffekte in der schweizerischen Industrie, Zürich, 1973.

58. *Bauer, H.*, Basel – gestern – heute – morgen. Hundert Jahre Baseler Wirtschaftsgeschichte, Basel, 1981.

59. *Christoffel, M.*, Die industrielle Ballung in der Schweiz, Diss. St. Gallen, Thusis, 1967.

60. *Grossmann, E.*, Die Finanzen der Stadt Zürich, Zürich, 1904.

61. *Kesselring, H.-Ch., u.a.*, Straßennetzausbau und raumwirtschaftliche Entwicklung. Eine Potentialanalyse am Beispiel ausgewählter schweizerischer Regionen, Bern, 1982.

62. *Stab für Gesamtverkehrsfragen des EVED*, GVK-Dateninformation, Bern, 1979 (GVG-Bericht 1/79).

63. *Stolz, P.*, Baseler Wirtschaft in vor- und frühindustrieller Zeit, Diss. Basel, Zürich, 1977.

(f)   Arts and Sciences, Churches

64. *Furrer, B.*, Das kommerzialisierte Entertainment in Zürich an der Wende vom 19. zum 20. Jahrhundert, Zürich n.d. (unpublished).

65. *Gesellschaft für Schweiz. Kunstgeschichte*, ed. INSA. Inventar der neueren Schweizer Architektur. Vol. 1–4 Zürich 1982–1986.

E.   Local Studies (a representative selection)

• Basel

66. *Meier, E. A.*, Basel anno dazumal, Basel, 1980.

● Bern

67. *Feller, R.*, Geschichte Berns, 4 vols., Bern, 1946–1968.
68. *Feller, R.*, Die Stadt Bern seit 1798, in Archiv des Historischen Vereins des Kantons Bern, Year 44 (1960), pp. 253–306.
69. *Menz, C.*, Bern im Bild 1680–1880, Bern, 1981.

● Geneva

70. *Guerdan, R.*, Histoire de Genève, Paris, 1981.
71. *Lescaze, B.*, Genève 1842–1942, Lausanne, 1976.

● Rapperswil

72. *Halter, E.*, Rapperswil im 19. Jahrhundert, Rapperswil, 1980.

● Winterthur

73. *Ganz, W.*, Geschichte der Stadt Winterthur vom Durchbruch der Helvetik 1798 bis zur Stadtvereinigung 1922, Winterthur, 1979.

● Zürich

74. *Fierz, J.*, Zürich, wer kennt sich da noch aus?, Zürich, 1971.

KATHLEEN NEILS CONZEN AND MICHAEL H. EBNER

The United States

A. Urban History Institutions

Urban history in the United States has evolved largely without the support of formal institutions or organisations, other than those common to the historical profession at large. An Urban History Group was organised in 1953 that met in conjunction with the American Historical Association and published its own newsletter, but this organisation, by the mid-1960s, proved unable to contain the divergent strands of the field, and dissolved. Since that time, the editorial board of the *Journal of Urban History* has taken some responsibility for proposing urban history sessions at major scholarly conventions, but the field remains without a formal organisation. Occasional special conferences conducted under a variety of different auspices at universities in the United States and Canada have proved important in bringing practitioners together and maintaining a sense of a common ongoing enterprise: at the Massachusetts Institute of Technology (M.I.T.) in 1961, Yale in 1968, University of Wisconsin in 1970, York University in 1973, University of Connecticut in 1979 and Guelph University in 1982. Also important in giving public shape to the field, were publications series in urban history issued by Oxford University Press (*Urban Life Series*, edited by R. C. Wade, 1967–1978, 25 books) and Harvard University Press (*Harvard Studies in Urban History*, edited by S. Thernstrom and C. Tilly, 1972–1979, 12 books), as well as continuing seminars (e.g. the Columbia Seminar on the City and its newly formed midwestern counterpart, the Chicago Historical Society Urban History Seminar) and large-scale research projects like the Philadelphia Social History Project (University of Pennsylvania, directed by T. Hershberg). There are no significant handbooks or atlases of American urban history.

B.   Aids to Research

(a)   Urban History Journals

1. *Journal of Urban History*, Beverly Hills, Calif., 1974 ff.
2. *Urban History Group Newsletter*, Washington, 1954–1975.
3. *Urbanism Past and Present*, Milwaukee, Wisc., 1975/76 ff.

(b)   Bibliographies

Up-to-date bibliographies appear regularly in the reviews, *Journal of American History* and *Urbanism Past and Present*.

4. *Artibise, A. F.*, and *G. A. Stelter*, eds., Canada's Urban Past: A Bibliography to 1980 and Guide to Canadian Urban Studies, Vancouver, 1981.
5. *Buenker, J. D., G. M. Greenfield* and *W. J. Murrin*, eds., Urban History: A Guide to Information Sources, Detroit, 1981.
6. *Glaab, C. N.*, The Historian and the American City: A Bibliographic Survey, in P. M. Hauser and L. F. Schnore, The Study of Urbanization, New York 1965, pp. 53–80.
7. *McKelvey, B.*, American Urban History Today, in American Historical Review, Vol. 57 (1952), pp. 919–929.
8. *Mohl, R. A.*, The History of the American City, in W. H. Cartwright and R. L. Watson, Jr., eds., The Reinterpretation of American History and Culture, Washington, D. C., 1973, pp. 165–205.
9. *Shunsky, N. F.*, and *T. Crimmins*, eds., Urban America: A Historical Bibliography, Santa Barbara, Calif., 1983.
10. *Weber, R. D.*, and *D. C. Belli*, Urban Studies: The Historical Dimension, Ann Arbor, Mich., 1976.

(c)   Handbooks on Urban History

—

(d)   Atlases on Urban History and Urban Development

—

(e)   Urban History Sources

11. *Glaab, C. N.*, ed., The American City: A Documentary History, Homewood, Ill., 1963.
12. *Still, B.*, ed., Urban America, New York, 1974.
13. *City Directories of the United States* (19th century), Research Publications,

Reading, Engl., 1970 ff.

14. *Historic American Buildings Survey*, Cambridge, Engl., 1982.
15. *Housing and Urban Affairs*, 1965–1976, New York, 1978 ff. (Microfilming Corp. of America).
16. *The Immigrant in America*, Research Publications, Reading, Engl., 1981 ff.
17. *A Microfilm Library*: Sources for the History of Social Welfare in America, Westwood, Conn., 1970.
18. *Photographic Views of New York City 1870s–1970s*, Ann Arbor, Mich., 1981 (University Microfilms International).
19. *Reform of Local Government Structures in the United States 1945–1971*, Millwood, N.Y., 1976.
20. *Sanborn Fire Insurance Maps in the Library of Congress 1867–1950*, Cambridge, Engl., 1985 ff.
21. *Schomberg Center for Research in Black Culture*, Millwood, N.Y., 1973–1974.
22. *Urban Documents Microfiche Collections*, Westport, Conn., 1972 ff.

C. Research Reports

(a)   General Surveys

23. *Brownell, B.*, After Ten Years: An Editorial, in Journal of Urban History, Vol. 11 (1984), pp. 3–7.
24. *Chudacoff, H. P.*, The Evolution of American Urban Society, New York, 1967.
25. *Glaab, C. N.*, and *A. T. Brown*, A History of Urban America, New York, 1967.
26. *Goldfield, D. R.*, and *B. A. Brownell*, Urban America. From Downtown to No Town, New York, 1979.
27. *Green, C. McLaughlin*, American Cities in the Growth of the Nation, London, 1957.
28. *Handlin, O.*, The Modern City as a Field of Historical Study, in ibid. and J. Burchard, eds., The Historian and the City, Cambridge, Mass., 1963, pp. 1–26.
29. *Hays, S. P.*, American Political History as Social Analysis: Essays, Knoxville, Tenn., 1980.
30. *Lampard, E. E.*, The History of Cities in the Economically Advanced Areas, in Economic Development and Cultural Change, Vol. 3 (1955), pp. 86–136.
31. *Lampard, E. E.*, The Nature of Urbanization, in D. Fraser and A. Sutcliffe, eds., The Pursuit of Urban History, London, 1983, pp. 3–53.
32. *Lampard, E. E.*, The Pursuit of Happiness in the City. Changing Opportunities and Options in America, in Transactions of the Royal History Society, Vol. 23 (1973), pp. 175–220.

33. *McKelvey, B.*, The Urbanization of America 1860–1915, New York, 1963.

34. *Miller, Z. L.*, Scarcity, Abundance, and American Urban History, in Journal of Urban History, Vol. 4 (1978). pp. 131–156.

35. *Miller, Z. L.*, The Urbanization of Modern America, New York, 1973.

36. *Mumford, L.*, The Culture of Cities, London, 1940.

37. *Park, R. E., E. W. Burgess* and *R. D. McKenzie*, The City, Chicago, 1925.

38. *Schlesinger, A. M. Sr.*, The City in American History, in Mississippi Valley Historical Review, Vol. 27 (1940), pp. 43–66.

39. *Schlesinger, A. M.*, The Rise of the City 1878–1898, New York, 1933.

40. *Wade, R. C.*, An Agenda for Urban History, in H. J. Bass, ed., The State of American History, Chicago, 1970, pp. 43–69.

41. *Wade, R. C.*, Urbanisation, in C. Vann Woodward, ed., The Comparative Approach to American History, New York, 1968, pp. 187–205.

42. *Warner, S. B., Jr.*, If All the World were Philadelphia. A Scaffolding for Urban History, in American Historical Review, Vol. 74 (1968), pp. 26–43.

43. *Warner, S. B., Jr.*, The Urban Wilderness. A History of the American City, New York, 1972.

44. *Wiebe, R.*, The Search for Order, 1877–1920, New York, 1967.

(b)   Surveys of Individual Fields of Urban Research/Historiographical Essays

45. *Conzen, K. N.*, Community Studies, Urban History and American Local History, in M. Kammen, ed., The Past Before Us. Contemporary Historical Writing in the United States, Ithaca, 1980, pp. 270–291.

46. *Conzen, K. N.*, The New Urban History. Defining the Field, in J. B. Gardner and G. R. Adams, eds., Ordinary People and Everyday Lives. Perspectives on the New Social History, Nashville, 1983, pp. 67–89.

47. *Conzen, K. N.*, Quantification in the New Urban History, in Journal of Interdisciplinary History, Vol. 13 (1983), pp. 653–677.

48. *Ebner, M. H.*, Urban History. Retrospect and Prospect, in Journal of American History, Vol. 68 (1981), pp. 69–84.

49. *Fogel, R. W.*, and *G. R. Elton*, Which Road to the Past? Two Views of History, New Haven, 1983.

50. *Frisch, M.*, American Urban History as an Example of Recent Historiography, in History and Theory, Vol. 18 (1979), pp. 350–377.

51. *Frisch, M.*, L'Histoire urbaine américaine: Réflexions sur les tendances récentes, in Annales Economies, Sociétés, Civilisations, Vol. 25 (1970), pp. 880–896.

52. *Gardner, D. S.*, American Urban History: Power, Society and Artifact, in Trends in History, Vol. 2 (1981), pp. 49–78.

53. *Hershberg, T.*, The Future of Urban History, in D. Fraser and A.

Sutcliffe, eds., The Pursuit of Urban History, London, 1983, pp. 428–448.

54. *Hershberg, T.*, The New Urban History. Toward an Interdisciplinary History of the City, in Journal of Urban History, Vol. 5 (1978), pp. 3–40.

55. *Hoover, D. W.*, The Diverging Paths of American Urban History, in The American Quarterly, Vol. 20 (1968), pp. 296–317.

56. *Lampard, E. E.*, American Historians and the Study of Urbanization, in American Historical Review, Vol. 67 (1961), pp. 49–61.

57. *Lampard, E. E.*, The Dimensions of Urban History. A Footnote to the "Urban Crisis", in Pacific Historical Review, Vol. 39 (1970), pp. 261–277.

58. *Lampard, E. E.*, Historical Contours of Contemporary Urban Society. A Comparative View, in Journal of Contemporary History, Vol. 4 (1969), pp. 3–25.

59. *McKelvey, B.*, American Urban History Today, in American Historical Review, Vol. 57 (1952), pp. 919–929.

60. *Mohl, R. A.*, The New Urban History and its Alternatives. Some Reflections on Recent U.S. Scholarship on the Twentieth-Century City, in Urban History Yearbook, 1983, pp. 19–28.

61. *Moehring, E. P.*, Public Works and Urban History. Recent Trends and New Directions, in Essays in Public Work History, Vol. 13 (1982).

62. *Schaffer, D.*, A New Threshold for Urban History. Reflections on Canadian-American Urban Development at the Guelph Conference, in Planning History Bulletin, Vol. 4 (1982), pp. 1–11.

63. *Sharpless, J. B.*, and *S. B. Warner, Jr.*, Urban History, in American Behavioral Scientist, Vol. 21 (1977), pp. 221–244.

64. *Smith, D. S.*, Modernization and American Social History, in Social Science History, Vol. 2 (1978), pp. 361–367.

65. *Stave, B. M.*, The Making of Urban History. Historiography Through Oral History, Beverly Hills, 1977.

66. *Stave, B. M.*, In Pursuit of Urban History. Conversations with Myself and Others – A View from the United States, in D. Fraser and A. Sutcliffe, eds., The Pursuit of Urban History, London, 1983, pp. 407–427.

67. *Thernstrom, S.*, The New Urban History, in C. F. Delzell, The Future of History, Nashville, 1977, pp. 43–52.

68. *Thernstrom, S.*, Reflections on the New Urban History, in Daedalus, Vol. 100 (1971), pp. 359–375.

69. *White, Dana F.*, "The Underdeveloped Discipline": Directions/Misdirections in American Urban History, in American Studies International, Vol. 22 (1984), pp. 122–140.

D. Literature on Individual Areas of Urban History Research

(a)   Concept and Definition of Town and Town Types

70. *Abbott, C.*, The New Urban America: Growth and Politics in Sunbelt Cities, Chapel Hill, 1981.

71. *Belcher, W.*, The Economic Rivalry between St. Louis and Chicago, New York, 1947.

72. *Blouin, F.X., Jr.*, The Boston Region 1810–1850. A Study of Urbanization, Ann Arbor, Mich., 1980.

73. *Bridenbaugh, C.*, Cities in Revolt: Urban Life in America, 1743–1776, New York, 1955.

74. *Bridenbaugh, C.*, Cities in the Wilderness: Urban Life in America, 1625–1742, New York, 1938.

75. *Brownell, B.*, The Urban Ethos in the South, 1920–1930, Baton Rouge, 1975.

76. *Conzen, M. P.*, The American Urban System in the Nineteenth Century, in Geography and the urban Environment, Vol. 4 (1981), pp. 295–347.

77. *Conzen, M. P.*, The Maturing Urban System in the United States, 1840–1910, in Annals of the Association of American Geographers, Vol. 67 (1977), pp. 88–108.

78. *Crowther, S. J.*, Urban Growth in the Mid-Atlantic States, 1785–1850, in Journal of Economic History, Vol. 36 (1976), pp. 624–644.

79. *Earle, C.* and *R. Hoffmann*, Urban Development in the 18th Century South, in Perspectives in American History, Vol. 10 (1976), pp. 7–80.

80. *Ernst, J. A.* and *R. Merrens*, "Camden's Turrets Pierce the Skies". The Urban Process in the Southern Colonies during the Eighteenth Century, in William and Mary Quarterly, Vol. 30 (1973), pp. 549–574.

81. *Glaab, C. N.*, Kansas City and the Railroads, Madison, Wisc., 1962.

82. *Goldfield, D. R.*, Cotton Fields and Skyscrapers: Southern City and Region, 1607–1980, Baton Rouge, 1982.

83. *Haeger, J.*, The Investment Frontier: New York Businessmen and the Economic Development of the Old Northwest, Albany, 1981.

84. *Hudson, J. C.*, The Plains Country Town, in B. W. Blouet and F. C. Luebke, eds., The Great Plains. Environment and Culture, Lincoln 1979, pp. 99–118.

85. *Lemon, J. T.*, Urbanization and Development of Eighteenth Century Southeastern Pennsylvania and Adjacent Delaware, in William and Mary Quarterly, Vol. 24 (1967), pp. 501–542.

86. *Lindstrom, D.*, Economic Development in the Philadelphia Region 1810–1850, New York, 1978.

87. *Lotchin, R.*, The Metropolitan-Military Complex in Comparative Perspective, in Journal of the West, Vol. 19 (1979), pp. 19–30.

88. *Lotchin, R.*, San Francisco, 1846–1856. From Hamlet to City, New York, 1974.
89. *Meyer, D. R.*, A Dynamic Model of Integration of Frontier Urban Places into the U.S. System of Cities, in Economic Geography, Vol. 56 (1980), pp. 120–140.
90. *Miller, R. B.*, City and Hinterland. A Case Study in Urban Growth and Regional Development, Westport, Conn., 1979.
91. *Mitchell, R. D.*, Commercialism and Frontier. Perspectives on the Early Shenondoah Valley, Charlottesville, Virg., 1978.
92. *Muller, E. K.*, Selective Urban Growth in the Middle Ohio Valley, 1800–1860, in Geographical Review, Vol. 66 (1976), pp. 178–199.
93. *Nash, G. D.*, The American West in the Twentieth Century: A Short History of an Urban Oasis, Englewood Cliffs, N.J., 1973.
94. *Pred, A. R.*, Urban Growth and the Circulation of Information, The United States System of Cities 1790–1840, Cambridge, Mass., 1973.
95. *Pred, A. R.*, Urban Growth and City Systems in the United States, 1840–1880, Cambridge, Mass., 1980.
96. *Price, J. M.*, Economic Function and the Growth of American Port Towns in the Eighteenth Century, in Perspectives in American History, Vol. 8 (1974), pp. 123–188.
97. *Rainbolt, J. G.*, The Absence of Towns in Seventeenth Century Virginia, in K. T. Jackson and S. L. Schultz, Cities in American History, New York, 1972, pp. 50–65.
98. *Rothstein, M.*, Antebellum Wheat and Cotton Exports. A Contrast in Marketing Organization and Economic Development, in Agricultural History, Vol. 41 (1966), pp. 91–100.
99. *Rubin, J.*, Urban Growth and Regional Development, in D. T. Gilchrist, ed., The Growth of Seaport Cities, Charlottesville, Virg., 1967, pp. 3–21.
100. *Scheiber, H. N.*, Urban Rivalry and Internal Improvements in the Old Northwest, in Ohio History, Vol. 71 (1962) pp. 227–292.
101. *Smith, D.*, Rocky Mountain Mining Camps. The Urban Frontier, Bloomington, Indiana, 1967.
102. *Vance, J. E., Jr.*, The Merchant's World, Englewood Cliffs, N.J., 1970.
103. *Wade, R. C.*, The Urban Frontier, New York, 1959.
104. *Ward, D.*, Cities and Immigrants, New York, 1971.
105. *Wheeler, K.*, To Wear a City's Crown. The Beginnings of Urban Growth in Texas, 1836–65, Cambridge, Mass. 1968.
106. *Williamson, J. G.* and *J. A. Swanson*, The Growth of Cities in the Northeast, 1820–1870, in Explorations in Economic History, Vol. 4 (1966), Supplement.

(b)   Politics, Law and Statutes

107. *Adrian, C. R.*, and *E. Griffith*, A History of City Government. The Formation of Traditions, 1775–1870, New York, 1976.

108. *Allswang, J. A.*, A House for All People: Ethnic Politics in Chicago, 1890–1936, Lexington, Ky., 1971.

109. *Anderson, A. D.*, The Origins and Resolution of Urban Crisis: Baltimore, 1890–1930, Baltimore, 1977.

110. *Bridges, A.*, A City in the Republic: Antebellum New York and the Origins of Machine Politics, Cambridge and New York, 1984.

111. *Buenker, J. D.*, Urban Liberalism and Progressive Reform, New York, 1973.

112. *Colburn, D. R.*, and *G. E. Pozzetta*, Bosses and Machines: Changing Interpretations, in History Teacher, Vol. 9 (1976), pp. 445–463.

113. *Ebner, M. H.*, Urban Government in America, 1776–1876, in Journal of Urban History, Vol. 5 (1979), pp. 511–520.

114. *Fox, K.*, Better City Government: Innovation in American Urban Politics, 1850–1937, Philadelphia, 1977.

115. *Funigiello, P. J.*, The Challenge of Urban Liberalism: Federal-City Relations during World War II, Knoxville, Tenn., 1978.

116. *Gelfand, M. I.*, A Nation of Cities: The Federal Government and Urban America, 1933–1965, New York, 1975.

117. *Griffith, E. W.*, History of American City Government: The Colonial Period, New York, 1938.

118. *Griffith, E. W.*, History of American City Government: The Conspicuous Failure, 1877–1900, New York, 1974.

119. *Griffith, E. W.*, History of American City Government: The Progressive Years and their Aftermath, 1900–1920, New York, 1974.

120. *Hammack, D. C.*, Elite Perceptions of Power in the Cities of the United States, 1880–1900: The Evidence of James Bryce, Moisei Ostrogorski, and their American Informants, in Journal of Urban History, Vol. 4 (1978), pp. 363–396.

121. *Hammack, D. C.*, Power and Society: Greater New York at the Turn of the Century, New York, 1982.

122. *Hammack, D. C.*, Problems in the Historical Study of Power in the Cities and Towns of the United States, 1800–1960, in American Historical Review, Vol. 83 (1978), pp. 323–349.

123. *Harris, C. V.*, Political Power in Birmingham, 1871–1921, Knoxville, Tenn., 1977.

124. *Hartog, H.*, Public Property and Private Power: The Corporation of the City of New York in American Law, 1730–1870, Chapel Hill, 1983.

125. *Hays, S. P.*, The Changing Political Structure of the City in Industrial America, in Journal of Urban History, Vol. 1 (1974), pp. 6–38.

126. *Holli, M. G.*, Reform in Detroit: Hazen Pingree and Urban Politics,

New York, 1969.

127. *Holli, M. G.*, and *P. d'A Jones*, eds., Biographical Dictionary of American Mayors, 1820–1980, Westport, Conn., 1981.

128. *Mandelbaum, S. J.*, Boss Tweed's New York, New York, 1965.

129. *Melosi, M. V.*, ed., Pollution and Reform in American Cities, 1870–1930, Austin, 1980.

130. *Miller, W. R.*, Cops and Bobbies: Police Authority in New York and London, 1830–1870, Chicago, 1977.

131. *Miller, Z. L.*, Boss Cox's Cincinnati: Urban Politics in the Progressive Era, New York, 1968.

132. *Platt, H. L.*, City Buildings in the New South: The Growth of Public Services in Houston, Texas, 1830–1915, Philadelphia, 1983.

133. *Rice, B. R.*, Progressive Cities: The Commission Government Movement in America, 1901–1920, Austin, 1977.

134. *Schiesl, M. J.*, The Politics of Efficiency: Municipal Administration and Reform in America, 1880–1920, Berkeley, 1971.

135. *Shefter, M.*, The Electoral Foundations of the Political Machine: New York City, 1884–1897, in J. H. Silbey *et al.*, eds., History of American Electoral Behavior, Princeton, 1978, pp. 263–298.

136. *Stave, B. M.*, A Conversation with Eric E. Lampard, in Journal of Urban History, Vol. 1 (1975), pp. 440–472.

137. *Stave, B. M.*, The New Deal and the Last Hurrah: Pittsburgh Machine Politics, Pittsburgh, 1970.

138. *Sutcliffe, A.*, New York, New York, in Reviews in American History, Vol. 12 (1984), pp. 99–103.

139. *Teaford, J. C.*, Finis for Tweed and Steffens: Rewriting the History of Urban Rule, in Reviews in American History, Vol. 10 (1982), pp. 133–149.

140. *Teaford, J. C.*, The Municipal Revolution in America: Origins of Modern Urban Government, 1650–1825, Chicago, 1975.

141. *Teaford, J. C.*, The Unheralded Triumph: City Government in America, 1870–1900, Baltimore, 1984.

142. *Watts, E. J.*, The Social Basis of City Politics: Atlanta 1865–1903, Westport, Conn., 1978.

(c) Population and Social Structure

143. *Baltzell, E. D.*, Puritan Boston and Quaker Philadelphia, Philadelphia, 1979.

144. *Barton, J.*, Peasants and Strangers: Italians, Rumanians, and Slovaks in an American City, 1880–1950, Cambridge, Mass., 1976.

145. *Blassingame, J. W.*, Black New Orleans, 1860–1880, Chicago, 1973.

146. *Blumin, S. M.*, The Historical Study of Vertical Mobility, in Historical Methods Newsletter, Vol. 1 (1969), pp. 1–13.

147. *Blumin, S. M.*, The Hypothesis of Middle-Class Formation in Nineteenth-Century America: A Critique and Some Proposals, in American Historical Review, Vol. 90 (1985), pp. 299–338.

148. *Blumin, S. M.*, The Urban Threshold: Growth and Change in a Nineteenth-Century American Community, Chicago, 1976.

149. *Bodnar, J.*, Immigration and Industrialization: Ethnicity in an American Mill Town, 1870–1940, Pittsburgh, 1977.

150. *Bodnar, J., R. Simon* and *M. Weber*, Lives of Their Own: Blacks, Italians, and Poles in Pittsburgh, 1850–1960, Urbana, Ill., 1982.

151. *Borchert, J.*, Alley Life in Washington: Family, Community and Religion, 1850–1870, Urbana, Ill., 1980.

152. *Boyer, P.*, Urban Masses and Moral Order in America, 1820–1920, Cambridge, Mass., 1978.

153. *Camarillo, A.*, Chicanos in a Changing Society: From Mexican Pueblos to American Barrios in Santa Barbara and South California 1848–1930, Cambridge, Mass., 1979.

154. *Chudacoff, H. P.*, Mobile Americans: Residential and Social Mobility in Omaha, 1880–1920, New York, 1972.

155. *Chudacoff, H. P.*, A New Look at Ethnic Neighborhoods, in Journal of American History, Vol. 60 (1973), pp. 76–93.

156. *Cinel, D.*, From Italy to San Francisco: The Immigrant Experience, Stanford, 1982.

157. *Conzen, K. N.*, Immigrant Milwaukee, 1836–1860: Accommodation and Community in a Frontier City, Cambridge, Mass., 1976.

158. *Couvares, F. G.*, The Remaking of Pittsburgh: Class and Culture in an Industrializing City, 1877–1919, Albany, N.Y., 1984.

159. *Cumbler, J.*, Working-Class Community in Industrial America: Work, Leisure, and Struggle in Two Industrial Cities, 1880–1930, Westport, Conn., 1979.

160. *Dawley, A.*, Class and Community: The Industrial Revolution in Lynn, Cambridge, Mass., 1977.

161. *Decker, P.*, Fortunes and Failures: White Collar Mobility in Nineteenth-Century San Francisco, Cambridge, Mass., 1978.

162. *Doyle, D. H.*, The Social Order of a Frontier Community: Jacksonville, Illinois, 1825–1870, Urbana, Ill., 1978.

163. *Faler, P.*, Mechanics and Manufactures in the Early Industrial Revolution: Lynn, Massachusetts, 1780–1860, Albany, N.Y., 1981.

164. *Frisch, M. H.*, Town into City: Springfield, Massachusetts, 1840–1880, and the Meaning of Community, Cambridge, Mass., 1972.

165. *Galishoff, S.*, Safeguarding the Public Health: Newark, 1895–1918, Westport, Conn., 1975.

166. *Garcia, M. T.*, Desert Immigrants: The Mexicans of El Paso, 1880–1920, New Haven, 1981.

167. *Griffen, C.* and *S. Griffen*, Natives and Newcomers: The Ordering of

Opportunity in Mid-Nineteenth-Century Poughkeepsie, Cambridge, Mass., 1978.

168. *Griswold Del Castillo, R.*, The Los Angeles Barrio, 1850–1890: A Social History, Berkeley, 1980.

169. *Guest, A. M.* and *S. Tolnay*, Urban Structure and Fertility: The Case of Large American Cities, in Journal of Interdisciplinary History, Vol. 13 (1983), pp. 387–410.

170. *Gutmann, H. G.*, Work, Culture, and Society in Industrializing America: Essays in American Working-Class and Social History, New York, 1976.

171. *Handlin, O.*, Boston's Immigrants: A Study in Acculturation, Cambridge, Mass., 1940.

172. *Handlin, O.*, The Uprooted, Boston, 1951.

173. *Hareven, T. K.*, Family Time and Industrial Time: The Relationship between the Family and Work in a New England Industrial Community, New York, 1982.

174. *Hershberg, T.*, ed., Philadelphia: Work, Space, Family, and Group Experience in the Nineteenth Century, New York, 1981.

175. *Hirsch, A. R.*, Making the Second Ghetto: Race and Housing in Chicago, 1940–1960, New York, 1983.

176. *Jaher, F. C.*, The Urban Establishment: Upper Strata in Boston, New York, Charleston, Chicago and Los Angeles, Urbana, Ill., 1982.

177. *Johnson, P.*, A Shopkeeper's Millennium: Society and Revivals in Rochester, New York, 1815–1837, New York, 1978.

178. *Katz, M. B.*, The People of Hamilton Canada West: Family and Class in a Mid-Nineteenth Century City, Cambridge, Mass., 1975.

179. *Katzman, D. M.*, Before the Ghetto: Black Detroit in the Nineteenth Century, Urbana, Ill., 1973.

180. *Kessner, T.*, The Golden Door: Italian and Jewish Immigrant Mobility in New York City, New York, 1977.

181. *Kusmer, K. L.*, A Ghetto Takes Shape: Black Cleveland, 1870–1930, Urbana, Ill., 1976.

182. *Lane, R.*, Policing the City: Boston, 1822–1885, Cambridge, Mass., 1967.

183. *Laurice, B.*, Working People of Philadelphia, 1800–1850, Philadelphia, 1980.

184. *Modell, J.*, The Peopling of a Working Class Ward: Reading, Pennsylvania 1850, in Journal of Social History, Vol. 5 (1971), pp. 71–96.

185. *Mohl, R.*, Poverty in New York, 1783–1825, New York, 1971.

186. *Nash, G.*, The Urban Crucible: Social Change, Political Consciousness, and the Origins of the American Revolution, Cambridge, Mass., 1979.

187. *Osofsky, G.*, Harlem: The Making of a Ghetto, New York, 1966.

188. *Pessen, E.*, Riches, Class, and Power Before the Civil War, New York,

1973.

189. *Philpott, T. L.*, The Slum and the Ghetto: Neighborhood Deterioration and Middle-Class Reform, Chicago, 1880–1930, New York, 1978.

190. *Pleck, E.*, Black Migration and Poverty: Boston, 1865–1901, New York, 1979.

191. *Rabinowitz, H. M.*, Race Relations in the Urban South, 1865–1890, New York, 1978.

192. *Romo, R.*, East Los Angeles: History of a Barrio, Austin, 1983.

193. *Rosenzweig, R.*, Eight Hours for What We Will: Workers and Leisure in an Industrial City, 1870–1920, New York, 1983.

194. *Ryan, M. P.*, Cradle of the Middle Class: The Family in Oneida County, New York, 1790–1865, New York, 1981.

195. *Schneider, J. C.*, Detroit and the Problem of Order, 1830–1860: A Geography of Crime, Riot, and Policing, Lincoln, Neb., 1980.

196. *Thernstrom, S.*, The Other Bostonians: Poverty and Progress in the American Metropolis, Cambridge, Mass. 1973.

197. *Thernstrom, S.*, Poverty and Progress: Social Mobility in a Nineteenth-Century City, Cambridge, Mass., 1964.

198. *Thernstrom, S.*, and *R. Sennett*, eds., Nineteenth-Century Cities: Essays in the New Urban History, New Haven, 1969.

199. *Trotter, J. W., Jr.*, Black Milwaukee: The Making of an Industrial Proletariat, Urbana, Ill., 1985.

200. *Tuttle, W., Jr.*, Race Riot: Chicago in the Summer of 1919, Boston, 1970.

201. *Vecoli, R.*, Contadini in Chicago: A Critique of "The Uprooted", in: Journal of American History, Vol. 51 (1964), pp. 404-417.

202. *Vinovskis, M.*, Fertility in Massachusetts from the Revolution to the Civil War, New York, 1981.

203. *Ward, D.*, Cities and Immigrants: A Geography of Change in Nineteenth Century America, New York, 1971.

204. *Warner, S. B., Jr.*, and *C. B. Burke*, Cultural Change and the Ghetto, in: Journal of Contemporary History, Vol. 4 (1969), pp. 173-187.

205. *Wilentz, S.*, Chants Democratic: New York City and the Rise of the American Working Class, 1788–1850, New York, 1984.

206. *Yans-McLaughlin, V.*, Family and Community: Italian Immigrants in Buffalo, 1880–1930, Ithaca, N. Y., 1977.

207. *Zunz, O.*, The Changing Face of Inequality: Urbanization, Industrial Development, and Immigrants in Detroit, 1880–1920, Chicago, 1982.

(d)   Town Planning, Housing

208. *Abbott, C.*, Portland: Planning, Politics, and Growth in a Twentieth-Century City, Lincoln, Neb., 1983.

209. *Arnold, J. L.*, The New Deal in the Suburbs: A History of the Greenbelt Town Program, 1935–1954, Columbus, 1971.

210. *Barrows, R. G.*, Beyond the Tenement: Patterns of American Urban Housing, 1870–1930, in Journal of Urban History, Vol. 9 (1983), pp. 395–420.

211. *Bauman, J. F.*, Safe and Sanitary without the Costly Frills: The Evolution of Public Housing in Philadelphia 1921–41, in Pennsylvania Magazine of History and Biography, Vol. 101 (1977), pp. 114–124.

212. *Birch, E. L.*, Four Perspectives on the History of Urban Planning, in Trends in History, Vol. 2 (1981), pp. 79–92.

213. *Buder, S.*, Pullman: An Experiment in Industrial Order and Community Planning, 1880–1930, New York, 1967.

214. *Caro, R. A.*, The Power Broker, New York, 1974.

215. *Condit, C. W.*, The Railroad and the City: A Technological and Urbanistic History of Cincinnati, Columbus, 1977.

216. *Conzen, M. P.*, The Morphology of Nineteenth Century Cities in the United States, in W. Borah, J. Hardoy and G. A. Stelter, eds., Urbanization in the Americas: The Background in Comparative Perspective, Special issue of the journal, Urban History Review, 1980, pp. 119–141.

217. *Fein, A.*, Frederick Law Olmsted and the American Environmental Tradition, New York, 1972.

218. *Fitch, J. M.*, American Building, 2nd ed., Boston, 1966.

219. *Hayden, D.*, The Grand Domestic Revolution: A History of Feminist Designs for American Homes, Cities, and Neighborhoods, Cambridge, Mass., 1981.

220. *Hines, T.*, Burnham of Chicago: Architect and Planner, New York, 1974.

221. *Jackson, A.*, A Place Called Home: A History of Low-Cost Housing in Manhattan, Cambridge, Mass., 1976.

222. *Kahn, J.*, Imperial San Francisco: Politics and Planning in an American City, 1897–1906, Lincoln, Neb., 1980.

223. *Lockwood, C.*, Manhattan Moves Uptown: An Illustrated History, Boston, 1976.

224. *Lubove, R.*, Community Planning in the 1920s: The Contribution of the Regional Planning Association of America, Pittsburgh, 1963.

225. *Lubove, R.*, The Progressives and the Slums: Tenement House Reform in New York City, 1890–1917, Pittsburgh, 1962.

226. *Lubove, R.*, Twentieth-Century Pittsburgh: Government, Business and Environmental Change, New York, 1969.

227. *Muller, E. K.*, Distinctive Downtowns, in The Geographical Magazine, Vol. 52 (1980), pp. 747–755.

228. *Peterson, J. A.*, The City Beautiful Movement: Forgotten Origins and Lost Meanings, in Journal of Urban History, Vol. 2 (1976), pp.

415–434.

229. *Peterson, J. A.*, The Impact of Sanitary Reform upon American Urban Planning, 1840–1890, in Journal of Social History, Vol. 13 (1979), pp. 88–101.

230. *Reps, J. W.*, The Making of Urban America: A History of City Planning in the United States, Princeton, 1965.

231. *Schaffer, D.*, Garden Cities for America: The Radburn Experience, Philadelphia, 1981.

232. *Schultz, S. K.*, and *C. McShane*, To Engineer the Metropolis: Sewers, Sanitation, and City Planning in Late Nineteenth Century America, in Journal of Social History, Vol. 12 (1978), pp. 389–411.

233. *Scott, M.*, American City Planning Since 1890, Berkeley, 1971.

234. *Sutcliffe, A.*, Towards the Planned City: Germany, Britain, the United States and France, New York, 1981.

235. *Tucci, D. S.*, Built in Boston: City and Suburb, 1800–1950, Boston, 1978.

236. *Tygiel, J.*, Housing in Late Nineteenth-Century American Cities, in Historical Methods, Vol. 12 (1979), pp. 84–97.

237. *Whitehill, W. M.*, Boston: A Topographical History, Cambridge, Mass., 1959.

238. *Wright, G.*, Moralism and Model Home: Domestic Architecture and Cultural Conflict in Chicago, 1873–1913, Chicago, 1980.

(e)   Economy and Transport

239. *Anderson, A. D.*, The Origins and Resolution of an Urban Crisis: Baltimore, 1890–1930, Baltimore, 1977.

240. *Barrett, P.*, The Automobile and Urban Transit: The Formation of Public Policy in Chicago, 1900–1930, Philadelphia, 1983.

241. *Berry, B. J. L.*, ed., Urbanization and Counterurbanization, in Urban Affairs Annual Review, Vol. II, Beverly Hills, Cal., 1976, pp. 7–30.

242. *Binford, H.*, The First Suburbs: Residential Communities on the Boston Periphery, 1815–1960, Chicago, 1985.

243. *Blackmar, B.*, Re-Walking the "Walking City", in Radical History Review, Vol. 21 (1979), pp. 131–150.

244. *Cheape, C. W.*, Moving the Masses: Urban Public Transit in New York City, Boston, and Philadelphia, 1880–1912, Cambridge, Mass., 1980.

245. *Conzen, K. N.*, Patterns of Residence in Early Milwaukee, in L. F. Schnore, ed., The New Urban History: Quantitative Explorations in American Urban History, Princeton 1975, pp. 145–183.

246. *Daniels, G. H.*, and *M. H. Rose*, eds., Energy and Transportation: Historical Perspectives on Policy Issues, Beverly Hills, Cal., 1982.

247. *Dolce, P. C.*, Suburbia: The American Dream and Dilemma, Garden City, N.J., 1976.

248. *Ebner, M. H.*, "In the Suburbes of Toun": Chicago's North Shore to 1871, in Chicago History, Vol. 11 (1982), pp. 66–77.

249. *Fogelson, R. M.*, The Fragmented Metropolis: Los Angeles, 1850–1930, Cambridge, Mass., 1967.

250. *Hoy, S. M.*, and *M. C. Robinson*, eds., Public Works History in the United States: A Guide to the Literature, Nashville, 1982.

251. *Jackson, K. T.*, Crabgrass Frontier: The Suburbanization of the United States, New York, 1985.

252. *Mallach, S.*, The Origins of the Decline of Urban Mass Transportation in the United States, 1890–1930, in Urbanism Past and Present, Vol. 8 (1979), pp. 1–17.

253. *Mayer, H. M.*, and *R. C. Wade*, Chicago: Growth of a Metropolis, Chicago, 1969.

254. *Miller, Z.*, Suburb: Neighborhood and Community in Forest Park, Ohio, 1935–1976, Knoxville, Tenn., 1981.

255. *Muller, P. O.*, Contemporary Suburban America, Englewood Cliffs, N.J., 1981.

256. *O'Connor, C. A.*, A Sort of Utopia: Scarsdale, 1891–1981, Albany, N.Y., 1983.

257. *Platt, H.*, City Building in the New South: The Growth of Public Services in Houston, 1830–1915, Philadelphia, 1983.

258. *Preston, H. L.*, Automobile Age Atlanta: The Making of a Southern Metropolis, 1900–1935, Athens, Ga., 1979.

259. *Schnore, L. F.*, Class and Race in Cities and Suburbs, Chicago, 1972.

260. *Schwartz, J.*, and *D. Prosser*, eds., Cities of the Garden State: Essays in the Urban and Suburban History of New Jersey, Dubuque, Iowa, 1977.

261. *Sennett, R.*, Families Against the City: Middle Class Homes of Industrial Chicago, 1872–1920, Cambridge, Mass., 1970.

262. *Simon, R. D.*, The City Building Process: Housing and Services in New Milwaukee Neighborhoods, 1880–1910, Philadelphia, 1978.

263. *St. Clair, D.*, The Motorization and Decline of Urban Public Transit, 1935–1950, in Journal of Economic History, Vol. 41 (1981), pp. 579–600.

264. *Stilgoe, J. R.*, Metropolitan Corridor: Railroads and the American Scene, New Haven, 1983.

265. *Stilgoe, J. R.*, The Suburbs, in American Heritage, Vol. 35 (1984), pp. 21–36.

266. *Tarr, J.*, Transportation Innovation and Changing Spatial Patterns in Pittsburgh, 1850–1934, Chicago, 1978.

267. *Teaford, J. C.*, City and Suburb: The Political Fragmentation of Metropolitan America, 1850–1970, Baltimore, 1979.

268. *Theodorson, G. A.*, ed., Studies in Human Ecology, Evanston, Ill., 1961.

269. *Warner, S. B., Jr.*, The Private City: Philadelphia in Three Periods of

Its Growth, Philadelphia, 1968.

270. *Warnner, S. B., Jr.*, Streetcar Suburbs: The Process of Growth in Boston, 1870–1900, Cambridge, Mass., 1962.

271. *Yago, G.*, The Decline of Transit: Urban Transportation in German and U.S. Cities, 1900–1970, New York, 1984.

(f) Arts and Sciences, Churches

272. *Barth, G.*, City People: The Rise of Modern City Culture in Nineteenth-Century America, New York, 1980.

273. *Bender, T.*, Toward an Urban Vision: Ideas and Institutions in Nineteenth-Century America, Lexington, Ky., 1975.

274. *Duis, P.*, The Saloon: Public Drinking in Chicago and Boston, 1880–1920, Urbana, 1983.

275. *Erenberg, L. A.*, Steppin' Out: New York Nightlife and the Transportation of American Culture, 1890–1930, Westport, Conn., 1981.

276. *Goist, P. D.*, From Main Street to State Street: Town, City, and Community in America, Port Washington, N.Y., 1977.

277. *Hales, P. B.*, Silver Cities: The Photography of Urbanization, 1839–1915, Philadelphia, 1984.

278. *Harris, N.*, Four Stages of Cultural Growth: The American City, in History and the Role of the City in American Life, Indianapolis, 1972, pp. 25–49 (Indiana Historical Society Lectures).

279. *Horowitz, H. L.*, Culture and the City: Cultural Philanthropy in Chicago from the 1880s to 1917, Lexington, Ky., 1976.

280. *Kaestle, C. F.*, The Evolution of an Urban School System: New York, 1750–1850, Cambridge, Mass., 1973.

281. *Kasson, J. F.*, Amusing the Millions: Coney Island at the Turn of the Century, New York, 1978.

282. *Lazerson, M.*, Origins of the Urban School: Public Education in Massachusetts, 1870–1915, Cambridge, Mass., 1971.

283. *Lees, A.*, Cities Perceived: Urban Society in European and American Thought, 1820–1940, New York, 1985.

284. *McCarthy, K. D.*, Noblesse Oblige: Charity and Cultural Philanthropy in Chicago, 1849–1929, Chicago, 1982.

285. *Morse, R. M.*, and *G. A. Stelter*, Cities as Cultural Arenas, in Journal of Urban History, Vol. 10 (1984), pp. 347–482.

286. *Pease, W. H.*, and *J. H. Pease*, The Web of Progress: Private Values and Public Styles in Boston and Charleston, 1828–1843, New York, 1985.

287. *Ravitch, D.*, The Great School Wars: New York City, 1805–1973, New York, 1974.

288. *Reiss, S. A.*, Touching Base: Professional Baseball and American Culture in the Progressive Era, Westport, Conn., 1980.

289. *Schultz, S. K.*, The Culture Factory: Boston Public Schools, 1789–

1860, New York, 1973.

290. *Siegel, A.*, The Image of the American City in Popular Literature, 1820–1870, Port Washington, N.Y., 1981.

291. *Story, R.*, The Forging of an Aristocracy: Harvard and the Boston Upper Class, 1800–1870, Middletown, Conn., 1980.

292. *Troen, S. K.*, The Public and the Schools: Shaping the St. Louis System, 1838–1920, Columbia, Mo., 1975.

293. *Tyack, D. B.*, The One Best System: A History of American Urban Education, Cambridge, Mass., 1974.

294. *Walters, R. G.*, Signs of the Times: Clifford Goertz and Historians, in Social Research, Vol. 47 (1980), pp. 537–556.

295. *Warner, S. B., Jr.*, The Management of Multiple Urban Images, in D. Fraser and A. Sutcliffe, eds., The Pursuit of Urban History, London, 1983, pp. 383–394.

296. *Warner, S. B., Jr.*, Province of Reason, Cambridge, Mass., 1984.

297. *White, M.*, and *L. White*, The Intellectual Versus the City: From Thomas Jefferson to Frank Lloyd Wright, New York, 1964.

E. Local Studies (a representative selection)

• Baltimore

298. *Olson, S. H.*, Baltimore: The Building of an American City, Baltimore, 1980.

• Buffalo

299. *Goldman, M.*, High Hopes Before the Fall: The Rise and Decline of Buffalo, New York and Albany, 1984.

• Chicago

300. *Pierce, B. L.*, A History of Chicago, 3 vols., New York 1937, 1940 and 1957.

• Everett

301. *Clark, N. H.*, Mill Town: A Social History of Everett, Washington, Seattle, 1970.

• Knoxville

302. *McDonald, M. J.*, and *W. B. Wheeler*, Knoxville, Tennessee: Continuity and Change in an Appalachian City, Knoxville, Tenn., 1983.

- Madison

303. *Mollenhoff, D. V.*, Madison: A History of the Formative Years, Dubuque, Iowa, 1982.

- Milwaukee

304. *Still, B.*, Milwaukee: The History of a City, Madison, Wisconsin, 1948.

- Nashville

305. *Doyle, D. H.*, Nashville in the New South, 1880–1930, Knoxville, 1985.

- New Haven

306. *Osterweis, R. G.*, Three Centuries of New Haven, 1638–1938, New Haven, 1953.

- New York

307. *Spann, E. K.*, The New Metropolis: New York City, 1840–1857, New York, 1981.

- Rochester

308. *McKelvey, B.*, Rochester on the Genesee: The Growth of a City, Syracuse, N.Y., 1973.

- Washington

309. *Green, C. M.*, Washington, 2 vols., Princeton, 1962 and 1963.

- Wilmington

310. *Hoffecker, C. E.*, Wilmington, Delaware: Portrait of an Industrial City, 1830–1910, Charlottesville, Virginia, 1974.

EVA HOLZ

Yugoslavia

Communal development in Yugoslavia in recent decades has tended to move towards a gradual balance between town and rural settlement. Town ways of life have been strengthening their grip, however, through the creation of industrial centres in smaller towns. Recent research on the most important aspects of the history of the modern city has mainly been concerned with tracing this development. One important facet of this change has been the appearance of the commuter. Alongside economic policy approaches (which are detailed in a series of newspaper articles), geographic and related statistical data have been given major attention. Cadastral registers, plan collections and appraisals of statistics are abundant and have been of great help in this work.

In addition to observations and descriptions of modern development processes, many publications have dealt with the problem of revitalising older sections of towns.

Literature on urban history published prior to about 1973 is listed in S. Vilfan's work (see No. 26). Most of the books and articles mentioned there are not repeated here.

The bibliography compiled below mainly contains a selection of works published in the last 10 to 15 years. For the most part, publications which are useful for purposes of comparison or which deal with the picture of the town or touch on area problems in any way have been included. Titles from the large number of works dealing with historical events have been included only in exceptional cases, e.g. when they are significant as a synthesis. Collections that are decidedly local in nature have not been listed although they have much of interest to offer.

Since the publication of various current bibliographies has been delayed, relatively few of them could be drawn on here. The bibliography in this publication is based mainly on direct inquiries which means that, unfortunately, certain omissions could not be avoided.

A. Urban History Institutions

—

B. Aids to Research

(a) Urban History Journals

1. *Arh. Časopis za arhitekturu, urbanizam, primijenjenu umjetnost i industrijsko oblikovanje*, Sarajevo, 1963 ff. (= Journal of architecture, urbanisation, applied art and industrial design).

2. *Arhitektov bilten. Glasilo društva arhitektov Ljubljane in ZDAS*, Ljubljana, 1964 ff. (= The architect's bulletin. Organ of the architects' association, Ljubljana).

3. *Bilten. Biro za regionalno prostorsko planiranje in Urbanistični inštitut SR Slovenija*, Ljubljana, 1967 ff. (= Bulletin. Office for regional planning and Urban Institute SR Slovenija).

4. *Bilten mednarodnega obveščanja in sodelovanja*, Ljubljana, 1969 ff. (= Bulletin for international information and co-operation for building).

5. *Bilten. Urbanistično društvo Slovenije*, Ljubljana, 1964 ff. (= Bulletin of the Society for Urbanism, Slovenija).

6. *Časopis za zgodovino in narodopisje*, Maribor, 1904–1939, new edition, 1965 ff. (= Review for History and Ethnography).

7. *Čovjek i prostor*, Zagreb, 1954 ff. (= Man and space).

8. *Geografski glasnik*, Zagreb, 1929 ff. (= Bulletin of geography).

9. *Geografski obzornik. Časopis za geografsko vzgojo in izobrazbo*, Ljubljana, 1954 ff. (= Geographic forum. Journal of geographic education).

10. *Geografski vestnik*, Ljubljana, 1925 ff. (= Bulletin of the society of geography of Ljubljana).

11. *Geografski zbornik*, Ljubljana, 1952 ff. (Acta geographica).

12. *Geographica Slovenica*, Ljubljana, 1971 ff.

13. *Komuna. Časopis za pitanja teorije i prakse komunalnih zajednica*, Belgrade, 1954 ff. (= The community. Journal for theoretical and practical urban matters).

14. *Kronika. Časopis za slovensko krajevno zgodovino*, Ljubljana, 1953 ff. (= Chronicle. Journal for local Slovenic history).

15. *Sinteza. Revija za likovno kulturo*, Ljubljana, 1964 ff. (= Fine arts review).

16. *Statistički godišnjak*, Belgrade, 1929, 1932–1940 (= Annual statistics).

17. *Statistički godišnjak FNRJ*, Belgrade, 1954–1962 (= Statistical yearbook of the Socialist Federal Republic of Yugoslavia).

18. *Statistički godišnjak SFRJ*, Belgrade, 1963 ff. (= Statistical yearbook of the Socialist Federal Republic of Yugoslavia).

In addition to the above, separate statistics are published in the individual republics.

19. *Varstvo spomenikov*, Ljubljana, 1948 ff. (= Protection of monuments, 1948–1973; Monument conservation, 1974 ff.).
20. *Zbornik radova Prirodno-matematičkog fakulteta*, Belgrade, 1954 ff. (= Anthology of works of the natural sciences-mathematics faculty).
21. *Zbornik za umetnosto zgodovino*, Ljubljana, new ed., 1951 ff. (= Art history records).

(b) Bibliographies

22. *Mihajčić, R.* and *V. Perić*, Contribution à la bibliographie de nos villes sous la domination turque, in Balcanica. Annuaire de l'Institut des Etudes Balkaniques, Belgrade, 1972, pp. 636–684 (The bibliography includes works from 1900–1970).
23. *Pak, M.*, Bibliografija del s področja urbane geografije od 1945 do 1982, Ljubljana 1983 (= Bibliography of works on urban geography, 1945–1982 – The bibliography includes works from all Yugoslavia. Published material only.)

(c) Handbooks on Urban History

24. *Enciklopedija Jugoslavije*, 1st ed., Vols. 1–8, Zagreb, 1955–1971; 2nd ed., 4 vols. to date, Zagreb, 1980–1986.

(d) Atlases on Urban History and Urban Development

25. *Nova Gorica v prostoru in času*, Nova Gorica, 1979 (= Nova Gorica in space and time).

(e) Sources of Urban History

—

C. Research Reports

(a) General Surveys

26. *Vilfan, S.*, Yougoslavie, in Guide international d'histoire urbaine. 1: Europe, Paris, 1977, pp. 505–528.

(b) Surveys of Individual Fields of Urban Research

—

D. Literature on Individual Areas of Urban History Research

(a) Concept and Definition of Town and Town Types

27. *Melik, V.*, Mesto (civitas) na Slovenskem, in Zgodovinski časopis, Year 27 (1972), pp. 299–316 (= The town (civitas) in Slovenija).
28. *Vilfan, S.*, Stadt und Adel. Ein Vergleich zwischen Küsten– und Binnenstädten zwischen der Oberen Adria und Pannonien, in Die Stadt am Ausgang des Mittelalters, Linz, 1974 (Österreichischer Arbeitskreis für Stadtgeschichtsforschung).

(b) Politics, Law and Statutes

29. *Društvo i razvoj gradova. Tribina. Naučno politička rasprava*, Belgrade, 1980 (= Society and the evolution of towns. Tribunes. A scientific, political debate).
30. *Kostić, C.*, Sociologija grada, Belgrade, 1973 (= Urban sociology).
31. *Marinović-Uzelac, A.*, Socialni prostor grada, Zagreb, 1978 (= Social space of the city).

(c) Population and Social Structure

32. *Demografska kretanja i projekcije u Jugoslaviji*, Belgrade, 1968 (= Demographic movement and trends in Yugoslavia).
33. *Demografska kretanja i karakteristike stanovništva Jugoslavije prema nacionalnoj pripadnosti*, Belgrade, 1978 (Centar za demografska istraživanja. Inštitut društvenih nauka) (= Demographic movement and special features of the Yugoslav population according to nationality).
34. *Jugoslovanski simpozij o stanovništvu*, Ohrid, 1973 (= Yugoslav symposium on the population from 20–23 April, 1973, in Ohrid).
35. *Melik, V.*, Demographische und ethnische Entwicklung der Städte in Slowenien im 19. Jahrhundert, in Internationales kulturhistorisches Symposion Modersdorf 4, Szombathely, 1974, pp. 237–248.
36. *Popis prebivalstva v letu 1971. Migracijska obeležja*, Belgrade, 1973 (= Census, 1971. Migration).
37. *Popis stanovništva, domaćinstva i stanova u 1981 godini*. Stalno stanovništvo, stanovništvo u zemlji i osnovni skupovi stanovništva u zemlji, po mestu stalnog stanovanja (SFRJ, SR i SAP, opstine i naselja), Belgrade, 1984 (= Census, households and housing, permanent residences).
38. *Prebivalstvo*. Vitalna, etnična in migracijska obeležja. Rezultati po republikah in pokrajinah, Belgrade, 1974 (= The population; vitality (birth-rates, age structure, life expectancy); ethnic groups and migration to republics and other areas).

39. *Simpozijum: prostorno i urbanističko planiranje u uslovima ekonomske stabilizacije*, Belgrade, 1982 (= Symposium: Spatial and urban planning in view of economic stability).

40. *Zbornik IX. kongresa geografa Jugoslavije u Bosni i Hercegovini od 24. do 30.IX.1972*, Sarajevo, 1974 (= Proceedings of the IX. Congress of Yugoslav Geographers in Bosnia and Hercegovina).

(d) Town Planning

41. *Janić, M.*, Osnove prostorne organizacije grada, Belgrade, 1979 (=The basis of spatial organisation of the city).

42. *Karanfilovski, D.*, Naselja u SFRJ, Skopje, 1975 (= Settlements in the Socialist Federation of Yugoslavia).

43. *Kojić, B. -D.*, Stari balkanski gradovi, varoši i varošice, Belgrade, 1976 (= Ancient towns, markets and villages in the Balkans).

44. *Kokole, V.*, Primerjalna študija ukrepov za izboljšanje okolja v izbranih mestih Jugoslavije, Ljubljana, 1982 (= Comparative studies on measures for ecological restoration in selected cities of Yugoslavia. Belgrade, Novi Sad, Zagreb, Ljubljana).

45. *Kokole, Vl.*, The Future of Urbanisation in Slovenija, in International Workshop of Comparative Ecological Analysis of Social Change, Vol. 2, Ljubljana, 1976, pp. 3–12.

46. *Kokole, Vl.*, Sodobni trendi urbanizacije, Ljubljana, 1968 (= Trends of urbanisation in Slovenija).

47. *Krajinsko planiranje.* Zbornik mednarodnega simpozija, Ljubljana, 1972 (= Landscape planning).

48. *Maksimović, B.*, Urbanizam, Belgrade, 1980 (= Urbanism).

49. *Marković, J. -D.*, Gradovi Jugoslavije, Belgrade, 1971 (= The cities of Yugoslavia).

50. *Mestno stanovanjsko okolje – urbanistično raziskovanje in planiranje – mednarodno posvetovanje*, Ljubljana, 1977 (= Urban housing environment. Symposium on research and planning strategies).

51. *Mlinar, Z.*, Urbanizacija, urbanizem, sociologija, Ljubljana, 1978 (= Urbanisation, urbanism and sociology).

52. *Mušić, V.*, Urbanizem – bajke in resničnost, Ljubljana, 1980 (= Urbanism – poetry and truth).

53. *Naučni skup: Sarajevo – grad i regija u vremenu i prostoru 2000 godine* (23. i 24.IV.1981), Sarajevo, 1982 (= Symposium: Sarajevo – town and region in time and space in the year 2000).

54. *Naučniot kolokvium "Kulturnoto nasledstvo i čovekiot životen prostor"*, Ohrid, 1981 (= Scientific colloquium "Cultural heritage and space to live" in Ohrid from 9–11. 11. 1981. Lectures and discussion).

55. *Piha, B.*, Osnove prostorskega planiranja, Belgrade, 1979 (= An introduction to spatial planning).

56. *Pogačnik, A.*, Urbanistično planiranje, Ljubljana, 1980 (= Town planning).

57. *Prelog, M.*, Prostor – vrijeme, Zagreb, 1973 (= Space – time).

58. *Problemi i tehnika zaštite historijskih gradskih centara.* Medunarodni simpozij, Split, 1970 (= Problems and Techniques of Preservation of Historic Urban Centers. International Symposium).

59. *Razvoj i planiranje gradova srednje velicine*, 2 vols. Belgrade, 1974 (= Evolution and planning of medium-sized cities).

60. *Stefanović, D.*, Specifičnosti procesa urbanizacije u Jugoslaviji u periodu 1948–1961, Diss. Belgrade, 1971 (= Special features of urbanisation processes in Yugoslavia 1948–1961).

61. *Tepina, M.*, Razsežnosti našega okolja, Ljubljana, 1974 (= The dimensions of our environment).

62. *Urbana in industrijska geografija / Urban and Industrial Geography.* Jugoslovanski geografski simpozij / Geographical Symposium of 8–10.11.1979, Ljubljana, 1980.

63. *Urbanističko i prostorno planiranje, retrospektiva i prospektiva*: Simpozijum u godini urbanizma u Srbiji. Symposium of 7./8.11.1980 in Belgrade, Belgrade, 1980 (= Town and spatial planning – review and preview).

64. *Urbanizacija prigradskog područja velikih i srednjih gradova*, 2 vols. Belgrade, 1980 (= Urbanisation of suburbs in large and medium-sized cities).

65. *Vresk, M.*, Osnove urbane geografije, Zagreb, 1980 (= An introduction to urban geography).

66. *Vresk, M.*, Razvoj urbanih sistema u svijetu. Geografski pregled, Zagreb, 1984 (= The evolution of towns throughout the world. Geographic outline).

67. *Vrišer, I.*, Regionalno planiranje, Ljubljana, 1978 (= Regional planning).

68. *Vrišer, I.*, Urbana geografija, Ljubljana, 1984 (= Urban geography).

69. *Vrišer, I.*, Vplivna območja jugoslovanskih mest in drugih središč, Ljubljana, 1972 (= The areas of influence in Yugoslav cities and towns).

70. *Žujić, S.*, Proces urbanizacije na području Jugoslavije, Zagreb, 1970 (= The process of urbanisation in Yugoslavia).

(e)   Economy and Transport

71. *Acta historico-oeconomica Iugoslaviae*, Vol. 5, Zagreb, 1978.

72. *Erceg, I.*, Trst i bivše habsburške zemlje u medjunarodnom prometu. Merkantilizam u drugoj polovini 18. stoljeća, Zagreb, 1970 (= Trieste and the former Habsburg countries in international traffic. Mercantilism in the second half of the 18th century).

73. *Gavrilović, S.*, Prilog istoriji trgovine i migracije Balkan-Podunavlje XVIII i XIX stoljeća, Belgrade, 1969 (= A contribution to the history of trade and migration from the Balkans in the area of the Danube).

74. *Jelinović, Z.*, Borba za jadranske pruge i njeni ekonomski ciljevi, Zagreb, 1957 (= The battle for the Adriatic railway lines and its economic objectives).

75. *Plovidba na Dunavu i njegovi, pritokama kroz vekove.* Zbornik radova sa medunarodnog naučnog skupa održanog 5. i 6. juna 1979 godine, Belgrade, 1983 (= Navigation on the Danube and its tributaries over the centuries. Anthology of papers presented at the international scientific conference of 5 and 6 June 1979).

(f) Arts and Sciences, Churches

76. *Gradska kultura na Balkanu (XV–XIX vek).* Zbornik radova, Belgrade, 1964 (= The Balkan Urban Culture [15th–19th Centuries]. Collection of Studies).

77. *Kunstdenkmäler in Jugoslawien*, 2 vols., Leipzig, 1981.

E. Local Studies (a representative selection)

● Bosnia and Hercegovina

78. *Kovačević-Kojić, D.*, Gradska naselja srednjevekovne bosanske države, Sarajevo, 1978 (= Urban areas in the medieval Bosnian state).

— Banja Luka

79. *Smlatić, S.*, Banja Luka – grad i njegove funkcije, Zagreb, 1974 (= Banja Luka – A city and its function).

— Mostar

80. *Ćupina, D.*, Mostar i okolica, Zagreb, 1977 (= Mostar and its surroundings).

— Sarajevo

81. *Sarajevo*, Sarajevo, 1976.

● Montenegro

82. *Kovačević, M.*, Srednjevekovni gradovi na teritoriji SR Crne gore. Problemi nastanka i razvoja obrambene arhitekture, Belgrade, 1978 (= Middle Ages towns in Montenegro. Problems of their origin and development of fortress architecture).

— Cetinje

83. *Martinović, D. J.*, Cetinje: Teritorialno-funkcionalni razvoj i turističke mogučnosti, Diss. Cetinje, 1973 (= Cetinje: territorial-functional development and possibilities for tourism).

● Croatia

84. *Centralna naselja i gradovi SR Hrvatske.* Geografska analiza, Zagreb, 1976 (= Main settlements and towns in the Socialist Republic of Croatia. Geographic analysis).

85. *Raduš, V.*, Spomenici Slavonije iz razdoblja XVI do XIX stoljeća / Razvoj arhitekture na području Slavonije u razdoblju od XVI do XIX stoljeća, Zagreb, 1974 (= Slovenic monuments from the 16th to the 19th century. Development of Slovenic architecture from the 16th to the 19th century).

— Dubrovnik

86. *Beritić, D.*, Dubrovnik i okolica, Zagreb, 1978 (= Dubrovnik and its surroundings).

87. *Foretić, V.*, Povijest Dubrovnika do 1808, Vols. 1–2, Zagreb, 1980 (= History of Dubrovnik up to 1808).

88. *Gattin, N.*, Dubrovnik, Zagreb, 1977.

89. *Planić-Lončarić, M.*, Planirana izgradnja na području Dubrovačke republike, Zagreb, 1980 (= Planned building in and about the Republic of Dubrovnik).

90. *Stulli, B.*, Dubrovačka republika, in Enciklopedija Jugoslavije, 2nd ed., Vol. 3, Zagreb, 1984 (= The Republic of Dubrovnik).

— Karlovac

91. *Karlovac 1579–1979.* Zbornik radova, Karlovac, 1979 (=Karlovac 1579–1979. Anthology).

— Varaždin

92. *Varaždinski zbornik.* Zbornik radova sa Znanstvenog skupa održanog u Varaždinu od 1. do 3. listopada 1981 godine povodom obilježavanja 800 godišnjice grada, Zagreb, 1983 (= Varaždin commemorative publication: Collection of articles from the scientific colloquium of 1.-3.11.1981 in Varaždin on the occasion of its 800th anniversary).

— Zadar

93. *Klaić, N.* and *I. Petricioli*, Zadar u srednjem vijeku do 1409., Zadar, 1976 (= Zadar in the Middle Ages up to 1409).

94. *Raukar, T.*, Zadar u XV stoljeću. Ekonomski razvoj i društveni odnosi, Zagreb, 1977 (= Zadar in the 15th century).

— Zagreb

95. *Blašković, V.*, Zagreb, Zagreb, 1981.

96. *Klaić, N.*, Povijest Zagreba u srednjem vijeku, Zagreb, 1982 (= The history of the city of Zagreb in the Middle Ages.)

97. *Krivočić, S.*, Zagreb i njegovo stanovništvo od najstarijih vremena do sredine XIX. stoljeća, Zagreb, 1981 (= Zagreb and its population from the oldest times to the middle of the 19th century).

98. *Ranitović, S.*, Zagreb 1900, Zagreb, 1974.

99. *Timet, T.*, Stambena izgradnja Zagreba do 1954. godine. Ekonomsko-historijska analiza, Zagreb, 1961 (= Housing in Zagreb up to 1954. Economic-historical analysis).

● Macedonia

100. *Čipan, B.*, Makedonskite gradovi vo XIX. vek i nivnata urbana perspektiva, Skopje, 1978 (= The Macedonian towns of the 19th century and their urban perspective).

101. *Stojanovski, A.*, Gradovite na Makedonija od krajot na 14. do 17. vek. Demografska proučavanja, Skopje, 1981 (= Macedonian towns from the end of the 14th century to the 17th century. Demographic studies).

— Skopje

102. *Arsovski, T.*, Skopje. Urban razvitok, Skopje, 1977 (= Skopje. Urban development).

103. *Galic, R.*, Skopje. Urbanistički plan, Skopje, 1968 (= Skopje. Plan of urbanisation).

● Slovenija

104. *Slovenska urbanistična bibliografija.* Kritični pregled knjig, periodike, študijskega gradiva in načrtov s področja urbanizma ter bliznjih panog, Ljubljana, 1966 (= Slovenic urban bibliography. A critical overview).

105. *Gosar, L.*, Procesi urbanizacije v SR Sloveniji. I faza, Ljubljana 1978 (= Urbanisation trends in Slovenija).

106. *Klemenčič, V.*, Industrialisierung und raumwirksame Urbanisierung in Slowenien – Jugoslawien, in Industrialisierung und Urbanisierung in sozialistischen Staaten Südost-Europas, Regensburg, 1981, pp. 27–35 (Münchener Studien zur Sozial- und Wirtschaftsgeographie, Vol. 12).

107. *Kokole, V.*, Gravitacijska območja slovenskih mest in centralnih krajev, Ljubljana, 1968 (= Spheres of influence of central places in Slovenia).

108. *Kranjec, S.*, Model metropolitanskega razvoja za slovenske razmere, Ljubljana, 1974 (= Model for the development of metropolises in

Slovenic conditions).

109. *Mihevc, P.*, Urbanizacija v Sloveniji. Politika razvoja naselij. Tipologija naselij, Ljubljana, 1979 (= General problems of development. Typology of the settlements).

110. *Pagačnik, A.*, Urbanizem Slovenije, Ljubljana, 1983 (= Urban planning in Slovenija).

111. *Sedlar, S.*, Vpliv urbanizacije na podobo in strukturo podeželskih mestnih naselij v Sloveniji, Ljubljana, 1974 (= The influence of urbanisation on the image and the structure of towns in rural areas in Slovenija).

— Celje

112. *Orožen, J.*, Oris sodobne zgodovine Celja in njegove okolice, Celje, 1980 (= Description of the modern history of Celje and its surrounding area).

— Izola

113. *Prenova starega jedra Izole*, Piran, 1981 (= A summary of the history of Izola).

— Kranj

114. *Žontar, J.*, Zgodovina mesta Kranja. Reproduciran ponatis iz leta 1939, Ljubljana, 1982 (= History of Kranj).

— Krško

115. Krško skozi čas 1477–1977. Zbornik ob 500 letnici mesta, Krško, 1977 (= Krško 1477–1977. Commemorative publication on the occasion of its 500th anniversay).

— Ljubljana

116. *Mihelič, B.*, Urbanistični razvoj Ljubljane, Ljubljana, 1983 (= The architectural development of Ljubljana).

117. *Šumi, N.*, Prenova Ljubljane. Spomeniško varstveni postopki pri izdelavi sanacijskih načrtov, Ljubljana, 1978 (= Modernisation of Ljubljana. Ways of preserving monuments when drawing up restoration plans).

118. *Valenčič, V.* and *R. Traven*, Ljubljanske ulice, Ljubljana, 1980 (= The streets of Ljubljana).

119. *Zgodovina Ljubljane*. Prispevki za monografijo, Ljubljana, 1984 (= The history of the city of Ljubljana).

— Maribor

120. *Pirkovič-Kocbek, J.*, Izgradnja sodobnega Maribora, mariborska arhitektura in urbanizem med let 1918–1976, Ljubljana, 1982 (= The development of present-day Maribor – Architecture and town planning 1918–1976).

— Murska Sobota

121. *Obal, F.*, Arhitektura v obdobju 1900–1941 v Murski Soboti, Murska Sobota, 1982 (= Architecture in Murska Sobota from 1900–1941).

— Piran

122. *Pahor, M.* and *T. Mikeln*, Piran, Piran, 1972.
123. *Prenova Pirana*, Piran, 1976 (= Modernising Piran).

— Ptuj

124. *600 let ustavne in upravne zgodovine Ptuja*, Ptuj, 1979 (= 600 years of statutory and administrative history of the city of Ptuj. An anthology).

— Škofja Loka

125. *Planina, F.*, Škofja Loka s Poljansko in Selsko dolino, Škofja Loka, 1972 (= Škofja Loka, Poljansko and the valley of Selsko).

• Serbia

126. *Marković, B.*, Idejni razvoj srpskoga urbanizma, pregled rekonstrukcije gradova do 1914, Belgrade, 1978 (= Ideological evolution of Serb urbanism 1861–1914).
127. *Šalipurović, V.*, Prilozi za istoriju gradjevinarstva u srednjem Polimlju u XIX. veku, Belgrade, 1979 (= Contributions to the history of construction in the Middle Polimlje region in the 19th century).

— Belgrade

128. *Istorija Beograda*, Belgrade, 1974 (= History of the city of Belgrade).
129. *Urbanizam Beograda*, Belgrade, 1968 (= Belgrade's urbanisation).

— Mitrovica

130. *Garvrilović, S.*, Mitrovica. Trgovište u Sremu XVIII i XIX veka (1716–1848), Belgrade, 1984 (= Mitrovica. Market areas in Srem in the 18th and 19th centuries (1716–1848)).

— Ruma

131. *Gavrilović, S.*, Ruma – Trgovište u Sremu 1718–1848/49, Novi Sad, 1969 (= Ruma. Market areas in Srem 1718–1848/49).

— Smederevo

132. *Pavlović, L.*, Istorija Smedereva u reči i slici, Smederevo, 1980 (= The history of Smederevo in words and pictures).

— Sombor

133. *Beljanski, M.*, Letopis Sombora od 1907 do 1917. godine, Sombor, 1983 (= Chronicle of Sombor 1907–1917).

— Vojvodina

134. *Gradovi i naselja Vojvodine u XXI. veku.* Naučni skup, Novi Sad, 1983 (= Towns and settlements in Vojvodina in the 21st century. Scientific colloquium).

135. *Mirić, S.*, Poljoprivreda i urbanizacija u Vojvodini, Novi Sad, 1974 (= Agriculture and urbanisation in Vojvodina).

— Zemun

136. *Dabižić, M.*, Staro jezgro Zemuna. Istorijska urbana celina, Zemun, 1967 (= The old city centre of Zemun. An historical–urban unit).

CHRISTIAN ENGELI AND HORST MATZERATH

International Comparative Urban History Research

A. Urban History Institutions

Commission Internationale pour l'Histoire des Villes
Planning History Group
International Group for Urban History

B. Aids to Research

(a)   Urban History Journals

There is no special journal for international comparative urban history research. Occasional articles on the urban history of other countries or international comparisons appear primarily in:

1. *Journal of Urban History*, Beverly Hills, Calif., 1974 ff.
2. *Storia della Città*, Milan, 1976 ff.
3. *Storia Urbana*, Milan, 1977 ff.
4. *Urban History Review*, Winnipeg 1972 ff.
5. *Urban History Yearbook*, Leicester, 1974 ff.

(b)   Bibliographies

6. *International Bibliography of Urban History*. Denmark, Finland, Norway, Sweden, Stockholm, 1960.
7. *Dawson, P.*, and *S. B. Warner*, Jr., A Selection of Works Relating to the History of Cities, in O. Handlin and J. Burchard, eds., The Historian and the City, Cambridge, Mass. 1963, pp. 270–290.
8. *Pfeil, E.*, Großstadtforschung. Entwicklung und gegenwärtiger Stand, 2nd ed., Hanover, 1972 (in particular in the bibliography pp. 391–410).

9. *Sutcliffe, A.*, The History of Urban and Regional Planning. The Annotated Bibliography, London, 1981.

10. *Wolff, P.*, ed., Guide international d'histoire urbaine, Vol. 1: Europe, Paris, 1977.

(c) Handbooks on Urban History

—

(d) Atlases on Urban History and Urban Development

—

(e) Urban History Sources

11. *Chandler, T.*, and *G. Fox*, 3,000 Years of Urban Growth, New York, 1974.

12. *Dyos, H. J.*, and *A. B. M. Baker*, The Possibilities of Computerising Census Data, in H. J. Dyos, ed., The Study of Urban History, London, 1968, pp. 87–112.

13. *Flora, P.*, Indikatoren der Modernisierung. Ein historisches Datenhandbuch, Opladen, 1975.

14. *Growth of the World's Urban and Rural Population.* 1920–2000, New York, 1969 (Population Studies. 44).

15. *Haufe, H.*, Die Bevölkerung Europas. Stadt und Land im 19. und 20. Jahrhundert, Berlin, 1936.

16. *Haus, W.*, and *A. Krebsbach*, eds., Gemeindeordnungen in Europa, Stuttgart 1967 (Series of the Verein für Kommunalwissenschaften, Vol. 17).

17. *Levasseur, E.*, Les populations urbaines en France comparées à celles de l'étranger, Paris, 1887.

18. *Mihov, N.*, Naselenieto na Turcija i Balgărija prez XVIII i XIX v. Bibliografski izdirvanija săs statističeski i etnografski danni, Vol. I–V, Sofia, 1915–1967 (= The populations of Turkey and Bulgaria during the 18th and 19th centuries).

19. *Mitchell, B. R.*, European Historical Statistics, London, 1975.

20. *Mols, R.*, Introduction à la démographie historique des villes d'Europe du 14e au 18e siècle, Vols. 1–3, Gembloux, 1954–1956.

21. *Weber, A. F.*, The Growth of the Cities in the Nineteenth Century, New York, 1899 (Reprint 1963).

22. *World Urbanisation 1950–1970.* Vol. I: Basic Data for Cities, Countries and Regions; Vol. II: Analysis of Trends, Relationships, and Developments, Berkeley, 1972.

23. *The World's Metropolitan Areas*, Berkeley and Los Angeles, 1959.

C. Research Reports and Anthologies on Urban History Research

(a)   Research Reports

24. *Carter, H.*, An Introduction to Urban Historical Geography, London, 1983.

25. *Castells, M.*, Structures sociales et processus d'urbanisation. Analyse comparative intersociétale, in Annales. Economies, Sociétés, Civilisations, 1970, pp. 1155–1199.

26. *Checkland, S. G.*, Toward a Definition of Urban History, in H. J. Dyos, ed., The Study of Urban History, London, 1968, pp. 343–361.

27. *Conzen, M. R. G.*, The Use of Town Plans in the Study of Urban History, in H. J. Dyos, The Study of Urban History, London, 1968, pp. 113–130.

28. *Dyos, H. J.*, Agenda for Urban History, in ibid., The Study of Urban History, London, 1968, pp. 1–46.

29. *Gokhman, V. et al.*, Characteristics of World's Urbanisation and its Features in Individual Countries, in Geographia Polonica, Vol. 37 (1977), pp. 7–18.

30. *Hammarström, I.*, Urban History in Scandinavia, in Urban History Yearbook, 1978, pp. 46–55.

31. *Handlin, O.*, The Modern City as a Field of Historical Study, in ibid. and J. Burchard, eds., The Historian and the City, Cambridge, Mass. 1963, pp. 1–26.

32. *Heineberg, H.*, Geographische Aspekte der Urbanisierung: Forschungsstand und Probleme, in H. J. Teuteberg, ed., Urbanisierung im 19. und 20. Jahrhundert, Cologne and Vienna, 1983, pp. 35–63.

33. *Hershberg, T.*, The Future of Urban History, in D. Fraser and A. Sutcliffe, eds., The Pursuit of Urban History, London, 1983, p. 428.

34. *Hershberg, T.*, The New Urban History: Towards an Interdisciplinary History of the City, in Journal of Urban History, Vol. 5 (1978), pp. 3–40.

35. *Lampard, E. E.*, Two Cheers for Quantitative History: An Agnostic Foreword, in H. J. Teuteberg, ed., The New Urban History. Quantitative Explorations by American Historians, Princeton, 1975, p. 12.

36. *Pfeil, E.*, Großstadtforschung. Entwicklung und gegenwärtiger Stand, 2nd ed., Hanover, 1972.

37. *Schöller, P.*, Einige Erfahrungen und Probleme aus der Sicht weltweiter Urbanisierungsforschung, in H. J. Teuteberg, ed., Urbanisierung im 19. und 20. Jahrhundert, Cologne and Vienna, 1983, pp. 591–604.

38. *Schöller, P.*, ed., Trends in Urban Geography. Reports on Research in Major Language Areas, Paderborn, 1973.

39. *Stave, B. M.*, The Making of Urban History. Historiography through Oral History, Beverly Hills, 1977.

40. *Stave, B. M.*, In Pursuit of Urban History: Conversations with Myself and Others – A View from the United States, in D. Fraser and A. Sutcliffe, eds., The Pursuit of Urban History, London, 1983, pp. 407–427.

41. *Teuteberg, H. J.*, Historische Aspekte der Urbanisierung: Forschungsstand und Probleme, in idem ed., Urbanisierung im 19. und 20. Jahrhundert, Cologne and Vienna, 1983, pp. 2–34.

42. *Veit-Brause, I.*, The Place of Local and Regional History in German and French Historiography: Some General Reflection, in Australian Journal of French Studies, Vol. 1 (1979), pp. 447–478.

43. *Walton, J., and L. H. Masotti*, eds., The City in Comparative Perspective. Cross-national Research and New Directions in Theory, New York, 1976.

44. *Warner, Jr., S. B.*, A Research Strategy for Urban History, in J. Hammarström and T. Hall, eds., Growth and Transformation of the Modern City, Stockholm, 1979, pp. 163–170.

(b)   Collections

45. *Dyos, H. J.*, ed., The Study of Urban History, London, 1968.

46. *Fraser, D., and A. Sutcliffe*, eds., The Pursuit of Urban History, London, 1983.

47. *Frech, R. A. and F. E. I. Hamilton*, eds., The Socialist Cities Spatial Structure and Urban Policy, Chichester, 1979.

48. *Friedrichs, J.*, ed., Stadtentwicklungen in West- und Osteuropa, Berlin and New York, 1985.

49. *Germani, G.*, ed., Modernization, Urbanisation and the Urban Crisis, Boston, 1973.

50. *Glettler, M., H. Haumann and G. Schramm*, eds., Zentrale Städte und ihr Umland. Wechselwirkungen während der Industrialisierungsperiode in Mitteleuropa, Ostfildern, 1985.

51. *Hall, P.*, ed., The Innercity in Context. The Final Report of the Social Science Research, London, 1981 (Council Innercities Working Party).

52. *Hammarström, I., and T. Hall*, eds., Growth and Transformation of the Modern City. The Stockholm Conference, September 1978, Stockholm, 1979.

53. *Handlin, O., and J. Burchard*, eds., The Historian and the City, Cambridge, Mass. 1963.

54. *Jäger, H.*, ed., Probleme des Städtewesens im Industriezeitalter, Cologne, 1978.

55. *Lees, A., and L. Lees*, eds., The Urbanisation of European Societies in the Nineteenth Century, Lexington, Mass., 1976.

56. *Matzerath, H.*, ed., Städtewachstum und innerstädtische Strukturveränderungen, Stuttgart, 1984.

57. *Nordisk lokalhistoria.* Mötesrapporter 1–4, Stockholm 1986
— Vol. 1 Nordens naere fortid. Lokalsamfundene i de seneste 100 år.
Foredrag och diskussioner på det første nordiske seminar i
lokalhistorie Sostrup slot, August 1973, Sostrup 1973
(= The recent past of the Nordic countries. Local administration in the last 100 years).
— Vol. 2 Den andra nordiska lokalhistoriska konferensen i Viitasaari
1976. Föredrag i diskussioner (= The second Nordic local
history conference).
— Vol. 3 By och bygd, stad och omland, Oslo, 1981 (= Town and
village, town and surroundings).
— Vol. 4 Lokal praxis på det sociala området i de nordiska länderna
1800–1920, Stockholm, 1986 (= Tasks of the community in
the social sphere in Nordic countries 1800–1920).
58. *Rausch, W.,* ed., Die Städte Europas im 19. Jahrhundert, Linz, 1983.
59. *Rausch, W.,* ed., Die Städte Europas im 20. Jahrhundert, Linz, 1984.
60. *Schmal, H.,* ed., Patterns of European Urbanisation since 1500, London, 1981.
61. *Schnore, L. F.,* ed., Social Science and the City. A Survey of Urban
Research, New York, 1968.
62. *Schnore, L. F.,* ed., The New Urban History. Quantitative Explorations by American Historians, Princeton, 1975.
63. *Stave, B. M.,* The Making of Urban History. Historiography through
Oral History, Beverly Hills, 1977.
64. *Stave, B. M.,* ed., Modern Industrial Cities. History Policy and Survival, Beverly Hills, 1981.
65. *Stave, B. M.,* and *S. A. Stave,* eds., Machines, and Progressive Reformers, Matabar, Fla., 1984.
66. *Stoob, H.,* ed., Die Stadt. Gestalt und Wandel bis zum industriellen
Zeitalter, 2nd edition, Cologne and Vienna, 1985.
67. *Thernstrom, S.,* and *R. Sennett,* eds., Nineteenth-Century Cities. Essays
in the New Urban History, New Haven and London, 1969.
68. *Walton, J.,* and *D. E. Carns,* eds., Cities in Change. Studies on the
Urban Condition, Boston, 1973, 2nd ed., Boston, 1977.
69. *Walton, J.,* and *L. H. Masotti,* eds., The City in Comparative Perspective. Cross-national Research and New Directions in Theory, New
York, 1976.

D. Literature on Individual Areas of Urban History Research

(a)   Urbanisation and Town Planning

70. *Authén Blom, G.*, ed., Urbaniseringsprosessen i Norden. Det 17. Nordiske historikermøte Trondheim 1977, 3 vols. Oslo, 1977 (= Urbanisation in Scandinavia).

71. *Beckinsale, R. P.*, and *J. M. Houston* eds., Urbanisation and its Problems. Essays in Honour of E. W. Gilbert, Oxford, 1970 (Reprint).

72. *Berry, B. J. L.*, The Human Consequences of Urbanisation. Divergent Paths in the Urban Experience of the Twentieth Century, London, 1973.

73. *Blumin, S. M.*, When Villages Become Towns: The Historical Contexts of Town Formation, in D. Fraser and A. Sutcliffe, eds., The Pursuit of Urban History, London, 1983, pp. 54–68.

74. *Bosl, K.*, Die mitteleuropäische Stadt des 19. Jahrhunderts im Wandel von Wirtschaft, Gesellschaft, Staat, Kultur, in W. Rausch, ed., Die Städte Mitteleuropas im 19. Jahrhundert, Linz, 1983, pp. 1–23.

75. *Castells, M.*, La question urbaine, Paris, 1972.

76. *Davis, K.*, The Origins and Growth of Urbanisation in the World, in American Journal of Sociology, Vol. 60 (1955), pp. 429–437.

77. *Davis, K.*, The Urbanisation of the Human Population, in Scientific American, No. 213 (1965), pp. 41–53.

78. *Dickinson, R. E.*, The West-European City. A Geographical Interpretation, London, 1951.

79. *Ennen, E.*, Die europäische Stadt des Mittelalters, Göttingen, 1972, 3rd ed., Göttingen, 1979.

80. *Flora, P.*, Modernisierungsforschung. Zur empirischen Analyse gesellschaftlicher Entwicklungen, Opladen, 1974.

81. *Geddes, P.*, Cities in Evolution, London, 1915.

82. *George, P.*, La ville. Le fait urbain à travers le monde, Paris, 1952.

83. *Germani, G.*, ed., Urbanisation, Social Change, and the Great Transformation, in ibid., ed., Modernisation, Urbanisation and the Urban Crisis, Boston, 1973, pp. 3–58.

84. *Golden, H. H.*, Urbanisation and Cities. Historical and Comparative Perspectives on Urbanising World, Lexington, Mass., 1981.

85. *Goldstein, S.*, and *D. Sly*, eds., Patterns of Urbanisation: Comparative Country Studies, 2 vols., Dolhain, 1970.

86. *Hall, P.*, The European City in the Year 2000, in Growth and Transformation of the Modern City. The Stockholm Conference September 1978, Stockholm, 1979, pp. 157–162.

87. *Harvey, D.*, Consciousness and the Urban Experience, Oxford, 1985.

88. *Harvey, D.*, The Urbanisation of Capital, Oxford, 1985.

89. *Lampard, E. E.*, The Nature of Urbanisation, in D. Fraser and A. Sutcliffe, eds., The Pursuit of Urban History, London, 1983, pp. 3–53.

90. *Lees, L. H.*, and *P. Hohenberg*, The Making of Modern Europe, Cambridge, Mass., 1985.

91. *Matzerath, H.*, and *H. Ogura*, Moderne Verstädterung in Deutschland und Japan, in Zeitschrift für Stadtgeschichte, Stadtsoziologie und Denkmalpflege, Year 2 (1975), pp. 228–253.

92. *Mohs, G.*, Urbanisierung – Geographische Aspekte ihrer weltweiten Entwicklung, in Geographische Berichte, Vol. 23 (1978), pp. 270 ff.

93. *Mumford, L.*, The City in History. Its Origins, its Transformations, and its Prospects, New York, 1961.

94. *Mumford, L.*, The Culture of Cities, New York 1938.

95. *Sjoberg, G.*, The Pre-industrial City. Past and Present, Glencoe, Ill., 1960.

96. *Stoob, H.*, Städtebildung in Mitteleuropa im industriellen Zeitalter, in H. Jäger, ed., Probleme des Städtewesens im industriellen Zeitalter, Cologne and Vienna, 1978, pp. 316–341.

97. *Vries, J. de*, European Urbanisation 1500–1800, London, 1984.

(b)   Definition of Town and Town Types

98. *Goldfield, D. R.*, Suburban Development in Stockholm and the United States: A Comparison of Form and Function, in J. Hammarström and T. Hall, eds., Growth and Transformation of the Modern City, Stockholm, 1979, pp. 139–156.

99. *Löwinger, I. D.*, Stadt und Land in der Statistik, Zürich, 1970.

100. *Stoob, H.*, Frühneuzeitliche Städtetypen, in idem ed., Die Stadt. Gestalt und Wandel bis zum industriellen Zeitalter, Cologne and Vienna, 1979, pp. 195–228.

101. *Summerson, J.*, Urban Forms, in O. Handlin and J. Burchard, eds., The Historian and the City, Cambridge, Mass., 1963, pp. 165–176.

(c)   Metropolises and Capital Cities

102. *Banik-Schweitzer, R.*, Berlin – Wien – Budapest. Zur sozialräumlichen Entwicklung der drei Hauptstädte in der zweiten Hälfte des 19. Jahrhunderts, in W. Rausch ed., Die Städte Mitteleuropas im 19. Jahrhundert, Linz, 1983, pp. 139–154.

103. *Banik-Schweitzer, R., et al.*, Zeit der Metropolen. Berlin – Wien – Budapest 1850–1914, Vienna, 1986.

104. *Braun, S. D.*, and *J. F. Williams*, eds., Cities of the World. World Regional Development, New York, 1983.

105. *Cacciari, M.*, ed., Metropolis: Saggi sulla grande città, Rome, 1973

(= Metropolis: Attempts at the large city).

106. *Creese, W. L.*, The Form of the Modern Metropolis, in O. Handlin and J. Burchard, eds., The Historian and the City, Cambridge, Mass., 1963, pp. 202–208.

107. *Eldridge, H. W.*, ed., World Capitals: Toward Guided Urbanisation, New York, 1975.

108. *Ewers, H.-J., J. B. Goddard* and *H. Matzerath*, eds., The Future of the Metropolis. Berlin – London – Paris – New York, Berlin and New York, 1986.

109. *Hall, P.*, The World Cities, London, 1966.

110. *Instituto Gramsci*, ed., Le città capitali in Europa, Rome, 1985 (= The capital cities of Europe).

111. *Jakobson, L.*, and *V. Prakash*, eds., Urbanisation and National Development, Beverly Hills, 1971.

112. *Mecking, L.*, Die Entwicklung der Großstädte in Hauptländern der Industrie, Hamburg, 1949.

113. *Miller Lane, B.*, Government Buildings in European Capitals 1870–1914, in H. J. Teuteberg ed., Urbanisierung im 19. und 20. Jahrhundert, Cologne and Vienna, 1983, pp. 517–560.

114. *Robson, W. A.*, and *D. E. Regan*, Great Cities of the World. Government, Politics and Planning, Vol. 1, 2, 3rd ed., London, 1972.

115. *Sagave, P. P.*, 1871. Berlin, Paris, Reichshauptstadt und Hauptstadt der Welt, Frankfurt/M., 1971.

116. *Ságvári, A.*, ed., The Capitals of Europe. Les Capitales de l'Europe, Munich *et al.*, 1980.

117. *Schnieder, T.*, and *G. Brunn*, eds., Hauptstädte in europäischen Nationalstaaten, Munich and Vienna, 1983.

118. *Schwarz, K.*, Die Zukunft der Metropolen: Paris – London – New York, Vol. 1: Essays, Berlin, 1984.

119. *Sutcliffe. A.*, ed., Metropolis 1890–1940, Oxford, 1984.

120. *Wendehorst, A.*, and *J. Schneider*, eds., Hauptstädte – Entstehung, Struktur und Funktion, Neustadt/Aisch, 1979.

(d) Politics, Administration

121. *Glum, F.*, Die Organisation der Riesenstadt. Die Verfassungen von Paris, London, New York, Wien und Berlin, Berlin, 1920.

122. *Goetz, H., et al.*, eds., Die Verwaltungsorganisation der Weltstädte Paris, London, New York, Wien. Ein Beitrag zur Berliner Verfassungsreform, Berlin, 1931.

123. *Havránek, J.*, Soziale Struktur und politisches Verhalten der großstädtischen Wählerschaft im Mai 1907 – Wien und Prag im Vergleich, in Politik und Gesellschaft im alten und neuen Österreich. Festschrift für Rudolf Neck, Vienna, 1981, pp. 150–166.

(e) Population and Social Structure

124. *Bairoch, P.*, Population urbaine et taille des villes en Europe de 1600 à 1970. Présentation de série statistique, in Revue d'histoire économique et sociale, Vol. 54 (1976), pp. 304–335.

125. *Bairoch, P.*, Taille des villes, conditions de vie et développement économique, Paris, 1977.

126. *Brogan, D. W.*, Implications of Modern City Growth, in O. Handlin and J. Burchard, eds., The Historian and the City, Cambridge, Mass. 1963, pp. 146–164.

127. *Castells, M.*, The City and the Grassroots. A Crosscultural Theory of Urban Social Movements, London, 1983.

128. *Glettler, M.*, Pittsburg – Wien – Budapest. Programm und Praxis der Nationalitätenpolitik bei der Auswanderung der ungarischen Slowaken nach Amerika um 1900, Vienna, 1980.

129. *Lampard, E. E.*, Urbanisation and Social Change. On Broadening the Scope and Relevance of Urban History, in O. Handlin and J. Burchard, eds., The Historian and the City, Cambridge, Mass. 1963, pp. 225–247.

130. *Legoyt, A.*, Du progrès des agglomérations urbaines et de l'emigration rurale en Europe et particulièrement en France, Marseille, 1867.

131. *Matzerath, H.*, Grundstrukturen städtischer Bevölkerungsentwicklung in Mitteleuropa im 19. Jahrhundert, in W. Rausch, ed., Die Städte Mitteleuropas im 19. Jahrhundert, Linz, 1983, pp. 25–46.

132. *Meuriot, P.*, Des agglomérations urbaines dans l'Europe contemporaine: Essai sur les causes, les conditions, les conséquences de leur développement, Paris, 1897.

133. *Niehuss, M.*, Arbeiterschaft in Krieg und Inflation. Soziale Schichtung und Lage der Arbeiter in Augsburg und Linz 1910–1925, Berlin and New York, 1983.

134. *Pahl, R. E.*, Concepts in Context: Pursuing the Urban of 'Urban' Sociology, in D. Fraser and A. Sutcliffe, eds., The Pursuit of Urban History, London, 1983, pp. 371–382.

(f) Town Planning, Housing

135. *Benevolo, L.*, Die Geschichte der Stadt, Frankfurt/M., 1983.

136. *Benevolo, L.*, The Origins of Modern Town Planning, Cambridge, Mass. 1971.

137. *Bollerey, F.*, Architekturkonzeption der utopischen Sozialisten. Alternative Planung und Architektur für den gesellschaftlichen Prozeß, Munich, 1977.

138. *Bullock, N.*, and *J. Read*, The Movement for Housing Reform in Germany and France 1880–1914, Cambridge, 1985.

139. *Cherry, G. E.*, ed., Shaping an Urban World: Planning in the Twentieth Century, London, 1980.

140. *Choay, F.*, The Modern City: Planning in the Nineteenth Century, New York, 1969.

141. *Czok, K.*, Vorstädte und Vororte im Sog industrieller Entwicklung im 19. Jahrhundert – Leipzig und Prag im Vergleich, in W. Rausch, ed., Die Städte Mitteleuropas im 19. Jahrhundert, Linz, 1983, pp. 103–120.

142. *Fishman, R.*, Urban Utopias in the Twentieth Century: Ebenezer Howard, Frank Lloyd Wright and le Corbusier, New York, 1977.

143. *Garden, M.*, and *Y. Lequin*, eds., Construire la ville, XVIIIe–XXe siècle, Lyon, 1983.

144. *Hall, T.*, Planung europäischer Hauptstädte. Zur Entwicklung des Städtebaues im 19. Jahrhundert, Stockholm, 1986.

145. *Lopez, R. S.*, The Crossroads within the Wall, in O. Handlin and J. Burchard eds., The Historian and the City, Cambridge, Mass., 1963, pp. 27–43.

146. *Miller Lane, B.*, Changing Attitudes to Monumentality: An Interpretation of European Architecture and Urban Form 1880–1914, in I. Hammarström and T. Hall, eds., Growth and Transformation of the Modern City, Stockholm, 1979, pp. 101–114.

147. *Millon, H.*, The Visible Character of the City, in O. Handlin and J. Burchard, eds., The Historian and the City, Cambridge, Mass., 1963, pp. 209–215.

148. *Simson, J. von*, Kanalisation und Städtehygiene im 19. Jahrhundert, Düsseldorf, 1983.

149. *Steinböck, W.*, Wien und Berlin in der Architektur des Klassizismus. Untersuchung über stilgeschichtliche und geistesgeschichtliche Voraussetzungen der Monumentalarchitektur Berlins und Wiens in der Zeit von 1780 bis 1830, phil. Diss. Graz, 1960.

150. *Sutcliffe, A.*, Environmental Control and Planning in European Capitals 1850–1914: London, Paris and Berlin, in Growth and Transformation of the Modern City. The Stockholm Conference September 1978, Stockholm, 1979, pp. 71–88.

151. *Sutcliffe, A.*, Toward the Planned City: Germany, Britain, the United States and France, Oxford, 1981.

152. *Sutcliffe, A.*, Urban Planning in Europe and North America before 1914: International Aspects of a Prophetic Movement, in H. J. Teuteberg, ed., Urbanisierung im 19. und 20. Jahrhundert, Cologne and Vienna, 1983, pp. 441–474.

153. *Tunnard, C.*, The Customary and the Characteristic: A Note on the Pursuit of City Planning History, in O. Handlin and J. Burchard, eds., in The Historian and the City, Cambridge, Mass., 1963, pp. 216–224.

(g) Economy and Transport

154. *Bairoch, P.*, De Jérusalem à Mexico: Villes et économie dans l'histoire, Paris, 1985.
155. *Fleischer, A.*, The Economics of Urbanisation, in O. Handlin and J. Burchard, eds., The Historian and the City, Cambridge, Mass. 1963, pp. 70–73.
156. *Gerschenkron, A.*, City Economies – Then and Now, in O. Handlin and J. Burchard, eds., The Historian and the City, Cambridge, Mass. 1963, pp. 56–62.
157. *Hambloch, H.*, Die moderne Stadt als zentraler Ort, in H. Stoob, ed., Die Stadt. Gestalt und Wandel bis zum industriellen Zeitalter, Cologne and Vienna, 1979, pp. 243–262.
158. *Hietala, M.*, Services and Urbanisation at the Turn of the Century. The Diffusion of Innovations, Helsinki, 1987.
159. *Kresse, J.-M.*, Die Industriestandorte in mitteleuropäischen Großstädten. Ein entwicklungsgeschichtlicher Überblick, Berlin, 1977.
160. *Mauersberg, H.*, Wirtschafts- und Sozialgeschichte zentraleuropäischer Städte in neuerer Zeit. Dargestellt an den Beispielen von Basel, Frankfurt a. M., Hamburg, Hannover und München, Göttingen, 1960.
161. *McKay, J. P.*, Tramways and Trolleys. The Rise of Urban Mass Transport in Europe, Princeton, 1976.
162. *Meier, R. L.*, The Organisation of Technological Innovation in Urban Environments, in O. Handlin and J. Burchard, eds., The Historian and the City, Cambridge, Mass., 1963, pp. 74–83.
163. *Rémy, J.*, La ville phénomène économique, Brussels, 1966.
164. *Tsuru, S.*, The Economic Significance of Cities, in O. Handlin and J. Burchard, eds., The Historian and the City, Cambridge, Mass., 1963, pp. 44–55.
165. *Warner, Jr., S. B.*, The Public Invasion of Private Space and the Private Engrossment of Public Space, in Growth and Transformation of the Modern City. The Stockholm Conference September 1978, Stockholm, 1979, pp. 171–178.
166. *Yago, G.*, The Decline of Transit. Urban Transportation in German and US Cities, Cambridge, 1984.

(h) Arts and Sciences, Churches

167. *Boulding, K. E.*, The Death of the City: A Frightened Look at Postcivilisation, in O. Handlin and J. Burchard, eds., The Historian and the City, Cambridge, Mass., 1963, pp. 133–145.
168. *Cityscape. 1910–39.* Urban Themes in American, German and British Art, London, 1977/78.

169. *Fanger, D.*, Dostoevsky and Romantic Realism, Cambridge, Mass., 1965.

170. *Faucher, J.*, Vergleichende Kulturbilder aus den vier europäischen Millionenstädten Berlin, Wien, Paris, London, Hanover, 1877.

171. *Freidel, F.*, Boosters, Intellectuals, and the American City, in O. Handlin and J. Burchard, eds., The Historian and the City, Cambridge, Mass., 1963, pp. 115–120.

172. *Klotz, V.*, Die erzählte Stadt. Ein Sujet als Herausforderung des Romans von Lesage bis Döblin, Munich, 1969.

173. *Lees, A.*, Cities Perceived. Urban Society in European and American Thought. 1820–1940, Manchester, 1985.

174. *Lees, A.*, Perceptions of Cities in Britain and Germany 1820–1914, in D. Fraser and A. Sutcliffe, eds., The Pursuit of Urban History, London, 1983, pp. 151–165.

175. *Moholy-Nagy, S.*, Matrix of Man – An Illustrated History of Urban Environment, New York, 1968.

176. *Olsen, D. J.*, The City as a Work of Art, in D. Fraser and A. Sucliffe eds., The Pursuit of Urban History, London, 1983, pp. 264–285.

177. *Schorske, C. E.*, The Idea of the City in European Thought: Voltaire to Spengler, in O. Handlin and J. Burchard, eds., The Historian and the City, Cambridge, Mass. 1963, pp. 95–114.

178. *Spears, M. K.*, Dionysos and the City: Modernism in Twentieth-Century Poetry, New York, 1970.

179. *Die Stadt*: Druckgraphische Zyklen des 19. und 20. Jahrhundert, Bremen, 1974.

180. *Wirth, L.*, Urbanism as a Way of Life, in The American Journal of Sociology, Vol. 43 (1938), pp. 1–24.

181. *White, M.*, Two Stages in the Critique of the American City, in O. Handlin and J. Burchard, eds., The Historian and the City, Cambridge, Mass. 1963, pp. 84–94.

182. *White, M.*, and *L. White*, The Intellectual Versus the City: From Thomas Jefferson to Frank Lloyd Wright, Cambridge, Mass., 1962.

E. Local Studies (a representative selection)

- Austria

183. *Hubbard, W. H.*, Der Wachstumsprozeß in den österreichischen Großstädten 1869–1910, in P. C. Ludz, ed., Sociologie und Sozialgeschichte, Opladen, 1973, pp. 386–418.

- France

184. *Evenson, N.*, Paris. A Century of Change. 1878–1978, New Haven and London, 1979.
185. *Sutcliffe, A.*, The Autumn of Central Paris. The Defeat of Town Planning 1850–1970, London, 1970.

- Federal Republic of Germany

186. *Ayçoberry, P.*, Cologne entre Napoleon et Bismarck – La croissance d'une ville rhénane, Paris, 1981.
187. *François, E.*, Koblenz im 18. Jahrhundert. Zur Sozial- und Bevölkerungsstruktur einer deutschen Residenzstadt, Göttingen, 1982.
188. *Marquardt, F. D.*, Sozialer Aufstieg, sozialer Abstieg und die Entstehung der Berliner Arbeiterklasse, 1806–1848, in Geschichte und Gesellschaft, Year 1 (1975), pp. 43–77.
189. *Miller Lane, B.*, Architecture and Politics in Germany, 1918–1945, Cambridge, Mass., 1968.
190. *Piccinato, G.*, La costruzione dell'urbanistica: Germania 1871–1914, Rome 1974.
191. *Sackett, R. E.*, Popular Entertainment, Class and Politics in Munich 1900–1923, Cambridge, Mass., 1986.
192. *Walker, M.*, German Home Towns. Community, State and General Estate 1848–1871, Ithaca and London, 1971.

- Great Britain

193. *Calabi, D.*, Il "male" città: urbanistica inglese del primo Novecento, Rome, 1979 (= The 'sick' city: English urbanism at the start of the 20th century).

- Soviet Union

194. *Bater, J. H.*, The Soviet City. Ideal and Reality, London, 1980.
195. *Hamm, M. F.*, ed., The City in Russian History, Lexington, 1976.
196. *Socialismo, città, architettura:* URSS 1917–1937, Rome, 1979 (= Socialism, city, architecture: USSR 1917–1937).

- USA

197. *Dal Co, F., et al.*, La città: americana dalla guerra civile al New Deal, Bari, 1973 (= The American city from the war of Independence to the New Deal).